D0324253

Personality Dynamics and Mental Health

Principles of Adjustment and Mental Hygiene

Personality Dynamics and Mental Health

Principles of Adjustment and Mental Hygiene

Revised Edition

Alexander A. Schneiders

Boston College

Holt, Rinehart and Winston, Inc.

New York · Chicago · San Francisco · Toronto · London

To my clients
who have been my best teachers concerning
mental health and adjustment.

Preface

It has been several years since the first edition of this book on mental health was published, but even in that relatively short period of time there have occurred many new ideas, new approaches, new emphases, and new research directed toward a better understanding of the problems encountered by the student of mental health and by the practitioner involved in the promotion of mental health. Diligent researchers have completed a number of excellent studies which have contributed greatly to the better understanding of the statistical characteristics, the ecology, and the dynamics of both mental health and mental illness. Several noteworthy publications have appeared that have provided a better understanding of the nature and dynamics of mental health, and there have been certain developments which have created various shifts in emphasis, not the least of which has been the growing relationship between religion on the one hand and psychiatry and psychology on the other.

In the present edition we have tried to take account of the various new developments, at the same time that we have attempted to reshape the book to the better advantage of the student. For example, there is a much stronger emphasis on mental hygiene (Part Four), there is a separate chapter on religion and mental hygiene (Chapter 15), and a chapter on the mental hygiene of the home, the school, and the community (Chapter 16).

Also in many parts of the text there have been extensive changes in the interest of simplifying its over-all structure and eliminating unnecessary duplication of material. In addition, there has been considerable reorganization of both the material and the various parts of the text, as well as a selection of new titles for many of the chapters and for the book itself. More emphasis has been given to the normal personality, to dynamic factors and determinants of adjustment and mental health, and particularly to the principles and application of mental hygiene. With these different emphases, the book will be more useful to teachers, counselors, and practitioners concerned with mental health and adjustment.

Structurally, the edition is different from its predecessor. In an effort to avoid repetitions, some chapters have been eliminated altogether and several new ones added. Throughout the text new material has been fitted into the content. Also, all footnotes have been eliminated and, taking their place, there is a master reference list at the end of the text.

The text has four essential parts. Part One leads off with three chapters that deal with the concepts of adjustment, normality, and mental health, followed in Part Two by three chapters on the dynamics and determinants of adjustment and mental health. This arrangement enabled the author to bring together many ideas that were scattered throughout the original text. Part Three, "The Process and Patterns of Adjustment," corresponds closely to the original text, although there has been considerable revision and updating of material. In Part Four, which includes six chapters, there has been a great deal of revision and reorganization under the heading of "Mental Hygiene and Treatment." This part includes the principles of mental hygiene, personal mental hygiene, the mental hygiene of work and marriage, religion and mental hygiene, mental hygiene of the home, the school, and the community, and the treatment of adjustment and mental health problems. Finally, as in the original text, there is a glossary and a listing of films relating to mental health.

As every author who has attempted it knows, a revision of his own text is an extremely difficult and time-consuming task. This revision depended greatly on the help of several people whose selfless devotion to the author's writing efforts was a principal factor in getting the job done. Particularly is the author grateful to his wife for her endless patience and tireless efforts in reading and checking the manuscript, to his secretary, Miss Martha McLaughlin, for countless hours spent in typing and checking bibliographical items, and to his assistant, Miss Rose Marie Dickson, for the many hours spent in library research.

The author wishes to express his sincere gratitude to Dr. John F. Kinnane, who read the manuscript in its entirety and offered many important and helpful suggestions for revision, and to Frank A. Melone, who also offered valuable suggestions after reading parts of the manuscript. The author is also grateful to the many persons who participated in a survey of users of the original text for their cooperation in completing the questionnaire and for their numerous valuable criticisms and suggestions. The author wishes also to express his thanks to the authors and publishers who so graciously permitted the reproduction of copyrighted material. Without the help of these many friends and colleagues, this book could not have been completed in its present form.

Boston, Massachusetts   A. A. S.
January 1965

Contents

PART THREE   THE PROCESS AND PATTERNS OF ADJUSTMENT

Personality
Dynamics
and Mental Health

Principles of Adjustment and Mental Hygiene

PART ONE

Adjustment, Normality, and Mental Health

1

Introduction

We begin our study of human adjustment and mental health with a statement of aims to be achieved and reasons for studying problems in adjustment. We will see that mental disorder and maladjustment are very prevalent and that these facts have many implications for individuals and society. We also will take a quick look at different approaches to adjustment and how it may be studied.

VALUES AND OBJECTIVES IN THE STUDY OF ADJUSTMENT

General Aims

The scientific study of adjustment is concerned with those human responses—mental as well as behavioral—by which you and I and all other people attempt to cope with different situations and problems of everyday life, with conflicts and frustrations that arise, with the stresses and strains that we encounter as we go about our daily tasks. For the moment, then, let us think of adjustment simply in terms of getting along well with ourselves, with others, and with our work. The idea of mental health fits in here too. It means being happy a good part of the time, having fun, being able to think effectively, and being more or less free of too much worry and anxiety, depression, hostility, and other feelings that make life difficult.

To illustrate these points, let us take the case of a young boy who was neither well adjusted nor happy. Walter is a sixteen-year-old boy who was referred to the psychologist because of chronic school failures and difficulties at home. He was described as being resentful, hostile, and antagonistic toward school, to his brothers and sisters, and to home discipline. His school record was spotty: some A's and B's, but mostly C's, D's, and a liberal sprinkling of F's. Walter comes from what would be called a good home. His parents are well educated, his brothers and sisters are seemingly well adjusted, and the social, moral, and economic level of the family is high.

Walter had done reasonably well in grade school and once had made the honor roll. Psychometric examination revealed an intelligence quotient of 130. Reading skill and grade achievements were well above

3

average. At the time of referral, Walter was a tenth-grade student in a private boys' school.

Interviews soon revealed that Walter was completely uninterested in, and actively disliked, most of the subjects he was studying. Further examination indicated an intense interest in mechanical subjects. Significantly, he had done well in arithmetic and mathematics, and his chief out-of-school interests were automobiles and model airplanes. In his third year, on the advice of the psychologist, Walter was transferred to a technical high school. Almost at once his grades took an upward turn, much of the resentment and hostility disappeared, and his home life improved considerably.

This is a relatively simple case of maladjustment, centering around Walter's inability to get along well in school. His failures, his lack of interest, and the prodding and criticism of his parents are what made Walter unhappy and caused a great deal of his resentment and hostility. Not all cases of maladjustment are this simple by any means. Some, as we shall see in later pages, are very complicated and difficult to deal with effectively. But cases like this one help us to understand quickly what adjustment and mental health are. Even in such simple instances, the elements of maladjustment are present: emotional turmoil, frustration, conflict, unhappiness, lack of achievement, sense of failure, and so on. And from this analysis it is easy to figure out what adjustment is. If Walter had got along well at school and at home; if he had liked his subjects and found them interesting and stimulating; if, instead of hostility and resentment there had been enjoyment, friendship, and affection, then we would have concluded that Walter was a well-adjusted boy.

The general aims of our study, then, are to understand adjustment and mental health, and such related concepts as normality and abnormality, maladjustment, and mental disorder. Fortified with such knowledge, we will be in a position to develop the principles of mental hygiene (Chapters 12–16) and to say something about the treatment of adjustment problems (Chapter 17).

Some Specific Aims

Adjustment and mental health, as we shall see, are a complicated business. They have many facets that have to be understood and that must be related to each other and to numerous personality and environmental factors as well. It is not enough to set down practical principles and rules by which adjustment can be achieved or maintained. Principles of this kind have much more meaning and practical significance when we understand the nature of the process and the conditions to which they refer.

For example, if you are told that regularity in personal habits is of considerable importance to personal efficiency and adjustment, you will want to know why, even though you are quite willing to accept the principle by itself. Furthermore, when you know why, the principle becomes more meaningful and, at the same time, more helpful.

Understanding human adjustment in this way means knowing what it is, its forms, and how these different forms are interrelated. We want to know also how adjustment is related to, and in what way it differs from, normality, mental health, and efficiency. Also, our understanding of the adjustment process will be furthered by a statement of the conditions that govern its development and the criteria by which it can be evaluated. And just as important to the understanding of adjustment is the effort to bring it in line with the concept of personality because of the role that each personality plays in the adjustment process.

This aim of understanding the nature and conditions of adjustment is basic to the achievement of other objectives. Quite naturally, a study such as this leads to practical results, and thus we may say that one of our aims is *personal self-improvement*. In more specific terms this aim is directed toward a healthier personality, the prevention of maladjustment, the elimination of disturbing or disabling symptoms, and the development of traits or habits that contribute to greater efficiency and better living. Put in another way, the psychology of adjustment naturally leads to the practice of mental hygiene. And it is good to remember that the rules and criteria of mental hygiene or personality development must be grounded in an empirically sound psychology of adjustment.

Anderson expresses this relationship clearly when he says (Anderson, 1949, p. 1):

> Why should we study ourselves? Why should we be interested in development from birth to maturity? First and foremost, in order to understand ourselves. All persons travel much the same road from infancy to old age, meet similar problems and pass through comparable periods of development. Knowing who we are, how we have developed, what our assets and liabilities are, and how we meet and solve problems is important for our own adjustment in life situations. Only by the study of development can we gain knowledge on the road we have already travelled, insight into our present situation, and awareness of our future possibilities.

This statement exemplifies well the attitude of psychologists and mental hygienists toward the study of human adjustment at the same time that it emphasizes its practical value.

Bringing together the general and specific aims of our study of adjustment and mental health we can define them specifically in this way:

1. To determine the relations between adjustment psychology and other fields, such as mental hygiene, abnormal and clinical psychology, psychiatry, and psychotherapy
2. To determine the nature of and relations between certain basic concepts, including adjustment and maladjustment, normality and abnormality, mental health and illness, mental efficiency, maturity, and morality
3. To define the general and specific criteria of adjustment and mental health
4. To outline and define the conditions and determinants of adjustment and mental health
5. To define the relations between adjustment and personality
6. To explain the basic dynamics of the adjustment process
7. To determine the relations between adjustment, conflict, frustration, and stress
8. To outline and explain the principal mechanisms of adjustment
9. To study the nature, conditions, and characteristics of personal, social, vocational, and marital adjustment
10. To develop basic principles of mental hygiene

Only to the extent that these aims are realized will it be possible for us to develop a complete psychology of adjustment and mental health and to define the nature of personality dynamics.

SOME BASIC REASONS FOR STUDYING ADJUSTMENT PROBLEMS

Extent of Maladjustment and Mental Disorder

The objectives of our study become more meaningful when we realize how widespread psychological difficulties are. No one knows the actual incidence of these difficulties, nor is there any exact method of determining what the figures are (Felix & Kramer, 1953). As we shall see (Table 1), there are fairly reliable figures regarding the extent of *mental disorder* because this type of difficulty is more likely to come to the attention of one or another person or agency, from whom such figures are available (Appel, 1946). But there are countless persons suffering from some form of personality disorder or maladjustment who do not come within the scope of statistical surveys (Srole, *et al.*, 1962). Many of these remain unknown to the psychiatrist, the medical practitioner, or the psychologist. Many other disturbed persons seek the help of a therapist, but no statistical records are kept; or, at best, the available figures constitute only a meager representation of the actual number. When to this large number we add the countless thousands who each year seek the help and advice of lawyers, priests, ministers, self-appointed counselors, and the ever-greedy lunatic fringe of phrenologists, soothsayers, palmists, and crystal-ball gazers, we begin to realize how impossible it is to obtain a truly representative statistical survey (Goldhamer & Marshall, 1953).

TABLE I

First Admissions to Hospitals for Mental Disease in the United States: 1946

(*By Diagnosis and Type of Hospital Control*)

DIAGNOSIS	ALL HOSPITALS		STATE HOSPITALS		COUNTY AND CITY HOSPITALS		VETERANS' HOSPITALS		PRIVATE HOSPITALS	
	No.	%	No.	%	No.	%	No.	%	No.	%
General paresis	6021	4.1	5367	6.0	121	4.0	275	1.2	258	0.8
Alcoholic (psychotic)	5713	3.9	3932	4.4	94	3.1	912	4.1	755	2.5
Alcoholic (non-psychotic)	9541	6.6	3742	4.2	76	2.5	1424	6.4	4299	14.1
Cerebral arterio-sclerosis	15,665	10.8	13,665	15.3	506	16.8	159	0.7	1335	4.4
Senile	13,543	9.3	11,345	12.7	791	26.2	52	0.2	1355	4.4
Involutional	6888	4.7	3898	4.4	66	2.2	112	0.5	2812	9.2
Psychoneurosis	11,677	8.0	2930	3.3	62	2.1	5261	23.6	3424	11.2
Manic-depressive	12,078	8.3	6951	7.8	188	6.2	820	3.7	4119	13.5
Dementia-praecox	29,753	20.5	16,918	18.9	456	15.1	8058	36.1	4321	14.1
Other	34,324	23.8	20,551	23.0	721	21.8	5241	23.5	7874	25.8
All patients	145,203	100.0	89,299	100.0	3018	100.0	22,314	100.0	30,572	100.0

Source: The Council of State Governments. *The mental health programs of the forty-eight states.* Chicago: 1950, p. 35.

The fact that mental illness is widespread is well known. More than half of all hospital beds in the country are occupied at any one time by mental patients (Table 2). It has been conservatively estimated that one out of every ten persons in the United States would benefit from some kind of mental health care or psychotherapy, which would mean that there are about 18 million persons suffering from some kind of psychological disorder (Fein, 1958). During World War II the United States Army was

TABLE 2

Patients Resident in State Hospitals for Mental Disease,
by Age at End of Year, and Sex, 1952

Age	MALE		FEMALE	
	No.	%	No.	%
Under 15	555	0.38	385	0.26
15–24	6204	4.29	4467	2.99
25–34	16,942	11.70	15,919	10.66
35–44	28,432	19.64	26,915	18.03
45–54	32,315	22.32	30,931	20.72
55–64	25,688	17.74	30,696	20.56
65–74	22,350	15.44	23,682	15.86
75–84	10,388	7.18	13,306	8.91
85 and over	1902	1.31	3003	2.01
Total	144,776	100.00	149,304	100.00

Source: Fein, R. *Economics of mental illness.* New York: Basic Books, 1958, p. 62.

deprived of 2,500,000 men, or the equivalent of 165 divisions, because of mental and emotional breakdowns. A total number of 1,767,000 draftees were rejected for mental and personality disorders; and in spite of selective service screening, about 40 percent of all men given medical discharges were declared unfit for service because of emotional disorders. These numbers do not include individuals who would benefit from counseling and guidance in their efforts to cope with personal difficulties, nor does it include many others who have significant emotional disturbances that do not call for hospitalization. Not too long ago one author (Steckle, 1949, p. 20) wrote:

> The extent to which emotional living handicaps mankind is demonstrated by the conservative estimate that from 12 to 13,000,000 men and women in the United States are in need of active psychotherapy. Unfortunately, some 10,000,000 of them are not receiving help. Further, almost 20 per cent of all draftees in the last war showed evidence of psychological disturbance. Add to this, the good statistical bet that one out of every ten youngsters alive today will have need of psychological care sometime during his life, and some idea of the serious magnitude of the problems may be gained.

We can see what has happened to the figures in the thirteen or fourteen years since this book was published.

To say that maladjustment is widespread (if not actually universal in our society) is not to accept the foolish dictum that "everybody is neurotic." But, human nature being what it is, we can expect that a great many people will, at one point or another in their lives, find the going rather difficult. Everyone can expect periods of unhappiness, tension, frustration, depression, worry, anxiety, or mental turmoil. Into every life the fine mist of minor maladjustment must fall, and one must always be careful that it does not become a downpour. If you want to look closely enough, you will see the mist very quickly. Perhaps the boy or girl next to you is a chronic worrier; the lad in the first row is a nail biter; the neighbor next door hates children; the couple on the other side are arranging for a divorce; your teacher is high-strung and irritable; your little brother is a bed wetter; and you yourself find it hard to get along with your parents!

Some of these difficulties are relatively minor, whereas others are very serious (Milt, 1957). But the important point here is that all of them fit into the general concept of *maladjustment*; that is, they are poor or inefficient ways of coping with reality. No one will ever go to hell or to jail for bed wetting, but it is certainly an undesirable response. It is a kind of behavior that reflects lack of control, anxiety, or some other disturbance in the child's personality. It is, in other words, a poor way of behaving. When these maladjustments are added to the large number of more serious disturbances, the total number of maladjusted people swells to extremely large proportions.

Specific Data on Maladjustment

Psychosomatic Disorders. The extent of maladjustment is exemplified also by the number of persons who seek help from physicians regarding ailments that are not actually physical in nature. It is reliably estimated by physicians themselves that between 50 and 75 percent of the patients who come to them for help have nothing physically wrong with them! True enough, these patients have aches and pains; they really suffer from headaches, sleeplessness, lack of energy, chronic tiredness, palpitations of the heart, and so on. But the most careful diagnosis fails to reveal any physical disturbance or pathology. The symptoms are real enough and cause a great deal of suffering and anguish; yet the underlying causes of these symptoms are not physical; they are, instead, psychological, and this fact brings such disturbances within the scope of the concept of maladjustment. In one study of such disorders, it is reported that 40 percent of 7000 children observed in a pediatric clinic presented problems involving psychosomatic symptoms, indicating how widespread these maladjustments are (Scull, 1952, pp. 285–292).

These disorders are referred to as "psychosomatic," to distinguish them from similar disorders that are the result of physical conditions. They are called psychosomatic to indicate that the symptoms are the result of psychological rather than physical causes. Thus the common headache may result from eye strain, constipation, or head injury, but it may also result from *emotional tension*. Similarly, high blood pressure may be a symptom of hardening of the arteries and chronic fatigue a sign of heart disorder, but they can also result from anxiety or conflict. Later on (Chapter 11) we shall have a great deal more to say about psychosomatic disorders. Here we wish to indicate simply that these reactions increase the already large number of maladjusted persons, since psychosomatic symptoms are a form of maladjustive response.

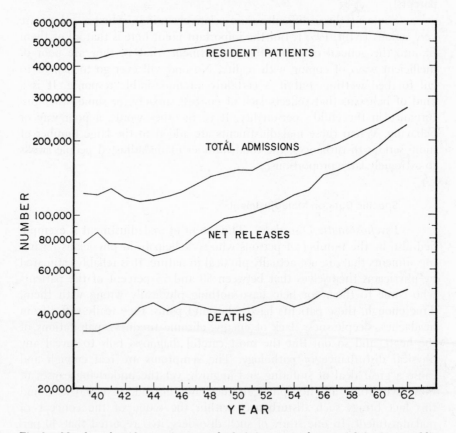

Fig. 1.   Number of resident patients, total admissions, net releases, and deaths in public mental hospitals in the United States, 1939–1962. (By permission from U.S. Department of Health, Education, and Welfare, National Institute of Mental Health. *Mental health statistics: current reports, January 1963*.)

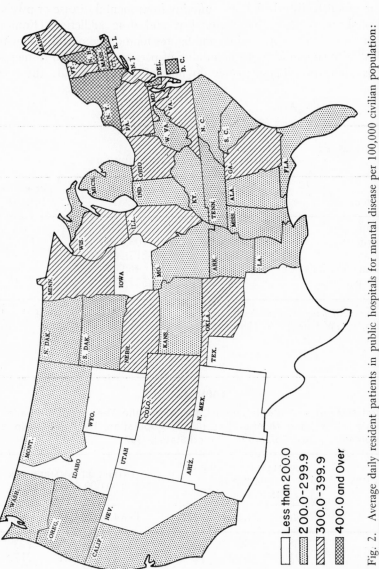

Fig. 2. Average daily resident patients in public hospitals for mental disease per 100,000 civilian population: 1957. (Based on provisional data, subject to later revision.) (By permission from U.S. Department of Health, Education, and Welfare, National Institute of Mental Health. *Mental health statistics: current reports, May, 1958.*)

Less than 200.0
200.0 - 299.9
300.0 - 399.9
400.0 and Over

Mental Disease. Many persons who seek medical help for the relief of psychosomatic symptoms are actually *neurotic*—victims of relative benign personality disorders. There are countless others who are far more seriously disturbed, those suffering from mental disease or psychosis, alcoholism, psychopathic personality, and drug addiction (Fromm, 1955, pp. 8–9). Some of the tables and figures reproduced on the following pages will give you an idea of the number of persons committed to mental hospitals each year. These figures do not, of course, include the even

TABLE 3

Patients in Public Mental Hospitals

Item	Actual 1960	Estimate 1961	Percentage Increase
First admissions	137,853	144,372	4.7
Readmissions	96,989	108,743	10.8
Net releases	191,755	215,566	12.3
Deaths in hospitals	49,774	46,975	−5.6
Resident patients	535,269	527,945	−1.4

Source: Facts on mental health and mental illness. U.S. Department of Health, Education, and Welfare. Public Health Service. Publication No. 543, 1962.

TABLE 4

Estimated Number of Patients under Care during the Year in all Outpatient Psychiatric Clinics and Number per 100,000 Population, by Age Group at Admission and by Sex, Continental United States, 1959

AGE GROUPS	ESTIMATED NUMBER OF PATIENTS (IN THOUSANDS)			ESTIMATED NUMBER PER 100,000 POPULATION		
	Total	Male	Female	Total	Male	Female
Under 18	208	138	70	327.4	427.1	223.7
18 and over	294	167	127	263.1	313.1	217.8
Total	502	305	197	286.4	356.2	219.9

Source: Facts on mental health and mental illness. U.S. Department of Health, Education, and Welfare. Public Health Service. Publication No. 543, 1962.

larger number of psychotics who are in private treatment or who are able to maintain their position in society despite their emotional handicaps.

Delinquency and Crime.   Each year we witness the tragic spectacle of thousands of school children running headlong into some kind of psychological difficulty (Newell, 1947). It is conservatively estimated that between 2 and 3 million school children in any single year require some kind of special help to stave off or to remedy some form of maladjustment. Some of these children cannot read, and others are handicapped by speech impediments. Some have difficulty with school subjects, whereas others are emotionally confused or distraught. A large number of them, torn by conflicts and frustrations, become truants and delinquents or turn to more serious forms of crime. That is why today every progressive school system and community employs psychologists, psychiatrists, and similar experts whose job it is to help children with these adjustment problems. The following case illustrates the kind of problem that often arises in school.

> An eight-year-old boy had remained for two years in the first half of the first grade without learning to write or to read. He reversed letters or sequences, made meaningless combinations of letters, and used peculiar punctuation marks. Other symptoms were solitary withdrawal from social relationships and wetting and soiling, the latter representing a regression after his mother placed him, at the age of three, in a foster home after the birth of a sister. Both children were illegitimate, but the mother married the father of the second one, and he did not want to take the patient into the home. . . .
>
> At the age of three, before he developed his neurosis, he achieved an IQ of 95. When tested by the same psychologist at five and at seven, he achieved IQ's of 75 and 74. At the end of therapy, after he recovered from his neurosis, his IQ was again 95.7 (Maslow & Mittelmann, 1951, pp. 344–345).

Many delinquent youngsters become increasingly maladjusted until, by late adolescence, they join the ranks of the habitual criminal. Here we have another large section of the population that is seriously maladjusted. All delinquents and criminals are morally and socially maladjusted, and many of them have serious emotional difficulties too. That these groups constitute a serious problem in adjustment and social welfare is clearly indicated by figures showing the increase in crime and juvenile delinquency for the past twenty years (Table 5).

From this table you can get a clear and quick impression of the staggering increase in juvenile delinquency during the past twenty years. Some of this increase is attributable, of course, to increase in population; but many statistical surveys show that delinquency is actually increasing

TABLE 5

Adolescent Crime in New York City during 1955–1957

Type of Crime	Total Arrested of All Ages	Total of 16–20 Group Arrested	Position of 16–20 Group
Destruction of property	950	288	1
Robbery	2195	721	1
Grand larceny from highway, vehicle, etc.	2384	1371	1
Burglary	2772	1175	1
Petit larceny from highway, vehicle, etc.	762	344	1
General criminality felonies	838	238	1
Homicide unclassified	107	26	1
Homicide by shooting	63	17	1
Assault on officer, felony	768	177	1
Kidnapping	53	13	2
Rape, age of female not reported	76	18	2
Rape, female under 18	560	144	2
Abduction	32	19	1
Sodomy	176	26	3
Impairing morals of children, misdemeanor	263	45	1
Arson	74	15	2
Malicious mischief			
Felony	41	15	1
Misdemeanor	835	258	1
Extortion, felony	74	12	2
Larceny of auto	1894	1262	1
Dangerous weapons	693	204	1
Burglars' tools	117	28	2

Source: Block, H., & Niederhoffer, A. *The gang: A study in adolescent behavior.* New York: Philosophical Library, Inc., 1958, p. 147.

faster than population growth. Table 6 gives a clear picture of how adolescent delinquency quickly turns into adolescent crime.

Vocational and Marital Maladjustment. While there is no sure way of determining the number of persons who are vocationally maladjusted, that is, deeply dissatisfied with their occupation, it has been reliably estimated that the figure may be as high as 50 percent! Whether this figure is correct or not, the number of persons unsuited to their jobs or emotionally frustrated in their work must be appallingly large. Even if the estimated figure were as low as 10 percent, the incidence of voca-

TABLE 6

Juvenile Delinquency—Police Arrests of Children Under 18—
Cases Handled by Juvenile Courts, 1940 to 1957

(Index, 1940 = 100)

| Year | CHILDREN UNDER 18 ARRESTED BY POLICE | | JUVENILE COURT CASES |
	Number	Index	Index
1940	35,332	100	100
1943	47,884	136	172
1944	46,690	132	165
1945	49,566	140	172
1946	37,833	107	148
1947	34,376	97	131
1948	31,750	90	127
1949	32,922	93	136
1950	34,599	98	140
1951	37,259	105	149
1952	86,128	—	166
1953	149,806	—	187
1954	163,666	—	198
1955	195,626	—	216
1956	234,474	—	260
1957	253,817	—	302

Source: *Statistical abstract of the United States.* U.S. Department of Commerce, 1958, p. 143.

tional maladjustment would be staggering. Many of these persons are simply dissatisfied with or disinterested in their work, while others keep shifting from one job to another; but the important point is that they do belong to the ranks of the maladjusted.

In a similar manner other persons have trouble coping with the responsibilities of marriage. This is understandable since marriage, like a job or a profession, makes heavy demands on the abilities of the two partners to cope with one another. In both situations, there are day-to-day problems that require careful handling, good judgment, emotional control, and adaptation. The incidence of marital maladjustment is extremely high. One out of every four marriages ends in divorce, and these figures do not take into account instances of separation, desertion, and marital discord in which there is a great deal of unhappiness, conflict, and hatred.

When we bring together all of these data, it is obvious that the number of persons with some degree of maladjustment runs into the millions. This statement is somewhat pessimistic, but it is also realistic since it reflects the problem of adjustment as it actually exists. You must understand that the concept of maladjustment extends all the way from a simple problem like reading disability to the most complex psychosis. We can expect so big a net to catch a great many fish. Furthermore, human existence is a complex affair, and it is difficult for children and adolescents, and men and women to meet all of the demands and problems they encounter with sureness, efficiency, or emotional stability. Human beings are limited in their capacity to adjust to every situation. In a crucial situation calling for just the right kind of response they may lack experience that is necessary; or perhaps some long-standing inhibition gets in the way; or it may be lack of tact, a bad habit, or a feeling of inferiority that prevents them from coping effectively with the situation. The possibilities for poor adjustment in a world as complex as ours are endless, and we need not wonder that so many persons develop symptomatic or maladjustive responses.

IMPLICATIONS OF OUR DATA

Importance of Mental Health and Mental Hygiene

The recognition that maladjustment and mental disorder are extremely widespread only serves to emphasize the serious implications that these facts have for all of us as individuals and as members of society. In one of its leaflets on mental illness, the National Association for Mental Health points out that (1) one out of every twelve children born each year will need to go to a mental hospital sometime during his lifetime; (2) at least 9 million Americans are suffering from a mental or emotional disorder; (3) in the current year about 250,000 people will go to mental hospitals for the first time; (4) mental illness costs over a billion dollars a year in tax funds; (5) about $1,750,000,000 is lost in earnings in one year by patients becoming ill for the first time; and (6) the 650,000 mental-hospital patients equal in number all other hospital patients combined. These facts certainly highlight the social implications of mental disorder (Fein, 1958).

It is something of a truism to assert that a society cannot be healthier than its individual members; and conversely that an unhealthy society has adverse effects on its individual members. It is this vicious circle that makes the study of mental health and mental ill-health so important. It is the same data that underscore the importance of an effective program of mental hygiene. Individually and collectively we cannot expect to live contentedly, nor can we hope to achieve personal or social goals, as long as we are hampered by maladjustments. For these reasons we should make every effort toward understanding the adjustment process, so that, in turn, by understanding we may come to a knowledge of the rules and conditions for healthy, effective living.

SCIENTIFIC STUDY OF ADJUSTMENT

Psychology of Adjustment

Psychological investigation is much the same regardless of what we happen to be interested in at any particular moment. There are some variations in aim, in point of view, and, at times, in methodology; but on the whole these variations are subordinate to the general interests and orientation of the psychologist, which may be stated simply as a knowledge of human behavior, personality, and interpersonal relationships. In every branch of scientific psychology, as distinct from the applied fields, we are always trying to find out more about human beings—how they behave, why they act that way, what their characteristics are, how changes in personality and behavior come about, and so on. The psychology of adjustment and mental health is no exception to this rule, so that it is closely related to general psychology.

Yet it is possible to emphasize certain aspects of personality, or of mental life and behavior, that give rise to a new point of view; and this is what we do in the psychology of adjustment. Adjustment is a quality of human behavior to which we direct our attention when we are interested in how well or how poorly mental activity and behavior are suited to the demands and problems that people encounter. Thus, in a given instance, we might be interested in the delinquency patterns of a group of young boys. We study their background, their personality development, and their motivations in order to find out where the delinquency came from. Or we can shift our point of view and study the behavior from the standpoint of its relation to adjustment. In this instance we analyze its value as an adjustive response and how it compares with other methods of coping with reality (Chapter 9). Adopting this point of view we are then working in the area of adjustment psychology.

The scope of this study is therefore very broad since so many types of response are related to the problem of adjustment. However, it is incorrect to imply that all behavior or all mental processes are directed toward adjustment. There are many instances of everyday behavior that do not come within the scope of the psychology of adjustment. One may light his pipe, take a stroll, play a tune on the piano, write a letter, and do countless other things that have no direct relation to the adjustment processes. Nor does the concept of adjustment apply to many mental activities such as solving a mathematical problem, planning the day's work, reminiscing about a recent trip, or learning a poem for the sheer joy of doing it.

The question of adjustment arises when there are certain demands or requirements that must be met, or when we are confronted with problems, conflicts, or frustrations that must be resolved in some way. The worker is required to meet the demands of his job; the student must face the responsibilities of academic life; the husband must somehow cope with the exigencies of marriage that stem from the needs of his children or his wife. In every area of human endeavor, there are some requirements that must be fulfilled, and there are situations or personalities to which we must adjust. It is in this context that the problems of adjustment arise.

Adjustment psychology is also intimately concerned with the problem of human personality. We shall deal with this relation in more detail later (Chapter 3), but here we wish to note the fundamental connection between personality and adjustment which revolves around the fact that in any adjustment situation *one's personality always plays a predominant role*. Adjustment processes are ways of behaving, and these responses are direct expressions of personality, so that their form or content will be determined to a large extent by the make-up or kind of personality they reflect. Thus, when confronted with a serious or tragic incident, like the sudden loss of both parents, expulsion from school, the breakup of the home, or a sexual attack, any two people can be expected to react quite differently in terms of their unique personalities.

The well-integrated, mature, and emotionally stable person may take such events in stride without any deep shock to his style of life. He has learned to function at a high level of efficiency, to discipline himself when necessary, and to tackle problems in a straightforward and intelligent manner. A second person may react in just the opposite manner because of his immaturity, emotional instability, self-centeredness, or lack of self-discipline. His inadequate personality determines the nature and level of his adjustment to such situations. In all such instances the deciding factor is the personality of each individual. This is why we must learn what we can regarding the structure of personality, the conditions of its development, and the principles that relate to personal integration.

Study of Adjustment and Mental Health

Where does the problem of mental health fit into this picture? Is it a part of adjustment psychology? Later on we will have a chance to discuss these relations more fully, but here we can indicate that the concept of mental health must be fitted into the study of adjustment. You are certainly aware from your own experience that a healthy mental life is an important part of good adjustment. From what you have read, or from personal observation, you know that a person with obsessive ideas, delusions of persecution, morbid fears, or chronic worry and anxiety is not well adjusted to reality. He may manage to hold a job, complete his schoolwork, or get along with members of his family, but there are always periods when his mental difficulties will interfere with good adjustment. Personality is an integrated whole, and it is not likely that harmony in one area of human response can be sustained when there is serious disharmony in another. Mental health, therefore, may be regarded as a special phase of the total adjustment pattern which must be investigated carefully for its relations to different aspects of adjustment.

ADJUSTMENT PSYCHOLOGY AND RELATED FIELDS

Abnormal Psychology and the Psychology of Adjustment

Our many references to maladjustment, mental illness, and personality disorder must have provoked the question, What is the relation between the study of adjustment and abnormal psychology? It is clear that these two fields touch at many points, but there are important differences which, when clearly defined, will help us to understand both fields better. For one thing, the scope of abnormal psychology is considerably broader than that of adjustment psychology. It studies abnormalities of all kinds, not just those that have adjustive significance. Moreover, the psychology of adjustment is oriented as much to normal as to abnormal responses since it is as much interested in understanding adjustment as it is in explaining maladjustment. There is also the fact that adjustment psychology, though basically empirical in nature, provides the groundwork for the development of practical principles that are utilized in psychiatry and mental hygiene. Abnormal psychology is purely empirical and is not in itself oriented toward the formulation of practical rules. Despite these differences, we wish to emphasize that abnormal psychology *is basic* to the study of adjustment. It provides many of the facts, theories, and interpretations necessary to an adequate psychology of adjustment.

Adjustment Psychology and Mental Hygiene

From what we have just said, the connection between adjustment psychology and mental hygiene is clear. The latter discipline is essentially an art directed toward the *prevention* of mental disorder and maladjustment. It comprises a set of practical rules and principles derived from the scientific study of adjustment and mental health (Chapters 12–16). In the same way, therefore, that abnormal psychology is basic to the psychology of adjustment, the latter is basic to mental hygiene. A careful study of the nature, conditions, and dynamics of adjustment and mental health generate the principles of mental hygiene. It is for this reason that the study of the adjustment processes precede the discussion of mental hygiene in this text.

Clinical Psychology, Counseling, and Psychiatry

The principles of mental hygiene are utilized most extensively in the fields of counseling, clinical psychology, and psychiatry, all of which are dependent on adjustment psychology for basic facts and interpretations regarding human behavior. In the nature of the case, the work of the counselor, or of the clinical psychologist and psychiatrist is directed toward the treatment or the remedy of mental disorder and maladjustment rather than their prevention, and therefore their aim is partially different from that of mental hygiene. But the dividing line between prevention and treatment is extremely thin, and the skilled clinician or therapist is well versed in all the necessary sciences, such as abnormal and adjustment psychology, as well as in the practical arts required for the treatment of personality disorders.

These are only a few of the relations between adjustment psychology and other fields of study. You must realize that, since adjustment pervades every area of human life, other important relations could be drawn. The facts and principles of our study have serious implications for education, for medicine, for religion, and for social work; and some of these implications will be brought out in subsequent discussions.

APPROACHES TO THE STUDY OF ADJUSTMENT

Some Important Theories of Behavior

There are many historical roots of adjustment psychology, which go all the way back to the beginnings of psychiatry and medical psychology, evolutionary biology, and the growth of the mental hygiene movement in this country and abroad. But it would take us too far afield to explore this background in any detail. What is more to the point is to take a close look at some of the more important developments in the history of psychology that have contributed directly to our understanding of adjustment and of the behavior disorders.

Foremost among these influences is the *theory of psychoanalysis* which, as everyone knows, is the creation of Sigmund Freud. According to this viewpoint, the interpretation of adjustment and maladjustment requires the acceptance of several basic concepts (Mullahy, 1948). The first of these is the *theory of the unconscious* according to which all behavior, mental processes, symptoms, and adjustment mechanisms are determined in large measure by psychic factors (instinctual drives, repressed wishes, complexes) of which the individual himself is unaware. This notion is complemented by the *theory of psychological dynamics*, which means that unconscious psychic factors function as powerful forces that demand expression in behavior or response of some kind. Thus the wish to kill or the desire for sexual expression may, because of strong repressive influences of a social or moral nature, "come to the surface" in the form of dreams, symbolic acts, neurotic symptoms, or adjustment mechanisms, such as sublimation, rationalization, and projection. As one can readily guess, the idea of psychological dynamics leads to *psychic determinism*, according to which the responses that result from unconscious drives are necessitated by the strength of the motivating conditions, thus leaving no room for freedom or self-determination. This part of the total theory is of particular significance for the principles of adjustment and mental hygiene because of the importance of self-discipline for the achievement and maintenance of adjustment.

These three principles of psychoanalysis are complemented by the theory of psychosexual development, the pleasure principle, the reality principle, and the idea of psychic formation or structure. All of these different parts of the total theory are fitted together into a coordinated whole. The *theory of psychosexual development* supposes different stages of sexuality, beginning in infancy and progressing through childhood and adolescence and dominated throughout by the factor of pleasure. If this development is normal and if the sexual urge (libido) is allowed adequate gratification, the person should remain free of conflicts, symptoms, or personality disturbances. If, in contrast, restrictive measures, originating in the environment or society, inhibit normal gratifications, some kind of distortion of personality or behavior will result.

These ideas can be understood better by studying the analytic interpretation of personality formation or *psychic structure* (Figure 3). The psychic structure has three parts: id, ego, and superego. The id is a personalized version of the unconscious; it is the hidden, primitive, pleasure-dominated, unmoral part of personality. The ego mediates between the id and reality; it is the conscious, knowing "I" which gradually emerges

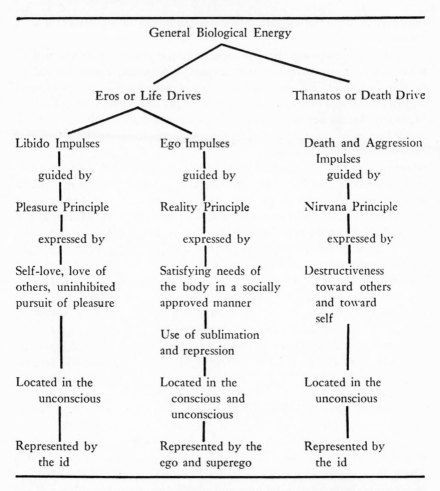

Fig. 3.   Schematic representation of some psychoanalytic concepts and their interrelations. (From Page, J. D. *Abnormal psychology*. New York: McGraw-Hill, 1947, p. 186. Used by permission of McGraw-Hill Book Company.

out of the conflict between the strivings of the id and the impositions of reality. The superego embodies the incorporated taboos, rules, laws, and proscriptions of culture and society; it is the "public conscience" incorporated within the structure of the personality. It is closely related to both the id on the one hand and reality on the other, acting to control strivings of the id through restrictions imposed by social or moral codes.

The connection between these concepts and the process of adjustment can be readily clarified. If, in the process of growing up, everything goes well, good adjustment is assured; if not, maladjustment results. In other words, if psychosexual development is normal and adequate, if pleasure does not become too dominating a force, if the ego achieves strength and security, if the id does not dominate the ego or the superego, if the relations between the ego and reality are adequate, if the superego does not become overdeveloped, and if need gratifications can be brought effectively into line with the demands of reality and of the superego, then the organism should remain relatively free of damaging conflicts, symptom formation, or personality disturbances. But let us suppose that the impulses of the id get out of hand. In that case the ego is weakened, relations with reality become impaired, and there is a strong likelihood of symptom formation or neurosis. Or, again, if the superego becomes overdeveloped, damaging guilt feelings and neurotic conflicts result, especially regarding sexual impulses and actions. Such guilt feelings and conflicts are almost certain to develop into personality disturbances.

Without going further into the many ramifications of this complex theory, let us ask ourselves what it means to the psychology of adjustment. Are its basic concepts and principles sound? Do they help us to understand the problems of adjustment more thoroughly? First of all, let us note that the classical psychoanalysis of the Freudian school has been partially abandoned or radically altered by many psychoanalysts themselves, including Carl Jung, Alfred Adler, Otto Rank, Karen Horney, and Erich Fromm (Mullahy, 1948). Their interpretations differ considerably from those of the Freudian group.

Here are the main criticisms of the classical school, made by one or another of these psychoanalysts: (1) the doctrine of the unconscious is difficult to substantiate scientifically; (2) there are too many gross generalizations based on restricted clinical experience, especially in the matter of symbolization and symptom formation; (3) the concept of infantile sexuality is purely inferential and based on clinical experience with adults rather than with children; (4) the unrestrained emphasis on sex and its role in the development of personality disorders is unwarranted; (5) normality is interpreted entirely in terms of abnormal behavior; (6) there is too little attention given to social determinants of personality and its disturbances; (7) the theory of psychic determinism is fatalistic and leaves no room for treatment that utilizes the patient's capacities for self-realization; (8) the emphasis on pleasure as the dominant motivating force is unrealistic and unwarranted; (9) the doctrine of psychic structure is purely conceptual and difficult to apply consistently; (10) there is little room in the total theory for the influence of either morality or religion in the achievement of adjustment and mental health.

The difficulties listed above are serious, and they limit the value of psychoanalytic doctrine for the psychology of adjustment. Still, as we have already intimated, parts of the theory are very useful, and some parts are indispensable. In our own interpretation of the adjustment process in succeeding pages, we shall take what is good in psychoanalytic theory and incorporate it with our interpretations; those elements that are unscientific or questionable we shall simply leave out.

A healthy antidote to the overstatements and unwarranted generalizations of psychoanalysis was the school of *behaviorism*, founded by John B. Watson, which also established a theoretical groundwork for the interpretation of adjustment. The contrast between these two viewpoints is extreme, and you may find it somewhat difficult to understand how both can be applied to the problem of adjustment. Behaviorism categorically denies every major doctrine of psychoanalysis and, in fact, most of the interpretations of classical psychology. Consciousness, mind, the unconscious, free will, morality, the soul—all cease to exist, as far as the behaviorist is concerned. There is no mind, and therefore there is no mental illness in the usual sense of the term. There is no unconscious, and therefore there can be no psychic determinism of the type posited by Freud. There is no consciousness and therefore no psychological freedom. It is obvious enough what these negations mean for the interpretation of adjustment and mental health.

According to behaviorism, all human responses fall into one simple category—behavior. There is no real difference between such divergent responses as walking, talking, thinking, "mental" conflict, frustration, visceral reactions, imagination, dreaming, and wanting. There are no innate responses (with the possible exception of reflexes) so that all responses are habitual, at least those that count in the adjustments of the organism. Personality is not a psychophysical entity, composed of mind and body or of mental and physical processes; it is rather an organized totality of habit responses acquired in the course of development, training, and learning. The organism begins life with an extremely simple repertoire of responses, and, through the mechanism of *conditioning*, it gradually acquires a wide range of responses by which it strives to meet the demands of its own nature or those imposed by the environment. In this view, then, adjustment is a process of adapting acquired behavior responses to the needs of the moment; maladjustment occurs when the habits formed are ill-suited to these requirements. Personality disturbances and maladjustment are simply a matter of bad habits. Habits are bad when they are inefficient, poorly formed, or not suited to the demands imposed on the organism. Thus the secret of effective living and good adjustment is proper conditioning from infancy. Everyone starts with the same equipment, but difficulties arise because of the inefficient application of methods of training.

In this doctrine, we have the opposite extreme in the interpretation of adjustment and personality. Where psychoanalysis is extremely subjective in its viewpoint, behaviorism is just as objective. For Freud the study of behavior is unimportant, and the study of psychic processes is of primary significance. For Watson, the only psychological reality is behavior and the study of psychic processes is a waste of time.

Watson's somewhat crude objectivism has been largely rejected by contemporary psychologists because it is so obviously unrealistic. However, there are contemporary viewpoints in psychology that still retain some of the essential qualities of behaviorism, such as the theories of Hebb, Skinner, and Snygg and Combs. Nevertheless, whatever a particular theory requires, the fact is that mental disease does exist, and there are numerous personality disturbances that cannot be interpreted in terms of inefficient learning connections or bad habits. No one has yet found a way successfully to dispense with such basic concepts as psychological needs, mental conflict, self-determination, feelings of guilt and inferiority, psychic trauma, and a host of other mentalistic concepts. The mind-body entity is a reality that has a way of forcing itself into the picture regardless of any theorizing.

However, the behavioristic emphasis led to a better understanding and interpretation of the role of environmental factors in the development of personality and its adjustments and to deeper appreciation of the significant part that learning plays in the process of adjustment. This emphasis also paved the way for the discovery of new methods and techniques for the better study of adjustment processes. Behaviorism promoted the idea that maladjustment consists of learned responses and that proper training is more important in human development than such "mystical" factors as psychic trauma, Oedipal relations, or castration anxiety. These attitudes of behaviorism were important in rescuing adjustment psychology and mental hygiene from the morass of confused thinking and terminology that had become a part of psychological theory.

There are other viewpoints of adjustment that could be described here, but for brevity we shall mention only one other type of interpretation, which we will call simply the *psychological viewpoint* of adjustment. Both behaviorism and psychoanalysis suffer from the limitation that they are theoretical rather than empirical interpretations of human personality. By "psychological" we mean a standpoint that is relatively free of theoretical preconceptions or special pleading, and that essays to study human nature empirically through methods of scientific investigation. In this view, personality is not conceived in terms demanded by theory but in terms of what it actually is or as it can be known through empirically devised methods and techniques. Mental disorder is not stubbornly interpreted as a faulty habit pattern, which it certainly is not, but simply as a kind of inadequate or abnormal response that exists in the psychological order.

From the psychological viewpoint, then, the study of adjustment and maladjustment requires that whatever scientific investigation has revealed about learning and conditioning, conflict and frustration, habit formation and personality development, or needs and emotions should be applied in a scientific manner. Contrast this attitude with the psychoanalytic appeal to infantile sexuality, the Oedipus situation, latent homosexuality, castration anxiety, or oral needs and you will see the difference between the highly theoretical and a scientific approach to human adjustment. We do not mean to deride such theoretical formulations since any one of them may be empirically valid. But from the standpoint of scientific psychology, it is better to take man as he is rather than as theory demands. In relating adjustment to the dynamics of personality, it is scientifically more correct to recognize the existence and influence of *all* motivating factors than to limit motivation to libido, the death instinct, or the feeling of inferiority.

It must be understood that any one of these ideas, as for example, the theory of inferiority, may be valid and distinctly useful when correctly interpreted and cautiously applied to clinical situations. In fact, many of the concepts of psychoanalysis can be incorporated with viewpoints and practices that are known to be empirically valid. It is certainly understandable that a child can be conditioned to inferiority or that unconscious incestuous relations with parents can be learned through faulty environmental conditions. But the validity of such interpretations should be tested by rigorous standards of investigation. We know that learning has much to do with the formation of personality and adjustment patterns; we do not know that all motivation is basically sexual or that every child passes through a narcissistic phase of development. In succeeding chapters we shall adhere to this empirical approach as closely as possible.

Methods of Investigating Adjustment Processes

An important aspect of the scientific approach that we have defined is its methodology; and we must frankly recognize that there are difficulties here not encountered in other fields of study. There are certain forms of adjustment, such as the academic and social or the vocational and marital, in which the gathering of data does not offer a serious problem. It is even possible to create experimental conditions by which one or another form of adjustment can be studied; but mental disorder and serious maladjustment do not lend themselves to the usual methods of science. Such processes can be observed and studied clinically, and this method has yielded a great deal of valuable data; but the experimental study of such problems is largely precluded by the nature of the problems themselves (Felix, 1952; Pasamanick, 1952; Weil, 1952).

The difficulties found in the study of adjustment are complicated by various factors that we should watch for. One may, for example, expect to encounter a great deal of *subjectivity* plus a priori reasoning and prejudice in the interpretation of adjustment problems. Such problems are deeply personal, and it is not easy to maintain a high level of objectivity in our thinking about them. Behavior symptoms, inadequacies of personality, and so on are likely to be interpreted in terms of our own feelings and prejudices rather than in terms of empirical data.

These biases are strongly supported by *uncritical attitudes*. In scientific investigation we must maintain a severely critical attitude toward theoretical interpretations or toward personal impressions and convictions that stand in the way of careful observation and logical thinking. The fact that a relative is in a mental hospital, or that divorce is contrary to our religious beliefs, or that homosexuality is socially repugnant cannot be allowed to affect our critical evaluation of abnormal behavior. We must learn to accept these phenomena and to understand them as special instances of maladjustment. There is no room for blame, censure, or moralization about such behavior.

In our study of these behavior phenomena let us be careful, too, of *unwarranted generalizations*. The fact that sexuality is prominent in some cases of neurosis does not mean that it is a primary factor in all. Nor can we argue conclusively that bad habits are the substance of maladjustment because we find them so often associated with poor adjustment. This kind of scientifically bad generalization is a constant companion of those formulations that seek to explain all behavior in terms of an oversimplified concept. Human nature and conduct do not readily fall into a pattern that is created in the image of a pet theory or belief.

There is one other thing that bears watching in the study of adjustment processes. That is the lavish and *uncritical use of such terms* as "cause," "effect," and "determinant." What exactly is meant by saying that parental rejection "causes" maladjustment, or that damage to the brain "causes" a psychosis? There are countless instances where these so-called causes do not produce the expected effects. We must be careful too of the jump from one order of reality to another. Brain damage or parental rejection, to use the same examples, may be only the *conditions* under which bad effects sometimes result. However important it may be, *a condition is not a cause*. Nor are so-called determinants to be interpreted always as causes. We know, for example, that broken homes are often determinants of juvenile delinquency, but that does not mean that broken homes cause delinquency. We can see that the whole question of the etiology (causes) of neurotic, psychotic, and other personality disturbances is bound up with the problem of the meaning of causality. Let us be careful therefore about the incautious use of such terms.

Methods of Observing Adjustment Processes

One may learn a great deal about adjustment by the simple expedient of closely observing the way in which people cope with their problems. Faced with the same difficulty or frustration, one person will make a headlong attack on the problem, a second will curse and swear, a third will sit down calmly to think it over, and a fourth will burst into tears. This kind of casual observation tells us something about the possible range of adjustive responses and about the effect of individual differences on adjustment. Discernible also is a link between the nature of the difficulty and the kind of response it calls for. Direct observations of this kind become scientific when we set up careful controls that tend to eliminate errors of judgment, subjectivity, or individual interpretation. With children, for example, we can easily arrange situations in which the nature and characteristics of social adjustment can be observed. In some instances, like marital adjustment, the situation cannot be manipulated, but other techniques can be brought into play for the study of such behavior.

A common adjunct to direct observation is *statistical analysis*. If we wish to examine the extent of maladjustment, for example, we study whatever statistics are available regarding the incidence of neurosis, psychosis, delinquency, etc. If we are interested in the magnitude of the marital problem, then the number of divorces, broken homes, or desertions can be used as an index. These statistical analyses are often complemented by empirical studies of adjustment that use the techniques of the interview, the rating scale, and the personality questionnaire to elicit whatever information is necessary for statistical treatment. These methods are common to all scientific observation of this kind and are not peculiar to the study of adjustment.

More closely identified with the psychology of adjustment is the *clinical method*. In the application of this method we are dealing almost entirely with instances of maladjustment since the normal person is not likely to become involved in clinical study. Much of our knowledge of human adjustment has been derived from clinical observations. By studying the manner in which patients react to the stresses and strains of adult living and by analyzing the nature of symptomatic behavior and its relation to personality determinants, we learn some very important facts about human adjustment. After all, the psychology of adjustment owes its very existence to the fact that there are so many persons who are poorly ad-justed. We may remind ourselves here that maladjustive responses, like those observed in the clinic, are merely peculiar or bizarre ways of ad-justing and that, therefore, the study of these maladjustments will lead directly to a better understanding of adjustment in all its different phases.

The clinical approach to the understanding of adjustment relies on the careful study, classification, and interpretation of symptoms or symp-tomatic behavior and the relations between these indicators of maladjust-ment and the causes or conditions that contributed to their development. An important adjunct to this approach, therefore, is *personality study* since, as we have already seen, all adjustments and maladjustments are directly related to personality make-up. There are many avenues to the analysis of personality, the most prominent being the *case history technique* by which the clinician brings together in considerable detail the background of the client (Bucklew, 1960). This history brings to light many factors that contributed to the client's pattern of adjustment, including parent-child relations, early schooling, sibling rivalries, marital strife, parental discipline, or economic deprivation.

The analysis of personality can be helped also by the use of *person-ality questionnaires, rating scales,* and *inventories,* along with the various *projective devices* such as the Rorschach Psychodiagnostic Test, the Thematic Apperception Test, and the Sentence Completion Test. All these instruments are designed for the appraisal of individual personality or adjustment level; and the data yielded by these appraisals can shed considerable light on the problems of personality and adjustment.

What about the *experimental approach?* Can this method be used at all for the study of maladjustment? We have already intimated that the application of experimental design to the study of human adjustment is limited because we cannot manipulate variables that involve human suffering (Hoch, 1952; Keys, 1952). We cannot, in other words, experi-mentally produce neurotic or psychotic symptoms in human subjects in order to test various hypotheses regarding the development of these re-sponses. This has been done in some instances, but the limitations are obvious (Lloyd & Heinstein, 1952). Some advances have been made along these lines by the use of animal subjects. Different investigators have produced what are called "experimental neuroses" in animals with results that have been useful to the better understanding of similar reactions in human subjects. These results must be used with considerable caution because of the gap between human and animal reactions. With animals we can only observe overt behavior; whereas, in the case of human sub-jects, it is usually the internal condition that is most significant from the standpoint of normality or adjustment.

Studies of animal behavior are particularly helpful in clarifying the relation between overt "neurotic" behavior and certain conditions that seem to favor its development, a relation that is of considerable importance in the interpretation of adjustment processes (Gantt, 1944; Masserman, 1943). There are other studies of an experimental nature concerning such factors as frustration and conflict that are also important to the analysis of adjustment. The results of these investigations have helped to clarify a number of problems in this area, and, in later chapters dealing with these problems, we shall have occasion to refer to these studies. When we bring all of these methods and findings together, we can see that the scientific study of adjustment has made considerable progress (Sarbin, 1961).

QUESTIONS AND PROJECTS FOR FURTHER STUDY

1. On the basis of your own experience, and without reference to any text, formulate ten basic rules for effective living.
2. Write a short essay on the importance of adjustment and mental health to academic performance.
3. Compare the concept of psychological adjustment with biological adaptation and explain the survival value of both.
4. Make a survey of the mental health facilities in your community.
5. Write a brief essay on the difference between clinical psychology and psychiatry.

SELECTED COLLATERAL READINGS

ANDREWS, M. F. (Ed.) *Creativity and psychological health.* Syracuse, N.Y.: Syracuse University Press, 1961.

DEUTSCH, A. *The mentally ill in America.* (2d ed., rev.) New York: Columbia University Press, 1949.

DYSINGER, R. H. (Ed.) *Mental health in the United States.* Ann. Amer. Acad. Pol. Soc. Sci., 1953, **286.**

FEIN, R. *Economics of mental illness.* New York: Basic Books, 1958.

FELIX, R. H., *et al.* *Mental health and social welfare.* New York: Columbia University Press, 1961.

GANTT, W. A. H. *Experimental basis for neurotic behavior.* New York: Harper & Row, 1944.

GURIN, G., VEROFF, J., & FELD, SHEILA. *Americans view their mental health.* New York: Basic Books, 1960.

HUNT, J. MCV. (Ed.) *Personality and the behavior disorders.* 2 vols. New York: Ronald, 1944. Vol. I, Parts II, III.

RIDENOUR, NINA. *Mental health in the United States: a fifty year history.* Cambridge, Mass.: Harvard University Press, 1961.

ROSE, A. M. (Ed.) *Mental health and mental disorder: a sociological approach.* New York: Norton, 1955.

SROLE, L., *et al. Mental health in the metropolis: the midtown Manhattan study.* (Vol. I.) New York: McGraw-Hill, 1962.

WHITE, R. W. *Lives in progress.* New York: Holt, Rinehart and Winston, 1952.

2

Some Basic Concepts
and Criteria
of Adjustment
and Mental Health

Adjustment is a word of many meanings, and it sometimes means different things to different people. This is because it is complicated and because sometimes it is good and sometimes it is bad. When it is bad, we usually call it maladjustment. Good or bad, it has many relations to mental health. We must try to decipher its meanings, and then decide what yardsticks we can use to test these qualities in any single personality.

THE CONCEPT OF ADJUSTMENT

Meanings of Adjustment

Adjustment is not an easy term to define, partly because it has many meanings, partly because the criteria for evaluating adjustment have not been clearly defined, and partly because adjustment and its contrary, maladjustment, have common boundaries which tends to blur the distinctions between them. Yet, if we are to aviod confusion and misunderstanding, we must clarify the basic concepts of our area of study. If we do not know what adjustment is, we are not going to get very far with determining its criteria, conditions, or principles. Similarly, we want to be sure that related terms, such as normality, abnormality, and maladjustment are clearly understood. As Tyson remarks (1951, p. 9):

> One of the first steps in solving a problem is to achieve a satisfactory definition of its nature, i.e., directions become clear once a clear perception of basic issues is achieved. In the field of mental hygiene, there has been some confusion concerning exactly what constitutes good personality adjustment. Laymen look to mental hygiene for practical

answers to the question of how to achieve mental health, success and happiness. In contrast, psychiatric conceptions of healthy adjustment stress deeper emotional factors on subconscious levels with success and happiness being regarded as symptoms rather than basic factors.

To illustrate these points, let us consider two cases that came to the writer's attention. Both youngsters (Peter and Helen) were about the same age and from much the same social and economic background. But Peter was a happy, carefree young man, who got along well in school, was liked by others, had a deep interest in sports and hobbies, was proud of his family, and had already decided what he wanted to be when he finished high school and entered college. Helen was just the opposite. She was a moody youngster, hostile toward her parents, jealous of other children in the family, uninterested in schoolwork or social activities, and almost without friends. She had twice run away from home and was showing definite signs of failure in school. Helen is emotionally disturbed, poorly adjusted to almost every aspect of her environment, and generally maladjusted. Peter, of course, would be described as a well-adjusted adolescent who will probably sail into adulthood with a minimum of conflict, frustration, or unhappiness.

What is the difference between these two young people? And why do we say that one is well adjusted and the other is maladjusted? Is it the relation between them and their environments? Is it the state of their own personal feelings? Is it the range or depth of their interests and goals? We could say very simply that adjustment is defined by how well you get along with yourself and with others—not a bad notion. But there are difficulties in this simple concept of adjustment. Strangely enough, the poor way in which Helen responded to circumstances and people must be regarded as adjustment. Hostilities, jealousies, moodiness, and so on were her way of coping with different situations. While these are not desirable ways of reacting to situations, they are nevertheless adjustive in quality. As one author says,

> From the biological standpoint all modes of response—direct or indirect, adequate or inadequate—are adjustive in aim. They represent the best of which the organism is capable under the total existing conditions. Presumably an attempt is being made in every case to preserve integrated functioning by the restoration of equilibrium (Rosenzweig, 1944, p. 384).

This is an important lesson to learn in the study of human adjustment. It is not the *kind* of behavior that determines whether we are dealing with adjustment processes, but *the way in which behavior is used*. Whether internal demands or environmental stresses are met by prayer, delinquency, neurotic symptoms, psychotic episodes, laughter, joy, or hostility, the concept of adjustment is applicable as long as the response serves to reduce or to mitigate the demands made on a person. When such responses are inefficient, detrimental to personal well-being, or pathological, they are designated as *maladjustive*.

Adjustment as Adaptation.   Historically, the meaning of the term "adjustment" has gone through many changes. Because of the strong influence of evolutionary thinking on psychology, adjustment was at first likened to adaptation, a process by which simpler organisms conform to the demands of the environment. While there are similarities between the two ideas, the complex processes of adjustment cannot be fitted into the simpler concept of biological adaptation. Human personality and environment are too complex to be explained in terms of adaptation (Hahn, 1962). Erich Fromm, in his provocative book, *Escape from freedom* (1941, pp. 15–16), offers an interesting and useful concept of adaptation that comes close to the idea of adjustment. Fromm distinguishes what he calls *static* from *dynamic* adaptation. He uses the term static adaptation to refer to relatively simple change in habit, as when a person moves from one country to another, and dynamic adaptation to refer to a situation where a person accepts things even when they are painful, as when a boy submits to the commands of a strict and threatening father. Fromm interprets neurosis as an example of dynamic adaptation. Interpreted in this way, as a dynamic response, adaptation is equivalent to adjustment.

Similarly, the notion of adjustment as self-maintenance or survival is applicable to physical well-being but not to adjustment in the psychological sense. Nor can we accept such oversimplified definitions as "satisfactory relation of an organism to its environment," or "adaptation to the demands of reality." While a satisfactory relation to one's environment is part of adjustment, who can tell exactly what satisfactory means in this connection? Similarly, the idea of adaptation to the demands of reality is too ambiguous for precise definition.

The idea of adaptation suggests conformity, and it is often emphasized that adjustment requires conformity to some norm so that the concept becomes bound up with the problem of normality. We shall deal with normality later, but now we wish to suggest that the interpretation of adjustment as conformity to social, political, or moral norms involves too many complications to be very useful. We recognize that there are strong pressures against deviating from moral, social, or legal restrictions, and we should note that between the norms or standards set by society and the process of adjustment there are certain set relations. However, we must not allow adjustment to become confused with conformity.

Adjustment and Individuality.   In defining adjustment we cannot ignore individual differences. Brilliant children or geniuses do not correspond to the "normal" pattern either in capacity or in behavior; yet we cannot label them as being maladjusted. Quite often social and cultural standards are too rigid for intelligent conformity. In some instances, like the law governing divorces or sterilization in the United States, it is not only a privilege but a responsibility for some members of the community to reject them. This failure to conform cannot be regarded as maladjustive.

Also, group standards vary considerably from one culture to another, as the data of cultural anthropology show very clearly. In the area of sexual adjustment, for example, social taboos and practices are so different in different societies that the concepts of good sexual adjustment acceptable to Western culture would be wholly unacceptable in other societies. This extensive variation in concepts of what is right or wrong, acceptable or unacceptable, puts a decided crimp in any effort to force particular criteria into the procrustean bed of cultural conformity. The following case illustrates the limits of conformity.

> Robert was an extremely shy, retiring young man of twenty-five when he first came for counseling. He had completed two years of college and was employed as a bookkeeper in a small firm. He was rated as a "good" employee by his supervisor. He adhered strictly to his duties and never violated company rules, but he lacked initiative and drive. Investigation showed that Robert was actually a bright young man who had potentialities for achievement far beyond the work he was doing. But his case history also showed that Robert had a domineering, punitive, and perfectionistic father who ruled Robert and his brothers with an iron hand. To his rules no exceptions were allowed. Contrary views and opinions were never tolerated. As a dutiful son, Robert had conformed to the rules laid down by his father, so that every issue, from the choice of clothes to the choice of college, was decided for him. He never had any opportunity to develop initiative, ambition, or independence of judgment and decision. Today Robert is a poorly adjusted person, primarily because the requirements of conformity to imperious parental rules made it impossible for him to achieve individuality of adjustment.

Adjustment as Mastery.   Good adjustment seems to imply some degree of mastery, which suggests the ability to plan and to organize personal responses in such a way that conflicts, difficulties, and frustrations tend to disappear in the wake of efficient or mastering conduct. It includes *mastery of self*, so that drives, emotions, and habits are brought under control. It also means *mastery of the environment*—the ability to cope with reality in an adequate and healthy manner and to manipulate the environment of people and events in a way that leads to adjustment. As one writer says, "If the need for mastery is completely or for the most part frustrated over a long period of time, the individual will inevitably become maladjusted" (Carroll, 1951, p. 116).

This idea is certainly useful, but it fails to take into account individual limitations. Most persons do not possess the ability that mastery requires. Leaders, geniuses, and above-average persons may be expected to exhibit considerable mastery, but even here there are failures. This reminds us that each person has his *own level of adjustment*, determined by innate capacities, acquired dispositions, and experience. Thus, many soldiers "cracked up" under the stresses of warfare; they became victims of battle fatigue or neuropsychiatric disabilities. Yet these same men, confronted with the much less rigorous trials and demands of ordinary civilian life, may never have developed disabling symptoms. Failure to adjust is often determined by the relation between the adjustment capacity of people and the nature of the demands made on them.

Definition of Adjustment.   From the strictly psychological point of view, adjustment means many things, such as need gratification, skill in dealing with frustrations and conflicts, peace of mind, or even the formation of symptoms. It means learning how to get along successfully with other people and how to meet the demands of the job. Tyson lists such things as adaptability, capacity for affection, balanced life, ability to profit from experience, frustration tolerance, humor, moderation, objectivity, and many others (Tyson, 1951, pp. 9–14). We will encounter other such qualities in our discussion of the criteria of adjustment and mental health. Obviously, this multiphasic character of the adjustive process makes it difficult to formulate a concise definition. We are also handicapped by the fact that adjustment in itself is neither good nor bad; it is simply an organism's individual or peculiar way of reacting to inner demands or external situations. In some instances this reaction is efficient, wholesome, or satisfying, and in others it is disabling, ineffective, or even pathological.

Since adjustment in itself is neither good nor bad, we can define it most simply as *a process, involving both mental and behavioral responses, by which an individual strives to cope with inner needs, tensions, frustrations, and conflicts and to bring harmony between these inner demands and those imposed upon him by the world in which he lives.* Taken in this sense, the majority of responses fit into the concept of adjustment.

Concept of "Good" Adjustment

With the general definition of adjustment, made above, in mind, it will be helpful to ask, What is the well-adjusted person like? What, in other words, is good adjustment? The well-adjusted person is one whose responses are mature, efficient, satisfying, and healthy. In contrast, for example, the neurotic person is characteristically inefficient and never manages to complete tasks that a well-adjusted person will complete in half the time. The emotionally disturbed student is notoriously inefficient in completing assignments. The term "healthy" implies that the response is wholesome, that is, suited to man's nature, to his relations with others, and to his responsibilities. Wholesomeness is one of the most characteristic features of good adjustment.

In brief, then, the well-adjusted person can, within the limitations of his own personality, react effectively to different situations and resolve conflicts, frustrations, and problems without the use of symptomatic behavior. He is, therefore, relatively free of such disabling symptoms as chronic anxiety, scruples, obsessions, indecision, or psychosomatic disturbances. He creates a world of interpersonal relations and satisfactions that contribute to the continuous growth of personality.

Adjustment Is Relative

Adjustment, as we have defined it, is relative in character since there is no such thing as a perfectly adjusted person. It must be judged or evaluated in terms of a person's capacity to change and to cope with demands that are encountered, and these capacities vary with personality and with developmental level. As one writer says (Anderson, 1949, p. 429),

> Good adjustment cannot be defined once and for all in any simple or complete fashion. It must be defined in terms of meeting the problem appropriate to the level of development—what is good adjustment at one age level may be poor adjustment at another. Viewed in this way, *growing up* is a process of meeting stresses and strains in succession and thus building the capacity to meet the problems of the next higher level.

Adjustment is relative also because it varies to some extent with social and cultural norms and because of individual variations in behavior. Even the well-adjusted person occasionally finds himself face to face with situations or problems that are beyond the scope of his adjustive ability. Then, too, good adjustment is not necessarily pervasive. The student sitting next to you may be well adjusted emotionally and socially but swamped by academic difficulties. Many husbands handle their jobs well but find it impossible to live happily with their family. However, maladjustment is a creeping paralysis that tends to spread from one part of the personality to another—a point to keep in mind.

Adjustment versus Morality

The use of such words as "good" and "bad" places the adjustment psychologist in the position of making value judgments regarding behavior, which no scientist is supposed to do. Yet it can be demonstrated very easily that value judgments are not peculiar to morality or to ethical science. Everyone speaks of good and bad health, or good and bad weather, without being concerned about moral implications. The objection, however, serves a point. We must not regard maladjustive behavior as morally bad, and, by the same rule, the well-adjusted person is not necessarily a paragon of virtue. Adjustment cannot be equated with virtue, nor maladjustment with sin (Mowrer, 1960). However, it often happens that immorality is at the root of maladjustment, and certainly wholesome adjustment in the widest sense must include moral soundness.

When, however, adjustment is characterized as good the reference is to psychological rather than moral well-being. Just as physical health is desirable, so mental health is good for people, and it is just as obvious that mental instability, neurotic symptoms, or psychotic episodes are psychologically bad. It is here that the distinction between morality and adjustment becomes clear. Sin is primarily a moral evil and only secondarily maladjustive, whereas maladjustment is primarily a psychological evil and is morally bad only when the response is moral as well as psychological. Let us keep this distinction in mind at all times (Schneiders, 1954).

CRITERIA OF ADJUSTMENT

Criteria and the Nature of Adjustment

We have seen that adjustment has many different qualities, each one of which can be developed into a *criterion* by which adjustment can be more clearly evaluated. As Levine, quoted by King puts it, definitions of normality in terms of the average "must be supplemented by definitions of normality in terms of health, happiness, good functioning, and maturity. This general fact calls for specific amplification. It calls for a detailed set of criteria of psychiatric health and good functioning" (King, 1951, p. 4). Erich Fromm goes one step further and insists that the concept of mental health requires universal criteria. He says (1955, p. 12): "To speak of a 'sane society' implies a premise different from sociological relativism. It makes sense only if we assume that there can be a society which is *not* sane, and this assumption, in turn, implies that there are universal criteria for mental health which are valid for the human race as such, and according to which the state of each society can be judged. This position of *normative humanism* is based on a few fundamental premises." A definition of such criteria will lead to a better understanding of other problems of adjustment that we will encounter later and will make it easier to develop the basic concepts and principles of mental hygiene and treatment that are also presented later in this book. In this analysis, we must not overlook the warnings of some writers who feel that ideals of adjustment may lead to excessive conformity or mediocrity (White, 1952; Lindner, 1952). Many of these writers seriously question the basic rationale of adjustment psychology.

Criteria of adjustment and mental health may be defined as the standards, norms, or yardsticks used to determine the quality as well as the degree of personal or social adjustment for any individual (Jahoda, 1958). By applying these criteria in a clinical situation, or when trying to help someone to a better understanding of his problems, we are able to get a clear picture of his adjustment level. They are, therefore, *practical guideposts* that can be used in both evaluation and treatment. When we know what the standards of good adjustment and mental health are, we are in a better position to direct our efforts intelligently and effectively when helping others. Also, they can be used as primary sources for the development of principles of mental hygiene and counseling. All such principles have been derived from a careful study of the nature and criteria of adjustment and mental health. In this way, science and clinical application join hands in furthering the knowledge and the effective treatment of adjustment problems.

General versus Specific Criteria of Adjustment

Is there a general norm or standard that we can use to evaluate man's behavior and thus determine whether it is adjustive or maladjustive? We have already seen that good adjustment is primarily conformity to a psychological norm rather than a moral one, and this psychological norm may be regarded as a general criterion of adjustment. This means simply that adjustive responses can be evaluated as wholesome or unwholesome by comparing them with what man should do in terms of his natural make-up and his relations to others. Thus we can say that delinquency, hostility, insomnia, or masturbation are all maladjustive since each one violates some aspect of the psychological criterion.

However, if we are ever to reach a point where we can evaluate less obvious examples of behavior, we must make explicit the implications contained in the general criterion. This we can do most effectively by defining a number of specific criteria that apply to adjustive behavior. For example, it is easier to see why insight is important to adjustment when we find out how it is related to psychological well-being. Insight is one of our criteria.

There are many criteria, similar to insight, and all of them will be found in a number of different sources (Tyson, 1951, pp. 9–16; Bernard, 1951, p. 18; Symonds, 1949, pp. 387–398; Thorne, 1958). Because there are so many of them, we have organized them into three categories: (1) criteria affecting self, (2) criteria affecting others, and (3) criteria for personal growth.

Criteria Affecting Self.   Let us begin with *insight* and *self-knowledge*. What is the significance of this criterion? All it means is that we must know our own capabilities and limitations if we are to deal effectively with adjustment problems. Self-knowledge requires an intelligent inventory of personal assets and liabilities. By knowing what our weaknesses are we can at least try to minimize or eliminate their influence on our lives, and by knowing what our strong points are we are in a better position to exploit them for personal growth. Personal improvement begins with the courage and determination *to face the truth about one's self.*

Self-insight also means an awareness of one's basic motivations and the effects that these motivations may have on thinking and conduct. Self-insight can make us aware that we often blame others for our own mistakes and weaknesses or that aches and pains are often an excuse for failing to meet responsibilities. Lacking such insight, people tend to find fault with others, to rationalize inadequate behavior, or to develop defensive mechanisms, all of which are inimical to good adjustment. In one study of seventy-nine male college students, for example, it was found that those who had poor insight into their own level of adjustment were more likely to be maladjusted than those who possessed good insight (Calvin & Holtzman, 1953). A note of caution: self-knowledge does not mean morbid introspection. The chronically introspective person is no more adjusted than the one who is totally lacking in self-knowledge.

Self-knowledge can lead to *objectivity* and eventually to *self-acceptance*, two additional qualities by which adjustment can be evaluated. As Allport says very succinctly, "Integration, for the neurotic or for the normal person, requires self-objectification. That is to say, it requires insight, a knowledge of one's values, a clear picture of one's assets and liabilities. Psychotherapy and religion agree on this point" (Allport, 1950, p. 95). This knowledge and objectivity are direct opposites of the subjectivity that is so characteristic of disturbed or maladjusted persons.

Personal limitations, feelings of inferiority, and similar handicaps can be looked at objectively and their damaging effects minimized by this frank appraisal. Failure to do so will cause a person to become a victim of his own limitations (Waldschmidt, 1960).

Objectivity is an important step to self-acceptance, a quality of adjustment that is regarded as essential for personal growth (Taylor & Combs, 1952; Sheerer, 1949; Zimmer, 1954). Self-acceptance is the opposite of self-alienation and the degrading of one's self often found in neurotics. It does not mean condonement of one's weaknesses which would actually hinder adjustment, but it does mean that feelings of worthlessness, failure, or despair are contrary to personal adjustment. To accept one's self is really the first step toward self-improvement. No well-integrated life is possible, says Fosdick (1943, p. 53),

> without an initial act of self-acceptance, as though to say: I, John Smith, hereby accept myself, with my inherited endowments and handicaps and with the elements in my environment that I cannot alter or control, and, so accepting myself as my stint, I will now see what I can do with *this* John Smith. When Margaret Fuller said, "I accept the universe," Carlyle's retort was "Gad! she'd better!" Accepting the universe, however, is for many people a simple matter compared with the far more intimate act of accepting themselves.

A third criterion of good adjustment is *self-control*, by which we mean the personal regulation of impulses, thoughts, habits, emotions, and behavior in terms of self-imposed principles or of requirements imposed by society. Thus compulsive, hysterical, or obsessive individuals, or those who are victims of worry, scruples, temper tantrums, or nervous habits, find it difficult or impossible to cope successfully with everyday tasks and problems. Magner says pointedly (1944, p. 53): "Emphasis must be placed on *self*-discipline, for it is only on this basis that a person can live *maturely and creatively*." And King (1951, p. 22) echoes the same idea when he states that "A characteristic of the emotionally mature individual is the possession of a sense of discipline which is very little dependent upon coercion."

Self-control is basic to *personal integration*, which is one of the most significant qualities of the well-adjusted person and one of the best yardsticks for determining adjustment level. It refers to the organization of the many different elements of personality into a closely knit and efficiently functioning totality. Integration precludes the emotionally disruptive conflicts that disturb the neurotic patient and the autonomous functions of the hysterical person. It insures a basic harmony of striving and of conduct, of thoughts, feelings, and impulses that make possible the resolution of conflict and of frustrations without the necessity of developing defense mechanisms or symptomatic behavior. As Allport says, "Psychology's chief contribution to mental health is the concept of integration, a term less Biblical, but meaning much the same as St. James's 'single-mindedness.' Integration means the forging of approximate mental unity out of discordant impulses and aspirations" (Allport, 1950, p. 92; also May, 1953a).

In the development of control and integration, the formation of *worthwhile habits* is an important feature since a great many of our day-to-day adjustments are effected through habitual behavior, and it is not uncommon for good adjustment to be impaired by inefficient or faulty habit systems. Habits are particularly important to both physical and mental efficiency, and efficiency itself is necessary to adjustment. We see this principle exemplified in work situations, in the home, in moral conduct, and in the classroom. Conversely, habits of laziness, indecision, tardiness, etc., preclude good adjustment. As Bernard says (1951, p. 80): "Mental hygiene has been defined as a way of life; and the manner of one's life is in no small way determined by the habits which have been formed. If man is to acquire control over his life that is fundamental to mental health, he must guide the formation and re-formation of the habits that constitute so large a part of his daily living." We might note in passing that the possession of good habits is related to the acquisition of virtues, which are themselves *habits of mind* that can be very important to mental health. Patience, charity, forbearance, courage, and integrity are typical of such virtues. Habits and virtues go hand in hand in promoting adjustment.

The relation between habits and adjustment makes it important to recognize another criterion, which may be defined as *adaptability* or the capacity for change. Adjustment is a *dynamic process*, and therefore some elasticity or resilience is necessary to keep pace with constantly changing conditions. Our emphasis on the importance of habits should not be interpreted to mean that rigidity of habit is not often detrimental to good adjustment. Such habits as cleanliness, good speech, neatness, punctuality, logical thinking, or charity are not likely to require much modification, whereas others *may have to be changed entirely* in order to meet changing demands.

For example, in adulthood the dependence of childhood must be replaced by independence, and when one loses or changes a job, the old way of doing things may have to be radically altered. Many marriages fail from the outset because of the reluctance of one or both of the partners to give up old response patterns and adopt new ones to fit the new situation. As we have indicated several times, adjustment is a dynamic process requiring almost constant change and adaptation, and therefore the more fixed responses are, the more difficult it is to meet changing demands. This fact explains the devastating effects on personality of old-age retirement. Persons so affected often find it impossible to adjust to the pattern of behavior that retirement requires.

The stress of daily living, with its problems, conflicts, and demands, can be softened to a great extent by a *healthy sense of humor*, which is therefore a criterion of healthy-mindedness. It is interesting to note how closely humor and happiness, and lack of humor and lack of happiness are correlated. As everyone knows, the emotionally distraught person, the neurotic, and the psychotic are characteristically deficient in humor, and they are generally unhappy people. For some persons, reality is threatening, hostile, and even overpowering, so there is little room for joy and laughter. Their prevailing mood is sadness, melancholy, timidity, anxiety, or chronic worry. On the contrary, the well-adjusted person has a zest for living, and while life has many serious aspects there is room also for joy and humor (Allport, 1950, pp. 92–93).

Criteria Affecting Others.   Some of the criteria by which we evaluate adjustment bear directly on man's relationships to other people, one of the foremost being a *sense of responsibility*. The well-adjusted person, while enjoying a zest for living and being able to appreciate the less serious aspects of life, nevertheless accepts his responsibilities. The father who fails to provide for his children, the student who neglects his studies, or the employee who is habitually late for work is certainly not reacting adjustively. The irresponsible adult is immature and childish in his attitudes toward what is expected of him, and this itself is a sign of inadequate adjustment. Responsibility is an essential part of *maturity* and is also essential to adjustment (Katzenelbogen, 1950).

In Chapter 3 we shall deal at considerable length with the quality of maturity, but it is clear to everyone that *maturity of response* is an essential criterion of effective adjustment (Cameron & Magaret, 1951; Warters, 1949; Symonds, 1949, pp. 385–386). Maturity implies adequate development of basic structures, capacities, and needs, acceptance of responsibility, and growth of personality toward a well-ordered, balanced, and satisfying adult life. Good adjustment requires maturity in every department of human conduct, including the emotional, social, moral, and religious, and, to the extent that there is failure or deficiency in any one of these areas, maladjustment is likely to occur. It does not require any great amount of reflection to see how these different maturities will affect our relationships to others (Saul, 1960; Barrett, 1962).

Speaking of social relations, good adjustment requires that we be able to get along with other people, which is the essence of social adjustment. In other words, *social consciousness* is a basic criterion of adequate adjustment. To get along with other people means the development of healthy, friendly relationships, the enjoyment of companionship, respect for the rights, opinions, and personalities of others, and especially a high regard for the personal integrity and worth of our fellow man.

Social consciousness requires also a sincere interest and even participation in the experiences, hopes, ambitions, disappointments, and failures of those with whom we live. We cannot afford to be merely passive spectators in the daily drama of social life; we must take an active interest in the lives of others. We must develop within ourselves the virtues of sympathy, of compassion, and of sincere altruism.

Criteria for Personal Growth. Many of the qualities of good adjustment have specific implications for personal growth. This idea is embodied in the criterion of *self-development which means the continuous growth of personality toward the goals of maturity and personal achievement.* Each step in the process of growth from infancy to adulthood should be a definite advance toward greater maturity of thought, emotions, attitudes, and conduct. Fixation at any level is contrary to adequate adjustment, as we see in nail-biting, thumb sucking, bed wetting, temper tantrums, or inordinate cravings for affection and attention. Self-development is in essence the gradual realization of maturity.

The growth of personality is furthered by *a wide range of interests in both work and play*. It is difficult to adjust well to the demands of work that is uninteresting or boring. Before long there is distaste and then revulsion. Moreover, our vocations have a way of changing, which requires a range of interests if we are to derive continued satisfaction from work. These vocational interests and changes are complemented by avocational or play interests, which can contribute greatly to working out satisfactory adjustments. Thus many housewives have found their reading and social interests of great value in filling hours that otherwise would have been wasted in frustration or self-pity. And everyone has discovered the value of play in the reduction of tension, boredom, and unhappiness. Healthy interests lead to healthy adjustment.

These vocational and avocational activities must also provide *satisfying experiences*. The chances are, of course, that where there is interest there will be satisfaction also, but interest is not the sole determinant since personal achievement, ambition, the nature of the activity, and the absence of frustration will also determine satisfaction. As one writer says (Magner, 1944, pp. 58–59):

> In most instances, the reason for an unmanageable imagination and for nervous hysteria is to be found, at least partially, in the failure to

develop positive outlooks through creative mental activity and intellectual interests. A person who is interested in the world of affairs, of books, of hobbies, and *above all in his own work*, is not likely to become the prey of every passing fancy, worry, or phantasm. A person with a well-stocked mind will not find it difficult to drive out mental weeds and cockles. . . . Persons who can coordinate their activities in line with their special work, and take their supreme interest and pleasure in their work, have learned the inner secret of this development.

Personal growth is dependent also on an *adequate scale of values* and *well-defined goals,* criteria by which one can always evaluate adjustment. By a scale of values or philosophy of life we mean simply the set of ideas, truths, beliefs, and principles that guide a person in his thinking, in his attitudes and relations to himself and others, in his perspective regarding reality, and in his social, moral, and religious behavior (Soddy, 1962). It is this set of values that will determine whether reality is threatening, hostile, overwhelming, or not worth trying to adjust to. Adjustment requires the effective handling of problems and stresses that occur in our daily lives, and the solution of problems will be determined by the values that we can bring to bear on the situation. We often hear of people being "mixed up" and therefore emotionally disturbed or unhappy. Such persons are not sure of what is good or bad, right or wrong, worthwhile or worthless. They lack the knowledge, values, or principles that would enable them to reduce the indecision, the vacillation, or the conflict that is so emotionally disturbing. King emphasizes the point that the ability to resolve conflicts and abide by long-term values is necessary to emotional maturity (King, 1951, pp. 80–81).

In the process of maturing, the development of a value system will include the formation of *intermediate* as well as life-long goals (Smith, 1961), the nucleus around which integration and adjustive behavior can be centered. The person with well-defined goals acts with direction and purpose and is seldom troubled by aimlessness, boredom, or lack of interest and incentive. In one study of the effects of goal attainment among college students, it was found that goal direction was associated with increased confidence, improvement of self-esteem, and renewed striving. The authors suggest that a general effect of goal attainment is reduction of tension (Child & Whiting, 1949).

As a final criterion by which to evaluate adjustment, we should consider briefly *attitudes toward reality.* Good adjustment requires a sound, realistic attitude that enables a person to accept reality as it is rather than in terms of what his wishes, beliefs, or feelings determine it to be. This applies to temporal as well as to spatial aspects of reality. There are persons who live in a dream world of past events, who cherish memories of their childhood, and for whom the present is an ugly reality and the future a frightening possibility. There are others who, through the mechanism of amnesia, blot out the past; there are also those who have no regard for the future. Adolf Meyer argued that hindsight, or the capacity to *use* the past rather than merely suffer from it, is necessary to adjustment, that insight should be used to cope with present realities, and that creative opportunities can be realized through a healthy foresight. Healthy attitudes toward the past, the present, and the future are of profound importance to healthy adjustment.

To the extent that these criteria are fulfilled, the end result is likely to be a healthy and well-adjusted personality *free of the disabling responses and symptoms* that characterize the inadequate, maladjusted, or neurotic personality. The presence of these negative signs is also a criterion for evaluating adjustment level. Maladjustment has a way of expressing itself noticeably in overt responses as well as in mental symptoms, and therefore the absence of such responses can be used as an index of adequate adjustment. This criterion is not absolute, but it is a good rule of thumb for the quick evaluation of adjustment level.

CONCEPT OF MENTAL HEALTH

What Mental Health Means

There is an obvious relation between the concepts of adjustment and mental health, but it is not easily defined. Certainly, mental health is a necessary condition of good adjustment, and vice versa, when a person is mentally healthy there is little likelihood of serious maladjustment. We can see, then, that *mental health is the key to wholesome adjustment* (Scott, 1961; Nunnally, 1961; Smith, 1961).

The two concepts, however, are not synonymous, any more than the psychology of adjustment is identical with mental hygiene. For one thing, the term "adjustment" is broader in scope. When we refer to academic, vocational, or marital adjustment we are not thinking in mental health terms. A person may be vocationally maladjusted even though he is mentally sound. However, if vocational difficulties lead to chronic frustration, unhappiness, resentment, or delusions of persecution, then there is a mental health problem. A typical case is that of Harold, who decided to become a teacher. His father, however, had planned for Harold to enter the real estate business that he owned. Rather than disappoint his father, Harold took a business course instead of one that would prepare him for teaching. All through college, the young man disliked his subjects and built up a deep resentment toward them. This resentment was transferred (unconsciously) to the father, so that in time the emotional wedge between Harold and his parent continued to expand, and Harold became a bitter, disillusioned, and hostile person.

Here we have a clear instance of the link between maladjustment and mental ill health. Reactions like bitterness, envy, jealousy, and hostility are mental symptoms of deep-seated conflicts and frustrations, in much the same way that aching muscles, tiredness, or headache may be signs of an infection. In one sense, then, mental health means *freedom from disabling and disturbing symptoms* that interfere with mental efficiency, emotional stability, or peace of mind (Maslow, 1954).

Mental Health and Mental Efficiency

The concept of mental health is closely related to mental efficiency, and sometimes the two ideas are confused. Certainly health of any kind is basic to efficiency, and Jones, for example, considers efficiency to be one of the three main aspects of mental health and normality, the other two being happiness and adaptation to reality (Jones, 1942). However, the concept of efficiency has its own meaning, referring to the use of capacities to the best possible effect under the circumstances that exist at the time. Mental efficiency refers to the effective use of our capacities for observation, imagination, learning, thinking, and choosing, as well as the continuous development of mental functions to a higher level of efficiency. It requires, for example, using principles and methods of learning in a way that promotes the rapid acquisition of knowledge or skills. It excludes excessive fantasy-thinking or distorted perception.

The highest form of mental efficiency, then, requires mental health. Deep-seated prejudices, hostilities, projections, or anxieties make it impossible to organize and control thinking in a way that is necessary to mental efficiency. Factors like these are the enemies of logic and truth. They stand in the way of effective studying and learning or of planning intelligently for the future. It can be seen that mental health stands in the same relation to mental efficiency that physical health does to physical efficiency. Just as the sick child cannot play or study well, so the emotionally disturbed person cannot observe, think, or learn effectively. As Babcock (n.d., pp. 4–5) says:

> This concerns the adequacy with which potential abstract-verbal ability can function and is related to the health of the neuro-physiological system. A weak neurological system decreases mental ability in varying degrees according to the extent of the weakness and the age at which the brain and developing mind are affected. Among normally function-

ing persons this phase is closely correlated with abstract-verbal level. . . . When the relation is substantially changed, however, there is either unusually quick mental functioning with poor control, or very slow functioning. Both kinds tend to cause difficulty in adjustment.

The Concept of Positive Mental Health

Just as physical health means more than the absence of disturbing symptoms, mental health also has a positive aspect. Where physical health implies energy, stamina, and adequate strength or resources for the requirements of work, mental health indicates strength of purpose, co-ordination of effort, steady pursuit of well-chosen goals, and a high degree of mental organization and integration. As defined in the Annual Report of the World Federation for Mental Health, mental health is "not merely the absence of mental disorder, but . . . a state in which the individual lives harmoniously with himself and others, adapting to, and participating in, an ever-changing social setting, and with the sense that he is achieving self-realization through satisfaction of his basic needs" (1950, p. 53). Similarly, the Expert Committee on Mental Health of the World Health Organization defined mental health as ". . . a condition, subject to fluc-tuations due to biological and social factors, which enables the individual to achieve the satisfactory synthesis of his own potentially conflicting, instinctive drives; to form and maintain harmonious relations with others; and to participate in constructive changes in his social and physical environment" (1951, pp. 27–28).

The concept of positive mental health is basically related to one's concept of the nature of man. As Fromm points out (1955, p. 67), the needs which man shares with the animals are very important, but their gratification is not a sufficient condition for sanity and mental health. They depend on the satisfaction of needs and passions which are specifi-cally human and which stem from the condition of the human situation. Earlier in this same book (1955, p. 14), Fromm states:

> The approach of *normative humanism* is based on the assumption that, as in any other problem, there are right and wrong, satisfactory and unsatisfactory solutions to the problems of human existence. Mental health is achieved if man develops into full maturity according to the characteristics and laws of human nature. Mental illness consists in the failure of such development. From this premise the criterion of mental health is not one of individual adjustment to a given social order, but a universal one, valid for all men, of giving a satisfactory answer to the problem of human existence.

Clearly, all these qualities of mental health are of fundamental importance to good adjustment. Reactions to environment, work, marriage, and to other interpersonal relations are constantly affected by our state of mind. A sense of well-being, emotional stability, and mental efficiency are of inestimable value in the resolution of personal difficulties and conflicts. Mental health or ill health, therefore, permeates the adjustment process and may be regarded both as a condition and as an integral part of adjustment (Jahoda, 1958; Peck & Mitchell, 1962).

CRITERIA OF MENTAL HEALTH

The Criterion of Mental Efficiency

From what we have just said about the relation between mental health and mental efficiency, it is clear that efficiency can be used to evaluate mental health. It is certainly significant that emotionally disturbed, neurotic, or inadequate personalities are characteristically lacking in this quality (Eaton, 1951; Smith, 1950).

Control and Integration of Thought and Conduct

Effective control is always one of the surest signs of a healthy personality, and this applies particularly to mental processes. An unbridled imagination, such as we see in excessive fantasy-thinking, is detrimental to mental health because it impairs the relation between mind and reality. Without such control, obsessions, fixed ideas, phobias, delusions, and other symptoms are likely to develop.

Important to mental health also is the integration of thought with conduct, a quality that is usually identified as *personal integrity*. The pathological liar, the swindler, the psychopath are all lacking in personal integrity and are often characterized by a pathological mentality.

Integration of Motives and Control of Conflict and Frustration

The integration of thought and conduct is paralleled in the mentally healthy person by the ability to integrate personal motivations and to maintain control of conflicts and frustrations. When motives are not integrated, serious conflict can result. The need for affection or security may conflict with independence; the sex drive may conflict with moral ideals or principles; the craving for amusement often conflicts with personal responsibility or integrity.

These divergent tendencies must be integrated with each other if conflicts and frustrations are to be controlled. It can be seen that control of conflict is an extension of the criterion of integration; however, it must be emphasized that it is necessary for the maintenance of mental stability.

Positive, Healthy Feelings and Emotions

The integration necessary to mental health can be strongly supported by positive feelings, and by the same rule negative feelings can act to disrupt or even to destroy mental stability. Deep feelings of insecurity, inadequacy, guilt, inferiority, hostility and hatred, jealousy, and envy are signs of emotional disruption and can lead to mental ill health (Schneiders, 1951, 1963a). Contrary to such feelings are those of acceptance, love, belonging, security, and personal worth, each one of which contributes to mental stability and serves as a signpost of mental health. Of these feelings, security is probably the most dominant because of its pervasive effect on the relation between the person and reality demands. Emotional health, therefore, is an integral part of mental health, and emotional adequacy, which may be defined in terms of the control, depth, and range of emotional life, is itself a criterion by which mental health can be evaluated (Arnold & Gasson, 1954, pp. 294–313; King, 1951).

Tranquillity or Peace of Mind as a Criterion of Mental Health

Many of the criteria of adjustment and mental health are oriented to peace of mind, which is often mentioned in discussions of mental health. Where there is emotional harmony, positive feeling, control of thought and conduct, and integration of motives there will be mental tranquillity. We cannot have the one without the other. This suggests that mental health, like adjustment, requires the absence of disabling symptoms. The development of symptomatic responses, like daydreaming, delusions, or hallucinations, is directly opposed to mental stability. These relations will become clearer when we analyze the nature and functions of symptomatic responses in a later chapter.

The Criterion of Healthy Attitudes

Attitudes are very similar to feelings in their relation to mental health. Invariably, in our encounter with maladjusted or disturbed personalities, we are forcibly reminded how important it is to maintain a healthy outlook regarding life, people, work, or reality. Mental health is impossible in a context of hatreds and prejudices, pessimism and cynicism, or despair and hopelessness. Attitudes such as these are to mental health what certain bacteria and toxins are to physical health (Anderson, 1952).

Healthy Self Concept as a Sign of Mental Health

If we are to believe the voluminous literature on the problem of the self concept, there is no doubt that mental health depends deeply on this quality. Just as a person must maintain a healthy orientation to objective reality, so must he learn to think of himself in a healthy manner. Feelings of personal inadequacy, helplessness, inferiority, or insecurity or worthlessness will undermine an adequate self concept. This condition will serve to disrupt the relations between self and reality so that it becomes more difficult to meet other criteria of mental health. This idea can be compared with the criterion of self-acceptance described earlier (Stock, 1949; Horney, 1950).

The effect of the self concept on mental health has received a great deal of attention in recent years. Writers in various fields have emphasized that a healthy concept of self is a desideratum of mental stability, as Karen Horney emphasizes in a negative way when she writes (Horney, 1950, pp. 64–65):

> Unlike Pygmalion, who tried to make another person into a creature fulfilling his concept of beauty, the neurotic sets to mold himself into a supreme being of his own making. He holds before his soul his image of perfection and unconsciously tells himself: "Forget about the disgraceful creature you actually *are*; this is how you *should* be; and to be this idealized self is all that matters."

Here Horney indicates how a distorted concept of self can lead to neurotic formation. Other writers also have defined the role of the self concept in mental health (Stock, 1949; Havighurst, Robinson & Dorr, 1946). Here, in this area of the ideal versus the real self, the virtue of humility and the destructive force of pride can play dominant roles in mental health or ill health. A healthy self concept leaves ample room for humility and banishes the foolish pride that leads to the development of egotism or neurotic defense mechanisms (Fosdick, 1943, pp. 52–53).

The role of such qualities as pride and humility indicates, as Mowrer has pointed out a number of times, that the problem of neurosis and mental disorder is to a grave extent a moral one. Nor is Mowrer alone in his opinion. In her last book, Horney devoted an entire chapter to the subject of neurotic pride (Horney, 1950). Allport also emphasizes the intrinsic relation between pride and neurosis (Allport, 1950, pp. 94–95).

> Any neurotic is living a life which in some respects is extreme in its self-centeredness. Even though many of his individual sentiments may

be altruistic, the region of his misery represents a complete preoccupation with himself. The very nature of the neurotic disorder is tied to pride. If the sufferer is hypersensitive, resentful, captious, he may be indicating a fear that he will not appear to advantage in competitive situations where he wants to show his worth. . . . If he is over-scrupulous and self-critical, he may be endeavoring to show how praiseworthy he really is. Thus, though involuntary, partially unconscious, and uncontrollable in any direct way, most neuroses are, from the point of view of religion, mixed with the sin of pride. A more becoming basic humility, held in the religious perspective, could not help but improve the state of the sufferer's conscience, and thus indirectly affect favorably his mental health.

Relations between such factors as pride and neurosis make the development of a healthy self concept one of the most important factors in the achievement of mental health (Herr, 1954; Hanlon, Hofstaetter & O'Conner, 1954).

Adequate Ego-identity

The growth of an adequate self concept, devoid of neurotic pride, unrealistic aims, and the tyranny of irrational superego demands, is an important step toward ego-identity. In the ceaseless struggle to cope with the requirements of self and of reality and to deal resolutely with threats, frustrations, and conflicts, we must have a firm grip on our own identity. *We must know who and what we are.* Disturbed, unhappy, or neurotic people are confused and isolated, lost in a vortex of complex, changing relations that undermine their personal identity (Soddy, 1962). As White says (1952, pp. 332–333):

> Ego identity refers to the self or the person one feels oneself to be. In infancy the sense of identity is little developed, but progressively experience brings sharper outline and clearer definition. . . . Gradually the sense of identity becomes a fuller and richer establishment, compounded of bodily sensation, feelings, images of one's body, the sound of one's name, the continuity of one's memories, and an increasing number of social judgments delivered through the words and behavior of others. During adolescence there is a time when ego identity becomes heavily dependent on the judgments of one's peers. . . . Once this difficult period has been traversed, however, ego identity can continue its development along less diffuse channels.

With some people ego identity does not seem to grow more stable during adolescence or adulthood. Fixations at immature levels of development occur, or there is regression to earlier ways of behaving, and the capacity for effective action is seriously handicapped. Conversely, "as ego identity grows more stably autonomous, the person becomes capable of having a more consistent and lasting effect upon his environment. The more sure he becomes about his own nature and peculiarities, the more solid is the nucleus from which his activity proceeds" (White, 1952, p. 334). For some writers, including Alexander, identification is the most important mechanism in the development of a mature ego (King, 1951, p. 25).

Adequate Relation to Reality

In discussing the criteria of adjustment, we identified one as an adequate orientation to reality. In evaluating mental health we encounter something very similar, the concept of contact, although the two notions are not exactly the same thing. Orientation refers specifically to one's attitude toward reality; contact refers to the manner in which or extent to which we accept reality, reject it, or run away from it. Thus a person who overemphasizes the past is poorly oriented to reality, whereas one who substitutes fantasy for reality has rejected it (Meyer, 1932). Poor orientation is most likely to be associated with maladjustment and neurotic disorders, whereas inadequate contact with reality is found characteristically in the more seriously disturbed patient such as the schizophrenic. The boundary lines are not sharp, and the distintcion must not be overdrawn. Rather, we should think of the organism's relation to reality as being on a continuum, with very good contact or orientation at the one extreme and complete disorientation or flight from reality at the other. Important here is the fact that both adjustment and mental health require a wholesome relation with the world of objects, people, and events with which a person comes into daily contact.

These are some of the most important criteria by which mental health can be evaluated. We do not pretend that this is a complete picture, and the student will find descriptions of many other criteria in the literature (Eaton, 1951, pp. 81–90; Smith, 1950, pp. 503–510). If nothing else, the criteria that we have defined will provide a good starting point for the student interested in the further study of mental health characteristics.

NORMALITY AND ABNORMALITY

The Meaning of Normality

Most people take for granted that good adjustment is very similar to being normal and that maladjustment is the same thing as abnormality.

These concepts are closely related, but they have distinct meanings of their own (Hahn, 1962). One major difficulty is the ambiguous use of the term "normal." Taken literally, the term means "conformity to a norm or standard of some kind." This standard is often a statistical average. For example, the normal height of American males refers to the average computed from a large sample of men. Abnormal in this sense means any deviation from the average or *central tendency*, determined for any particular set of data. Thus, in America, a 7-foot man is abnormally tall because the average height of men is 5 feet, 9 inches. In this connection see the articles by Maeder (1941), Thibaut (1943), Mowrer (1948), and Binder (1956).

The statistical concept of normality can also be applied to human behavior and adjustment, but the results are sometimes startling and confusing. For example, it has been determined statistically that the "average" boy has begun the practice of masturbation by the time he is fifteen years old, and from this fact some writers conclude that the practice is normal. Then, to add to the confusion they allow the implication that whatever is normal is natural, and argue that statistically normal behavior is to be accepted regardless of its social or moral defects. There are many other instances of this statistical normality that refer to undesirable conditions. Six-year-old children normally have four to five dental cavities, and it is normal for the average man to smoke a pack of cigarettes a day. In other words, what is normal can be very undesirable.

Following the same line, it can be shown that abnormality is sometimes desirable. Reference to Figure 4 will illustrate this point. There you

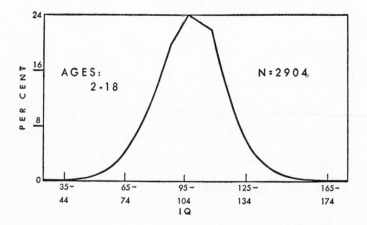

Fig. 4.   A curve plotted from sampling the IQ's of a large group of college students. (Modified from Terman, L. M., & Merrill, Maude A. *Measuring intelligence.* Boston: Houghton Mifflin, 1937, p. 37.)

see plotted, in the form of a curve, the results of sampling the intelligence quotients of a large group of students. In the center are the average scores, those that cluster around the statistically determined mean. To the extremes of the curve are those scores that are higher or lower than the average. If average students in this group are normal, those with high IQ's are abnormal, since abnormal, statistically, means deviation from the average. But it is better to have a high IQ than an average or low IQ; therefore, it is desirable in some instances to be abnormal.

From the standpoint of adjustment, the difficulty with the statistical concept of normality is the fact that the norm is derived from what people are or do rather than from criteria for adequate behavior. It may be statistically normal to quarrel with one's wife, but it happens to be psychologically bad. For this reason we must develop a norm or standard that is suited to the problems of adjustment.

Individual versus Group Normality

The statistical concept of normality implies that it is determined by reference to what the group is like. To be like the group in capacity or behavior is to be normal. But normality can also be determined by reference to personal standards. *This is a norm of consistency.* It would certainly be regarded as abnormal if a person who had never taken a drink in his life were suddenly to go on a one-day drinking spree. This concept of consistency in behavior is more acceptable than a group standard, but it falls short of an adequate standard for adjustment because it is limited to one person. However, it should not be overlooked in defining the concept of normality.

The Psychological Concept of Normality

In order to make use of the concept of normality, we must develop a norm or standard that does not yield always to exceptions. We know that good adjustment is desirable and maladjustment is undesirable, but we ask, good or desirable in what way, from what standpoint? What standard is there to help us to determine the good or bad quality of adjustment?

The answers to the questions raised above are implicit in the definition of adjustment. Good adjustment is that type of response that is in agreement with man's nature or capacities, that promotes healthy relations with his fellow man, and that is in accord with his dependence on a Supreme Being. Such behavior is wholesome, satisfying, and mature. And each one of these qualities is derived from the nature of man and his relations to reality. This is what we should mean when we refer to a person as being normal. This standard is psychological rather than statistical, moral, individual, or pathological. In other words, some responses are psychologically worthwhile and beneficial, and they are normal and adjustive. Also there are just as many that are damaging to personality, or to man's interpersonal relations, and these are abnormal and maladjustive. The psychology of adjustment, therefore, needs to become self-conscious and to evaluate itself correctly as a normative as well as an empirical science (Schneiders, 1954a).

The relations between normal and abnormal, adjustive and maladjustive, subnormal and superior are indicated schematically in Figure 5. In the center we have placed normality, both in the sense of good adjustment and statistical average. Extending from this center are the subnormal and the supernormal categories, which include the dull and deficient, the mentally defective, the bright, and the superior groups. Similarly, extend-

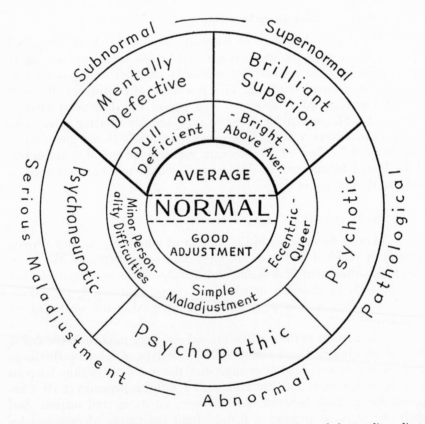

Fig. 5.   Schematic representation of relations between normality and abnormality, adjustment and maladjustment. Explanation in text.

ing from the point of normality as good adjustment are, first of all, the minor personality difficulties, the simple maladjusted, and the eccentric categories; farther out (away from normality) are the psychoneurotic, psychopathic, and psychotic groups. This arrangement has the advantage of bringing together all varieties of abnormality in relation to the normal, and of indicating *qualitative* as well as *quantitative* deviations. The greater the distance from the center, the greater is the quantitative deviation, whereas around the peripheries of the circle are indicated the qualitative variations. The outermost rim of the figure, then, represents abnormality in all its different phases.

ABNORMALITY AND MALADJUSTMENT

The Nature of Abnormality

Normality can be clarified, as we just saw by reference to Figure 5, by defining more precisely the meaning of abnormality. Starting from the statistical concept of abnormality, we can see that it embraces both the subnormal and the supernormal deviations, the one category subsuming those factors that are "below" the normal or average, and the other category embracing those that are "above" the average. Thus, if the average man can lift one hundred pounds, his lifting two hundred pounds indicates supernormal strength. A person who has an IQ of 80 is classified as subnormal because the average is 100. But there are also persons who are *just different* without being above or below average—the eccentric person who wears three overcoats on a summer day, or the hobo who ekes out an existence without regard for obligations of any kind. These persons also come within the scope of adjustment psychology.

Findings reported by Moore (1944, p. 5) support this interpretation of abnormality. In a study of the character traits of 110 normal individuals and the prepsychotic character traits of 112 patients in mental hospitals, it was found that the symptom "different from others" correlated most significantly (.814) with the prepsychotic character of mental patients. Other traits that showed a significantly high correlation were churlishness, peculiar personality, gloominess, reluctance to laugh, peculiar ideas in early life, poor mixer, reluctance to make friends, and preference for being alone. Klein cites the experimental findings of Maier on abnormal behavior in animals and the studies of sexual development in the human female by Landis in support of the hypothesis that normal and abnormal represent a bimodal rather than a continuous distribution. Quoting several authorities, he concludes that "with all due respect to the fetish of the normal distribution curve, it is our belief that both a quantitative and a qualitative dichotomy between the wholesome and the pathological is justified" (Klein, 1944, p. 14).

In his discussion of abnormality, Thorpe also refers to eccentricity and difference as a criterion. One concept, he writes, "considers inadequate health as constituting a combination of traits which are out of balance and in conflict with one another. On this basis, certain behavior characteristics may be exceptionally strong or unusually weak, causing the individual to be 'different' or 'eccentric'." *

The Pathological Concept of Abnormality

The concept of abnormality is often linked with the notion of pathology, but certainly not all abnormality of the kind described as eccentric is pathological, nor is all maladjustment pathological. Pathology indicates disease or morbidity of some kind. A heart beat that is too rapid, a body temperature of 103 degrees, ulcers, or tuberculosis are regarded as indicative of pathology and therefore abnormal from the medical point of view. Mental diseases (the psychoses) fall into the same category, and therefore there are many instances of maladjustment that are clearly abnormal from the pathological or medical point of view as well as from the statistical viewpoint (Marzolf, 1947; Bucklew, 1960; Szasz, 1960, 1961). But let us remember that there are numerous instances of simple and nonpathological maladjustments that cannot be characterized as truly abnormal. Reading deficiencies, truancy, disobedience, and aggression are maladjustive, but they are not abnormal in the sense that physical illness and mental disease are.

Here, then, are some of the concepts and criteria fundamental to our study of human adjustment. There are others, like personality, conflict, and frustration, that are just as important, but we will define these in later chapters. In this chapter we have singled out those concepts that we must understand at the outset of our investigation. They are the key concepts for adjustment psychology.

QUESTIONS AND PROJECTS FOR FURTHER STUDY

1. Make a careful analysis of your own day-to-day behavior for a period of one week, and list those responses that are (a) indicative of wholesome adjustment; (b) maladjustive; (c) eccentric or different.

* Thorpe, L. P. *The psychology of mental health.* New York: Ronald, 1950, p. 118.

2. Write a brief term paper on the topic, "Adjustment Psychology as a Normative Science, and Its Relation to Ethics."
3. Critically evaluate the concept of statistical normality as it applies to moral and social conduct.
4. Discuss and relate the criteria of adjustment and mental health to the following areas: (a) marital adjustment, (b) vocational adjustment, (c) school adjustment.
5. Explain and exemplify the statement that orientation to reality is essential to adjustment and mental health.
6. Explain in your own words the influence of healthy feelings and emotions on mental stability and adjustment.

SELECTED COLLATERAL READINGS

DEUTSCH, A., & FISHMAN, HELEN (Eds.) *Encyclopedia of mental health.* 6 vols. New York: Franklin Watts, 1963.

FOSDICK, H. E. *On being a real person.* New York: Harper & Row, 1943.

HORNEY, KAREN. *Neurosis and human growth.* New York: Norton, 1950.

LINDNER, R. *Prescription for rebellion.* New York: Holt, Rinehart and Winston, 1952.

MASLOW, A. H. *Motivation and personality.* New York: Harper & Row, 1954.

MAY, R. *Man's search for himself.* New York: Norton, 1953.

NUNNALLY, J. C. *Popular conceptions of mental health: their development and change.* New York: Holt, Rinehart and Winston, 1961.

OVERSTREET, H. A. *The mature mind.* New York: Norton, 1949.

SAUL, L. J. *Emotional maturity.* Philadelphia: Lippincott, 1947.

WARTERS, J. *Achieving maturity.* New York: McGraw-Hill, 1949.

WHITE, R. W. *Lives in progress.* New York: Holt, Rinehart and Winston, 1952.

WYLIE, RUTH C. *The self-concept: a critical survey of pertinent research literature.* Lincoln, Nebr.: University of Nebraska Press, 1961.

3

The Normal Personality

Personality is the key to adjustment and mental health. A healthy, well-developed, and well-integrated personality is a guarantee of effective adjustment, whereas an inadequate personality is just as much a guarantee of poor adjustment. Human behavior takes its character from the personality which it expresses, and therefore it is important for us to study the characteristics of personality. It is also important to determine the characteristics of the normal personality.

THE NATURE OF PERSONALITY

Personality and Adjustment

The problems of adjustment and of mental health are inseparably bound up with the problem of personality. Every process of adjustment is a distinctly personal affair and involves a relation between personality and some aspect of reality. Adjustment and mental health, therefore, are always influenced and conditioned by the kind of personality that is involved in a person's attempts to cope with reality. Thus the normal personality reacts to problems, situations, and events in a distinctively *normal* fashion, whereas the neurotic personality reacts in a characteristically *symptomatic* way to the stresses of everyday living. If, for example,

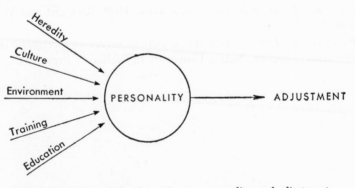

Fig. 6.   Relations among determinants, personality, and adjustment.

anxiety is a prominent characteristic, every reaction will be colored by this dominating anxiety (Krasner, 1953; Plunkett & Gordon, 1960, p. 31).

Furthermore, conditions and determinants of adjustment are "routed" as it were through the personality of the individual (see Chapter 4). Such factors as heredity, environment, and education influence adjustment and mental health in terms of the individual make-up of the personality that is always at the center of the adjustment process. Thus the effects of parental discipline or rejection will be different for a timid or withdrawn child than for a secure, emotionally stable one (Vroom, 1959). These relations are depicted schematically in Figure 6.

Personality, a Psychosomatic Reality

The most useful concept for the interpretation of personality is the psychosomatic concept (Hunt, 1944; Eysenck, 1951; Dunbar, 1947). This viewpoint stresses the fact that, however we regard human nature, man in his daily life gives evidence of both physical and mental functions which are intrinsically related and joined to each other. Between mental functions like thinking, willing, and feeling on the one hand, and such physiological functions as breathing, glandular secretions, and nerve reactions on the other, there are relations of mutual dependence and influence (Wolff, 1961). Thus the mental condition of anxiety can affect pulse rate, digestion, perspiration, and other physical functions, and conversely, physical processes can exert a strong effect on mental functions as when thyroid imbalance is reflected in emotional tension or hyperexcitability. In this view, then, *man is not a mind plus a body, but a psychosomatic unity in which the different processes of mental life and physical responses are complexly intermingled* (Dunbar, 1938, 1942; Cannon, 1929).

The concept stated above explains the current idea that many physical disorders, such as peptic ulcer, high blood pressure, or cardiac disturbances, are psychosomatic rather than organic in nature. The symptoms themselves are physical, but the real cause of the difficulty is traceable to such reactions as worry, fear, or anxiety. The implications of this concept for mental hygiene and personal adjustment are obvious; and therefore the psychosomatic principle is indispensable to understanding human adjustment and mental health.

Reciprocal Influence of Mental and Physical Processes

It may be difficult to think in psychosomatic terms at first because we are used to thinking of mind and body as being so different. So let us study some typical instances of the reciprocal influence of mental and physical processes, for example, the influence of fatigue on mental functioning. We know from our own experience as students that fatigue interferes with efficient concentration, often disturbs emotional stability, and may contribute to failures in memory and learning. We know, too, that the situation is often reversed; chronic fatigue is the result rather than the cause of mental conflict or anxiety. Here we have a clear example of the reciprocal influence of mental and physical functioning.

Other physical agents also impair mental functions. We all know of the effects of alcohol and of the opiates, such as morphine and cocaine, on mental processes. The excessive intake of alcohol impairs memory, judgment, reasoning, emotion, and perception. Similarly, dietary deficiencies are known to affect psychological processes, especially when the deficiency is closely related to nerve functioning (Sherman, 1950). It is a generally accepted principle that all physical conditions that affect the mental functions of the organism do so through the medium of the nervous system because this system is the immediate basis of psychical processes. Thus, whenever the functioning of the nervous system is impaired or interfered with we can expect some change in the psychological picture.

This fact is brought out clearly in cases of disease, injury, or surgical interference with the nervous system. Cerebral tumors, surgical removal of parts of the brain, damage to the cortex resulting from head injury, or degeneration of cortical fibers coincident with old age are all paralleled by mental symptoms of one kind or another. These effects range from complete loss of consciousness to impairment of memory or speech, failure of judgment, hallucinations, and illusions. We do not mean to imply that there is a one-to-one relation between cerebral conditions and mental functioning. Even in the organic psychoses there is variation in mental symptoms from one patient to another, but the basic fact remains that physical conditions in the organism can seriously affect mental functioning (Cobb, 1944, pp. 550–581).

Additional evidence of this relationship comes from the study of glandular influences on mental activity. In extreme cases, like cretinism, the impoverishment of mental life due to inadequate glandular development or malfunctioning is quite obvious. Even in less severe cases the effects are often discernible. There is also a close relation between endocrine functioning and emotional responses in both normal and disturbed persons. The pervasive effects of the adrenals, the thyroids, and the sex glands on emotional responses are well known. Here again the relation is reciprocal since mental and emotional factors can affect glandular function. It is this relation that helps us to understand the psychosomatic disorders referred to earlier. Chronic worry or anxiety can disturb physical functioning just as surely as glandular imbalance can interfere with emotional or mental processes (Shock, 1944, pp. 582–618). These are some of the striking instances of the effect of physical factors on mental processes. They should help us to grasp the significant implications of these facts for adjustment and mental health. Many instances of poor adjustment, such as failure in school, conflicts at home, or misbehavior, can be traced to glandular disturbances, incipient pathology, or some other physical condition (Dolores, 1951).

Psychogenic Influences on Physical Conditions

Of even greater importance to the understanding of adjustment is the extent to which mental (psychogenic) processes affect physical conditions. This relation is even more difficult for the layman to understand because he is not accustomed to thinking in psychogenic terms. If Johnny complains of a stomach ache, his mother is likely to think of such causes as overeating or constipation rather than frustration or mental conflict. Similarly, headaches are likely to be referred to eye strain, sleeplessness to too much coffee, vomiting to an upset stomach, or paralysis to poliomyelitis. Yet each one of these symptoms can result from psychological disturbances such as frustration, conflict, or anxiety. This is what the term "psychosomatic illness" means—one that is caused by psychological rather than physical factors. The following case of migraine is illustrative.

> The patient, a 33-year-old seaman, was admitted to the neuropsychiatric ward of a large naval hospital with tentative diagnosis of migraine, after he had reported to sick bay complaining of severe incapacitating headaches which he had experienced from time to time during the past 13 years. He had been drafted into the naval service approximately 10 months before, but had failed to reveal the history of his headaches during his induction physical examination because of a strong patriotic drive and the fear of being rejected and classified as 4F. He had been assigned to duty in this country only, and had made a fairly satisfactory adjustment; however, during his period of naval service, he had experienced attacks of headache which were so intense that it ultimately was necessary for him to report to his medical officer for symptomatic relief. Physical findings were essentially negative. The patient's mother was described as "high strung" and an older sister as "nervous." The patient's maternal aunt had similar headaches (Burton & Harris, 1947, pp. 281–282).

There are many instances of this relation between psychological processes and physical conditions. Take, for example, the influence of emotional states. When a person is frightened his heart beats faster, he begins to tremble and perspire, and he feels shaky all over. Much the same thing happens when he gets angry. Worry and anxiety also act in the same way. Chronic worry can cause indigestion, high blood pressure, insomnia, or nervousness; anxiety can result in colitis, peptic ulcer, or essential hypertension. Let us keep in mind that emotional reactions are *psychophysical* and therefore naturally involve some kind of physical reaction (McKell & Sullivan, 1950; Shock, 1950). The following case is illustrative:

> A 37-year-old male barber complained of fear of death, suffocating sensations, numbness of hands and lips, and panic attacks. His symptoms had begun about one year prior to his first visit after a saphenous vein ligation. At first he had a great deal of preoccupation with the possibility of embolism about which he had read, but gradually his anxiety became generalized. A generalized foreboding and apprehension developed which were present constantly, becoming irregularly worse in attacks of panic during which he would show all the somatic manifestations of acute anxiety, such as dilated pupils, tremor of the facial muscles and the hands, pallor of the face, tachycardia, and hyperpnea. During such attacks he would be impelled to run from his shop into a doctor's office. Physical examination was essentially negative. Psychodynamic studies revealed that the patient's nuclear anxiety was related to a strict and forceful father who compelled the patient to leave school and take a job as a barber, which he detested, in the father's shop. . . . No defensive maneuvers against the anxiety were possible. In spite of all methods of treatment the chronic anxiety state persisted for years (Grinker & Robbins, 1954, pp. 56–57).

Like emotion, thinking and imagination can also affect physical reactions, as we see clearly in the process of suggestion. Suggestion is a common experience, and all persons are to some degree suggestible. By means of suggestion it is possible to induce many kinds of physical changes and behavioral reactions. Thus, if you are told by your doctor that you are in excellent health, your sense of physical well-being is considerably enhanced, whereas the reverse is likely to happen if you read an article describing the symptoms of a physical disorder, particularly one that you have always dreaded. Through hypnosis and the medium of suggestion, it is possible to induce sleep, cataleptic rigidity, paralysis, anesthesia, and other physical conditions. These effects are obviously important for the psychology of adjustment since many symptoms are the result of direct or indirect suggestion. Similarly, suggestion can be used in removing symptoms, as exemplified in the techniques of hypnosis and hypnoanalysis (Wolberg, 1945).

The effects of suggestion remind us of the part that imagination plays in determining physical reactions. In some instances physical illness or disability is the result of too vivid an imagination, although we must understand that the aches and pains of the maladjusted person are not purely imaginary. They are very real, but it is true that physical symptoms often have their source in the imagination. In normal persons, the effects of imagery are clearly exemplified in the case of sexual functions, since sexual fantasies can cause erections, nocturnal emissions, and sexual excitement.

Finally, let us recognize that psychological processes interact among themselves, as we see again in the case of chronic anxiety. Not only does anxiety produce psychosomatic symptoms, but it can act in a negative way on other aspects of psychic life, such as concentration, judgment, and reasoning. Similarly, obsessive thoughts, compulsions, and delusions can seriously interfere with efficient mental functioning. In the understanding and interpretation of symptom complexes or syndromes, these relationships must be known.

Personality and Behavior

The interpretation of personality as psychosomatic, involving an interdependent relation between mental and physical processes, can be clarified further by explaining the relation between personality and behavior. This is particularly useful here because adjustment processes occur at several different levels. In one situation the reaction to a conflict, frustration, or problem may be on a distinctly *mental level,* as we see in the various adjustment mechanisms like projection, egocentrism, and rationalization (Chapter 8). Or it may take the form of a psychosomatic response, as exemplified in hysteria and neurasthenia. In addition, there are many responses that occur primarily at the behavioral level which bring a person into more direct and immediate contact with the environment. The student preparing for an examination, the worker cleaning his tools, or the young boy apologizing for his bad conduct are all meeting certain demands in the environment and are thus reacting adjustively (Bertocci, 1945).

In the majority of situations several levels of adjustment are involved and become closely intermingled with the total behavior pattern. However, *from a strictly objective point of view,* personality is expressed in the behavior of the organism. The concept "behavior disorders," which is often used for personality disturbances, derives from the identification of personality and behavior. Into this category would be brought such typical clinical symptoms as reflex disorders, convulsions, compulsive behavior, stereotyping, and personal mannerisms. From the standpoint of adjustment psychology, these objective expressions of adjustment or maladjustment are important in the development of a theory of personality that will fit into the framework of a satisfactory explanation of behavior.

Personality-Environment-Culture Relations

In addition to the relation between personality and adjustment, there is an important connection between adjustive behavior and the environmental and cultural milieu within which the personality develops. We must understand that personality is as intimately bound up with objective reality as mental and physical processes are bound up with each other. Thus between personality and such factors as the home, the neighborhood, and school there is a constant interplay, and within this network of relations many adjustments occur. The quality of adjustment in any single instance, therefore, will be determined in large measure by this relationship. As Kraines (1948, p. 45) says, the total personality

> is a function of a *socio-psycho-biologic unity in a given setting at a given time,* and can be understood only if studied as such. These five elements must be studied with reference to each other. It is not possible to draw general conclusions from a study of any *one* of the parts, even if the time and situation are considered; and in like manner, social analysis, psychological analysis, and biologic analysis are inadequate to explain a person's symptoms unless reference is made to the other analyses; i.e., of time and circumstance . . . *personality is a complex whole* responding to, being conditioned by, determining as well as being determined by the environment.

PERSONALITY FACTORS IMPORTANT TO ADJUSTMENT

Modifiability and Resilience

Our study of the relation between personality and adjustment prompts the question whether certain qualities of personality are particularly significant for adjustment and mental health (Thorpe, 1950, pp. 242–256). Certainly, since adjustment is a continuous process and constantly requires changes in behavior, attitudes, and values, we can assume that both modifiability and resilience are necessary conditions of adequate adjustment. Modifiability refers to the capacity for learning and for personal growth, and tends to exclude rigidity and inflexibility, characteristics that we often find in neurotic and psychotic personalities. Through learning the organism acquires the traits and responses by which new problems, conflicts, and situations can be effectively resolved. Adjustment, then, becomes more and more difficult as the quality of modifiability is reduced by the rigidity of habits, psychological mechanisms, or neurotic traits and attitudes.

The quality of resilience is similar to modifiability. It is defined as "the capability of a strained body to recover its size and shape after deformation," and this is pretty close to what the word means in the psychology of adjustment. In everyday language it is the ability of the healthy human organism to "bounce back" when buffeted by the trials and difficulties of daily living. There are countless persons who constantly "suffer the slings and arrows of outrageous fortune," and for whom every difficulty is a major tragedy or unsurmountable obstacle. The sting of a chance remark is never forgotten, ordinary human failures are regarded as personal affronts. Persons without resilience never quite recover from a broken love affair, the death of a cherished relative, professional failures, or the loss of a good job. Resilience is important to help us to recover from difficult or damaging experiences.

Personal Freedom and Adjustment

Equally important to good adjustment and mental health is the quality of freedom or self-direction (Mailloux, 1954, pp. 264–280; Tyson, 1951). Significantly, this is getting considerable emphasis in several contemporary viewpoints of counseling and psychotherapy on the assumption that successful treatment of personal difficulties depends to an important extent *on what the patient is able to do for himself*. In an older and largely mechanistic viewpoint of personality, neuroses and other maladjustments were supposedly caused by heredity, early environment, emotional trauma, conflicts, and frustrations, a drama in which the person himself plays only a passive role. Now, however, it is felt by many therapists that treatment depends as much on the inner resources of the patient as on the ingenuity and skill of the therapist (Rogers, 1942, pp. 28–30). Psychopathic conditions are resistant to treatment because the psychopath is characteristically lacking in self-control.

In normal personalities, by way of contrast, self-control makes it possible to form worthwhile habits and to break undesirable ones; to use ideals and principles to support healthy conduct; to bring feelings and emotions under control (Schneiders, 1963a), and to direct thinking toward socially and morally desirable goals. On this point Mowrer states,

> An objection I have commonly encountered in connection with the position I have taken in this paper is this, that in stressing the ethical rather than the biological nature of neurosis, I seem to be saying that if a person is neurotic, it is his *fault*, his *responsibility*. To this I assent, and willingly. We are excused from blame, from responsibility, only for events or conditions over which we have no control. Do we, as psychotherapists, wish to imply that neurosis and the lesser states of

unhappiness are such that nothing can be done to avoid or correct them, without our special intervention? Or would we not rather see human beings in general take the point of view that neurosis is lawful, not capricious, and that by observing certain principles, by accepting certain responsibilities it can be both cured and prevented? *

Self-Realization and Adjustment

The quality of self-control implies also the potentiality for personal self-realization or self-actualization. Neurotics, psychotics, and other maladjusted persons are notably deficient in this potentiality, which sets a serious limit to their ability to meet the criteria of adequate adjustment. Both adjustment and mental health are dependent on healthy personality development, and when this development proceeds normally throughout childhood and adolescence there is a continuous emergence of individual potentialities and a gradual accretion of traits, skills, and other personal characteristics which together constitute the total adult personality. It is this unfolding and accretion that underlie self-actualization. Impediments to this process of development result in immaturity, and immaturity is directly opposed to self-realization (Maslow, 1950, pp. 11–34; Ausubel, 1952).

Intelligence and Adjustment

The qualities of maturity, self-control, and self-actualization are determined to an important extent by the degree to which rational understanding and judgment are applied to personal goals and to problems that are encountered. Quite often the difference between good and bad adjustment is determined simply by how intelligently (or unintelligently) we attack personal difficulties, frustrations, and conflicts. As one writer says, "An individual with an inadequate personality is one who deals with virtually all of his problems and difficulties with an apparent lack of intelligence. Such a person seems unable to do what is expected of him" (Thorpe, 1950, p. 273).

Take, for example, the student who fails in his work because he does not apply his talents. The resulting academic maladjustment is due simply to an unintelligent approach to responsibilities. Similarly, the housewife who plods along doing her household duties and tasks in the same inefficient way is courting frustration and discouragement. This does not mean that all personality disorders can be explained by lack of intelligent application, but it is significant that effective treatment is often

* Mowrer, O. H. Pain, punishment, guilt, and anxiety. In P. H. Hoch & J. Zubin (Eds.), *Anxiety*. New York: Grune & Stratton, 1950, p. 39. Used by permission.

contingent on the development of rational insight into problems and their causes. The criterion of self-knowledge which we described earlier is also dependent on the factor of intelligence. The quality of rationality is necessary to intelligent choices and decisions, and these decisions form the groundwork for intelligent self-control and self-actualization. The same quality plays a leading role in the development of ideals, principles, and goals that play so important a part in self-realization. In many ways, then, intelligence and rationality have an important bearing on adjustment and mental health.

Maturity, Adjustment, and Mental Health

Of the several qualities of personality that we have singled out as being particularly important to mental health and adjustment, there is none more basic than maturity (Saul, 1960). In fact, the interdependence is so close that the criteria for the one are often indistinguishable from the criteria for the other. King, for example, emphasizes the following indices of maturity: acceptance of reality, assimilation of authority, responsibility, self-dependence, objectivity, anxiety control, ability to accept unpleasant aspects of life, mental health, and complete development (King, 1951, pp. 26–27, 49, 93–94). Barrett emphasizes that a mature person is one who is open to experience, who is genuine and congruent, and who trusts and depends on his own capacities to organize and interpret the data of his experience. The mature person is a naturally helping person, and other persons become more constructive in their own interpersonal relationships through significant associations with him (Barrett, 1962).

McKinney lists complete physical growth, emancipation from the home, heterosexuality, appreciation of others, delay of responses, controlled and directed emotionality, control of environment, and philosophy of life as indicative of maturity (McKinney, 1949, pp. 672–682). Overstreet (1949, pp. 42–75) lists continuing interests in a wide range of knowledge, acceptance of responsibility, the ability to articulate verbally, ability to communicate with others, creative sexual relations, growth from egocentricity to sociocentricity, adequate perspective, and a philosophy of life as criteria of maturity. Compare all these criteria with those for adjustment and mental health in the preceding chapter, and you will see how closely adjustment, maturity, and mental health are related (Allport, 1937; Meyer, 1932).

From the many criteria of maturity discussed above it is clear that adjustment at the adult level requires a high level of maturity, and even at earlier stages of development adjustment will vary with the degree of maturity. The following case illustrates this point.

Paul M. is just seven years old. He was referred to the clinic because of repeated difficulties in school, both of an academic and behavioral kind, and because of his obvious babyish mannerisms. Examination revealed that Paul is of average intelligence (95 IQ), but definitely below average in reading skill and readiness for schoolwork. His speech is retarded, his relations with adults are babyish, and there is serious lack of emotional control shown in his crying and temper tantrums. Psychiatric diagnosis indicated that Paul is operating at the level of a three- or four-year-old, and that his difficulties are traceable to this failure of development, or immaturity.

The reason for this close relation between adjustment and maturity is easy to see. Each age level brings with it new demands and responsibilities, and maturity is the factor that supplies the organism with the skills, traits, or responses that are necessary for meeting these demands. The adult world does not tolerate behavior of a childish kind in a person who is supposed to be grown up.

If we are to understand social deviation, we must extend our concept far beyond the small circle of those whom a society or rigid convention labels misfits. We must include the indecisive, ineffectual person whose search for security carries him repeatedly back to childlike dependence on others, and the pleasant, ingratiating, often successful adult whose interpersonal relations are a chain of superficial contacts. We must include . . . the timid, inadequate person who never quite succeeds in achieving the vocational, economic, or marital status of the average adult. To the behavior pathologist, all of these persons illustrate social deviation, and they all show in their behavior the unmistakable signs of biosocial immaturity (Cameron & Magaret, 1951, pp. 188–189).

Such terms as "adult" and "mature" have multiple meanings and should not be used carelessly. Maturity may be regarded as a single personal quality, but there are many facets to it, four of which are of particular importance: physical, intellectual, emotional, and social maturity.

Physical maturity is the bedrock of development and requires at least *normal growth* in size, height, and weight; a degree of strength, skill, and coordination required for everyday tasks; and such physiological development as is necessary to maintain health, stamina, and energy. Similarly, *intellectual maturity* requires a degree of development that enables a person to achieve a reasonable amount of education, to profit by learning and experience, and to make some progress in understanding, judgment, and reasoning. When these qualities are absent, the person will certainly be regarded as intellectually immature.

Permeating all aspects of adjustment and mental health is the factor of *emotional maturity*. Maturity requires, more than anything else perhaps, the adequate development and control of feelings and emotions, and it is small wonder that emotional instability or pathology lies at the core of every neurotic, psychotic, or other maladjustive personality. Thus the ill-tempered, high-strung, jealous, timid, hating, or anxious person is neither emotionally mature nor well adjusted. This emotional maturity requires at least three qualities: (1) *adequacy of emotional response,* which means that such responses must be consonant with developmental level; (2) *emotional range and depth,* which is an aspect of adequate development—the person in whom feelings are superficial (for example, the oversympathetic person), or one who is lacking in feelings of friendliness, consideration, love, and compassion (the apathetic person) is emotionally immature; and finally (3) *emotional control,* by which we can identify as immature those persons who are consistently victimized by their own anxiety, anger, rage, jealousy, or hatred (Saul, 1960).

The three facets of maturity, listed above, pave the way for the development of *social maturity.* As we have seen in discussing the criteria of maturity, the well-adjusted person must be able to relate effectively to others, develop creative heterosexual relations, move away from egocentrism toward sociocentric responses, and to communicate and share with other people. If, in the course of development, the achievement of these various aspects of maturity force the emergence of the general quality of maturity, effective adjustment and mental health are likely to be assured.

BEHAVIOR CHARACTERISTICS OF THE NORMAL PERSONALITY

The Quality of Normal Adjustment

For any single problem arising in the course of human experience there may be several possibilities for solution. The outcome depends on experience in the handling of problems, availability of substitute responses, adaptability, level of maturity, and similar factors. Some of these responses are normal and healthy and thus fulfill the criteria of adequate adjustment; others are abnormal or maladjustive and may contribute to the breakdown of personality and mental health or to the disruption of the relations between the individual and reality.

Suppose, for example, that a boy's father is offered a position in another city, which means a change of residence for the entire family. This would involve breaking up old friendships, changing schools, learning to live in a new and strange environment, relinquishing family ties, and so on. A situation like this can be deeply frustrating and may lead to a number of adjustment problems. Whether or not it does depends on the boy's reactions, and it is these reactions that will determine the quality of adjustment. The boy could, for example,

> Accept the change in a spirit of adventure
> Plead with his father not to accept the position
> Become resigned to a situation over which he has no control
> Accept the situation in a mature and realistic fashion
> Elect to remain in his home town and live with relatives
> Refuse to make the change
> Fail in school subjects as a protest against the change
> Develop resentment, hostility, and aggression
> Become moody and depressed
> Exploit his mother's reluctance to make the change
> Rejoice over his father's good fortune in getting a better position
> Develop hysterical symptoms in an effort to prevent the change
> Threaten self-destruction if forced to change residence
> Accuse his father of ruining his life
> Develop symptomatic disorders that would preclude the change of residence

The possibilities are numerous, and no one could tell for sure what the outcome is going to be. Some of these possible reactions would promote good adjustment, and others would just as surely lead to adjustment difficulties. The question then arises whether the quality of adjustment varies in a straight line, or whether it is discontinuous. Is all adjustment (good and bad) essentially the same, varying only in degree or in accidental characteristics? Or are adjustment processes discrete, so that we can draw a sharp line between those that are normal and adequate and those that are abnormal or maladjustive in character (Shoben, 1957).

Continuum of Adjustment Processes

The precise quality of any adjustment process has a lot to do with the essential nature of adjustment. The more fully we understand the difference between good and bad adjustment, the more certainly will we grasp the basic nature of the adjustment process. In the sense that all adjustment processes, regardless of individual characteristics, represent attempts by the person to secure the gratification of basic needs and desires, and to reduce conflicts, frustrations, and tensions associated with these motivations, we may say that *they are all essentially alike*. From this viewpoint the difference between adjustment and maladjustment is a matter of degree, which could be determined in any single instance by applying some reliable criterion such as maturity. As one writer says, "The pathological individual does not differ from the normal in some quality or essence which he possesses but the normal person does not. Nor does the normal possess certain qualities that the poorly adjusted person does not. The difference is merely one of degree. . . . The only difference between the normal person and the abnormal is a quantitative one" (Symonds, 1949, p. 384).

In other words, therefore, the more that any response fulfills the selected criterion, the greater the degree of adjustment. Pathologically immature responses, then, would represent the extreme of maladjustment. Using the example described earlier, we could say that acceptance of the father's change in position in a realistic and mature fashion is an instance of very good adjustment, whereas the development of symptomatic disorders, or of resentment, hostility, and depression exemplifies gross maladjustment. Figure 7 is a simple diagrammatic representation of this

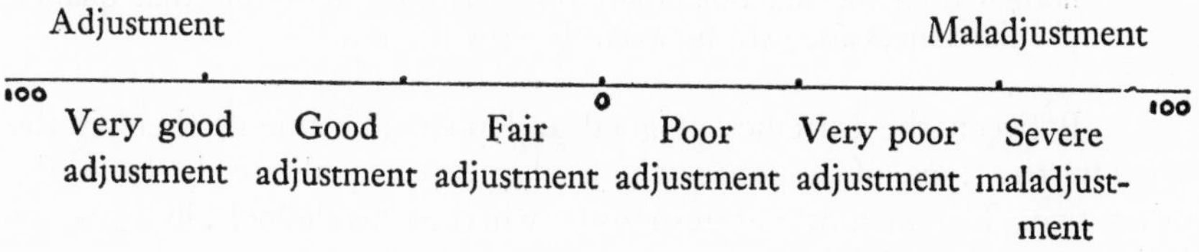

Adjustment   Maladjustment

100 ————————————•————————————o————————————•————————————•————————— 100

Very good   Good   Fair   Poor   Very poor   Severe
adjustment adjustment adjustment adjustment adjustment maladjust-
                                                              ment

Fig. 7. Continuum of adjustment processes.

continuum of human adjustment, which extends from the extreme of unusually good adjustment to that of severe maladjustment. Human nature being what it is, the majority of responses would tend to cluster in the middle range.

From another point of view, maladjustive responses may be said to differ fundamentally from those that are adjustive. Between the normal person's rational, healthy acceptance of reality and the complete rejection or distortion of reality by the psychotic patient, there is a gap that cannot be readily bridged by the concept of quantitative variation. There seems to be, in other words, *a qualitative difference* between responses that are essentially normal and those that are essentially abnormal. This distinction was anticipated in our earlier discussion of psychological normality. This argument is based on the character or quality of the response itself. There is *a real qualitative difference* between the acceptance of reality and its distortion or rejection. Thus complete maladjustment, from the *quantitative* point of view, would mean maximum failure in attempting to meet the demands of self or of reality, whereas *qualitatively*, it would signify pathological distortion of one's relation to self and to reality. Expressed concretely, the paranoid patient is severely maladjusted because of the pathological quality of his delusions which distort his relation to reality, whereas the person who consistently fails to meet the requirements of daily living, in academic, social, or marital situations, is also poorly adjusted even though no pathology is involved. In the latter case, however, it is the *degree of failure* rather than the nature of the response that determines the quality of adjustment.

Some writers recognize qualitative as well as quantitative differences between normality and abnormality. Pointing to the fundamental difference between physical health and disease, Page says:

> This viewpoint, which is known as the *pathological criterion* of abnormality, is also applicable to certain forms of mental disorder. For example, normal individuals do not appear to have the same kind of emotional and thought disturbances that are observed in some mental patients. . . . The pathological criterion does not differentiate the normal from the superior group, but it is not improbable that qualitative differences also exist between these two groups.*

Between the extremes of good and poor adjustment, there is the *nonadjustive* type of response which also varies qualitatively from the other two. The majority of responses, whether psychologically good or bad, are adjustive in the sense that they reduce tension, frustration, and conflict; however, there are some responses that seem to have no adjustive significance. To this class belong many mannerisms, eccentricities, and peculiarities of conduct or expression, such as continuous humming, wearing odd-looking clothes, speaking with an affected accent, habitually squinting, or pursing one's lips. These responses have little to do with adjustment and thus merit no further consideration (Shaffer, 1936, p. 257).

Classification of Adjustive Responses

The wide range in complexity of adjustive responses makes it somewhat difficult to set up a satisfactory classification that would serve all purposes. But several possibilities can be studied to advantage.

First of all, adjustive responses can be classified by *symptoms and causes*. Here the categories of neurotic, psychotic, psychopathic, and epileptic are used. This classification is more suited to the aims of abnormal psychology and psychiatry than to those of adjustment psychology, since our primary purpose is to study the process of adjustment, whether normal or abnormal. Adjustments can also be grouped in terms of the *kinds of response* involved. This classification is particularly useful to

---

* Page, J. D. *Abnormal psychology*. New York: McGraw-Hill, 1947, pp. 14–15. Used by permission of McGraw-Hill Book Company.

the study of adjustment because it centers attention on the mental and behavioral processes involved in adjustive behavior. Within this classification we can distinguish (1) normal adjustment, (2) adjustment by means of defense reactions, (3) adjustments by escape and withdrawal, (4) adjustments by illness, and (5) adjustments by aggression. For these different forms we have adopted the general term "patterns of adjustments," which are described in Part Three.

Finally, adjustments can be classified in terms of the *problems or situations* involved. In this category would be included personal, social, family, academic, vocational, and marital adjustments. This grouping is also consonant with the aims of adjustment psychology, which describes the adjustment process in all of its different phases. These we will study in the section on mental hygiene (Part Four). There are, of course, many interrelations between these two groupings, and we shall find that the different patterns of adjustment condition the varieties of adjustive behavior in a complex and intricate manner. By studying such relations we can bridge the gap between the more abstract study of adjustment processes and their occurrence in everyday, concrete situations.

NORMAL ADJUSTMENTS

Characteristics of Normal Adjustments

The term "normal adjustment" is used here to denote those ways of behaving or reacting that do not involve the difficulties or negative characteristics associated with maladjustive and abnormal responses. Everyone recognizes the difference between a calm, deliberate attack on a problem and one that is disorganized, overemotional, and lacking in direction. For example, the worker who calmly accepts criticism and sets about correcting whatever deficiencies exist is responding normally, and the student who redoubles his efforts in order to overcome low grades, instead of rationalizing his poor performance or blaming his teachers, is making a normal adjustment. Examples like these could be multiplied endlessly; it is probable that the majority of human responses belong in this category.

These responses are characterized in certain ways that enable us to identify them without too much difficulty. First of all, they can be identified by a relative *absence of excessive or damaging emotionality*. In persons who respond normally to problems or reality demands, there is always a certain degree of emotional tranquility and control, which enables them to size up the situation intelligently and to go about resolving the difficulty.

Normal adjustments are characterized also by a relative *absence of psychological mechanisms*. A straightforward approach to a problem, conflict, or frustration is more clearly indicative of normal response than the devious route of such mechanisms as rationalization, projection, sour grapes, or compensation (Chapter 8). Falling back on the specious reasoning of rationalization is less a normal adjustment than the frank admission of personal weaknesses or lack of adequate effort.

Normal adjustments are also largely *free of the sense of personal frustration*. A feeling of frustration, as we will see later, makes it difficult or even impossible to react normally to problem situations. If, for example, a student feels hopelessly frustrated in his academic efforts or social aspirations, it becomes increasingly difficult for him to organize his thinking, feelings, or behavior effectively in those situations in which he feels frustrated. Therefore, instead of reacting normally, he is likely to use outmoded responses, psychological mechanisms, or other nonadjustive responses.

From a more positive point of view, normal adjustments are characterized by *rational deliberation and self-direction*. The basic human ability to think through problems, conflicts, or frustrations, and to organize thinking and behavior so that difficulties can be resolved is the surest guarantee of normal adjustment. This characteristic is illustrated daily in the efficient handling of economic problems, marital difficulties, responsibilities in school, social relations, sex conflicts, vocational frustrations, disappointments, and tragedies. Conversely, the absence of rational deliberation and self-direction is a sure sign of inadequate adjustment.

Normal adjustment is further characterized by the *ability to learn*. This point is clearly exemplified in marital adjustment which demands continuous growth. Personal, selfish aims must be relinquished, at the same time that necessary habits, skills, attitudes, and interests are developed, without which adjustment is impossible. In situations like this, therefore, normal adjustment is characterized by *continuous learning*.

The ability to learn reminds us of another characteristic of normal adjustment, which is the *utilization of past experience*. This of course is one of the ways in which we learn. It is often noted that the psychopathic personality, with a high degree of maladjustment, is characterized by the inability to profit from past experience. This inability lies at the basis of many other adjustment difficulties as well. Normal adjustment, then, requires effective use of past experience. For example, the worker who finds that he cannot meet the responsibilities of his job with less than seven hours' sleep is adjusting normally when he arranges a schedule that will insure adequate rest. Inadequate personalities are notoriously lacking in this ability.

Finally, we may note that normal adjustments are consistently associated with a *realistic, objective attitude,* one that, based on learning, past experience, and rational deliberation, *enables us to evaluate a situation, problem, or personal limitation as it actually is.* Suppose, for example, that the loss of a job, a serious injury, or the death of one's parents is regarded as an irreversible catastrophe, from which recovery is impossible. In such a case, the chances of adjusting normally to the situation are pretty slim. Similarly, to appraise one's own personal qualities unrealistically is likely to impede good adjustment. To view one's self realistically and objectively is one of the clearest signs of the normal personality. It acts as a protection against distortions of the self concept and the damaging influences such distortions can have on adjustment and mental health.

Here, then, are some of the characteristics of normal, healthy adjustments. Understanding them thoroughly will pave the way to a clearer understanding of the behavior characteristics of the normal personality.

THE FORMS OF NORMAL ADJUSTMENT

Adjustment by Direct, Frontal Attack

Under the heading of normal adjustments would first come those responses that involve a direct, decisive approach to everyday problems. As Tyson says, "Most important: always attempt to meet a difficult situation in a frank, straightforward manner, no matter how disagreeable, without evasion" (Tyson, 1951, p. 27). This kind of response is illustrated daily in many different situations, and, if we search our own experience carefully, we should have little difficulty in finding some good examples. Suppose, for example, that because of transportation difficulties you are going to be late for an important engagement. This situation is not helped any by becoming angry, cursing the transportation system, or feeling sorry for yourself. A much better way to reduce the frustration is to get a taxicab to your destination as soon as possible and explain the cause for delay to whomever is involved, or to telephone the person and let him know that you have been delayed. This is a direct, frontal attack on a frustrating situation. It is intelligent and it meets the demands of the situation efficiently.

The same kind of approach can be used effectively with more serious adjustment problems. It is much better for a youngster having school difficulties to go to his teacher for help and advice, and then to apply the information in a decisive manner, than to become emotionally upset, quit school, or rationalize his failure. Similarly, the young housewife is better off when she brings her budget problems directly to her husband for help than when she blames herself for inefficiency, secretly blames her husband for not allowing her enough money, becomes angry or sullen whenever there is mention of the household budget, or, in sheer desperation, "goes home to mother." The following case illustrates the direct mode of adjustment.

> Mary Jane was married to a young doctor whose growing professional responsibilities kept him away from home a great deal. At first, Mary Jane was busily occupied with household duties, social affairs, etc. But before long time began to hang heavy on her hands. She resented her husband's intense preoccupation with his work and his enjoyment of it; and she began to resent the fact that there were no children to give more meaning and purpose to her life. When Mary Jane became aware of these danger signals, she decided to do something about the situation. Having already completed an undergraduate major in psychology, she enrolled in a graduate school for a Master of Arts degree, and after several years secured a position in a child-guidance center. She made a good adjustment by partly matching her husband's professional interest and by creating the opportunity to work with children, thus effectively reducing several sources of frustration with one decisive stroke.

You can see that the direct, frontal approach to problems is effective just because it embodies the characteristics of normal adjustment. It is realistic, intelligent, unemotional, self-directed, and escapes the sense of personal frustration by effecting a solution to the problem. This relatively simple lesson is seldom learned by inadequate personalities, which is one of the strongest reasons why their responses to conflict or frustration are inadequate and symptomatic.

Adjustment by Exploration

Where the direct approach to problems of adjustment is precluded by lack of experience or insufficient learning, the adjustment process may be furthered by *behavioral exploration*. This type of response is likely to occur in young children or in persons lacking the experience or skills necessary for coping behavior. A child, for example, may explore various modes of response that will lead to the gratification of basic needs, and older persons explore the field of work or of social relations until they find something that conforms to their abilities, strivings, or special interests. Adjustment by exploration is, therefore, a special instance of the principle of varied response which we will study later (Chapter 7). Behavior sampling could of course lead to inadequate as well as to normal adjustments, but the point is that good adjustment is often effected through the medium of exploratory behavior.

Adjustment by Trial and Error

Allied to behavioral exploration is adjustment by trial and error, the only difference being that exploration is more random, trial and error more select. For example, a student may discover that the curriculum he has chosen does not fit either his abilities or his interests, and therefore its selection was an error. If recognition of this mistake is followed by the choice of a more suitable curriculum, we have the situation of trial-error-new trial, and the student has effected a good adjustment. It is obvious how much better these responses are than would be giving up, blaming others, rationalizing, self-pity, or many similar responses that only serve to aggravate the tensions aroused by the situation. Trial and error may of course lead to other frustrations or to responses that are ineffective and even damaging to adjustment, but in most instances it is better to chance the uncertainties of an untried response than to succumb to the frustrations of an inadequate adjustment. We may note here that adjustment by exploration and by trial and error is similar to the concept of "reality testing" used by some writers. In their attempts at adjustment, children will often pit their resources against the demands and restrictions of reality in an effort to find out what will work, that is, to bring about adequate or maximum satisfaction.

Adjustment by Substitution

Very similar to the three foregoing modes of normal adjustment is adjustment by substitution (Lindgren, 1953, pp. 89–102). The case of Mary Jane partly illustrates this mode of behavior, as does that of the student who chose a new curriculum. Substitution, like exploration, is a special instance of varied response. Here, however, there is a deliberate effort to ward off or reduce frustration by the expedient of *changing one's direction.* There are countless instances in which the expression of a need, desire, or interest is blocked by some personal defect or limitation, or by some extraneous impediment. A young man with extremely poor eyesight would find it impossible to enlist in the Air Force and must of necessity relinquish his ambitions along such lines. Similarly, there are persons who fail to attract a mate, others who cannot have children, and still others who, because of various limitations or obstacles, cannot hope to achieve their most cherished ambitions. Such persons often effect a good adjustment by substituting another goal for the one that is permanently blocked (Figure 8).

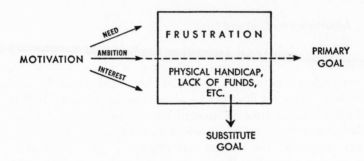

Fig. 8.   Adjustment by substitution.

One can substitute a career for marriage, dentistry for medicine, a lucrative job for an education, or teaching children for raising a family of one's own. In the interest of normal adjustment, one should always be prepared to make substitutions of this kind, which is why *availability of substitutes* is an important determinant of response to frustration. The student should study the section on sublimation and compensation in Chapter 8. Both of these mechanisms may be used for purposes of substitution. Some authors interpret substitution as a psychological mechanism (Kaplan & Baron, 1952, pp. 315–317).

Adjustment by Exploiting Personal Capabilities

The use of substitution depends on one's potentialities. Obviously, where there is a decided lack of mechanical aptitude the development of mechanical skill does not offer itself as a possible substitute for some other ambition. However, those potentialities that do exist should be exploited in the interest of achieving normal adjustment (Tyson, 1951, pp. 25–30). As Tyson remarks, "Most *normal* people are capable of learning to behave more efficiently by maximizing intellectual resources." Our own concept of adjustment by intelligent planning, described in this chapter, is very similar to his idea. In the areas of social, marital, academic, and vocational adjustment, there are numerous possibilities for maximizing personal resources for purposes of effective adjustment. The student who doubles his academic efforts in order to gain admission to a professional school, and the housewife who exploits her natural talents to become a good wife and mother are adjusting effectively by this method. These are only two of many instances that could be used as examples.

Adjustment by Learning

The process of learning is, naturally, basic to effective adjustment. Actually exploration, and trial and error are merely special techniques by which the organism learns responses that are important to normal adjustment. Learning, of course, reaches far beyond these two methods; it constitutes one of the most effective means of coping with the demands of daily living. The adolescent who fails to learn the responsibilities of adult living cannot be expected to adjust normally to adult situations, nor can the psychologist meet the demands of his profession if he fails to learn essential facts about human nature. In every instance, normal adjustment is furthered by the acquisition and development of responses that are required to meet the demands of various situations.

Adjustment by Inhibition and Self-control

There are times when the purposes of normal adjustment are better served by the blocking or inhibition of responses than by the acquisition or development of new ones. We have already noted that the right amount of inhibition and an effective degree of self-control are fundamental to normal adjustment (Mailloux, 1954, pp. 264–280). In the matter of sexual adjustment, for example, particularly before marriage, exploration, trial and error, and even learning are for the most part precluded by social and moral restrictions. Hence effective adjustment can only be secured by means of intelligent control of such responses. Here we see the close relation between inhibition and self-control, the one serving to block the expression of a drive or motive, the other making possible the direction of mental processes or behavior into acceptable channels of expression. Sexual adjustment is only one situation requiring inhibition and control. Normal adjustment demands *control of all appetites* at one time or another (as we see in weight control), and control also of thought, imagination, emotions, and behavior. The normally adjusted person sets limits to such needs as hunger, thirst, and rest, directs his thinking along logical lines, excludes excessive daydreaming, and prohibits violent expression of feelings and emotions. Such control is a sign of normal adjustment.

Adjustment by Intelligent Planning

Finally, we may note that normal adjustment is reflected in the consistent application of intelligence to problem situations. Nowhere is this more evident than in the process of intelligent planning, whether it be directed toward future economic security, health, the education of one's children, marital happiness, or the responsibilities of a job. As Allport says, "Intelligent and perspicacious *planning* for the future is always a significant feature of any mature life" (Allport, 1937, p. 219; also Tyson, 1951, p. 28). Many students get into academic difficulties because they fail to plan their course of studies intelligently, to budget their time efficiently, or to organize their study habits. Many teachers court maladjustment by their failure to organize their daily activities in terms of a carefully devised plan that will enable them to complete their work with a minimum of fatigue and frustration.

Intelligent planning is particularly important for adjustment because it is *oriented toward the future* and thus helps to insure continuous adjustment by anticipation of difficulties that may arise. This anticipation affords an opportunity to organize personal resources for meeting the demands and problems that arise and for initiating whatever changes or learning may be necessary. One can readily see that if intelligent planning were not used in complex positions of leadership and social responsibility, frustration and maladjustment would be the common lot of outstanding men and women.

THE NORMAL PERSONALITY AND ADJUSTMENT MECHANISMS

Nature of Psychological Mechanisms

We have alluded several times to the use of psychological mechanisms for adjustment purposes, and we have implied that these mechanisms stand in contrast to normal adjustive responses, such as those we have just described. Yet it would be difficult to say that all such mechanisms are abnormal, even though some of them are detrimental to healthy adjustment. This difficulty arises because psychological mechanisms stand midway on the continuum of adjustment between normal (good) adjustment and severe maladjustment. Some of them, at least, *are nearly normal* and often appear as a compromise between direct, decisive handling of a problem and serious maladjustment. Thorpe (1950, p. 145) advances four criteria for evaluating adjustment mechanisms: (1) extent of progress toward original objective, (2) maintenance of prestige or social status, (3) social significance or the extent to which the mechanism helps in maintaining satisfactory school, home, vocational, or community relations, and (4) ability to adjust or the extent to which the mechanism helps in meeting future problems. Such criteria are helpful in evaluating mechanisms, but we must be careful not to overlook their effect on mental health, morality, and personal development. Mechanisms are merely special ways of adjusting and therefore subject to the same criteria that govern any adjustment process (Chapter 2).

As an example of the compromise involved in mechanisms we may take the person who is frustrated in his work. Rather than give up his job and look for work that is more congenial to his ability and interest, he compromises by the development of a compensatory reaction (mechanism) that tends to offset or mitigate the disagreeable features of his work. By thus reducing the sense of frustration and the accompanying tension, he effects a degree of adjustment, but note that he does so by avoiding the direct, frontal approach to the problem which could set him completely free of frustration and also provide an opportunity for a more adequate development of personality.

Page (1947, p. 39) gives us a good definition of the concept and purposes of such mechanisms:

> When psychological equilibrium is threatened by severe emotional traumata, frustrations, or conflicts, the mind resorts to a variety of subterfuges and detours called *mental mechanisms* or *dynamisms*. Since mental mechanisms usually are forms of self-deception, the individual is not fully aware of their presence or purpose and resents having his attention called to them.
>
> These balancing devices are desirable in moderation and are frequently utilized by normal individuals. They soften failure, preserve inner harmony, and permit some degree of adaptation to distressing experiences. In exaggerated form they are indicative of abnormality in that undue reliance on defense-escape mechanisms interferes with real achievement, fosters social maladjustment, and makes for personal unhappiness.

From this we can see that the adjustment mechanism is a deep-seated, indeliberate, and more or less permanent response tendency that develops in the course of a person's efforts to achieve personal adjustment. Like all adjustments, it is oriented to the gratification of needs and to the reduction of tension and frustration, often without the effort required by more normal adjustments. In brief, then, worthwhile personality traits can be developed in the interest of more effective living (normal adjustment), or they can be introjected from other persons (adjustment mechanism). Thus mechanisms can be utilized for achieving the aims of adjustment, even though the route taken *is a devious one.*

Characteristics of Adjustment Mechanisms

Let us take a brief look at the essential characteristics of adjustment mechanisms in order to understand them better. First of all, they *function mechanically*, which means that they function without conscious or deliberate intent and independently of self-control. Like reflexes and autonomic responses, psychological mechanisms are nonvoluntary and indeliberate. There is a great deal of difference between the mechanism of rationalization, for example, and the deliberate falsification of reasons for bad or unacceptable conduct, even though both responses follow the same pattern. The person who consciously excuses his own behavior does so in the knowledge that it needs some justification, whereas the piling up of excuses in the process of rationalization goes on without the person knowing that he is trying to justify his conduct.

Psychological mechanisms are also characterized by *unconscious functioning.* Whereas voluntary conduct is determined largely by the purposes, aims, or goals that are consciously formulated on the basis of rational evaluation and deliberation, mechanisms are formulated unconsciously on the basis of needs, tensions, conflicts, and frustrations. The aim of voluntary conduct is the realization of a purpose or the achievement of a goal; the aim of a mechanism is the achievement of adjustment, that is, the reduction of the tension, conflict, or frustration generated by basic motivations. Most persons, certainly, are unaware of the functioning of such mechanisms. Tell the egocentric person that he is egocentric and that this mechanism functions as a protection against inferiority, and he will be the loudest in his denials and the last one to discover the fact that he is utilizing a psychological mechanism as a protective device.

Determinants of Psychological Mechanisms

While mechanisms are oriented toward adjustment, this does not explain their origins. Mechanisms are characteristically determined by the functioning of basic needs like affection and security and such feelings as inferiority, inadequacy, and guilt. Typically, therefore, the mechanism of egocentrism or superiority is an overexpression of the craving for ego security and the feeling of inferiority; rationalization is the expression of guilt feelings or the need for personal status. Mechanisms develop then as manifestations of frustration and conflict that arise from the *inadequate* gratification of needs and from the expression of feelings. A fundamental requirement of the human organism is *ego integrity*, and mechanisms are formed for safeguarding this requirement. These determinants function for the most part at an unconscious level, and thus the mechanism itself develops unconsciously. For this reason, psychotherapy is oriented toward the achievement of self-insight.

Varieties of Adjustment Mechanisms

The widely accepted dichotomy of *defense* and *escape* mechanisms, while useful, should not be overemphasized. As we have noted, symptom formation of any kind is unconscious and not deliberate and therefore not unlike the development of typical adjustment mechanisms such as sublimation and rationalization. In each case, there is an attempt to meet the demands of reality, to escape the limitations of self, or to reduce conflict and frustration by unconscious adoption or development of responses that serve the purposes of adjustment. We see this point clearly illustrated in adjustment by the adoption of illness or disease symptoms (Chapter 11). The development of such symptoms is also "mechanical" in the sense indicated earlier in this chapter, and just as alcoholism can be described as a flight from reality (escape mechanism) so neurasthenia may be regarded as a flight into illness, which may be then interpreted as either defense or escape, depending on the point of view. Prominent among adjustment mechanisms are those oriented to the psychological defense of the personality. These include compensation, rationalization, sublimation, egocentrism, projection, and introjection, which we will describe in Chapter 8.

QUESTIONS AND PROJECTS FOR FURTHER STUDY

1. Explain in your own words the relations between normal personality, normal adjustment, and mental health. What are the essential characteristics of normal adjustment, and how are these related to the criteria of normality explained in Chapter 2?
2. On the basis of your own experience, describe ten different situations that involved normal adjustments. Then describe five situations that involved the use of psychological mechanisms.
3. Describe in your own words the difference between neurotic inhibition on the one hand and adjustment by self-control on the other.

4. Explain the psychosomatic concept of personality, and relate this concept to the category of psychosomatic disorders referred to in the text.
5. Cite several examples of the influence of mental on physiological processes.
6. Write a brief essay on the importance of personality to adjustment and mental health.
7. What is your understanding of the relation between intelligence and adjustment? Why is intelligent planning a sign of adequate adjustment?

SELECTED COLLATERAL READINGS

ALLPORT, G. W. *Pattern and growth in personality.* New York: Holt, Rinehart and Winston, 1961.

ANDREWS, M. F. (Ed.) *Creativity and psychological health.* Syracuse, N.Y.: Syracuse University Press, 1961.

ARNOLD, MAGDA, & GASSON, J. A. (Eds.) *The human person.* New York: Ronald, 1954.

DUNBAR, H. F. *Mind and body: psychosomatic medicine.* New York: Random House, 1947.

HALL, C. S., & LINDZEY, G. *Theories of personality.* New York: Wiley, 1957.

HONIGMANN, J. J. *Culture and personality.* New York: Harper & Row, 1954.

HORNEY, KAREN. *Neurosis and human growth.* New York: Norton, 1950.

JUNG, C. G. *The integration of the personality.* New York: Holt, Rinehart and Winston, 1939.

LAZARUS, R. S. *Adjustment and personality.* New York: McGraw-Hill, 1961.

MASLOW, A. H. *Motivation and personality.* New York: Harper & Row, 1954.

MC KELL, T. E., & SULLIVAN, A. J. *Personality in peptic ulcer.* Springfield Ill.: Charles C Thomas, 1950.

ROYCE, J. E. *Personality and mental health.* Milwaukee: Bruce, 1954.

SARNOFF, I. *Personality dynamics and development.* New York: Wiley, 1962.

SENN, M. J. E. (Ed.) *Symposium on the healthy personality.* New York: Josiah Macy, Jr. Foundation, 1950.

SMITH, H. C. *Personality adjustment.* New York: McGraw-Hill, 1961.

PART TWO

Determinants of Adjustment and Mental Health

4

Conditions and Determinants
of Adjustment

There are literally hundreds of factors—causes, conditions, determinants, influences, forces, whatever you want to call them—that have some bearing on the course of adjustment and mental health. Some of these are internal or intrapersonal, and others are external, that is, they come from the person's environment or culture. We shall have to study both if we want to understand the course of adjustment and mental health. We will begin with those determinants that are physical in nature and then will study those that stem from the environment and culture.

SOME GENERAL CONSIDERATIONS

Personality as a Determinant

In the preceding chapter we discussed the relations between personality and adjustment, primarily because of the importance of these relations to a knowledge of adjustment and also as a prelude to studying the determinants of adjustment and mental health. In the one instance we emphasized the role of personality itself and in the other those specific factors within the personality, or external to it, that condition and determine the process of adjustment in day-to-day situations. Taken as a whole, without regard for specific factors, *personality itself functions as a primary determinant of adjustment and mental health.* In other words, reactions to conflict, stress, frustration, or threat are determined to an important extent by the kind of personality we have. For this reason it is important to recognize that personality *transcends its own characteristics* or traits and functions as an independent variable in adjustment situations.

This fact is recognized implicitly in the use of such terms as neurotic, psychotic, and psychopathic as applied to different personality "types." In such personalities the quality of adjustment and mental health is determined by the distinctive organization of personality rather than by individual factors within or external to it. As we have suggested before, personality is the medium through which different determining factors are channeled into the process of adjustment.

One may argue that the relation of personality to adjustment is itself determined by the combined influence of internal and external determinants. Thus the neurotic or psychopath reacts to demands and conflicts in his peculiarly abnormal way because of defective discipline, inferiority, parental rejection, or some other determinant. This view is certainly correct, but it does not go far enough. It fails to take into account that personality is essentially *an emergent phenomenon* and therefore possesses properties and characteristics, peculiar to itself, that transcend the determining factors from which it arises. As an example of this development, let us consider the trait of inferiority in relation to adjustment. There are many normal persons in whom there is a strong feeling of inferiority, but, when such persons are faced with a problem or a conflict, the inferiority at most makes them hesitant, curious, or timid. In the neurotic, in contrast, inferiority is likely to have a damaging effect. His sense of inferiority is, as it were, routed through the neurotic structure, with the result that he finds it difficult to adjust adequately to situations that evoke his feelings of inferiority. This explains why the reactions of the abnormal personality are so excessive and intense even in situations that cause only a mild response in normal persons.

Kinds of Determinants: Native versus Acquired Responses

The determinants of both personality and adjustment can be grouped conveniently in the following way:

1. *Physical factors,* including heredity, physical constitution, the nervous, glandular, and muscular systems, health, and illness
2. *Development and maturation,* particularly intellectual, social, moral, and emotional maturation
3. *Psychological determinants,* including experiences, learning, conditioning, self-determination, frustration, and conflict
4. *Environmental conditions,* particularly the home, family, and school
5. *Cultural determinants,* including such factors as tradition, ethnic practices, etc.

We are using the term "determinants" here to mean any factor that sets the stage for, influences, or exerts a determining effect on adjustment and mental health. Thus we can say that the physical constitution sets the stage for certain kinds of social adjustment, that the broken home is often a condition of social maladjustment, and that religion often exerts a strong influence on mental health. To know what these determinants are and how they function in adjustment and mental health is an important step in understanding the process of adjustment itself. It will also help us to understand the problem of mental health.

In trying to determine how personality is formed and what determines the process of adjustment, some psychologists have held to the view that the organism begins life with little more than a group of reflex responses which become conditioned and cross-conditioned in a complex manner, leading in some instances to good adjustment and in others to maladjustment. In this view, even though reflexes are themselves innate (that is, inborn), the emphasis is placed on acquired behavior since conditioned responses will in time far outnumber original reflex behaviors. The embryological viewpoint, which emphasizes prenatal determinants of behavior, may be regarded as an extension of this reflex hypothesis. These viewpoints, while limited in value, serve to emphasize the extent to which human responses are the result of learning rather than of innate endowment.

Undue emphasis on innate behavior patterns was the besetting sin of the instinct psychologists, who never seemed to tire of inventing long lists of innate behavior patterns with which the organism is supposedly endowed (Beach, 1955). The implications of instinct theory for the psychology of adjustment and mental health are clear. The more that responses are innate, the greater is the degree of rigidity imposed on the organism. Instinctive responses are not easily modified; they are predetermined and stereotyped, involving a behavior sequence that is more or less invariable. For this reason lower organisms have far less adjustive capacity than humans. Their ability to learn is limited, nor do they possess the capacity to manipulate behavior in the interest of achieving future aims and goals (Nissen, 1953).

A familiar example of this fact can be observed in sex behavior. The sex drive is certainly innate and instinctive and thus tends to dominate behavior in situations where it is aroused. Everyone knows that it is difficult to make good sex adjustments, and the more that the sex drive is allowed to function on a purely instinctive level, the more difficult it becomes to meet the demands that society and morality impose. Sexual responses can be modified; they can be sublimated and controlled. The large number of sexually maladjusted persons, however, is testimony to the fact that it is not easy to bring this drive into line with the criteria of good adjustment.

This critical evaluation of the instinct theory should not be interpreted as a denial of instincts nor as approval of the reflex and embryological hypothesis. The human organism is endowed at birth, and innately, with reflexes and instincts but not to the extent that some hypotheses claim (Bolles, 1958). In addition, there are innate patterns of affective response, including feelings of pleasantness and unpleasantness, a primitive emotional excitement, and, in all probability, an innate temperamental disposition peculiar to the organism. To this list should be added the natural capacities for sensory experience, imagination, thinking, and language, with which every human organism is endowed by nature.

Groundwork of Adjustment and Mental Health

The innate factors given above constitute the basic groundwork for adjustment and mental health and thus create a pattern for the influence of other determinants (Figure 9). It is easy to illustrate this fact.

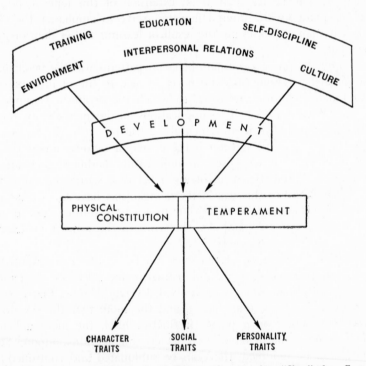

Fig. 9. The manner in which basic conditions of personality "filter" the effects produced by the determinants of personality and adjustment.

Let us suppose that a person is born without the use of one of his senses, such as vision. The fact that he cannot see will alter his adjustments to reality throughout the entire course of his life. Moreover, his blindness will set a limit to the effects of certain determinants like education, interpersonal relations, and self-determination. The adjustments of the blind person, therefore, cannot ever parallel those of the sighted person, even though in any single instance he may be the better adjusted person. Similarly, variations in temperament, intelligence, and imagination will condition adjustment and mental health in various ways.

Although the course of adjustment and mental health is charted by these primary conditions, we must recognize that the great majority of responses, as well as the more important personality traits, are acquired and that the potentialities for change and growth are practically unlimited. This fact implies that the determinants of adjustment carry a great deal more weight than the primary conditions and that if these determinants, particularly family living, discipline, education, religion, and self-discipline, are applied in an efficient and healthy manner, good adjustment and mental health will most certainly be assured. Out of these relations can be expected to emerge a well-balanced, normal personality, with behavior patterns and traits that will enable the person to cope effectively with tension, conflict, and frustration. Conversely, where the determinants of adjustment exert a damaging influence, maladjustment is a likely result.

PHYSICAL DETERMINANTS OF ADJUSTMENT AND MENTAL HEALTH

The Influence of Heredity

There have been a great many arguments over the influence of heredity on adjustment, mental health, and mental disorder (Cameron & Magaret, 1951, pp. 28–32; Sontag, 1950; Levine, 1963, pp. 20–25). What exactly does heredity have to do with these factors? We all know of instances where abnormality of one kind or another seems to run in families, which the pedigree studies of Goddard and Galton support (Levine, 1963, pp. 22–23; Shields & Slater, 1961, pp. 313–318). There is considerable statistical evidence to show that the incidence of abnormality is higher in the families of neurotic and psychotic persons than in those of normal individuals, but the data must be sifted carefully. We must remember that the entire question of genetic influence is inseparably bound up with the factor of physical condition because heredity as a physical process must transmit its effects through the physical mechanism.

The pedigree studies have given us a clue to understanding the possible if indirect influence of heredity. We may accept the general principle that the more that personal capacities, traits, or dispositions are linked to or grounded in physical constitution, the more likely are they to be influenced by heredity. Therefore in some instances tendencies toward maladjustment may be transmitted genetically, particularly through the medium of temperament, which, it is generally agreed, both as an innate disposition and as a developmental phenomenon, is linked to physical constitution and is, for that reason, genetically determined to a degree. As a primary component of personality, temperament may be regarded as the matrix from which arise some of the most basic characteristics of personality, characteristics that have much to do with the later adjustments of the organism, especially in view of the close connection between emotions, adjustment, and mental health. It is highly probable, therefore, that fundamental dispositions such as cheerfulness, moodiness, and sensitivity, all of which are important to adjustment, are in part genetically determined; it is in this *indirect* way that heredity may condition the adjustments and mental health of the human organism (Gates, 1952; Ostow, 1959).

This connection between emotion and genetic factors reminds us of the influence of heredity on specific personality factors such as intelligence, special abilities, and learning capacity. The point is of special importance in this connection because adjustment and mental health are conditioned to a notable degree by intellectual level and special abilities. Thus, after reviewing the evidence from a number of sources, Shields and Slater frankly state (1961, p. 311):

> The genetical background of intellectual abnormality can thus be regarded as determined polygenically for the greater part. The same is probably largely true on general grounds for the genetical background of personality abnormality. The situation, however, is more complex than in the case of intelligence. Personality is more difficult to assess or measure, it is a much less unitary character than intelligence, and its manifestation throughout life is subject to quite wide fluctuations depending on a variety of circumstances.

Much the same could be said for learning capacity and perhaps even for imagination, both of which are important determinants in the adjustment process.

When we turn to specific mental disorders, particularly the functional psychoses, the evidence clearly suggests genetic determination. The best example is Huntington's chorea, a disease that usually occurs in middle life and that involves progressive personality changes and continued intellectual deterioration to the point of severe dementia some fifteen or twenty years after initial onset. Among the earlier signs are personality changes such as increased irritability, aggressiveness, unreliability, lack of control and slovenliness (Shields & Slater, 1961, pp. 304–305). Other diseases in this class would probably include *Pick's* and *Alzheimer's* disease, both of which probably are influenced genetically.

Empirical studies clearly indicate that there is a genetic factor in psychoses, particularly manic-depressive psychosis and schizophrenia, that have been traditionally regarded as functional or psychogenic. Kallmann (1952, 1953), who has studied this relationship perhaps more intensively than any other investigator, concludes that these two rather widespread disorders are genetically determined. Essentially, Kallmann's method consisted in a study of the comparative incidence of these disorders in monozygotic and dizygotic twins, full siblings, half-siblings, and parents. After a painstaking analysis of the data, Kallmann states (1952, p. 290):

> With respect to the other two diagnostic categories, schizophrenia and manic-depressive psychosis, which generally occur before the involutional period of life, the available evidence is conclusively in support of specific and basically single-factor types of inheritance. According to an analysis of age-corrected expectancy rates, the chance of developing either psychosis increases strictly in proportion to the degree of blood relationship to the respective type of index case.

This viewpoint is well supported by other investigators (Shields & Slater, 1961).

After a careful review of a great amount of evidence, Shields and Slater drew an interesting parallel between the genetic determination of psychoses and the environmental determination of neuroses. Hypothesizing that single genes of a large specific effect are involved in the etiology of schizophrenia and manic-depressive psychosis, they suggested that in the etiology of anxiety states and hysteria any genetic factors are probably polygenic and not very specific in their effects (Shields & Slater, 1961, p. 314):

> This fits in well with the observation that neurotic modes of behavior are within the compass of all of us, and can be regarded as non-pathological, whereas schizophrenic behaviour is beyond the normal range. If large numbers of individuals are subjected to physiological and psychological stress, such as occurs in war-time, the incidence of neurosis increases *pari passu* with the increase of stress, while the incidence of schizophrenia remains practically constant.

Therefore, heredity seems to be more important in the etiology of psychotic disorders than in the background of neuroses.

Constitutional Factors in Adjustment

Our earlier comment that heredity, being physical in nature, works through the mechanism of the body prompts a second question in this connection: To what extent are adjustment and mental health determined by constitutional factors? In the article referred to previously, Kallmann (1952, p. 284) strongly suggests that there is reason to believe that some persons are carriers of a specific type of predisposition or potential vulnerability and thus have the biologic capacity to react to precipitating external stimuli with some type of psychosis. Presumably, this capacity is not possessed by ordinary people. Such a biologic capacity would clearly establish a relationship between genetics, body constitution (physique), and adjustment processes (Rees, 1961, pp. 378–380). Throughout the centuries there have been a number of theories to account for the relation between body build or physique and personality, on the assumption that two such closely related and interdependent factors should have some bearing on each other (Cabot, 1938; Sheldon & Stevens, 1942). Two of the most prominent viewpoints in this area are those of Kretschmer and Sheldon. Sheldon claims to have found high correlations between his "somatotypes" and temperament types. For example, his ectomorphs— delicate, poorly muscled, fragile persons—are characterized by restraint, inhibition, and aversion to social activity, whereas the more muscular and sturdy mesomorphs are described as typically active, vigorous, and assertive. Kretschmer, starting with psychotic and potentially psychotic patients, described four basic body types (asthenic, athletic, pyknic, and dysplastic), with which he attempted to correlate psychic dispositions, particularly manic-depressive and schizophrenic types (Rees, 1961, pp. 346–347).

That there are significant possibilities for a theory of adjustment and mental health in the relation between psychic disposition and body type is beyond argument, but there are difficulties that stand in the way of fully accepting such interpretations. As Cameron and Magaret point out in reference to Sheldon's method (1951, p. 28), even if we disregard the serious criticisms that have been aimed at the method,

> we may still question whether a given somatotype represents a constitutional predisposition toward a particular temperament type. Perhaps the individual with one variety of body build calls forth reactions from others which train him in characteristic ways of behaving. Thus the biological fragility of the ectomorph may make him unacceptable to his peers and unable to compete with them; he may then acquire, in social interaction, the techniques of withdrawal and isolation which characterize the "cerebrotonic" temperament. Conversely, the strong and stalwart mesomorph may learn, in successful competition with his peers, the techniques of vigorous assertiveness which define the "somatotonic" temperament. In studies of body type, as in the case of the biochemical investigations, the critical question of interplay between constitution and social learning remains unanswered.

As we have already noted, there are other factors in personality linked to physical constitution, such as intelligence and imagination, but the influence here is more indirect than in the case of emotional factors. As we move away from factors that are clearly linked to physical constitution and toward traits or dispositions that are more psychological and social in nature, the influence of heredity and body physique on adjustment and mental health diminishes. The role of genetic and constitutional factors diminishes even more in such important traits as responsibility, truthfulness, courage, and unselfishness, each of which has significant implications for good adjustment.

Body Systems and Adjustment

Because physical constitution is a primary condition of all behavior responses, the nervous, glandular, and muscular systems have a direct bearing, and often an important one, on adjustment and mental health. Furthermore, because these systems are the physical groundwork of both psychic processes and behavior, their condition and development are basic to effective adjustment. Disorders of the nervous system, associated with severe head injury, encephalitis, brain tumor, spinal and cerebral meningitis, syphilitic infection, senile deterioration, and toxic conditions, are expressed symptomatically in mental, behavioral, and personality disorders. In other words, a healthy, intact, and normally developed nervous system is a *sine qua non* of adequate psychological functioning and therefore of both adjustment and mental health (Meyer, 1961, pp. 557–559).

Physical Health and Disease in Relation to Adjustment

The foregoing discussion prompts the question whether physical health or illness has any precise relation to adjustment. Certainly we can assume that adjustment and normality are more easily maintained under conditions of physical well-being than when illness is a constant companion or when there is physical debilitation of any kind. As one writer says, "The maintenance of good physical health is a step in the direction of mental health. Physical health and vigor must be given attention in order for one to be a happy, efficient, harmonious person—a person who is living a full life" (Bernard, 1951, p. 46). It is certainly evident that excessive fatigue, dissipation, chronic illness, and indiscretions in eating or sleeping are poor habits with which to meet the demands and stresses of daily life, as any students with such habits who have attempted to carry on their studies are well aware.

Perhaps even more important to adjustment are the *indirect* effects of physical conditions, particularly health, chronic illness, and physical deficiencies. Buoyant health has a strong salutary effect on the self concept, on feelings of well-being, self-confidence, and self-acceptance. To the contrary, chronic illness can stimulate feelings of inadequacy and inferiority, morbid self-concern that leads to hypochondria, self-pity, or feelings of persecution. Physical deficiencies, such as partial deafness, structural defects, unsightly skin conditions, often produce similar psychological effects. Cruickshank reports a study in which a sentence-completion test was administered to 264 physically handicapped children and to a similar group of children without handicaps, both with similar social and economic backgrounds. The children with disabilities, including poliomyelitis and cerebral palsy, see themselves as having more fears and more feelings of guilt than do children of normal physical structure. Moreover, the presence of these feelings has a direct impact on the less satisfactory social adjustments that the handicapped children feel they are making (Cruickshank, 1951; Wiener, 1952; Morgan, 1944; Solomon, *et al.*, 1961).

Similarly, Barker and his associates, on the basis of an analysis of personal documents of physically disabled persons, list the following characteristics as being most commonly mentioned: feeling of inferiority, compensatory behavior, fear, aggressiveness, feeling of being mistreated, and nervousness and anxiety. Numerous other characteristics are also mentioned but with decreasing frequency. These authors state that, while the inventory type of personality test does not differentiate physically disabled and physically normal persons, nevertheless, "studies by means of interview, observations, and reports of informants indicate rather consistently that physically disabled persons are more frequently 'maladjusted' than physically normal persons, although this is far from universal; instances of excellent adjustment in spite of both major and minor disablement are not infrequent" (Barker, Wright & Gonick, 1946, pp. 72–73). According to these same authors (1946, p. 73), maladjustment appears in many different forms, including the following:

1. Withdrawing, retiring, reticent behavior
2. Shy, timid, self-conscious, fearful behavior
3. Serious, thoughtful behavior
4. Refusal to recognize real condition; concealment, delusions
5. Feeling of inferiority
6. Emotional and psychosexual immaturity
7. Friendless, isolated, asocial behavior
8. Paranoid reactions, sensitivity, suspiciousness
9. Craving for affection, love of praise, seeking of attention
10. Too high goals
11. Extremely aggressive, competitive behavior
12. Anxiety, tension, nervousness, temper tantrums

All such conditions resulting from physical illness or deficiency, whether expressed directly in symptoms or in personality traits, or indirectly in the person's reactions to the difficulties, have important implications for adjustment and mental health. This does not mean that the effects are invariable or necessary, but there is always a possibility that adjustment will be affected by the physical conditions described (Garrett, n.d.; Washburn, 1962).

Nutritional Factors and Adjustment

Closely allied to physique, physical systems, health and illness, and their influence on adjustment and mental health is the question regarding the influence of nutritional factors. Quite obviously, if the various systems of the body are denied the nutritional elements necessary to health or to good adjustment, emotional and behavioral problems are likely to develop. As one prominent investigator points out (Keys, 1950, 1952), most scientists would agree that it is valuable to recognize the influence of mind on body, but it is equally important to recognize the influence of body on mind. As he says (p. 516), "Somatopsychics must not be neglected."

To support this position Keys refers to one of the best known experiments on the effect of nutrition and starvation on psychic and behavioral processes, the Minnesota experiment. This experiment consisted primarily of a detailed study of thirty-six normal young men during three months of control on a good diet, six months of semistarvation, and a period of nutritional rehabilitation. The subjects were all volunteers, and each man could at any time escape from the rigors of the semistarvation diet. Various tests were used at different points of the experiment to determine the influence of starvation on intellect, frustration, personality, and behavior.

Without going too much into detail, it may be noted that while there was no change in intellectual capacity at any time, *voluntary* intellective effort progressively diminished. There was no loss in the capacity of the visual senses, nor was there anything of significance derived from the Rorschach or from the Rosenzweig frustration test. However, there were marked tendencies for behavioral changes to follow uniform patterns resembling those reported from natural starvation, although there was quite a bit of individual variation in both behavior and emotional changes (Keys, 1952, pp. 519–520).

In his report of the experiment, Keys states that during the semistarvation period the subjects became not only progressively emaciated, but "increasingly quiet, somber, apathetic, and slow in motion." In his evaluation of himself, the starved man "states that he is depressed, moody, apathetic, that he is not alert mentally and has lost ambition. His self-judgment of inability to concentrate and to comprehend is explained by his assertion that he finds nothing interesting except questions of food and eating" (Keys, 1952, pp. 520, 521). Of greatest interest was the marked rise during the starvation period in the neurosis triad of hysteria, depression, and hypochondriasis on the MMPI and the full return to normal after nutritional rehabilitation. Significantly, the scores for the psychosis scales showed essentially no real change. Four of the men evidenced a character neurosis, including inability to maintain former standards of morals and honesty. Eventually the neurotic tendencies regressed and at the end of the year there were few traces left. It is interesting to note that observations of prisoners in German concentration camps also showed loss of normal moral standards and a sense of responsibility. These experiments on nutrition and starvation demonstrate conclusively the basic relation between mental and physical processes to which we referred earlier. *Mens sana in corpore sano* still remains the fundamental principle of mental hygiene.

Hormones, Drugs, and Behavior

This relation can be given added emphasis by defining the role of the glandular and muscular systems in adjustment. Spastic paralysis is a good example of the latter relation, whereas hyperthyroidism, cretinism, and pituitary deficiencies are clear instances of the effects produced by glandular malfunction (Ingle, 1935; Lawrence, 1942; Beach, 1948; Margolese, 1948; Cleghorn, 1952). Here again the effects may be distinctly psychological, or they may show up in behavior or personality disorders. Regardless of the particular nature of the symptomatology, the symptoms themselves indicate that the glandular and muscular mechanisms function as a condition of healthy adjustment and mental stability. This does not mean that every glandular disorder results in mental or behavioral symptoms, but only that such disorders can lead to adjustment difficulties. As Thorpe says (1950, p. 214):

> Endocrinologists also have demonstrated that, although deviations from normal behavior are associated with endocrine imbalance more often than chance would permit, such association is not necessarily causal. Many abnormalities of behavior occur without a demonstrable connection with glandular disorders. Both endocrine dysfunctions and personality deviations occur frequently and may thus often be associated in the same person by chance. Furthermore, there is evidence that glands themselves are subject to the influence of both physiological factors and external agents of a tension-arousing nature.

In his definitive study of hormones and behavior Beach cites the work of a number of investigators which demonstrates the relation between hormones and emotion in both animals and man (Beach, 1948, pp. 110–116). However, while the evidence is strongly suggestive of such a connection, the author cautions that the emotional aspects of mental life are "exceedingly difficult to estimate from the available evidence" (p. 113). Very little is known concerning the mechanisms whereby the endocrines exert their effects, but there is considerable knowledge concerning the relationship between hormones and behavior. Beach (1948, p. 279) summarizes this viewpoint, which corresponds with that of many other investigators:

> From the anthropocentric point of view it must be apparent that in man as in all animals the impact of hormonal influences upon behavior is pronounced. At the same time the extreme difficulties of investigating scientifically the basic nature of such effects in humans are obvious. Throughout this survey it has been repeatedly demonstrated that differences in the hormone-behavior relationships of man and lower forms are more frequently quantitative than qualitative. It seems beyond question that progress toward an explanation of the effects of hormones in other animals will inevitably result in a better understanding of similar effects in the human.

The interested student will find an excellent summary of generalizations regarding the relationship between hormones and behavior in the source just quoted on pages 250–261.

There remains just a brief consideration of the possible relation between drugs and behavior, especially in view of the recent emphasis on the pharmacological treatment of neurotic and psychotic disorders. In recent years Trouton and Eysenck made a thorough study of the experimental and clinical literature relating to the effects of drugs on behavior, but came up with very few positive results (Trouton & Eysenck, 1961, pp. 631–696). They state that the data available are too divergent to permit of any useful summary and that little in the way of general descriptive or causal relationships between personality and drug effects has emerged (p. 683). This does not mean that the various tranquilizing drugs, alcohol, or narcotics do not produce noticeable effects on behavior and personality, but rather that there are so many intervening variables that no one has yet determined exactly what is producing which effects. Nevertheless, following the principle of the mental-physical relationship defined earlier, and using the data that are available from experimental and clinical studies, it is clear that drugs can have a pervasive effect on psychological functioning (Miller, 1956). Mental hygiene would certainly require the sensible use of drugs of various kinds. By the same rule, drugs can be used for therapeutic purposes if for no other reason than to support the therapeutic process.

From the foregoing analysis of the different physical determinants of adjustment and mental health, it is abundantly clear that these two qualities of human personality depend importantly on the physical state of the organism. For this reason mental hygiene begins with physical hygiene, and it thus becomes necessary to make a careful survey of physical factors in order to determine their possible effects on adjustment and mental health.

PERSONALITY DEVELOPMENT AND ADJUSTMENT

The Process of Maturing and Adjustment

As the organism matures physically, and passes from one stage of growth to another, the gradual achievement of adjustment is conditioned at every point by development and maturation. We know, for example, that the young child is poorly equipped to meet the demands of his environment. Sometimes the best that he can do is cry, stamp his feet, or sulk, none of these responses being adequate for purposes of adjustment. As the child grows older, these immature and infantile ways of behaving are likely to disappear, not only because of increased learning, training, and conditioning but also because he is becoming more mature (Havighurst, *et al.*, 1962; Hesterly, 1963). Similarly, the adolescent who seems incapable of accepting ordinary responsibilities will, when he reaches adulthood, show much greater capacity for coping with the demands of adult life. This growth varies a great deal from one person to another, but the important fact is that *the pattern of adjustment and mental health will vary always with the developmental level that the organism has achieved* (Kagan & Moss, 1962; Allport, 1961).

This fact is further exemplified in those instances where development is *impeded* or *distorted*, or where there is *overdevelopment*. For example, intellectual, social, or sexual precocity affords a striking instance of the way in which overdevelopment affects adjustment. Intellectually precocious children are for the most part better equipped to meet the demands of their environment than are average children. This is certainly true of academic requirements, but in other areas of behavior precocity may have bad effects. The intellectually superior child often runs into behavior difficulties because our society is geared largely to the needs and interests of the average child. Garrison, for example, points out that the percentage of gifted children referred to child guidance clinics is higher than the percentage of such children in the general population (17.3 as against 11.9). Nevertheless, studies also show that gifted children are more likely to have high moral character traits than average children, and they are far more likely to be chosen as leaders. Thus their adjustment capacity is high, but they often come into conflict with accepted standards and norms (Garrison, 1950, pp. 216–218).

Adjustment is seriously affected by failures in development. In the case of feeble-minded children, the ability to cope successfully with problems, conflicts, and frustrations is considerably limited. This statement does not mean that subnormals are for the most part maladjusted. On the contrary, various studies indicate that when demands are pitched to their intellectual level, many subnormal children are able to make good adjustments. They fulfill the responsibilities of the jobs for which they are suited, make friends readily, and often are free of the adjustment difficulties that are found in their intellectual superiors. But because intelligence influences adjustment in many different situations, it can happen that the requirements imposed by the environment or by their own personal needs are beyond the capabilities that subnormals possess. This fact should serve to warn us against the mistake of thinking that all persons, regardless of their abilities or level of maturation, can be expected to reach the same level of adjustment.

Because there are as many kinds of development as there are different aspects of personality—physical, emotional, intellectual, social, and moral—we can expect the relations between adjustment and development to vary always *with the kind of development involved*. While there is ordinarily some correspondence among the various forms, it can happen that intellectual development may lag behind physical maturation, and quite often emotional maturation is far below the level of other stages of development. Also, some aspects of maturation are more important to adjustment than others. Moral growth is more important than social maturation, and emotional maturity is the most important of all, it being impossible to cope adequately with problems and conflicts under conditions of emotional immaturity. The relation between failures in development and adjustment or mental health, therefore, can be understood only when we take into account the differential effects of various phases of development.

Personality an Emergent Phenomenon

It is important to note that personality is essentially *a continuously emerging reality*, which begins in the prenatal stage and continues throughout the life span (Montague, 1962). This emergent quality means that the organism starts out in life with the barest essentials of personality and, through such processes as learning, discipline, and maturation, acquires the majority of its characteristics and behavioral responses, both good and bad. It means also that personality is *a constantly changing phenomenon* and is therefore in a sense ready for the constantly changing demands imposed by the requirements for good adjustment. If personality becomes fixed or rigid, as in some psychoses, the possibilities of adjustment are very limited, and even readjustment by means of psychotherapy may become almost hopeless.

The principle of emergence also serves to de-emphasize certain predetermining factors such as heredity and to emphasize the role that maturation and learning play in personality growth (Soddy, 1956). If personality characteristics are largely an outgrowth of experience, learning, and other nongenetic factors, the successful application of principles of mental hygiene and of techniques of counseling and psychotherapy is a more likely possibility than would be the case if personality were largely determined by genetic factors or physical constitution. From this viewpoint of personality as being emergent, the maladjusted and the neurotic personalities are the results of a growth process *that is in itself reversible*. If maladjustive responses are learned, they can be avoided (mental hygiene); also, if they are learned, they can be unlearned (psychotherapy). The acceptance of this principle does not require the exclusion of genetic or constitutional factors; it serves merely to emphasize the fact that personality is primarily a developmental phenomenon and only remotely determined by genetic and constitutional factors (Stagner, 1948).

Characteristics of Personality Development

In its broadest meaning, *development is a steady progression toward maturity*, and maturity, as we have seen, is a basic criterion of adjustment. In other words, adequate development is necessary if the growing organism is to reach a point where it can deal effectively with problems, conflicts, and frustrations. When development or maturation fails to occur, becomes fixed at some point, or becomes distorted, the organism invariably shows signs of poor adjustment, inadequate personality integration, mental instability, or emotional impoverishment.

A prime feature of personality development is that it is *gradual and continuous* and that it starts from a point of immaturity. As we have noted, the infant possesses only the barest rudiments of personality and is very poorly equipped to meet the requirements of adjustment. These facts are of particular significance for mental hygiene because they imply that by the right application of good principles of training and by provision of the right kind of milieu for normal development, there is every likelihood of healthy personality growth and good adjustment. The potentialities for such growth are present in every child, but if the child's potentialities are to be actualized there must be a careful nurturing by parents and teachers to whom the development of personality is ordinarily entrusted.

Development, therefore, is *a gradual evolution of inner potentialities*, which find expression in overt characteristics. Within the general framework of this development the special process referred to as *maturation* may be distinguished. The organism *develops* when it actualizes inherent potentialities; it *matures* when these potentialities are brought to a state of growth whereby the demands of reality, and of sensible, adult living can be dealt with in an effective and healthy manner. It is this quality that makes the process of development so important to adjustment and mental health.

Development and maturation must be complemented by external influences which serve to stimulate and nurture the entire process. Thus development is always complemented by learning which results from conditioning, training, experience, and education. These influences, along with the environmental and cultural setting within which development takes place, serve to foster the expression or actualization of basic potentialities and the subsequent growth of personality characteristics. Personality development takes a wrong turn when one or another of these factors is "misapplied," as happens with inadequate or punitive discipline, traumatic experiences, faulty training, or a distorted educational procedure. In short, then, every personality reflects a *balanced combination* of the natural evolution of individual potentialities and the influence of external factors that serve to promote, hinder, or distort the emergence of personal characteristics.

Emphasis on personality development must not be taken to mean that genetic or constitutional factors have little to do with personal growth, adjustment, or mental health. Actually, these factors often set the stage for the emergence of individual characteristics, and therefore the problem of personality growth and adjustment must be brought into line with the concept of genetic and constitutional determinism. This interpretation is required by the psychosomatic principle described earlier, in terms of which the physical and mental aspects of personality are regarded as intrinsically related to each other. The clearest example of this relation is temperament, which everyone agrees is determined in large measure by physical make-up and heredity. Thus such personal traits as excitability, emotional stability, or apathy, which are important to adjustment and mental health, could well be the indirect expression of physical or genetic factors. While the evidence we have is not conclusive, we must admit the possibility that innate temperament constitutes the groundwork in some instances for the emergence of neurotic and psychotic characteristics, always, of course, *within the limits* set by nongenetic influences.

Segmental versus Integrative Development of Personality

Our reference in the foregoing section to the emergence of individual characteristics will give us a one-sided view of personality development if we fail to recognize that *development is integrative as well as segmental.* The term segmental refers to the emergence of such separate traits and characteristics as timidity, introversion, honesty, shyness, or sociability. From the standpoint of adjustment and mental health, therefore, the symptom of chronic anxiety could be related to timidity or sensitiveness, just as withdrawal reactions are often related to introversion. In such instances the diagnosis and perhaps the treatment of the difficulty may depend upon the identification and evaluation of the personality trait.

But personality is not merely the totality of individual characteristics peculiar to a person; it is also an *emergent synthesis or integration* of these characteristics, which is as much a feature of development as are the separate traits. Integrative development, in fact, permeates every aspect of the human organism. Muscular responses that at first are clumsy and disorganized in time become integrated into a smoothly functioning, co-ordinated pattern of movement. Speech becomes integrated with thought, and thought with other mental processes. We have reason to believe, too, that the nervous system, in the course of its development from conception to maturity, achieves an increasingly higher level of integrative functioning. This is manifested in the remarkable executive control that the nervous system exercises over sensory and motor functions. In every department of personality, development tends toward integration.

The implications of this synthesizing characteristic for adjustment and mental health are clear. A certain degree of personal integration is necessary to both, and therefore, *the higher the level of integrative development, the more likely is the individual to achieve adequate adjustment.* Correlated with this is the important fact that maladjustment, especially in its severest form, *is characterized by disintegration of personality.* The person who is torn between conflicting motives, or whose mental life is disrupted by anxiety, fear, or rage is going to find it difficult to tackle his problems in an integrated manner.

Integrative development is related also to *the essential unity or oneness of personality,* which means that, in crucial situations, it is not some part but rather the whole of the personality that is involved. For this reason maladjustment tends to reach into every aspect of personality. In the last analysis it is the person himself, not some abstracted trait or quality, who is called upon to solve a problem, overcome frustrations, or adjust to the demands of daily living. Thus, whenever there is a disruption of personality in the direction of autonomous functioning, as happens typically in hysteria, maladjustment already exists. To achieve a high level of personal integration, it is of considerable importance to create the most favorable setting for personality development, one in which training and education, environment and culture, discipline and precept strongly favor integrative development. It is to these factors that we direct our attention in the following section (Allport, 1961).

ENVIRONMENTAL INFLUENCES ON ADJUSTMENT AND MENTAL HEALTH

Home and Family Influences

Of the many factors conditioning adjustment and mental health, it is generally agreed that none is more important than the home and family. As one writer expresses it (Allen, 1942, p. 23):

> The actual living reality of the child at birth consists of two fused and inseparable realities: the reality *with* which he is born (genetic and biological), and the reality *into* which he is born (the social). These two realities can never exist apart from each other but constitute a totality from which growth, as a process of individuation, always proceeds. The infant has a sense of oneness with his outer reality, which is not experienced by him as outer but as a part of the whole. . . . An inseparable and dynamic relation between the inner (biological) and the outer (social) realities constitutes the growth picture. The child, emerging through the process, can be understood only as we perceive the constant relation that his inner organization bears to the larger whole (mother or culture) in which he discovers himself. In this discovery, and as he moves toward maturity, the child experiences both his relatedness to others (parents, siblings, friends) and finds at the same time the values of his own individuality and difference.

This relationship between the two realities is emphasized by Steckle, who points out that during the London blitz in World War II it was found that children from psychologically good homes, where there was acceptance, affection, and sympathy, showed relatively little shock effect from the bombings, whereas other children, from psychologically bad homes, developed neurotic symptoms as an aftermath of the attacks (Steckle, 1949, pp. 83–84). There are several family characteristics of particular importance for adjustment. Among them are peculiarities in the family constellation, social roles within the family, the character of group membership, and the degree of cohesion or disruption that characterizes the family (Schneiders, 1954c, pp. 157–170). We cannot study each one of these factors in detail, but we can emphasize certain facts that will serve to highlight the relation between family living and adjustment (Mangus, 1957).

> That parents should make provision for the physical care and nourishment of their children is a commonly accepted principle. It is not so universally recognized that satisfactory family life is indispensable to adequate emotional development of the child. It is in the home that the child encounters the initial experiences which are to determine whether he will be characterized by a feeling of personal security and of being loved and accepted. It is in the home also that the child meets the situations which will determine the extent of his sense of personal adequacy (Thorpe, 1950, pp. 463–464).

Family Constellation.   What an individual does, and the manner of his response to internal needs or external demands, will always be determined in part by the character of the primary group to which he belongs. The family may be large or small, predominantly male or predominantly female, with the children clustered together in age or spread over a period of twenty years. Each one of these characteristics gives rise to a distinctive family constellation. The effect of the constellation on the adjustment of children can be exemplified by the situation of the only child. Here the constellation is very simple. The only child has no siblings to relate to and must look to adults for the source of his experiences, play activities, amusements, security, recognition, rivalry, and so on. He can easily get lost in a world of adult concepts, expectations, and demands, so that when he enters the world of childhood in school or kindergarten, he may find it difficult to make the proper adjustments. Remember, however, that this is merely illustration; there are many only children who are well adjusted, and often more so than persons from families with two or more children (Schneiders, 1960b, pp. 389–397; Thorpe, 1950, pp. 486–489; Partridge, 1938, pp. 217–221; Maller, 1931).

In more complex family organizations, the members must adapt their behavior to the rights and expectations of others. This situation may be conducive to adjustment, learning, and a high degree of socialization, or it may lead to intense rivalries, fighting, jealousy, envy, aggressiveness, or hostility (Vogel & Lauterbach, 1963). Where there is a preponderance of males, the only girl may identify strongly with the mother or become tomboyish in her outlook and behavior; the boy in a feminine environment may become effeminate or react negatively in the direction of excessive masculinity. The oldest child tends to assume the position of authority held by the parents and may become dominant and aggressive with the younger children, and the youngest child characteristically seeks to dominate the family by exploiting his position as the "baby" of the family. The possibilities are almost endless, but these few examples will give some idea how the pattern of human adjustment can vary with family organization.

Social Roles Within the Family. The effects of family constellation will depend a great deal, of course, on other factors, especially *parental attitudes and expectations.* For example, if the father wanted a boy but a girl was born, he may expect and even demand that the girl assume the role of a son, setting the stage for the development of interests, attitudes, and adjustments of a typically masculine quality. Sometimes, foolish parents reinforce this role playing by giving the girl a nickname that is definitely masculine. The following case illustrates this point very clearly.

> "Billy," a girl of sixteen, was arrested with a gang of boys for armed robbery, and was referred to the psychological clinic for examination. Billy was markedly masculine in speech, mannerisms and dress, and showed the typical callousness of youth bent on a life of crime. Her mother explained that Billy was given her unusual name because "her father wanted a boy," and did everything in his power to make a tomboy out of Billy. Evidently, he succeeded far beyond his expectations.

The attitudes and expectations of parents are clearly reflected also in the roles they create for children through *sex and age patterning* (Mead, 1947). More often than not, parents foist their preconceived notions of what a girl or boy should be like on the children and influence the pattern of their behavior in various situations where the sex of the child makes a difference. In this way, girls assume the characteristics and behavior that are expected of girls rather than those that the situation objectively calls for. These expectations of parents are given added strength by similar expectations on the part of society, and so the pattern of adjustment is rigidly set until or unless the child rebels and begins to act on his own.

Age patterning works in the same way. The older child is expected to assume roles of authority and responsibility for which the younger child is not even considered. This attitude often helps the process of maturation, unless the child becomes envious of the greater freedom of the other children or is so immature that responsibility has a damaging effect. Younger children also come in for their share of age patterning, being denied the privileges and responsibilities that most parents automatically link with age. This attitude may be carried so far that the youngster is smothered in anxious overprotection, usually by the mother, into adolescence and even adulthood. Studies show that overprotected children may reject the parent and rebel openly, or sink to pathological immaturity, which completely incapacitates them for adult responsibilities and adjustments (Merrill, 1952, pp. 402–409).

Group Membership. The effects of family living are particular instances of the influence of group membership, which begins almost as soon as the child is born and continues in one form or another for the remainder of his life. As a member of the family, community, gang, fraternity, social organization, or society in general, the individual is always a part of some group, which influences or determines his style of life, his individual behavior, and his adjustments (Davis, 1949). Any group, such as the family, is internally organized in a way that affects each and every member—for good or ill. It is well known, for example, that gangs have a way of so patterning the behavior of their members that they are often led to delinquent (maladjustive) conduct. The group can also be the source of strong socializing influences, of high ideals, of strict moral codes, and of attitudes and interests that condition adjustment in many ways.

> All the arrangements for human living in the neighborhood are such as to favor the transmission of custom and tradition. The family, the playgroup, and the neighborhood become the first school for the child. He acquires here the social traditions, social attitudes, and social values of his group. They make him what he is, socially, and in order to understand him we must study him in this setting. . . . The ideals of freedom, justice, and good citizenship originate largely in the experience of neighborhood life. Culture patterns are formed, diffused, and transmitted through direct association (Sullenger, 1936, p. 74).

This relation between group membership and individual behavior is a special instance of the general principle in psychology that the whole determines the character or functions of the parts that belong to it. We took note of this principle in another way in the preceding chapter when we studied the relation between personality and the environment within which it develops.

Family Cohesion. Because of the relation between personality and environment, family cohesion and disruption are of fundamental importance to adjustment and mental health. Everyone working with dependent children recognizes that the breakup of the home can be the most damaging influence on the psychological well-being of children. Patterns of maladjustment, from simple symptomatic behavior like nail biting and thumb sucking to the most serious delinquencies, are associated with the breakup of the home. For the child to achieve wholesome adjustment and psychological stability, it is indispensable that he develop a deep sense of inner security and belonging, and this the natural home alone seems able to provide. Foster homes, boarding homes, and cottage-plan institutions are welcome and necessary substitutes when families break up; yet it is generally agreed that none of them is able to provide the psychological climate that is characteristic of the natural home. As Thorpe says, "Mental hygienists and others are, however, largely agreed that institutional care, no matter how systematic, is inadequate for the fulfillment of the psychological needs of either infants or older children" (Thorpe, 1950, p. 464; also Torrance, 1945; Goldfarb, 1947, 1943).

Numerous studies dealing with behavior disorders and delinquency in relation to family disorganization clearly illustrate the potency of this factor. Outland, for example, found that, of 3352 boys listed as transients, 57 percent came from broken homes. Sullenger also states that, of 808 delinquent boys in Omaha, fully 54 percent were from broken homes; and of another 337, 64.1 percent came from broken homes (Outland, 1938; Sullenger, 1936). It is the tragedy of modern society that in many respects it has encouraged the widespread dissolution of the home and family through its lax attitudes toward marriage, divorce, and the sanctity of the home (Toby, 1957).

Parent-Child Relations and Adjustment

The environmental factors so far considered form the background for a network of relations between parents and children that are of primary significance for psychological well-being. Outstanding among these relations are acceptance, identification, idealization, negative identification, cross-identification, punitiveness and overdiscipline, jealousy, hostility, overindulgence and overprotection, and rejection (Glidewell, 1961). To understand the impact of these relations on adjustment and mental health we must keep in mind the basic needs of the human personality, a topic to which we shall turn in the following chapter. As we have already noted, such needs must be adequately gratified for the achievement of psychological well-being (Brown, Morrison, & Couch, 1947; Stagner, 1948).

Let us take a brief look at some of these parent-child relations in order to grasp more fully their implications for adjustment and mental health. For example, a home situation in which parents accept the child, make him feel wanted, and give him the kind of affection he needs is obviously conducive to healthy growth. Such relations breed security, self-confidence, respect, obedience, healthy emotional reactions, and other qualities that contribute to good family life and a happy childhood. The outcomes of rejection, in contrast, are written in hostility, hatred, rebellion, and delinquency.

Symonds, for example, found that rejected children are more often delinquent and more aggressive than overprotected children, whereas Steckle lists "withdrawn" as the primary characteristic of rejected children, with distractibility, hyperactivity, subject to night terrors, sullen, and likely to run away as additional characteristics (Symonds, 1939, pp. 54-103, 146-147; Steckle, 1949, p. 146). On the basis of a number of studies, Radke lists the following characteristics as being associated with parental rejection: submissive, aggressive, maladjusted, insecure, sadistic, nervous, shy, stubborn, and noncompliant (Radke, 1946, p. 11). Thus parental rejection, whether expressed by overprotection or lack of care, by punitive discipline or a broken home, is one of the most damaging experiences to which children are subjected; it is seriously detrimental to both mental health and adjustment (Sears, Maccoby, & Levin, 1957).

The effects of any parent-child relations will always vary to some extent with the kind and degree of *identification* that characterizes the relationship. It may also be the other way around, namely, that acceptance or rejection determines the pattern of identification that develops (Mussen & Distler, 1959). In any case, when a boy identifies with his father, as often happens, the effects of acceptance are more readily and more firmly implanted (Stagner, 1937, pp. 101-102, 305-307). Also, the child tends to assume the qualities (good or bad) of the parent and to be more amenable to the parent's influence (Bandura, Ross, & Ross, 1961). Identification smooths the way for effective and wholesome parental discipline because the child is ready to accept the ideas and the commands that the parent feels he must impose. If the parent is a good model, the positive effects of identification on adjustment can be considerable, but identification can also lead to the assumption of traits or adjustment patterns that are detrimental to coping behavior. The following case is a good example (Stagner, 1937, p. 306):

Henry, a bright-faced boy of 13½ years, had a chip on his shoulder. He was said to be very ill-tempered, treating his younger brother harshly and cruelly, and fighting with his mother. He had even attempted to beat her. . . . His father had died a few years before, and gradually Henry had come to regard himself as the head of the home. In accordance with this belief he had attempted to discipline his brother along lines that his experience with his father had made familiar. The brother resented this attempted domination and naturally appealed to the mother for protection. Henry was actually jealous of his mother's position in the home, and resented her domination.

Here we have a clear example of the bad effects of identification, but a great deal depends on circumstances and the exact nature of the relationship. As Virginia Robinson says (quoted by Allen, 1942, p. 40).

> Enlargement and enrichment of the self can be seen as the result of the process of identification as the individual takes into his own psychological structure aspects of the different wholes of which he has become a part. As the self becomes organized through separation and deprivation experiences it gains greater awareness of its own wants as inside and the objects which satisfy, oppose, deny or punish as outside.

These differential effects of identification have been studied by many investigators (Symonds, 1949; Cava & Raush, 1952; Sopchak, 1952). White makes the point, following the theory of Erikson, that ego identity, which we classified earlier as a criterion of good adjustment, "develops out of a gradual integration of all identifications" (White, 1952, p. 316).

In some instances, far too many in fact, a relation of *negative identification* develops between parent and child, which results in traits and behavior patterns that are opposite to those of the parent. Thus there is the typical instance of the learned scholar whose son would rather tinker with a 1925 Ford than study or do research of any kind. Again, it is common to see a dominant, overbearing father with a timid, frightened child. If this negative identification leads to the rejection of undesirable characteristics, it can have a beneficial effect on the child's adjustment. Ordinarily, however, positive identification with the parent is more beneficial because it provides a source of security and confidence for the child that he cannot readily secure in any other way (Bandura & Huston, 1961).

Negative identification is ordinarily less damaging than the relation of *cross identification*. In this relation the girl identifies with the father, and the boy with the mother. Numerous studies have indicated that this type of relation is almost invariably associated with adjustment difficulties. The reason is simple: the girl who identifies with the father rather than with the mother, who is a more natural object of identification, is clearly seeking need gratification in an inadequate manner. It is natural for the boy to identify with his father; therefore identification with the mother requires rejection of the father. This rejection is usually unconscious, which makes it all the more damaging, and it leads to the development of response patterns that are inimical to effective adjustment. Rejecting the father, the boy is likely to assume feminine characteristics, and there are some writers who believe that this is often the beginning of a homosexual tendency. The same thing can happen to girls who identify with the father. In general, therefore, positive, like-sex identification is most conducive to wholesome adjustment.

As we have already noted, identification of the right kind can be salutary to effective parental discipline, a relation that has its own implications for healthy adjustment. On the negative side, it is clear from numerous studies that lax or inconsiderate discipline is always detrimental to healthy personality growth, although the relations between adjustment and *different forms* of discipline are not invariable (Korner, 1949, pp. 160–162). Poor discipline robs the child of one of the means by which the eventual control of behavior is achieved, and it fosters the development of such negative personality characteristics as impulsiveness, indecision, compulsiveness, and scrupulousness, all of which are inimical to good adjustment.

Even more damaging in its effects on adjustment than lax or inconsiderate discipline is punitive and harsh discipline (Radke, 1946, p. 12), as is indicated by the large number of delinquents who report that harsh discipline is one of the major causes of their antisocial attitudes. Punitive

TABLE 7

Children's Reported Feelings as a Result of Parental Punishment

Response to Punishment	Percentage of Cases
Feelings of penitence or resolutions for better behavior	14
Feelings of sadness, unhappiness, pain	63[a]
Feelings that punishment was unjustified	7
Do not feel better or worse	5
Do not know how they feel	11

Source: Radke, M. J. *The relation of parental authority to children's behavior and attitudes.* Minneapolis: University of Minnesota Press, 1946.

[a] Despite this high percentage, 83 percent of this same group of children reported that the punishment was justified.

discipline alienates and degrades the child. It threatens his security, depletes his sense of personal worth, and creates hostility and aggression. Parental discipline, therefore, can be an instrument of good for the child, but it can also be extremely damaging. A great deal of the animosity toward authority shown by disturbed children can be traced to the inexpert and even savage use of discipline by inadequate parents (Meyers, 1944).

Punitive discipline grows out of hatred, jealousy, and rejection. There are many parents who (perhaps unconsciously) hate their children, and there are others who are jealous of the affection between the children and the other parent. There are also many children who hate and are jealous of their parents. Such feelings in parents lead ineluctably to harsh and punitive discipline, and in children they lead to withdrawal, hostility, aggression, and open rebellion. It is clear to everyone that a program of child training, aimed at healthy adjustment and mental health, cannot be predicated on relations of this kind. Children need affection, security, a sense of belonging and personal worth in order to achieve happiness and well-being, and it is impossible to gratify these needs in an atmosphere of hatred and rejection. The following case illustrates the point (Steckle, 1949, p. 110):

> A seven-year-old son of a violent and abusive father spent his time staring into space, biting his nails and playing with pieces of string. He showed an indifference toward people, was very quiet in school and demonstrated marked fear and suspicion of advances made toward him. He was extremely withdrawn and attempts to talk with him met with absolute silence. Since understanding and sympathy were indicated, he was placed in a foster home in which he developed into a sociable, normal lad.

Ineffective or damaging discipline is often paralleled in inadequate parents by overindulgence and overprotection, and numerous empirical studies show that both of these parental failures prevent children from achieving healthy personality growth or effective adjustment (Levy, 1952; Symonds, 1939; King & Henry, 1961). The parent who is too protective reflects his own inadequacies and anxieties which are soon communicated to the child. The only way to learn to meet the demands, frustrations, and difficulties of daily living is to meet them, and this the overprotected child never learns to do for the simple reason that he is never given the chance. Children learn to solve problems by being thrust into the middle of them, not by being shielded whenever a difficultly arises. This principle applies to such diverse things as the choice of a school, earning one's own spending money, buying clothes, selecting friends, deciding to live away from home, or engaging in a fist fight. One of the fundamental needs of children is a sense of independence, which is thoroughly frustrated by overprotection, as the following case clearly illustrates (Steckle, 1949, p. 109):

> A boy, age ten, was anxiously obedient to his mother. He accepted her domination without protest and her slightest sign of disapproval was highly effective in controlling him. He tried to do exactly

as his mother wished and was overresponsive to her demands. He was breast fed for the first three years of his life and his mother slept with him until he was six. During these years they lived alone with a minimum of social contacts. She prevented him from playing with other children until he was eight because of her fear of "roughness." She had also hired a "body guard" for the lad because he reported that other children molested him.

Investigations by Grant, Hattwick, Witmer, and others indicate that overprotection and "babying" may result in feelings of insecurity, aggressiveness, jealousy, nervousness, submissiveness, withdrawal, and other impediments to adjustment (Radke, 1946, p. 12). If nothing else, over-indulgence leads to a poor scale of values, self-centeredness, self-indulgence, and other negative personality traits. Worse than that, it often acts to alienate the child, who interprets parental indulgence as a type of rejection. This is not difficult to understand, for too much generosity naturally leads to the suspicion that the indulgent person is "covering up" some deficiency in his relation to the recipient. The unconscious reasoning is something like this: He doesn't really like me although he's supposed to, and he gives me all these things to convince himself and me that he likes me. Children are extremely sensitive to the actions and the attitudes of the significant persons in their environment; and this sensitivity sharpens their perceptions to a considerable extent.

Sibling Relations and Adjustment

As a natural social unit the family can help the child achieve a high level of socialization which is so important to the adjustments required by society. The degree of this socialization will vary with the character of the relations children build among themselves (Smart & Smart, 1953; Thorpe, 1950, pp. 485–494). If there is friendship, a spirit of give and take, mutual respect, cooperation, and affection, there is every possibility that these qualities will be communicated to other situations involving interpersonal relations, which is the essence of socialization. But in an atmosphere of deep-seated jealousy, intense rivalry (especially for affection), mutual dislike, and so on, socialization is greatly impeded. This, of course, is not the only possible effect of sibling discord, but it is one of the most prominent. Hostile relations can lead to serious emotional instability, damaging personality traits, suspiciousness, and many other inhibiting characteristics that stand in the way of good adjustment. While sibling relations are not as profound nor as important ordinarily as those that bind the child to the parent, their impact on adjustment should not be ignored (Vogel & Lauterbach, 1963).

CULTURAL DETERMINANTS OF ADJUSTMENT

The Community and Adjustment

The fact that the family exerts so pervasive an influence on adjustment suggests that any group, including the neighborhood and community, may exert a similar, if less profound, influence. Many studies of gangs, of different kinds of neighborhoods, and of whole communities have shown unmistakably that individual adjustment varies according to membership in one group or another (Srole, *et al.*, 1962). This influence is to be expected in view of the general principle outlined earlier that the whole (the group) determines to some extent the character of its parts (individual members). Investigations of neighborhood influences, for example, have indicated a definite relation between neighborhood and delinquency; other studies have shown that the pattern of sexual behavior among adolescents, often including sexual deviations, seems to be determined by the make-up of the community. And it is well known that peer group membership sets the style of behavior for its members. It should be understood that this influence is not limited to the overt adjustments of group members; it extends to their thinking, beliefs, attitudes, and interests, all of which have an important bearing on social and moral adjustment (Schneiders, 1960d, pp. 410–423; Hollingshead, 1949; Pratt, 1952).

The School and Adjustment

The school as a social agency can also be expected to influence the pattern of adjustment. It is universally recognized as a powerful medium for influencing the intellectual, social, and moral lives of students. While it is the primary agent of the educational process, it must not be thought of simply as an intellectual mill (Biber, 1955). It is much more than that. It reaches deeply into the social and moral aspects of daily living, contributing its own distinctive effects in shaping the interests, beliefs, attitudes, and values of young people from nursery school through college and university. Rasey states it clearly in this way (1947, p. 55):

> The children who sit on the little red chairs are called beginners, but they are beginners neither in structure nor in function. They are beginners merely in that they have entered a new turn of their cycle. They are not without their attitudes or knowledges. They have closed off the brief epoch of babyhood wherein they were nourished by the

single-flavored diet of their family's attitudes and beliefs. They are weaning themselves from this simple milk to which they were born. They are beginning to subsist upon the heartier, more varied diet afforded them by experiencing new people and new places. Through such experiencing, their world expands. School is not an essential to this process. It has been demonstrated frequently enough that a child may grow to manhood an ardent humanitarian and fellow man, without benefit of school. But school is the expedient designed by society to shorten the time and ease the strain incident to the passing of an individual from helpless, inadequate infancy to helpful, adequate maturity.

Buhler emphasizes the same point (1952, p. 22):

> For many years of his childhood and youth, everyone who grows up in the traditions of the Western civilization spends half or more of his day within the orbit of school. School represents, dynamically speaking, an impact second only to the home in the individual's childhood. What important mission it could fulfill, if teachers were given more clinical understanding and training to equip them to exercise that beneficial influence.

Here again the empirical evidence is unmistakable, many studies showing clearly how interests, attitudes, and beliefs change at different levels of educational achievement. These changes are not only significant for the here-and-now adjustments of youngsters in school; they have important implications for vocational, marital, social, and religious adjustments in the postschool period (Kanner, 1944).

Other Cultural Determinants of Adjustment

As the child moves away from the immediate family circle into the play group or the gang, the school, and the community, and therefore into an ever-widening circle of experiences and relations, we may well ask whether his pattern of adjustment is not affected also by the broad cultural framework which transcends these environmental factors. Do individual adjustments or mental conditions reflect cultural peculiarities? Do cultural values, traditions, mores, standards, and practices have anything to do with mental health and disease? (Horney, 1936). The answers to these questions are partly expressed in the fact that the incidence of mental disorder varies a great deal from one cultural organization to another. As the child reflects family traits and peculiarities in his thinking and behavior, so members of society reflect the cultural pattern. A disordered, morally corrupt, or psychologically unhealthy cultural organization will just as surely affect its members adversely as will a drunken, punitive father, or a broken home disturb the behavior and emotional equanimity of a child. There are many empirical studies to support this interpretation (Honigmann, 1954; Weinberg, 1952; Shaw & Ort, 1953; Kardiner, 1953, pp. 157–179; Klineberg, 1953).

Moreover, there is more than a general relation between culture and personal adjustment. Not only does the incidence of mental disorder or maladjustment vary with cultural factors, but the character of these disorders seems to be affected also. There are societies in which neurotic patterns of behavior are practically unknown. There are others that seem to be permeated with a neurotic, or even psychotic, pattern of thinking and behaving. In our own society, alcoholism, sexual promiscuity, anxiety neurosis, and neurasthenia are prominent patterns of behavior that seem to be linked to our peculiar culture. Often, too, the particular content of behavior and personality disorders reflects cultural peculiarities (Benedict, 1934; Bateson, 1944, pp. 714–735).

These relations are partly explained by the fact that cultural characteristics are transmitted to individuals through the mediums of the family, school, neighborhood, and community and partly also by the effect that particular cultural demands and prohibitions have on human behavior. Many personal conflicts, frustrations, anxieties, and behavior peculiarities stem, directly or indirectly, from cultural influences. A good example of this is the anxiety we mentioned earlier as characterizing so many individuals in contemporary society that it can be described as a mass phenomenon. The influence of culture is reflected also in the many personal conflicts engendered by the puritanical philosophy that permeates American thinking. Admittedly, the mechanisms by which cultural influences are transmuted into behavior or mentality are not always known, but the facts themselves are unmistakable.

The Church and Adjustment

Needless to say, the Church as a social institution is an important part of the cultural determinants that help to shape personality, or that determine adjustment and mental health (McCann, 1962). Since, however, in Chapter 15 we will study in some detail the relation between religion and mental health, involving the influence of the Church, we need not consider this relationship at the present time.

EPIDEMIOLOGY AND MENTAL HEALTH

In this far-ranging discussion of the causes and determinants of maladjustment, mental disorder, and personality difficulties, we cannot escape encounter with the question whether the concept of epidemiology can apply to the problem of mental health. We have taken careful note of the widespread incidence of personality difficulties, and certainly the figures available to us would suggest a condition of epidemic proportions. As stated succinctly by Plunkett and Gordon (1960, p. 5):

> Mental illness is a problem of massive proportions. It has been estimated that 17,500,000 Americans are suffering from mental illness severe enough to warrant treatment. Slightly more than 10 per cent of these, approximately 1,814,000, are recognizable during the course of a year; this is the number treated in hospitals, clinics, or by private psychiatrists. Nearly 90 per cent of mental illness escapes recognition and, consequently, any possibility of treatment, control, or prevention.

It is the task of epidemiology, say these investigators, to define the size and content of this enormous problem. Epidemiology is a study of the health status of a total population. It is "a body of knowledge about the occurrence and behavior of disease in populations and, also, a method of study to determine causes and courses of diseases affecting the individual and the community. . . . It is an important diagnostic and research discipline of public health" (Plunkett & Gordon, 1960, p. 11; also Jaco, 1960). This important approach, joined to medical ecology, promises to shed a great deal of light on the causes, particularly those of a social and cultural nature, of mental disorder. Epidemiology is essentially a recognition of the basic principle that no disease process or disorder is exclusively individual in nature, that the extent and the severity of disease or maladjustment depends on conditions within the organism, and on the relation between the organism and the environment (Hollingshead & Redlich, 1954). It is also an outgrowth of a basic and generally accepted principle that any disorder is likely to have multiple causes and that in our search for the understanding of health and disease we should be wary of limiting our investigation to single causes. In a brilliant summation of this point of view, Plunkett and Gordon state (1960, pp. 42–43):

> Female patients outnumber males, and frequency of attack increases with age. Marital status is clearly associated with occurrence of mental disease; the unmarried are more susceptible than the married, and the widowed and divorced have high attack rates. Race and nativity are suggestive determining factors (in recent years, hospital admission rates of Negroes in the United States have exceeded those of whites, a shift probably related more to altered social conditions than to race). Residents of rural areas tend to have more mental disorders than do urbanites. Migration within a country and between countries appears to contribute to the frequency of psychosis and other mental disorders. Variations in the economic welfare of a society influence frequency of mental disease to the extent, at least, that admissions to mental hospitals increase during times of financial stress.

This trenchant statement serves to remind us and to emphasize very strongly the importance of varied approaches to mental health and to mental disorder. As Ewalt says in his introduction to *Epidemiology and mental illness* (Plunkett & Gordon, 1960, p. xii):

> Epidemiology reminds us that no man is sufficient unto himself, that mental illness—perhaps more so than any other scourge of humanity—is a by-product of man's social existence in a complex environment of his own making. Much, of course, can be gained by studying the pathological process in the individual; but complete understanding can be approached only as mental illness is viewed in the light of man's eternal striving to adapt himself to the demands of his destiny.

This statement needs no additional comment.

PSYCHOLOGICAL DETERMINANTS OF ADJUSTMENT AND MENTAL HEALTH

Experience and Adjustment

In our study of the determinants of adjustment and mental health thus far we have examined the influence of physical conditions, development, and environmental and cultural determinants. Is there also a category of psychological determinants? Since both adjustment and mental health are themselves psychological phenomena, this category might seem a bit strange. But just as the general welfare and efficient functioning of the body can be influenced by the glands, the nervous system, or the musculature, so adjustment and mental health can be influenced by various psychological factors. Among these factors are experiences, learning, conditioning, psychological needs, self-determination, frustration and conflict, and psychological climate.

It is not an easy task to keep the different psychological factors distinct from each other. Experience, for example, is so broad a concept that it could be used to include things like learning and frustration. But there is an advantage in treating them separately, especially since there are countless everyday experiences that have little to do with the way in which a person copes with problems, conflicts, or environmental stresses. There are some experiences, however, that are of deep significance to a person's adjustment and mental health (Beach & Jaynes, 1954; Weininger, 1956; Levine, 1957). These may be *salutary*, or they may be *traumatic*. Of particular importance are experiences in the latter category, as the following case illustrates.

Joanne came to the psychologist with the complaint that she had considerable difficulty in getting along with young men. Already twenty-four years of age, attractive and pleasing in her personality, Joanne had very few "dates," and had never succeeded in going steady with any man she had known. In other words, they never asked her for a second date. Asked about the cause of this situation, Joanne remarked that it was probably because she never allowed them to touch her in any manner. In fact, she reported, she once slapped her escort very soundly when he tried to hold hands with her.

Analysis soon brought to light the underlying cause of this completely negative attitude toward physical contact with the opposite sex. When she was twelve years old, Joanne had experienced a traumatic incident with a favored uncle. Of deep moral sensibilities, she was greatly shocked when her uncle made sexual advances. The shock was so great, in fact, that for years it had lain buried in the unconscious recesses of her mind; and it was only the questioning of the psychologist that brought it to the surface of consciousness. Joanne was quick to see the connection between this unfortunate experience and her attitude toward physical contact and, after a few interviews, was able to modify her attitudes and become more responsive to the opposite sex.

Here we have a striking incidence of how a single experience can affect adjustments and psychic processes over a long period of time. This relation has received considerable attention in recent years, particularly because of the emphasis that psychoanalysis has given to early experiences (Ribble, 1944, pp. 621–651; Murphy, 1944, pp. 652–690; Blanchard, 1944, pp. 691–713; Fredericson, 1951).

We must not overlook the fact that some experiences have a striking salutary effect. The experiences of receiving a reward for a job well done, of a generous act of kindness, of being helped to overcome a difficulty, and so on often serve to influence attitudes and adjustments in a positive manner. Salutary effects of experience should be exploited fully in the application of mental hygiene principles to the education and development of children.

Learning and Adjustment

From what has already been said concerning adjustment, it should be clear that learning is an all-important determinant. The simple fact that the majority of responses and personality traits are acquired rather than innate indicates the pervasive influence of this process. Even when responses and characteristics are determined by innate or genetic factors, the influence of learning is unmistakable.

Regardless of the innate factors which may underlie them, personality characteristics develop in relation to the experiences of the individual in the social and physical world. As the individual meets the situations of life and reacts to them, he finds that certain modes of behavior afford him satisfaction. To him they represent adequate adjustments to specific situations. Faced again with similar situations, the person employs the same type of behavior once more. In this way habits develop. Once established, such habits become to some extent self-perpetuating and lend consistency to behavior. Habits of dress, of manner, of speech, of cleanliness or orderliness, and so on come to form important and consistent elements in the personality of the individual (Kaplan & Baron, 1952, p. 73).

As a process of modification, learning begins in the earliest stages of development (even prenatally) and, in conjunction with maturation, reaches into every aspect of personality and adjustment. Let us note, too, that *learning produces undesirable and maladjustive responses as well as those that bring the organism into a wholesome and efficient relation with reality*. Learning coupled with maturation will give final form to an innate capacity or disposition toward some response or trait. From a strictly psychological point of view, therefore, the different patterns of adjustment, from normality to the severest types of maladjustment, and including symptomatic responses and traits, are in large part outcomes of changes brought about through learning and maturation.

The influence of learning on adjustment will vary to some degree with the kind of learning involved. For example, during childhood the response made to a situation, whether good or bad, may be the result of *behavioral exploration* or *trial and error*. The child, faced with a problem or a frustration that is unfamiliar and for which no response is available, strikes out blindly in an effort to reduce the tension he feels. Refusal to eat, destructiveness, sulking, running away, and attention-getting behavior are familiar instances of exploratory responses. When such responses are successful or satisfying, *they tend to become fixed and gradually emerge as stabilized habits or as personality traits*.

Learned responses may also be the outcome of *conditioning*, a process by which different stimuli *become functionally equivalent in evoking different responses*. Typically, a child will react to frustration in an emotional manner, usually with anger. If another stimulus is linked to the frustrating situation, such as a dark room, the child may become emotionally conditioned to the room or to darkness in general. Thus what was originally an ineffective stimulus becomes functionally equivalent to another stimulus that produces the response. Undoubtedly, many responses, good and bad or normal and abnormal, are the result of conditioning. Certainly many abnormal fears (phobias), compulsive acts, negativistic behavior, and everyday habits can be traced to early conditioning.

Conditioning may lead to *inhibition,* which is another form of learning important to adjustment. The blocking or control of responses may be as necessary to good adjustment as is wholesome expression. In fact, inhibition is the beginning of *self-control,* which is one of the most significant determinants of adequate adjustment. In the early formative years, the child must be inhibited with respect to the free exercise of bodily functions, play activities that interfere with more important requirements, unnecessary soiling of clothes, aggressive behavior, fighting, and so on. Such inhibition, the mechanism of which is conditioning, leads to the establishment of inner controls by which undesirable or nonadjustive behavior is eliminated or at least modified to conform to existing requirements.

> Effective learning requires good discipline in the external process of education, and in the learner. It requires effort and sustained application. No device will substitute for these requirements, although it may help to implement learning activities.
>
> Good discipline promotes achievement. Good discipline and achievement promote mental health; one's view of oneself hinges to a great extent upon how one meets the demands and expectations of daily living (Phillips, *et al.,* 1960, p. vi).

Just as ordinary conditioning can lead to the development of inadequate responses, so excessive inhibition can result in the development of tendencies poorly suited to good adjustment. Too much inhibition, like too much of anything, is not a good thing; it fosters *rigidity.* Overinhibited persons cannot express themselves freely or act "naturally" in any situation. They are typically characterized by hesitancy, timidity, distance in social relations, frigidity in sexual relations, and other personality traits that reflect the excessive inhibition and external control to which they have been constantly subjected. They are rigid and stylized in their reactions to ordinary events. When a joke or story is told, they manage a polite, frozen smile when others are laughing out loud. At a dance or party, they are the last to enter into the activity. In the matter of clothes, they are as outdated as last week's newspaper. In conversation, they are stilted, formal, and extremely careful in the choice of words, never permitting themselves a lapse from grammatical correctness, or the easy grace of a rich colloquialism. In nearly all situations the overinhibited person reflects the rigidity that is an essential characteristic of his personality. Rigidity, as we have noted, is contrary to the adaptability and resiliency that are necessary to effective adjustment.

In later stages of development, learning becomes more typically rational in character and the *mechanisms of association* begin to play an important part. However, association is much more pervasive than this statement would indicate since it permeates the learning process from the earliest beginnings and therefore has an important relation to adjustment at all levels. To understand adjustment in all of its phases we must realize that quite often the response a person makes to a situation is determined by the *peculiar meaning* that the situation evokes rather than by the objective characteristics of the situation itself (Sherman, 1941, pp. 191–199). This personal meaning is often the result of association. Many persons, for example, have associated particular characteristics or ways of behaving with certain racial or national groups, and they react to these groups in terms of the associations they have formed rather than in terms of actual characteristics or behavior. To others, social affairs or competitive activities are distasteful because they have become associated with fear, failure, or chronic frustration. The possibilities for association, through which a great amount of adjustive learning takes place, are legion, and thus the understanding of individual adjustments often hinges on a thorough knowledge of the kinds of associations that have been formed.

In the relation of learning to adjustment, the *law of effect* is of considerable importance in determining the effect that learning will have. Stated simply in the terms of adjustment psychology, this law holds that *whenever a response is satisfying, and reduces tension or frustration, it is likely to be learned and to become fixed within the general pattern of personal responses*. If it is dissatisfying and fails to reduce tension, it is likely to be forgotten or eliminated. This principle applies generally to *all* modes of learning, for it involves satisfaction and tension reduction. Thus, if a child finds that he can realize his purposes or reduce frustration by the adoption of symptoms of illness, running away, temper tantrums, sucking his thumb, attention-getting behavior, and so on, these responses are likely to become fixed and permanent. This gives us a clue to the meaning of symptomatic behavior, which often seems senseless and lacking in purpose. Why, for example, does the hysteric become paralyzed? Why does the neurasthenic cling to his headaches, backaches, and fatigue when obviously such symptoms are undesirable and annoying? Why does the child bite his nails, or persist in bed wetting? Questions like these could be asked interminably, but the answer would always be the same: *because such symptoms and ways of behaving serve a purpose,* because in one way or another they have been found to satisfy and to reduce tension and frustration. That is why they become a fixed and permanent part of the person's adjustments to himself and to the demands imposed by the environment.

Finally, let us note the relation between *rational learning and adjustment.* By means of rational learning human beings acquire numerous responses and personality characteristics that exert extensive influence on everyday adjustments and mental health. It is also the means of acquiring knowledge that can be used for adjustment purposes. Rational learning lies at the basis of intellectual, moral, and religious growth. It is the process by which a person acquires values, principles, ideals, and goals, all of which are significant for adequate adjustment and mental stability. As we noted previously, a sound scale of values is an important criterion by which to determine the level and quality of adjustment; and goals, we noted, are necessary for the effective organization of human effort. It is a generally accepted rule that conduct determined by values and regulated by selected principles and goals is ordinarily superior in adjustment value to that which results from poorly disciplined needs, frustrations, inadequate conditions or excessive inhibition. This interpretation is an extension of the theory of personality described earlier. Human nature being what it is, the quality of rationality must permeate behavior if people are to reach or maintain a high level of adjustment and mental health.

Training, Education, and Adjustment

Learning may be regarded as the subjective counterpart of the processes of training and education. But these two processes have characteristics of their own that are important to the understanding of adjustment. Essentially, the process of training or discipline is a means, externally imposed, *by which an organism acquires certain responses necessary for adequate functioning in the environment in which it lives.* Its relation to adjustment, therefore, is fundamental. These responses usually take the form of deeply ingrained habits and skills which the organism uses repeatedly in its day-to-day adjustments. The very young child is trained in toilet habits, eating, dressing, cleanliness, obedience, speech, and numerous other forms of behavior necessary to daily living. The school child is further trained in writing, reading, drawing, fundamentals of arithmetic, habits of regularity, orderliness, and the like. This kind of training continues throughout adolescence, when new habits and skills are added to those already developed, and, at the higher levels of development, specialized training is often used to acquire skills necessary to such occupations as dentistry, surgery, auto mechanics, and accounting.

On all levels, the aims of training are essentially the same because they are determined by the demands inherent in certain situations. The child cannot get along in school without the skills of reading and writing, anymore than the doctor can perform an operation successfully without the techniques of surgery. These points may seem obvious, but the important fact is that many parents and teachers fail to exploit this basic relation between training and adjustment. They seem not to realize that effective training and discipline, especially in early childhood, *are requirements of healthy adjustment and personality development*. As Mowrer says, in referring to the use of punishment as an educative measure, "Childhood discipline is a necessary prelude to the self-discipline and social discipline of responsible adult life" (Mowrer, 1950, p. 35). A little later on he states (Mowrer, 1950, p.36):

> Just as the capacity to feel pain and to learn fears appears to have evolved in living organisms because of their survival value, so does it seem that the use of punishment has become a recognized technique of socialization and social control in all known human cultures because, again, of its survival value. Societies which do not make use of punishment are unknown, presumably for the reason that they cannot exist.

Too often parents attempt to make up for defective discipline by using precept, example, or formal instruction, without realizing that the young child is better adapted by nature to the process of training than to other methods of shaping personality. Moreover, training is the gateway to formal education and to self-discipline, which also enhances its importance to the process of adjustment (Mowrer, 1947).

Both training and discipline are complemented by the process of education. Where training is directed toward the acquisition of skills and habits, education is directed primarily to the growth of knowledge. Education is the objective complement of rational learning. However, the acquisition of knowledge is not the sole benefit of education, important as knowledge is to adjustment and mental stability. On all levels of education, ideals, values, principles, and attitudes are inculcated in the minds of young people. We have noted several times how important an adequate scale of values, a sound philosophy of life, and wholesome attitudes are, for which education is the primary instrument of development.

Self-determination and Adjustment

To what extent, if any, does the individual himself determine the pattern of his own adjustment? During this era of determinism (which is waning to some extent), it is customary to think of maladjustment and mental illness as the outcomes of heredity, innate disposition, home environment, faulty training, traumatic experiences, and similar influences. Seldom do we come across the notion that the difficulties encountered by persons in the areas of adjustment and mental health might be their own doing. We are willing to grant that some men are "self-made," but we are not so willing to accept the idea that neurotics and psychotics are self-made. Yet it is difficult to ignore the argument that within the make-up of human personality there is a powerful factor that can be utilized for good or ill, for the achievement of mastery and high level of adjustment, or for self-destruction and mental deterioration. *This factor is self-determination.* As one writer says "It is very important for mental hygiene that we realize that the strings of our destiny are in our own hands, and that no blind fate cuts through the strands of our mental health with a shears of a fatal heredity or the steel of the mechanics of the unconscious" * (also Mowrer, 1950, p. 39; Hogan, 1952, p. 424).

To avoid misunderstanding and senseless quibbling, let us grant that the patterns of adjustment and personality are determined early in life and to an important extent by the many factors discussed in this chapter. We all know that parental rejection, the broken home, bad heredity, economic and social deprivation, negative identification, and a large number of other determinants can seriously damage personality and the chances for good adjustment. And there is no sure way of telling how much of the undesirable effect is attributable to these sources, whether it is 50, 75, or 99 percent. However, these facts do not preclude the possibility that the individual himself has a say about how he will react in various situations. Parental rejection may be damaging to psychological health, but it does not have to be! Many normal adults have experienced rejection in childhood without lasting damage to their personalities. Similarly, many persons have, through their own self-determined efforts, overcome the bad effects of faulty training, and many others have emerged from under-privileged environments with adequate personalities.

It is important to realize that the philosophy of determinism contradicts the principles of mental hygiene and of effective living. From the standpoint of mental health it is helpful to realize that we *can* regulate our own conduct to an important extent, that we *can* rid ourselves of undesirable traits or habits that stand in the way of good adjustment, and that we *can* encourage the development of those responses that are beneficial to adjustment (Oppenheimer, 1952). The tragedy of neurotic and inadequate personalities is that this natural ability is stifled by an overlay of traumatic experiences, unwholesome parent-child relations, developmental anomalies, and generally bad environments. For this reason, the principles of mental hygiene and the techniques of psychotherapy must be used to break through and liberate the forces of self-realization that are inherent in every personality. This notion is the particular virtue of the technique of nondirective counseling or client-centered therapy, which, unlike other therapeutic philosophies, supports the idea that human nature

---

* Moore, T. V. *Personal mental hygiene.* New York: Grune & Stratton, 1944, p. 309. Used by permission.

contains within itself the capacities for psychological growth and rehabilitation of personality. No set of principles or treatment techniques can be wholly effective unless this basic idea is used as a starting point. On this point May makes an interesting observation regarding the treatment of tuberculous patients (May, 1950, p. 41n):

> In observing numbers of tuberculous patients, the writer noted that the sick persons were often reassured by well-meaning friends and medical personnel that the disease was due to an accident of infection by the t.b. bacilli. This explanation on the basis of fate was supposed to be a relief to the patient. But actually it threw many of the more psychologically sensitive patients into greater despair; if the disease were an accident, how could they be certain that it would not occur again and again? If, on the other hand, the patient feels that his own pattern of life was at fault and that this was one of the causes of his succumbing to the disease, he feels more guilt, to be sure, but at the same time he sees more hopefully what conditions need to be corrected in order to overcome the disease. From this point of view, guilt feeling is not only the more accurate attitude, but it is also the one yielding the more genuine hope.

If this is true of patients who are physically ill with diseases that have physical causes, how much more important is it for the maladjusted person or the neurotic to realize the part he can play in his own rehabilitation and return to normality and mental health!

Psychological Climate and Adjustment

Because adjustment and mental health are primarily psychological in nature, it is helpful to study the effects of the psychological setting within which they develop. By psychological climate we mean the complex of beliefs, taboos, prohibitions, emotional stimuli and relations, neurotic characteristics, and similar factors to which and within which a person reacts in an effort to cope with demands and to solve his problems. It is well known that neurotic or emotionally immature parents are likely to generate maladjusted children, simply because of the climate that they create by their own inadequacies. Similarly, where there are healthy relations of respect, trust, and mutual affection, or unhealthy conditions of jealousy, hatred, suspicion, envy, or bickering between the parents, or between parents and children, we can expect adjustments and mental stability to be directly affected. In some situations there is a general atmosphere of anxiety, timidity, or hostility; in others, there is a climate of confidence, security, comradeship, and happiness, and this atmosphere will be reflected in the psychological makeup of the persons subjected to it over a period of time. Mental health or adequate adjustment cannot readily flourish in an unhealthy psychological climate, which is one reason why the mental hygiene of the family and of society is as important as the mental hygiene of the individual (Senn, 1948; Schneiders, 1954b, pp. 52–61).

Symonds, citing a study by Hall on the effect of domestic discord on the personality development of children, points to a marked difference between the problems of children from homes where there was friction and those from homes where there was little or no friction (Symonds, 1939). Similarly, a study by Lewis on the influence of parental attitudes on children's lying showed that "ninety per cent of the nonliars came from stable, harmonious homes, as contrasted with twenty-five percent of the other group. All the nonliars were wanted children while of the twenty liars eight were definitely unwanted and seventy-five percent of the liars suffered from inconsistent discipline at home" (Lewis, 1930, p. 403). Using his own data on the marital relations of parents of accepted and rejected children, Symonds concludes that "marital disharmony is much more frequently found in homes where children are rejected than in homes where children are accepted. . . . The opposite finding which our data do not bring out, namely, that parents who accept their children have favorable, stable, and happy marital relations, is undoubtedly true . . ." (Symonds, 1939, p. 95). These results are supported by many other studies reported in the literature (Kanner, 1949; Winder & Rau, 1962; Korner, 1949).

We should not suppose that psychological climate is limited to the home. Right now we are witnessing the effects of what has been called "mass anxiety," a generalized fear that is national and even international in scope, and to which large groups of people are subject. Today, because of atomic weapons, international tensions, and the constant threat of global war, we are living in an atmosphere of dread and insecurity, and its effects on the mental condition and adjustments of individuals are clearly evident. We are on the verge of a mass psychosis, and it is small wonder that the incidence of neurotic and psychotic disorders continues to increase precipitously from year to year. Especially are these effects noticeable among young people who are faced with the calamitous uncertainties of an age in which the stable values, ideals, and goals of an earlier era have been crushed by the onslaught of materialism, universal military training, atomic destruction, and the internal dissolution of contemporary society, particularly the family (Kisker, 1951). Here we see how the psychological climate spreads into the cultural framework within which personality develops and adjustments are made, and why it is important to study these relationships. We are reminded here of the formula adopted by UNESCO, "Since wars begin in the minds of men, it is in the minds of men that defenses of peace must be constructed."

QUESTIONS AND PROJECTS FOR FURTHER STUDY

1. Name and describe the symptoms or characteristics of three psychological disorders that are clearly organic in nature. Explain what is meant by the term "organic."
2. Using whatever scientific data you can find, write a documented term paper on the influence of heredity on mental disorder.
3. From your own experience, or from biographical data, describe several "cases" that illustrate the influence of physical deficiencies on personal adjustment. Can you explain what happens psychologically in such instances?
4. Now that you have studied the conditions and determinants of adjustment and mental health, do you think that most instances of maladjustment or mental disorder are reversible? Why? From this same line of evidence, would you conclude that the future of treatment lies in tranquilizers and shock treatment, or in counseling and psychotherapy?
5. State the psychological law of effect and cite examples to show how it relates to the development of good and poor adjustments.
6. Write an essay, supported by authority, on the importance of discipline to mental health.
7. Explain in your own words the limits of personal freedom with relation to adjustment and mental health. Is a neurotic responsible for his neurosis? Explain your answer.
8. Write a comparative, critical evaluation of any two books or six journal articles that deal with the problem of family influences on adjustment.

SELECTED COLLATERAL READINGS

BARKER, R. G., et al. Adjustment to physical handicap and illness. Bull. No. 55, rev. New York: Social Science Research Council, 1953.

FRY, C. C., & ROSTOW, E. G. Mental health in college. New York: Commonwealth Fund, 1942.

HOCH, P. H., & ZUBIN, J. (Eds.) Comparative epidemiology of the mental disorders. (Vol. XVI of the Psychopathological Association Series) New York: Grune & Stratton, 1961.

HOLLINGSHEAD, A. B. Elmtown's youth. New York: Wiley, 1949.

HOLLINGSHEAD, A. B., & REDLICH, F. C. Social class and mental illness, a community study. New York: Wiley, 1958.

KALLMANN, F. J. *Heredity in health and mental disorder.* New York: Norton, 1953.

LEIGHTON, K. H. *My name is legion.* New York: Basic Books, 1959.

MC CANN, R. V. *The Churches and mental health.* New York: Basic Books, 1962.

MYERS, J. K., & ROBERTS, B. H. *Family and class dynamics in mental illness.* New York: Wiley, 1959.

ORR, W. H. *Hormones, health, and happiness.* New York: Macmillan, 1954.

PHILLIPS, E. L., WIENER, D. N., & HARING, N. G. *Discipline, achievement, and mental health.* Englewood Cliffs, N. J.: Prentice-Hall, 1960.

PLUNKETT, R. J. & GORDON, J. E. *Epidemiology and mental illness.* New York: Basic Books, 1960.

RADKE, M. J. *The relation of parental authority to children's behavior and attitudes.* Minneapolis: University of Minnesota Press, 1946.

REISSMAN, F. *The culturally deprived child.* New York: Harper & Row, 1962.

SHAW, F. J., & ORT, R. S. *Personal adjustment in the American culture.* New York: Harper & Row, 1953.

SLOTKIN, J. S. *Personality development.* New York: Harper & Row, 1952.

SMART, M., & SMART, R. *An introduction to family relationships.* Philadelphia: Saunders, 1953.

SYMONDS, P. M. *The psychology of parent-child relationships.* New York: Appleton, 1939.

WEINBERG, S. K. *Society and personality disorders.* Englewood Cliffs, N. J.: Prentice-Hall, 1952.

WEINSTEIN, E. A. *Cultural aspects of delusion: A psychiatric study of the Virgin Islands.* New York: Free Press, 1962.

WHITE, R. W. *Lives in progress.* New York: Holt, Rinehart and Winston, 1952.

WILNER, D. M., et al. *The housing environment and family life: A longitudinal study of housing, morbidity, and mental health.* Baltimore: The Johns Hopkins Press, 1962.

WRIGHT, BEATRICE. *Physical disability—a psychological approach.* New York: Harper & Row, 1960.

5

Dynamic Factors in Adjustment and Mental Health

Nowhere in the broad field of psychological science is the question "Why?" more important than in the area of mental health and adjustment. It is not so hard to understand normal adjustments just because they are normal; but as we saw, some adjustments are very unusual, strange, and even bizarre; and to understand them we must figure out why people behave this way. We must understand why mental health can break down and be replaced by delusions, silly thinking, symptoms, and syndromes. Are these things expressive of needs? Of desires? Of feelings and emotions? Or do we have to appeal to some other dynamic principles to explain what is happening? Let us see.

ADJUSTMENT AND MOTIVATION

Determinants of Behavior versus Behavior Dynamics

This chapter on the dynamics of adjustment is in a sense a continuation of the preceding discussion of personality determinants which, as we said, set the stage for, influence, or determine the course adjustment takes. The dynamic factors that make up human motivation also have much to do with the course of adjustment. However, needs, motives, and goals—the dynamic factors underlying behavior—have a special relation to adjustment and mental health that distinguish them from behavior determinants. This relation can be described by saying that the essential purpose and content of adjustive behavior are determined by needs and motives. If we think of learning, self-determination, training, and education as the compasses by which the course of adjustment is charted, then motivation can be interpreted as the propeller that initiates and sustains the course that is followed.

From one point of view, the essential purpose of adjustive response is to set up an adequate relation between the organism and reality; from another, and more fundamental point of view, its purpose is the expression and gratification of dynamic factors within personality (especially needs), and the reduction of tensions, frustrations, and conflicts to which these factors often give rise (White, 1952, pp. 3–25). In the achievement of this purpose, the content of behavior and of response in general is determined primarily by the character of the motivation and only secondarily by the qualities of the situation in which the behavior occurs. Thus, if a child is deprived of affection, his behavior will reflect the dynamics of this basic need. However, the situation in which he finds himself will determine whether he invests his interest in a dog, a drunken father, an overprotective mother, or an indulgent uncle (Schneiders, 1960d, pp. 145–170; Lewin, 1946).

Adjustive Responses and Human Needs

Is all adjustive behavior directed toward the reduction or expression of basic needs and motives? This is part of the broader question whether or not all responses fit into the concept of adjustment (Symonds, 1949, Chapter II). First of all, we must recognize that there is a large category of reactions, physiological and neuromuscular in nature, to which the term "adaptive" is more appropriate than the term "adjustive." Circulatory, digestive, respiratory, and eliminative functions fit into this category. And perhaps the entire range of pure reflex responses should also be included here since they have little relation to motivation.

Then there are those responses that stem from and serve the purpose of gratifying basic needs, including physiological drives like hunger and sex, and those that are psychological or social in nature, such as security and affection. These responses fit into the concept of adjustment as it is used and interpreted in current psychological thought. Needs may be defined as *internal demands*, and adjustment is consistently interpreted as a kind of response directed toward meeting the demands that the organism is confronted with in daily living (Crow & Crow, 1963c).

There are of course other demands that arise from *external sources*, which the organism is required to resolve by an effective organization of behavior; responses to these demands are also adjustive. As we have seen many times, family life, marriage, one's job, social relations, military life, and education make demands that must be met adequately and efficiently; and in meeting these demands the organism is correctly described as adjusting. In these instances the behavior is characteristically voluntary or habitual in nature, rather than need-determined. Hence we can say that *all responses, whether habitual, voluntary, instinctive, or emotional, are adjustive when they are directed toward meeting internal or external demands.*

This relation to the demands imposed on the organism distinguishes typically adjustive responses from others that are more correctly interpreted as *rational* and *goal-directed*. Let us suppose, for example, that a person decides, on graduation from high school, to become a physician. With this selection of a distant goal, he sets in motion a long series of responses directed toward its achievement. He registers at a university, consults advisers, buys textbooks, goes to classes, travels long distances, writes to medical schools, and does many other things that will help him realize his ambition. Yet no one of these actions is really a form of adjustment. If at any point he decides to relinquish the career of medicine for something less distant or ambitious, we could not say that he was failing to adjust to life.

Similarly, for other persons, the purchase of a house, establishing a savings account, joining a book club, buying insurance, trading in the old car for a new one, taking a trip, and so on, are sensible and rational ways of behaving, and often contribute to the enrichment of life, but they are *not* forms of adjustment. However, if any of these situations brings along with it certain demands that must be met for the sake of propriety, justice, or efficiency, then we are dealing with a problem in adjustment. For example, the medical student must meet academic requirements, and the person who buys an automobile must conform to the limitations of his budget. But these demands are incidental to the main course of the behavior, which is rational and goal-directed, and whatever adjustment problems arise in this type of situation are quite accidental, even though they may at any point disrupt the pattern of healthy adjustment to a noticeable degree.

The idea that all behavior or conduct is adjustive stems from the assumption that responses invariably reflect basic urges or needs. Thus Symonds states, "The argument of this book is based on the hypothesis that all behavior originates in response to urges within an individual. His frustrations and conflicts, his modes of adjustment and all of the details of daily conduct follow in response to certain fundamental motivating forces within him." Moreover, "the basic understanding of human behavior is rooted in biology and physiology" (Symonds, 1949, p. 11). The implication of such statements is that all conduct is determined by needs or drives, leaving little room for rational control. In fact, in the preface to the first edition of this book, Symonds had stated, "reason and intellect are dethroned as the principal factors in adjustment." However, he modified his position in the newer edition (Symonds, 1949, Chapter XX).

If our interpretation is correct what are we to say about earlier statements to the effect that rationality and goal direction are basic to the process of adjustment and to mental health? Actually, the one interpretation supports the other. Although goal-directed behavior is not itself a kind of adjustment, the chances for meeting the demands of self or environment are much better when our behavior is oriented toward goals than when it is impulsive, disorganized, or lacking in direction. Similarly, adjustive responses that are controlled by the factor of rationality have a better chance of succeeding than are those dominated by blind impulse, needs, frustrations, or conflicts (Schneiders, 1963a). If all human responses were rational or goal-directed, which they most certainly are not, the problems of adjustment would simply disappear. This is not likely to happen as long as there are human needs and environmental situations that impose demands on human beings.

THEORIES OF MOTIVATION

Mechanical Theories

The way in which we interpret the relation of human responses to adjustment will depend on how we interpret the nature of motivation (Koch, 1951; Allport, 1953; Littman, 1958). For example, if all motivation is fundamentally sexual or unconscious, as some Freudians maintain, then all behavior, whether normal or abnormal, must be regarded as a collective effort to reduce the tensions, conflicts, or frustrations engendered by these motivations. In such a scheme there is little room for deliberation, choice, or goal-directed activity. In this view, all behavior is adjustive (Brown, 1953; Maslow, 1954; Bindra, 1959).

Much the same limitation is inherent in mechanistic theories of motivation, including the *stimulus response* hypothesis and the *physiological* theory (Fuller, 1962). In the former view all behavior is determined by stimuli, and it is either reflexive or the result of conditioning, so that such categories as needs, desires, and motives are regarded as nonexistent. While this view can explain adaptive responses and account for conditioned reactions, it is essentially of little value to the psychology of adjustment. Only when conditioning is applied more broadly as a part of the learning process can it help us to a better understanding of the development of adjustive or maladjustive patterns (Vinacke, 1962).

The physiological hypothesis of human motivation is not much of an improvement over the reflex theory (Stellar, 1954). The reduction of all motivations to physiological drives, tensions, or disequilibrium is as much at fault in its oversimplification as the notion that all responses are determined by stimuli. Psychological needs, desires, motives, and goals, all of which are profoundly significant to adjustment, must be integrated into any theory of motivation, and this the physiological hypothesis cannot do for the simple reason that it leaves no room for them. Thus, according to Symonds, "all behavior arises from drives for the alleviation of organic needs, whether these be nutritive deficits in the body, the need to excrete waste products, the stimulation of chemical or glandular agents in the blood and tissues, or the need to protect the organism against injury. . . . [Admittedly,] this stimulus-response psychology is deficient in that it does not take into account the dynamic processes of the organism itself and the fact that an organism behaves in response to its own needs. . . . [Nevertheless,] in these fundamental terms happiness may be traced back to the satisfaction of physiological needs" (Symonds, 1949, p. 17).

We may grant, of course, that some of our most basic motivations are physiological, but to understand the peculiarities and intricacies of adjustment and mental health, we must go considerably beyond the physiological needs of the organism. Of much greater signficance are the psychological and social needs, spiritual desires, feelings and emotions, complexes and mechanisms, goals, motives, and attitudes that underlie human responses. These factors constitute the real dynamics of adjustive behavior (Seward, 1956; Morgan, 1957; O'Kelly, 1963).

Instinct Theory

The physiological hypothesis, in its turn, is closely related to the instinct theory, since many physiological drives (hunger, thirst, and sex, for example) are among the most clear-cut examples of instincts. Among the different forms of the instinct hypothesis, the *hormic* viewpoint of William McDougall is one of the most prominent. It holds that all behavior is in the service of a number of basic instincts, and therefore these instincts are the primary internal determinants of adjustive behavior (Maslow, 1954). This theory, once widely held, has been largely abandoned by psychologists because it contains too many broad and indefensible generalizations and because it does not give enough credit to learning, maturation, and cultural determinants (Fletcher, 1957).

Much hardier than the hormic theory are the doctrines of Sigmund Freud, collectively referred to as psychoanalysis, of which there are many good accounts in the literature (Hendrick, 1939; Mullahy, 1948; Rado, 1946). In this view the instinct hypothesis took an entirely different turn. First of all, Freud reduced the number of instincts to two: eros, or the life (love, sex) instinct, and thanatos, or the instinct of death and self-destruction. Freud also gave much more prominence to the importance of sex in determining adjustment and maladjustment than had McDougall. Further than that, with his passion for systematizing, Freud integrated his instinct theory with his philosophy of the unconscious and of hedonism. This system was expanded into a psychology of personality which is expressed succinctly in the tripartite division of id, ego, and superego, the whole being rooted in the theory of instincts. To understand this viewpoint completely, the theory must be brought into relation with Freud's concept of the reality principle because the expression of the instincts is "conditioned" by the impositions of reality (Gill, 1959; Rapaport, 1960).

Freud begins and ends his theory of behavior, mental life, and mental disorder with the sexual instinct. Breast feeding, thumb sucking, and smoking are interpreted as instances of oral or infantile sexuality. Dreams are the distorted expressions in mental life of repressed sexuality. The mental life and adjustments of women are conditioned throughout by penis envy. Neurotic symptoms are the overt expression of unresolved sexual conflicts. Homosexuality is the result of fixation at an early level of psychosexual development. Aggression toward the parents represents the hatred or fear that is part of the Oedipus complex or, more specifically, castration anxiety (Blum, 1949).

This is an all too brief synopsis of the Freudian theory of psychosexual development as it relates to adjustment and mental health, but we may note that there is much in Freud's theory that is useful to the psychology of adjustment. The same applies to his psychology of personality and to his theory of the unconscious. Freud's theory of repression, symbolism, and symptom formation has gained almost universal acceptance. His interpretation of dreams, while not altogether acceptable from a scientific point of view, is one of the most brilliant theories in the history of abnormal psychology and psychiatry. And even the concept of psychosexual development and the pansexual theory, along with hedonism, receive a great deal of support from clinical and therapeutic observations. The brilliance of many of Freud's discoveries has not dimmed to any great extent with the passing years, although there have been many of his disciples who have tried to improve on Freud's basic ideas (Munroe, 1955; Horney, 1950; Fromm, 1941, 1950).

Despite wide acceptance of his theories, and a durability that suggests that they have much truth in them, Freud's interpretation has been severely criticized by many careful investigators and completely rejected by not a few others. Following are some of the more prominent criticisms: (1) It is grossly unscientific because it generalizes from limited data. (2) It interprets the normal completely in terms of the abnormal. (3) Its doctrine of infantile sexuality is entirely gratuitous and based on inferences from adult experiences. (4) It is oversimplified, putting nearly all its emphasis on sex and failing to recognize that there are other basic drives of equal or greater importance. (5) It makes the mistake of forcing data to fit the theory, instead of developing the theory in terms of the data, a point that is clearly exemplified in the uses made of castration anxiety and penis envy. (6) Its interpretation of dreams and neurotic symptoms is forced, since they can often be accounted for more adequately in terms of other postulates (Salter, 1952; Sears, 1943; Mullahy, 1948, Part II; Nuttin, 1953; Stern, 1954).

These criticisms can apply with equal force to Freud's theory of self-destruction, which Freud developed to explain suicide, criminal acts, pathological drinking, drug addiction, and other self-destructive behavior. Yet all the facts of development, growth, and organic repair are contrary to the idea of the death instinct. So, too, are the universal will to live, the interest in living, the zest for life found in many people, and the general repugnance to death and self-destruction found everywhere. Arguing from instances of self-destruction is again the mistake of interpreting the normal in terms of the abnormal, although it can be argued that in some instances, such as pathological drinking, it would seem that the victim is intent on his own destruction. One writer has argued that Freud's theory of life as a step toward the goal of death is a projection of his own unresolved terror; that Freud's theoretical prejudices became a defense against the outward toler-ance that reflected the rejection pattern of a lifetime (Levin, 1951).

Hedonistic Theory

We will leave for later study (Chapter 6) the theory of unconscious motivation because it has become an essential part of dynamic theory, but there is one other aspect of the Freudian dynamics that is of considerable importance for the psychology of adjustment, and that is the *pleasure principle*. This notion is generally referred to as *psychological hedonism, which means that conduct is dominated and determined by the quality of pleasure.*

> In the psycho-analytical theory of the mind we take it for granted that the course of mental processes is automatically regulated by "the pleasure-principle": that is to say, we believe that any given process originates in an unpleasant state of tension and thereupon determines for itself such a path that its ultimate issue coincides with a relaxation of this tension, i.e. with avoidance of "pain" or with production of pleasure (Freud, 1948, p. 1; also Symonds, 1949, pp. 15–16).

This view, whether correct or not, is consistent with Freud's sexual theory, since sexual activity is certainly dominated by pleasure. However, it is seriously questionable whether pleasure is the motivating force behind *all* human conduct.

Here again we see the danger of oversimplification and unscientific generalization. Granted that numerous responses, both normal and abnor-mal, can be explained by reference to the pleasure they afford, there are just as many that can be accounted for by reference to other factors, including rational desires and motives, goal seeking, frustrations, psychological needs, habits, effect, emotions, attitudes, and the like. Hedonism is particularly cumbersome in the explanation of abnormal behavior and mental difficulties because so many of these responses are extremely unpleasant and distasteful to the patient. Here the law of effect, described in the preceding chapter, is a much better principle of explanation than is pleasure because it emphasizes the fact that satisfaction determines the repetition or continuation of a response. A response may be pleasant or not, but if it is satisfying, that is, if it gratifies some need, desire, or motive, or reduces tension and conflict, it is likely to be repeated. Similarly, many unpleasant acts as well as pleasant ones are undertaken in striving toward a goal. A serious student will endure many hardships and disagreeable tasks in order to complete his education. Here, too, the element of ultimate satisfaction is much more influential than the pleasure or pain of the moment. In the explanation, therefore, of ordinary conduct, of adjustment and maladjustment, of symptoms and mechanisms, we must be careful not to overwork one principle to the exclusion of others, particularly those that are better suited by reason of their greater explanatory value (Brown, 1955; Young, 1955).

Voluntaristic Theory

In a measure opposed to all of the preceding hypotheses of motivation is the viewpoint that conduct can be best explained by reference to voluntary or volitional antecedents. What a person does is determined by what he *wants* to do, that is, by rational motives and desires operating under the principles of self-determination, deliberation, and choice. Here there is little room for unconscious motivation, pansexualism, stimulus-response behavior, or hedonism. Not that these possibilities are completely excluded; rather *the emphasis is placed on man as a volitional, self-determining organism*, capable of deliberating on, and choosing for himself different courses of action. This notion was implied in our earlier discussions of man's rationality and his capacity for self-determination.

In normal persons, certainly, a good share of ordinary conduct is determined by rational motives, deliberation, and intelligent decisions. Such conduct is often goal-directed, and the striving toward goals is both voluntary and rational. These capabilities are of major importance in reducing conflicts, in overcoming irritating or inhibiting frustrations, in breaking bad or inefficient habits, and in developing consistent patterns of response that are both beneficial and necessary to achieving healthy adjustment. However, it is just as serious a mistake to overwork this idea, because *the dynamics of adjustment and mental health reach far beyond the boundaries of deliberate, voluntary conduct* (Schneiders, 1963a).

There are many responses, particularly in abnormal and maladjusted persons, that cannot be accounted for in terms of the voluntaristic hypothesis. Symptoms are not voluntary; psychological mechanisms are not voluntary; nor are neurotic, psychopathic, and psychotic response patterns voluntary. These symptom complexes and abnormal ways of behaving are the expressions of dynamic factors within the personality and of the relations between personality and the objective world in which it functions. This notion, too, was implied in our discussion of the conditions and determinants of adjustment in the preceding chapter. Thus, if we are to understand the dynamics of adjustment and mental health, these various theories of motivation must be integrated into a total and consistent dynamics of behavior.

RANGE OF MOTIVATING FACTORS

In the light of the difficulties encountered with various theories of motivation, it is important to determine the range and the classes or types of motivating factors. Table 8 is a simple diagram of factors ordinarily described in the literature and encountered in any effort to interpret the dynamics of behavior.

TABLE 8

Classification of Motivating Factors

Conscious motivations	*Unconscious motivations*
Needs	Feelings
Desires and wants	Experiences
Motives	Wishes
Interests	Complexes
Attitudes	Instinct
Goals	Habits and mechanisms

Admittedly, there are limitations to any system of classification, and the one shown in Table 8 is no exception. It has the virtues of simplicity and of being particularly well suited to studying the relation between dynamics and adjustment, but there are certain implications that would be misleading if they were not carefully pointed out. This is usually the case with simple dichotomies. For example, needs, desires, and attitudes are not always clearly conscious; sometimes they are definitely unconscious. Similarly, the class of unconscious motivations means only that *some* feelings, experiences, wishes, and the like, are unconscious. The important point is that some adjustments are determined by conscious motivations, and among them the factors we have included are most significant; other adjustments are determined by unconscious motivations, and here repressed feelings, wishes, traumatic experiences, and complexes play a dominant role. As long as we are aware of the limitations of this dichotomy, it should serve well as a basis for interpreting the relations between motivation and adjustment.

HUMAN NEEDS AS MOTIVATING FACTORS

Nature and Classes of Needs

Of all dynamic factors in personality, there is none more important to the understanding of adjustment and mental health than human needs because, by their very nature, *needs are internal demands that must be gratified in order to achieve adjustment.* Needs are dynamic tendencies oriented toward objects, qualities, or experiences that are required for the physical, psychological, or social well-being of the organism (Cameron & Magaret, 1951, pp. 32–37; Maslow, 1948). It is this fact that certain experiences (like love) and certain objects (like food) are *required* that explains the dynamic characteristics of human needs. Whenever one or more of these basic tendencies is frustrated, inhibited, or not allowed adequate expression, the organism gravitates toward mental reactions or forms of behavior that are inadequate, distorted, bizarre, symptomatic, or pathological. To take a simple example, the child who is denied a sense of security or belonging by parental rejection or a broken home will show symptoms of anxiety, withdrawal, aggressiveness, or hostility because, needing security and not knowing how to achieve it, he strikes out blindly in a desperate effort to reduce the tension created by the frustrated need (Raths, 1963). If needs could be consciously inhibited or willed out of existence, this development would not occur, but, because they represent *actual organic requirements*, the tensions they create must be reduced in one way or another. If the situation is favorable to the gratification of the need, normal behavior results; if not, abnormality or maladjustment may be the outcome (Thorpe, 1950, Chapter II).

Physiological Needs

There are different classes of needs, corresponding to different facets of personality. Of these, physiological needs clearly exemplify the dynamic relation between needs and adjustment (Symonds, 1949, pp. 28–30). Everyone knows that, for physical well-being and integrity, the organism requires air, food, liquid, rest, shelter, activity, elimination of waste products, and freedom from noxious stimuli. Without these requirements the organism tends toward physical weakness, ill health, disease, or death. The end result, then, of frustration or privation of these needs is physical maladjustment.

The sexual impulse, which is certainly physiological in nature, does not fit well into this category, because its denial does not produce the same consequences that the deprivation of the needs mentioned above would. Since sexual need is directed primarily to the preservation of the species rather than the individual, it is clearly different from other physiological needs. For the same reason, it is the one need whose gratification is *not* *required* for adjustment. Sexual functioning is dominated by group requirements or pleasure and not by the demands for adequate personal adjustment. These characteristics do not make the sex drive less dynamic than other needs, nor do they make the problem of sexual adjustment less severe or important. The inhibition or chronic frustration of sexual impulse, or the failure to exercise control over or to sublimate sexual desire can lead to damaging conflicts and behavior disturbances. The only point we wish to make here is that sexual need functions differently in relation to adjustment than do other physiological needs, not that the problem of sexual adjustment is insignificant.

Physiological needs bring out clearly why needs are referred to as *requirements* and why their gratification is basic to the process of healthy adjustment. But it should be understood that the gratification of physiological needs ensures only the physical adjustment of the organism; therefore, *in themselves*, they have little do with *psychological* well-being or mental health. This is particularly true in a society such as our where the standard of living is relatively high, and basic physical requirements are usually well taken care of. However, we must note an important relation between the gratification of physical needs and the achievement of psychological adjustment (Kaplan & Baron, 1952, pp. 148–149). Good physical care, particularly in early childhood, can contribute greatly to satisfying the psychological needs for affection, security, and a sense of belonging (Wilner, 1962). This fact is clearly illustrated in the differential effects of breast feeding and bottle feeding in early infancy. Psychologists and psychiatrists generally agree that natural breast feeding lays a more secure groundwork for the psychological well-being of the child. In this natural physical relation between mother and child, the seeds of affection and security are more firmly planted and more readily nurtured than in the unnatural situation of bottle feeding. Similarly, in later years, the psychological requirements of the child can be healthily nutured in a setting in which his physical needs are well cared for (Ribble, 1943, pp. 621–651).

An excellent discussion of the relation of physical to psychological well-being is given in Bowlby's well-known monograph on maternal care and mental health. Bowlby states that "prolonged deprivation of the young child of maternal care may have grave and far-reaching effects on his character and so on the whole of his future life" (Bowlby, 1951). Although the relation of breast feeding to character formation is supported in a number of places (Goldman, 1950), this viewpoint has been disputed by different investigators (Thurston & Mussen, 1951). Whatever the final outcome of these different studies, the important fact is that physical well-being is important to the total adjustment of the individual.

Psychological Needs

Because the human organism is psychological as well as physical, its mental life and adjustments are dominated by a number of psychological requirements or needs, satisfaction of which is fundamental to adjustment. These requirements are generally referred to as psychological needs, although the terms "emotional needs" and "adjustment needs" are also used (D'Evelyn, 1957; Gardner, 1948, pp. 69–90). Technically, *a psychological need is defined as a tension resulting from the absence or deprivation of a quality, experience, or relation that is necessary to the psychological well-being (adjustment) of the organism.*

But what is "psychological adjustment"? This condition is the equivalent, in the psychological order, of physical well-being. It denotes a sense of inner security, emotional tranquillity, happiness, peace of mind, self-satisfaction, and personal worth. Contrast these qualities with the psychological condition of the typical neurotic person, and you will see what is meant by psychological well-being. The neurotic is emotionally disturbed, unhappy, dissatisfied with himself, and almost completely lacking in a sense of security and personal worth. This is what is meant by saying that such persons, although physically sound, are psychologically disturbed (Thorpe, 1950, pp. 35–44).

Among the psychological needs are several that stand out prominently in their relation to adjustment and mental health. These are affection, belonging, security, achievement, independence, self-identity, and status or personal worth (Sears, 1963). So pervasive and profound are the effects of these needs that they are universally regarded as the *primary internal determinants* of mental health and adjustment, a viewpoint that is thoroughly substantiated by clinical experience with disturbed and maladjusted children and by observations of children in institutional settings who are suffering from need deprivation of one kind or another (Frank, 1938; Ribble, 1943; Goldfarb, 1945; Reik, 1963).

The allied needs for affection and belonging provide excellent illustrations of the close connection between psychological needs and adjustment. Children need to be loved, and they need to feel that they belong to someone or to a family group (Beller, 1959). When they are given affection in a healthy manner, the sense of belonging quickly develops. When these needs are stifled by rejecting, hating, selfish or jealous parents, or by the breakup of the home, the child feels unwanted (Suttie, 1952). He becomes insecure and frightened and feels that there is no one to whom he can turn to help him push back the threats or terrors of reality —a reality, incidentally, that he little understands and for which he is poorly equipped. The child who is secure in affection and the feeling of being wanted reflects this security in a happy disposition, affectionate behavior, and a healthy relation with other people in his environment; similarly, the child in whom these needs are stifled shows withdrawal, resentment, hostility, anxiety, or aggressiveness. Here we have a clear example of how the dynamics of basic needs find expression in behavior, the quality of which is determined by how well or poorly the needs themselves are gratified.

Denial of affection and a sense of belonging seriously affect the satisfaction of the demands for security and status (Bennett, 1959). A feeling of security is fundamental to good adjustment because it provides the individual with the psychological means necessary to cope with the conflicts and frustrations, and the demands and difficulties that arise every day. This kind of security is not achieved through economic or physical well-being, although later on these factors may contribute to its development; rather, it is the basic conviction of one's own intrinsic value and capability, a conviction that helps to establish status with reference to self and to others (Maslow, 1942).

Erich Fromm, in his *Escape from freedom* (1941, p. 19) expresses very clearly the need for belonging:

> To feel completely alone and isolated leads to mental disintegration just as physical starvation leads to death. This relatedness to others is not identical with physical contact. An individual may be alone in a physical sense for many years and yet he may be related to ideas, values, or at least social patterns that give him a feeling of com-

munion and "belonging." On the other hand, he may live among people and yet be overcome with an utter feeling of isolation, the outcome of which, if it transcends a certain limit, is the state of insanity which schizophrenic disturbances represent.

And in a later book, *The sane society* (1955, p. 31), Fromm defines the power of love:

> There is only one passion which satisfies man's need to unite himself with the world, and to acquire at the same time a sense of integrity and individuality, and this is *love*. *Love is union* with somebody, or something, outside oneself, *under the condition of retaining the separateness and integrity of one's own self*. It is an experience of sharing, of communion, which permits the full unfolding of one's own inner activity.

The feeling of personal worth and of status is determined by a number of factors, some of which we discussed under the heading of behavior determinants. For example, the internal cohesion of the family, healthy parent-child relations, adequate discipline, worthwhile experiences, opportunities for achievement, and group acceptance can foster both security and the conviction of personal worth (Jayasuriya, 1950). In the absence of such factors, a sense of security or status cannot easily develop, with the result that behavior and mental stability ofen become disrupted. The insecure child typically becomes anxious, timid, withdrawn, and unhappy, whereas children lacking in a sense of personal worth often show symptoms of hostility, aggressiveness, seclusiveness, or sometimes an almost pathological superiority.

Psychological needs, particularly security and status, are reflected in the craving for attention that children (and some adults) consistently manifest, hence the reference to "attention-getting mechanisms" in the literature. Gaining the attention of others is especially a boon to feelings of personal worth because, temporarily at least, it divests the child of feelings of inadequacy and thus contributes to the enhancement of his ego. Children who feel insecure in their own capacities or who have strong feelings of inferiority are most likely to utilize behavior that secures attention; therefore, the more persistent attention-getting behavior becomes, the more certainly can we conclude that the need for affection, security, or status is being inadequately gratified.

The young child's craving for security is tempered in later years, particularly during adolescence, by the need for independence (Gardner, 1947). Once the child breaks away from the narrow confines of the family circle to establish relations with playmates, schoolmates, friends, and occasional companions, the striving for independence begins, and it continues to grow in intensity until the end of the adolescent period, when often there is a complete break with the family. This process is sometimes referred to as *psychological weaning* or emancipation from the home. During these years, the need for security also keeps its grip on the child—a situation, incidentally, that makes for conflict and emotional uncertainty—but its hold is gradually weakened as the child approaches the threshold of mature living and adult responsibilities Then young people want to go away to school, join the service, establish a "home" of their own (even if it is only one room in a boarding house), or simply run away (Finesinger, 1944; Johnson, 1938; Morgan, 1939; Vinacke, 1960).

This craving for independence shows itself in many ways in the behavior of children, affecting their adjustments to themselves and to other persons. Where the family situation is adequate, and parent-child relations are good, independence expresses itself normally in the personal selection of friends, individual preferences for clothes, for school, demands for freedom of action, and so on. In the overprotected or severely disciplined child, in contrast, independence often leads to conflict, confusion, aggression, or open rebellion.

A balance must be carefully maintained in gratifying such needs as affection, security, and independence. Extremely close emotional ties of affection with the parents can seriously blunt the normal development of independence, so that in adulthood the person is clinging, immature, and poorly adjusted. Similarly, too much security (overprotection) or too little (the rejected, unwanted child) will inhibit or distort the growth of independence. The insecure child, like the one smothered with affection, cannot successfully achieve emancipation from the home, and thus the realities of adulthood stand as a constant threat or barrier to mature, efficient living. Insecure persons shy away from the responsibilities of marriage or an important job; or, if they venture into marriage, their marital relations are constantly tortured with hesitation, fear, uncertainty, the intrusion of parental images, and desires for separation so that they can return to the security and affection of their childhood. *Mature living and good adjustment require ego security, but they also require a healthy measure of independence in judgment, decision, and conduct.*

The dynamic craving for independence is closely joined to another primary psychological need—*self-identity*. The struggle for self-identity and the achievement of selfhood are the most striking characteristics of the late adolescent period. The clamor that the adolescent sets up for independence is partly a reflection of this need for identity since identity can only be achieved by emancipation from dependence on parents. The adolescent must literally *become himself*; he must discover what this self is and how it is related to the present and to the future. Here we see again why goal direction is so important to adjustment and to mental health. The more goal-oriented the young person becomes, the easier it is for him to achieve self-identity and certify his own selfhood. These two needs functioning together—independence and self-identity—explain much of the conflict, frustration, and difficulties of the adolescent period (Erikson, 1959; Strauss, 1959; Mussen, 1962).

The functioning of independence and self-identity is complemented by another psychological requirement, the *need for achievement*. This may be simply a special instance of the need for status because the higher the level of achievement the greater the feeling of personal worth. In any event, the craving for personal achievement is reflected in the behavior of many people. Its frustration can lead to real personal difficulties (McClelland, 1953), for parental lack of interest in a child's accomplishments, or the deep conviction of failure that children experience when their best efforts prove inadequate, can give rise to deep feelings of inferiority or worthlessness. This is especially likely to happen when parents are perfectionistic or hypercritical and strive to realize through their children the achievements of which they themselves were incapable. The child may develop compulsive tendencies toward achievement (later to become the adult with excessive drive or ambition to succeed), or a chronic sense of frustration and failure, and a habit of giving up too easily. Or he may rebel against standards of achievement and refuse to rise above mediocrity even if his natural capacities are well above average (Broverman, Jordan & Phillips, 1960). This *commitment to mediocrity* helps us to understand why some very capable students consistently underachieve in high school and in college. There are other factors at work in this situation, but this is one of the most important. Conversely, satisfying the need for achievement enhances the feelings of security and status and fosters the development of healthy attitudes toward self and toward others (Sears, 1957).

Finally, we may note the relations between adjustment and the *need for experience*. This primary requirement of human nature, too often ignored or unrecognized is one of the most dynamic factors influencing human behavior. From birth on, the organism is not only receptive to experience, but actively seeks situations that provide experiences of various kinds (Hill, 1956). Thrill seeking among adolescents is one of the more obvious illustrations of this need, which is sometimes referred to as the "craving for novelty." Not all experiences gratify this craving, since the experience itself may be very ordinary or dull. But experiences that are unusual, or different, or peculiarly satisfying in some way will gratify this need. Thus the typical youngster wants to live on a farm for the summer, paddle a canoe by himself, drive a car at eighty miles an hour, ride the back seat of a motorcycle, smoke a cigarette, or have a date—just "to see what it is like."

Quite often the need for experience takes a peculiar twist, especially when blocked by parental restrictions, social demands, or by lack of opportunity for normal expression. Then patterns of maladjustive behavior are likely to emerge—joy riding, truancy, nomadism, illicit sex relations, stealing, experimenting with narcotic drugs, or predatory gang behavior. The need for experience is not as deeply related to psychological well-being as are other needs, but it must be carefully channeled in the right direction, and it should not be chronically or excessively thwarted in young people. Parents and teachers should provide many and diverse opportunities for expression of this need in a normal, acceptable, and healthy way that contributes to personality growth and to adequate adjustment.

Psychological Needs and Emotional Adjustment

So far we have indicated the influence of psychological needs on both mental and behavioral adjustments. Equally important are the effects of need gratification or deprivation on emotional stability, especially in view of the basic relation between this factor and mental health. For this reason the term "emotional needs" is sometimes used as a substitute for psychological needs. Certainly healthy gratification of such needs as affection, security, personal worth, and belonging can do a great deal to promote emotional development and expression in children. Children whose emotional needs are gratified usually are happy, free in their emotional expression, and quick to establish good affectional relations with others (Schneiders, 1951). Unburdened by feelings of rejection, inadequacy, hatred, inferiority, or jealousy, they are seldom given to emotional outbursts or to fits of moodiness and depression. How unlike the fate of those children whose emotional needs are chronically frustrated and forced into modes of expression that stand in the way of mental health and adjustment. As one writer states,

> The causation of emotional disturbance can be fully understood only in relation to the attitudes and motives of the individual who experiences the emotion. . . . It should be made clear that appetite is one of the underlying factors in the affective life. Appetites are the basis of a large group of organically determined desires and in the satisfaction and frustration of these appetitive impulses arise feelings of comfort and discomfort, as well as emotional upsets (Young, 1943, p. 115).

The following case illustrates clearly the influence of emotional blunting or impoverishment.

Janie was a young girl of nineteen, referred to the psychologist because of academic failure and poor social adjustment in college. Interviews revealed that the client's mother had died when the client was only four years old and that she had been raised by the maternal grandmother, who was incessantly critical and belittling of Janie's efforts to succeed. Her father, an emotionally and vocationally inadequate person, showed little interest in the daughter and was only too anxious to shift the responsibility to the grandmother. Janie was constantly reminded that "she was just like her father" and would, like him, grow up into a worthless human being. In this setting, Janie had received almost no affection, was extremely lonely and unable to establish worthwhile social contacts, and was deeply convinced of her own inadequacy. Emotionally starved, she resorted to excessive daydreaming and autoerotic practices, which heralded a complete disintegration of her personality. Psychotherapy was largely ineffective.

In cases like Janie's, the emotional structure is seriously damaged. These are the children who hate, or whose emotional makeup is shot through with jealousy, hostility, anger, temper tantrums, sulkiness, or anxiety, and who find it impossible to set up adequate and healthy emotional relations with other members of society. Redl and Wineman have described these children in their well-known book, *Children who hate* (Redl & Wineman, 1951). From this category are recruited the inadequate personalities, the neurotics, the delinquents, and the psychopaths, in all of whom emotional distortion or impoverishment is a typical characteristic. The relation between needs and emotions, incidentally, is not limited to psychological needs even though they are the most important. Gratification or frustration of any motivational factor always has emotional concomitants (McCabe, 1950).

Social Needs and Adjustment

While psychological needs condition the personal and emotional adjustments of the organism, other dynamic factors—the social needs—exert a more direct influence on *interpersonal* adjustments. We do not mean by this that such needs as affection, security, or status have no implications for social behavior, nor that such social needs as approval and recognition do not affect psychological well-being. The process of adjustment cannot be fragmented in this way. Whatever happens to a person's ego security or emotional stability is certain to affect his social relations, and these relations, in turn, will affect his internal make-up. This interrelation was emphasized earlier when we discussed the intimate relations among personality, environment, and culture. The point is that some dynamic factors have more meaning for one aspect of adjustment than for others, even though all of them are complexly intermingled. The social needs of primary importance for adjustment are communication, participation, recognition, approval, and conformity.

The first two needs, communication and participation, are the most significant in this category. These needs impel the organism toward the sharing of experiences and activities and thus play a major role in the process of socialization. Whenever damaging social experiences, unhealthy emotional ties to the parents, or the overdevelopment of contrary motivations block the natural expression of communication or participation, the organism tends toward some form of social maladjustment. Children who find it difficult or impossible to participate in social experiences and activities have few friends (if any) among either sex, tend toward solitary activities to an abnormal degree, shun parties, dances, and games involving participation, and often manifest a decided antisocial attitude. In extreme cases, such tendencies are reflected in homosexuality or schizophrenia. Conversely, the normal development and expression of these needs lead to behavior patterns that ensure the social adjustment of the organism.

Effective communication, participation in social life, and the development of interpersonal relations will be influenced to some extent by other social needs such as recognition. Because man is by nature a social animal—which is why social needs exist—the recognition of his abilities, achievements, and personal qualities by his fellow human beings is of considerable value and importance to him. *The opinions and evaluations of others are an objective reflection of personal worth*, and it may be that the dynamics of recognition is determined by its intrinsic relation to the need for status. Here we have a good example of how psychological and social needs are intermingled, the expression of one being determined in many instances by the dynamics of the other. Whether the blocking of recognition has serious effects on adjustment is difficult to say, for many persons seem to get along without recognition; but it is well known that the gratification of this need has a definite salutary effect on adjustment. Feelings of inadequacy, inferiority, or discouragement, and a sense of failure or lack of achievement can be mitigated by healthy doses of recognition. This fact can be exploited to advantage in promoting normal adjustment.

Closely allied to recognition is the desire for social approval, but where recognition is based on evaluation of traits or behavior, social approval involves social values (Barthel & Crowne, 1962). The drive for recognition often finds expression in conduct that is morally or socially undesirable, as in delinquency and criminality. Thus one might recognize a criminal as being the outstanding member of his group, without condoning or approving his behavior. More often, perhaps, recognition and social approval go hand in hand. Like recognition, social approval reflects the status of personal worth of an individual. Social disapproval can have a damaging effect on the self concept, on feelings of adequacy, achievement, and personal worth, and can, in extreme cases, lead to serious social maladjustment. These effects will vary a great deal with such factors as personal make-up and developmental level. An extremely sensitive person will react more disastrously to social disapproval than will the person who is emotionally well-adjusted; and we may expect the adolescent to react more strongly than the young child. As a general principle, the satisfaction of needs will be determined or in some way conditioned by the context within which the need strives for gratification.

In much the same way that approval is linked to recognition, the need for conformity is linked to social approval (Beloff, 1958). This relation is especially noticeable in adolescence, when conformity seems to be consistently evaluated in terms of the approval or disapproval of friends or of the peer group. Very few things seem as painful to the adolescent as the frustration of this need, whether in the matter of styles of dress, staying out late at night, or dating; it is during this period that the drive for conformity reaches the peak of intensity (Walker & Heyns, 1962). Here again it is questionable whether uninhibited expression or blocking of the drive has any profound or lasting effects on adjustment. In some instances, parental restrictions on conformity lead to emotional upsets, hostility, or rebellion, but usually these effects are temporary and disappear as the youngster reaches a higher level of maturity or develops a better scale of values (Crutchfield, 1955). However, since we are interested here in the dynamics of adjustment, whether these adjustments are temporary or permanent, the functioning of the need for conformity, like that of any other need, must be considered. Not all needs have the same dynamic value for adjustment, but, more important than their varying impact is the fact that all of them influence the course of adjustment to some extent (Schneiders, 1960b, Chapter 8).

DESIRES AND WANTS AS MOTIVATORS

Desires and Adjustment

In addition to basic needs, we must recognize also the influence on adjustment of a large number of desires or wants that give rise to tensions, conflicts, and frustrations. These wants may spring from basic needs, or they may represent previous experience or evaluation. Where they come from is important because the more closely they are linked to needs the more dynamic will they be (Nuttin, 1953, pp. 242–246). For example, the desires for an education, social position, fame, fortune, or political power may stem from the cravings for security, status, recognition, or achievement. Consequently, the effects of such desires on adjustment will be similar to those produced by the original needs. Other desires have little or no reference to personality needs, either physical or psychological, and thus have little to do with the problems of adjustment. The desires to play golf, take a trip, read a book, go to a movie, or visit friends belong to this category (Nowlis, 1953; Seward, 1953).

Desires and Motives

While some desires originate in basic needs, others are simply tendencies to action that we experience whenever there are motives or reasons for acting in a certain manner. As Young says, a desire "is a conscious experience. It is the subjective aspect of a motive and is always oriented. In so far as desires rest upon the physicochemical state of the organism, they are the conscious aspect of appetites; but the concept of desire is broader than this. The anticipated goal of a desire may refer to any object or activity under the sun. Desires range in degree from those that are felt very mildly to the most intense cravings. . . . A person may desire anything from a beefsteak to a place in heaven" (Young, 1943, p. 152).

Thus a person wants (desires) to buy a car because of the difficulties of transportation he would encounter without one. These difficulties, as he sees them, are his reasons (or motives) for wanting to buy a car. *Motives, therefore, constitute the dynamics of reasonable, voluntary conduct* in much the same way that needs constitute the dynamics of adjustive responses. This ability to evaluate a course of action and to act reasonably has important implications for adjustment and mental health since it can be used to reduce the pressure of needs, tensions, and frustrations. For example, reason can be used to reduce the influence of feelings of inferiority, inadequacy, or guilt. Similarly, the capacity for rational behavior can be applied to the problems of marriage, home, school, or a vocation and thus can promote the process of adjustment to an important degree (Schneiders, 1963a).

Motives are the values or reasons for rational behavior and are the groundwork for the development of permanent values or value systems, and for principles, ideals, interests, attitudes and goals. The importance of these motives for effective adjustment and mental health has already been indicated in our discussion of the criteria of adjustment, self-determination, and goal-directed activity. In adult life particularly, the functioning of rational motives is indispensable to the achievement of adjustment and to the maintenance of mental and emotional stability. Whereas needs dominate the adjustive responses of children, the pattern of adult life should be dominated by rational motives and behavior. The more that adults gravitate toward childish, immature ways of behaving, the more unstable and maladjusted they become.

Rational Conduct and Habit

Behavior initiated by motives is referred to as *voluntary conduct*, which means that it is self-directed and controllable. The frequent repetition of such voluntary responses is the basis of habit formation, and habits are important to adjustment because they promote facility and efficiency of response. Once they are well established, habits acquire the property of *functional autonomy*, a term first coined by Allport to apply to motives, but which has since been generalized to apply to other factors that influence adjustment (Allport, 1937, Chapter 7). Functional autonomy means that habits become independent of their motivational origins and develop a dynamic quality of their own. Thus, in many situations requiring adjustive response, behavior is not determined by needs, motives, or desires, but simply by habit. Smoking, social drinking, conversation, leisure reading, play, and many similar activities can be explained in this way (Oppenheimer, 1947; Rethlingshafer, 1943). These statements do not mean that habitual behavior is purely autonomous and completely independent of dynamic tendencies. They serve merely to emphasize the important fact that habits acquire a force of their own; and that this dynamic quality of behavior must also be controlled.

Also important to adjustment is the fact that habits are mechanical, facile, and functionable with little provocation, and because of these qualities, they can contribute much to the efficiency and ease of adjustment. This is the reason we say that the possession of worthwhile habits is a criterion by which adjustment can be evaluated. By the same rule, of course, these qualities can militate against adequate adjustment, first because adjustment requires a certain degree of adaptability and resilience, and, second, because many habits are in themselves impediments to good adjustment. This applies with equal force to mental, moral, and emotional habits, as well as to habits that are more objective and behavioral in character. Thus, habits of lying, procrastination, laziness, tardiness, gossiping, slovenliness in speech or work, and so on, are as detrimental to good adjustment as worthwhile habits are beneficial. Here we are reminded of the importance of effective training, especially in early childhood, for training plays a leading role in the development of habits.

FEELINGS AND EMOTIONS, ADJUSTMENT, AND MENTAL HEALTH

Feelings as Dynamic Motivators

The dynamics of adjustment and mental health is influenced to an important extent by feelings and emotions (Tyson, 1951, Chapter 3). Among the feelings important in this connection, and which occupy a prominent place in the literature of psychopathology, are feelings of inferiority and inadequacy, insecurity, guilt, rejection, worthlessness, resentment and hostility, hatred, anxiety, dependence, and frustration.

Each one of these feelings listed above plays a prominent role in determining the course of adjustment and mental health. Any one of them, or any combination of them, is likely to impair psychological health, especially if it becomes a permanent feature of motivation. However, it is important to understand that such feelings are only *secondary* reactions that stem from more basic dynamic tendencies. Since none of them is observable in infancy or early childhood, they must result from something that happens to the organism in the course of experience and development. Their relation to basic needs is clear. They may, in fact, be defined as affective derivatives of the thwarting or frustration of needs, particularly those that are psychological in nature. In other instances, they result from the mental conflicts that are engendered by different motivations.

Figure 10 is a schematic picture of the relations between such dynamic factors as affection, security, or achievement and the process of adjustment. Needs and desires are represented as being blocked by such factors as parental rejection, social taboos, and punitive discipline which give rise to feelings of various kinds. These feelings function as intermediary dynamic influences in the development of inadequate adjustive responses, restrictive personality characteristics, or mental instability (Young, 1959). Let us note that the primary causes in these situations are the motivations and frustrations that arise in the course of adjustment. However, feelings, as secondary causes, are just as important in understanding and interpreting the dynamics of the situation. In fact, if these feelings did not develop, the adjustment picture would be quite different (Kaplan & Baron, 1952, pp. 242–246; Spitz, 1952, pp. 490–495).

The responses that result from situations like the one described in Figure 10 will be determined by many different factors, but in general we can predict that there will be behavior disturbances, mental symptoms

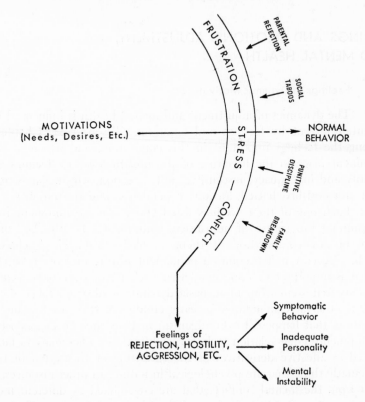

Fig. 10.   Illustration of the connections between motivation, feelings, frustration, conflict, and adjustment.

of various kinds, and inadequate or crippling personality characteristics. For example, feelings of hostility or hatred are typically expressed by aggressive behavior, insecurity through anxiety reactions, dependence by immature responses, and guilt in compulsive behavior. There are no hard and fast rules governing the development of abnormality or maladjustment, and in each case the diagnosis and interpretation of symptomatic responses must be made in the light of whatever knowledge can be brought together regarding the patient's history, personality make-up, developmental level, and other factors that bear on his difficulty. Nevertheless, it is important to recognize that between personal characteristics and dynamic tendencies on the one hand, and the development of symptoms and syndromes on the other, there are significant relationships (Schneiders, 1958, 1963a). In Chapter 7 we shall consider the problem of etiology and symptomatology, which will shed additional light on the problem of behavior dynamics.

Emotions and Behavior Dynamics

The damaging and disruptive effects of negative feelings give us an idea of how important emotional reactions can be to the dynamics of behavior, as can be seen if we take as typical examples the reactions of fear and anger. Emotions of this kind are psychophysical in nature, and they are often disruptive of both mental and behavioral responses. To say that emotions are psychophysical means that they are prone to influence physical processes as well as to disturb the mental stability of the organism. This is particularly the case with the primitive and sometimes violent reactions like fear and anger. In the etiology and development of mental symptoms and psychosomatic disorders, therefore, emotions play a prominent role.

The disruptive effects of intense emotional reactions on psychic processes are equally well known. Rage, fear, depression, jealousy, and hatred interfere with the efficient functioning of psychic processes of all kinds, such as attention, perception, judgment, and reasoning. Typical symptoms, such as disorders of association, delusions, hallucinations, and illusions develop under the influence of intense emotional reactions. These disruptive effects are carried over into the behavior of the organism and thus impair its adjustment to reality. The enraged or jealous person is not only affected mentally but is hampered also in the efficient organization of behavior necessary to meet the demands of his environment (Meltzer, 1933).

Emotional reactions, especially those that fail to find adequate expression, often lead to psychosomatic disorders. Peptic ulcer, high blood pressure, and digestive disturbance are typical symptoms of emotional disturbance. The reason for these effects is that emotions involve deep-seated reactions in the glandular and autonomic nervous systems, which, when not allowed to take a normal course, often lead to serious physiological disturbances. Thus chronic worry, which is essentially a fear reaction, is likely to lead to digestive upsets or to symptoms of cardiac disease because the reaction of fear normally involves these mechanisms. The effects of normal fear quickly wear off, but chronic fear (or worry) continues to stimulate physiological reactions that cannot be properly utilized by the organism. It is then that psychosomatic symptoms develop.

Pathological Feelings and Mental Health

It must be understood that we are referring here only to excessive, abnormal, or pathological emotions, not to normal emotions. We have already indicated that emotional adjustment depends as much on the capacity for *normal* expression as it does on control or inhibition and that the complete suppression of emotion is itself pathological. In any case, whether normal or pathological, emotions play a dominant role in reinforcing the dynamics of behavior. Like feelings, they are intermediary elements in the process of adjustment, resulting from the expression or frustration of other motivational tendencies. As such they give rise to various behavior patterns, personal characteristics, and expressive symptoms. Here again we see how diverse motivational factors come together to effect the particular adjustments of the human organism.

QUESTIONS AND PROJECTS FOR FURTHER STUDY

1. Explain in your own words the difference between the determinants and the dynamics of adjustment. Compare the influence of psychological needs with parent-child relationships.
2. Compare the concept of hedonism with the instinct theory of behavior.
3. Write a critical essay on Freud's classical treatise, *Three essays on the theory of sexuality.*
4. In a short term paper, discuss the implications of different needs for physical, psychological, and social adjustment.
5. On the basis of experience with people whom you have known, write up several case histories that exemplify the frustration of psychological needs.
6. Write a term paper comparing the instinct theory of McDougall with that of Freud.

SELECTED COLLATERAL READINGS

BERG, I. A., & BASS, B. M. (Eds.) *Conformity and deviation.* New York: Harper & Row, 1961.

BROWN, J. F. *The psychodynamics of abnormal behavior.* New York: McGraw-Hill, 1940.

BROWN, J. S. *The motivation of behavior.* New York: McGraw-Hill, 1961.

COLEMAN, J. C. *Personality dynamics and effective behavior.* Chicago: Scott, Foresman, 1960.

FREUD, S. *The psychopathology of everyday life.* (Trans. by A. A. Brill). New York: Macmillan, 1914.

HALL, J. F. *Psychology of motivation.* Philadelphia: Lippincott, 1961.

LINDNER, R. *Prescription for rebellion.* New York: Holt, Rinehart and Winston, 1952.

LINDZEY, G. (Ed.) *Assessment of human motives.* New York: Holt, Rinehart and Winston, 1958.

LYND, HELEN M. *On shame and the search for identity.* New York: Harcourt, 1958.

MADSEN, KRISTEN B. *Theories of motivation.* Cleveland, Ohio: Howard Allen, Inc., Publishers, 1963.

MASLOW, A. H. *Motivation and personality.* New York: Harper & Row, 1954.

MC CLELLAND, D. C., *et al. The achievement motive.* New York: Appleton, 1953.

MOWRER, O. H. *Learning theory and personality dynamics.* New York: Ronald, 1950.

PETERS, R. S. *The concept of motivation.* New York: Humanities Press, 1958.

REDL, F., & WINEMAN, D. *Children who hate.* New York: Free Press, 1951.

SOROKIN, P. A. *The ways and power of love.* Boston: Beacon Press, 1954.

SYMONDS, P. M. *Dynamic psychology.* New York: Appleton, 1949.

TUTTLE, H. S. *Dynamic psychology and conduct.* New York: Harper & Row, 1949.

WALKER, E. L., & HEYNS, R. W. *An anatomy for conformity.* Englewood Cliffs, N.J.: Prentice-Hall, 1962.

WHITE, W. *Beyond conformity.* New York: Free Press, 1961.

WOODWORTH, R. S. *Dynamics of behavior.* New York: Holt, Rinehart and Winston, 1958.

YOUNG, P. T. *Motivation and emotion.* New York: Wiley, 1961.

6

Some Basic Principles
of Motivation

It is not enough to indicate what the factors are that influence behavior and adjustment, or the mental stability of individuals. We must also determine how, and why, and under what circumstances. To what extent is behavior unconsciously determined? How does the present situation fit into the picture? How is motivated behavior influenced by conflict and frustration, by stress and threat? Where do symptoms come from and what do they do for adjustment? These are some of the questions that prod us for answers and around which we will develop some basic principles of motivation.

SIX BASIC CHARACTERISTICS OF MOTIVATION

The facts brought out so far in our discussion of the dynamics of adjustment and mental health can be combined into a set of principles that will give us a fuller understanding of the problem. Other principles will emerge as we study more closely the nature of unconscious motivation, symptom formation, and other characteristics of motivated behavior.

Motivations are dynamic. The motivators of behavior and adjustment do not function as static "entities" but exert their influence by reason of an inherent or acquired power to bring about changes in human response. It is important to understand this principle because it means that the organism will make *some kind* of adjustment under the pressure of needs or motives, even when the possibility of adequate response is to a large extent limited by personal weaknesses or environmental restrictions. Motivational dynamics, therefore, is as important to the understanding of maladjustment and abnormality as it is to normal, everyday behavior (Maslow, 1943).

Motivations influence mental life as well as objective behavior. This principle helps relate the problem of adjustment to that of mental health. Needs, desires, and emotions significantly affect our perceptions, imagination, thinking, attitudes, and beliefs, and, under the influence of

160

frustration, conflict, or stress, they can seriously distort mental functions, giving rise to mental symptoms, such as delusions and obsessions, and generally disrupt mental health (Sarnoff & Katz, 1954; Nissen, 1954; Taylor, 1956; Vogel, Baker, & Lazarus, 1958).

Motivations are closely interrelated. Dynamic factors more often than not function together in determining both normal and abnormal responses. Thus the functioning of such needs as affection, security, and status is determined by their relation to each other and also by their relation to physiological and sociological drives. By the same rule, desires, motives and goals are often derived from basic needs, and the functioning of needs may be conditioned by such processes as deliberation and choice.

Motivations are conditioned by the social context in which they function. This concept is part of the broader principle that governs the relation between personality and environment. It is well known that affection, security, status, and similar needs will be more readily stimulated and gratified in one environmental setting than in another; similarly, the blocking or expression of motivations will vary with the environmental setting or the social milieu within which the motivaton occurs (Barker, 1960). These phenomena are expressed succinctly in the principle of *social facilitation,* according to which the expression or inhibition of motivations and of behavior is facilitated by the nature of the social context in which they take place.

Motivations follow the principle of individual variation. The dynamics of adjustment and mental health is determined also by the peculiar personality organization within which it functions. Each personality is a unique phenomenon, and general principles are always limited by this individuality. To the extent, therefore, that the pattern of motivation is unique and individual, we can expect the pattern of adjustment and mental health to be similarly unique, and in this sense all problems of adjustment must be regarded as distinctive and to some extent as transcending the general principles that govern adjustive behavior.

Not all motivations are known either to the person involved in the adjustment or to an external observer. This principle is derived from the facts regarding unconscious motivation to which we shall turn in the following section. The understanding of all adjustment and mental health, of normal behavior and abnormal personality, of symptoms and syndromes, hinges on a thorough appreciation of the extent to which the behavior and mental life of the human person reflect unconscious experiences or tendencies. Adequate diagnosis, the interpretation of symptoms, and the development of therapeutic and remedial measures must take into account whatever relations exist between unconscious, dynamic factors and the quality of individual adjustment. The application of these six basic principles to the dynamics of adjustment and mental health should be of considerable value to a better understanding of the discussions that follow in this and succeeding chapters (Erickson, 1939).

CONSCIOUS VERSUS UNCONSCIOUS MOTIVATION

Conscious Motivation and Adjustment

The emphasis on unconscious motivation, in this text as well as in the literature, must not lead to the one-sided position that all behavior reflects unconscious drives or feelings. In our analysis of adjustment, we must leave room for the influence of conscious desires and values, interests and attitudes, ideals and goals. In our work as teachers and counselors of children and youth, we must not assume the role of psychotherapists always searching in the background of behavior for hidden motivations. Nor must we lose sight of the fact, pointed out in an earlier chapter, that some thinking and behavior does not fit into the concept of adjustment, that people can act rationally on the basis of deliberation and choice, thus determining the pattern of their behavior independently of the demands of adjustment. Following a career in science, counseling high school students, or seeking the high office of the Presidency of the United States can hardly be regarded as instances of adjustment. These are instances of behavior that are value-determined rather than need-oriented.

The Concept of Unconscious Motivation

The recognition of value-oriented motivation, or of rational choice, does not preclude the possibility that in many instances behavior and adjustment are strongly influenced or even completely determined by psychic factors (needs, wishes, impulses, complexes, experiences) of which the victim is himself unaware. The discovery of this "hinterland of the human mind" is one of the great contributions of Freudian theory, according to which personality development and organization, mechanism formation, and behavior dynamics are dependent on the concept of the unconscious. Such factors as oral needs, castration anxiety, oedipal fixation, repressed wishes, and infantile experiences would have little meaning or influence if they were consciously known and recognized. Their power to influence behavior or the formation of symptoms stems from the fact that they are unknown, repressed, and hidden from conscious awareness. Because they are generally opposed by moral and social restrictions and the demands of the superego in their striving for expression, they surreptitiously make their way into the symbolism of dreams, errors, or neurotic reactions (Robbins, 1956; Ericksen, 1958).

The objections often voiced against Freud's sexual theory, or the concept of the death instinct, do not carry over into his theory of the unconscious. Even moral theologians, and members of the clergy, who find considerable difficulty accepting Freud's pansexualism, or his hedonistic determinism, have accepted the theory of the unconscious. As one writer says (O'Brien, 1950, p. 57):

> Previous to Freud's contribution to the understanding of the dynamic development of unhealthy emotional patterns, there was relatively little known that was really useful in the prevention or treatment of delinquency, crime, the neuroses and psychoses.
>
> Many of the basic techniques of psychoanalysis have made far-reaching contributions not only in such specific areas as juvenile delinquency, adult crime, the neuroses and psychoses but also to the increased proficiency of many professional fields such as child guidance, child psychiatry, clinical psychology, education, juvenile and adult court practices, religious education, business and industry, physical medicine and modern social case work.

An even stronger statement is the following (Hayden, 1950, p. 65):

> It might be truthfully stated that those who firmly hold to a psychology of consciousness would find it quite impossible to interpret human conduct without the inclusion of unconscious phenomena. There is an abundant literature to support this contention and it would be fatuous to call it into question. The influence of ideas and memories in the mental life may be real and extensive and yet the relation of cause and effect between ideas and memories and their resonance in the mental life may be utterly unknown to the subject.

While it is difficult, because of the nature of the concept of the unconscious, to establish its empirical validity, there is an abundance of evidence from both clinical and experimental studies to support the idea of unconscious motivation (Miller, 1942; Nuttin, 1953, Chapter 3; Dalbiez, 1941, Volume II, Chapter 1). Clinical experience with disturbed and maladjusted persons reveals that the motivations underlying their symptomatic behavior are often unknown to them. Careful analysis of compulsive behavior, anxiety states, neurasthenia, stuttering, and similar difficulties often brings to light traumatic experiences, feelings of guilt, desires, or fears, of which the patients themselves seem unaware but which are causally related to the symptoms (Kilby, 1948; Mowrer, 1953). The proof of this relation lies in the fact that, when such factors are brought to light and the patient develops insight into their existence and how they function, the symptoms often disappear.

Unconscious determinants that express themselves in the behavior or thinking of human subjects may also be implanted experimentally. The procedure involves suggesting some idea for future conduct to a hypnotized subject and inducing amnesia for the suggested idea. Carefully controlled observations show that such ideas will be carried out post-hypnotically, even though the subject is totally unaware of the "reason" for his conduct. In other words, the suggested idea acts like an unconscious motivation.

The implications of unconscious motivation for adjustment and mental health are extremely important. The development of an explanatory etiology, the understanding of mental symptoms and behavior disturbances, the interpretation of psychological mechanisms, mental conflicts, and frustrations, the value and limitations of self-determination, the successful application of mental hygiene and of methods of treatment— all hinge on the existence, the extent, and the correct interpretation of unconscious motivation. Whether normal adjustments are much affected by unconscious factors is problematical and of relatively little importance; however, the evidence seems to indicate clearly that abnormal responses often are affected, and these offer the greater challenge to adjustment psychology.

The Content of the Unconscious

By the term unconscious is not meant an entity or some mysterious "part" of the human mind that "lies below" the realm of normal consciousness. Concepts like these are ill-suited to the interpretation of mental phenomena because of their spatial and topographical implications. The unconscious is simply *the aggregate of processes or experiences of which at the moment we are not aware, or which, because of strong inhibiting and repressive factors, are not accessible to awareness by the ordinary mechanisms of recall* (Nuttin, 1953, Chaper 3). Thus many of the feelings we have referred to earlier, such as guilt, inferiority, hostility, and anxiety may be unconscious and inaccessible to introspection or to recall because of their disagreeable nature. Similarly, experiences that are damaging to the self-concept or emotionally repugnant are often relegated to the unconscious by the mechanism of repression. There are also certain wishes and desires that are contrary to moral, spiritual, or social values and ideals and for that reason are not consciously acceptable. This concept of the unconscious and its contents is based upon the simple fact that the human mind naturally turns away from or actively rejects (represses) experiences and tendencies that cannot be readily harmonized with a healthy outlook on life. What is more important than repression is the fact that this repressed content retains its dynamic quality and tends to force its way back into the stream of psychic life and behavior (Mowrer, 1959).

The Formation and Dynamics of the Unconscious

The key to the understanding of unconscious formation is the *mechanism of repression,* which Freud used to explain the mechanics of unconscious development (McGranahan, 1940). The term repression refers to the exclusion from consciousness of processes and experiences that are frightening, disagreeable, damaging to ego security, or intolerable for any other reason. It is a special kind of forgetting, a forgetting that is not induced in the usual manner by lapse of time, disuse, or lack of practice.

> Repression represents a flight of the ego from danger. It represents an endeavor on the part of a person to escape from tendencies within himself that he finds dangerous and untenable. Freud has likened repression to the process in the body of building up a wall of protective tissue, which will isolate the tumor or diseased part from the rest of the organism. Repression has a comparable function of isolating from the conscious part of the mental life that which is not acceptable because it is dangerous or repulsive or bad. Repression takes its place as one of the measures that the ego can adopt in defending itself against unacceptable and dangerous tendencies within. It is probably the most important defense against unacceptable impulses (Symonds, 1949, p. 184).

Repression, therefore, is a dynamic process directed toward preserving the integrity of the mind by excluding factors that threaten its internal harmony or integration. This is understandable and in line with the generally accepted axiom of psychology that disagreeable or disturbing experiences and tendencies are likely to be pushed out of mind and forgotten (Sears, 1943; Gould, 1942).

As we have already noted, because of their inherent motivational force and their strong affective quality, repressed feelings, wishes, and experiences tend dynamically to express themselves in the psychic life and behavior of the organism, often in symbolic form. The following cases illustrate this fact quite clearly (Lindgren, 1953, pp. 49–50):

Miss Primrose, the English teacher, finds it necessary to assure her classes at least once each day that she has their best interests at heart. The very fact that she finds it necessary to reassure them is a clue to her students that something is amiss; and, if this in itself were not revealing, her cold and hostile tone makes it doubly clear how she feels about students. She further reveals herself by her defensive attitude whenever she believes that her motives are being questioned by parents, her fellow teachers, or her principal.

Mrs. Larkspur is always saying, "My family comes first in everything." Yet she is "up to her ears" in club work to the extent of spending afternoons, evenings, and week-ends in the service of her organizations. Her very behavior is a clue pointing to the strong probability that, unconsciously, she either dislikes her family or despises her role as a wife and mother, or, at best, really prefers organizational activities to homemaking.

The unconscious wishes, ideas, and feelings reflected in the two cases above have been shut out of consciousness because to experience them would be intolerable; hence they are expressed *indirectly and symbolically.* In some cases, these tendencies are expressed in the person's reactions to others or to the role he supposes them to play; in others, they find their way into dreams, unaccountable errors, peculiarities of behavior, and pathological symptoms. Thus unconscious guilt is expressed in the form of a compulsion, a traumatic experience as a phobia for high places or as an obsession regarding purity, a wish for the death of an enemy as a dream of his traveling to a distant land; a forbidden sexual desire as frigidity. There is nothing very strange in this symbolic expression, since symbolism is a natural function of the human mind. When a situation exists that precludes direct expression of wishes and feelings, we are most likely to resort to symbolic formulation.

IMMEDIATE DETERMINANTS OF ADJUSTMENT AND MENTAL HEALTH

Situational Factors

The repeated reference in foregoing pages to basic needs, impulses, feelings, and unconscious determinants could easily lead to the conclusion that all adjustments as well as all mental disorders are primarily the result of personal factors. There are many psychologists and psychiatrists who believe that no disorder is without a personal history to account for it, and the psychoanalysts pay particular homage to this viewpoint by insisting that the basic personality structure is determined for good or ill in the first six years of life.

But the issue is not this simple. A thoroughgoing interpretation of maladjustment, symptom formation, or personality disturbance must take into account the role of other factors that are not so clearly bound to personality make-up or development. There are at least four such factors that enter into the dynamics of adjustive behavior and mental health: conflict and frustration, stress and threat. Notably, there are several schools of thought—particularly the client-centered group—that de-emphasize the role of early background in the development of personality disturbances in favor of what we might call a *situational approach*. In this view, adjustments are determined more by the exigencies and forces operating at the present time than by the personal background of the client. This would certainly be true where the pressures exerted against mental stability and healthy adjustment are so great as to break through the most highly developed resistance. Combat soldiers, for example, are often subject to psychological stresses and traumatic experiences that even the best adjusted person cannot cope with successfully (Grinker & Spiegel, 1945; Janis, 1951). If in such situations there is symptom development or mental breakdown, it would be attributed far less to faulty training, overprotection, and similar factors in the patient's background than it would be to the overpowering effect of stress or threat. Similarly, other situations, such as the loss of limbs, the sudden death of one's parents, or the failure to pass an examination for medical practice after years of grueling effort, could precipitate a personality disorder without benefit of predisposing causes. However, even in such instances there are personality differences, and it is probable that in the majority of cases of maladjustment, predisposing factors play an important part (Eriksen, Lazarus, & Strange, 1952).

Stress, Adjustment, and Mental Health

The concept of situational maladjustment is closely related to the idea of *stress* which has received a great deal of attention in recent years in connection with the study of adjustment and abnormality. Stress is linked up with several important etiological factors, particularly that category referred to as *precipitating causes* (Vogel, Baker, & Lazarus, 1958). In his discussion of stress as a determining influence in neuroses and psychoses, Kraines refers to it as a precipitating factor, and certainly in many situations it functions in that way (Kraines, 1948, p. 157). White tells the story of a young man in the air force who was referred to his flight surgeon because, on his tenth and eleventh bombing missions, he had fainted at 10,000 feet. Careful investigation brought out that the stress of combat evoked a latent anxiety that had its roots in his early childhood (White, 1956). In this case, personality factors were clearly the *predisposing* causes, and stress the precipitating cause. In other instances, particularly where stress is excessive, it may be the sole cause of symptom formation or break-down (Pronko & Leith, 1956; Davis, 1956; Schaffer, 1954; Korobow, 1955).

> Adjustment to stress and strain can be made in a variety of ways. Some people are able to meet and survive very great amounts of stress without damage to themselves, while others break in meeting small amounts. Where stresses are in proportion to the capacity of the person, adequate adjustment is achieved; if the stresses are greater than capacity, adjustment is inadequate; and if stresses are much too great, the person evolves behavior which, while it enables him to maintain some sort of equilibrium between what is within and what comes from without, necessitates special care and often detention (Anderson, 1949, pp. 421–422).

In other words, stress-producing situations function always in terms of individual personality factors (predisposing causes), although "an amount of stress can be produced that will break almost any person" (Anderson, 1949, p. 422). Kraines also, as well as many other writers, emphasizes personal factors. "In general, it may be said that stress produces tension in proportion to the person's attitude toward it; that is, stress tends to be as bad as he feels it to be" (Kraines, 1948, p. 158). This idea, as we shall see later on, is very similar to the concept of frustration tolerance. As Anderson remarks, "It is quite clear that it is the feeling of stress rather than the actual measurable amount of stress which is often in question in distinguishing between serious and temporary stresses" (Anderson, 1949, p. 158). This distinction is similar to our own distinction between frustration and the feeling of frustration discussed later in this chapter.

Each individual reacts to stress within the limits of his capacities and development. As Kaplan and Baron remark (1952, pp. 288–289):

> In the psychological realm as in the physical there are limits to the capacity of the individual to adjust to the varying conditions which place him under stress. Within these limits, such conditions encourage constructive effort. When stresses become too great, effectiveness is impaired. The individual is unable to make adequate adjustments.

Just as one must learn to cope with conflicts and endure a certain degree of frustration, he must also mature to the point where he can tolerate some stress.

> Development toward mature levels of behavior involves the expansion of our limits of tolerance of stress, a progressive increase in ability to function comfortably and adequately under increasing degrees of frustration and conflict. This process is fostered when we augment our

ability to endure stress without harmful effect and when we develop more adequate methods to successfully overcome or reduce tension (Kaplan & Baron, 1952, p. 289).

Moreover, it is not enough to simply endure stresses and frustrations; like conflict, they can be exploited to the advantage of personal growth and adjustment (Fisher & Noble, 1960). Stress is harmful only when it interferes with adjustment or causes breakdown of inner controls or personality integration. "The experience of stress not only adds zest to living but also is essential to the development of the mature personality. It is through contact with reality and through growth in ability to adapt to stress that the individual matures socially and emotionally" (Kaplan & Baron, 1952, p. 283). Thus the student who learns to face up to the stresses of daily studies, examinations, and assignments will become better equipped to meet other and heavier responsibilities in later life (Cowan, 1952a, 1952b; Davids & Oliver, 1960). Similarly, the young adolescent girl who accepts the responsibilities of housework and child care in the family will find it easier to stand up under the stresses of married life later on. Adjustment, as we have said often, *is living,* and *learning to live* under conditions of stress is one of the essential conditions of good adjustment (Funkenstein, King, & Drolette, 1957).

Let us inquire briefly into the relation between stress and frustration since they are often linked in discussions of adjustment. Stress is a condition in which the organism is faced with certain demands and pressures from without that tax its ability to a greater or lesser degree in effecting an adjustment. Thus we speak of the stress of daily living, academic work, marital adjustments, and vocational responsibilities (Vogel, Raymond & Lazarus, 1959). In these instances, the word "strain" is often used as a synonym for stress. Frustration is a condition in which the motivation or behavior of the organism is blocked by some internal or external factor. Conflict is a contention between opposed motivations or between motivations and external demands. Cameron and Magaret distinguish stress and frustration in a similar manner.

> Let us define stress as a situation in which a person's ongoing behavior is altered from its customary pattern, because of continuing pressure from others or from his own reactions.

And by frustration we shall mean

> a situation in which a person's ongoing motivated behavior is temporarily or permanently prevented from reaching consummation (Cameron & Magaret, 1951, pp. 44, 47).

That stress and frustration influence each other is well known, but it is not always clear which one exerts the greater influence. The more important fact is that, under certain conditions and motivations or because of personality factors, conflicts, stresses, and frustrations can give rise to various behavior difficulties and maladjustments and thus become part of the etiology of mental ill health and personality disorder (Sharma, 1955; Lazarus & Baker, 1957).

Adjustment and the Factor of Threat

The relation between frustration and stress is paralleled by a similar relation between frustration and the concept of threat interpreted as a determinant of adjustment and mental health. Rosenzweig, for example, identifies primary frustration with privation, by which he means the absence of an end situation that is necessary for the satisfaction of an active need. When obstacles are active they become dangerous, and frustration then develops *as a threat to personal security.* "In other words, whereas passive obstructions entail only the need which is frustrated, active ones invoke additional needs pertaining to the immediate security of the organism. This distinction serves to indicate that frustration includes situations both of satisfaction and of danger" (Rosenzweig, 1944, Volume I, p. 381).

Other writers take a similar view to that given above. Maslow states, "The one concept that is important is neither conflict nor frustration, but the essential pathogenic characteristic of both—namely, threat of thwarting of the basic needs of the organism." Furthermore, "All the following are felt as threatening in our sense; danger of thwarting of the basic needs, or the conditions upon which they rest, threat to life itself, threat to the general integrity of the organism, threat to the integration of the organism, and threat to the organism's basic mastery of the world" (Maslow, 1943, p. 82; also Maslow, 1941, 1954; Zuckerman, 1951; Eriksen, 1952). Similarly, Maslow and Mittelmann (1951, p. 68) state that

> The serious psychopathological reaction arises if the patient feels severely deprived of one of his vital needs. He perceives this blocking of a vital need as an extremely serious threat, one which endangers his whole existence; at least potentially he feels catastrophically threatened.

Hogan offers a different interpretation of threat, but one that is also directly related to the problem of adjustment (Hogan, 1952). In his view, threat occurs when the self perceives its experiences as being inconsistent with the structure of the self. Threat relates to concepts or values regarding the self. Nevertheless, "at different levels of theoretical importance or interest one may speak of threat to concepts and values, threat to the self, threat to the security, adequacy, or worth of the self, or threat to its need satisfaction. In other words, interpretation of the meaning of threat will be determined by one's frame of reference, but regardless of this fact, threat, like frustration, "is a motivating factor of prime importance" (Hogan, 1952, pp. 418, 419). This viewpoint, as the author points out, is clearly related to the interpretation suggested by Snygg and Combs. According to these authors (Snygg & Combs, 1949, p. 118), threat is defined as

> the individual's awareness of menace to his phenomenal self. Since his need is to maintain and enhance it, the only thing he can do under threat is to defend the organization which exists. This may or may not result in a removal of the threat he feels. If it does, the crisis has been met and the organism's need is satisfied. On the other hand, if the individual cannot solve the threatening situation the threat may persist and continue to frustrate need for long periods of time. Such threats to the phenomenal self are the most characteristic aspects of persistent tension states.

Note that this interpretation of threat and tension is basically different from others that try to explain the nature of frustration. Admittedly, as Hogan states, one can approach the problem from different points of view, but there is a real difference between the idea of threat as the blocking of vital needs, and threat as the disruption of the "phenomenal self." In the latter view needs and need gratifications are subordinate in importance to the integrity of the self. Frustration as threat is not directed against the satisfaction of vital needs but against the inner security of the self. As Hogan states (1952, p. 423):

> At the root of threat, to be sure, lies the possible thwarting of needs. Yet, if need satisfaction were of prime importance in maladjustment, need-persistive reactions would usually predominate; and occasions when they did to the detriment of cherished values would be viewed with less concern. Yet the conditions established for need satisfaction seem predominant in maladjustment. The individual is absorbed with defending his system of defenses. It appears that deprivation involving threat and not deprivation alone is responsible for maladjustment.

Thus the self is injected into the center of both frustration theory and the concept of stress, so that however it is interpreted stress becomes an essential part of frustration theory. In attempting to understand the significance of immediate determinants of adjustments, we should keep these different viewpoints in mind.

CONFLICT, ADJUSTMENT, AND MENTAL HEALTH

The Nature of Mental Conflict

One of the most prominent and important determinants of mental health and adjustment, both from a theoretical and a practical standpoint, is the element of mental conflict. There is much interest in the problem of conflict (Horney, 1945; Luria, 1932; Guthrie, 1938; Miller, 1944, pp. 431–465). The reason for this interest is that many adjustment situations are characterized by the simultaneous development of *contrary* motivators, a condition that arouses mental conflict unless the issue is resolved immediately by an impetuous decision or recourse to habit. Some of these conflicts are *intramental* in nature, and stage their battle within the personality of the individual; others are *interpersonal,* and thus involve two or more individuals (Miller & Swanson, 1956; Epstein, 1962).

Conflicts are very common experiences, mainly because of the opposition between desires and principles, interests and responsibilities, and between impulses and moral ideals. As St. Paul said many centuries ago, "I see another law in my members, fighting against the law of my mind, and captivating me in the law of sin" (Rom. 7:23). The same conflict was expressed by Goethe when he cried, "Two souls within my bosom dwell," the one pulling him toward the material order and the other toward spiritual values. These are clear instances of intramental conflict, whereas conflicts between parental demands or restrictions and children's wishes, or between social rules and personal desires, are examples of the interpersonal type. Speaking of conflict in childhood, Moore says, "There is a double conflict—one without, with nature and its inexorable laws and man and his unbending will; the other within, with his own ideals of conduct" (Moore, 1948, p. 253).

Actually, the development of conflicts is much more complicated than has been indicated above. Symonds, for example, lists the following types of conflict: conflict between basic drives, between immediate wishes, between immediate and remote drives, between two ideals or ambitions, between two duties, between duty and ambition, between two antagonistic beliefs, between drives and external frustration, between drives and inner restraints, between drives and anticipated self-punishment, between drives and thoughts of one's own limitations, between introjected systems, between ego ideal and superego, between inner restraining systems and outer encouragement, and between two restraining systems (Symonds, 1949, pp. 255–265; also Cameron & Magaret, 1951, pp. 254–260).

Regardless of type, however, *the mechanism of conflict is always essentially the same: a contention or opposition between opposed motivations or courses of action, which is fought out on a psychological level.* In other words, all conflicts, no matter how they get started, are essentially psychological. Cameron and Magaret state the issue very simply:

> By *conflict* we mean the *mutual interference of incompatible reactions.* The interference, as we have seen, may occur between simple responses, attitudes, roles, or self-reactions. The contradictory reactions may be overt or covert, easily identified or altogether inaccessible. They may be sharply circumscribed or widely inclusive. Whatever the character of the mutually interfering reactions, however, conflict has one necessary consequence: *it alters the smooth flow of ongoing behavior* (Cameron & Magaret, 1951, p. 252).

The effect of conflict on behavior will depend partly on the nature of the conflict. Normally, the immediate outcome of conscious conflict is deliberation (or discussion, which is a type of deliberation on the verbal level). Deliberation is a process of comparative evaluation by which we weigh the good and bad points of different courses of action against each other and thus determine which one we should choose. It is the clearest instance of the application of intelligence and reason to a problem of adjustment. The outcome of deliberation, if successful, is an act of decision or choice, which enables us to resolve the conflict by accepting one of the possibilities and rejecting all others. The disposition of conflicts by deliberation and choice is of considerable importance to mental health and adjustment; it is this approach to human problems that distinguishes the inadequate and neurotic personality from the normal one. The neurotic finds it impossible to resolve or to cope with conflicts. This is why we said earlier that integration of motives and resolution of conflicts are essential criteria of mental health (Lesser, 1958; Berlyne, 1960).

Implications of Conflict for Mental Health

The keystone of mental health and adjustment is the *effective resolution* of mental conflicts, not their existence. Conflicts of one kind or another are inevitable in the course of experience and are therefore a constant challenge to personal fortitude and moral strength (Janis, 1959). As one writer says, it is equally important from the standpoint of mental health that "many such battles should be lost" in order to learn that we cannot have everything that we want in this life (Moore, 1948, p. 252). Victories cannot be won unless there is a struggle or conflict to begin with, and each mental victory over conflict is a further step toward moral strength and personal integration. As Sherman says (1941, pp. 286–287):

Psychiatric reports usually imply that all conflicts are detrimental. It is known, however, that a person may have many conflicts without detrimental results. Indeed, some conflicts may be useful in motivating a person to greater activity. Conflicts may be detrimental or useful depending upon their number and intensity and the issues they involve. They are likely to be detrimental when they either become so intense that the emotional balance of the individual is upset or when they involve an undesirable change in behavior. . . . *The way in which a person resolves his conflicts is probably the most important criterion of their benefit or detriment.* A person may solve his conflicts by increased energy toward the attainment of a socially valuable goal. On the other hand, he may attempt to solve his conflict by escape, especially into neurotic symptoms of illness.

This writer goes on to say that "it is commonly believed that creative work is impossible without the stimulating effects of conflicts. A person who does not have some systematized conflicts is not sufficiently energized to attempt to attain accomplishment beyond those specifically required by his environment" (Sherman, 1941, p. 287). This viewpoint is not shared by all writers. The psychoanalytic school, especially, finds it difficult to admit the value of conflict. The following quotation emphasizes the damaging effects of conflict (Maslow & Mittelmann, 1951, pp. 57–58):

Conflicts are painful for several reasons. They give the individual a feeling of lack of integration and of threatening disorganization. They further lead to a feeling of hesitation and indecision. They may also represent threats to the self-esteem and to the feeling of adequacy. They are problems that we are unable to solve and they therefore represent a lack of power in us and inferiority.

Other writers list additional bad effects of conflict, including tension, emotional impoverishment, and distortion of behavior. Such effects, however, are due mainly to *unconscious* conflicts, and it is generally agreed that conflicts that cannot be consciously dealt with are damaging in their effects, as we shall see in the following section.

Outcomes of Mental Conflict

The outcomes of mental conflict will be determined by a number of factors, two of which are of primary importance—*personality make-up* and *type of conflict* (Sherman, 1938, pp. 280–283). Regarding the first factor, there are some persons in whom drives, desires, or motives are so *weak and underdeveloped* that they seldom experience a struggle between contrary tendencies. Obviously, these persons have little opportunity to use life conflicts in the development of personal integration. They present the picture of a weak, flabby personality with little drive or ambition.

There are persons in whom mental conflicts are conspicuously absent also, but for a different reason. These are the persons *dominated by basic needs and impulses.* For them, contrary motivations, such as principles and ideals, have little psychological meaning. The compulsive, psychopathic person is an extreme example of this group. Obviously, where one or another motivation is persistently dominant, there is little room for the functioning of other tendencies, and therefore little possibility of conflict. Thus the psychopath, unlike the neurotic, is relatively free of mental conflict and is characteristically lacking in mental organization and character development.

A third kind of personality organization reacting differently to conflict is represented by the neurotic, who is characterized by an almost *complete inability to resolve mental conflicts,* especially those that have serious implications for emotional stability or mental health. The neurotic person is constantly torn by inner conflicts between right and wrong, impulse and principle, responsibilities and desires, ideals and practicality. Because of immaturity, lack of experience, emotional interference, or failures in training, he is incapable of efficient deliberation and decision. Not knowing which way to turn or how to direct behavior and thinking efficiently, he is in a state of constant mental turmoil, hesitation, and uncertainty. Hence there is little integration of motives and just as little integration of personality and character. The failure of the neurotic to resolve indecisions and conflicts, robs him of the victories over motivation that he needs for peace of mind, emotional stability, and ego security. These inadequacies constitute the immediate basis of neurotic symptom formation.

Finally, there is the kind of personality characterized by *a high level of maturity and integration* in whom mental conflicts are resolved with relatively little difficulty. Such persons have a background of rich experience in making decisions, effective discipline, healthy development, and the satisfaction of having achieved numerous victories in their conscious deliberations and choices. Here we encounter the importance of such determinants as effective parental discipline, self-determination, and goal-directed activity. Also, growth in independence, in feelings of security, in personal worth, and in habits of decision are significant for learning how to cope with mental conflicts. This is a good example of how the nature, criteria, determinants, and dynamics of mental health fuse into one picture, each part of which contributes to the character and appearance of the whole.

The nature of the conflict itself is important to mental stability. Some conflicts are superficial and easily resolved; others are deep seated and often hopelessly mixed up with emotions, which makes them much less amenable to deliberation or reason. Thus the problem of deciding whether to study or go to a movie is more easily solved than the conflict that often rages between sexual desire and moral responsibility. Similarly, intramental conflicts are generally more severe in their effects than those that arise between one person and another, or between the individual and society. Intramental conflicts readily disturb emotional equanimity, whereas those of an interpersonal nature are more likely to interfere with the social adjustments of the individual. Of the two effects, the former has more serious implications for mental stability.

We must note, finally, that some conflicts develop at an unconscious level and are generally more damaging in their effects than those that are conscious. Admitting that conscious conflicts may be "extremely severe," Maslow and Mittelmann point out that such conflicts "rarely breed neurosis (even though there may be some 'symptom' results), whereas unconscious conflicts, even when they are apparently less severe or important . . . are much more likely to eventuate in general psychic illness or character change" (Maslow & Mittelmann, 1951, p. 53). As we have said, the normal outcomes of mental conflict are deliberation and decision, but these outcomes are precluded in the case of unconscious conflicts since they are not accessible to deliberation. Typical of such conflicts are those between security and independence, sexual desire and superego demands, hatred and love of parents, inferiority and the need for achievement. Any one of these contentions may at times be conscious, but often they develop and function without a person's knowledge of them, a condition that is conducive to serious disturbances of mental stability.

Whenever mental conflicts cannot be resolved because of personality factors, or the nature of the conflict, they are likely to disrupt adjustment and mental health (Thorpe, 1950, p. 113). Such conflicts disturb mental and emotional equanimity, and thus interfere with effective control of emotional or mental processes. They also militate against the organization and direction of behavior and personality integration. They tend to produce a state of continuous frustration because they interfere with the normal expression of motivational tendencies. And they lead to the development of disabling symptoms, which function as symbolic efforts to reduce the tension that results from conflict. These difficulties occur only when there is a failure to resolve conflicts in an intelligent and effective manner.

By the same rule, the ability to resolve conflicts, both mental and interpersonal, along with repeated experiences in resolving them, particularly during the stress period of adolescence, will produce just the opposite effect. In place of maladjustment and symptom formation, there will develop control of behavior, a higher level of integration, and healthier adjustment. The end result of conflict will depend always on the manner in which the person responds to it.

FRUSTRATION AND ADJUSTMENT

Nature of Frustration

One of the more important immediate determinants of adjustment and mental health is the phenomenon of frustration, a factor which has attracted a great amount of attention in recent years (Maier, 1949; Rosenzweig, 1938; Dollard, et al., 1939; Miller, et al., 1941). Theories of frustration should be brought into line with experimental approaches to the problem (Korner, 1949, Chapter VI; Cameron & Magaret, 1951, Chapter II; Maier, 1950). One may think, from our ready use of the term in preceding paragraphs, that it is an easy matter to decide what frustration is; actually, however, frustration is very complex in nature, and there are many opinions to take into account in trying to define its essential characteristics. Symonds, for example, considers any blocking of behavior or motivation a frustration, even when there are means available for adequate adjustment (Symonds, 1949, Chapter III). Shaffer regards frustration as involving a situation in which accustomed reactions fail to bring satisfaction; thus situations to which one can readily adjust are not thought of as frustrating (Shaffer, 1936, p. 117). Maier defines a frustrating situation as one in which learning is inhibited and other forms of response are adopted (Maier, 1949, pp. 123–129), whereas Maslow and Mittelmann (1951, pp. 61, 67–70) conceive of frustration as involving danger to the integrity of personality, the lowering of self-esteem, or damage to the feeling of security. Finally, there is the viewpoint that frustration occurs only in those situations in which the individual is actively striving to reach a goal that is important and attainable. Interference with this striving is interpreted as frustration (Lawson & Marks, 1958).

Definition of Frustration

All the foregoing interpretations contain something of value for the definition of frustration, but there are several points that must be clarified. First of all, frustration applies to the blocking or hindrance of behavior as well as motivation or mental activity. A child trying without success to reclaim a toy from a playmate shows typical signs of frustration such as crying, hitting, or disorganized and aimless behavior. So, too, does the motorist whose car stalls on slippery pavement; he curses, spins the wheels, or rails angrily against the vicissitudes of fate. On the mental and motivational level, frustration is clearly manifested by the teacher who fails to arouse interest in her students, by the adolescent faced with a serious mental conflict that resists solution, and by the mathematician who cannot solve a certain problem (Yates, 1962).

An interesting experimental study of the effects of frustration on the hunger drive is reported in Cameron and Magaret (1951, p. 48). Existing on a severely restricted diet for six months, the subjects gave many indications of being thwarted that were both behavioral and mental; some chewed gum incessantly; others collected recipes, talked and fantasied about food during the day, and dreamed of food at night. Some of the behavior assumed an almost pathological form. In all such instances, the existence of frustration is determined by objective signs or criteria rather than in terms of a preconceived notion of what frustration should be. What these signs are we shall note later on.

Second, an acceptable definition of frustration should be predicated on a clear distinction between *subjective* and *objective* frustration. To *be* frustrated is not the same thing as to *feel* frustrated. The subjective feeling of frustration is more important to adjustment and is manifested unmistakably in the external signs of frustration. The mere blocking of motivation, behavior, or mental activity is certainly a kind of frustration, but if the person does not react subjectively (emotionally) to the blocking, it has little psychological meaning, especially where adjustment is concerned. Thus, if a person is hungry and dinner has not been prepared, he is temporarily frustrated in the gratification of this need, but, if he does not feel frustrated, the chances are there will be no aftermath of the objective frustration and hence no effect on adjustment. Note, however, what happens when this situation produces subjective frustration. The person becomes angry and irritable, complains about the dinner not being ready, or prances aimlessly about until it is served. Failure to recognize this distinction between objective and subjective frustration leads to different and sometimes confusing definitions of frustration. If the various viewpoints described earlier are reviewed, it can be seen that many of the differences could be reconciled on the basis of this distinction (Yates, 1962, p. 175).

Third, it is important to note that the character of frustration and its subsequent effects on adjustment vary considerably with the kind of motivation or response involved and with the psychological context in which it occurs. For example, the blocking of basic needs, such as the need for affection, security, or status, has a great deal more frustration significance than interference with casual desires or motives. Similarly, the frustration of behavior directed toward important goals has deeper meaning for adjustment than the blocking of incidental responses. The student who fails a course required for graduation or for entrance to medical school is more apt to show signs of frustration than one who cannot take notes because he forgot to bring his pencil to class. The context of behavior is important too. In situations where substitution can be easily made, or where learning can be readily exploited for purposes of eliminating any hindrance to effective adjustment, frustration may be temporary and may remain at the objective level (Britt & Janus, 1940).

In the light of these considerations, and for the special purpose of adjustment psychology, *frustration may be defined as the subjective reaction to the blocking or hindrance of significant behavior or motivation that leads to interference with adequate and effective adjustment.* Interpreted in this way, it is clear that frustration is an essential element in the progression of human responses from initial motivation to whatever adjustments the organism can accomplish (Snygg & Combs, 1949, p. 116; Marx, 1956).

Kinds of Frustration

Besides objective and subjective frustrations, there are also external impersonal frustrations, and those that are internal and personal in nature. The distinction is important because the effects of frustration vary considerably from one kind to another.

Impersonal frustrations are those originating in some aspect of the environment or cultural setting. They include *privations*, such as poverty, lack of cultural or recreational advantages, absence of playmates, and inadequate funds for education; also included are *deprivations*, such as the sudden loss of wealth or social position, the breakdown of one's means of transportation, or the death of parents on whom one is dependent; furthermore there are *obstructions*, such as parental restrictions, social conventions, and moral laws that stand in the way of personal gratifications.

It should be understood that privations or deprivations by themselves do not bring about negative effects; rather, the frustrations to which they give rise come about only when they cause loss of prestige, status, or security, failure of achievement, and the like. Poverty or sexual deprivation may be borne without any difficulty until it begins to imply inferiority, lack of personal status, isolation, or rejection, which reminds us that frustration is basically a *personal* affair, to which external factors contribute only when certain conditions already exist. As Snygg and Combs (1949, p. 17) point out: "The degree of frustration felt by the individual will be a function of the meaning of the frustrating event in his field and, in particular, how he perceives that event as affecting the satisfaction of need."

Internal or *personal* frustrations generally affect adjustment more than those externally determined. Since, as we have said, the significance of frustration increases in proportion to the degree of subjective reaction

to frustrating conditions, we may expect that personal privations, deprivations, or barriers will have a more direct and damaging effect on adjustment
than those that are impersonal. Poverty, for example, can be very frustrating when one wants an education, position, or power; however, it will
seldom exert as much influence on adjustment as bodily deformity, lack
of intelligence, or sudden loss of sight. Poverty can be attributed to the
weaknesses or failures of others, but personal defects are peculiarly one's
own and for that reason have much greater power to produce a deep and
crippling sense of frustration. It is these frustrations that we come across
most often in studying the etiology of behavior disorders.

The following case illustrates the potency of real and imagined personal defects in producing personality disorders.

> The client, an attractive youngster nineteen years old and a
> sophomore in college, was referred to the clinic because of a serious
> speech handicap. He complained of difficulties with his studies, being
> laughed at in class, not being popular with girls, lack of manly qualities,
> extreme fatigue, various aches and pains, poor sleep habits, and of
> course the habit of stuttering. He thought of himself as being physically,
> socially, and emotionally inadequate, and vastly inferior to his classmates
> and friends. He was deeply convinced of his inability to attract girls or
> to continue to stimulate their interest if he should manage an initial
> attraction. His self-concept included feelings of inferiority, particularly
> in the areas of social communication and masculinity, and a body image
> that centered around visual deficiency, physical weakness and unattrac-
> tiveness, and chronic fatigue.
>
> The client's difficulties had begun early in life with the onset
> of stuttering at the age of seven. From that time on, he had felt socially
> and personally inadequate and "queer," feelings that were strengthened
> by the rude jibes of classmates directed at his speech handicap. The
> situation worsened considerably in late adolescence when the goal of
> becoming an officer in the air force was shattered by a rejection based
> on visual deficiency. Already burdened with inferiority and inadequacy,
> his self-concept suffered additional damage by this failure, which he
> interpreted illogically as being his own fault, thus adding feelings of
> guilt to an already severely damaged ego.
>
> Interview therapy, directed toward the development of insight
> into the causes of his feelings and reactions, growth of a healthier self-
> concept and a better evaluation of his own shortcomings and potentiali-
> ties, had a marked effect on the client's personality. He now sees himself
> in a much healthier light, the feelings of inferiority and guilt have been
> greatly reduced, and social adjustment has improved.

Personal privations include any defects, *real or imagined,* in a person's physical, mental, moral, spiritual, or social make-up, the effects of
which will vary with the part of the personality involved. Generally, it may
be assumed that mental defects will be felt more keenly than those of a

physical nature and that moral defects will be regarded more seriously than either of the other two. These reactions will be conditioned by individual peculiarities, particularly one's personal scale of values, but in assessing the relation between personal defects and frustration, we must first determine the special meaning they have for the person and where they stand in his scale of values. We must take account of the fact, too, that imagined defects can be just as potent in the development of frustration as real ones. The personal conviction of moral inadequacy, physical unattractiveness, or intellectual deficiency, even though it does not correspond to objective fact, is often the cause of deep-seated frustrations, and it should be noted that the effects on adjustment are no different nor less severe than the effects of real defects. In fact, the ultimate effects may be more damaging to stability because it is impossible to properly evaluate imagined defects. They are nurtured in a psychological soil that is in itself unfavorable to healthy mental development and are therefore less amenable to adequate evaluation than defects that are real and fully apparent.

These principles can be applied just as well to *personal deprivations*, or loss of abilities and characteristics, as in cases of chronic illness, injury, sensory incapacitation, or structural impairment. But there is an important difference that may affect frustration noticeably. Privations or defects are usually regarded as *congenital*, and thus an integral part of personality, whereas deprivations are *adventitious* and only accidentally related to personality make-up. There is quite a difference, for example, between being born blind and becoming blind through injury or disease. In the one case, blindness is an integral part of the personality, and the feeling of frustration gets off to an early start, with possible damaging effects on the person's adjustment. Yet we know, too, that it may work the other way around. The person who suffers the loss of a vital capacity may become more seriously frustrated because he realizes much more keenly what this deprivation means. Similarly, it often happens that persons born with a structural defect are less seriously affected in their adjustments to the demands of reality than those who suffer physical loss later in life. Never having known the virtues of physical wholeness, they may experience little frustration in situations where this factor is important. Furthermore, in congenital cases there is more likelihood of effective compensation than when the deprivation is adventitious. The deeper implications of these facts will receive fuller treatment in our discussion of the mechanisms of defense in Chapter 8.

The external obstructions described in connection with impersonal frustrations are paralleled by *internal barriers* that play a definite part in the development of personal frustrations. In fact, the moral, social, and cultural taboos and regulations that function as external obstructions are often the same factors that become internalized (introcepted) as subjective barriers leading to frustration. At this point, frustration and mental conflict merge as co-determinants of adjustment (Rosenzweig, 1944, p. 382; Maslow, 1943). Internal barriers in the form of moral prohibitions and principles, conventional codes, cultural taboos, and so forth, come into conflict with other motivations of an instinctual or habitual character and thus create frustration. Again, however, the depth and possible damage of such frustrations depend largely on the level of personality integration, the ability to cope with conflicts by rational deliberation and choice, the extent of moral development, the level of maturation, and similar factors. In some instances, there is relatively little subjective frustration; in others, it becomes so intense as to cause severe personality disturbances. Differences like these point to the need for extreme caution in interpreting the effects of frustration. It can mean radically different things in different persons.

The quality of internal frustrations may be expected to vary also with the *character of the motivation* involved, including its innate strength, its relation to other dynamic factors, and particularly its emotional connotations. The greater the strength of a need or drive, the more imperatively does it lead to some form of expression; hence the frustration is more deeply felt when strong drives come into conflict with internal barriers than when weaker motivations are functioning. Similarly, mental conflicts and frustrations are deepened by the interplay among different motivations. The sex drive, for example, is often reinforced by ego needs such as status and recognition, in which case sexual frustration more decisively affects adjustment than when it is functioning alone. If, in addition, there are strong emotional components such as fear or anxiety, as is usually the case, the frustration is still further deepened and behavior more markedly affected. For these reasons, the chronic frustration of basic needs, such as affection, security, achievement, and independence, often leads to damaging personality characteristics and disturbed behavior. Pathological aggressiveness, hostility, destructiveness, delinquency, and numerous mental and behavioral symptoms can be traced to these intrapersonal frustrations.

It is worth noting also that external and internal frustrations are *closely interrelated.* The deprivations or obstructions that arise in a person's environment are often the occasion for serious personal frustration. The death of parents, for example, may be regarded by the young child as rejection; the superiority of others is often taken as a reflection of personal inferiority; punishment may enhance feelings of guilt that already exist. Conversely, intrapersonal frustrations have a way of influencing external determinants. To a person in whom the feeling of personal worth is stifled by the feeling of inferiority, such a factor as parental rejection can be a much more serious handicap in making adjustments than it is to a person who has not experienced inferiority. Here, again, we are reminded of the dynamic relations between personality and environment described earlier.

Frustrations in Childhood

Before continuing with the analysis of frustration, it might be helpful to pause for a moment and study some of the typical frustrations that occur in the course of daily experience (Kaplan & Baron, 1952, pp. 256–260). Since they vary considerably with developmental level, we begin with those that characterize early childhood. At this stage in life, frustrations are most closely linked to basic needs since the child has not reached the motivational level where rational motives, ideals, or goals play a significant part in determining behavior. Nor, perhaps, are frustrations as yet a threat to the phenomenal self. Typically, the very young child is frustrated by loss of love, restrictions of behavioral exploration, family rivalries, sex and age patternings which force him into socially accepted but undesirable modes of behavior and parental restrictions which interfere with a growing independence.

Segel (1951, pp. 29–30) cites a study by Baldwin, Kelhorn, and Breese on preschool and first-grade children that illustrates very clearly the effects of parental attitudes on frustration and adjustment.

> Their results show the amount of consideration given to the child in his early years has a definite bearing on whether or not he will be frustrated. The type of psychological atmosphere seemed to have more to do with frustration than the physical environment at this level. The main classifications of behavior of parents toward their child and the general resulting behavior of the child, frustrated or otherwise, which they found are as follows:

PARENTAL BEHAVIOR	CHILD BEHAVIOR
1. *Rejection of children*	
a. Passive or ignoring	A desperate seeking for affection and attention; expression in near social or near delinquency type of behavior
b. Active or repressing	Withdrawn, shy and stubbornly resistant in situations demanding response; retreats into self
2. *Casual autocracy*	
a. Casual autocracy (as a policy)	Rebellious, earning a certain grudging respect; sometimes anxious compliance
b. Casual autocracy (as an expediency)	Rebellious, almost uncontrollable at times; insistent in wanting to command a situation

PARENTAL BEHAVIOR	CHILD BEHAVIOR
c. Casual indulgence	Develops conflicts, shy outside the home situation—aggressive through refusing contacts with others
3. *Acceptant*	
a. Indulgent	Learns to fool parents and get his own way by wheedling actions; tends toward emotionality
b. Pseudo-democratic	Tends to develop intellectual abilities; aloofness developed; unpopular with other children
c. Scientifically democratic	Learns a lot, open to new ideas, tends to reason, but does not understand other children too well
d. Warmly democratic	All-round development of the child

The majority of childhood frustrations, then, are external, resulting from the blocking of needs and desires by the imposition of external rules, demands, and restrictions, and by the failure of adults to provide situations and relations that lead to the wholesome gratification of needs. We can easily see why broken homes, working mothers or mothers too busily occupied with social affairs, fathers who never find time for the children, the only-child situation, severe punishment, rigid discipline, lack of opportunities for play and free expression, lack of playmates, and poverty are prolific sources of frustration for the young child. Small wonder that "warmth," acceptance, and permissiveness figure so prominently in current therapeutic efforts to reduce the effects of chronic frustration.

Frustrations in Adolescence

Many of the childhood frustrations are carried over into adolescence, but there are motivational changes that alter the picture. Adolescents, too, are affected by interference with independence, school failures, sex patterning, and the like. Yet there is a noticeable shift from external to internal frustrations. The adolescent is more subject than the child to mental conflicts revolving around sex desires, the need for experience, moral principles, social expectations, and the needs for conformity, recognition, and social approval. He is more clearly conscious of his personal limitations, particularly when they have social implications, and he is more likely to be seriously affected by the lack of achievement. On the threshold of adult responsibilities, the adolescent is yet denied the privileges of holding a job, voting, joining the armed forces as a volunteer, living away from home, or getting married. In other words, plagued with a growing number of internal frustrations, the adolescent is also faced with new restrictions and regulations to which the young child is seldom subjected. For these reasons, adolescence is often singled out as a period of considerable stress and conflict, when both internal and external frustrations reach their peak. Because of immaturity and lack of experience, the average youth is poorly equipped to deal efficiently with frustrations. His intellectual, moral, and social perspectives and values have not developed sufficiently to help him resolve conflicts and frustrations in an efficient and wholesome manner. Thus in adolescence the groundwork is often laid for maladjustments that appear later in adulthood (Segel, 1951).

Frustrations in Adulthood

Adulthood brings with it its own store of frustrations, both internal and external, mainly because of increasing responsibilities. Added to the personal frustrations that arise from conflicts, and the chronic failure to gratify needs and desires, are the stresses and threats associated with vocational and marital responsibilities. Because there are many opportunities for frustration in marriage it is not surprising to find a high incidence of maladjustment among married couples. Imagine the depth of frustration and threat that results from wanting children and not being able to have them; or, conversely, having too many children, closely spaced! In the sexual sphere, too, marriage, which is supposed to provide opportunities for normal and wholesome expression of sexual desire, often leads to the most serious frustrations and conflicts, because of fear of pregnancy, sexual immaturity, or inhibitions stemming from childhood and adolescence. In addition, the young housewife is often frustrated in her social inclinations, in her desire for freedom of expression and activity, or in her ambition to achieve a high level of efficiency in homemaking; while the husband is frustrated in his desires for male companionship, participation in sports, and freedom in the use of family funds. These are only a few of the numerous possibilities that could be cited, but they are good examples of the kinds of frustration that the responsibilities of marriage bring.

The frustrations and tensions of marriage are similar in many respects to those associated with a job or a career since both marriage and vocations impose demands and restrictions that cannot always be handled successfully. The limitations of a job may seriously frustrate functions and abilities, as when a person with good intellectual capacity is required by circumstances to do work far below his natural abilities. Or ambition may be frustrated and goals blocked either because the vocational situation does not afford opportunities or because the vocation is not suited to a person's ambition. The facetious remark that all dentists are frustrated doctors, and all psychologists frustrated psychiatrists, while not necessarily true, serves nevertheless to exemplify the possibilities of vocational frustration. Sometimes, too, in the vocational sphere, there is a great deal of frustration of beliefs, attitudes, and convictions. The progressive-minded teacher, for example, may find himself in a school or a community where his convictions are frowned upon and his methods not tolerated by the school board or the principal. The young social worker, fresh from professional school, may find scant opportunity to put into practice the new ideas and theories propounded by her teachers. Here again you can see that there are many possibilities for frustration, some of which can seriously affect the personal and vocational adjustments of individual workers (Marquart & Arnold, 1952).

We must take note also of the serious frustrations that occur because of impediments or failures in work and marriage. For the majority of adults, both work and marriage are necessary to adequate adjustment; therefore, when illness, injury, forced retirement, divorce, separation, or spinsterhood make either one or both impossible, frustration is the inevitable outcome. It is largely through the medium of work that persons utilize their time and efforts productively, realize ambitions, express their talents and capacities effectively, and gratify their needs for achievement, status, security, and recognition. For most men, there is nothing so frustrating and threatening as forced idleness, whatever the cause; it is small wonder that the practice of retirement brings so many problems of adjustment. Any effective program of mental hygiene and psychotherapy must seek the elimination of idleness and provide opportunities for productive effort, regardless of the age or condition of the person. The need for such programs is highlighted by the emphasis put on occupational therapy in mental hospitals and by the increasing interest shown in recent years in the problems of adjustment posed by the aged (Gilbert, 1953).

Even greater than the frustrations of forced idleness are the frustrations caused by impediments to marital happiness. While there are some people who successfully sublimate natural desires for children, sexual gratification, and companionship, by means of special vocations, they are relatively few, and certainly this number does not include those who have failed at marriage or who have been forced into a state of "single blessedness." Any person who fails to find a mate, or to keep one, is frustrated, no matter how adept he is at sublimation or rationalization, and this frustration, which is always serious because of the character of the motivations involved, will be reflected in personal characteristics and behavior. Nature, it is said, will not be denied or mocked. Where marital inadequacy exists, there is small chance of mental stability or wholesome adjustment. Only if one's life and work are dominated by the highest ideals and spiritual goals can this pitfall be avoided.

That these typical adolescent and adult frustrations involve serious threat to the integrity of the self and the self ideal is a fact that requires little emphasis. For the adolescent faced with the intense moral conflicts engendered by sexual desires, for the young housewife subjected to the stresses of family life, or for the older person who is informed that his usefulness has ended, there can be no more serious threat to the structure of the self. In the face of such damaging frustrations, it is almost psychologically impossible to escape the development of avoidant, defense, or escape mechanisms. Once the inner integrity of the self concept is breached, the road to maladjustment is laid wide open.

Characteristics of the Frustrated Personality

Whenever subjective frustration develops the person shows several typical characteristics. Prominent among them are *tenseness, stiffness,* and *rigidity.* Marital and vocational failures evoke these characteristics in a striking manner. Frustration necessarily creates tension, and because it interferes with natural expression, it causes the person to become stiff and rigid in his responses, especially those that are in any way related to the cause of the frustration. Thus the maritally frustrated person is tense and rigid with persons of the opposite sex, in contacts with children, in discussions about marriage, or in work that repeatedly evokes the feeling of frustration. The degree of tension and rigidity will be determined by the depth of the frustration, whether it is chronic or merely temporary, and the kind of motivation involved. Frustrations involving basic psychological needs, marital desires, or vocational aspirations are likely to be deep and chronic and may be expected to produce considerable tension and rigidity.

Frustrations are also characterized by a strong *emotional quality,* which serves to reinforce the subjective feeling of frustration. Both the hindrances involved and the resulting tension are unpleasant, and there are likely to be other emotional concomitants such as irritability, annoyance, anger, resentment, envy, and jealousy. The quality of feeling will vary with the nature of the frustration. Anger and aggression, for example, are common results of the frustration of needs in childhood, whereas resentment, envy, or jealousy are familiar concomitants of adult frustrations relating to work, marriage, or social position. In every instance, however, unpleasantness is the invariable component (Symonds, 1949, pp. 47–48).

Because frustrations represent failure and inadequacy, there is one characteristic especially common to frustrated persons: *a strong tendency toward projection*, the mechanism whereby one's failures and inadequacies are attributed to a source outside oneself. This does not occur in every instance of frustration, but it is likely to occur when the frustration involves significant motivations. The student, for example, who is blocked in his efforts to achieve a degree will tend to project his own inadequacies onto the teachers, the school system, examinations, and so forth. Similarly, the housewife, frustrated in her desires for exciting romance, efficiency in homemaking, or freedom of action, will often find the causes of her failures in her husband, too many children, or the unreasonable demands of the marriage state. Other mechanisms may also be utilized to take the edge off frustration, including *sublimation, rationalization,* and *a sour-grapes attitude*, all of which serve to reduce the tension and unpleasantness associated with frustration (Chapter 8).

Signs of Frustration

The dynamics of frustration leads to the development of symptomatic behavior or external signs that betray its existence. Some of these manifestations are very common and well known, especially since everyone experiences frustration at one time or another in the course of his daily strivings. When, for example, you wait interminably for someone to answer your phone call, you know what happens. You begin to doodle or scribble. These are *meaningless responses* occasioned by the inability to do anything else in a completely frustrating situation. Here one can detect, too, the presence of annoyance, anger, and irritation. Sometimes these meaningless responses are actually *behavioral explorations*, which function as an effort to break out of a frustrating situation. Similar to these responses is *stereotypy*, or the meaningless repetition of responses, as exemplified in the endless pacing back and forth of a person completely frustrated in his efforts to solve a problem. The expectant father often manifests this kind of behavior because of his inability to help in any way.

Also likely to occur in cases of frustration is *emotional disruption*, leading to explosive discharge of tensions and pent-up feelings, or to confusion. A small child, frustrated in his efforts to reach a toy, may suddenly burst into tears or loud wailing until the situation is changed in his favor. An adolescent girl, denied the privilege of dating or staying out late at a party, angrily rejects the wiser decisions of her parents. Where the motivation is little understood and the usual expressions of frustration are unavailable, there is likely to be *emotional confusion*, involving simultaneous stimulation of feelings such as anger, annoyance, envy, jealousy, or anxiety. In much the same way as abnormal conflict precludes rational deliberation or thinking about a problem, so frustration makes it difficult to express feelings in a normal and wholesome manner.

Emotional disruption is reflected, in part, in the *unusual energy* and the almost *dogged application* to tasks that characterize the frustrated person. We might compare this reaction to Steckle's concept of "flight into reality" (Steckle, 1949, p. 45). Symonds states bluntly that "the person who burns the most energy in some enterprise is the person most frustrated" (Symonds, 1949, p. 58). Vocationally and maritally frustrated persons usually show these qualities. The devotion of the spinster to her work and the ceaseless social activity of the childless wife are good illustrations. Because frustration sets off emotional reactions that cannot find normal expression, the energy of these reactions is expressed in *excessive activity* of one kind or another. Devotion to work serves this purpose also, and, in addition, it helps to reduce the feeling of frustration through the sense of accomplishment that work produces. This does not mean, of course, that all persons showing a great deal of energy and serious application to duty are frustrated, any more than calm deliberation always indicates conflict. However, we must recognize that in many such instances it is neither drive nor high purpose that motivates energetic application or accomplishment, but rather the existence and dynamics of a deep-seated frustration (Rosenzweig, 1935; Singer & Feshbach, 1959).

It is to be expected, of course, that frustrations, particularly those that resist all efforts at reduction, will often lead to *acceptance of failure* and that chronic frustration will generate *a habit of giving up easily*. The attitude, so often observed, in "What's the use, I couldn't succeed no matter how hard I tried" is a clear sign of chronic frustration. Domineering or perfectionistic parents who never afford children the opportunity for achievement, or who fail to recognize ability and effort are often the cause of these damaging attitudes. For this reason, the imposition of adult standards on the efforts and aspirations of children can lead to the most detrimental effects on adjustment. Once the conviction is established that no amount of effort will serve to overcome obstacles to achievement, success, affection, or any other goal or quality of mind, the sense of frustration becomes an integral part of the mental structure, and there is little hope that the demands of reality or of inner strivings can be met in an efficient or healthy manner.

It is small wonder that chronically frustrated people show *reluctance to assume responsibility*. The conviction that certain failure is in store for them, regardless of the degree of effort expended, causes them to shy away from tasks or positions that involve serious responsibility. The willingness to accept responsibility is always determined in part by the inner conviction that one possesses the abilities and personal qualities to meet whatever demands arise and also that the cards are not stacked against one. If a student graduating from high school were convinced that he had reached the upper limits of educational achievement, there is little chance that he would undertake a college education. Responsibilities demand ability, effort, and achievement, which a sense of frustration can block very effectively. Thus we can understand why a frustrated housewife and mother, convinced that success in marriage is unattainable, develops fatigue, headache, backache, and similar symptoms, so that she can dodge the responsibilities that marriage imposes.

Factors Determining Response to Frustration

Now we may ask, what determines the responses made to a frustrating situation? We know that there are many possibilities—emotional outburst, tolerance, symptomatic behavior, or even delinquency. But why do people react in different ways, even when the motivations and the situations are similar?

One source lists only three factors determining the effects of frustration: (1) the degree of frustration, (2) nature of the impulse that is frustrated, and (3) personality structure (Maslow & Mittelmann, 1951, p. 64). These factors are of primary importance, but there are others that should be noted. As a starting point, we can be sure that the frustration-adjustment pattern will be affected by the character and strength of the motivations involved. Casual or insignificant motivations, when frustrated, will not affect behavior in a serious way, while the blocking of needs, like affection and security, is very likely to influence adjustment adversely, depending always on the strength of the motivation. Even ordinary desires, if they are strong enough, can cause behavior difficulties when thoroughly frustrated. Much depends on the special meaning these desires have. To some persons, clothes, social position, or amusement mean more than affection, security, or achievement, so that the response to frustration is quite different from what we would normally expect.

The *kind of barrier or privation* causing frustration will affect responses to an important degree. Children will react differently to parental discipline and restrictions than to the regulations imposed by teachers or other persons in authority. In the one instance there may be frustration tolerance, in the other open rebellion or aggression. It makes a difference who imposes frustrating conditions. Similarly, the restricting influence of moral principles may be expected to affect responses differently than will social codes or cultural traditions. If, for example, sexual behavior is self-regulated in terms of a healthy morality, frustration will have little adverse effect on adjustment; whereas a puritanical code of sexual behavior often produces damaging effects on mental stability and adjustment. Here, too, the strength of the barrier is important. Where parental, social, or internal restrictions are completely unyielding, so that there is no possible alternative to frustration, the effects on behavior will be apparent. Maladjusted persons often have a set of rigid codes and principles from which they cannot allow the slightest deviation. In such cases, the outcome of frustration will include strong guilt feelings, scruples, obsessions, compulsive behavior, anxiety, and phobias.

The *psychological context* in which frustration occurs is another important factor determining response to frustration. Where there is a high level of emotional security and maturity, frustration is not likely to have a damaging effect. One can readily see, for example, that a physical or mental privation such as poor eyesight, illness, or intellectual weakness will be more frustrating and cause maladjustment more quickly in the emotionally immature person than in one who is emotionally stable. Similarly, the loss of one or both parents in childhood can be adjusted to effectively by the emotionally secure child, whereas it might precipitate a serious disorder in one already insecure in his emotional relations.

The factor of emotional security is closely related to *personality structure*. We have pointed out several times that adjustment is routed through personality, and therefore the peculiar make-up of personality will condition the outcome of frustration. Included in personality structure are developmental level, organization of motives, drives, attitudes, and sentiments, the extent of symbolic functioning, existence of predisposing factors, extent and influence of unconscious determinants, level of intellectual functioning and self-determination, and fund of available habits. Thus, to take one example, response to frustration will be more adequate where there is a high level of intellectual functioning and self-determination than would be the case where responses are determined by unconscious factors. The student who reacts to academic failure by more intensive study is adjusting far more adequately than one who reacts with inferiority and compensatory mechanisms.

The *degree of ego involvement* and ego integrity will also affect reactions to frustration. If, in the example just mentioned, academic failure is regarded as a reflection of inherent personal weakness (ego involvement) the effect on adjustment might be damaging. Referring to the differences and similarities in the content of individual egos, Sherif and Cantril (1947, pp. 117–118) point out:

> These contents of the ego, these things, persons, ways of conducting oneself, social norms of various kinds, provide for the individual the standards of judgments or frames of reference which determine to

such an important degree his social behavior and reactions. And when any stimulus or situation is consciously or unconsciously related to them by the individual, we can say there is "ego-involvement." Thus, the ego in its various capacities enters in as an important determinant which may color, modify, or alter our experiences and behavior in almost any situation. For *our* standards, *our* values, *our* goals and ambitions, *our* ways of doing things have become involved. *We* feel elated, restricted, gratified, supported, disturbed, or insecure, in these ego-involving situations.

This ego-involvement can and does range from what may be a temporary moderate involvement in a laboratory experiment with some task to be performed where we feel that somehow *our* capacities or abilities are at stake, to complex social situations in which we feel involved, because of some threat to, or enhancement of, *our* position as a member of some gang, group, or class we identify ourselves with.

Such possibilities make ego integrity important, as well, because the integration of motives, attitudes, feelings, and so on into a well-knit organization precludes, or at least offsets, the damaging effects of frustration. In fact, as we noted earlier, personal integration is a necessary condition for the achievement of adjustment and mental health. Where this condition exists, frustration is not likely to evoke inadequate responses (Klein & Schoenfeld, 1941).

Finally, we may note that frustrations will be conditioned by how readily available substitutes are. If a young lady, frustrated in a love affair by the death or desertion of her fiancé, can in a short while develop an interest in someone else, or temporarily direct her energies and interests toward a satisfying activity, she will make a good adjustment. However, if no substitute is available, she will probably become maladjusted. Similarly, the housewife who finds romance in loving and caring for her husband and children quickly offsets the frustrations that inevitably arise in marriage. We have noted that frustrations of one kind or another are inevitable in the course of daily experience. Where some of them are concerned, tolerance is the only answer, but, in many instances, detrimental effects on adjustment can be forestalled by being able to turn to a substitute, especially in situations where tolerance is not easily developed. Thus the student who, failing to qualify for the study of medicine, elects a career in dentistry or pharmacy is taking a long step toward the reduction of what might have become a chronic frustration. Similarly, it is much better to place a child who has lost his parents in a boarding home than to commit him to an institution for child care. In many crucial situations involving frustrations, some kind of substitution is possible, and good mental hygiene requires that we avail ourselves of this possibility in order to offset the damaging effects of frustration.

Frustration Tolerance

From what has been said about frustration so far one might get the impression that it almost invariably leads to personality disorder or symptom formation. But let us recall that it is the subjective, emotional, and chronic reaction to objective frustration that is most significant for adjustment and mental health. Some frustration *is unavoidable* because it is impossible in our society and with our limitations to secure the gratification of all needs, to realize all personal ambitions or goals, or to avoid all stresses and strains. For every motivation there are many internal or external barriers that stand in the way of fulfillment, and it would require an excision of most human motivations or a complete revamping of our society and culture before the majority of frustrations could be eliminated.

> There are many causes of tension and distress: quarrels, misunderstandings, loneliness, rain on Sunday, furnace fire going out during a cold snap, defeat, failure, handicaps, a stalled car, a mosquito circling the pillow, accidents, sickness, shocks, waiting for a phone booth, long-winded speakers, traumas, bereavement, being cut in on when you're dancing with *the* adorable one, boredom, "standing room only," "the line is busy," incompetent help, unpaid bills, no letter in the mail, not being invited, breaking one's glasses, broken promises, ants at a picnic, pain, etc. Every human being has to face such hardships. The mature person develops frustration tolerance, inuring himself to upsetting events so that they do not disturb him overmuch (Vaughan, 1952, p. 49).

Frustrations, once they exist, cannot always be reduced, and therefore, to maintain emotional tranquility and peace of mind, some degree of frustration tolerance is necessary. *Frustration tolerance means simply the capacity to accept inevitable frustrations,* as against trying to overcome them or reacting to them in a subjective, emotional, or damaging way. Cameron and Magaret define tolerance for stress and frustration as *"the ability to endure pressure, delay, thwarting and conflict without developing maladaptive reactions"* (Cameron & Magaret, 1951, p. 50). According to Rosenzweig, "frustration tolerance may be defined as an individual's capacity to withstand frustration without failure of psychobiological adjustment, i.e., without resorting to inadequate modes of response. In its broadest implications the concept is related to resistance in the medical sense" (Rosenzweig, 1944, Volume I, p. 384).

Obviously, the person deprived of an arm or hand simply cannot become a surgeon no matter how much he wants to; the youngster with poor eyesight cannot become an aviator; the child whose father dies cannot have the love of both natural parents. There are countless instances like these, some of major and others of minor significance, some temporary and some permanent, but all of them make frustration inevitable. It is therefore important to appreciate that *a certain degree of frustration tolerance is an essential part of adequate adjustment and mental health.*

Both lack of frustration and too much frustration are inimical to good adjustment and stand in the way of the development of frustration tolerance. Indulgent, lenient, and overprotective parents are the primary causes of the first difficulty. The only way to learn how to live with frustrations is to experience them, and sooner or later the parents can no longer stand between the child and reality, can no longer provide gratifications for every need and impulse or protect the child from the realities of daily life (Hybl & Stagner, 1952). Then lack of experience in dealing with frustration is going to have a damaging effect. Learning to accept or to cope with frustrations is as much a part of growing into maturity as learning how to speak and write; without such learning there is little chance of dealing adequately with the demands of self or of reality. Rosenzweig (1938, p. 153) goes so far as to suggest that frustration tolerance might even provide—

> . . . a working definition of the difference between the psychotic—in whom a generalized low frustration tolerance would be said to obtain; the neurotic—in whom certain circumscribed areas of low frustration tolerance (complexes) might be posited; and the normal individual— in whom relatively high frustration tolerance would usually be found throughout the personality.

In their experimental study of frustration tolerance, Hybl and Stagner (1952, p. 170) found that normal subjects and schizophrenics showed high frustration tolerance and in this respect were significantly different from neurotics, alcoholics, and psychopaths. These results partly conflict with Rosenzweig's formula, even though the low frustration tolerance of neurotics is in the expected direction. The unexpectedly high tolerance of the schizophrenics to frustration is explained by Hybl and Stagner as being attributable to a drastic restriction of the phenomenal field. The schizophrenic "denies that it is important for him to succeed on the task, he also denies that it matters if he fails. By drastically restricting his phenomenal field, he protects himself against any disturbance" (Hybl & Stagner, 1952, p. 169). This interpretation is probably correct since frustration cannot exist when the necessary conditions of frustration are removed.

Excessive frustration inhibits learning of the kind necessary to adjustment. If a child is told occasionally that he cannot go out and play because there is work to be done, or if recognition is sometimes postponed because of circumstances that cannot be avoided, the child can learn to defer gratifications or even give them up altogether; however, if he is continuously or repeatedly frustrated in his efforts to achieve gratification of needs and desires, it is impossible for him to learn tolerance of frustration since no one can give up important desires all of the time. Play, for example, is natural and necessary to children; no child can accept giving up play altogether, but he can learn to defer such activity for a time, and it is this learning that is important to adjustment. Where frustration of important motivations is continuous, subjective frustration rather than frustration tolerance is the inevitable result.

Apart from those instances wherein circumstances preclude the realization of certain motives and desires, the *essence of frustration tolerance consists in the capacity to postpone action or satisfaction* until opportunities are more favorable. When a child can say, "Okay Mother, I'll wait until next week, or next month, or next year for what I want," we know that he has reached a point where he can deal with frustrations adequately. *Frustration tolerance is a clear sign of maturity*, and maturity is one of the most important criteria of good adjustment. The important fact for personal maturity and adjustment is the realization that, from time to time, some activities and gratifications must be deferred, and the realistic acceptance of this fact is one of the best indications of the ability to deal effectively with demands that arise in the course of daily living.

We must, however, enter a note of caution. *Too much frustration tolerance can be as bad as too little.* There are some persons who relinquish desires and activities too easily; they get into the habit of giving up, which is one of the signs of frustration. After a while, rather than making the effort, such persons regularly yield to restrictions, demands, or limitations imposed on them and thus never learn the important lesson of *reducing frustrations.* Where frustration tolerance is necessary to effective adjustment, it is wholesome and beneficial; however, where it is used to escape from effort or to win the affection and esteem of others, it can be detrimental to both adjustment and maturity.

Outcomes of Frustration: The Principle of Varied Response

Frustration is the springboard for the development of adjustive and maladjustive behavior. The child frustrated by school may adopt the simple expedient of truancy; the adolescent who is denied recognition or status may redouble his efforts to move to the head of the class; the adult frustrated in the realization of personal ambitions drifts from one job to another until there are no jobs left for him. The responses may very from increased effort to aggressiveness, antisocial behavior, defense mechanisms, hostility, or crime. The response to frustration can tip the scale toward normality or abnormality, adjustment or maladjustment.

In this effort to escape frustration, varied response is one way of trying to achieve gratification of basic needs or reduction of the tension produced by frustration. Varied response is simply the exploration of different response possibilities that may serve to reduce tension. They may be overt or symbolic, depending on the degree of learning, tendencies toward symbolic functions, or character of the frustration. *Overt responses* are objective and behavioral in character and usually result from learning. Thus, as we saw, learning is basic to adjustment since it supplies various possibilities for utilizing varied response. An infant frustrated by hunger can only cry or writhe, whereas an adult has at his command a number of behavioral possibilities for the reduction or control of the frustration. Thus varied response bears a direct relation to the efficiency of adjustment and is the mechanism by which effective substitution is often made. In many frustrating situations, the organism, by the simple expedient of trial and error, hits upon a solution that is satisfying and efficient and thereby effects an adjustment that otherwise would have been impossible. This process is analagous to experimental research, where various hypotheses are subjected to experimental tryout until the problem is solved.

In frustrating situations, where expressive behavior is precluded or unavailable because of deficiency in learning, the organism turns to *symbolic responses* for the reduction of tension. The child deprived of a playmate falls back on daydreaming and fantasy thinking and creates a dream world of his own, peopled with the playmates he needs to gratify his wishes. Symbolic functioning is often expressed in overt behavior, too, but the behavior is only indirectly related to the motivation. The normal person with soiled hands "adjusts" to the situation by washing them, whereas the hand-washing compulsion of some neurotics is a symbolic expression of unconscious guilt. Symbolic functioning, then, may express itself in various mental symptoms such as obsessions, delusions, and fantasy thinking; or it may take the form of overt responses exemplified in compulsive behavior mannerisms and the like.

The theory has been developed that frustration invariably leads to aggression (Dollard, *et al.*, 1939). However, other investigators have found that *the response to frustration assumes many different forms, ranging from subjective feelings of inferiority, guilt, and shame, to regression, personality disorganization, and overt aggression.* In some instances it has been found that frustration even leads to an increase both in effort and in the efficiency of cognitive functions (Barker, 1938). Some of the more important of these findings have been brought together in Table 9.

Important to note is that frustration itself does not necessarily lead to undesirable or maladaptive response. The outcome will vary with the determinants that influence frustration (Sears, 1951; Sargent, 1948; Frederiksen, 1942).

TABLE 9

Outcomes of and Reactions to Frustration

Investigator	Outcomes of Frustration
Dollard, *et al.* (1939)	Aggression, later modified to include other responses
Britt & Janus (1940)	Aggression, withdrawal, regression, resistance, anger, guilt and remorse, shame and embarrassment
Rosenzweig (1944)	Need-persistive and ego-defensive reactions, the latter subdivided into extrapunitive, intropunitive, and impunitive responses
Page (1947, pp. 33–37)	Direct approach (increased effort, variation in attack, change of goals), feelings of inferiority, aggressive behavior, mental mechanisms, mental symptoms
Korner (1949, p. 93)	Hostility, compliance, evasion, withdrawal, inhibition, regression, rationalization, acceptance
Symonds (1949, pp. 58–66)	Aggression and rage, learning, withdrawing, resignation, fantasy, repeating behavior, abandoning of goal, regression, personality disorganization, "social outcomes"
Thorpe (1950, pp. 43–44, 50–60, 108–110)	Ego-defensive (autocorrective) reactions, hostile reactions, symbolic (neurotic) reactions, insulation, aggressive behavior
Segel (1951, pp. 25–28)	Aggression, regression, fixation

The Solution

The process of adjustment, which begins with motivation and involves the immediate determinants of stress, threat, conflict, and frustration, is terminated by a response that serves to reduce these several factors and the motivation that underlies them. *This response constitutes the solution.* In perhaps the majority of instances of human behavior, the solution hit upon is adequate for the purposes of adjustment. Frustration or conflict is satisfactorily reduced, tension disappears, and the response is relatively efficient as well as socially acceptable. There is no noticeable damage to personality or to mental and emotional stability. In many other instances, far too numerous for the good of society, the response to frustration is not adjustive in the good sense of the term, as some of the entries in Table 9 clearly indicate. In place of efficient, healthy, and satisfying responses, there occur such reactions as rage, withdrawal, worry, anxiety, delinquency, lying, nail biting, enuresis, psychosomatic disorders, and a host of other symptomatic reactions detrimental to personality, to mental health, and to emotional stability. These are the nonadjustive and maladjustive reactions described in Part Three.

QUESTIONS AND PROJECTS FOR FURTHER STUDY

1. The text describes a number of principles of motivation. Could you add four or five principles of your own?
2. Dr. Hans Selye has developed a widely accepted theory of stress in relation to behavior. Write a short essay describing Selye's theory.
3. What is meant by the statement that some behavior does not fit into the concept of adjustment? Document your answer with reference to the literature cited in the text.
4. Write a research paper on the theory of unconscious motivation, citing experimental and clinical evidence to support your hypotheses and conclusions.
5. Select any two books on the phenomenon of conflict, and write a critical and comparative evaluation of them.
6. Explain in your own words why frustration is often related to aggressive behavior. What evidence is there to support this relationship?
7. Discuss the interrelations of conflict, frustration, and stress, and indicate how they are related to motivation on the one hand and to adjustive behavior on the other.

SELECTED COLLATERAL READINGS

BARKER, R., DEMBO, T., & LEWIN, K. *Frustration and regression: an experiment with young children.* Iowa City, Iowa: University of Iowa Press, 1941.

BASOWITZ, H., PERSKY, H., KORCHIN, S. J., & GRINKER, R. R. *Anxiety and stress: an interdisciplinary study of a life situation.* New York: Mc-Graw-Hill, 1955.

BOULDING, K. E. *Conflict and defense: a general theory.* New York: Harper & Row, 1962.

BROWN, J. F. *The psychodynamics of abnormal behavior.* New York: McGraw-Hill, 1940.

DOLLARD, J., *et al. Frustration and aggression.* New Haven: Yale University Press, 1939.

GRINKER, R. R., & SPIEGEL, J. P. *Men under stress.* New York: McGraw-Hill-Blakiston, 1945.

HORNEY, KAREN. *Our inner conflicts.* New York: Norton, 1945.

JANIS, I. *Psychological stress.* New York: Wiley, 1958.

LEIBMAN, S. *Stress situations.* Philadelphia: Lippincott, 1955.

MAIER, N. R. F. *Frustration: the study of behavior without a goal.* New York: McGraw-Hill, 1949.

MASLOW, A. H. *Motivation and personality.* New York: Harper & Row, 1954.

MILLER, J. G. *Unconsciousness.* New York: Wiley, 1942.

MOWRER, O. H. Motivation. In *Ann. Rev. Psychol.,* 1952, 3, 419–438.

SAPPENFIELD, B. R. *Personality dynamics.* New York: Knopf, 1954.

SELYE, H. *The stress of life.* New York: McGraw-Hill, 1956.

SHERMAN, M. *Mental conflicts and personality.* New York: McKay, 1938.

STACEY, C. L., & DEMARTINO, M. F. (Eds.) *Understanding human motivation.* Cleveland, Ohio: Howard Allen, 1958.

SYMONDS, P. M. *Dynamic psychology.* New York: Appleton, 1949.

YATES, A. J. *Frustration and conflict.* New York: Wiley, 1962.

PART THREE

The Process and Patterns of Adjustment

7

The Adjustment Process

Now that we have defined both the determinants and dynamics of adjustment we should take a look at the process itself. What are the essential factors that enter into the adjustment process, and what is it that distinguishes adjustment from other behavioral responses? We know that conflict and frustration, stress and threat are involved in the process, but we want to determine exactly how. In other words, we want to study the basic pattern of adjustment. We want also to determine the relation between adjustive behavior and reality and the essential criterion of adequate adjustment. And finally, we wish to fit symptomatology into the total picture because so many adjustive processes involve symptom formation.

ELEMENTS OF THE ADJUSTMENT PROCESS

Behavior Dynamics and Adjustment

In our survey of the dynamics of adjustment in the preceding chapter, it became increasingly clear that motivation is the keystone for understanding the process. Needs, motives, feelings, and emotions are internal forces that cause tension and lack of equilbrium within the organism. Both of these conditions are unpleasant and repugnant because freedom from tension and an equilibrium of internal forces are more natural to the organism than their opposites. For the same reasons, conflicts and frustrations are unpleasant and repugnant, opposed as they are to the natural tendency of the organism toward internal harmony, peace of mind, and the satisfactions derived from the expression of needs or motives. This is particularly true when tension and disequilibrium represent the disruptive influence of pathological feelings and excessive emotions, or the failure to realize healthy need gratifications because of abnormal conflicts and frustrations (Schneiders, 1963a).

Adjustive response, then, whether good or bad, may be regarded simply as an effort on the part of the organism to reduce or escape from tension and to restore the more natural conditions of equilibrium. The *quality* of the response, that is, whether it is healthy, efficient, damaging, or pathological, will be determined by such factors as personality make-up, the quality of the motivation, environmental determinants, the peculiar

203

character of the frustration or conflict, and the individual's relation to reality. The first of these factors we have already studied at considerable length; in this chapter we will direct our attention to the structure of the adjustment process and the functioning of the reality principle (Filer, 1952; Hartly, 1943; Wright, 1943).

Basic Pattern of Adjustment

Whether we are dealing with a simple, everyday adjustment or a highly complex one, such as a neurosis, there is a basic pattern in which certain elements can always be distinguished. Let us suppose that a young child wants affection from a mother too occupied with other duties to meet the child's need. The child will be frustrated and will strike out in one direction or another to find a possible solution to the problem and thus reduce the tension of the need and the frustration. He may temporarily abandon the effort, turn to some other activity, seek affection elsewhere, or indulge in thumb sucking. Similarly, an adult frustrated in his desire for affection, children, or achievement, seeks and ultimately hits upon some form of activity or expression, often of a symptomatic kind, that serves to gratify the desire and to reduce tension. Thus, typically, the frustrated desire for children is redirected (sublimated) into welfare work, clinical psychology, teaching, or boarding care of children. Whenever adequate outlets *are unavailable,* because of situational or personality limitations, the outcomes of frustration (or conflict) are likely to assume a neurotic or psychotic character (Yates, 1962).

In all situations of frustration, conflict, or stress we can readily discern essential and common elements. These are (1) *motivation,* (2) *frustration,* conflict, or stress, (3) *varied response,* and (4) *solution,* that is, reduction of the problem, frustration, conflict, and tension by the adoption of some form of response. This sequence, adapted from Shaffer (1936), is essentially the same as that defined by a number of writers (McKinney, 1949, pp. 14–19; Page, 1947, pp. 30–31; Thorpe, 1950, pp. 106–114). Remember, however, that this applies only to situations in which some kind of blocking or frustration occurs. If a child is hungry and avails himself of cookies that are handy, the sequence of events can be very simply diagramed:

motivation   →   satisfying behavior

However the same child, hungry for affection, security, or belonging, may turn to gluttonous eating as a substitute response when these needs are not adequately gratified (Figure 11) Sherman makes the observation that frustration only occurs with significant behavior. "Frustration does not occur when an activity, with which there has been interference, is of little importance" (Sherman, 1941, p. 88). The point is well taken, but it narrows the meaning of frustration. The reader is referred to our distinction between subjective and objective frustration in the preceding chapter.

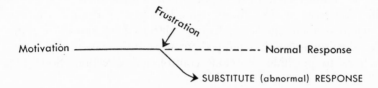

Fig. 11.   Illustration of the influence of frustration.

In some instances, substitute responses are not readily available. Then the person casts about for a response that will gratify the motivation and thus reduce tension. This situation is pictured in Figure 12, in which

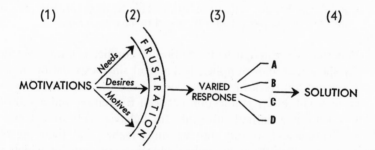

Fig. 12.   Illustration of the elements involved in a typical adjustment process in which frustration is a determining factor. The same sequence would occur if conflict were the immediate determinant of varied response.

the four elements of the adjustment process are indicated. This diagram may be applied to the example just cited and to many other situations that are considerably more complex. It indicates that motivation assumes a variety of forms, any one of which may be subjected to blocking by conflict or frustration resulting from some aspect of reality—parental restrictions, physical barriers, social codes, or discipline. Because of the tensions that this blocking causes, the organism "explores" different modes of response (A, B, C, D in the diagram) until it hits upon one that is satisfying because it reduces tension and frustration. This response, then, constitutes the solution of the difficulty. The case of the child whose hunger for affection is gratified by eating is a good example of this mechanism, particularly because eating is a natural symbolic substitute for the gratification of hungers that are not physiological in nature.

There are several characteristics of the frustrating situation that should be emphasized. First of all, when motivation is denied natural gratification or expression, the response hit upon as a solution is a substitute and may therefore be inadequate, distorted, or abnormal, especially if the organism is poorly equipped for substitution, or if the motivation is such as to preclude conscious control and direction. Segel remarks (1951, p. 24):

> The individual who is frustrated tends to act in a different manner from what he does in a nonfrustrating situation. This is an important point. He reacts in a way which is detrimental to himself and often to those about him. Furthermore, the type of reaction which takes place in one frustrating situation not only tends to appear every time that situation is presented, but also tends to spread to other situations, so that the individual reacts to other (more normal) situations through a frustrated type of behavior. This tends eventually to become a pattern and the individual is then said to have a *neurosis*.

Whether the reaction to frustration or conflict is always detrimental, as the statement above implies, is doubtful since exploration and substitution do not always lead to behavior difficulties. We must note also that there is no necessary connection between frustration and a substitute response. Eating is a natural substitute for behavior determined by such needs as affection and security, but we must realize that there are other possibilities for substitution in such a situation, any one of which may serve to reduce tension. However, *the more a substitute response deviates from the aim of the motivation, the more distorted and abnormal it becomes.* Let us note, too, that varied response is itself conditioned by the intensity of the motivation and the character of the frustration. In many situations, the blocking of a drive or motive terminates the process; there is neither varied response nor solution. If a child is forbidden to go swimming, he may do nothing more than sit down and read a book. This is a substitute response, if you wish to call it that, but it is indifferently related to either the motivation or the frustration. You can see from this that the quality of adjustment will always be determined by the kind of motivation involved and by the degree of frustration or conflict in the situation. Characteristics like these are important to the understanding of what adjustment is actually like.

Frustration and Conflict as Dynamic

The point is often made that frustration and conflict function as dynamic factors in the determination of behavior. Whether this viewpoint is correct or not, it is certainly true that these immediate determinants of adjustment are an integral part of a series of events that culminate in some form of overt expression. The initial and more basic factor is the motivating condition (needs, goals, etc.); yet, without the frustration or conflict, this particular, culminating response would not occur. Moreover, the frustration itself is dynamic insofar as it functions as a tendency within the organism toward expression in the psychic reactions or in the behavior of the individual. As we noted earlier with respect to habit, once the frustration is well established and becomes chronic, it tends toward *functional autonomy* and thereafter will influence various responses independently of its motivational origins (Mohsin, 1954; Filer, 1952; Hartley, 1943; Child & Waterhouse, 1952).

ADJUSTMENT AND REALITY

Attitudes toward Reality and the Adjustment Process

As we have noted several times, the processes of adjustment and mental health are determined in large measure by the attitude toward, and the manner in which, the individual reacts to the world of people, things, and relations that constitute reality. For this reason it is widely assumed that a healthy attitude toward and adequate contact with reality are indispensable to healthy adjustment. This point was emphasized in our definition of specific criteria of mental health in Chapter 2. Thus, excessive daydreaming and introversion, antisocial attitudes, solitary amusements, lack of interest in activities or other persons, pathological drinking, cynicism, selfishness, hostility, and delinquency are all disruptive of a healthy relation to reality. Even the individual himself is a part of reality, and for this reason self-acceptance and a healthy self concept are also necessary to good adjustment. It is reality that poses the demands, restrictions, codes, and mores with which the individual must learn to cope effectively. Hence adjustment can be defined simply as *a process by which the internal demands of motivation are brought into harmonious relation with the external demands of reality*. It is in this setting that conflict, stress, and frustration arise, and the organism is driven to explore different behavior possibilities in order to secure relief from tension.

Motivation, Perception, and Adjustment

In defining the relation between adjustment and reality, it is important to keep in mind that *the "reality" to which a person strives to adjust will be determined in large measure by his distinctive needs and values*. Thus, in a well-known experiment by Bruner and Goodman, poor children over-estimated the size of coins more than did rich children, suggesting that the children's need had an effect on perceptual adjustment. In other words, reality is changed, enlarged, or distorted by the influence of different motivations (Bruner & Goodman, 1947; Carter & Schooler, 1952, pp. 246–252; Pepitone, 1950; Postman & Bruner, 1948; McClelland, Atkinson, & Clark, 1949).

This relation between motivation and the perception of reality has been known for a long time, but its implications for adjustment and mental health must be carefully spelled out. If an adequate orientation to reality is regarded as a basic criterion of adjustment, and if reality is determined to a degree by subjective factors, the problem of adjustment becomes even more complicated. Whatever the implications of this fact, there is unmistakable evidence that the perception of reality is subjectively influenced, and therefore, in evaluating the particular adjustments of different persons we must consider the manner in which they perceive reality. As one writer says (Steckle, 1949, pp. 105–106):

> Whatever be the individual's basic attitude toward life, whether it be grounded in rational or emotional processes, he tends to perceive the world in terms of his personal outlook upon it. A maxim attributed to the French equivalent of our FBI is appropriate here: "The eye sees what it looks for, but it looks for only what is already in the mind." If a person views the world as a place in which security is to be found only through reliance upon others, through a vigorous "striking back" or through retreat into himself, he behaves accordingly. In any event, his behavior is conditioned by the way he *feels* about things; he never has learned that his feelings are relatively unimportant, that it is only what he *does* that counts. Kant has said: "We see things not as they are, but as we are."

This viewpoint regarding the perceiver's contributions to the thing perceived is echoed in many places. In his definitive book on client-centered therapy, for example, Rogers states as an essential proposition, *"The organism reacts to the field as it is experienced and perceived. This perceptual field is, for the individual, 'reality.' "* Expanding this principle, he writes, "This is a simple proposition, one of which we are all aware in our own experience, yet it is a point which is often overlooked. I do not react to some absolute reality, *but to my perception of this reality*. It is this perception which for me *is* reality" (Rogers, 1951, p. 484). To the child, therefore, parents, school, teachers, and playmates are somewhat different from what they are to an adult who cannot see with the eyes of a child. The following case illustrates this point very well.

> Mary was a fourteen-year-old girl who was having considerable difficulty adjusting to the home situation. She was in almost constant conflict with her mother because she refused to come home after school hours, rebeled at doing housework, quarreled with other children in the family, resented the father's discipline, and was generally unhappy when at home. Yet Mary's teachers reported her to be a model student. She was happy and carefree at school, got along well with classmates, was always willing to help the teachers in school chores, and maintained a high scholastic average. It is not difficult to understand Mary's adjustment problem. To her, school meant everything that her home did not. She perceived the school as a place of achievement, acceptance, security, and social equality. Actually, Mary's home was a very good one; but it was her different perception of the two situations that caused the adjustment difficulties. As she grew older and more mature, these perceptions changed, and today Mary is a well-adjusted girl, both at home and at school.

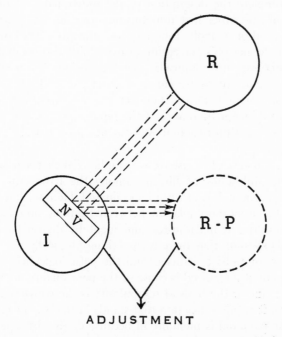

ADJUSTMENT

Fig. 13. How needs and values influence perception and alter the process of adjustment. I = Individual; N-V = Needs and Values; R = Reality; R-P = Reality as perceived.

Here, then, we have another factor to consider in trying to understand the process of adjustment. It is not enough to know the determinants and dynamics of human response and a person's objective relation to reality; we must also ascertain the manner in which and the degree to which needs, values, and other motivations condition his reaction to reality. (Levine, Chein, & Murphy, 1942). Only when this peculiar reaction is known and understood can we adequately evaluate or interpret individual adjustments. Subjective perception applies to all aspects of reality, including the individual himself. Hence the influence of the self concept on adjustment and mental health should be brought into line with this view. How a person regards himself is just as important to the process of adjustment as how he perceives objective reality. The interested student will find many articles in the literature dealing with these various relationships (Fensterheim & Tresselt, 1953; Postman, 1953; Erikson, 1954; Klein, Schlesinger, & Meister, 1951; Cattell & Wenig, 1952; Chodorkoff, 1954; Lazarus, Yousem, & Arenberg, 1953).

Thinking, Imagination, and Adjustment

To complete the description of the individual's relation to reality we have to fit one other fact into the picture, the influence of thinking and imagery, and of symbolic functions, on adjustment and mental health. It is not only the person's perception of reality but also *his evaluation of it,* how he symbolizes it to himself, that determines his reactions. These several processes are of course closely interrelated, and we must not overwork the distinctions between them. However, perception and thinking, or thinking and imagination are not the same thing, nor do they function in the same way within the total adjustment process (Hastorf & Knutson, 1949).

Above, on several occasions, we emphasized that a person's scale of values, or his philosophy of life are among the basic criteria by which adjustment and mental health can be evaluated. Here we have the clearest instance of the important relation between thinking and mental health. The hypochondriac is maladjusted and mentally disabled because of his fixed idea or obsession that there is something physically wrong with him. The obsessive-compulsive neurotic, and the pathologically scrupulous person are mentally disorganized because of the poor quality of their thoughts and beliefs. Lying at the basis of scrupulosity is the conviction of personal worthlessness; it is this conviction that stands in the way of mental health. Similarly, the paranoid is mentally ill because of the discrepancy between his ideas or beliefs and what is actually true. In all these instances the essential difficulty involves a distortion of the relation between thinking and reality. If this relation were straightened out, if, in other words, the patient could be made to "think straight," the maladjustment would disappear (Levitt, 1950).

The distortion of the relation between thinking and reality is paralleled in other symbolic functions, particularly imagination, and is expressed most clearly in symptom formation (Bucklew, 1960). We see this illustrated normally in daydreaming, and abnormally in the fantasy thinking of the schizophrenic. We see it also in normal night dreaming and in the bizarre, terrifying qualities of the nightmare. In all these instances, some of which are not only symbolic but symptomatic in nature, imagery is being manipulated in such a way as to distort the picture of reality. In the mind of the schizophrenic, or the child having a nightmare, reality is represented as a frightening caricature. Everyone knows that a distorted or overworked imagination will cripple the human mind. In such cases, the zone of defense, which we will describe more fully in Chapter 10, tends to break down, and the patient becomes victimized by the thrusts or demands of reality (Korchin & Basowitz, 1954).

It is clear that symbolic processes of the kind described above are subject to the same motivational influences as the process of perception. In a number of places, but particularly in the *Interpretation of dreams* and *The psychopathology of everyday life* (Freud, 1913, 1914), Freud emphasized again and again the fact that thinking and imagination are often determined by dynamic factors, particularly those that function at an unconscious level. Every student of Freud is well aware of the theory of wish fulfillment as applied to the content of dreams and of the equally important notion that symbolism and distortion, as reflected in both thinking and imagery, are the outcomes of powerful needs, feelings, or emotions. This point is not in dispute. What we are emphasizing here is the fact that the relation between adjustment and reality, and between mental health and reality, is always conditioned by the kind of thinking a person does, and by the content of his imagery.

ETIOLOGY AND SYMPTOMATOLOGY

Determinants, Dynamics, and Etiology

The foregoing analysis of the determinants, the dynamics, and the principles of motivated behavior brings us to a widely accepted principle among behavioral scientists to the effect that the understanding, interpretation, and treatment of adjustment problems require an intensive study of the causes and conditions that underlie them. The study of such causes and conditions, as they relate to disease, mental disorder, or maladjustment, is referred to as *etiology*. Thus much of the preceding discussion of the determinants and dynamics of behavior has as much to do with the etiology of maladjustment as with the explanation of adjustment itself. However, it must be understood that the investigation of the dynamic background and the determinants of behavior is not the same thing as etiology. These factors underlie *all human response*, normal as well as abnormal, and we deliberately followed this broader line of investigation, consonant with our general purpose of studying adjustment in all of its phases. Etiology, therefore, is only one part of this broader study, and behavior dynamics or motivation is a special area that must be understood as a necessary background to the study of etiology. In and by themselves, dynamic factors such as needs, desires, or motives do not cause maladjustment or abnormality; they function merely as the origins or mainsprings of human behavior. It is when they are interfered with or distorted by frustration, conflict, or environmental stress that maladjustment may result. Similarly, the conditions and determinants of adjustment and mental health outlined in Chapter 4 have as much or more to do with *normal* behavior and personality development as with maladjustment.

Causes versus Conditions

It is important also to distinguish between causes and conditions of adjustment and maladjustment. A condition is some factor, internal or external, that functions as a determining influence on, or as a prerequisite for, the appearance of certain effects. For example, a broken home or drunkenness is a condition and not a cause of delinquency. If it were a cause, delinquency would be much more widespread than it actually is. However, if a drunken father beats a child, the beating may act as a cause of rebellion, running away, or violence against authority. Causes, then, are the immediate antecedents (agents, principles, originators) of certain effects, without which these effects would not occur. Thus dynamic factors, such as needs and motives, are true *causes* of *normal* behavior, whereas such factors as frustration, conflict, traumatic experiences, and pathological feelings are *causes* of *abnormal* response.

Predisposing versus Exciting Determinants

The distinction between causes and conditions is not unlike the distinction often found in the literature of abnormal psychology regarding *predisposing* and *exciting* causes of maladjustment and personality disorder. Predisposing causes (determinants is a better term here) are those factors that incline a person toward some form of mental disorder or maladjustment. By themselves, they never precipitate the difficulty, but they serve, as it were, to prepare the soil for the development of the disorder or maladjustment. Heredity, faulty development, inadequate parent-child relations, poor environment, occupational hazards, chronic illness or disease, punitive discipline, broken homes, and chronic frustration or failure are examples of predisposing determinants of maladjustment. Note that any one of them, or any combination, may exist without the development of abnormality; where they do exist, however, the chances for such development are greatly increased.

Exciting or precipitating causes are those elements in the situation that ignite or touch off the difficulty, like a match applied to a trail of gunpowder that leads quickly to an explosion. Let us suppose, for the sake of illustration, that a person is extremely introverted, sensitive, and withdrawn. Perhaps, as a child, he was rejected or ridiculed by parents and friends and experienced a succession of failures. This person is predisposed to the reaction of schizophrenia. The soil is well prepared. Now, let us suppose further that, in a fatal accident, this person suddenly loses his wife, on whom he had been greatly dependent. The traumatic shock of her death, the loss of support, and the imminent threat of a reality that he fears act to precipitate the psychosis. Already withdrawn because of his fear of reality and a long history of rejection, mistreatment, and personal failure, he now loses contact with reality completely and sinks into a complete psychosis. Great catastrophes, loss of a job, traumatic experiences, death of near relatives, business failures, loss of one's fortune, accidents, serious physical injury, incurable disease, and failure in school are examples of events that serve to precipitate mental disorder or maladjustment.

The Development of Symptomatic Responses

Behavior maladjustments and mental disorders are characteristically reflected in the development of symptoms or symptomatic responses. Between etiology and symptomatology, therefore, there are basic relations of paramount importance (Rubins, 1959). As we have already noted, however, *symbolic* response is not alien to the normal, well-adjusted personality. It is, rather, a natural part of thinking and behavior. Language, for example, is a system of symbols for the communication of thoughts, experiences, and attitudes, and symptoms, we may note, are the language of the disturbed personality—symbols whose meaning can be read and interpreted by experts as precisely as can the writings and sayings of an author or poet. In the normal course of development, symbols of one kind and another come to be used consistently as substitutes for both stimuli and responses and thus figure prominently in ordinary adjustments. A flashing light is a symbol of danger, and tipping one's hat is a symbol of respect, in much the same way as words are symbols of ideas or feelings. This capacity for, and tendency toward, symbolic expression, common to all normal persons, constitute the psychological basis for symptom formation in disturbed personalities. Symptoms and symbols, however, are not identical. Both function as *signs*, but symptoms are regarded as *special* signs of illness or disability. Thus the night terror is symptomatic of disturbed emotion, whereas the content of the dream is symbolic of hidden fears or other mental processes. Hence it is possible to speak of symbolic symptoms (Kraines, 1948, pp. 33–40).

In many instances of maladjustive behavior, the symptomatic response is determined by some one element in the total situation, and this element functions symbolically to touch off the total response. A student, having failed an examination in a certain classroom, fails again in the same room, not because of inability or lack of preparation but because the situation symbolizes failure, and he reacts to the situation in terms of its special meaning (symbolism) rather than its objective characteristics. Often our failure to react adequately to other persons is determined by the symbolic meanings they evoke and not by their actual qualities. In interpreting the behavior or mental reactions of maladjusted persons, then, we must try to find out the special significance of their behavior and the symbolic meanings that they attach to different situations (Strecker & Appel, 1944, Chapter XX).

The Nature and Teleology of Symptoms

Symptoms are forms of behavior or response that signify (1) the existence of illness or pathology, (2) disturbed psychogenic conditions, (3) stress, frustration, or conflict, and (4) tension. Thus fatigue may be a symptom of neurasthenia, which is a neurotic reaction to stress or frustration. These signs are not the disorder itself—they merely signify the existence of the disorder, in much the same way that fever signifies the existence of a physical illness. And, just as physical symptoms often represent the organism's efforts to cope with illness or pathology, psychological symptoms are an effort to meet the demands of adjustment. In this characteristic we can discover the true meaning and economy of psychological symptoms. As Page expresses it (Page, 1947, p. 98),

> . . . the symptoms of the psychoneurotic usually provide a solution to his problems, and for this reason the patient may cling to his symptoms and resist treatment. Loss of memory is an inconvenient neurotic symptom, but as long as it persists, the patient is protected from thinking

about the disturbing experience that was initially responsible for the loss of memory. . . . The compulsion to count steps and read signs is annoying, but by concentrating on this senseless task the patient perhaps avoids more disagreeable thoughts. The soldier torn between duty and fear finds in a neurosis a solution to his dilemma. If he is unwittingly overtaken by chronic fatigue, a paralysis, or some other psychosomatic disturbance, he will be removed from the battlefield without loss of self-respect.

There is no implication here, of course, that symptoms are consciously formulated as a solution to a problem; nor are they faked any more than the symptoms of high blood pressure are simulated by the patient. In some instances, there is malingering (faking of symptoms for conscious purposes), but in the typical neurotic adjustment this is not the case. *Symptoms are unconsciously formed for the purpose of adjusting to the demands of a frustrating or stressful situation* (Moore, 1944, pp. 18–20; Brown, 1940, pp. 71–75; Rubins, 1959).

Symptoms and Syndromes

Symptomatic responses sometimes occur more or less in isolation, as when a relatively normal person develops a twitch of the eyelid (tic), a phobia, or an obsessional idea. This is not uncommon and reminds us of the important difference between a person with one or two neurotic symptoms and a person with a *neurotic personality*. The neurotic personality is characterized by a definite group of symptoms called a "syndrome." This distinction is similar to the hypothesis developed by Marcuse (1953, pp. 151–152). He suggests that "in certain cases symptoms may be of an autonomous nature and should therefore be attacked directly. An autonomous symptom may be defined as one which is not deeply imbedded in the psychic structure of the individual and one which does not reflect an underlying conflict." Autonomous symptoms are distinguished from "true" symptoms which are always signs of something else, for instance, an underlying conflict. This hypothesis, as Marcuse points out, is essentially the same as Maslow's distinction between coping and expressive behavior.

A syndrome is an organized pattern of symptoms that are related to each other in definite ways, a fact that enables us to distinguish classes of personality disorder. For example, hysteria, which is a neurotic disorder, manifests itself systematically in a variety of symptoms, including functional paralysis, anesthesia, and somnambulism. But in each of these manifestations there is discernible a common quality—autonomous functioning in some aspect of behavior or mental reaction. *Syndromes, therefore, are patterns of responses that are determined in their organization by the pathological aims that dominate the personalities of maladjusted individuals* (Wittenborn & Holzberg, 1951; Wittenborn, 1951).

Symptoms and Causes

Symptomatic responses will be determined also by other factors, including personality make-up and background, experience and success in the exploitation of symptomatic behavior, the peculiarities of the present situation, and principally, the causes and conditions that underlie the maladjustment. To illustrate, compulsive behavior is typically a symptom of guilt feelings because the person feels compelled to expiate or undo in some way the wrong he feels he has committed. Thus he may wash repeatedly in the course of each day—an obvious symbol of the desire to be cleansed of guilt. Similarly, hysterical paralysis symbolizes an unconscious desire to escape from or avoid an intolerable situation, and scruples represent a deep conviction of moral uncertainty and inadequacy. These few examples indicate that symptoms are not accidental or haphazard but are determined by the causes and conditions underlying the particular difficulty. This is the logic of symptom formation and symbolism that Freud developed so brilliantly in his theory of dream interpretation and of the psychopathology of everyday life (Freud, 1913).

Let us not forget, however, the other factors mentioned. The kind of personality disposed to neurosis will develop symptoms different from those of the prepsychotic personality, just as the psychopathic person manifests symptoms peculiar to his type of maladjustment. Furthermore, those symptoms that have proved to be of value in realizing the aims of the patient will recur and become fixed. For example, if a child discovers through trial and error that illness brings him the attention or affection he craves, illness in one form or another is likely to become a permanent part of his adjustment pattern. Similarly, symptomatic behavior that is peculiarly suited to the situation that requires some kind of adjustment will take precedence over other forms. Thus the neurotic housewife, who is bored with the routine of housework or child care develops a fatigue syndrome, and the student who is terrified by an examination faints just as the examination begins. In each instance, symptomatic behavior is "chosen" with the same idea in mind: to dominate or control a situation by the exploitation of symbolic expression. The student who learns to interpret the logic of symptomatology will have taken a long step toward the understanding of maladjustment and mental disorder (Schneiders, 1963a, Chapter X).

QUESTIONS AND PROJECTS FOR FURTHER STUDY

1. Explain in your own words the structure of the adjustment process, with particular emphasis on behavior dynamics and varied response.
2. What is the connection between perception, thinking, and adjustment? Explain briefly the role of needs and values in determining perception, thinking, and fantasy.
3. In what manner are symbolic processes and symptom formation related to adjustment and mental health?
4. Write a term paper on the logic or teleology of symptom formation, stressing the role of symptoms in the process of adjustment.
5. In what way does frustration enter into the dynamics of adjustment?
6. Define the meaning of etiology and explain its relation to the determinants of adjustment.
7. Discuss the difference between predisposing and exciting causes of maladjustment, and cite examples to illustrate the difference.
8. Why do unconscious motivations lead to symbolic formulation? Can you cite any personal experiences that exemplify this relation?
9. Write a book report on Freud's *The psychopathology of everyday life.*

SELECTED COLLATERAL READINGS

BLAKE, R., & RAMSEY, G.   *Perception, an approach to personality.* New York: Ronald, 1951.

BUCKLEW, J.   *Paradigms for psychopathology: A contribution to case history analysis.* Philadelphia: Lippincott, 1960.

GIBSON, J. J.   *The perception of the visual world.* Boston: Houghton Mifflin, 1950.

SHERMAN, M.   *Basic problems of behavior.* New York: McKay, 1941, Chapter II.

STECKLE, L. C.   *Problems of human adjustment.* New York: Harper & Row, 1949.

TAGIURI, R., & PETRULLO, L.   *Person perception and interpersonal behavior.* Stanford, Calif.: Stanford University Press, 1958.

TAUBER, E. S., & GREEN, M. R.   *Prelogical experience: An inquiry into dreams and other creative processes.* New York: Basic Books, 1959.

TAYLOR, J. G.   *The behavioral basis of perception.* New Haven, Conn.: Yale University Press, 1962.

8

Adjustment by Defense—
The Flight from Self

So far we have taken a long, hard look at the nature and criteria of adjustment and mental health, at the dynamics and determinants of adjustment processes, at the normal personality, and at the process of adjustment itself. We even made a brief excursion into symptoms and symptomatology, and into some of the adjustment mechanisms. Now we wish to study the patterns of adjustment that border more closely on the abnormal. We begin with defense reactions because they are closest to normal responses. Here we must examine the dynamics of inferiority, inadequacy, failure, and guilt, and see how these factors are expressed in adjustive behavior.

NATURE OF PSYCHOLOGICAL DEFENSE REACTIONS

Among the adjustment mechanisms referred to earlier are those identified in the literature as "defense" reactions, although the term "protective" might be more appropriate in some instances. To understand the nature and purposes of these adjustments, we must relate them to the psychic structure of the human organism and its relation to reality. As we well know, human beings are constantly beset with numerous demands and pressures, either from within themselves or from external reality, that threaten ego security; against these threats the organism must protect or defend itself if it is to avoid anxiety, emotional imbalance, or maladjustment. This theory of defense is different in some respects from that of the psychoanalytic school since it admits of *external threat* as well as internal pressure, as when defense is necessary. The psychoanalytic view is well developed in Anna Freud's book, *The ego and the mechanisms of defense* (Freud, 1946). In this view, defense is regarded largely as "the ego's struggle against painful or unendurable ideas or effects" or as "the protection of the ego against instinctual demands" (Freud, 1946, pp. 45, 46). In the broader view, defense mechanisms are erected against stresses and threats from without as well as from within (Hogan, 1952; White, 1952, pp. 312–318; McCall, 1963).

218

The human organism must protect itself against stresses and threats because it cannot function efficiently when its sense of inner security is threatened or damaged. To understand the importance of this fact, we need only realize that every poorly adjusted person, every psychologically disturbed individual is suffering to some extent from a sense of insecurity. Sometimes this insecurity is conscious and produces anxiety; at other times, it is unconscious and produces overt symptoms of one kind or another. It is always present, however, playing its role in the development of symptomatic, inefficient, and maladjustive response (Crow & Crow, 1963b).

Because insecurity is psychologically intolerable, it is to be expected that the organism will erect protective barriers and defenses against those factors that threaten ego security, as is well known. The person who is physically handicapped by poor hearing, small stature, weakness, and so forth, protects himself from the implications of his handicaps by excelling in school achievement, dress, wealth, or social position. This method of defense is referred to as *compensation*, one of the most common of all protective mechanisms. Similarly, the person with a strong feeling of inferiority will often attempt to reduce the resulting anguish and frustration by the simple expedient of acting in a superior or arrogant manner—the so-called *egocentric* mechanism. In each such instance you will note that the behavior or mechanism functions as a protective device against the encroachment of some threat to security or psychological well-being (King & Schiller, 1960). Hogan conceives of threat as the immediate cause of defense, which he defines simply as "a response to threat," and defensive behavior therefore is activated "to restore feelings of security." (Hogan, 1952, p. 420.) Such factors as inadequacy, inferiority, and guilt, which form the background of defensive mechanisms, leave their impress on personality because of the insecurity they generate (Thorpe, 1950, pp. 266–269).

Varieties of Defense Reactions

Just as there are many ways to defend oneself physically against the elements, diseases, or enemies, there are different ways of defending oneself psychologically against personal weaknesses and limitations or the encroachments of a threatening reality. When the threat to personal security originates in reality, there is set up a tendency toward the development of reactions that involve a *flight from reality*, whereas personal limitations tend to stimulate the development of defense reactions or what might be called *flight from oneself*. One might compare this idea with Horney's concept of "alienation from self" which she says "is furthered through processes, likewise compulsive, which can be described as *active moves away from* the real self. The whole drive for glory is such a move, particularly through the neurotic's determination to mold himself into something he is not" (Horney, 1950, p. 159).

Similarly, unresolved difficulties based on relations with other persons favor the development of reactions involving a *flight into illness.* These distinctions should not be overworked because difficulties and frustrations have a way of expressing themselves differently in different persons, but, if used cautiously, they help us to gain a better understanding of the variations in adjustive response. We can see that there is a certain logic in reacting to the thrusts of reality by developing mechanisms that insure an escape from reality, just as personal weaknesses tend logically to force the emergence of defense reactions. As we noted previously in our discussion of the nature and purpose of symptoms, the selection or formation of response patterns is generally determined by the nature of the difficulty and the serviceability of the response in reducing the psychic pain, frustration, or tension associated with it. What is more natural, then, that illness should be used to effect control of relations between oneself and other persons? Here again the logic of the relation between adjustive difficulty and mechanism is apparent (Schneiders, 1963a).

While all mechanisms are in some measure directed toward the protection of personal security, there are some that are generally regarded as being most typically defensive (Maslow, 1956). Prominent among this group are compensation, sublimation, rationalization, repression, egocentricity, projection, blaming, introjection, and identification (Freud, 1946, p. 47). All these reactions and mechanisms are fundamentally alike in one respect: *They serve as a defense against real or imagined personal failures and inadequacies.* It is psychologically possible, of course, to utilize some of these reactions as defenses against reality or other persons, but as will become apparent in our discussion of each one, the primary groundwork of their development lies in the individual himself rather than in reality. These mechanisms are developed in the first place to overcome or reduce the sense of frustration and pain that accompanies personal weaknesses. In fact, it is only *because of* the existence of personal weaknesses that reality begins to assume a threatening aspect, so that the relation between these mechanisms and the encroachments of reality is largely incidental (Shaffer and Shoben, 1963). This personal basis is one of the principal reasons why adjustive reactions, whether good or poor, vary so much from one person to another—from direct attack on a problem to excessive withdrawal, from defensive reactions to flight into illness. As we pointed out earlier, all adjustive responses are filtered through the personality structure.

PSYCHOLOGICAL BASIS OF DEFENSE REACTIONS: INFERIORITY

Nature of Psychic Inferiority

From the foregoing discussion, one can see that the understanding and interpretation of defense reactions depend on a careful evaluation of those intrapersonal threats against which psychological defenses are erected. The most important and prominent is *psychic inferiority, which may be defined as a feeling or attitude, usually unconscious, that stems from a real or imagined personal deficiency.* Note that it makes little difference to the development of psychic inferiority whether the defect is real or not. In fact, imagined deficiencies often cause more damaging inferiority feelings than those that are real, just as the physical symptoms of neurasthenia are likely to be more distressing to a patient than symptoms based on actual physical pathology. Real personal deficiencies are easier to evaluate objectively and often exist without a trace of psychic inferiority, whereas the conviction of personal deficiency in the absence of any condition corresponding to the conviction is itself indicative of poor adjustment and is fertile soil for the development of inferiority feelings. To exert their maximum effect and cause the outcropping of defense reactions, feelings of inferiority must be unconscious; that is, their existence must be unknown to the person himself. Whenever such feelings are consciously recognized, the tendency toward defense mechanisms still exists, but there is less likelihood of mechanism formation and a greater possibility of successfully coping with the disturbing feelings. For this reason, treatment of patients whose basic difficulty is inferiority is directed toward a conscious realization by the patient of the part that inferiority has played in the development of his adjustment difficulties—in other words, *growth in self-insight.*

Theory of Inferiority

Analysis of psychic inferiority based on casual and clinical observation of the relations between inferiority and adjustment should be carefully distinguished from the *theory* of inferiority as developed by one of Freud's pupils, Alfred Adler (Adler, 1917, 1930; also Allers, 1943; Nuttin, 1953, pp. 259–275). Freud attempted to interpret all behavior and adjustment difficulties in terms of the dynamics of sex, pleasure, and the death instinct; Adler sought the explanation of all such phenomena in what he termed *organ inferiority.* According to this viewpoint, the source of personal peculiarities, neuroses, and maladjustments is the feeling or attitude of inferiority, which stems from some organic deficiency. On the basis of this notion, Adler formulated the hypothesis of *psychic compensation*, a mechanism by which the effects of organ inferiority are reduced through the development of behavior or traits that serve to overshadow it (Adler, 1927). Like the Freudian sex concept, the Adlerian theory of inferiority is an oversimplification, but it has served the twofold purpose of de-emphasizing sexual causes of maladjustment and of focusing attention on the important factor of inferiority. It has also provided psychology with several basic concepts, particularly compensation, that have proved of great value in understanding adjustment mechanisms. However, apart from oversimplification, the theory is weakened internally by its insistence on the organic basis of inferiority. As we shall see, many factors besides defective organs lead to feelings of inferiority.

Social and Environmental Conditions of Inferiority

While inferiority is in itself a personal affair and largely caused by subjective factors, we must note that it can originate in several sources. Indeed, if inferiority were invariably tied to an organic condition, as Adler maintained, it would present much less of a clinical problem than it does. But careful clinical diagnosis requires us to recognize a number of general conditions as well as specific causes in the development of inferiority. Among the conditions are such factors as sex status, age patterning, social position, faulty training, negative intrafamily relations, economic inadequacy, and racial status. These are referred to as *conditions* because, though they favor the development of inferiority, in many instances they produce no noticeable effect. More dynamic causes must be at work for inferiority to develop. Female sex status, for example, often generates or at least contributes to inferiority since women are relegated to an inferior position by the traditions and taboos of society. The double standard governing sexual activities of men and women is a good example. Restrictions on style of dress, play, professional and vocational aims, and so forth, all serve to emphasize the "inferiority" of feminine status. Recognizing this fact, we are then able to understand the intense drive on the part of women for social, economic, and political equality, which Adler aptly designated the "masculine protest," and which is a striking example of compensatory functioning. A similar concept, the "feminine protest," is developed in the author's recent book, *The anarchy of feeling* (Schneiders, 1963a).

Inferior ethnic status, whether real or imagined, is another condition that contributes to inferiority. Minority groups, such as the Jews, Negroes, and Italian immigrants, and national groups, such as the Germans and

Japanese, have given unmistakable evidence of feelings of racial inferiority. In some of these instances, we note the typical signs of sensitivity to criticism, seclusiveness, shyness, and timidity; in others there appear the equally typical symptoms of aggressiveness, an attitude of superiority, poor reaction to competition, or the tendency toward excessive criticism. "Inferior" racial status produces the expected tendency to reduce feelings of inferiority by the development of defense reactions (Brachfeld, 1951; Katz, 1949).

Poor economic and social status also favors the growth of inferiority attitudes, especially in marginal environments where there is repeated contact with persons in the "upper strata" of society. It is difficult, especially for children, not to feel inferior when one is constantly reminded of inferiority. You will note that all the conditions of inferiority we have cited are special examples of the principle that personality functions within a general social matrix which conditions its growth and development at every stage. The family, too, is part of the social matrix, and there are many intrafamily relations that may stimulate inferiority. Favoritism, parental rejection, scorn, ridicule, harsh punishment, and the like, are typical instances of actions that often lead to inferiority. In fact, these conditions so dynamically influence a person's attitude toward himself, and may exert so damaging an effect on the self concept that they can be regarded as remote causes of psychic inferiority.

The Basic Cause of Inferiority

However, that even dynamic conditions of inferiority can exist without causing inferiority indicates that an intrinsic factor is necessary to touch off its development. In other words, social, cultural, and economic factors can affect personality only to the extent that it is susceptible of being influenced by them. There are some hardy souls who in some way manage to remain untouched by ridicule, scorn, inferior sex status, parental rejection, and the like, and thus escape feelings of inferiority and the adjustment mechanisms they tend to provoke. *Psychologically, the basic cause of inferiority is damage to the self concept brought about by continuous frustration of basic needs.* When, for example, a child fails to develop a sense of belonging and is blocked in his efforts to win status, affection, achievement, recognition, or social approval, the psychological groundwork of inferiority is securely laid; damage to the concept of self and ego security is unavoidable, and the feeling of inferiority gets off to a good start (Turek & Howell, 1959).

Blocking of emotional needs and the subsequent damage to the self concept, then, may be regarded as the immediate, intrinsic determinants of psychic inferiority. To this state of affairs the general conditions just described can contribute a great deal. Certainly, constant belittling and ridicule of a child will go a long way toward blocking achievement of status, security, and recognition; under such conditions, a healthy concept of self cannot be expected to develop. Yet, important as emotional needs are, these are not the only factors at work; we have yet to take into consideration the mental and physical characteristics of the person himself that have a bearing on inferiority.

Physical Determinants

Considering the close connection between the self concept and the body image, which includes, in time, all physical characteristics, potentialities, and limitations, it is obvious that physical deficiences can easily lead to inferiority. In fact, when we study the issue closely, we see that the sense of inferiority is difficult for anyone to avoid. Consider, for example, the young child's smallness in a world geared largely to the range of adult potentialities. Because of this smallness, and its attendant weakness, it is difficult to escape the impression of inferiority. Actually, when we take into account the real physical limitations of childhood, there is a great deal of *actual* inferiority. This inferiority exists not only in the physical order but in the mental and psychological order as well. In other words, inferiority of one kind or another is a universal condition to which all humans are subject. However, the more important fact is that many persons do not react to these natural human limitations with a feeling of inferiority; and it is this feeling only that gives rise to defense mechanisms.

Physical smallness and weakness are perhaps of less importance in causing inferiority feelings than such deficiencies as chronic illness, ugliness, repulsive skin conditions, structural defect, and organ deficiency or pathology. Undoubtedly, the child finds it easier to accept smallness than he does any factor that he feels impairs others' judgments of him or that impairs his concept of himself. In a society like ours, where a premium is placed on physical attractiveness, skill, and prowess, it is not an easy matter to accept one's own ugliness or clumsiness. Similarly, it is difficult not to react with psychic inferiority under conditions of structural defect, like deformity, blindness, deafness, or a missing limb. Chronic illness and pernicious pathology, too, can be expected to contribute to psychic inferiority in many instances. In all such cases, the effects will vary with the extent to which the person's self concept is damaged or basic needs are frustrated. Therefore, when this does not occur—and there are many instances in which it does not—the feeling of inferiority is avoided (Calden, Mundy, & Schlafer, 1959).

These facts have been clearly recognized and strongly emphasized by persons working with physically handicapped persons. As Barker and Wright state, the physically handicapped person

> is faced with greater uncertainty in building a consistent attitude toward himself. He meets the same difficulties others have in forming a stable, consistent attitude toward him. He receives the same ambiguous stimuli as others do when he views his own physique. He, too, must separate his perception of his imperfect body from the stimuli that reveal his less imperfect person. He is also faced with a conflict between the cultural values concerning physique and those relating to the dignity of the individual. He fluctuates between feeling ashamed when the physical values are high and feeling an inner strength when the human dignity values are most potent. Moreover, in the case of acquired disability, his new body image conflicts with that of his former self. The anguish that can arise from this uncertainty and conflict about the self is effectively described by Katherine Butler Hathaway who suffered from a tubercular infection of the spine and was bedridden throughout her middle childhood. She says:
>
> "When I got up at last . . . and had learned to walk again, one day I took a hand glass and went to a long mirror to look at myself, and I went alone. I didn't want anyone . . . to know how I felt when I saw myself for the first time. But there was no noise, no outcry; I didn't scream with rage when I saw myself. I just felt numb. That person in the mirror *couldn't* be me. I felt inside like a healthy, ordinary, lucky person—oh, not like the one in the mirror! Yet when I turned my face to the mirror there were my own eyes looking back, hot with shame . . . when I did not cry or make any sound, it became impossible that I should speak of it to anyone, and the confusion and the panic of my discovery were locked inside me then and there, to be faced alone, for a very long time to come (Barker & Wright, n.d., p. 26).

This poignant statement by one who has experienced the anguish and conflict of physical disability epitomizes in the clearest way its potentialities for psychological damage. In a recent study on the relation of adjustment to physical handicap published by the Social Science Research Council, the effect of this factor on inferiority and similar feelings is pointed up by the authors (Barker, Wright, & Gonick, 1953). In an analysis of personal documents written by disabled persons, they found that feelings of inferiority were mentioned most often, followed closely by compensatory behavior, fear, and aggressiveness. These are only a few of the numerous negative feelings and reactions that these investigators report as being consistently associated with physical disability. However, as we ourselves have already pointed out, good adjustments are also possible in such cases, depending always on the significance attached to the disability (Faterson, 1931).

Mental and Moral Determinants of Inferiority

More important than physical weaknesses or limitations in the growth of psychic inferiority are the mental and moral deficiencies common to human nature. Their greater importance stems from the fact that mental and moral qualities are generally more highly evaluated than are physical characteristics, and rightly so, since they are more important to human personality. This statement applies particularly to factors like intelligence and moral rectitude. It is surprising how readily people will admit being musically or artistically ignorant but will deeply resent any implication that they are intellectually deficient. There are few things more damaging to self-evaluation than the charge of stupidity. The knowledge or conviction, therefore, of intellectual inferiority is very likely to lead to psychic inferiority, especially when this deficiency interferes with achievement, recognition, or a sense of personal worth.

Self-evaluation is strongly affected also by the conviction of moral weakness. Children with bad moral habits, such as lying, stealing, or masturbation, are easy prey to the feeling of inferiority since the concept of self is readily impaired by the conviction of moral inadequacy. This fact serves to remind us that, in the development of self ideals, special emphasis is always placed upon those factors that are most distinctively human, and among these the intellectual and moral characteristics of human nature stand out prominently.

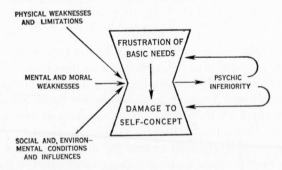

Fig. 14. Causes and conditions in relation to the development of psychic inferiority.

The several relations between the conditions and causes of psychic inferiority and its gradual development are illustrated in Figure 14. It will be readily seen from this diagram why the frustration of basic needs and damage to the self concept are interpreted as the immediate, intrinsic determinant of inferiority, whereas all other factors function for the most part as necessary conditions. Once established, inferiority itself becomes a cause of further frustration and ego damage.

Development of Inferiority Attitudes

From what we have said, it is clear that *psychic inferiority is developmental rather than organic or innate,* a fact of considerable importance to understanding as well as treatment. It means that inferiority is not in any sense necessary, and with insight into its causes and relation to defense reactions, both inferiority and its effects can be dispelled. Inferiority feelings, as we have seen, are the result of damaging experiences and frustrations; they are learned reactions that, if not corrected in their early stages of development, will eventually lead to the formation of deep-seated attitudes of inferiority. These attitudes tend to dominate or condition the majority of a person's reactions, especially those that involve his concept of self and his relations with others. It is this more pervasive inferiority that stands out prominently in the growth of defense reactions.

Symptoms of Inferiority

It is easy to detect the existence of attitudes of inferiority because the overt symptoms are clear-cut indicators.

Sensitivity to Criticism. The person who feels inferior rebels at having his weaknesses or mistakes pointed out to him. Every criticism is another dose of salt in an open wound. Criticism, whether objective and constructive, or unwarranted and harsh, stands as proof of his inferiority and only serves to accentuate the pain associated with it.

Overresponse to Flattery. The person with inferiority feelings will grasp at any straw that will help to rescue him from the uncertainty and insecurity these feelings constantly engender. Praise and flattery are testimony against inferiority, and this implicit denial the inferior person persistently strives to evoke.

Hypercritical Attitude. A hypercritical attitude serves the purpose of directing attention away from one's own limitations. This is especially likely to occur when inferiority is projected into other persons. Where overresponse to flattery is defensive in character, hypercriticism takes the offensive and is used as a means of warding off the implications of inferiority. In other words, it creates the illusion of superiority and relies on this illusion to belie inferiority.

Tendency toward Blaming. Whenever personal weaknesses and failures are projected into others, it is easy to fall into the habit of finding in them the causes of one's own failures, leading directly to the response of blaming. Quite typically the inferior student will blame the teacher, his parents, or anyone else available, for his weaknesses and failures.

Ideas of Reference and Persecution. It is only one step from blaming others for one's own personal misfortune to the position that they are actively seeking his downfall. Thus the student may blame the teacher's incompetence for low grades, or go one step further and charge the teacher with waging a personal vendetta against him. As a teacher, the author has been the butt of such reactions many times, and in numerous instances the existence of deep-seated inferiority was unquestionable (Saul, 1951).

Poor Reaction to Competition. The person with inferiority feelings, although most desirous of winning in competition, is convinced that success is always beyond reach. He reacts to competition as would a person who knows that he does not have the knowledge or skills necessary for successful competition. The psychologically inferior person in the office, on the football field, in the classroom, or in a friendly card game, complains about the breaks, rails at his opponents' good luck, makes oblique references to favoritism, deserts the game in a fit of temper, or blames his poor showing on outside factors. In some instances, this attitude toward competition is so extreme that the person refuses to be a part of any competitive situation; he shies away from such situations in a timid and hestitant manner.

A General Tendency toward Seclusiveness, Shyness, and Timidity. The feeling of inferiority will generate a certain amount of fear, particularly in situations involving other people. While this fear may, in some cases, be suppressed by one or another defense reaction, it is more common for it to express itself in timidity and shyness, or, more actively, in a withdrawal from or avoidance of situations that threaten to evoke the feeling of inferiority.

It is instructive to note how these symptoms of inferiority are bound up with one another. Timidity, as we have just seen, tends to bring about the avoidance of competition; it will also tend to make one more sensitive to criticism. In contrast, sensitivity to criticism is likely to lead to the blame of others or overresponse to flattery. All these symptoms spring from the basic sense of inferiority, and therefore one tends to influence the other.

Inferiority and Defense Reactions

The symptoms of inferiority should be regarded merely as telltale signs of its existence. In some instances, they resemble defense reactions, as in the case of hypercriticism or blaming. For the most part, however, they are clearly distinct from such overt reactions as compensation or rationalization. Psychic inferiority provides the psychological groundwork for both symptoms and defense mechanisms, and between them we may well find some important relations. But symptoms are primarily *indicators* of inferiority, whereas defense mechanisms are *positive efforts* to reduce or obscure inferiority feelings and to overcome the frustrations and tensions they produce. Typically, the timid, shy person compensates for his inferiority by intense social activity, in which we see the attempted reduction of inferiority by a defense reaction that is contrary to the symptoms themselves.

PSYCHOLOGICAL BASIS OF DEFENSE REACTIONS: INADEQUACY, FAILURE, AND GUILT

The Feeling of Inadequacy

Closely allied to, but not to be confused with, inferiority is the feeling or conviction of inadequacy, which often serves to touch off the development of defense reactions. However, *where inferiority, whether conscious or unconscious, implies unfavorable comparison with others, inadequacy suggests personal inability to meet the demands of a situation.* Because of this difference, the former is likely to have more damaging effects. In addition, the feeling of inadequacy is normally conscious, whereas psychic inferiority is usually unconscious. Inadequacy is clearly exemplified in the case of many housewives who complain chronically of their inability to cope with the requirements of housekeeping or raising a family. Many students, too, make the same complaint about the demands of academic life. Once this sense of inadequacy takes firm hold, defense reactions are likely to follow in quick succession (Bucklew, 1960).

The feeling of inadequacy touches off defense reactions for the same reason that inferiority does: frustration of basic needs and damage to the self concept. The needs for security, achievement, recognition, or independence are not easily gratified when one is convinced of his own inadequacy. It is also difficult to maintain the integrity of the self concept against the sense of inadequacy. Thus, the person's ego strives for completeness, protection, or security by the development of protective mechanisms, which reduce the sense of inadequacy and the frustration it causes. In this way, the self ideal can be maintained without too much effort, and the pain of self-criticism avoided.

Do defense mechanisms in any way reflect these psychological conditions? Although there is considerable variation from one person to another, there are certain relations to which we can point. Inferiority, for example, is most naturally and forcibly expressed in superiority and egocentricism because these reactions are most effective in obscuring inferiority. Similarly, the feeling of inadequacy is most effectively mitigated by the mechanism of introjecting the desirable qualities of other persons. Hence we may expect the inadequate person to identify strongly with other persons or groups that can supply the qualities necessary to ego integrity. This is in keeping with the general principle that behavior is at least partly determined by the nature of the drive or frustration that sets its off. This principle makes it easier to understand the peculiarities of individual responses to different situations. Anna Freud quotes Freud to the effect that " 'there is an intimate connection between special forms of defence and particular illnesses, as, for instance, between repression and hysteria.' " Again, "The considerations which determine the ego's choice of mechanism remain uncertain. Perhaps repression is preeminently of value in combating sexual wishes, while other methods can more readily be employed against instinctual forces of a different kind, in particular, against aggressive impulses" (Freud, 1946, pp. 46, 54–55; also Dodge & Kahn, 1931).

The Sense of Failure

Inadequacy, whether real or imagined, is likely to lead to failure because, when someone is already convinced of his inability to meet the demands of a task or situation, he greatly lessens the possibility of success. The sense of failure, therefore, is closely linked to the feeling of inadequacy. But there are other determinants as well. This conviction that one is inadequate often has its source in actual chronic failure—a basic inability to succeed in whatever tasks or relations confront the person. In such cases, failure is a reality that stems, in part at least, from actual inferiority or inadequacy, and the sense of failure is its psychical counterpart. In other instances, the sense of failure is less securely grounded, stemming from imagined inferiority or inadequacy. There are many persons who, judged by objective standards, are eminently successful and yet are constantly plagued by the conviction that they have failed in the most important tasks of life. No amount of logic or reason serves to dispel this deep conviction. In such cases, we see inferiority feelings at work—feelings that preclude the acceptance of achievements (White, 1959).

Failure, whether as a reality or as a personal conviction, can be extremely damaging to the ideal of self and to the gratification of the needs and the realization of the aims that empower and stabilize one's efforts at adjustment (Postman & Brown, 1952; Miller, 1951). It is difficult to meet the demands of reality effectively when there is a moral certainty of failure. The feeling of frustration runs extremely deep in cases of this kind. Because of these damaging effects, every effort will be made to offset failure, and especially the conviction of failure, through the development of protective mechanisms. Here we may expect to find the mechanisms of repression, rationalization, and compensation, each one of which has qualities that are particularly suited to the reduction of failure and its effects. How often have you witnessed failure being rationalized out of existence by the whole-

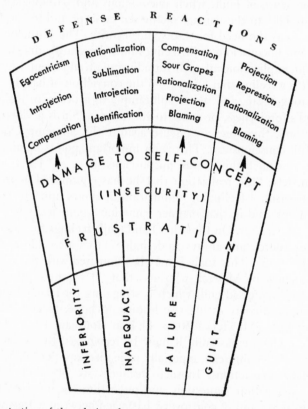

Fig. 15. Illustration of the relations between the psychological determinants of defense reactions and the reactions themselves.

sale manufacturing of excuses? And if this does not work, there is always the possibility of covering up failures by the expedients of compensation, sour grapes, or repression. Here again the kind of reaction is partly determined by the character of the difficulty. These relations between psychological bases and the development of defense reactions are illustrated in Figure 15. It should be understood that not all such relations can be indicated in this way. The diagram in Figure 15 serves merely to highlight some of the more important relations that are known to exist. Actually, any defense reaction can be grounded in any one or any combination of factors described. However, the relations indicated can be expected to emerge in the majority of cases.

The Sense of Guilt

There is, finally, the important relation between guilt and defense. Clearly, the sense of guilt, when unconscious and pathological, can contribute materially to the damage of the self concept and to the frustration of such needs as the need for status and security. The distinction between conscious and unconscious guilt feelings must be sharply drawn because of the different implications of each for adjustment and mental health. *Conscious guilt* is a feeling that arises from the conviction of having committed a moral wrong, a sin, and may result simply in a desire to make amends, asking God's forgiveness, or going to confession. "Sin is a violation of the moral law and, therefore, an offense against the Supreme Lawgiver. Sin supposes full consciousness. This is an important point, because it means that there is no such thing as an unconscious sin. . . ." Far from creating neurotic anxiety, "the realization that he has committed a sin may well create in a person a feeling of humiliation; it shows him his imperfection and limitations, and in that manner [conscious] guilt feelings may have a constructive character. On the other hand, guilt feelings that stem from an unconscious source are always undesirable" (Vanderveldt & Odenwald, 1952, pp. 187–188). This analysis may be compared with the statement on guilt and anxiety by Mowrer, who says that "if we are right in assuming that anxiety is repressed guilt which is struggling for recognition, then we may look upon anxiety as likewise leading to hope, to change, and to a new way of life" (Mowrer, 1950, p. 40; also Hoffman, 1952). Despite the emphasis on unconscious guilt, it must be recognized that even conscious, defensible guilt feelings can, especially in inadequate personalities, lead to strong defensive reactions. In such instances we often note tendencies toward rationalization, repression, and projection (Schneiders, 1960a).

A great amount of controversy has raged between writers who accept the principle that guilt is necessary in vanquishing sin and those who hold that guilt of any kind is damaging in its effects (the psychoanalysts especially). A good example of the latter viewpoint is Symonds, who says, "Guilt, like anxiety, is an intolerable state of affairs, one which the individual goes to any extreme to avoid or to disguise. Guilt is probably more intolerable than hate . . ." (Symonds, 1949, p. 277). The author mitigates this extreme viewpoint by stressing the social values of guilt later on (pp. 293–294). A useful analysis of the psychological implications of guilt can be found in a number of sources (Cameron & Magaret, 1951, pp. 284–289; Jenkins, 1950, pp. 353–361; Johnson, 1948, 126–143). Of one thing we can be sure and that is that only when the fear and anxiety of conscious guilt are dispelled by forgiveness or love can negative psychological effects be avoided.

The real damage, therefore, is brought about by *unconscious, neurotic guilt*, which, like inferiority, lies beyond the borders of insight and rational self-direction. Because of the threat that guilt of this kind signifies for personal integrity, defensive mechanisms of one kind or another are almost certain to develop. Here especially can we expect a great deal of intensive repression and projection. The tendency to repudiate guilt is old in human history. St. Augustine points out that Adam tried to shift responsibility for his fault onto God Himself: "The woman, whom Thou gavest me to be my companion, gave me of the tree." The sense of guilt is difficult to tolerate because it is laden with anxiety and fear, and thus there is an understandable tendency to repress it into unconsciousness or to rid oneself of it by projecting it into other persons or causes. The husband who feels guilty for having committed a sexual wrong easily projects this guilt to his wife, complaining that she is the real cause of his wrongdoing. *Excessive blaming* is usually a reliable sign of unconscious, repressed guilt.

It should be understood here that guilt is not necessarily expressed in defense reactions; in fact, it is widely recognized that anxiety, obsessive-compulsive tendencies, aggression, and other reactions are also grounded in these feelings. The important point here is that some defensive reactions are determined by guilt, and it is these reactions that we are interested in at the moment (Symonds, 1949, pp. 280–284).

In determining the psychological groundwork of defense reactions, we have selected four factors which, because of their effects on the self concept and the frustration of basic needs, are prominent in the development of defense reactions. This selection does not mean that other psychological factors have no part in setting up defensive mechanisms. Feelings of hostility, insecurity, rejection, and the like may also enter the picture at one point or another, although their relation to defense reactions is not as clear as those we have studied. Nor should our interpretation force the conclusion that feelings of inferiority, inadequacy, failure, and guilt invariably express themselves in defense reactions. We have noted already that guilt is manifested in compulsive tendencies, whereas inferiority may lead to paranoid delusions, and the sense of failure to severe depression. There are no absolutes governing the development of adjustment mechanisms or pathological symptoms, and the most that we can do in the present state of our knowledge is to point up certain significant relations that are important to the better understanding of adjustive behavior.

DEVELOPMENT OF DEFENSE MECHANISMS

Defense Mechanisms, Fear, and Insecurity

Let us now consider briefly the pattern of development of defense mechanisms. First of all, the setting up of defenses always implies a certain amount of fear or insecurity in the internal make-up of the self. Only a weakly structured ego reacts defensively to life's difficulties. Somewhere in the course of development, some personalities fail to achieve the strength and inner security necessary to withstand the buffeting of reality and to deal effectively with the frustrations and conflicts that arise from day to day. These persons feel an inner necessity to erect barriers that will protect them from their own limitations and from the pressures exerted against them by the demands of reality. This failure in development is, of course, one aspect of the immaturity that characterizes inadequate personalities and those that are prey to symptom formation and maladjustment. To be secure within oneself so that defensive reactions are not necessary, one must achieve maturity in emotional, social, moral, and intellectual reactions and relations. Thus the weakly disciplined child, who invariably shows signs of immaturity, tends to fall back on defensive mechanisms in any crucial situation because he does not have the ego strength or security necessary to solve conflicts or frustrations in a direct, intelligent, and normal fashion.

Defense Mechanisms and Varied Response

The development of defense reactions will be governed by the general principles of adjustive response outlined in Chapter 7. One of these principles was that of varied response, according to which the organism tries out different responses until it hits upon one that reduces frustration and tension. The selection of such a response will not be a purely hit-or-miss affair since the reduction of tension is determined at least partly by the suitability of the response selected. As we have seen, egocentricity is well suited to suppressing inferiority, and the tension aroused by guilt feelings is particularly susceptible to reactions like projection and rationalization. Once the discovery is made that tension and frustration can be reduced or eradicated by means of one or another mechanism, there is a tendency to fix the effective response until it reaches the stage of a well-organized habit. It should be recalled, however, that such "habits" (that is, defense mechanisms) are not the usual kind developed in the course of normal, everyday practice or learning. Defense mechanisms are formed unconsciously and indeliberately and are accepted by the person himself as definitely normal. This acceptance clearly indicates a lack of insight into the relations between the response and its causes, as well as into the defensive quality of the response itself. If the response were a conscious, deliberately formed habit, this lack of insight would not exist.

This lack of insight requires emphasis because it is important to understanding the development of defense reactions and to evaluating their moral and social qualities. Rationalization, blaming, projection, and the like are, as defense mechanisms, psychological reactions directed toward adjustment; they should not be confused with moral responses such as lying, and making false accusations, which are conscious and deliberate. In brief, then, *defense mechanisms are indeliberate responses that develop in terms of individual personality structures and become fixed because they reduce tension and frustration and thereby satisfy the demands of adjustment.*

THE MECHANISM OF COMPENSATION

Nature of Compensatory Reactions

We may begin our survey of typical defense reactions with the mechanism of compensation because it is so obviously defensive and because it is one of the most common defense reactions. In everyday language, compensation means to make amends, to remunerate, to "pay off." Used in a more subtle sense, it means to "make up for," as when we say that the leisure of a free day compensates for the loss of wages or working time. This is essentially the meaning of compensation as a defense mechanism. Adler, in his theory of inferiority, noted that nature tends to compensate (make up) for deficiencies; for example, if a person is blind, there is compensation in the greater acuity of other senses; if one side of the body is weakened by paralysis, the other side becomes stronger than normal; if one lung is impaired by disease, the other compensates by greater effort. In other words, weakness, deficiency, inferiority, or inadequacy initiate processes that function as compensatory mechanisms in the organic as well as in the psychological order. *The mechanism of compensation, therefore, may be described as a psychic effort, usually unconscious, to offset personal weaknesses and limitations by the development of qualities or responses that reduce tension and frustration and thus serve to promote the adjustment of the organism.* Note that the first part of this definition indicates the defensive nature of compensation, and the second part its relation to adjustment, that is, its peculiar value in helping the organism meet whatever demands are imposed on it (Symonds, 1949, Chapter XVII).

General Aims of Compensation

A better understanding of the mechanism of compensation may be gained by studying the aims toward which it is directed.

Substitution for Achievement. First of all, compensation can be used to substitute for real achievement. For example, if a young boy finds it difficult to achieve success in school, or to measure up to the standards set by his parents, he may direct all his interests, time, and energy to a hobby. Becoming proficient in this activity gives him a sense of achievement, thus reducing the tension of frustration, but without the effort and sacrifice that more worthwhile achievements require. This sort of defense is most likely to occur in cases where the ability to achieve is good, but the will and effort, or at times the interest, are lacking. The substitute achievement made possible by compensation not only reduces frustration tension but serves also to mitigate the sense of guilt that stems from the failure to use abilities in the right way.

> The student, a junior, twenty-one years of age, was referred to the clinic because of impending failure in several subjects, one of which was his major. Analysis revealed that the student was suffering from a deep sense of inadequacy, which was expressed most forcefully in "examination anxiety." This anxiety made it difficult for him to do well in examinations; hence the low grades. Interview indicated that during his high school career, the young man had aspired to become a member of the baseball team and to achieve a letter. He did not make the team. In his own words, he compensated for this failure by the determination to succeed well in school. This determination was realized during his high school years and in the first two years of college. The sting of failure was increased by the father's attitude which was expressed by the statement, "You can't even make the baseball tem." The father had been successful in athletics and was a man of physical prowess. The boy's failure, coupled with the belittling attitude of the father, created a deep sense of inferiority and inadequacy, which carried over into his academic effort.

Direction of Attention Away from Deficiency. Compensation also serves to direct attention away from personal deficiencies. It is as though the person were proclaiming, "Pay no attention to my weaknesses or failures, note instead, my (substitute) achievements." These achievements can take a variety of forms: hobbies, sports, group membership, social leadership, or participation in reform movements. In every instance, compensation must direct the attention of others toward some accomplishment or quality that serves to obscure personal deficiency.

Maintaining Status, Self-respect, and Integrity. Undoubtedly, one of the foremost functions of compensation is to maintain or even enhance status, self-esteem, and integrity. We know how damaging inferiority, inadequacy, and guilt can be to personal status or ego security and also how these factors can frustrate basic needs so that tension continues to mount to a point where it becomes unbearable. Any mechanism, therefore, that acts to mitigate these feelings and rescue the self concept from destruction becomes an important tool of adjustment.

Is compensation an unconscious mechanism? Is it not possible that the person, recognizing his own deficiencies, chooses to compensate for them by substitute achievement? This latter possibility cannot be excluded altogether. Undoubtedly, there are instances in which persons try to make up for apparent deficiencies by consciously striving to excel along other lines in a way that serves to soften the effects of their deficiencies. A husband, for example, might compensate for economic inadequacy by helping his wife with household chores, knowing that he cannot afford to hire help. Normally, however, inadequacy is not frankly recognized or admitted to onself, and thus the compensatory reaction takes shape without a conscious realization of its relation to personal deficiency. The aim of preserving ego integrity is begun when the individual fails to recognize, or represses, inadequacy, and is realized more fully by such mechanisms as compensation. The more successfully this process can be carried out "in the dark," the less threat will there be to ego-integrity at any point in its evolution.

Varieties of Compensation

The characteristics of compensation are brought out more sharply when we study its different forms.

Overreaction. There are many well-known examples of overreaction to or overdevelopment in a function where deficiency exists. Helen Keller, handicapped by blindness and deafness, proved to herself and the world that she was not really handicapped at all. The great orator Demosthenes began his career with a speech impediment. Beethoven, the genius in music, became deaf. Theodore Roosevelt, perhaps the most robust president we have had, was a physical weakling in his early years. Glen Cunningham, one of the world's great distance runners, was burned so badly as a child that it was thought that he would never walk again. Andy Devine, the movie actor, made a fortune out of misfortune—the "gravel voice" caused by a serious accident. In cases like these, which are certainly good examples of compensation, it would be foolhardy to say that compensation developed unconsciously. All these people were certainly aware of their physical deficiency. And in all of them there is noticeable a marked volitional determination to offset their peculiar handicap. Here, then, we have examples of deliberate, consciously directed compensation. Note, however, that there is no attempt in such cases to obscure the deficiency; rather, there is a concerted effort to utilize it as the basis of achievement.

Substitute Activity.   There are instances in which indirect compensation takes place—that is, compensation by substitute activity or achievement. This is the second form, in which unconscious determination is more likely to be exemplified. Napoleon with his small stature, Hitler with his artistic failure, and Franklin Roosevelt with his physical infirmity are good examples of this type of compensation. In such cases, the dominant attitude seems to be "pay no attention to my weaknesses or failures; regard, instead, my superior accomplishments." The fact that the achievement is along substitute lines suggests a tendency to obscure the deficiency, and it is unlikely that the deficiency and the achievement would be linked together in the mind of the person himself. We can well imagine Napoleon's resentment on being told that his military greatness hinged upon the fact that he was physically inferior. Yet one can observe many instances in which physical and other inferiorities are overcome or obscured by excelling in some other quality or activity. To test this hypothesis, note the people of small stature. In their excellent style of dress, personal appearance, social position, loudness of voice, persistent aggressiveness, gastronomic feats, or attitude of superiority, compensation stands out most prominently. In all cases, the unconscious attitude is the same, "I may be small, but . . .". It is rare indeed that the quality or achievement is properly related to the inferiority by the person himself. On the contrary, he will actively reject any such implication.

We do not wish to become victims of the Adlerian error that bases all indirect compensation on organic or physical defect. These compensatory reactions merely provide the most striking and familiar examples. Any kind of inferiority or inadequacy—social, intellectual, and moral, as well as physical—can serve to touch off the development of compensation.

The self-made business executive, feeling the lack of a formal education, may boast an impressive library. The academically weak student may be a master of the forward pass.

Development of Particular Abilities. In compensation by the development of particular abilities and special qualities the expression of inadequacy and frustration is also *indirect*, but it is along special lines. For example, among the author's acquaintances is a man who considers it quite an accomplishment to stand on his head and will do so at the least prompting from his audience. Other persons develop skill in hypnosis, rope tricks, magical arts, flagpole sitting, and so on. In each case, you will note, the peculiar skill serves to direct attention away from personal deficiencies. Similar to this type of reaction is the development of special qualities. The person with intellectual or moral deficiencies takes special pride in physical strength, chest size, well-developed muscles, or seductive feminine characteristics. Conversely, the physically inadequate person tends toward the development of outstanding moral, social, and intellectual qualities. In all such instances, the person has little insight into the connection between the compensatory reaction and whatever deficiencies are being covered up; thus the mechanism is developed at an unconscious level.

Identification. Indirect compensation may be secured through the achievement of others. This is illustrated most clearly in the pride with which parents often regard the accomplishments of their children. In fact, it is not at all uncommon for parents to stimulate and foster achievement in their children in order that their own limitations and deficiencies may thereby be obscured. You are familiar with the attitude "I never accomplished much, but look at my son—he's a doctor." Here we see another mechanism at work—identification. Frequently, one adjustment mechanism is complemented by another. Compensation often involves superiority, and introjection is dependent upon identification. In all such instances, however, you will find that the one mechanism is dominant and the other supportive. In the example just cited of parents realizing a sense of achievement through their children, the dominant mechanism is compensation, which, however, is only made possible through a certain amount of identification.

Reforming Activities. While the above are the main forms of compensation, compensatory aims can be realized in other ways. Where, for example, the defense reaction is based on guilt, we often see a strong compensatory tendency toward reform of one kind or another. So-called "reformers," bent on changing the wicked policies or actions of others, are often motivated by personal guilt and attempt to screen this guilt by their reforming activities. In such cases, there is likely to be also a certain amount of projection, repression, and blame; and it may be difficult to determine which is the primary mechanism.

Play and Fantasy. Finally, play activities and fantasy can be exploited for compensatory purposes. It is well known that play is an effective means of reducing frustration and sometimes of restoring ego integrity or status and thus serves well as a defense mechanism. When play is of such a nature as to obscure inadequacies, lack of status, or insecurity, it takes on the character of a compensatory reaction. For example, a little girl seven years of age seemed obsessively devoted to play activities. Investigation revealed a strong craving for affection, which the parents seemed unable to gratify. Her play activities invariably involved another girl of about the same age in whose company she seemed to be completely contented and happy. Undoubtedly, this relation served a compensatory purpose. Children can realize these aims also in wishful thinking and fantasy, which provide unlimited possibilities for overcoming personal limitations and the frustrations associated with them. In the realm of fantasy, all inferiorities and inadequacies can be made to vanish.

> In all societies, one of the most inexhaustible sources of compensatory substitution is that of covert fantasy—the fleeting thought, the dream, the daydream. What one cannot have to eat one can talk of eating, silently imagine oneself enjoying, or realize to the point of fulfillment in a dream at night. . . . in thinking, dream and daydream, one can enjoy all manner of forbidden fruit, achieve every imaginable satisfaction, witness pageants of triumph and parades of disaster, turn light into darkness and night into day, bring contradictions together side by side, violate the arrangements of time and space, and make an unlikely beginning lead irresistibly to an impossible end (Cameron & Magaret, 1951, p. 378).

Adjustment Value of Compensation

The linking of compensation to frustration, inadequacy, or ego damage will naturally create the impression that it is maladjustive. In fact, all defense reactions give that impression at first glance. But what are we to say of instances in which it seems to serve the purpose of worthwhile adjustment? Certainly, Helen Keller was better off by reason of her compensatory reactions; and the little girl frustrated in her craving for affection was happier because of compensatory play activities. The adequate handling of this issue is of basic importance to the understanding and evaluation of all adjustment processes.

To be of maximum value to good wholesome adjustment, compensatory reactions should

1. Reduce frustration and tension without damage to self
2. Be consciously and deliberately developed
3. Be based on a clear awareness of personal limitations
4. Not interfere with, but promote achievement
5. Not function as a substitute for worthwhile effort
6. Promote general psychological welfare

To the extent, therefore, that any compensatory mechanism falls short of these criteria, the closer it comes to an inadequate adjustment. If you go back over the examples cited in this section you can easily pick out the unwholesome compensations by simply applying these criteria.

What of other defense reactions? Cannot they be evaluated in much the same manner? We selected the mechanism of compensation for evaluation because it is one of the best examples of a defense reaction that can be both normal and abnormal, adjustive and maladjustive. However, it does not stand alone in this regard, as we shall see, and it should be understood that the foregoing criteria can be applied to any of the mechanisms discussed in this chapter. Let us note, however, that the more any response fulfills these criteria, the more it loses its character as a mechanism and as a defense and the more it tends to fit into those responses described in the preceding chapter as normal. By this time, we should be aware that the dividing line between the normal and the abnormal can be very thin.

THE MECHANISM OF SUBLIMATION

Nature and Defensive Quality of Sublimation

At times, it is almost impossible to determine whether a reaction is one of compensation or sublimation, so close are the relations between them (Cameron & Magaret, 1951, pp. 376–379). But, whereas compensation is essentially a masking of deficiency, *sublimation is the unconscious redirection of the energies of a drive or motive into socially and morally acceptable channels of activity*. This is a broader meaning than Freud gave the term, who restricted the use of the mechanism to sexual motivation. The term, however, has more meaning and wider significance for adjustment when applied to different forms of motivation. Moreover, there is no psychological reason why other drives than sex cannot be sublimated just as effectively as the sex drive. For these reasons, psychologists generally use the term in its broader sense (Moore, 1948, Chapter XXVI; Symonds, 1949, Chapter XVI; Davies, 1948).

The defensive implications of sublimation are somewhat different from those of compensation because the motivation is different. Of course, the primary purposes of the reaction are to reduce the tension of frustration, to avoid conflict, and to preserve ego integrity, in all of which it strongly resembles compensation. But compensation is founded on some kind of inadequacy, whereas sublimation is directed toward the reduction of guilt feelings associated with such motives as aggression, sex, curiosity, cruelty, and the maternal drive. In other words, it serves to protect the person psychologically from the possible damaging effects of certain drives or from the sense of failure and inadequacy that comes from the frustration of others. The classic example of sublimation is the redirection of the maternal drive into teaching, social work, and other activities that provide opportunities for a wholesome expression of the desire for and love of children. Maternal tendencies are extremely dynamic in the majority of women; if these tendencies are denied expression or gratification altogether, the sense of frustration runs very deep and can cause a great deal of damage to the self concept. Sublimation of these tendencies into a kind of work that is socially and morally acceptable reduces the tension of frustration and protects the self ideal from damage.

Expressions of Sublimation

There are many ways in which drives can be sublimated. Friendships, hobbies, social work, professional work, teaching, artistic productions, scientific research, sports, and religious activities are typical instances (Dalbiez, 1941, Volume I, Chapter VII). For example, curiosity, which often expresses itself in undesirable ways (voyeurism, peeping, sexual conversation, gossip, and so forth) that lead to feelings of guilt, can be sublimated into art and medicine; in both fields the human body can be viewed without conflict or reprisal. Curiosity is often sublimated also, and in a more striking way, into the area of scientific research. Aggression is another tendency that undergoes considerable sublimation in our society. Sports provide an exceptionally good outlet, although many examples also come from the field of business. We see in these cases how a tendency that could be very destructive of mental stability and adjustment is directed into activities that are not only acceptable but actually productive, and, at the same time, are a material contribution to the psychological well-being of the organism (Symonds, 1949, pp. 300–302).

How far can we go with this idea of sublimation? Is it true that interest in surgery is sometimes an expression of cruelty or sadism? That religious aspirations and activities are sublimations of the sex drive? That art is an expression of perverted sexual tendencies? That friendships are often sublimated forms of hostility? These interpretations are seriously maintained by many writers in the field of human adjustment, and we should face squarely the question of their truth or validity. To maintain perspective, let us recall the definition of sublimation, which states that it is the redirection of the *energies* of a drive into acceptable channels of activity. Certainly there is nothing repugnant in the notion that the energies of the sex drive, of hostility, and so on, are utilized for the purpose of artistic or religious expression.

This is much different from saying that all religion and art are the expression of sex. The latter statement carries the implication that the motivation for religion and art is sexual, whereas the former notion merely suggests a redistribution of the energies of the organism in the interests of achievement and adjustment. This notion is similar to the idea that the energies and frustrations associated with sex during adolescence can be most effectively handled by intensive activity in sports, hobbies, or work. This practical principle, as you can see, is closely related to the idea of sublimation. It would seem that, in the intersts of economy and efficiency, some such utilization of released energies would be necessary. Magner (1944, p. 80) states that strong passion "is often found in persons of intensely generous instincts, and, as sublimated into noble action, may well be one of the driving forces of creative expression in art, literature, social uplift, and of religious impulse itself. History is full of examples of persons, like St. Augustine, who have turned *their energy* from the pursuit of sensual gratification to that of the highest ideals in the service of mankind."

Value of Sublimation

Since sublimation is essentially a means of working off unusual energies and of reducing frustrations and possible conflicts, in a way that contributes to achievement, it fulfills several of the criteria of adjustment. One cannot say that sublimation is consciously and deliberately developed, for very few persons are aware of the connection between sublimated responses and their basic motivation; yet it promotes adjustment because in so many instances the only alternative to sublimation is complete and chronic frustration or pathological development of neurotic and psychotic response patterns. In this sense, therefore, sublimation may, like compensation, be regarded as a sort of safety valve for adjustment. For the most part, it would be better if needs could be expressed more directly; since that is impossible in some cases, however, sublimation is a good alternative.

THE MECHANISM OF RATIONALIZATION

There are many ways to defend oneself against the implications of inadequacy, guilt, inferiority, and failure. One of the most common is rationalization, long recognized although not always by that name. The Bible enjoins us not "to seek excuses for sinning," and this, essentially, is what rationalization implies, for *rationalization is the inventing of excuses or reasons for behavior and conduct that is inadequate, unacceptable, or damaging to personal integrity and status.* By making such conduct appear rational, the person protects himself from the effects of self-criticism as well as the criticism of others and thus preserves his ego integrity. Feelings of inadequacy, failure, and guilt (Figure 15) are the psychological groundwork of rationalization, although it is utilized in any situation where the demands of adjustment require it (Vaughan, 1952, pp. 346–360). The tendency to rationalize inadequacy and failure is exemplified in numerous adjustment situations. The schoolboy cannot recite because he forgot his book; the worker is late because of traffic conditions; the dinner is not ready because the children got in the way; the student fails the examination because he does not feel well; and so on. Each case reveals an inability to face the issue squarely, admit the weakness, and accept the responsibility. Here again we see the pervasive influence of low-level maturity, which is always indicated by failure to accept responsibility.

Inadequacy and failure are likely to involve guilt, and rationalization is often a defense against guilt feelings. In some instances, where the unacceptable behavior is clearly wrong, guilt becomes the primary determinant of rationalization and is conditioned, in turn, by feelings of inadequacy or failure. The student who neglects studying for an examination or puts off preparing a required research paper not only rationalizes his failure but also the guilt that is associated with not fulfilling a moral responsibility. This need to rationalize becomes more dynamic in proportion to the degree of guilt associated with the conduct. Thus we often hear sexual immorality rationalized as being necessary, natural, or only mildly sinful, because of the deep-seated guilt feelings characteristically associated with sexual delinquency. Against such damaging feelings the individual must protect himself at all cost if personal integrity is to be maintained. Incidentally, the fact that rationalization is so widespread indicates how common the psychological factors underlying it are.

Although in a measure protective, rationalization is always inadequate and maladjustive. It is a weakness indicative of inadequate maturity and a poor sense of responsibility, and it is a striking example of what we called earlier a flight from self. While compensation and sublimation can contribute to psychological welfare, the more rationalization is utilized, the poorer adjustment becomes. It serves to effect a kind of adjustment but at a cost to personal integrity and wholesomeness that is seriously detrimental to effective living.

Psychologists are generally agreed that rationalization is damaging to personal integrity and good adjustment. As one writer remarks (Vaughan, 1952, pp. 356–357):

> Rationalizing probably does more harm than any of the other methods of ego-defense because it is used more extensively and because it is *so subtle a foe to the life of reason.* Two very damaging effects of rationalization may be cited, by way of evaluation.
>
> First, using our wits to excuse our mistakes is to sacrifice the value of intelligence as an instrument for planning action in a rational manner. . . . Rationalization involves a costly waste of one's mental resources.
>
> Second, rationalizing is harmful because it *undermines the rationalizer's integrity.* Being dishonest with oneself is one of the subtlest ways of disintegrating, since the personality must dissociate to some extent in order for one part to fool another part. . . . Putting something over on oneself requires some degree of disintegration; in so far as the hoodwinking succeeds, the individual goes that much further to pieces. Kidding oneself is fun but it is fraught with psychological danger.

We may compare this evaluation with that of Cameron and Magaret (1951, p. 380):

> Rationalization, like deliberate lying, may paradoxically lead to inconsistency, self-contradiction, and, in extreme instances, even to incoherence. This happens because, in both rationalization and lying, an attempt is being made to preserve the integrity of a personal fiction against the attack of socially organized facts.

It is noteworthy that both of these evaluations emphasize the damaging effect of rationalization on the quality of integrity (Symonds, 1949, pp. 333–335).

THE MECHANISM OF SOUR GRAPES

Not much can be said in support of the reaction referred to as "sour grapes." You know the story of the fox who, when he could not reach the luscious fruit he desired so much, contented himself with the thought that it was much too sour anyway. This mechanism is similar to rationalization in so far as it involves a certain amount of self-deception. It is a deceptive, spurious way of giving up, of relinquishing all effort, and then avoiding the pain of defeat and frustration by adopting the conviction that the goal was not worth the effort anyway. The student who fails in school, the worker who loses his job, the husband divorced by his wife, and the writer who cannot find a publisher may utilize this mechanism to assuage their feelings of defeat and frustration. The sour-grapes attitude reveals a basic immaturity, and inherent personality weakness that favors the development of psychological defenses against the realities of a situation in place of determination, renewed effort, and a realistic acceptance of the situation as it actually exists. Because it distorts reality, the sour-grapes reaction must be regarded as a poor adjustment.

EGOCENTRISM AND SUPERIORITY AS DEFENSE REACTIONS

Nature and Determinants of Egocentrism

One of the most effective means of protection against the damaging effects of feelings of inferiority and failure is an attitude or "air" of superiority, or egocentrism. *Egocentrism is the unconscious pretension to superior qualities and traits that serves to belie or obscure the existence of a basic inferiority.* So close is the relation between them that psychologists generally assume that where spurious superiority exists there inferiority is likely to exist also. Needless to say, in egocentrism there is often a generous complement of other mechanisms including introjection, rationalization, sour grapes, and blame, which serve to support the egocentricity and to further obscure the feelings of inferiority they reflect.

A complete understanding of the development of egocentrism, however, requires us to take into account other contributing factors. There is, first of all, the factor of *insecurity*, which often stems from inferiority, yet plays its own part in generating superiority as a defensive measure. Secondly, there is *parental overindulgence*, which creates a spurious superiority in children by giving them the impression that they possess qualities that entitle them to special treatment. Allied to this is *parental favoritism*, which also creates the impression of superiority, since to be singled out for favored treatment is always taken as a sign of superiority. *Overevaluation of accomplishment*, by parents and others, leads to attitudes of superiority or egocentrism, particularly when the accomplishment is achieved in a competitive situation. A proper evaluation of achievement gives the youngster encouragement and perspective, but overevaluation puts undue emphasis on the achievement. *Effortless success* may also give rise to egocentrism.

It is problematical whether all cases of superiority are defensive in quality; perhaps we should distinguish between the two concepts of egocentrism and superiority. The attitude of superiority is, by and large, generated by the feeling of inferiority and is manifested in loudness, boasting, unending references to personal (although doubtful) achievements, and an almost desperate effort to belie inferiority of any kind. Egocentrism, in contrast, stems from such factors as favoritism, success, and overindulgence and is indicated by arrogance, superciliousness, and a condescending attitude. Egocentrism is surrounded by the "air of superiority," which we referred to earlier. In egocentrism, the attitude of superiority outruns actual abilities or achievements and thus creates a situation unfavorable to healthy adjustment. It is a defensive reaction of sorts—a defense against the loss of superior status—but it is different from the defensive superiority that is based on inferiority. This distinction is useful in evaluating the adjustive qualities of superiority.

Superiority and Attention-winning Mechanisms

Lying behind many instances of superiority and egocentrism is the desire for attention and recognition. The mechanisms devised for winning attention are built up as defenses against thwarting egocentrism; at the same time, they serve to gratify basic needs, such as the need for recognition, status, and approval, and thus foster a certain degree of ego security. Among these mechanisms are several that will be readily recognized: refusing to eat, showing off, disobeying, wetting the bed, running away, talking incessantly, and behaving in a delinquent manner. Each one of these reactions secures the attention of others, reduces frustration, and protects as well as develops feelings of superiority. Small wonder that these behavior patterns are so frequently manifested by children, in whom there is so much inferiority, and by adults who have failed to overcome their youthful capitulation to feelings of inferiority.

Psychological and Social Effects of Superiority and Egocentrism

As with the contrasting attitude of inferiority, superiority prevents good adjustment. It leads, as we have already intimated, to the development of other defensive reactions. One of these is *projection,* by which undesirable qualities are expunged from oneself and attributed to others. This, in turn, leads to carping, egoistic *criticism* and to the mechanism of *blaming.* Superiority also involves *introjection,* or the assumption of laudable qualities, which serves to bloster the attitude of superiority. And, when carried to an extreme, these tendencies often result in *delusions* of grandeur, persecution, and reference. At the core of the disorder of paranoia there is an impregnable egocentrism that is fed and constantly supported by the mechanisms of projection and introjection. Egocentrism, therefore, is not only damaging to personal adjustment and integrity; it erects a barrier to social adjustment that precludes wholesome social relations and behavior. It therefore stands in the way of adequate vocational and marital adjustments, which depend upon good social relations.

OTHER DEFENSE REACTIONS

Introjection and Identification

Reference has already been made to several defense reactions that often play an auxiliary and supportive role in the development of major defense mechanisms. Two of these, introjection and identification, are particularly prominent in helping to maintain the defense of the organism against internal weaknesses. *Introjection is a mechanism by which the desirable qualities of other persons or groups are assimilated to oneself,* a psychological ruse by which inadequacies and inferior characteristics are pushed into the background. The efficiency of this assimilation will depend upon the degree to which one can identify himself with the desirable person or group since *identification is the process by which psychological equivalence with others in capacities and traits is established.* Defensive aims can also be realized through the mechanism of *negative identification, a device that enables one to expel or reject the qualities of others that he regards as undesirable.* Boys ordinarily identify strongly with their fathers and thus introject qualities of manliness, courage, maturity, and the like, that the father is thought to possess. Less frequently, we encounter negative identification, in which the boy fails to identify with the father and expunges those qualities in himself that liken him to the parent. If identification leads to the assimilation and further development of worthwhile traits, it can have a salutary effect on adjustment. Similarly, negative identification (with undesirable persons, gangs, and so forth) can have good effects. The end results will depend on the extent to which defensive reactions are needed to preserve ego integrity.

Projecting and Blaming

The opposite of introjection is *projection, a defense mechanism by which the organism rids itself of undesirable qualities by attributing them and their causes to other persons or things.* Thus the inefficient worker projects his inefficiency onto the machine, and the young delinquent attrib-utes the cause of his difficulties to his parents or society rather than to himself. Projection is invariably associated with the mechanism of blaming and reflects a deep-seated sense of inadequacy and guilt. Whenever a per-son blames others for his own deficiencies and failures it is a good indication that he feels guilt and is thus indirectly blaming himself for his weaknesses. Obviously, the extent to which one is successful in shifting the blame for personal inadequacies will determine the effectiveness of projection in bringing about a reduction of the tension of frustration and in protecting the self concept. Admittedly, the ends of adjustment are thus served but at the cost of self-delusion and impairment of one's relations with others. Both projection and blaming, therefore, must be characterized as essentially mal-adjustive reactions against personal inadequacies (Norman & Ainsworth, 1954).

Repression and Segregation

Finally, we must take note of the mechanism identified by Freud as *repression*, which is described as *the unconscious suppression of experiences, wishes, desires, or thoughts that conflict with moral and social principles or ideals, and thus threaten ego security.* Repression is essentially a defense against unpleasant and disturbing ideas and motivations; it is one of the clearest examples of the flight from self. It is a means by which we "forget," that is, push into unconsciousness, ideas, tendencies, and feelings that are intolerable from the standpoint of personal ideals or ethical principles. Thus we might expect repression of guilt feelings associated with sexual transgressions, of experiences that had a traumatic effect on personal secu-rity and integrity, and of ideas of lust, murder, and incest because of their objectionable moral qualities. Repressions are protective in so far as they safeguard the organism against tension, frustration, and ego damage; but they also provide a starting point for the development of unconscious moti-vations that lead to symptom formation and behavior disturbances. More-over, they preclude self-insight and self-knowledge and thus make it difficult for the organism to react in a wholesome way to the demands of reality. Repression, therefore, must be regarded as essentially maladjustive (Freud, 1946, Chapter IV).

To repression is allied the mechanism of *segregation, which serves to protect ego security by the process of isolating ideas, feelings, and attitudes that are inappropriate to or in conflict with immediate and expedient wishes and aspirations* (Strecker & Appel, 1944, Chapter XVI). The mechanism of segregation underlies moral and political expediency and fosters the development of logic-tight compartments that exclude the intrusion of unwanted thoughts or beliefs, especially those that are in any way restrictive or embarrassing. The shrewd business man who is interested always in making an "honest" dollar manages by segregation to skirt moral principles and obligations. In other words, when it comes to business dealings, he shunts morality into a compartment of its own where it can have no effect on "hard-headed," "realistic" business affairs. In this way, of course, personal integrity is maintained without damage to the self concept. Similarly, the racial bigot segregates thoughts about the equality granted by the Constitution whenever a question arises regarding the rights of minority groups. This mechanism is usually complemented by a great deal of rationalization and at times involves other mechanisms, such as superiority, projection, and blaming. Because it prevents self-insight and objectivity and involves prejudicial thinking as well as other damaging mechanisms, segregation is clearly maladjustive in character.

GENERAL STATEMENT ABOUT DEFENSE REACTIONS

Defense Mechanisms as Normal

Our evaluation of defense reactions has provided us with an answer to the question regarding their normality. In a statistical sense, of course, all of them are normal occurrences, but, from a psychological point of view, the majority have to be regarded as maladjustive and abnormal. In their defensive and protective quality, they help to reduce the tension of frustration, prevent mental conflicts, and preserve the integrity of the ego. In this respect, they serve the purpose of adjustment in somewhat the same way as an antitoxin vaccine wards off disease or an amputation stops the progress of gangrene. However, it would be better if the general condition of the organism were such that defense mechanisms, vaccines, or amputations were not at all necessary. But people being what they are, with all their weaknesses and susceptibilities to disease and maladjustment, it is unlikely that mechanisms of defense can be avoided. Perfect mental health, like physical health, is only an ideal toward which we can aspire but which we cannot expect to achieve in all its fullness.

Defense Reactions in Relation to Severe Maladjustments

What is the relation between defense reactions and the more serious maladjustments, especially the neuroses? For one thing, neuroses are always abnormal and maladjustive, whereas defense mechanisms hover between the normal and the abnormal. Because defense reactions serve the aims of adjustment by reducing conflict and frustration, and particularly because they prevent damage to the self concept, they function *as a bulwark* against more serious disturbances. We might liken them to the rise in body temperature (fever) that accompanies certain physical diseases and in some cases is deliberately induced for therapeutic purposes. The fever itself is not a good thing and may indicate a dangerous physical ailment; yet it can be exploited for therapeutic purposes to stave off the development of more serious and disabling diseases. Defense mechanisms often function in a similar way (Tyson, 1951, pp. 15–16; Thorpe, 1950, pp. 147–150).

QUESTIONS AND PROJECTS FOR FURTHER STUDY

1. Explain in your own words the relation between sublimation and compensation, between introjection and identification, between projection and blame, between superiority and egocentrism. Illustrate the differences between these mechanisms.
2. To what extent are defense reactions normal? What is it that makes them abnormal or maladjustive?
3. Critically evaluate Alfred Adler's theory of inferiority and psychic compensation. Explain what Adler meant by the masculine protest.
4. Compare the aims of egocentrism and compensation. Discuss the significance of these aims for adjustment.
5. Is there any relation between social, economic, racial, and sex status on the one hand, and defense mechanisms on the other? Explain. Discuss the differential effects of inferiority, inadequacy, and failure on adjustment mechanisms.
6. Explain in your own words the difference between repression and segregation. How does repression cause symptom formation?

SELECTED COLLATERAL READINGS

ADLER, A. *The neurotic constitution.* (Trans. by B. Glueck & J. E. Laird). New York: Dodd, Mead, 1930.

ALLERS, R. *The psychology of character.* (Trans. by E. B. Strauss). New York: Sheed & Ward, 1943.

BARKER, R. G., *et al.* Adjustment to physical handicap and illness. Bull. No. 55, rev., New York: Soc. Sci. Res. Coun., 1953.

BRACHFELD, O. *Inferiority feelings in the individual and the group.* New York: Grune & Stratton, 1951.

DAVIES, J. T. *Sublimation.* New York: Macmillan, 1948.

DODGE, R., & KAHN, E. *The craving for superiority.* New Haven: Yale University Press, 1931.

FREUD, ANNA. *The ego and the mechanisms of defense.* (Trans. by C. Baines). New York: International Universities, 1947.

GARRETT, J. F. (Ed.) *Psychological aspects of physical disability.* Washington, D.C.: U.S. Office of Vocational Rehabilitation. n.d.

HORNEY, KAREN. *Neurosis and human growth.* New York: Norton, 1950.

MADISON, P. *Freud's concept of repression and defense: its theoretical and observational language.* Minneapolis: University of Minnesota Press, 1962.

VAUGHAN, W. F. *The lure of superiority.* Boston: Boston University Press, 1928.

9

Adjustment by Aggression and Delinquency

There are many ways that children and adults adjust to the drives and conflicts within themselves and to the demands and stresses imposed on them by reality. Some persons find the going too difficult and withdraw into the strange dream world of the schizophrenic or perhaps the stuporous world of the alcoholic. Others attempt to meet crises and demands by defensive mechanisms; others by flight into illness; and still others by lashing out violently against the world in which they live. These latter are the aggressive and delinquent persons, who resolve their frustrations and conflicts by bold, assertive thrusts against society. They are the ones who adjust by aggression and delinquency.

GENERAL CHARACTERISTICS OF AGGRESSION

Aggression versus Defense

In the preceding chapter we saw how adjustment is achieved by the development of defense mechanisms which are used to mitigate feelings of inferiority, inadequacy, insecurity, and guilt, as well as the negative effects produced by these feelings. The frustration to which these conditions give rise sometimes produces a different effect; in place of compensation, rationalization, and similar reactions, there is aggression, in which the organism, by means of attack, destructiveness, bullying, and brutality, seems intent on overcoming or destroying anything and everything related to the frustration. This reaction is seen even in young children who express a great amount of aggression in the common responses of biting, scratching, name calling, teasing, fighting, and rebellion.

On the theory that "the best defense is a strong offense," it is not unlikely that aggressive reactions of this kind are also defensive in quality. Certainly, aggressive behavior often serves to reduce the tension of frustration, and by its direct, frontal attack on the causes and conditions of frustration, it serves to maintain ego security. It is clear that the weakness and timidity so commonly associated with inferiority, inadequacy, or ego impairment are not among the characteristics of the aggressive person.

253

There are basic differences, however, between defense reactions and aggression that are important to the understanding of aggression. For one thing, defense reactions characteristically imply inadequacy and weakness, and the prevailing emotional tone is one of anxiety and timidity. The defensive person gives the impression of anxiously striving to keep others from discovering how inadequate he really is, and he even seeks to hide the fact from himself. Aggressive reactions, in contrast, imply a certain amount of ego strength and seem to be based on fearlessness and anger. The defensive child makes excuses for his poor showing; the aggressive child reacts angrily to his frustration by hostility, destructiveness, or rebellion. In both cases, the underlying immediate cause is frustration and the tension that accompanies it; but the personal characteristics, emotional accompaniments, and overt expression are strikingly different (McKellar, 1949).

Moreover, there are motivational differences that distinguish these reactions. Where the reactions of the defensive person are typically defenses against feelings of inadequacy or inferiority, those of the aggressive person typically reflect a great amount of insecurity, which he seeks to reduce or control by aggressive behavior. Defensiveness is expressed most characteristically in egocentrism, whereas aggressiveness tends toward self-assertiveness. Furthermore, just as superiority mitigates feelings of inferiority, self-assertiveness effectively reduces feelings of insecurity. "Insecurity is generally considered to be one of the basic causes of aggressive attitudes and behavior" (Sherman, 1941, p. 176).

Finally, there is the fact that defensive reactions are primarily oriented toward self; they develop out of the need to obscure personal weaknesses, and for that reason we have referred to them as a flight from self. Aggressive reactions *are directed mainly toward others* or toward reality in general as the source of the difficulties and encroachments that cause frustration and threaten ego security.

The difficulties that provoke defense reactions originate largely within oneself and are only conditioned and aggravated by external factors. Rejecting parents can cause a child to feel inferior and thus contribute to the development of defense mechanisms, but the primary cause of the adjusment difficulty is the frustration and ego damage that the feeling of inferiority leads to. In the case of aggression, the primary cause of the difficulty in adjustment lies outside the person, or so it seems to him (Shapiro, 1957). For example, restrictive or punitive measures on the part of parents and others in authority directly frustrate the interests and needs of the child. If the child reacts with anger, rebellion, or hatred, his behavior will be explosively aggressive. If he reacts with feelings of inadequacy or inferiority, his behavior will be defensive.

These several relations are diagramed in Figure 16. Note that the insecurity is an offshoot of the frustration caused by parental restrictions, just as anxiety is an offshoot of inferiority, neither one of these reactions is an immediate cause of defense or aggression (Siegel, 1956). It should also be noted that the defense reaction is directed against the inferiority, whereas aggression is normally directed against the original source of the frustration. Thus, while the frustration-aggression situation tends to create insecurity, there is a great deal more ego strength here than in cases where inferiority is the core of the reaction. The defensive person feels the need to defend himself against his own weaknesses; the aggressive person seeks to defend himself against the encroachments of outside forces.

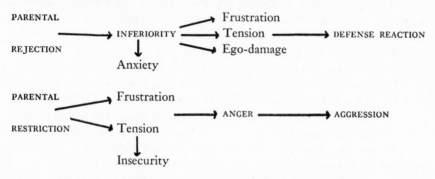

Fig. 16. The differences between defense reactions and aggression.

Definition of Aggression

Aggression is essentially a form of response that seeks the reduction of tension and frustration through the medium of behavior that is demanding, overpowering, or possessive. A peculiar feature of aggressive response, as this definition implies, is that, unlike so many forms of adjustment, it does not contribute to the solution of problems. To react aggressively to the demands and restrictions of parents or society is more likely to complicate and compound a problem than it is to afford a solution. The child who talks back to his parents or glares sullenly at them, while muttering under his breath at the unfairness of it all, is reacting aggressively and attempting in his own way to overcome or reduce the difficulties that are causing him to be frustrated; however, the behavior is such that it bars the way to an adequate solution of the problem. It is in the nature of aggressive responses to bring the organism into conflict with some aspect of reality, to tread, as it were, on somebody's toes. Aggression is always directed against some thing or person, and it is this quality that serves to complicate rather than to solve the problems in which aggression takes its roots (Graham, Charwat, Honig, & Weltz, 1951).

Aggression versus Aggressiveness. Aggression represents an attempt to reduce or overcome frustrating conditions and in that way bring about a reduction of the tension that these conditions stimulate; it is therefore an attempt at adjustment. But in so far as it impairs the organism's relations with reality and fails to solve the problem that initiated it, aggressive behavior must be regarded as poorly suited to the adjustive needs of the organism. This charge, of course, can be brought against many responses that represent attempts to secure personal adjustment, but it is particularly applicable in the case of aggression. Moreover, aggressive response often tends to disturb emotional equanimity and to heighten feelings of guilt and uncertainty, thus impairing still further the adjustive aims of the person. For the most part, then, aggression must be counted as inadequate to achieving wholesome adjustment.

However, there are times when aggressive behavior seems to fit the concept of normality (Bergler, 1946; Watson, Pritzker, & Madison, 1955). Here we need to introduce a distinction between aggression and aggressiveness. There are many persons whose behavior, although aggressive, does not disrupt their relations with other persons nor their feelings regarding themselves. We ordinarily think of these persons as having great drive and initiative, qualities, incidentally, that are common to all leaders. These qualities lead to aggressiveness, or self-assertiveness, and are manifested by many normal, well-adjusted persons in all walks of life. Often they are necessary to the realization of great aims and to the successful completion of important tasks. Whereas aggression is no more than an angry thrust at existing conditions, aggressiveness may lead to a determined, successful attack on a difficult problem. Aggression represents anger, hostility, and frustration; aggressiveness indicates determination and the feeling of self-confidence. At times, of course, aggressiveness disrupts interpersonal relations. There is not always a sharp line dividing aggressiveness and aggression; indeed, it is not unlikely that a great deal of aggressiveness is the expression of deep-seated aggression. Yet the two forms of behavior are different, and therefore we suggest that some aggressive responses, taking the form of aggressiveness, fit into the concept of normal adjustment.

This point is well brought out by Atkin (1950, p. 6) in her instructive pamphlet on aggressiveness in children. Here is her answer to the question, "What is aggressiveness?"

Aggressiveness is that force within us that gives strength and vitality to our actions. Aggressiveness isn't always evil and destructive;

it can be good and useful and healthy. It spurs us on to overcome obstacles and to strike out against dangerous or unpleasant situations. At its best, it makes for initiative, enterprise and healthy competitiveness. The scientist who seeks to conquer disease and the statesman who fights against poverty and injustice are aggressive in a socially useful way.

Aggressiveness propels children to grow and learn and master their environment. The newborn baby reaching out for food, the toddler tugging at the challenging electric cord, the little girl learning to skate, the schoolboy hitting a home run—are all displaying healthy aggressiveness. . . .

Indeed, every step the child takes to free himself from his dependence on his parents and stand on his own feet is an expression of healthy and desirable aggressiveness.

But aggressiveness has another face—one that is hostile and destructive. We all know the harm it can do. Some people believe we are born with it, as with the sex drive. Others believe it is not inborn, but is the way people respond to frustration, disappointment and fear.

The quotation above is only one of many statements on the nature of aggression and aggressiveness. There is a considerable body of research literature on aggressive behavior, particularly in children (Bailey, 1946; Graham, *et al.*, 1951; Bender, 1953; Scott, 1958). The idea that aggression is normal and innate is very widespread and is of course most popular with psychoanalysts. One writer states plainly, "I need not emphasize that the human organism is endowed by nature with the drive to be aggressive toward its environment" (Gardner, 1948, p. 78). This writer gives a good account (pp. 78–83) of the idea that aggression is a normal impulse.

Signs of Aggression

Unlike certain defense reactions that are subjective in character, such as introjection and identification, *aggression is characteristically outgoing and behavioral*, manifesting itself unmistakably in signs or expressions that help to identify it. Some of these signs are verbal, others are nonverbal. This statement should not be taken to mean that all aggression is obvious or outwardly directed (Berkowitz, 1958). According to accepted theory, some aggression is turned inward and thus at times gives rise to psychosomatic disturbances. See Chapter 11 on the flight into illness (Mussen & Naylor, 1954; Atkin, 1950, pp. 17–24).

Among the verbal signs of aggression are abusive language, frequent quarreling, name calling, rude answering, biting sarcasm, and vicious criticism. In the heat of a political campaign, among voters and candidates alike, these verbal signs of aggression erupt on the body politic like the rash of a bad case of chicken pox. In the relations of children to parents, of pupils to teachers, of labor to management, there are countless instances of verbalized aggression. The author once heard a young child, when asked why she liked horses so much, retort, without a moment's hestitation, "Because they are so different from people!" Wrapped in this simple expression was all the hostility, hatred, and rebellion engendered by her negative experience with other persons.

Verbal aggression has distinct advantages over more direct and overt forms, such as attack and destructiveness, and is therefore more common. It is economical and facile, more easily retracted, and does not cause the anxiety or guilt that goes along with more overt forms; at the same time, it achieves the psychological aims of aggression. If a child ruthlessly destroys another child's toy or hits him with a rock, it is difficult to undo the damage; however, "sticks and stones may break my bones, but words can never hurt me," shows how the child devaluates verbal aggression as compared with physical attack.

The limits of verbal aggression are determined by the degree of frustration and the nature of the aggression determinant. For example, a political candidate is usually just the butt of verbal rancor, booing, heckling, or criticism; but once in a while overt aggression bursts forth, and the candidate becomes the target of eggs and tomatoes instead of words. So intense and dynamic does the frustration-aggression mechanism sometimes become that the authority of the parent or the dignity of the high office of President of the United States is brushed aside as of no importance. It is both interesting and instructive to sit in on a religious or political discussion and inventory the examples of verbal aggression; we then realize how extensive aggression is and how closely it is tied in with frustration (Allison & Hunt, 1959).

Among the nonverbal signs of aggression may be included resistance to discipline and direction, rebelliousness, excessive disagreement with other persons, grudge carrying, sullenness, extreme irritability, tendency toward inconveniencing others, vengefulness, and domination. These qualities, of course, underlie or are characteristically associated with the more overt expressions of aggression, such as destruction and attack. The first of these qualities, resistance to discipline, is one of the most outstanding and significant features of the aggressive personality. It expresses most forcibly the basic hostility and antipathy toward others that dominate the thinking and conduct of the aggressive person. By resisting discipline and control, the person hopes to overcome the external sources of his frustration and in that way destroy at once the frustration and the insecurity associated with it (Jensen, 1957). Thus the adolescent boy, annoyed and hampered by the frustrating rules set up by his parents, stays out later than he should, indulges in forbidden pleasures, bullies his brothers and sisters, uses abusive language, and in general breaks every rule in the book. The connection between the frustration and the aggressive responses is clear; since the frustration is caused by restriction and discipline, the aggressive behavior serves to disrupt or to break down the forces that stand in the way of free expression, leading to at least a temporary reduction of frustration.

Not all expressions of aggression bear this precise functional relation to frustration. Sometimes, as in grudge carrying, vengefulness, and irritability, it is difficult to see the functional value of the response. Yet, if we follow the general principle that all responses have some functional significance, however remote, we must assume that these ways of behaving do reduce the tension of frustration. Carrying a grudge can do more harm than good to the aims of wholesome adjustment; but grudges nevertheless serve the purposes of aggression and so mitigate frustration and insecurity. Other characteristics of aggression may be interpreted in a similar fashion.

Functions of Aggression

To understand the nature of aggression we must define its basic functions, particularly in view of the fact that its relation to adjustment is somewhat ambiguous. Symonds (1946, pp. 83–84) states that aggression

> has two main functions: first to wrest satisfaction from the outside world; and second, to destroy the source of pain. Both functions are related to the need of the organism to maintain itself in an environment where the process of nourishment requires effort, and to protect itself from harm or destruction in an environment full of potential danger or enemies.

These functions can be fitted into the picture of aggression drawn in preceding pages with little difficulty; but there is more to aggression than satisfaction and the avoidance of pain. As Maier says (Maier, 1949, pp. 105, 106):

> If our contention is correct that aggression is solely a response to frustration and that the response expression is an end product rather than a means to an end, then we may expect the frustration-instigated response to be a relief of a tension rather than a solution to a problem. . . . It appears, therefore, that regardless of goals achieved, aggression relieves frustration tensions. . . .

In other words, then, *aggression is not goal-directed, nor is it directed toward the solving of a problem; rather it is aimed at the relief of tension associated with frustration.* This, it would seem, is the primary aim of aggressive response. We must remind ourselves, however, that frustration always represents, either directly or indirectly, the functioning of basic motivations, and therefore aggression may also be regarded as an attempt to ensure the free expression of these motivations. The contention that aggression is solely a response to frustration only means that aggression is not goal seeking or problem solving; it cannot mean that motivation is not involved since frustration always has some reference to needs and drives (Wurtz, 1960; Feshbach, 1961; Berkowitz, Green, & Macaulay, 1962).

FORMS OF AGGRESSION

The Continuum of Intensity

If we take aggression in its widest meaning to include aggressiveness as well as neurotic aggression, we see that there are many ways in which it expresses itself, ranging from simple self-assertiveness to extreme cases of destruction and brutality. These variations are determined by the motivation involved, the character and strength of the frustration, and by the emotional factors that dominate the frustration-aggression response (Symonds, 1949, pp. 70–71).

The forms of aggression, as here presented, can be arranged on a continuum of intensity, ranging from relatively mild manifestations to the most violent and explosive reactions. These relations are indicated in

Self-assertion	Teasing	Attack	Revenge
Dominance	Bullying	Destruction	Brutality
Possessiveness	Hostility	Violence	Sadistic fury

CONTINUUM OF INTENSITY

Aggressiveness ⎯⎯⎯⎯⎯⎯⎯⎯→ *Extreme Aggression*

Fig. 17.   Continuum of aggressive response.

Figure 17. Each one of these responses shades almost imperceptibly into the next, until we reach the violent expressions of revenge, brutality, and sadistic fury. In bullying we see something of self-assertion and dominance on the one hand, and hostility and attack on the other. Revenge is typically characterized by violence and destruction and is often the motivating force behind brutality and sadism. These relations are readily identified; yet it must be recognized that the different forms of aggression are distinct in themselves. They differ partly in their intensity, in the degree of frustration that touches them off, in the emotional accompaniment of the frustration, and in the character of the overt response by which the aggression is manifested.

For example, in bullying there is resentment, in destruction and violence there is anger or hatred. Hostility may be expressed verbally, whereas destruction and brutality more often involve a direct physical assault on the cause of the frustration. These differences in behavior result, of course, from the depth or amount of frustration tension, the emotional reaction that occurs, and the nature of the frustration determinant. Children seldom react with violence, destruction, or brutality to the restrictions imposed by parents; but nations at war or in ideological conflict run the entire gamut of aggressive response. We need but recall the brutality and wanton killing of World War II to exemplify this fact.

Self-Assertiveness, Dominance, and Possession

Among the more common and milder forms of aggression are self-assertiveness, dominance, and possession, responses that are more normal than neurotic. Nevertheless, there are features of such responses that pave the way to an understanding of the more severe forms of aggression. Self-assertiveness, for example, may represent nothing more than initiative, drive, or the will to succeed; yet there are numerous instances in which this forward thrust of self has distinctly aggressive characteristics, suggesting a background of frustration. In situations like these, we should not overgeneralize, that is, assume frustration is the cause in every case. Nevertheless, the fact that aggression is so closely linked to frustration suggests caution in ruling out the possibility that even these milder instances of aggression reflect a certain amount of frustration.

Frustration is even more likely to be present in situations involving domination of others since dominance offers excellent opportunities for reduction of the tension of frustration. We often see dominance exhibited in sibling relations, and usually there is a background of frustration caused by parental discipline or restriction. How natural it is for a boy to lord it over his younger brothers and sisters when his own desires and aspirations have been thwarted by parental commands. In work situations, husband-wife relations, and so on, one can point to many instances where dominance reflects a great amount of frustration. This is particularly true when the dominance-submission relation is the reverse of what is normally expected. Many wives dominate their husbands and children in an effort to mitigate frustrations that arise within the family situation. In this way they strive to re-establish the sense of security that chronic frustrations tend to destroy.

Similarly, gaining possession, and the quality of possessiveness (often illustrated in marital relations) are indicative of aggression founded on frustration. The child who claims possession of all playthings regardless of ownership, or angrily wrests objects away from playmates, or finds it difficult to share his possessions with others is exhibiting aggression. Intense desire for possession usually indicates considerable insecurity. The marital partner whose possessiveness precludes sharing of husband or wife with friends, relatives, or outside interests of any kind is revealing insecurity, frustration, and aggression. On a much larger scale, this form of aggression is reflected in the aggrandizement and the possessiveness of entire nations whose insecurity and frustration have led to aggressive reactions. Conversely, the security afforded by great wealth, national growth, and military victories has made aggression less necessary for other groups.

Teasing and Bullying

It is obvious from the words themselves that teasing and bullying are aggressive, although we should not take this to mean that occasional, playful teasing is aggressive. To tease a person jokingly about a slip of the tongue or some small peculiarity of appearance is hardly to be interpreted as aggressive; but the constant, provoking type of teasing that leads to angry protest is certainly a form of aggression that bespeaks a sense of frustration. Thus, the first-born child, frustrated in his efforts to secure maximum attention and affection after the arrival of the second child, turns to teasing as a means of reducing the tension he feels. This teasing may be directed toward the sibling (withholding a toy, snatching the baby's bottle, pinching his toes, and so forth) or toward the parent, since both are part of the frustrating situation. Here we see aggression in one of its earliest forms, and the relation between the response and the frustrating situation is unmistakable.

Teasing is not limited to early childhood. It is common among school children and can be detected often in the social relations of adults. It is surprising how many husbands and wives seem never to tire of directing sly verbal barbs at one another in the presence of friends and relatives, remarks that indicate a pattern of hostility and aggression in their attitudes toward one another. This social play is passed off as teasing, sometimes even as a mark of affection; but this interpretation does not obscure the underlying frustration and aggression.

The relation between frustration and aggression is even more obvious in bullying. Whereas some teasing is playful, the intent and the effects of bullying are always on the side of aggression and interfere seriously with adequate adjustment. Bullying may be verbal, but it often takes the form of hostile attack. It is a common phenomenon, and the bully is a typical example of the frustrated, aggressive personality. In his actions toward other persons, especially those younger and weaker than himself, one can readily discern the hatred, anger, resentment, and hostility that have been engendered by rejecting or punitive parents, a broken home, damaging rivalries, and similar conditions. In international relations as well as in industry there are many instances of this form of aggression; indeed, wherever deep-seated aggression exists, we may expect bullying to appear if the conditions are favorable.

Open Hostility and Attack

Open hostility and attack are common manifestations of aggression; they may assume a verbal as well as a nonverbal form. In our national elections the deep-seated frustration of a party kept out of office for many years shows itself unmistakably in the attacks directed against the opposition. Nothing is more frustrating to a politician than to be kept out of office. We may suppose, too, that the anticipated frustration coincident with defeat is felt almost as keenly and will therefore give rise to a great deal of aggression, which explains the bitter attacks of the party in power. These reactions are mixed up with many other causes and reasons, but frustration is one of the primary sources. The frustration caused by broken homes, by strike-breaking techniques used in industrial conflicts, by faithless wives or husbands, and so on, invariably leads to hostility or attack in one form or another (Palmer, 1960). Verbal lashings are all too common a phenomenon; but equally familiar are the physical assaults against persons and objects in situations dominated by the frustration-aggression mechanism. Children from broken homes, especially homes disrupted by desertion, separation, or divorce, are likely to show strong aggressive tendencies, literally biting, scratching, and kicking their way to a reduction of unbearable tension. As Sherman points out (1941, p. 177):

> Sociologists have shown that children from broken homes or from homes in which there is a great deal of quarreling or other disturbances tend to be aggressive and openly hostile. Sociologists have also emphasized the effect of conflicts of insecurity resulting from parental rejection on the development of hostile and aggressive behavior.

Strikers show similarly powerful aggressive reactions whenever someone threatens to wreck their aims by strike-breaking techniques. In every situation of this kind, the intensity of the reaction reflects the degree of tension and the emotional feeling that is aroused. In this connection see Redl & Wineman (1951, pp. 20–26).

Violence and Destruction

Open hostility and attack are but one step removed from violence and destruction. The behavior of lynch mobs is an example of extreme violence and destruction directed against a person or a racial group. There are killings and destruction of property in industrial conflicts, but these effects are incidental to the main purpose of the strikers' behavior, which is to prevent interference with their attainment of a highly cherished goal. In mob behavior, however, violence and destruction are an integral part of the act of aggression; the intent is to destroy what is regarded as the source of the frustration. Individuals or groups that have come to symbolize the causes of frustration are treated as scapegoats. In our own southern states, the Negro is blamed for all economic and social frustrations and therefore is the object of aggression. It is interesting to note that the number of lynchings varies in direct relation to economic conditions in the various southern states (Berkowitz & Holmes, 1959).

Scapegoating, which is common to all groups of people, provides an interesting sidelight to the frustration-aggression mechanism. Whenever the causes or conditions of frustration are unknown or cannot be directly attacked, there is a tendency to substitute some other person or thing as the cause, especially if there is some connection, however remote or specious, between the frustration and the substitute "cause." As one writer remarks (Sherman, 1941, p. 179):

> In many instances the person against whom aggression takes place may not have been responsible for the frustrations. This is a form of displaced aggression when an individual shows his aggressive tendencies toward the person or group from whom retaliation is not anticipated. The use of a scapegoat in political situations has been pointed out by some psychologists as an instance of displaced aggression. An individual or a group, having been seriously frustrated, unconsciously seeks some release for the inhibited aggressions. Frequently such individuals or groups find a national, racial or political minority against whom they can release their aggressions without fear of retaliation.

The southerner thinks of the "lowly" Negro as the cause of his difficulties, just as Hitler attributed all of Germany's difficulties to the "inferior" Jews. Similarly, but on a smaller scale, displacement occurs when a person slams the door of his car when it "refuses" to start or when a child destroys a toy that does not provide the satisfactions expected of it or because it belongs to a hated rival. It is easier to express aggression when there is available some "cause" to which it can be directed. Since aggression results from external frustration, the effort to reduce frustration is directed toward external conditions (Durbin, 1939; Berkowitz, 1959).

Displaced aggression is not unlike what might be called "vicarious aggression," in which the aggression is worked out by means of identification and imaginative projection. Children witnessing violence and death on the movie or television screen have an opportunity to vent their aggressive feelings against the "bad guys" who, by displacement, take the place of persons who have frustrated them and thus aroused their hostility. Similarly, an adult can let loose his aggressive tendencies in watching a bloody boxing match or a brutal football game. "Only relatively few people would go to a prizefight for the purpose of seeing the scientific skill of the boxers, but large numbers attend these fights to see the 'fighting' rather than the boxing" (Sherman, 1941, p. 176). The keen enjoyment with which people watch the wholesale mauling and slaughter in crime movies and westerns is testimony to the existence and the vicarious expression of a great amount of aggression. That vicarious expression of aggressive tendencies may have beneficial effects on adjustment and mental stability is a point well worth considering (Maslow, 1954).

Revenge

Aggression may reach its climax in the fury of destruction and violence, but there are several other expressions that also reveal the frustration-aggression relation. These are revenge, brutality, and sadistic fury. Revenge is an unusually good example of aggression because all aggression involves to some extent the attitude of retribution or retaliation, which is the essence of revenge. The reduction of tension by acts of revenge is a well-known phenomenon reflected in the simple aphorism "revenge is sweet." Revenge is sweet because of the feeling of satisfaction that comes with the lessening of frustration and tension. Revenge begins, of course, with injury, either real or imagined, physical, psychological, or moral. This injury thwarts personal satisfactions and the normal expression of needs and desires; it casts a reflection on self and thus may severely damage the self-concept, disrupting the feeling of pride and of security in status and achievement. In the football rivalries so common in this country, revenge phenomena are frequent. If feelings of pride and achievement suffered a setback in the previous season, the team comes roaring out for revenge, and aggression is evident in every move and play. Penalties against the revenge-motivated team are likely to run high, unless they have been carefully schooled to hold their aggression in check. In many instances of delinquency there is clearly discernible an attitude of revenge against parents or society for some real or imagined wrong, and delinquents are notoriously aggressive. In fact, in all walks of life, there are times when injury spurs the feeling of revenge and leads to some form of aggression.

Revenge can be satisfied in many ways, ranging from a tongue lashing to murder. According to Maier (1949, p. 106), the important thing in revenge behavior is the reduction of tension not the destruction of the hated object. Revenge

> relieves tensions and this relief makes revenge sweet and satisfying. No problem is solved, however, and no wrong is corrected by revenge. The fact that revenge behavior, rather than what revenge does to another, supplies the relief is born out of common experiences. Many persons have felt relief by writing a letter and telling a person just what they thought of him. Before the letter is written, tensions are unrelieved; after the writing there is relief, and it is unnecessary to send the letter to experience the relief.

The validity of this interpretation, however, depends partly on the demands for retribution inherent in the revenge. Revenge for a defeat suffered at the hands of a rival, as exemplified so often in sports, can only be satisfied by victory over the enemy. In such cases, and in others as well, vicarious revenge, as when a hated rival is beaten by another opponent, makes the victim feel better, but complete satisfaction can only come when the victim himself can vanquish the opponent. Similarly, letters to the editor concerning the evils and weaknesses of the opposing political party assuage feelings of tension and frustration, but the fullness of revenge is not experienced until the opposition candidates are soundly defeated at the polls.

Brutality and Sadistic Fury

Feelings of hostility and revenge, based on injury to the self concept and the threat to security posed by a frustrating environment, often lead to extreme aggressive behavior, such as brutality and sadistic fury. It is a common experience to see children from broken homes indulge in brutality to other children and to animals. Under the Nazi regime, and under the present communist regimes throughout the world, brutality is common. The psychological pattern is clear: frustration-tension-aggression. But why brutality? Why pick on minority groups, defenseless individuals, or animals? In some cases of aggression, the source of the frustration is regarded as personally injurious, and therefore the only kind of behavior that can reduce this hurt involves injury to another person. Hostility engendered by the feeling of having been injured is projected and generalized to include many things that may be directly, or only remotely, connected with the source of the frustration. The brutality of the enemy in the recent war is a clear instance of aggression based on hostility and hatred engendered largely by imagined wrongs. Brutality toward animals is based on hostility toward any living thing and is spurred on by the satisfaction derived from witnessing distress and pain such as the person himself experienced with other living things. Brutality is a positive sign of deep-seated frustration and aggression and requires careful therapeutic treatment.

The extreme of brutality is sadistic fury, a type of unrestrained, uncontrollable aggression that is expressed in a vicious, physical attack against another person. Psychoanalysts interpret sadism in a restricted way as the stimulation of sexual excitement by the infliction of pain or injury on another person. This definition is technically correct, but many writers have broadened the meaning of the term "sadism" so as to make it more useful. In the broader sense, sadistic behavior includes aggressive responses in which satisfaction is derived from inflicting pain or injury, a satisfaction that need not be sexual at all but that derives from the reduction of tension. In sadistic fury, all the elements of aggression are present. There are many instances on record of fathers mercilessly beating their children and seeming to derive a great deal of relief and satisfaction from their heinous behavior. Now everyone is aware that children are often a source of frustration to parents. They stand in the way of the parents' freedom, they rob one or the other parent of attention and affection, they are financially thwarting, and so on. Some unfortunate parents react to these frustrations with resentment, anger, and hatred, and these feelings act as immediate determinants of sadistic punishment. We must recognize the possibility also that sadistic fury often expresses unconscious guilt, which the sadistic person projects onto others whom he then uses as scapegoats.

Sadistic aggression is manifested in many other situations. In the fury of vandalism, in the beatings administered to innocent victims by gangs of delinquent boys, in the fury with which a husband beats his wife, in the tortures used against the victims of lynch mobs, in the physical degradations imposed on their enemies by the Communists and the Nazis—in these and countless other situations, sadistic fury is clearly evident. Here again we see how closely related are the different forms of aggression and how easily one form shades off into the other (Berg & Fox, 1947).

CAUSES AND CONDITIONS OF AGGRESSION

Biological Determinants of Aggression

In our analysis of aggression we have already indicated several factors that underlie aggressive response. We know that frustration, tension, insecurity, and similar feelings are the bases of aggression. But there are other internal and external causes and conditions to which attention should be directed because they shed considerable light on the development of the aggressive personality. Analysis of these factors will help us to gain a better understanding of why aggression is used in an effort to adjust to varying demands and situations.

If we start again with simple aggressiveness, we see that such behavior may simply be a reflection of unusual energy, a release of forces associated with buoyant health, good assimilation of food, rapid metabolism, healthy exercise and physical activity, and a wholesome diet. In persons characterized by these qualities, we may expect a great deal of "drive," energy, ambition, and self-assertion. They appear aggressive because the supply of available energy demands expression, and release is sought in a round of activities that easily give the impression of aggressiveness. Undoubtedly, there are many seemingly aggressive children whose only fault is an excess of energy that clamors for direct expression, a fact that should be carefully considered before any judgment is made regarding the existence of frustration and tension. It is obvious that aggressiveness (as distinct from neurotic aggression) requires a fund of available energy that surpasses the average supply.

Psychological Determinants of Aggression: Basic Needs

More to the point where actual aggression is concerned is the role played by the basic needs of the organism, particularly those of a psychological nature. We have seen that defense mechanisms are determined by the frustration of needs, such as status and achievement, and the situation is not basically different where the motivation of aggressive behavior is concerned. The distinction to be observed is that, in the matter of defense reactions, the frustration is primarily internal and personal, whereas aggression is largely a reaction to external frustration. In both cases, psychological needs play a prominent role, as they do in all human adjustments. Aggression seems particularly to reflect interference with the need for security, affection, independence, and recognition. The need for status is involved because external frustration endangers status and thus stands as a threat to personal integrity and security and to the development of a healthy self concept. In our discussion of motivation and adjustment in Chapter 5, we noted that the functioning of a need is always conditioned by the free expression or frustration of other needs, particularly those such as status, affection, and security; therefore any aggression based on needs will tend to reflect their interrelationships. It is to be understood that the frustration of needs by rejecting, dominating, or punitive parents, or by a neglectful society, leads to strong *feelings of hostility and hatred*, and it is these feelings that are the immediate precursors of aggression (Bender, 1948; Korner, 1949; Parsons, 1947; Hewitt & Jenkins, 1946).

Frustration-Aggression Theory

There has been considerable theorizing regarding the relations between frustration and aggression. In the well-known viewpoint of Dollard and his associates, aggression is the result of interference with goal-directed behavior, this interference causing frustration (Dollard, *et al.*, 1939; also Miller, 1941; Bateson, 1941). Typically, a frustrated person either verbally or physically attacks the source of frustration, and this attack is regarded as aggression. The aim of aggression would then be the removal or destruction of the frustrating object. Unfortunately for this simple explanation, there are too many instances in which the frustration-aggression equation does not hold. Sometimes, there is wanton attack or destruction in which no perceptible goal is achieved. Or persons and objects unrelated to the frustration may suffer attack, in which case the aim of aggression seems to be reduction of tension rather than elimination of frustrating conditions (Korner, 1949, p. 4; Segel, 1951, pp. 25–26; Maier, 1949; Berkowitz, 1960; Horanson, 1961).

Because of the difficulties mentioned above, other theories have been proposed to account for aggressive behavior. Maier, for example, argues that aggression is simply a product of frustration and is not to be interpreted as goal-oriented behavior (Maier, 1949, pp. 102–103).

> Thus when a frustrated person strikes an opponent he is not doing so to remove an obstacle or to injure someone. Rather we would contend that he strikes because he is frustrated, and if the obstacle is removed or if injury is done it is secondary or incidental. Although frustration frequently produces aggression against the barrier or the source of frustration we would not call such acts goal-oriented responses. Instead it seems that barriers and obstacles often are attacked because they are convenient objects to attack. . . . Although the consequence of behavior may alter the course of aggression or modify the state of frustration (for better or for worse), we do not consider it a part of the frustration-aggression sequence.

This interpretation has much in its favor, especially in view of the random, nonselective character of many aggressive responses. Yet there are several difficulties that must be taken into account.

First, a great deal of aggression is specifically directed against the source of the frustration and not only because the source is convenient. When status is injured by an insulting remark, and the injured person gives the offender a verbal dressing down, the aggression is clearly directed against the source of frustration. Many children aggressively disobey or rebel against their parents as the source of frustration of independence in order to wear down parental control and thus reduce the frustration.

Second, in many instances random attack is not as haphazard as it seems because the object of the attack is accepted as a symbol of the frustrating condition. As we have already noted, this is the essence of scapegoating, and though the attack does not eliminate the source of frustration, it has a symbolic value that helps in the reduction of tension.

Finally, we may note that the emotional accompaniments of frustration, such as anger, resentment, and hatred, are often so intense and disrupting as to interfere with the direction of the response; hence any object that comes within the scope of the aggression may feel the brunt of its attack. From this analysis we may conclude that, although some aggressive responses are random attacks determined solely by frustration, a great many (and perhaps the majority) are directed toward overcoming or reducing the source of frustration so that the free expression of basic needs becomes possible.

Inferiority, Inadequacy, and Aggression

Before we leave the subject of internal determinants of aggression we should inquire whether there are any relations between the primary determinants of defense mechanisms and aggressive responses. Do feelings of inferiority, inadequacy, and failure ever give rise to aggression? It is clear that bullying, dominance, and self-assertion have a great deal in common with the mechanisms of superiority and egocentrism; in many instances, in fact, we note varying degrees of superiority and aggression in the same person, the reaction of the moment depending largely on circumstances or on the force of the motivation and the character of the frustrating conditions. It is equally obvious that inferiority feelings can be effectively mitigated by aggression. Although inferiority and similar feelings are most likely to stimulate defense reactions, they may lead to aggression when the causes and conditions that underlie them are external and when aggression may be exploited as a defense mechanism. For example, a youngster born and reared in an economically underprivileged environment will often react aggressively toward children in a more favorable social and economic position. Here the reaction is clearly defensive and serves as a displacement of other defense mechanisms which would be inappropriate or ineffective in such situations. Similarly, a child made to feel inferior by a dominating, perfectionistic parent may turn to aggression as a means of defense and also as a means of attacking the source of the frustration. In cases like these the basic needs that we singled out as determining aggression are again involved, and it is only the surrounding conditions that cause responses to be channeled in the direction of aggression at one time and defense at another. On the relation between physical handicap and aggression, see

Barker, Wright, and Gonick (1946, pp. 72, 73). These writers report that aggressiveness against normal persons as a measure of revenge was one of the most frequently mentioned items in the personal diaries of handicapped persons.

The Feeling of Guilt and the Need for Punishment

The relation between guilt and aggression is even closer because guilt feelings stimulate the need for punishment, and aggressive behavior is often a guarantee of punishment. This fact is exemplified most clearly in aggressive delinquencies, to which we will turn in a later section of this chapter. Many delinquent acts are perpetrated even when there is certainty of apprehension and punishment. This fact indicates an underlying need for being punished. Punishment is the surest and most widely accepted means for the expiation of wrongs with which the sense of guilt is connected, and aggressive acts are usually punishable. This set of relations explains why children will persist in bullying, teasing, destruction, and other aggressive reactions, knowing all the time that the eventual outcome will be some form of punishment. Whenever such behavior is ignored or condoned, aggression may reach the limits of violence, brutality, and sadistic fury.

The influence of guilt and the need for punishment on hostility and aggression has been brought out in many studies. Korner, for example, in her intensive study of hostility in young children, found that "guilt over hostility set in motion further hostile acts as a punishment-provoking device aiming at the alleviation of anxiety" (Korner, 1949, p. 136). The same idea is expressed by Sherman in another way (Sherman, 1941, p. 180):

> Aggressions toward others are at times, however, displacements of a tendency for self-aggression. In some cases the displacement of self-aggression to aggression toward others is a substitute for a sense of guilt, frequently resulting in an attitude of persecution. Instead of feeling guilty because of his own behavior, the person now blames others for his misfortunes. Some sociologists have maintained the theory that aggressions by one nation toward another may in some cases be primarily the result of a tendency for aggression toward the "in-group." The strength of a drive toward self-aggression is displaced by aggressive acts toward outsiders.

This fact is bolstered by careful studies of the motivations underlying aggressive delinquencies. According to Healy and Bronner (1952, p. 488), in a substantial number of cases the sense of guilt directly or indirectly activated the delinquency "through the individual's feeling of the need of punishment." As we have said, punishment helps to destroy the sense of guilt and the anxiety associated with it.

External Determinants of Aggression

From the examples of aggressive behavior cited, it becomes increasingly clear that aggression goes hand in hand with *lack of control*, control that should be exercised in the form of discipline by persons in authority or control that should be self-imposed. Aggression is an explosive, irrational form of behavior, determined by strong feelings and frustrations (Livson & Mussen, 1957). Like defense reactions, it is largely the expression of unconscious determinants, which leave little room for the functioning of self-discipline. But, as we know, self-discipline has its start in external discipline; therefore, aggression is often a reflection of the failure to apply proper and effective methods in the training of children. As Gardner says (1948, p. 78):

> The first controlling mechanism in respect to aggression is the external control exercised by parents and others about us. The control is acquiesced in by the young child because of his fear of loss of parental love. In short, his first "conscience" is the *person* who stands beyond him in the figure of the mother and father.

Discipline of the right kind is a means of gratifying needs, such as the need for affection and security, and thus may ward off the very frustrations that lead to aggression. At the same time, it provides the child with a tool for self-control that will obviate the need for punishment. It is an empirical fact that children accept discipline as long as it is administered in a sensible and wholesome manner.

The intelligent use of discipline and the development of self-control in the child are precluded to a large extent by such factors as *excessive love and overprotection*. It is impossible to maintain good disciplinary relations when the emotional attachment to the child creates a horror of using controls, and when the child is given the impression that he can have whatever he wants. In point of fact, indulgence, overprotection, and excessive love are themselves signs of lack of discipline in the person in authority. And lack of self-discipline is a poor basis for control over the child. More than that, overindulgence and overprotection may be taken by the child as indicators of rejection since they reflect insecurity or guilt on the part of the person in authority. Furthermore, rejection, which violates the need for affection and security, is often the starting point of aggressive behavior. In his various studies and reports on maternal overprotection, Levy has consistently emphasized its basic relation to aggression. He says, "The behavior of the indulged overprotected children was featured by disobedience, impudence, tantrums, excessive demands, and varying degrees of tyrannical behavior. The characteristics described were thought to represent *accelerated growth of the aggressive components* of the personality, and related directly to maternal indulgence" (Levy, 1943, p. 196. Italics supplied). In an earlier study, quoted by Moore, Levy listed the following effects of overprotection: disobedience, impudence, refusal, excessive independence, and rebellion against authority. The relation between these qualities and aggression requires little emphasis (Moore, 1944, p. 196; also Symonds, 1939, pp. 12, 13, 15).

The reference to overprotection, indulgence, and rejection raises other issues regarding the extent to which aggression is determined by *family situations and relationships.* We already know that any factor that alienates the child, such as favoritism, rejection, negative identification, and severe punishment or mistreatment, will act as a spur to inadequate adjustment. In such cases, aggression is a likely outcome because the frustration is external and because these factors arouse feelings of resentment, anger, and hatred, all of which are favorable to the development of aggressive tendencies. Numerous investigators have found that inharmonious homes, rejective homes, and the like, are consistently productive of aggressive responses. Radke (1946, p. 103) reports that aggressiveness is connected with inharmonious and rejective homes, and aggressive traits (such as quarrelsome, uncooperative, and noncompliant) with dominating and autocratic parents. Korner (1949, p. 151) indicates that the homes of one aggressive group of children were markedly inharmonious. Symonds (1939, pp. 15, 16, 18, 121, 143–147) cites studies by Zimmerman, Figge, and Knight, as well as his own findings, to show that aggression is consistently associated with rejecting and dominating parents. Steckle indicates that aggression may also result from too much favoritism on the part of parents (Steckle, 1949, p. 145). It would seem, as Korner suggests, that "a given very aggressive child could have almost any type of parent, rejecting, oversolicitous, ambivalent, or any other" (Korner, 1949, p. 152). One writer goes so far as to suggest that it is not because of any particular attitude or condition that children become aggressive but just because parents are parents. However this may be, the significant fact is that aggression finds root in many different types of family soil.

Among the various factors stimulating aggression, punishment and strict home discipline stand out prominently also. Watson, in a study cited by Maier (1949, p. 117), found a definite relation between strict home training, degree of frustration, and incidence of aggressive traits. In the group of subjects characterized by the most confining home situation, it was found that the incidence of aggressive response was much higher than for the subjects from a less confining situation. These relations are indicated in Table 10. Strict home training is but one step removed from severe discipline and punishment, both of which are known to be closely correlated with aggressive reactions. In studies of delinquents showing aggressive tendencies, it has been found repeatedly that harsh, punitive treatment foments rebellion and antisocial attitudes (Levin & Sears, 1956; Lesser, 1957).

TABLE 10

Differences in Aggressive Behavior in Persons Having Different Degrees of Childhood Frustration

| | HOME SITUATION | |
BEHAVIOR TRAITS	Group 1 (most frustrated) %	Group 4 (least frustrated) %
Rude answering to parents	76	29
Irritated by parents	98	72
Feeling that teachers are unfair	36	12
Carry grudges	55	26
Frequent quarreling with friends	93	71
Broken engagements	26	7
Average	64.0	36.2

Source: By permission from Maier, N. R. F. *Frustration: The study of behavior without a goal.* New York: McGraw-Hill, 1949, p. 117.

Other family situations conducive to the development of the frustration-aggression mechanism include sibling rivalries, jealousy, and father's presence or absence from the home. The relation between aggression and the last-named factor is illustrated in Figure 18. Evidently, for this group of 126 children, the *presence* of the father had a stimulating effect on aggressive reactions in many instances. It has also been found that the absence of the mother, owing to death, work, and so forth, is often correlated with strong delinquency trends, in which aggression is a major factor. Regarding other home factors, Healy and Bronner (1952, pp. 487–488), in a study of 152 delinquents, found that forty-six cases reported feeling rejected, deprived, and insecure; thirty-four cases indicated intense feelings of discomfort about family disharmonies, parental misconduct, and poor parental discipline; and 31 cases reported bitter feelings of jealousy

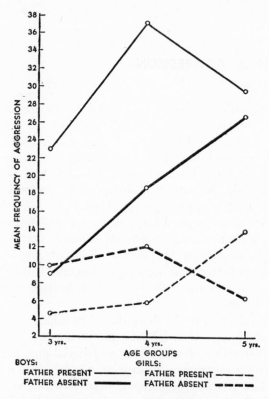

BOYS:
FATHER PRESENT ──────
FATHER ABSENT ━━━━━

GIRLS:
FATHER PRESENT ─ ─ ─ ─
FATHER ABSENT ━ ━ ━ ━

Fig. 18. Total aggression. Mean frequency of total aggression by each sex with father present or absent. (By permission from Sears, R. R., Pinter, M. H., & Sears, Pauline S. The father's influence on children's behavior patterns. In R. G. Kuhlen & G. G. Thompson (Eds.), *Psychological studies in human development*. New York: Appleton, 1952, p. 400.)

toward one or more siblings. Not all of these cases showed aggression, but aggressive behavior was one of the most common symptoms of the group.

The family situation is the most common determinant of aggression, but we must not overlook the fact that many other situations play a part in stimulating aggressive behavior (Sears, 1961). The frustrations of school life, negative teacher-pupil relations, restrictive or damaging work conditions, frustrations in marriage, in social experiences, and in vocational aspirations—all may serve as the spark to set off aggressive reactions. However, we should note that aggression is the distinguishing mark of an aggressive personality, and in the majority of instances the groundwork of this type of personality is laid in early childhood. Where family relations have been adequate and wholesome, later frustrations are not likely to produce aggression. Instead, there is variability of response, proper evaluation of problems and situations, and tolerance of frustration.

EVALUATION OF AGGRESSION

Earlier in this chapter we considered briefly the question of the normality and adjustive value of aggression, and we saw that for the most part it is disruptive and maladjustive. That some aggression is necessary to adjustment may be argued on the grounds that it is impossible to avoid all hostility, anger, and the kinds of frustration that lead to aggressive response. As one writer points out in discussing the prevention of neurosis, allowing some aggressive, even hostile, behavior is safer than trying to prevent all of it, the assumption being that the complete stifling of aggressive feelings is likely to damage emotional stability (Lott, 1951). There is some truth in this viewpoint; but, for the most part, intelligent control of aggression is much better than overt expression; and it is this control that children must learn in the early years when feelings of insecurity and hostility first take root.

To the evaluation made above should be added several other characteristics of aggression. It is laboring the obvious to say that neurotic aggression is destructive of wholesome social relations, but the point is worth emphasizing. Aggression is nearly always detrimental to friendship, comradeship, love relations, wholesome social activities, sympathy, family solidarity, and all other relations that make it possible for people to live together happily and harmoniously. It is also detrimental to the moral virtues of kindness, charity, altruism, self-restraint, patience, consideration, respect, and obedience. It is difficult for a healthy morality to flourish in an atmosphere of rebellion, hatred, violence, and similar characteristics associated with aggressive behavior. Finally, it should be noted that aggression is psychologically damaging. It is emotionally disrupting; it eats away at the roots of self-control; and it causes feelings of guilt, remorse, and antipathy. The most, therefore, that can be said for aggressive response is that it tends toward the reduction of tension and frustration but at a cost to wholesome adjustment that far exceeds its psychological value (Schneiders, 1963a).

It is because of these effects that we were careful, at the start of this discussion, to distinguish damaging aggression from useful and even productive aggressiveness. It is interesting to note that the latter quality represents drive, along with such correlates as ambition and energy; whereas aggression reflects frustrated need. This relation to frustration determines the character of aggression more than any other feature.

DELINQUENCY AS A MODE OF ADJUSTMENT

Nature and Forms of Delinquency

The relation between aggression and delinquency is very close because delinquency, of its nature, is a thrust against conditions that frustrate the needs and interests of individuals. We must not, of course, think of all delinquency as aggressive; there are some delinquent acts that fit better into the category of defense reactions, and others that remind us of withdrawal. Lying, for example, is defensive, and truancy is essentially a withdrawal or flight from reality. You can see, therefore, how well the concept and the problem of delinquency fit into this discussion of the different psychological mechanisms.

We can organize our thinking about this problem better if we consider first the different forms that delinquency assumes; by abstracting the common features of all delinquent acts we should be in a position to formulate a definition. The following forms of behavior are usually considered delinquent: lying, stealing, truancy, joy riding, drug addiction, arson, burglary, sex aggression, gangsterism, running away, and vandalism. It is not difficult to spot the essential features that run through and identify these delinquent activities. They are all socially or morally unacceptable and are clear-cut violations of rules, standards, or laws that have been established for the individual and the common good. *Delinquency, therefore, is essentially a thrust against society and may be described as any act or series of acts of an individual or a group that violates accepted social or moral standards and brings individuals into conflict with society.* Whenever such activities exhibit the characteristics of self-assertion, hostility, revenge, brutality, and the like, and most of them do in one degree or another, they assume the quality of aggression (Sherman, 1941, p. 181).

Delinquency as Adjustment

The difference and distance between the concepts of delinquency and adjustment probably make it difficult to perceive any identity between them. Yet, in the same way that defense and aggression are interpreted as (inadequate) efforts at adjustment, delinquent behavior may be regarded as an attempt to meet the demands of reality and to reduce the tensions, frustrations, and conflicts occasioned by these demands. Referring to the study on delinquents by Healy and Bronner, reported in their *Psychological studies in human development*, Kuhlen and Thompson remark (1952, pp. 480–481):

The results point to frustration, conflict, and emotional insecurity as the roots of delinquency, with the delinquency turning out to be a psychologically meaningful mode of adjustment, when in the individual case the whole picture is unveiled. This study, one of the most significant investigations of delinquency made so far, thus emphasizes personal psychological factors in the causation of delinquency.

Healy and Bronner themselves, in a summary statement on the meaningfulness of delinquency, describe its adjustive qualities (Healy & Bronner, 1952, p. 488).

We can, in summary, describe the types of reactions represented by delinquency as follows:

1. Attempt to avoid, even as a temporary measure, the unpleasant situation by *escape* or *flight* from it.
2. Attempt to achieve substitutive *compensatory satisfaction* through delinquent activities. . . .
3. Attempt to strengthen or *bolster up the ego* wounded by feelings of inadequacy or inferiority. The aim then is to obtain *recognition* and *status* with the delinquent crowd. . . .
4. Attempt to get certain ego-satisfactions through direct and conscious or even unconscious expression of *revenge attitudes* —perhaps through hidden desire to punish parents or others by conduct that will make life difficult for them.
5. Attempt to gain a *maximum of self-satisfaction,* to inflate the ego, by generally aggressive, antisocial attitudes, that is, by the exhibition of definite hostilities and antagonisms to authority.

This precise statement of the aims of delinquency serves several purposes. First of all, it brings into sharp relief the adjustive characteristics of delinquent behavior since the aims here are no different from those of any other adjustive reaction. The bolstering of the ego, gaining of satisfaction, and so forth, are so many means of reducing tension and frustration and re-establishing feelings of security and status. Second, the statement substantiates the view expressed earlier that delinquency may be aggressive, defensive, or withdrawing, depending on the character of the delinquent response. Third, it points up the importance of basic needs, such as the need for security, status, and recognition, in the development of delinquent behaviors (Cattell & Scheier, 1961, p. 9; Jenkins, 1957). And fourth, it emphasizes the important role of feelings, such as inadequacy and inferiority, in the determination of delinquency. These relationships have appeared many times in our analyses of the causes of maladjustive behavior.

CAUSES AND CONDITIONS OF DELINQUENCY

Psychological Factors

What causes delinquency? In general, we may say that the same causes and conditions that stimulate aggression furnish the psychological background for delinquency. This is to be expected because of the close relation between the two kinds of adjustment. From the examples used, it is apparent that many acts of aggression violate social and moral standards just as surely as do the various forms of delinquency; similarly, delinquency damages the moral, social, and psychological well-being of the organism to the same degree that aggression does. These similarities suggest a common basis for both, even though they are expressed in different ways (Glueck & Glueck, 1959; Herzog, 1960).

The emphasis on psychological causation, which has gained ground in recent years, is thoroughly justified by the facts (Cameron & Magaret, 1951, pp. 210–213; Sherman, 1941, pp. 312–317; Neumeyer, 1949, pp. 79–83; Reckless, 1943, pp. 16–20; Furstenheim, 1954). Delinquency results from the frustration of basic needs, particularly the need for status and the need for security, and from the conflicts that arise in certain environmental settings. Numerous empirical studies of delinquents show that inferiority, insecurity, lack of status, loss of affection, failure to win achievement or recognition, and the loss of a sense of belonging constitute the essential psychological bases of delinquent behavior. On the basis of their careful study, Healy and Bronner list the following factors as causes: (1) deep feeling of being rejected, deprived, insecure, not being understood, and unloved; (2) feeling of being thwarted in desires for self-expression and emancipation; (3) real or imagined inferiorities or inadequacies in relation to home life, school, sports, and so forth; (4) intense feelings of discomfort about family disharmonies, conditions of family life, and parental errors in management and discipline; (5) bitter feelings of jealousy toward siblings and feelings of discrimination; (6) deep-seated mental conflicts; and (7) conscious or unconscious sense of guilt and a feeling of the need for punishment (Healy & Bronner, 1952, pp. 487–488; also Durea, 1937a, 1937b, 1939). Since all these causes are psychological, we can say that delinquent behavior represents a desperate effort to mitigate the tension and frustration that these feelings bring about, and to develop a more effective relationship (for the individual himself) with the environment.

TABLE 11

Contrasts between 105 Delinquents and 105 Nondelinquent Controls from the Same Families with Respect to Personality and Emotional Characteristics, Mental Capacity and School Performance, and Sociality and Interests

Characteristic	Delin-quents	Con-trols
Personality and Emotional Characteristics and Deviations		
Diagnosed personality deviation (neurosis, mild or early psychosis, etc.)	25	2
Individuals Showing Such Nervous Habits as Food or Sleep Idiosyncrasies, Nail Biting, etc.	44	24
Enuresis after 8 years	22	4
Hyperactivity, overrestlessness, etc.	46	0
Control notably quiet, placid, subdued, etc.		41
Distinctly submissive tendencies	2	15
Marked feelings of inferiority	38	4
Mental Capacity and School Performance		
IQ 90 or above	69	78
Poor scholarship record	34	18
Strong dislike for school in general	40	4
Repeated, excessive truancy	60	0
Sociality and Interests		
Great urge for crowd membership	31	11
Prior club connection	47	28
Marked interest or activity in sports	73	37
Excessive movie attendance	33	10

Source: By permission from Healy, W., & Bronner, A. F. Delinquency as a mode of adjustment. In R. G. Kuhlen & G. G. Thompson (Eds.) *Psychological studies of human development.* New York: Appleton, 1952. P. 483.

Personality Factors

An important part of the question regarding the determinants of delinquency has to do with the role of personality in the development of delinquent behavior. Is there a delinquent personality that predisposes the individual to such conduct? If not, is there a pattern of distinguishing characteristics that functions in this way? One can see that we are converging here on the broad problem of predisposing causes or conditions of abnormal behavior. In many instances of abnormality or maladjustment it has been found that psychological make-up acts as a predisposing cause, which means simply that the personality is slanted or biased toward the development of some disorder (Trese, 1962; Siegman, 1962).

A number of studies indicate the existence in delinquents of a pattern of personality characteristics that set them off as a group from normal persons. In the study of Healy and Bronner cited earlier it was found that personality differences were prominent. Their findings are indicated in Table 11. Commenting on the results, the authors say (Healy & Bronner, 1952, p. 483):

> The role that personality deviations play in the genesis of delinquent behavior stands out most strongly. When a young individual, abnormal according to any of the above classifications and hence lacking in normal inhibitory powers, encounters the stressful conditions and thwartings that most of our delinquents had to meet through family life, companionship, or school failure and develop from any source ideas of delinquency evidently delinquent conduct is almost bound to ensue.

Emotional characteristics deserve special emphasis, particularly emotional immaturity (Peterson, Quay, & Cameron, 1959). To this observation should be linked emphasis on the attitudes of delinquents toward school and their obvious interest in group membership and activities, factors that also play a part in generating delinquent behavior. All these facts, which are supported by the results of many other studies, indicate that personality plays a decisive role in the peculiar adjustments of delinquent individuals (Durea, 1937a; Bromberg, 1947; Lansky, *et al.*, 1961; Dahlke, 1952).

Environmental Determinants

The tensions, conflicts, and frustrations that touch off delinquent behavior have their source also in environmental conditions. In other words, while psychological and personality factors are the *primary* and *immediate* determinants of such adjustments, home and family background, community influences, and so on, may be regarded as the *remote* determinants (Peterson, Quay, & Cameron, 1955). These remote determinants create frustrations and conflicts, and foster the development of inadequate personality characteristics. In much the same way, therefore, as the frustration-aggression mechanism is determined by external factors, delinquency also results from external conditions. Prominent among these determinants are the home and family, which often fail to provide the ego security, the need gratification, and the sense of achievement and personal worth that are necessary to effective adjustment and mental health.

As we noted earlier in discussing the psychological determinants of delinquency, parental rejection and the failure of parents to understand and accept the child contribute to delinquent response. The perfectionistic parent who creates feelings of inadequacy and inferiority in the child, and the neurotic parent who causes family dissensions also foster poor adjustment; there is, of course, the hating, punitive parent who alienates the child by his harsh attitudes and behavior. In all such situations the child feels isolated and unwanted and may turn to the security afforded by gang membership and to the achievements of delinquent behavior. Here he secures some measure of recognition, status, and approval. In a recent study of 500 delinquents carefully matched with nondelinquents in IQ, ethnic derivation, age, and residence area, it was found that family background and home climate of the delinquent group were markedly inferior (Glueck, 1953; also Cass, 1952; Jenkins, 1943, pp. 144–147; Sullenger, 1934).

Other factors in the environment also tend to disrupt ego security and to frustrate children in such a way that delinquency results. It is well known that the broken home is a prolific source of delinquent youngsters as are those communities in which the social, moral, and religious atmosphere is poor. Similarly, unstable neighborhoods, characterized by a shifting population and by shifting values, ideals, and traditions, foster delinquency. This is not the place to go into all the factors related to the growth of delinquency, but the few examples we have used will give us an idea regarding the possibilities. In general, we may say that any external factor that causes serious frustration and mental conflict, and that leads to a great deal of insecurity, lack of status, failure, and ego damage can contribute to delinquency. The form that the behavior takes will depend on circumstances, on the nature and depth of the frustration, on availability of courses of action, and similar factors that constitute the setting in which the frustration occurs (Sellin, 1938).

It is apparent that delinquency, like aggression, is socially, morally, and psychologically inadequate as a mode of adjustment (McCann, 1957). Yet there are circumstances in which it would have to be regarded as the more desirable of several alternative courses of action. As we have seen, it serves certain aims of adjustment, including the reduction of the tension of frustration, the gaining of satisfaction, the development of ego strength, and so on, which might occur as the alternative to severe personality disturbances. This idea is expressed by Healy and Bronner in their evaluation of delinquency. "Under certain circumstances it may be healthier and more normal to join in with the activities and imbibe the ideas of a delinquent crowd than to be a withdrawing, soft, effeminate 'mother's boy' or, as in instances already mentioned, to mope at home and develop an abnormal fantasy life" (Healy & Bronner, 1952, p. 489). Admittedly, the alternatives here are bad; yet there are many situations in which a person may be forced to choose the lesser of two evils.

QUESTIONS AND PROJECTS FOR FURTHER STUDY

1. Explain the difference between aggressive and defensive reactions. Are they ever motivated by similar factors? Do they ever serve the same adjustive purposes?
2. Are delinquency and aggression related to needs and to frustration in the same way? Explain any differences that might exist.
3. Write a short review of Dollard's book, *Frustration and aggression*. In your report critically evaluate the frustration-aggression theory.
4. What is meant by the statement that aggression, although adjustive in nature, does not always contribute to the solution of problems?
5. Name and describe in your own words five forms of aggression.
6. Write a short essay on internal and external determinants of aggression, with particular emphasis on the role of parent-child relations.
7. Explain what is meant by the "need for punishment." Is there any relation between this need and delinquency?
8. Write a critical comparison of any two standard books, or five journal articles, on the causes of delinquency. Comment on the relation between personality and delinquency.

SELECTED COLLATERAL READINGS

ATKIN, E. L. *Aggressiveness in children*. New York: Child Study Association, 1950.

BANDURA, A., & WALTERS, R. H. *Adolescent aggression*. New York: Ronald, 1959.

BERKOWITZ, L. *Aggression: A social psychological analysis*. New York: McGraw-Hill, 1962.

BETTELHEIM, B., & JANOWITZ, M. *Dynamics of prejudice*. New York: Harper & Row, 1950.

BUSS, A. H. *The psychology of aggression*. New York: Wiley, 1961.

DOLLARD, J., *et al*. *Frustration and aggression*. New Haven: Yale University Press, 1939.

KORNER, A. F. *Some aspects of hostility in young children*. New York: Grune & Stratton, 1949.

NEUMEYER, M. H. *Juvenile delinquency in modern society*. Princeton, N.J.: Van Nostrand, 1949.

RADKE, M. J.   *The relation of parental authority to children's behavior and attitudes.* Minneapolis: University of Minnesota Press, 1946.

RECKLESS, W. C.   *The etiology of delinquent and criminal behavior.* Bull. No. 50, New York: Soc. Sci. Res. Coun., 1943.

REDL, F., & WINEMAN, D.   *Children who hate.* New York: Free Press, 1951.

REDL, F., & WINEMAN, D.   *The aggressive child.* New York: Free Press, 1957.

SHERMAN, M.   *Basic problems of behavior.* New York: McKay, 1941.

WORCHEL, P.   Hostility: theory and experimental investigation. In D. Willner (Ed.). *Decisions, values, and groups.* New York: Pergamon Press, 1960, I, pp. 254–266.

10

Adjustment by Withdrawal—
The Flight from Reality

There are many ways to cope with the demands of self or of reality. We can meet them head on in a logical, intelligent, straightforward manner; we can erect defensive barriers against them; we can fight our way through and in that way destroy conflicts and frustrations; or we can run scared. There are a lot of people who just run away from the demands or threats of reality. They use what are called escape or withdrawal mechanisms in place of defensive or aggressive responses. When things get too difficult they daydream themselves into a world of fantasy, sleep reality away, drink themselves into a stupor, or even destroy themselves. These self-destructive behaviors are also part of the adjustment process; and we will now study them in some detail.

GENERAL CHARACTER OF ESCAPE MECHANISMS

Escape versus Defense Mechanisms

Just as aggression is sometimes identified as a defense mechanism, so it is not uncommon to find similarities drawn between escape and defense mechanisms. The reason for this is that escape often bears the mark of defense, and conversely, defense reactions are at times escapist. This fact serves to remind us that all these mechanisms are *basically alike;* that is, they represent individual efforts to solve problems, reduce tensions, conflicts, and frustrations, and meet the demands of self and reality. They are, as we have noted several times, different ways of adjusting. In any particular instance, the form assumed for effecting adjustment is determined by many things: personality traits, availability of responses, successful experience with different responses and the circumstances surrounding the adjustive situation. The interested reader will find many discussions in the literature on the essential connection between different patterns of adjustment (Sherman, 1941, pp. 182–184). Speaking of negativism, this writer says it "functions at times as an aggressive form of behavior and at other times as a withdrawal type of adjustment." Again, "Negativism as withdrawal is considered to be a defense reaction, that is,

285

a defense against those whom the individual believes are forcing him to adjust to situations which he fears" (pp. 183, 184). Other investigators relate withdrawal to both aggression and to invalidism, or what we have called the flight into illness (Cameron & Magaret, 1951, pp. 230–245). These writers define invalidism as a withdrawal reaction. The student will find an interesting parallel between this interpretation and the discussion of flight into illness in the next chapter. Along the same lines, the discussion of mental illness as a flight from reality in Vaughan (1952, pp. 66–68) would provide still another useful comparison.

It is apparent, of course, that defense reactions are developed in reference to the self, whereas escape mechanisms are reactions against reality. Hence we designated the former as a flight from self and the latter a flight from reality. *Escape or withdrawal, therefore, is essentially a means of defense against the demands, stresses, or threats of the world in which the individual lives.* In a typical instance, the young schoolboy, frustrated in school achievements or completely bored by the educational process, turns to daydreaming as an escape from the tedium of his existence. He withdraws from the world of reality and seeks ego gratifications in a world of dreams. He imagines himself in a world that is full of all the good things his humdrum existence denies him—achievement, renown, wealth, strength, prowess, and, above all, thrilling, satisfying experiences. Just as the mechanism of compensation covers up the inadequacies or weaknesses of the ego, escape rescues it from the despair of complete frustration. Similarly, the housewife, caught up in the deadening routine and drudgery of her daily life, turns longingly to the lusty novel, the soap opera, or the blissful oblivion of the afternoon nap as a means of escape.

The simple examples given above raise the question whether there is a distinction between escape and withdrawal reactions. It is probably unwise to force too sharp a distinction on these terms since both reactions are determined by one's attitude toward reality. However, escape is more typically related to the *frustrations* that reality imposes, whereas withdrawal is generated by the *threats* of reality. Escape reflects the feelings of boredom, discouragement, or despair; withdrawal indicates anxiety, fear, or terror. Thus the young schoolboy mentioned above seeks to escape from the boredom or discouragement of daily affairs, as does the housewife, whereas the alcoholic or drug addict withdraws from a reality that causes fear or anxiety. Both reactions, as one can see, are efforts to offset the internal difficulties that stem from the individual's inadequate relation to reality, by the flight into some mode of response and away from reality. But the different motivational backgrounds stimulate adjustive responses that are distinguishable. Escape into literature is different from withdrawal into fantasy.

Zone of Defense against Reality

It should be understood at the outset that between the individual and reality there is always some conflict. This situation exists because reality —the environment of people, events, experiences, and relations within which we live—comprises endless demands, strictures, laws, standards, obligations, customs, and the like that impinge on the individual's freedom, and force him to make some kind of an adjustment. The more complicated the social order becomes and the more that social and moral values shift in a constantly changing society like ours, the more difficult it is to make a good adjustment. These characteristics of reality are threatening to many persons.

This situation, moreover, is complicated to an important extent by conflict within the social and cultural order. Society imposes its own demands and regulations; the church enforces another set; the home and family still another. At times these standards correspond; at other times, they are fundamentally opposed, and the cultural conflict often victimizes the individual caught between opposing values. The devout Catholic rejects the practices of divorce and contraception, although living in a society that accepts both. Similarly, the southerner is caught between the principle of democratic equality and the idea of white supremacy. To complicate the situation still further, social and moral ideas, ideals, and values are constantly changing, so that the reality of yesterday, which seemed to provide a secure anchor for one's ideas and conduct, today assumes a new aspect that is strange and baffling. This sort of thing is bound to happen in a complex civilization that lacks the unifying quality of a single race, nationality, or faith; as a result, behavior disorders have been rapidly increasing.

Because of the complex and demanding character of reality, everyone builds around himself a zone of defense, which serves to protect him from the pressures and encroachments of reality. This defense perimeter includes personal and social ideas, beliefs, attitudes, ideals, traditions, and practices that serve as a buffer against the forces in reality that threaten ego security (Figure 19). In many instances, this zone of defense is securely structured. Whenever difficulties, conflicts, or frustrations arise, the integrity and security of the individual are maintained and the sense of defeat and acute anxiety held off by the strength of the defense perimeter. In other instances, the zone of defense is weakly structured and permeable, and the pressures of reality force a retreat or withdrawal, a situation that is most likely to happen when events in reality are severely threatening.

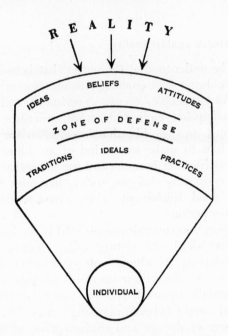

Fig. 19.   The zone of defense against reality.

Normal Withdrawal

To what extent is withdrawal normal? Or is it always pathological and symptomatic of personality disintegration? To answer these questions we must fall back on the criteria of normality and adjustment outlined in Chapter 2. We recall that among these criteria were adequate orientation to reality, and adequate contact with reality; thus we are forced to conclude that withdrawal or escape from reality is not in itself a normal reaction. These criteria, however, outline the *ideal* adjustment process and are never fully realized in all situations by even relatively normal persons. As we have noted repeatedly, it is impossible to avoid all frustrations, stresses, and conflicts, nor is it always possible to resolve problems and difficulties and meet the demands of reality in a perfectly satisfying and highly integrated way. The weaknesses and foibles of human nature preclude perfect adjustment. There are times, therefore, when escape or withdrawal gives the organism a chance to regroup its forces in order better to withstand the encroachments of reality. Temporary flight from reality by means of books, movies, and other entertainment is much more desirable than being engulfed or destroyed by it. We have seen that the same interpretation can be applied to certain defense reactions.

Withdrawal, as an adjustive technique, is by no means necessarily pathological, or even undesirable. On the contrary, innumerable situations arise in everyday life for which withdrawal is both the simplest and the most appropriate reaction. Such is the case, for example, when a person is faced with overwhelming odds, and when to retire from the immediate scene of the struggle seems to hold the promise of a more successful defense elsewhere, or at another time. The same can be said of situations which . . . appear almost certain to lead toward greater complexity, increased tension and ultimate failure. To withdraw, under these circumstances, is to escape the consequences of eventual defeat.

As compared with aggressive attack, withdrawal has some unquestionable advantages. It does not usually arouse hostile opposition, alienate sympathy, or invite retaliation. It protects the individual from fruitless expenditures of time and effort under conditions of unconquerable adversity and irresistible restraint. It shields him from humiliating defeat and personal injury, and if adroitly managed, it guards him from threats of damage to his social status (Cameron & Magaret, 1951, p. 230; also Tyson, 1951, p. 37).

Pathological Withdrawal

The pathology of escape and withdrawal is determined by a number of factors including (1) the extent to which such reactions become necessary and habitual, (2) the amount of ego gratification derived from them, (3) their relative permanence, (4) the nature of the response used as a means of escape, and (5) the extent to which reactions of escape and withdrawal are utilized as a substitute for reality. Evidently, the more habitual, satisfying, and permanent such reactions become, and the more they are exploited as a substitute for reality, the higher the degree of pathology. Excessive movie going, for example, is known to correlate with other indexes of maladjustment. Similarly, excessive daydreaming, alcoholism, and the fantasy thinking of schizophrenia are all instances of abnormal, pathological flights from reality. Extreme escape and withdrawal are distinctly abnormal responses that signify a complete breakdown of the zone of defense and a pathological substitution of the unrealities of a dreamworld for a world of reality to which one must adjust if normality is to be maintained (Vaughan, 1952, Chapter II).

Characteristics of Withdrawal

The person in whom escape and withdrawal mechanisms develop exhibits certain characteristics that betray the existence of such tendencies. First of all, there is noticeable a quality of *seclusiveness*, exhibited in lack of sociability and participation, and a positive effort to avoid the company of others. Some persons actually withdraw from society and social relations of all kinds. The withdrawing person is easily disturbed or frightened by social contacts and responsibilities. Secondly, therefore, one can observe qualities of *timidity, shyness,* and *overt anxiety.* Buffeted by a reality he cannot adequately cope with, he becomes hesitant and fearful. He is easily stirred to anxiety by the harsh, relentless demands of daily living, by the easy success of others in his group, and by the frightening necessity of making decisions, resolving conflicts and difficulties, and accepting the overwhelming responsibilities of adult living. Especially disturbed by the demands of social adjustment, of meeting and getting along with people, of establishing social relations, and assuming an active role in society, he becomes shy and reticent, preferring the safety of his own company to the uncertainties of social experience.

This shyness, timidity, and seclusiveness lay the groundwork for the emergence of other characteristics, notably *daydreaming, listlessness, apathy,* and *absent-mindedness.* In other words, the withdrawing person tends to exhibit characteristics that serve to shut out reality. Instead of taking an active, vigorous part in the affairs of life, meeting demands, and resolving conflicts and problems by a determined attack, he tends toward solitary occupations and activities and sometimes seeks the escape provided by inaction and the substitution of fantasy for reality. One can see that it would be difficult for a traveling salesman or business executive to be seclusive, shy, or timid, whereas research or writing might be just the thing for the seclusive, withdrawn personality.

PSYCHOLOGICAL BACKGROUND AND DETERMINANTS OF WITHDRAWAL

Personality Characteristics

The foregoing summary of the characteristics of withdrawal leads directly into the question of the kind of personality associated with such behavior. In fact, the characteristics described are themselves a part of the personality picture. But there are other features that bear mentioning. Typically, the withdrawn person is strongly *introverted, extremely sensitive, asocial,* and *autistic.* His basic attitudes and orientation are directed toward self. His thinking and feelings, therefore, are self-centered (autistic); he has a marked tendency toward preoccupation with ideas and with personal experiences and toward reflection, self-analysis, and chronic introspection. He is extremely sensitive, and tends to avoid or actively reject social relations. Part of this is due to the fact that his ego is weakly structured, so that the impositions and threats of reality create considerable anxiety.

All these things taken together, then, favor escape or withdrawal, and a substitution of fantasy thinking for reality thinking.

It is instructive to compare this type of personality with the defensive and aggressive types. The person who utilizes defense reactions is also unrealistic, self-centered, timid, and anxious, but his difficulty lies within himself rather than in his relation to reality. He therefore seeks to remedy the difficulty by the development of reactions that will obscure or make up for the deficiency. The aggressive person also has difficulties with reality since his frustrations come chiefly from external sources, but instead of withdrawing from reality he sets out to modify it by attacking what he thinks is frustrating him.

Immediate Determinants

Frustration and Conflict.   Withdrawal gives evidence of deep-seated frustration and, in many instances, great mental conflict, both of which serve to touch off the flight from reality. Withdrawal reactions are typified by the attitude, "I just can't face it any more" and often reflect the kind and degree of frustration or conflict that initiates them. For example, when frustration is relatively mild and temporary, the reaction may be nothing more than a brief escape into literature, sleep, movies, or social entertainment. In contrast, a damaging moral conflict in adolescence may lead to running away from home or even to suicide. Always, however, there is the basic inability to face reality.

Fear of Reality and Sense of Oppression.   But there is more to escape and withdrawal than frustration or conflict. Superimposed on these basic conditions are an intense fear of reality and a deep sense of oppression caused by the breakdown of the defense perimeter. Here we have a deeper reason for the inability to face reality. The alcoholic and the suicide, for example, are not bothered so much by their frustrations and conflicts, bad as they may be, as they are *by the fear of being overwhelmed* by the stresses of life. Their defenses shattered by the onslaughts of reality, they feel that there is no alternative to running pell-mell away from it. They are like the hunter who has used his last shell on the beast coming toward him; all he can think of is taking to his heels and running (Funkenstein, King, & Drolette, 1957; Selye, 1956).

Here again the distinction between escape and withdrawal can be used to advantage. Ordinarily, frustration and conflict will lead to mechanisms of escape, whereas fear of reality and the sense of oppression are more clearly reflected in headlong flight from reality, or withdrawal. The lowly clerk who is frustrated by the drudgery and boredom of daily existence seeks escape in some activity or relation that will reduce the sense of frustration. But the businessman who is overwhelmed by his responsibilities, worries, or losses dives headlong into alcoholism or self-destruction. In all instances of escape or withdrawal, mental conflict may play a decisive role. A teacher may not only be frustrated; she may also be torn between the ideal she has set up for herself and her actual accomplishments. Similarly, the adolescent boy may be seriously frustrated in striving toward a moral goal while he is also caught in a conflict between moral ideals and conduct. In cases like these, the conflict enhances the sense of frustration and pushes the individual farther along the road of withdrawal.

Emotional Impoverishment. Finally, emotional impoverishment or debilitation can bring about escape and withdrawal reactions. Emotional impoverishment is reflected in escapist reactions to boredom, discouragement, lack of adequate love relations, and the like. The person who fails to derive adequate satisfaction from his work, the wife whose marriage has turned out unhappily, the student who fails chronically in his efforts to achieve, the ugly duckling who cannot stimulate the interest of other persons—all become emotionally starved and seek through vicarious experiences some of the emotional gratifications they crave. It is clear, of course, that this emotional impoverishment is the outcome of frustration and that therefore the two factors work together to stimulate and encourage escape reactions. At other times, because of circumstances or the nature of the frustration, emotional flatness or apathy results, an attitude of "what's the use of trying? I can't succeed." By not trying, *failure is avoided*, and the tendency to escape into inactivity and daydreaming may therefore become securely established.

Where there is deep-seated conflict or a sense of oppression, emotional debilitation or panic is likely to occur, and the end reaction takes the form of withdrawal rather than mere escape. The following case illustrates this point.

> Helen, a graduate student in psychology, came to the psychologist voluntarily with the complaint that she had "blacked out" for a period of twenty-four hours after attending Sunday Mass. Theater ticket stubs found in her pocket accounted for part of her activities, but the rest of the time was blank. She reported an intense desire to "get away from it all," although she said she had no place to go.
>
> Helen is an attractive girl of twenty-two, who had graduated with honors the year before. She was doing well in her studies, and was considered to have a promising career. However, for the six months prior to the amnesic episode, she had been quarreling violently with her father, whom she had previously idolized, was having some difficulty with her mother, and wanted to leave home. Although attractive, she had no

male friends and few female acquaintances, and felt she was doomed to spinsterhood because of her intellectual gifts. More than anything, she wanted to get married and have children. She felt greatly oppressed by her present way of life, friendless, alone, not liked by others, and emotionally starved. Her strongest impulse was to get away and start a new life.

One can see in this unhappy girl's life the tremendous impact of a private world that to her seemed hostile, friendless, and oppressive. The amnesic episode was symbolic of her desire to withdraw completely from reality, to literally forget her unwelcome past and her present existence. Her future, too, seemed totally uninviting, and thus thoughts of self-destruction crossed her mind. In all respects, her life was dull, oppressive, and emotionally intolerable, and complete withdrawal seemed the only possible solution.

Temperamental Factors

The case of Helen illustrates the part that temperamental factors play in escape and withdrawal. As we have noted, withdrawing persons are extremely sensitive, particularly to the attitudes, conduct, and remarks of other people. They are easily hurt, and chronically, almost pathologically, disposed to interpret the behavior of others as being abusive, rejecting, or hostile. If they should also have a strong feeling of inferiority or inadequacy or a keen sense of failure, as often happens, it is very difficult for them to believe that they are accepted or loved by friends and relatives. They may even develop delusions of worthlessness, reference, or persecution.

Part of this sensitivity is traceable to early conditioning in which fear and anxiety played dominant roles. Children are easily conditioned to fear responses by timid and anxious parents who themselves regard the world and reality as threatening, hostile, and dangerous. The child of anxious parents learns to react with fear to many aspects of reality that are not inherently fearful. Thus there is established a generalized phobia toward reality that induces a great deal of timidity, shyness, anxiety, and sensitivity. For these persons life is filled with constant danger, threats, and aggressions against their security. Hence it is understandable that they should seek the relative safety of an unreal world devoid of all these frightening aspects.

The same emotional disposition can result from traumatic experiences. One can imagine the emotional impact on a child of his parents' desertion, the loss of the two people who make up the most important and secure aspect of his world, or the impact of witnessing the violent death of one of the parents, or the impact of a brutal attack by an older person. Experiences like these have a damaging effect on ego security and leave the child afraid, timid, and overanxious in a world that seems harsh and cruel. Ego security is a fragile flower in the early, formative years of development, and it is easily destroyed by the unkind, thoughtless treatment accorded some children. To be laughed at, scorned, ridiculed, mistreated, or deserted by older persons often leaves a scar that is never completely obliterated.

Parent-Child Relations

Overprotection. Poor emotional development often stems from inadequate relations between parents and children. One of these is over-protection of the child, so often observed in parents who are themselves timid, fearful, and overanxious. Learning to adjust to reality, to meet demands, difficulties, and stresses in a forthright and courageous manner requires experience. We can never learn to solve problems except by working with them. Overprotected children are not given this opportunity. Their weaknesses are sheltered (and thus allowed to grow) by the protective wall that parents build around them. They develop the impression that the world of reality is all beauty and softness and comfort. Then, struck by the impact of harsh, unpleasant events, they recoil in fear and try to shut out the reality that is so painful and frightening. Children, in other words, must learn to become realistic and to accept and work with the world as it actually is rather than as they would like it to be.

Rejection and Abusiveness. Timidity, fear, and withdrawal reactions may be prompted also by rejection and abusiveness. Some children react to parental abuse with aggression, as we have already noted. Others, however, are frightened and cowed by such treatment and are thus emotionally conditioned to respond to the exigencies of daily life with timidity and fear. They remind us of the little dog that, beaten and mistreated, slinks away whenever anyone approaches him. In cases involving reaction to abusive treatment, there is a tendency to generalize the attitude of fear toward persons and situations until it becomes habitual. The child abused by punitive or sadistic parents will react with fear and timidity to any person in authority and tend to withdraw from situations involving authority. Since there are persons of authority in almost every kind of situation, the abused child may withdraw almost completely.

Severe Discipline. Similarly, severe discipline can create timidity, especially when it is directed against the efforts of the child to adjust to his environment. For example, if a child has developed egocentric tendencies as a protection against inferiority, and discipline is directed against the egocentric behavior, withdrawal is likely to result. In the same way, severe disciplinary treatment of other defense reactions can lead to withdrawal. Parental discipline must be handled with a great deal of skill and wisdom if fear, timidity, and similar reactions are to be avoided. In his intensive study of parent-child relations, Symonds found clear-cut relations between parental attitudes and treatment, on the one hand, and withdrawal tendencies of children on the other. Overprotective, rejecting, and dominant parents stimulated withdrawal reactions in some of the children in this study (Symonds, 1939, pp. 18, 139, 143, 146).

Persistent Frustration and the Habit of Withdrawing

All of the causes and conditions so far described contribute in some measure to the sense of frustration, which we identified as one of the immediate determinants of withdrawal reactions. Thus, when such conditions are chronic and persistent, as often happens, for example, in the case of parental discipline, the frustration itself is persistent, and the tendency to withdraw becomes habitual. Here again the attitude of "what's the use of trying" is clearly exhibited. It is a common human tendency to fall back on habitual ways of behaving in crucial situations, since it requires a great deal less effort than working out new solutions. Particularly is this likely to happen when the habitual reaction is satisfying or contributes to the feeling of security and other ego gratifications. For the timid, anxious person, withdrawal is often this kind of response.

Personal Limitations and Failure

Besides such factors as timidity and sensitivity, there are other personal characteristics that contribute to withdrawal behavior, especially in so far as they cause reality to assume frightening and oppressive proportions. There are, for example, traits such as physical weakness and smallness and lack of skill and ability, which can make it extremely difficult to cope adequately and successfully with demands, problems, and difficulties that arise. The soldier in battle who lacks necessary equipment is forced to withdraw, and for much the same reason the person poorly equipped to handle the problems of daily living will often withdraw. The exigencies of life can be appalling to one who is not fitted to meet them. Many persons quail before the responsibilities of holding a job, of marrying, of making important decisions, of having children, of undergoing a major operation, and so on. Many bachelors and spinsters are testimony to this fact, and there are just as many married persons who shrink noticeably from the responsibilities of raising a family. This, unquestionably, is part of the explanation of postpartum psychosis; the new mother feels that she cannot cope with the responsibilities of motherhood. It is also part of the reason why people suddenly quit their jobs, refuse to look for work, drop out of school, desert their families, or abandon a career. They lack, or think they lack, the abilities and skills necessary to meet the demands of a reality situation.

For much the same reason, failure encourages withdrawal tendencies. To many persons, failure is convincing proof of lack of ability, especially when it is chronic and occurs against an emotional background of fear, anxiety, and timidity. Typically, the withdrawn person who has once failed refuses to try because by refusing he can most successfully avoid failure. With his inadequate perspective, and terrified by the prospect of failing again, the unreal world of fantasy, alcoholic stupor, or functional narcolepsy, which he substitutes for reality, is far more desirable. Here he can escape the pain of frustration and the awful conviction that he is wholly inadequate or worthless. Success is an important ingredient in the formula for wholesome adjustment and happiness in living; without it there is a strong tendency to withdraw from a reality that is always competitive and requires so arduous a struggle.

> Withdrawal behavior is usually considered to be the result of a type of frustration which does not involve the individual in aggressive retaliation. It also occurs when the individual evaluates his desires and the obstacles to their fulfillment in terms of some personal defect or inadequacy. It is essentially a form of adjustment as the result of a fear of involvement in a situation from which the person anticipates undesirable consequences. The child who believes, for one reason or another, that he is physically inadequate and inferior to his playmates is likely to withdraw from normal play activities as a way of avoiding failure or criticism. The adult who has failed, say, in attempting to make wide social contacts, may interpret his failure by a belief that he has some basic inadequacy. As a result, he may withdraw and occupy himself with personal and sedentary interests. This mechanism has been considered the basis for the development of hobbies which enable a person to be continually occupied without the necessity of sharing his interests with other people (Sherman, 1941, pp. 181–182).

FORMS OF ESCAPE AND WITHDRAWAL

Vicarious Experience

As we noted earlier, not all escape and withdrawal mechanisms are pathological, even though they may not be the most desirable ways of meeting a problem. There are, for example, many activities that utilize *vicarious experience* as a means of escape. Leisure reading, movies, television, sports, and other amusements are means by which reality can be temporarily shut out and the frustrations, conflicts, and oppressions of daily living greatly reduced. Because these aspects of life cannot be entirely avoided, it can be argued that these mechanisms of escape are not only helpful but necessary to the maintenance of mental and emotional stability. Every person is subject to emotional strain, annoying frustrations, anxieties, oppressive doubts, or weighty responsibilities from which he feels the need to escape, at least for a brief period. Respite provides an opportunity for regrouping one's emotional forces so that the issues of daily living can be faced with renewed confidence, free of accumulated tensions. Moreover, escapist activities bring into play ideas, feelings, activities, and attitudes that are often stifled in ordinary reality situations, and this too helps in the reduction of tension. We need hardly point out, however,

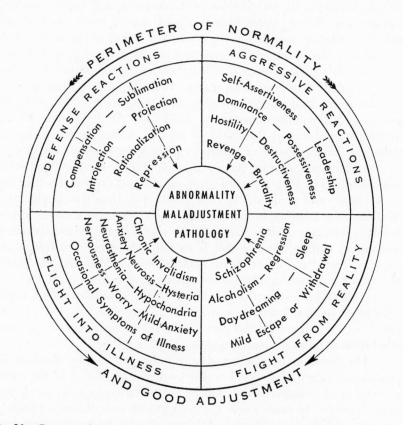

Fig. 20. Patterns of adjustment in relation to normality, abnormality, and pathology. The more that behavior deviates from the perimeter of normality, the closer it comes to pathology.

that the use of vicarious experience for escape purposes can be detrimental as well as helpful. If such experiences are utilized as a substitute for reality, if they are resorted to frequently at the expense of obligation or responsibility, and if they become the primary source of ego gratification, then they are detrimental to wholesome adjustment. As in the case of defense reactions, escape mechanisms must be carefully evaluated in terms of selected criteria before their adjustive significance can be known (see Figure 20).

Daydreaming and Fantasy Thinking

The use of vicarious experience as a means of escape from reality requires a certain amount of imaginative projection, and in this respect it is very similar to the mechanisms of daydreaming and fantasy thinking. The voracious fiction reader or movie goer deserts reality for a dream-world in much the same way as the young boy shuts out the reality of the classroom by daydreaming. The gratification of needs and motives and the reduction of the tension of frustration are accomplished by substituting imagination or fantasy for reality (Feshbach, 1955). Here again we must recognize that everyone daydreams, temporarily abandoning the burdens and difficulties imposed by reality for the more pleasant and satisfying experiences of the world of fantasy. And, just as reading and movies can be the source of fruitful, enriching experiences, the efficient use of imagination can be the starting point of great and worthwhile achievements. The biographies of great men record consistently that they were dreamers and visionaries in their youth. Yet, from the standpoint of adjustment, we must apply the same criteria in this case as in the others. The stern demands of daily living require that we hold such responses to a minimum; fantasy thinking that is regulated by needs and frustrations cannot be offered as a substitute for reality thinking. The child who prefers the solitude and seclusion of his dream world, peopled with figures conjured up out of his imagination, to the world of real people and live events is making a poor adjustment. Carried to an extreme, this sort of withdrawal behavior becomes the core of schizophrenia, one of the most pathological of psychotic reactions (Singer & Rowe, 1962).

The question of whether daydreaming and fantasy thinking are normal or abnormal is answered in part by their background, by the nature and content of imagery evoked, and by their relation to other psychological mechanisms. In cases where the background includes such factors as traumatic experiences, abusive treatment, chronic frustration, and emotional starvation, rather than temporary frustration or tension, the chances are that fantasy thinking will take a pathological turn. Such factors are likely to stimulate systematic fantasies in place of the casual daydreaming that characterizes lesser frustrations. The content of fantasy will also give a clue to its role in adjustment. Fantasies centered around death, revenge, grandeur, and the like, are more symptomatic of deep-seated difficulties than are daydreams of the conquering-hero or success variety. The more, too, that pathological or abnormal fantasies become bound up with such mechanisms as identification and introjection, the more they will promote withdrawal. All these factors must be known in order to evaluate this type of withdrawal as an adjustive mechanism (Feshbach, 1955).

Sleep and Narcolepsy

The contraction and narrowing of consciousness that make day-dreaming an effective means of escaping reality are realized even more fully in sleep and various allied states, such as fugues and narcolepsies, all of which can be utilized to shut out reality. Sleep, of course, is a normal phenomenon and is ordinarily used to overcome the effects of fatigue and to restore energy to a point where the organism can again function efficiently. Yet even normal sleep has escapist qualities, for it is a means of getting away from frustrations, conflicts, and tensions. It is nature's way of providing a temporary escape from the demands and difficulties of daily living.

Sleep, however, may be used for purposes of escape and withdrawal. There is little doubt that the person who finds it extremely difficult to awaken after eight or nine hours' sleep is often loath to face reality. Unconsciously, he realizes that, in the blissful oblivion of sleep, reality can hold few threats or terrors. Such persons often resort to sleep when reality becomes oppressive, even though they are not really tired at the time. The author has heard many persons remark, "When the going gets tough, I just knock off and take a nap." Even such slightly oppressive conditions as a boring lecture or movie can induce sleep.

In some cases, sleep, or what might better be called the reduction of consciousness, assumes a pathological quality, resulting in periods of sudden or prolonged unconsciousness. These conditions are referred to as *narcolepsies*. When caused by organic factors, as in encephalitis lethargica, prolonged unconsciousness is obviously not a mechanism of escape; but there are many cases on record in which there is no evidence of organic causes, and it is safe to assume that at least some of these are determined by psychogenic factors, including the desire for escape. Similarly, *fugue states*, in which there is loss of consciousness or of memory of one's past life, may be interpreted as an escape mechanism. In these states of narcolepsy or fugue, the disturbance involves the consciousness of the organism; that is, there is a reduction of, or interference with, conscious awareness, the means by which the organism maintains contact with reality. In the absence, therefore, of physical or organic causes, it is logical to suppose that the reduction of awareness is determined by this relation. Certainly, the most effective way to shut out reality that has become oppressive or threatening is to forget it or become unaware of it; this seems to be the mechanism at work in sleep and the conditions to which it is allied.

Alcoholism, Drug Addiction, and Self-destruction

Alcoholic stupor and the euphoric condition produced by other narcotics are well-known means of escape from reality. In these states of reduced or clouded consciousness, worry, anxiety, frustration, conflict, fear, problems, and disappointments can be made to disappear. If reality is not entirely shut out, it is at least changed to such a degree that its relation to the organism is completely altered (Miles, 1932; Spalding & Montague, 1949; Pfeffer, 1958). No longer is it oppressive, threatening, or damaging; the old tensions and anxieties fade away in the unreal world created by narcosis. As one writer says (Vaughan, 1952, p. 63):

> Some people drink to drown their sorrows or to ease themselves over trying situations. Inebriation offers an attractive escape to the individual who is vulnerable to stress, who is in the habit of evading responsibility, who "can't take it," who reacts poorly to deprivation, who is overwhelmed by defeat, who is self-conscious and consequently ill at ease in company, who is subject to guilt feelings because of a strict upbringing, who suffers extremely from a sense of insecurity aggravated by fear of losing the parental love, etc.

Strecker expresses the pathology of drinking in language that is even more forceful (Strecker, 1952, pp. 261–262):

> Anything which has persisted through the ages, defying all efforts to eradicate it, either by legislation or moral suasion, must be motivated by a powerful driving force. Alcohol is. It has the quality of blurring rosily the hard, unpleasant and forbidding aspects of reality. If taken in sufficient quantity, it has the magical power of effacing reality altogether. *It is a quick solvent of reality. It is phantasy in a bottle.*

Here again reality is brought under control by the simple expedient of dimming one's awareness of it. You can see, therefore, why self-destruction is the most complete expression of withdrawal, since by this means awareness of reality is completely obliterated, and all problems and frustrations cease to exist. Even the stuporous alcoholic must sooner or later again face reality, but the suicide abolishes temporal reality completely (Shneidman & Farberow, 1957, Part I).

Negativism, Regression, and Fixation

Many escape and withdrawal mechanisms represent efforts to get away from or shut out reality completely; others involve retreat into an earlier form of behavior or a refusal to react at all to the requirements of the present situation. Refusal to react is called "negativism" and is manifested in stubbornness, contradictoriness, and quiet rebellion. It is essentially an effort to control oppression and frustration by not responding to situations in which these factors are involved. Reality is shut out by acting as if it does not exist, and in extreme cases it is impossible to establish contact of any kind with the person. Negativism is the last emotional resort in situations involving restraint, interference, or frustration. In it there is discernible a great deal of insecurity, seclusiveness, and resentment against the encroachments of external forces. This resentment often gives negativism the quality of rebellion and aggression, making it appear as an aggressive rejection of reality. The insecure and already seclusive child, forced against his will or inclinations to react in a certain way (to eat, to go to bed, to recite a poem), refuses to act at all, becomes stubborn, or quietly rebellious. Frustrated by the pressures exerted against him, he attempts to control the situation by a withdrawal into negativism. In many psychotic cases, negativism assumes serious proportions; contact with reality may be completely lost.

Another way to withdraw from reality is to retreat to an earlier (and more secure) mode of response. This is the mechanism of regression. Here the intent is to escape the frustrations and tensions of reality situations by utilizing responses that were successful in the past in securing the gratification of needs and in keeping frustration at a low level. For example, a child five or six years old, frightened and insecure because of family difficulties, rejection, and the like, reverts to baby talk, soiling his clothes, or other babyish responses, because these responses had once been successful in gaining the attention and affection he craved. Similarly, the homesick student, troubled by the demands and frustrations of school, "goes home to mother" to resume a relation free of more adult responsibilities. Very old persons, too, regress sometimes to "second childhood," because they are no longer equipped to deal with the difficulties of adult living.

The background of regression provides a ready answer to its use. In the majority of cases there is a history of parental overindulgence and overprotection, which made it impossible for the child to face reality in a secure and wholesome manner. In addition, and partly because of these relations, the person has persistently failed to come to grips with adjustment problems, and has tended to fall back on earlier successful habits whenever frustration became too severe or intense. Such persons tend to remember and to emphasize to themselves only the pleasant aspects of early experiences; therefore, their past life has a special attraction for them. Furthermore, the background of overprotection and overindulgence often includes parental fostering of regressive behavior (one of the primary sources of mother-in-law trouble) and a serious lack of preparation for independent living. When all these factors are added together, regression becomes almost a certainty whenever reality becomes frustrating and oppressive.

Some writers interpret most neurotic behavior as regressive since it is characteristically immature and childish (Lindgren, 1953, p. 96). Certainly the pathological immaturity that one sees in certain neurotics is indicative of either fixation or regression. Cameron and Magaret (1951, pp. 217–230) discuss regression in relation to both fixation and retrogression. These investigators define regression as the recurrence or the new occurrence of behavior that is biosocially immature, and retrogression they define as the recurrence of a technique or relation that had earlier been given up. Fixation, in contrast, is the premature termination of some aspect of personality development or a delay in maturation. Obviously, all three modes of adjustment are closely related.

Both regression and fixation are strikingly immature patterns of behavior and are commonly found among overprotected persons. Whereas the immaturity of the regressive person causes him to retreat, under pressure, however, to the security of earlier relationships, fixation makes such a retreat unnecessary since the person who fixates never outgrows his childish or adolescent ways of meeting problems. His behavior becomes fixed at an early level of development. It is not uncommon to see adults exhibit childish temper tantrums, indulge in puppy-love romances and infatuations characteristic of adolescents, or affect the dress and mannerisms of people half their age. In every respect, fixation is wholly unrealistic. It is a special kind of flight from reality, a flight that is executed by the simple expedient of *freezing reality* at a point that is safe, convenient, and comfortable. Note that both regression and fixation provide maximum security, and freedom from dangers, threats, or oppressions. Because for many persons childhood represents security and freedom, in their thinking it becomes a haven of refuge from an intolerable reality. It is this basic attitude that sets in motion the mechanisms of regression and fixation.

Schizophrenia and the Mechanisms of Withdrawal

In the everyday behavior of people there are countless instances of flight from reality, some transient and relatively normal, and others almost pathological in their intensity and show of fear regarding reality. Certainly, such reactions as regression and alcoholism are extremely unhealthy and maladjustive. In general, the more completely reality is shut out or the more desperate the effort to escape from it, the more abnormal the response becomes. The complete development and expression of the flight from reality are realized in schizophrenia, a pathological disorder of mind and personality that is the most common functional psychosis.

Schizophrenia fits into the picture at this point particularly well because it embraces several of the withdrawal responses already described, including loss of contact with reality, fantasy thinking, regression, negativism, and emotional debilitation. Because the very core of this disorder is pathological fear of reality, it serves as the clearest example of the extremes to which the human organism can be driven in its efforts to cope with the demands and stresses of daily living. There is, of course, a wide gap between the milder forms of withdrawal and escape and the morbid condition of schizophrenia; yet it is important to realize that all withdrawal responses are linked together in a common attitude toward reality and its demands. When this attitude deepens, from boredom and a mild sense of oppression to fear and extreme feelings of oppression, the more severe forms of withdrawal, including schizophrenia, begin to take form.

The interpretation given above is supported by the fact that the causes and conditions that underlie schizophrenia are basically no different from those assigned to other withdrawal reactions. In every case of this disorder there are indications of extreme sensitivity, seclusiveness, the habit of withdrawal, emotional impoverishment, childishness and immaturity, introversion, traumatic experiences, frustration, and mental conflict. And, as usual, lying behind these causes are inadequate parent-child relations, failure, and other conditions that encourage the habit of escape and withdrawal.

How are we to evaluate this type of response? We have noted that the simple, common forms of escape can hardly be regarded as abnormal or maladjustive, especially since they serve a useful purpose in providing temporary respite from the tensions and conflicts of daily living. Yet, in the interest of adequate adjustment and mental health, it is necessary to insist on a healthy, thoroughgoing, realistic attitude toward human problems and frustrations. The extreme, pathological instances of escape and withdrawal teach us in the most convincing manner that it is dangerous to treat lightly our attitudes toward reality. Whether we like it or not, the fact remains that our lives are immersed in reality, and therefore we must learn how to cope with its demands and stresses in an effective manner. We may at times allow ourselves the luxury of temporary escape, but we must accept the fact that reality is always there and that sooner or later we must face up to it. The person who cannot accept this basic truth is doomed to maladjustment, or worse still, mental disorder.

QUESTIONS AND PROJECTS FOR FURTHER STUDY

1. Write a brief term paper on the nature and causes of schizophrenia, and explain why it was once referred to as dementia praecox.
2. Explain the dynamic relationship between daydreaming, movie going, excessive drinking, schizophrenia, and suicide.
3. What criteria can we use to determine the pathology of escape or withdrawal reactions? Are these reactions ever normal? Explain.
4. In what manner do parent-child relations determine children's attitudes toward reality? Give examples.
5. Define what is meant by vicarious experience, and explain how this kind of experience is related to daydreaming.
6. Explain in your own words what is meant by "the zone of defense." How is this defense perimeter developed, and which growth factors are most important in its development?
7. Compare treatment procedures of any kind for alcoholism and schizophrenia.
8. Write a term paper comparing Alcoholics Anonymous with Recovery, Incorporated.

SELECTED COLLATERAL READINGS

CAMERON, N., & MAGARET, A. *Behavior pathology.* Boston: Houghton Mifflin, 1951.

MOUSTAKAS, C. E. *Loneliness.* Englewood Cliffs, N.J.: Prentice-Hall, 1961.

PFEFFER, A. Z. *Alcoholism.* New York: Grune & Stratton, 1958.

SAPPENFIELD, B. R. *Personality dynamics.* New York: Knopf, 1954.

SHNEIDMAN, E. S., & FARBEROW, N. L. (Eds.) *Clues to suicide.* New York: McGraw-Hill, 1957.

STRECKER, E. A. *Basic psychiatry.* New York: Random House, 1952.

SYMONDS, P. M. *The psychology of parent-child relationships.* New York: Appleton, 1939.

11

Adjustment by Flight into Illness

Of all of the unusual and abnormal ways of trying to cope adjustively with situations, none is more interesting or challenging than the flight into illness. Here we encounter the neuroses and the neurotic personality, which so consistently use illness and psychosomatic symptoms for purposes of adjustment. These neurotic reactions, which we must distinguish clearly from psychotic ones, range all the way from worry and scrupulosity to such bizarre reactions as hysterical blindness or paralysis. It is these reactions we now wish to study— their frequency, their causes, and their characteristics.

THE PROCESS OF ADJUSTMENT AND THE NEUROTIC DISORDERS

Nature and Characteristics of Neurosis

Reference in the preceding chapter to such phenomena as regression and schizophrenia brings up the issue of the relation between adjustment and the more prominent personality disorders, including the psychoses and the psychoneuroses. The latter term, incidentally, is equivalent nowadays to the shorter term "neuroses," since it is now recognized that all neurotic disorders are functional or psychogenic, and thus the prefix "psycho" is not actually necessary. A neurosis may be defined as *a personality disorder of relatively mild form that results from chronic tensions, conflicts, frustrations, and personal inadequacies, and that expresses itself in fairly clear-cut symptom complexes or syndromes.* We will discuss what these syndromes are later on in this chapter (Cattell & Scheier, 1961, p. 7).

The relation between the neurotic pattern and the process of adjustment is substantially the same as that between adjustment and all the other reactions we have considered; that is, neurotic syndromes are attempts to resolve tensions, conflicts, and frustrations by means of responses that are inadequate and inefficient. As Thorpe (1950, p. 376) expresses it, neurosis "is a condition of emotional maladjustment in which both the symptoms and inefficiency involved are associated with deprivations or other environmental stresses. The symptoms manifested are regarded as autocorrective reactions designed to alleviate the individual's

305

problems in threatening and intolerable situations with which he is unable to cope." In other words, then, neurotic behavior, like so many human reactions, is a type of inadequate adjustment, an inefficient and unwholesome effort to meet the demands and responsibilities of daily living (Horney, 1950; Saul, 1950).

Neurosis has certain definite characteristics that enable us to identify it without much difficulty (Cattell & Scheier, 1961, pp. 8–11).

1. *Neurosis is more or less chronic,* that is, it is a disorder that continues even when there is no immediate frustration or conflict. For this reason, among others, it is customary to refer to the neurotic personality, the implication being that, regardless of individual maladjustments or symptoms, there is an underlying psychological make-up that runs through and conditions the responses of the neurotic person. This notion must be used with caution, and we shall attempt to evaluate it when we turn to the characteristics of the neurotic personality.

2. *Neurosis protects the neurotic from the dangers or failures that have contributed to his neurosis.* For this reason, illness is a common neurotic symptom.

3. *Neurosis is inseparably linked with immaturity, inadequacy, and childishness.* This is another reason why illness is so prominent in this disorder.

4. *Neurosis causes the patient to cling to his symptoms even though he is disturbed by them and seeks help from a psychiatrist or psychologist.* The reason for this is that the symptoms serve a protective purpose; the patient will not relinquish them until he develops insight regarding their morbidity and inadequacy (Marcuse, 1953).

5. *Neurosis is functional.* None is determined by organic damage of any kind. As Strecker says, neurotics "seek to attract attention, unconsciously, to gain 'a place in the sun' by a display of functional symptoms. Thus the normal desire to be of some importance in the social scheme being blocked, there is an 'illegitimate' (psychopathologic) attempt to seize a small measure of power" (Strecker, 1947, pp. 232–233). Nevertheless, related to this characteristic is the presence in neurotics of a great amount of organic morbidity, including endocrine malfunctions, organic heart disease, anemia, sinusitis, gastric and duodenal ulcer, and the like. Strecker explains this point clearly (Strecker, 1947, p. 232):

> It is not our conclusion that these and other conditions are causal; certainly they are not directly so. It is more likely that they play precipitating roles, perhaps by lowering resistance, but chiefly by providing a psychological opportunity of unconsciously adding functional symptoms to the clinical picture, without insult to the personality. In other words, the individual being organically sick. . . . there is provided the op-

portunity to secure psychopathologic compromises of long endured underlying emotional conflicts. Functional symptoms now may develop and present themselves clinically without "loss of face." This is one of the reasons why in everyday practice situations presenting organic disease with an overlayer of functional symptoms are so very common.

6. *Neurosis is characterized most strikingly by the development of symptoms.* This process is unconscious and nonvoluntary ("autocorrective" in Fisher's terms) and always serves the aim of ego defense; the symptoms are meaningfully related to the patient's difficulties and to the situation in which the difficulty emerges (Fisher, 1937). Much of this symptom development is expressed in the form of illness, and therefore neurosis is closely identified with adjustment by flight into illness and with the development of psychosomatic disorders of various types, a phase of the problem to which we shall turn later on. The student should compare the concept of "flight into illness" with the notion of "withdrawal into invalidism" defined by Cameron and Magaret (1951, pp. 231–242). Another investigator, Ruesch, uses the term "flight into illness" in a narrower sense to refer especially to cases of delayed recovery from actual injury or illness, although the motivation is very similar to that which determines neurotic illness (Ruesch, 1951, pp. 48–52).

Neuroses and Psychoses

Because neurosis is an identifiable reaction pattern, we must distinguish it clearly from psychosis (Bowman & Rose, 1952; Page, 1947, pp. 100–103). The differences between the two forms of personality disorder are set forth in Table 12. It is easy to see that there are important differences. Neuroses are essentially reactions to conflict or frustration that stay within the boundaries of socially accepted behavior patterns. They do not totally destroy the adjustive capacities of the organism and therefore do not require the close supervision or hospitalization that psychotic patients require. Nor is there the marked emotional and intellectual debilitation that is so often found in psychotic persons. It is not wise, however, to push these distinctions too far. There are neurotic persons who are extremely unrealistic, who have little insight into personal difficulties or their causes, whose emotional life is seriously disturbed, and who are markedly incapacitated for daily responsibilities. As stated by O'Kelly and Muckler (1955, p. 203),

a large area of overlapping conditions in which it is difficult to make a clear distinction. Indeed, one of the most prevalent problems of the clinical psychologist and of the psychiatrist is that of making a differential diagnosis between psychosis and neurosis. Examples can be found

TABLE 12

Comparison of Neurotic and Psychotic Disorders in Terms
of Primary Characteristics

NEUROSES	PSYCHOSES
Reactions less severe	Reactions much more severe and disturbing; disruptive in character
Less pervasive, involving only several areas of personality	Extremely pervasive; tend to involve the whole personality
Fairly good contact with reality	Generally poor contact with reality; may involve total abandonment of reality
Emotions fairly flexible; little impoverishment	Considerable emotional debilitation; often seriously diminished or abolished altogether
No intellectual deterioration; some impairment	Often serious intellectual deterioration or impairment
Generally fairly good insight; capacity to be objective regarding self	Generally lacking in insight; little understanding of difficulty
Not incapacitated; able to live in society	Incapacitated; often dangerous to self and society
Seldom require hospitalization	Require hospitalization

of persons who, on the basis of other considerations, are clearly neurotic, who show symptoms more intensely than many psychotics, whose total personality seems clearly involved, and who are distinctly in need of hospitalization for their own protection . . . it should be expected that many individuals will behave in ways that combine features of both neurosis and psychosis.

The Neurotic Personality

The many similarities and distinctions between neuroses and psychoses make it especially desirable to determine the structure of the neurotic personality. Let us emphasize at the start that the existence of neurotic symptoms is not in itself evidence of the existence of a neurosis. *There is a great difference between the truly neurotic personality and the person with neurotic symptoms.* Probably everyone behaves neurotically at one time or another. There are many persons, otherwise quite normal, who are mildly hypochondriac, who harbor a phobia or compulsion, who are overscrupulous, or who develop psychosomatic symptoms. The flight into illness is a common tendency in a culture where the problems of illness have been so greatly emphasized. Thus, it is not the presence of neurotic symptoms that bespeaks a neurotic personality; rather *it is the existence of a peculiar constellation of traits and characteristics that distinguishes the neurotic from the normal person*. Babcock makes a similar distinction. "While the behavior of given persons with neuroses may logically (or tautologically) be assumed to be neurotic, all persons who are pronounced neurotic do not necessarily have a basically neurotic personality." Thus, "the essential requirement for understanding the personality of neurotics is to determine whether there is a basic mental weakness or whether apparently neurotic behavior is superficial and the result of unfortunate circumstances" (Babcock, 1947, p. 61; also Sherman, 1941, p. 349).

A survey of the characteristics of the neurotic impresses us with the extent to which they are opposed to the criteria of good adjustment and mental health described in Chapter 2. The interested student will find a more intensive study of the neurotic personality and its characteristics in many sources (Abrams, 1953). Following are some of the more prominent characteristics of the neurotic personality.

Immaturity and Sensitivity.   In the neurotic personality there is, first of all, immaturity and sensitivity, both of which make it difficult for the neurotic to face up to the demands and stresses of daily living in a straightforward and healthy manner. Immaturity makes all problems and frustrations look large and menacing, and it favors the development of the typical neurotic symptoms of illness and inefficiency. Sensitivity makes the stresses and threats of reality almost unbearable. The treatment of neurotics, therefore, is directed toward raising the level of maturity and reducing sensitivity so that the patient will be better able to withstand the pressures and frustrations imposed by reality.

Self-centeredness.   The quality of sensitivity is complemented by self-centeredness. In the neurotic person there is always a great deal of self-concern, reflected in a characteristic tendency toward morbid self-scrutiny, a quality that is but one step removed from self-pity. Persons who are easily hurt are quick to pity themselves because self-pity is a means by which the effects of sensitivity can be reduced. As Allport remarks, "any neurotic is living a life which in some respects is extreme in its self-centeredness. Even though many of his individual sentiments may be altruistic, the region of his misery represents a complete preoccupation with himself" (Allport, 1950, p. 94).

Unrealistic Ego Ideal. The neurotic harbors an almost pathological ego ideal that prevents him from achieving a realistic attitude toward the issues and problems of daily life and leads to such typical symptoms as scruples, obsessions, and compulsions. He sets up a standard of conduct, attitudes, and ideals that is impossible to realize not only because it is a purely idealized goal but also because he lacks the talents and abilities.

Rigidity and Anxiety. This morbid idea of self causes a rigidity of response in the neurotic person since it does not allow him to adapt his behavior to changing situations. His sensitivity makes the neurotic timid and anxious, so afraid of problems, decisions, social relations, and so on, that he is immobilized, and his morbid ego ideal strengthens this rigidity (Horney, 1950, Chapters I–IV). It is factors like these that breed intense anxiety in the neurotic personality. As Klein remarks, "The hallmark of a neurosis is the existence of anxiety."

Isolation. Because of his anxiety, sensitivity, rigidity, and impossible ego ideal, the neurotic personality characteristically presents a picture of helplessness and isolation. Being immature, dependent, and afraid, the neurotic hesitates to grapple with problems and conflicts and often prefers to isolate himself from the world of people and social events. Thus there may be a certain amount of hostility in the neurotic make-up, and an inability to get along with others.

Aggression against Self. The neurotic's asocial traits are not like those of the aggressive person. In place of the verbal or physical attack of aggression, there is a great deal of petulance, annoyance with others, sensitivity to their attitudes and behavior, readiness to quarrel and find fault, and so on. Neurotics, like others who have emotional difficulties, experience a considerable amount of frustration and conflict that might lead to aggression. But, as many writers suggest, in the neurotic the aggression is directed inward rather than toward society and reality. This characteristic helps us to understand why so many neurotics develop illnesses and psychosomatic symptoms of various kinds; the frustration-aggression mechanism, having little outward expression, turns in upon itself. This quality corresponds with the tendencies toward self-pity, sensitivity, and self-scrutiny mentioned earlier and throws light on the neurotic's preoccupation with ill health so that symptoms of illness are the constant companion of neurotic disability.

Mental Conflict. Unlike cases in which frustration dominates the person's reactions and determines the formation of symptoms and mechanisms, the neurotic personality is more characteristically dominated by mental conflict, which is one of the reasons why there is so much automatic functioning in neuroses. More than frustration, mental conflict tends to disrupt the organization of personality since it is in the nature of conflict to pull the organism in different directions at the same time. Typical of neurotic conflicts are those between conduct and principles, between drives and ideals, between personal wishes and authority, between conscience and impulses, and between actual achievement and the goals set by the self ideal. Such conflicts may be conscious or unconscious, but they are always deep seated. Because of his immaturity and rigidity, the neurotic finds it difficult to cope with his conflicts, and he may revert to the development of psychosomatic symptoms in an unconscious effort to reduce the tensions they generate. Since some of these conflicts are centered around persons—parents, friends, children, wives—the neurotic often shows strong ambivalent attitudes of liking and disliking, loving and hating, approving and disapproving toward the people who make up his world. This attitude, which is not limited to personal relations, makes it more difficult to deal with conflicts and difficulties and reinforces other neurotic characteristics, including anxiety, hostility, and inability to get along with others.

Lack of Control. As one writer expresses it, "the common denominator of all neurotic phenomena is an insufficiency of the normal control apparatus" (Klein, 1951, p. 434). That the neurotic lacks control of his feelings, attitudes, ideas, and functions is not surprising; ambivalence, chronic conflict and frustration, immaturity, and anxiety are all unfavorable to the exercise of self-control. Particularly is this true of the factor of immaturity since the development of self-control hinges on adequate maturation. The young child is notably lacking in the quality of control just because he is immature; the immature adult neurotic is like a child in this respect. Chronic conflict, especially unconscious conflict, weakens self-control to a great extent, although here we cannot be sure that it is not lack of self-control that favors the development of conflicts. In any event, we can see in this characteristic the *raison d'être* of the autonomous functioning that distinguishes the neurotic personality. In obsessions, it is ideas that get out of hand; in compulsions, it is behavior; in hysteria, it is somatic functions. Whatever the form that neurosis assumes, there is always some evidence of failure in control and integrative functioning.

Suggestibility. Suggestibility and lack of control go hand in hand because the suggestible person is controlled by an idea or by someone else rather than by himself. This combination is fertile soil for the development of psychosomatic disorders, neurotic symptoms, and autonomous functioning. Suggestion is often the starting point for various symptoms, and lack of integration and self-control foster their development. Extreme suggestibility is most strikingly exemplified in hysterical and neurasthenic personalities.

Irresponsibility. Because of deficiency in self-control and maturity, the neurotic person is characteristically lacking in responsibility, and for that reason is generally unreliable. The sense of responsibility and the willingness to accept obligations are dependent to a great extent on maturity; and the carrying out of obligations requires considerable self-control. Typically, therefore, neurotics find it difficult to hold a job, to keep appointments on time, to meet the responsibilities of home and family, to make the family budget work efficiently, to get work done according to schedule, and so on. In other words, their many personality weaknesses make it extremely difficult for neurotics to meet the ordinary, normal demands of daily living, and thus the stage is set for maladjustment. In their helplessness, and baffled or frighened by the responsibilities imposed on them, they soon turn to symptomatic responses in an effort to cope with situations. Here again it is easy to see why illness is so often a part of the neurotic picture, it being one of the most expedient means of avoiding the stigma of irresponsibility. Cameron and Magaret (1951, pp. 238–239) imply this in their analysis of the value of psychological invalidism. They point out that

> any incapacitated patient is obliged to live as a comparatively helpless individual while his incapacitation lasts. He is dependent for his security, and for the satisfaction of even his simplest needs, upon the helping hand of stronger and more competent persons. This is essentially a repetition of the normal situation in infancy; and it tends to evoke infantile attitudes and responses from the relatively helpless adult. Some individuals discover a new and welcome satisfaction in their dependent status, and develop anxiety and insecurity when they face the necessity for regaining independence. Their reactions of anxiety and insecurity in convalescence may then contribute to the foundations of new complaints, or of an exaggeration of old complaints—which often increase, paradoxically, as the patient's general condition shows improvement.

In other words, even when invalidism begins as a bona fide physical illness, the patient often discovers that symptoms can be used to evade responsibility and to maintain a secure, dependent status, with the result that the illness extends far beyond the normal period of convalescence and often becomes chronic.

Lack of a Sense of Humor. The preoccupation of the neurotic with illness and with disturbing psychosomatic symptoms is reflected in his singular lack of a sense of humor. A good sense of humor we listed as one of the criteria of mental health and adjustment. As a personality trait, it possesses many virtues for wholesome living. It takes the edge off disappointments, bitter experiences, failures, and frustrations; it contributes to a better perspective regarding the basic issues of life; it sets a natural limit to the seriousness of problems and difficulties that come up from day to day; and it helps in the realization of a goal that is common to everyone and diametrically opposed to maladjustment, that is, human happiness (Allport, 1950, pp. 92–93). The neurotic person, because of his characteristics, is largely denied this saving grace. His pathological ego ideal, self-pity, extreme sensitivity, rigidity, chronic frustration and conflict, and constant anxiety make it difficult for him to develop a sense of humor. To him life is bleak, uninviting, and oppressive. Every issue and every problem is something of a calamity that taxes capacity, strength, and endurance to the utmost and leaves little room for joy or gaiety. If, on occasion, he manages to break out of his oppressive condition and really enjoy himself, the next crisis sends him spinning back into his neurotic gloom. He comes to regard joy and humor as temporary illusions that only serve to deepen his feelings of helplessness, frustration, and inadequacy. Thus his life becomes a humorless, drab affair dominated by illness, conflict, frustration, dissatisfaction, and discouragement.

Emotional Instability. In the neurotic reaction to demands and responsibilities, there is, of course, a great deal of emotional instability, although this characteristic is by no means peculiar to neuroses. Emotional disturbance is common to all forms of maladjustment, as we have noted many times, but it is a dominant feature of the neurotic personality, and a primary determinant of the neurotic's difficulties. Clearly, if the neurotic person did not react with fear, uncertainty, or anxiety to conflicts, difficulties, and the demands imposed on him, there is little chance that he would develop neurotic disabilities. Such emotions as fear and anxiety are the cue to an understanding of psychosomatic development, and it is the constant emotional turmoil of the neurotic that makes such development inevitable. As we noted earlier, emotional disturbance is the core of all abnormalities of behavior and personality, and neurotic disability is simply another expression of this basic relation.

Neurotic Traits and Illness

Throughout this discussion of the neurotic personality we have emphasized the relation of neurosis to the development of symptoms of illness. Not all neurotics develop symptoms of this kind; yet it is generally recognized that there is a special connection between neurosis and the flight into illness. The reasons for this have already been indicated—neurotic traits are particularly favorable to the development of such symptoms and to the exploitation of illness for personal aims. There is hardly a trait we have described that does not fit into this pattern. Immaturity, sensitivity, helplessness, conflict, anxiety, morbid self-examination, self-pity, suggestibility, and emotional instability—all of them dispose the neurotic to the use of illness as a means of adjustment.

In other words, to the limited perspective of the neurotic patient illness appears (subconsciously) to be the most effective means of reducing the tensions of conflict and frustration and of gaining what every neurotic craves—attention, affection, special consideration, and security. As Horney (1950, p. 41) remarks:

> The neurotic feels entitled to special attention, consideration, deference on the part of others. These claims for deference are understandable enough, and sometimes obvious enough. But they are merely part and parcel of a more comprehensive claim—that all his needs growing out of his inhibitions, his fears, his conflicts, and his solutions out to be satisfied or duly respected. Moreover, whatever he feels, thinks, or does ought not to carry any adverse consequences. This means in fact a claim that psychic laws ought not to apply to him. Therefore he does not need to recognize—or at any rate to change—his difficulties. It is then no longer up to him to do something about his problems; it is up to others to see that they do not disturb him.

One can see what a fitting background these claims provide for the development of symptoms and illnesses. Furthermore, it should be noted that once developed they are not readily relinquished.

From early childhood, many neurotics have learned the special value of illness, which can be an important part of the background of neurotic development. In this development, the law of effect plays a decisive role, for the neurotic soon learns that illness can be very satisfying, and it is not long before he acquires considerable skill in the exploitation of illness for its satisfying effects. The mechanism of this development is not essentially different from that of other forms of adjustment already studied. Regardless of their nature or acceptability from a social standpoint, those responses are repeated and fixed that serve to reduce tension and bring about a satisfying state of affairs.

Varieties of Neurosis

The relation between illness and neurotic development is exemplified in the different patterns that neurosis assumes. Prominent among these are (1) nervousness, worry, scrupulosity, accident proneness, and traumatic neuroses, (2) anxiety neurosis and psychomotor disturbances, (3) obsessive-compulsive reactions, (4) organ neuroses, (5) neurasthenia and hypochondria, and (6) hysteria. In nearly all these patterns of neurotic adjustment, there is an element of illness, so that it is customary to expect such symptoms whenever a diagnosis of neurotic disability is made. This relation will be brought out more clearly in our detailed discussion of the forms of neurosis.

Causes and Background of Neurosis

From the foregoing analysis it is clear that neurosis is essentially a personality disorder rather than an isolated group of symptoms or mechanisms. It is, therefore, a developmental phenomenon, the causes of which lie to a great extent in the early history of the person. Mowrer interprets neurosis as a learning deficit in which the ego remains immature, asocial, and id dominated (Mowrer, 1952; also Fromm, 1944).

Inadequate Parent-Child Relations. Especially prominent in the background of neurosis are neurotic attitudes and behavior on the part of the parents, inadequate training, overprotection and indulgence, jealousy and rivalry for affection, rejection and perfectionism, and faulty discipline. All such conditions stand in the way of healthy ego development and make impossible, in the majority of cases, the realization of personality integration. These are the reasons why the neurotic personality is stamped with inadequate control, extreme suggestibility, and a tendency toward autonomous functioning (Steckle, 1949, pp. 107–114).

Satisfying Experiences with Illness. In the history of many neurotics there is evidence of a great deal of illness, much more than occurs normally, and there is evidence also of an overprotective and unduly solicitous parent who causes the child to regard illness as a powerful weapon of control over the environment. Quite often, too, the parent is neurasthenic or hypochondriacal, so that illness becomes an essential and accepted part of family living. Repeated visits to the doctor, pills, bromides, remedies, patent medicines, and endless conversations regarding illness are common features of the armamentarium of the neurotic personality.

Failure to Mature. We have noted repeatedly that immaturity is the most common feature of maladjusted personalities and one of the most prominent traits of neurosis. This immaturity is itself determined by such factors as those just described. Adult living requires maturity of judgment, feelings, and conduct, and because the neurotic is immature, he falls back for his adjustments on symptoms and responses that provided satisfactions and release from tension in his early years. The use of headaches, pains, and psychosomatic disturbances for personal gain is essentially childish. Again, because of his basic immaturity, the neurotic is easy prey to suggestion, to conflicts and frustrations, to emotional tensions and disabilities. Like the child, the neurotic is poorly equipped to deal efficiently and forthrightly with either the demands of self or of reality. He is easily confused and made to feel helpless in situations that involve tension or conflict. In this condition of emotional turmoil, he readily turns to symptoms and behavior that, *subjectively*, are worthwhile because they help to reduce tensions; but, *objectively*, they are extremely inefficient, unhealthy, and damaging to personality.

Conflicts, Frustrations, and Emotional Tensions. Owing to his inadequate development and immaturity, the neurotic has never learned how to cope with conflicts, frustrations, and emotional tensions, and it is this chronic state of affairs that is more responsible for his difficulties than the simple fact of conflict itself. Mowrer generalizes this idea of inadequate learning into a philosophy of neurosis. "It is the very fact of learning that gives us our freedom, and it is the functional loss of learning capacity . . . that constitutes the very core of neurosis" (Mowrer, 1950, p. 31). It is out of this background, then, of inadequate, unhealthy parent-child relations, satisfying experience with illness, immaturity, and chronic conflict and frustration that the neurotic personality emerges and expresses itself in the variety of neurotic symptoms and behaviors to which we now direct our attention (Kardiner & Spiegel, 1947).

SIMPLE NEUROTIC SYMPTOMS AND BEHAVIOR

Nervousness

At the outset of this discussion we made a distinction between persons with neurotic symptoms and the neurotic personality. Among the former are those persons characterized by symptoms of nervousness, including such common reactions as thumb sucking, nail biting, jitters, chronic tenseness, and similar manifestations. No one of these symptoms is particularly significant in itself, nor are they necessarily indicative of a neurotic personality. They are, however, properly classified as neurotic symptoms and often exist as isolated indicators of frustration and tension. Thumb sucking and nail biting cannot be regarded as normal reactions, since there are countless normal persons who never manifest such behavior.

Nor is it normal to be jittery. Such reactions occur only under conditions of tension. For example, the ignored or rejected child discovers that thumb sucking reduces the tension created by the frustration of being unwanted or ignored. Similarly, the child frustrated by the demands of a task, or by the requirements imposed by a severely disciplinary or perfectionistic parent, works off the accumulated tension by biting his nails or by some ritualistic act like doodling or tearing paper off the wall. The jittery person smokes endless cigarettes or paces nervously around the room. These activities give evidence of tension, and of a drive to reduce this tension (and the underlying frustration) by some form of behavior. The same effects could be achieved more efficiently by vigorous physical exercise, though this would require more time and energy. (A good discussion of nervousness will be found in Whiles, 1951; Strecker & Appel, 1944, Chapter III.) Strecker and Appel discuss and dispose of the idea that nervousness is a disease of the nerves.

Worry

Worrying is a symptomatic response closely allied to nervousness. Generally, the chronic worrier is a nervous person and is likely to manifest the typical symptoms of nervousness. Worrying should be clearly distinguished from *concern*, which is a *rational* awareness of the threatening potentialities of a situation. The student who is sensibly concerned enough about an examination to study intensively in order to pass is not to be regarded as a worrier. The chronic, neurotic worrier is typically exemplified in the well-known story of the man who complained of getting gray hair from worrying, and then, when asked what he was worrying about, answered "getting gray hair."

Worrying is essentially the emotionalizing of an intellectual process directed toward a problem and its solution. It is an emotional rather than a rational concern and involves fear, anxiety, and tension. Behind chronic worrying are some of the typical characteristics of the inadequate or neurotic personality. There is inability to deal adequately with problems and conflicts, feelings of insecurity and helplessness, immaturity, morbid self-concern and self-pity, sensitivity, rigidity, and emotional instability. Thus, in a typical situation, the worrier becomes concerned about his health. There may be little evidence of ill health, and even a doctor's certificate to the effect that everything is in order. Yet he cannot be sure. He has palpitations of the heart, aches and pains of an unknown source, and perhaps an occasional blurring of vision. These are enough to set off the chain reaction of worrying. Because of such factors as self-concern and insecurity, there is little possibility of objective, intellectual evaluation in such a situation. Instead, there is a subjective, emotional reaction of fear and anxiety, which precludes a rational evaluation of symptoms and a deliberate, well-calculated attack upon the problem. Worrying, therefore, blocks normal adjustment to the situation and effects nothing more than a continuously increasing tension, which defeats its own purpose.

Scrupulosity

Still another common neurotic manifestation closely allied to worry is scrupulosity. It may be characterized as a special kind of worry directed toward the morality of actions. It is an emotional concern regarding the sinfulness of conduct that in itself is usually not sinful and, like worry, involves a great deal of anxiety. The writer recalls the case of a student who insisted that he was not entitled to the mark he had received on an examination because he had guessed at some of the true and false items and that, since some of the guesses would be right, it was sinful for him to accept the mark. No amount of reassurance that guessing was not sinful would convince him that he had not committed a wrong. Here again are betrayed the traits of the inadequate and neurotic personality. In the scrupulous person there is fear, anxiety, insecurity, and an almost pathological sense of guilt. Like the worrier, he cannot evaluate conduct objectively and rationally. Obsessed with the fear of committing sin, and convinced that he will do so, he is wholly unamenable to rational argument. In such cases, there is often discernible a background of parental perfectionism and constant emphasis on the wrongness or sinfulness of even the smallest acts. The scrupulous person is also immature and has a poorly developed moral perspective. Out of these conditions grows his sense of guilt, which tends to spread to every act regardless of its morality or immorality. He is preoccupied with sinfulness much as the hypochondriac is preoccupied with ill health, and both have characteristics in common with the obsessive-compulsive neurotic, whom we shall study later in this chapter (Moore, 1944, Chapter IV).

Accident Proneness

The flight into illness so characteristic of the neurotic personality is exemplified in a special way in the common trait of accident proneness, or what Dunbar has quaintly termed "accidentitis." While many neurotics express their inadequacies and conflicts in aches and pains or some form of functional disability, many others unconsciously attempt to resolve their difficulties and overcome their shortcomings through the medium of accidents. The number of such persons is much larger than is ordinarily suspected. As Dunbar states, "people hurt themselves more often than they are hurt by others or by fate or by the impersonal failure of machines." The disease of the broken-bone habit "covers a definite personality type whose sound bodies get damaged in mishaps brought on in the course of a state of mind which is far from strong, although not at all what we usually mean by 'unsound.' At least 80 percent of the millions of major accidents which happen every year are due to this ailment" (Dunbar, 1947, p. 96; also Krall, 1953).

This is indeed a large percentage, but it is strikingly similar to some estimates that have been made of patients whose illnesses are diagnosed as psychosomatic rather than organic. The statistical fact can be better understood when causes and personality factors involved in accident proneness are taken into account and related to the figures regarding the recurrence of accidents among individuals. The concept of accident proneness, as the term suggests, refers to a definite tendency in some persons to experience many more than the usual number of accidents. It implies that many such accidents are self-imposed rather than truly accidental, that is, owing to "fate," to the failure of machines, or to the faults of other people. "The studies of a good many authorities in recent years have established the conclusion that only about 10 to 20 percent of all these injuries, fatal or otherwise, are caused by really accidental accidents. The rest are linked to the personality of the victim" (Dunbar, 1947, p. 98).

The statement above is supported by the findings of a number of studies on accidents and accident proneness. For example, when workers suspected of accident proneness are shifted from one job area to another, the accident rate in the first area declines to a notable extent, indicating that the accidents are determined by personality factors rather than job conditions. In a study of hospital patients reported by Dunbar, the same conclusion is justified. As she points out (Dunbar, 1947, p. 100):

> The statistics gathered through our hospital study showed that fracture patients (even including the victims of accidental accidents) had fourteen times greater a tendency to have disabling mishaps than the average of all other groups in hospital patients studied. The fracture cases had averaged four accidents, even including those with their first; the other groups averaged less than three-tenths of an accident per person. The percentage of injuries among the other patients was in no group more than the 10 to 20 per cent which are believed on the basis of insurance and other statistics to be real accidents. . . . We found that 80 per cent of our fracture patients had two or more accidents.

The conclusion, from this and other studies, is inescapable: Persons vary in accident proneness and this characteristic is determined by other personality factors, some of which are clearly neurotic.

Outstanding among the characteristics of the accident-prone personality is *self-aggression*, which we noted earlier to be one of the basic traits of the neurotic personality. It has, in fact, been suggested that the aggression that the delinquent and criminal direct against society is of the same kind and has the same background as that found in the accident-prone personality. In this background are strict parental authority, stern religious upbringing, rejection, punishment, and similar factors that also characterize the history of the delinquent. Associated with these elements, as might be expected from our analysis of delinquency, are strong feelings of guilt, the need for punishment, and the desire for affection and attention. The behavior characteristic of the persistent lawbreaker, says Dunbar (1947, p. 102),

> is virtually identical with that of the persistent breaker of bones right up to the point where the one commits a crime and the other has an accident. It is a fact that few criminals get sick. They find release from their emotional conflict in what society has chosen to regard as an unsocial act, just as their counterpart in the accident wards of hospitals find their release in the accident habit.
>
> In both, the early history has been one of poor adjustment to a strict authority in the home or school, usually accompanied by a story of parental rejection. They have had the same childhood neurotic traits, and in both groups these tend to disappear as the child grows older. Their parallel development diverges when the one carries the early record of lying, stealing and truancy into a broader field and becomes a criminal, while the other begins to hurt himself instead of the community.

This parallel is interesting and provocative, even though it would be a mistake to emphasize too strongly the aggressive features of accident proneness. Primarily, the tendency toward self-injury is a form of the flight into illness and has much the same motivation and background as other forms of neurotic expression. It makes little difference to the neurotic whether he secures his aim to reduce tension by aches and pains, psychomotor disturbances, organic illnesses, or bruises, cuts, and broken bones. In all cases the pattern is similar and involves the use of physical ailments and disabilities for the purpose of effecting an "adjustment." In this view, having an accident is the same as developing a headache or essential hypertension, the purpose being to effect a reduction of emotional tension brought on by frustration and conflict, and by the general helplessness of the neurotic in the face of everyday demands. Here again we see clearly how the logic of symptom formation is expressed in the neurotic effort to effect adjustment.

The Traumatic Neuroses

Between the neurotic tendency to exploit self-injury or accidents for neurotic aims and the psychosomatic disturbances identified as organ neuroses, there is a clear-cut symptomatology that has its basis in *real* injury or in the *threat* of injury and death. Collectively, these symptoms are referred to as the traumatic neuroses, so called because the neurotic pattern springs from a traumatic situation. Typically, the syndrome occurs after some event that is interpreted by the person as a threat to his physical existence—a serious automobile accident, war experiences, an explosion in the home, bombings, or great catastrophes. All such experiences may result in mental shock or psychic trauma; hence the familiar terms "shell shock" and "war neuroses." The symptoms that result are not the expression of physical damage of any kind; that is, they are not caused by injury to the brain, as happens in the traumatic psychoses where symptoms are the result of damage to brain cells; rather, the symptoms of traumatic neuroses are a result of the disruption of personality brought on by mental shock or the threat of death. There may be real physical injury, but the symptoms occur just as readily in persons who are physically unharmed in any way (Page, 1947, pp. 149–150; Steckle, 1949, pp. 136–137).

The syndrome of traumatic neurosis is very complex and includes a large variety of symptoms. In milder cases, where symptoms often disappear after a short time, there are the common signs of excessive perspiration, trembling, irritability, sensitivity, dizziness and fainting, and less frequently, nausea and vomiting. General efficiency is impaired, and the patient tires easily. In more severe cases, such as the war neuroses, there may be disturbances of speech and walking, paralyses, mental confusion, and even convulsions. Among the purely mental symptoms, perhaps the most characteristic are the terrifying nightmares in which the patient relives again and again the traumatic experience that touched off the neurotic syndrome. Almost everyone has had traumatic experiences at one time or another; usually the symptoms disappear after a short period, but in the traumatic neuroses they persist for years or even for the lifetime of the patient.

What is the psychological basis of this differential reaction to shock? Clearly, since it is not physical injury that acts as a cause, the basis must lie in the personality of the patient. The traumatic event is interpreted by the potentially neurotic person as *a threat to personal security*. Suddenly, the world appears dangerous, threatening, full of impending death. The trauma seems to force a realization that he is entirely incapable of coping with the forces of life and death. The world is no longer a safe place in which to live, as he had previously believed; the trauma demonstrates that there is no real security; life is filled with danger. From this reaction, we can see that the neurosis is based on personal insecurity that existed long before the traumatic incident. The trauma served merely to bring it to the surface. Here is exemplified in the most striking way the neurotic characteristic of helplessness referred to earlier in this chapter. Faced with a situation resembling or reminding him of the traumatic incident, he recoils with fear and anxiety, and his symptoms become distressingly acute and disabling. As Maslow and Mittelmann point out (1951, p. 416):

> There is no substitute for walking, standing, sleeping, or eating, the functions that are inhibited or destroyed in traumatic experiences. The individual is deprived of the fundamental abilities upon which rest the most primitive feelings of self-esteem and security. Hence it is easy to understand why he perceives the world as overwhelmingly hostile and dangerous and himself as helpless. This is the meaning of the catastrophic dreams. In fact, we may think of the traumatic neurosis as an actual catastrophic breakdown. Furthermore, the patient feels resentful toward the world that threatens him; as a result, he fears counterattack. He may revert to childlike mechanisms and in severe cases may have to be cared for like an infant. This type of device, together with the care received, gives him a measure of security but perpetuates his helplessness.

THE ANXIETY NEUROSES

Nature and Characteristics of Neurotic Anxiety

You will have noted that one of the most constant features of neurotic behavior is anxiety. Anxiety is a consequence of the neurotic's helplessness, insecurity, immaturity, and sensitivity in the face of the demands of reality and the difficulties and stresses of everyday living. You are likely to feel anxious when you are unsure of yourself, when you feel incapable of coping successfully with problems, or when the world appears harsh and threatening. In fact, because such conditions are common, anxiety is a universal reaction, one to which everyone is subject at some time or other in his life. Some situations and events *are* frightening, and it would be strange if we did not experience anxiety in the face of them (Cattell & Scheier, 1961, pp. 10–18).

Anxiety is a kind of fear. It is fear projected toward future contingencies. It is normal when fear-laden contingencies actually exist (May, 1950, pp. 190–193; Hoch & Zubin, 1950; De Michele, 1954). A person may experience anxiety when faced with the necessity of a dangerous operation that may be fatal; the student feels anxious about an examination that means the difference between graduation and failure; the passenger in an automobile experiences anxiety when the driver races along a slippery highway at eighty miles an hour. These are instances of normal anxiety. As May points out (1950, p. 194):

> *Normal anxiety* is, like any anxiety, a reaction to threats to values the individual holds essential to his existence as a personality; but normal anxiety is that reaction which (1) is not disproportionate to the objective threat, (2) does not involve repression or other mechanisms of intrapsychic conflict, and, as a corollary to the second point, (3) does not require neurotic defense mechanisms for its management, but can be confronted constructively on the level of conscious awareness *or* can be relieved if the objective situation is altered.

Normal anxieties are very different from neurotic anxiety. This is a state of fear that is out of proportion to the cause, or that exists without any discernible cause (May, 1950, pp. 197–200; Schwartz, 1954). For example, a mother experiences intense anxiety about the safety of her children, knowing all the time that they are in no unusual danger. Here the feeling of anxiety is out of proportion to the cause. In other instances, the anxiety is of the "free-floating" type for which no cause can be found. The patient complains of waves of anxiety flooding over him, a deep sense of foreboding regarding the future, but there is nothing to which he can relate the feeling. Some persons experience a sudden state of intense fear—the anxiety attack—which only lasts a few moments and then subsides. Such attacks vary a great deal in frequency from person to person (Berg, 1951; Christie, 1951).

The focal points of neurotic anxiety of the first type are variegated. The attack may be precipitated by fear of dying, diseases like cancer or tuberculosis, loss of work, failure in school, and so on. In each case, however, the cause is not adequate to explain the intensity of the attack. In cases of free-floating anxiety, the patient frequently complains that things "are closing in on him," that he feels trapped by some gigantic, threatening force, or that he feels alone in a world that is hostile and destructive. Typically, anxiety attacks are accompanied by a variety of bodily symptoms—more rapid breathing, feelings of suffocation, palpitation, perspiration, increased heart beat, choking sensations, dizziness, nausea, headache, and the like. In other words, the patient manifests the symptoms brought on by reactions of the autonomic nervous system and the glandular mechanism to intense fear. Sometimes these symptoms occur even when there is no conscious feeling of anxiety, in which case the attack is unconscious and often more disturbing to the patient. Or the symptoms may be circumscribed, involving only difficulties in breathing or more rapid heart beat (Hodgins, 1951).

Anxiety Equivalents: Psychomotor Disturbances

Symptoms such as those we have just described are sometimes referred to as *anxiety equivalents, that is, they are the somatic equivalents of the feeling of anxiety.* This relation is important to understanding the nature and function of the anxiety neuroses because quite often the somatic equivalent is a means by which the patient rids himself of anxiety. The feeling of fear becomes displaced to the trembling, the rapid heart beat, or the feeling of suffocation. The symptom takes the place of the anxiety state. This mechanism is common to a number of neurotic reactions, as we might expect, since it is an economical way of getting rid of undesirable emotional states, conflicts, or frustrations. In hysteria, for example, the basic conflict is resolved by the adoption of some disability or disease symptom. Tension is relieved by the expedient of symptom formation in much the same way as the dynamics of needs and desires is expressed in daydreaming or fantasy thinking.

Like the condition of fear from which it springs, anxiety disturbs or disrupts a number of functions apart from those that are purely physiological. Everyone is aware that strong fear can twist the tongue or interfere with skilled movements. Similarly, anxiety is often reflected in psychomotor disturbances, such as stammering and stuttering. In every respect, the typical stutterer is like the anxious neurotic who trembles internally or externally in the face of problems and conflicts. Disturbances of speech are the psychomotor equivalent of the fear and helplessness that some persons experience in the presence of other people or in situations that are, in their minds, fraught with danger. If a child has been made to feel inadequate or inferior in vocal expression, his anxiety about his adequacy may become displaced to the speech function itself. This is also likely to happen when traumatic experiences involve social relations because speech is primarily a social function. We do not pretend, of course, that this is a complete explanation of functional speech disturbances; but in the background of patients exhibiting such symptoms we find traumatic experiences and a great deal of anxiety; for that reason, the explanation of these disturbances as a type of anxiety neurosis is one of the most probable that has been offered.

Dynamics of Anxiety Neurosis

It is clear from the nature and symptoms of neurotic anxiety that it is not an isolated neurotic manifestation; rather the anxiety reflects deep-seated and pervasive personality characteristics. The dynamics is very complicated, involving predisposing factors like fear conditioning and unfavorable parent-child relations, repressed feelings of guilt and hostility, frustration and conflict, and other causes and conditions that play a part in the development of neurosis (Cattell & Scheier, 1961, pp. 19–21). The interpretation of causes and background of anxiety will depend in part on theoretical convictions. Freud linked anxiety to the repression of sex impulses; Mowrer sees it as "the conscious manifestation of unconscious, repressed, repudiated guilt"; Horney relates it to repressed hostility, and Berg interprets it as a reaction to the suppression of aggression. In one of the best general statements of the causes and background of anxiety neurosis, May outlines a background of inadequate security patterns, hostility, conflict, and adverse cultural factors (May, 1950, pp. 206–223; Mowrer, 1950, pp. 27–40; Levy, 1950, pp. 140–149; Leavitt, 1953). All these writers recognize that frustration, conflict, and repression are basic determinants of neurotic anxiety.

In brief, neurotic anxiety is the sign of a neurotic personality in which such traits as helplessness, immaturity, sensitivity, and insecurity are prominent. The feeling of helplessness, engendered by chronic fear conditioning, creates an expectation of danger, annihilation, or catastrophe. There may also be a feeling of abandonment, of complete loss of love and emotional isolation in hostile and destructive surroundings. Sometimes the patient fears humiliation or social disapproval and ostracism, but fears of abandonment or loss of love are more prominent in the complex of fears that constitutes anxiety neurosis. Because of the inadequate social relations that these feelings represent, the anxiety neurosis may also involve unconscious anger and hostility. If these feelings were not repressed, but were expressed openly, anxiety would not develop. It does develop when the patient fears that he would be overwhelmed by such powerful emotions. Free-floating anxiety is the most common reaction to repressed fears. Similarly, the repression of impulses like sex, aggression, and guilt often leads to anxiety attacks for the same reason noted in the case of anger and hostility. The relation between hostility, aggression, and anxiety is very close. According to Horney (1950), repressed hostility is a specific source of anxiety. May, however, tries to show that the hostility would not have to be repressed except for the already existing anxiety, and therefore it is the anxiety that first gives rise to hostility, which in turn increases the anxiety (May, 1950, pp. 222–223).

Chronic anxiety reveals an early history of fear conditioning. Usually, the anxious adult was at one time an anxious child whose personality was of a typically neurotic character. Often, therefore, the anxiety attack stimulates regression to earlier, childish forms of behavior. Above all, the anxiety neurotic needs reassurance, protection, and the feeling of being safe and secure. His attack, therefore, is a signal of his helplessness, a distress signal calling for help. This seems to be the primary adjustive import of the anxiety attack. Just as the young child calls loudly for the protective security of his mother or father when threatened with danger or catastrophe, the anxious neurotic reaches out by means of his distressing symptoms for similar protection and security. This aim is seen most clearly in such symptoms as cardiac failure, suffocation, or constriction of the chest cavity that occur so often in anxiety attacks; they are a direct appeal for rescue from the appalling helplessness that neurotics typically experience.

OBSESSIVE–COMPULSIVE REACTIONS

Hysterical Phobias

Between anxiety reactions and those that are obsessive or compulsive in nature is the *hysterical phobia*, which may be characterized as a persistent, irrational, and sometimes overwhelming fear of certain situations or objects like closed and open spaces, great heights, germs, the dark, subways, and crowds. These phobias are usually designated by special terms such as "claustrophobia," "agoraphobia," "microphobia," and the like. Phobias resemble anxiety states in so far as they too are a special variety of fear. They are also linked to obsessive-compulsive tendencies, because they tend to dominate conduct in situations where the special fear is evoked. In an older terminology, therefore, they were subsumed under the general category of psychasthenia, along with obsessive-compulsive reactions. *Psychasthenia is a neurotic pattern characterized, as the symptoms indicate, by inadequate mental synthesis, in which feelings, ideas, or actions are beyond the control of the individual.* Here again we see exemplified some of the outstanding characteristics of the neurotic personality, particularly immaturity of development, lack of control, and autonomous functioning (Bucklew, 1960, Chapter 4).

Like the anxiety attack, the phobia represents a reaction to conflict and stress, but once fully established, it is difficult at times to determine its precise relation to the real causes underlying it, or its adjustive significance. For one thing, phobias are generally, if not always, *symbolic*, the fearful object or situation merely standing as a symbol of that which is the real cause of the obsessive fear. Thus, if a person fears his own moral weakness or the strength of his sexual urges, he may develop a phobia for high places, a phobia that may symbolize a fear of "falling" morally or spiritually. Similarly, microphobia may represent an unconscious fear of contamination of any kind. The phobia itself is not directly connected with the difficulty or conflict that caused it; the original fear has been displaced or projected onto some external object or situation. In this way, the phobia serves as a protective device against powerful impulses and their consequences. Typically, the patient's attitude is one of helplessness in the face of an uncontrollable fear. Like the anxiety neurotic, he appeals to others for help and he develops strong dependency feelings. Treatment requires an understanding of the psychogenic background and the function of the phobia, and the development of a more mature attitude toward those reality situations to which the phobia is unconsciously related.

Obsessions and Compulsions

In the neurotic pattern characterized by obsessions and compulsions, the patient's difficulty centers around certain ideas or thoughts that, despite every effort to dispel them, force themselves upon him. Or the difficulty may center around certain actions that he cannot resist performing. The patient may regard them as ridiculous, painful, or humiliating but finds it impossible to control them. In the case of compulsive acts, resistance may give rise to a severe attack of anxiety, whereas obsessions, because of their domination of consciousness, lead to indecision, hesitation, and uncertainty. As a result, obsessive-compulsive neurotics are often severely incapacitated for normal activities, especially as they become more and more preoccupied with the obsessions or the compulsive ritual (Maslow & Mittelmann, 1951, Chapter XXVII; Kennedy, 1951).

Obsessions and compulsions are manifested in many ways. There may be obsessive thoughts of one's own death or of killing someone, of sex, or health, or imminent catastrophe, of anything at all, in fact, that serves to symbolize or repress the inner conflict and emotional turmoil. Obsessive thoughts, by fastening attention to themselves, may also serve the adjustive aim of preventing even less agreeable ideas and impulses from gaining admission to consciousness. Typical of all compulsions is hand washing, which is usually determined by feelings of guilt or sinfulness and is sometimes carried to such an extreme that the hands become severely irritated. Another compulsive tendency is manifested in persons who retrace their steps several times to be sure that the car door is locked or that the oven burners have been turned off. Some obsessions and compulsions are relatively minor and very common and are not to be regarded in the same light as those that seriously disturb or incapacitate the person.

Obsessions and compulsions are, of course, mental, but it should be noted that here, too, there may be organic disturbances, although these symptoms are not exploited by the obsessive-compulsive personality in the way that is characteristic of other neurotic personalities. Along with obsessions and compulsions may be found disturbances of appetite, head-ache, dizziness, and so forth, brought on by the tensions that result from the obsessive condition. Although such symptoms may be nothing more than aftereffects of psychic tension, their psychosomatic qualities cause the obsessive-compulsive neuroses to fit into the general picture of neurotic illness.

The psychodynamics underlying these neuroses is complex and not always easily determined. Partly responsible is the personality of the patient, although it may be that both the neurotic pattern and the personality reflect deeper causes. The obsessive-compulsive neurotic is often characterized by a strong social conscience and an idealistic attitude, which lead to unusual or extreme sympathy for and consideration of others and a tendency to settle all issues in a purely rational and idealistic manner, free of anger, hostility, or rancor of any kind. These traits in moderation are beneficial, but in the obsessive neurotic they are carried to an extreme. Other common traits are excessive orderliness and cleanliness, exemplified by many housewives who make a fetish of housekeeping and insist that everything must be in its proper place at all times. Combined with these characteristics in many instances are miserliness and stubbornness, both of which reflect the rigidity of the obsessive-compulsive personality. When such traits are combined with their opposites, as frequently they are, the psychodynamics becomes more involved and extremely difficult to fathom.

Undoubtedly there is *a great deal of insecurity* in the personality of the obsessive-compulsive neurotic, which explains his extreme orderliness, perfectionism, idealism, and his need to be on the right side of things. These qualities serve to protect him from his own feelings of insecurity and helplessness in the face of difficulties and threatening impulses. In compulsive persons, there may be the additional factor of *guilt*, which serves to heighten the feeling of insecurity. Such feelings as insecurity and guilt may also lead to hostility because the patient fears being overcome by forces beyond his control or being morally criticized. This hostility may explain why obsessive thoughts so often center around acts of violence. These several characteristics and their underlying causes fit well into the general picture of the neurotic personality. If the patient can develop insight into the nature and causes of his obsessions and compulsions the possibilities of remedy are good. But the counselor or therapist must always remember that all adjustive behavior, whether normal or neurotic, is the person's solution to a problem or conflict, and he will tend, therefore, to resist any effort to dislodge his obsessions or compulsions. Insight must be supported by other approaches that will act to reduce the need for neurotic symptoms.

ORGAN NEUROSES AND PSYCHOSOMATIC DISTURBANCES

The Psychosomatic Theory

Many of the symptoms manifested in nervousness, worry, and anxiety attacks are *psychosomatic,* which means simply that they are physical disturbances with a psychogenic (psychic, mental, emotional) background or causality. While the term itself has been dropped from the official nomenclature of the American Psychiatric Association, it is too firmly entrenched in the literature and in the thinking of psychologists and psychiatrists to be materially affected by this change. The most common psychosomatic disturbances, peptic ulcer and essential hypertension for example, are the results of such emotional disorders as chronic worry and anxiety. Psychosomatic disturbances are called "organ neuroses" because they involve disorder or pathology of some organ of the body brought on by causes functioning in a neurotic personality. Today it is customary to regard the majority of human physical ills as psychosomatic rather than purely organic, not excluding such truly pathological conditions as heart trouble and tuberculosis. This interpretation is based on the conception that *the human organism is a mind-body entity in which the two aspects of human nature are so intimately conjoined that whatever occurs in the one area is likely to have repercussions in the other.* Psychosomatic illnesses are typical illustrations of this relation (the same thesis was developed at considerable length in our discussion of personality and adjustment in Chapter 3). This viewpoint has tremendous implications for the study of both physical and mental health and brings the fields of medicine (including psychiatry) and psychology so close together that at times they are indistinguishable.

The literature on the psychosomatic problem is very extensive. The student will find a number of these sources in the list of collateral readings and references at the end of the chapter. One should note particularly Dunbar (1947), Saul (1944, pp. 269–305), Brown, Preu & Sullivan (1938), Strecker (1952, Chapter X), and Mile, Cobb, & Shands (1952). An exhaustive bibliography of 2336 references on this problem will be found in Altschule (1953).

The Organ Neuroses

The organ neuroses *involve actual impairment or disorder* in one or another of the bodily organs. The range of such disorders is very broad, since every major system of the body may become involved. There are psychosomatic disturbances of the gastrointestinal system, the respiratory system, the endocrine glands, the cardiovascular apparatus, the skin, the genitourinary organs, and the skeletomuscular system.

Essential Hypertension. Prominent among psychosomatic disorders, and very common in occurrence, is the condition of essential hypertension, or high blood pressure (Hambling, 1951). Dunbar (1947) estimates that about 25 percent of all people beyond the age of fifty die of emotionally induced hypertension. It is, as we have indicated, a condition of high blood pressure, which may become chronic and irreversible if not corrected in time. In a sense, hypertension represents an effort of the heart and arteries to adapt themselves to the patient's emotional conflicts and difficulties. The only remedy, therefore, is a reduction of the emotional reactions expressed in the altered cardiovascular condition.

The personality picture in hypertension is typically neurotic, and it is customary to refer to the "hypertensive personality." There is often, of course, a chronic state of anxiety induced by the failure to achieve perfectionistic goals or by a conflict between a basic hostility toward people and an outward effort to respond to them in a socially acceptable manner (Dunbar, 1942). In other words, besides the anxiety there is the characteristic neurotic trait of ambivalence. "The emotional constellation most frequent in patients with essential hypertension is anger, often completely repressed, mingled with anxiety and depression" (Maslow & Mittelmann, 1951, p. 466).

> A well-known scientist has suffered from hypertension for the past several years. The man is a study in contrasts being deferential and polite to his peers and superiors but inconsiderate of his subordinates. Superficially he presents a picture of the quintessence of charm and courtesy, although a somewhat sarcastic tone often underlies his conversation. He obtains "sick leave" with some regularity and often is forced to ask his assistants to substitute for him in meeting professional obligations because of headaches and general feelings of illness. To date, no organic cause has been discovered to account for his elevated blood pressure and since he presents almost a clinical picture of the essential hypertensive personality, one suspects that behind his façade of politeness there lurks a rather supreme contempt for his fellow man (Steckle, 1949, p. 67).

Migraine. Closely allied to hypertension, and often associated with it as the foregoing case illustrates, is migraine, which consists of recurrent severe headaches, usually on one side and often accompanied by other symptoms such as nausea, constipation, and scotomata. The attack varies in length from a few hours to as long as several days and is thought to involve a spasm of the blood vessels supplying particularly the meninges of the brain. Migraine is a typical neurotic reaction to tension-producing situations, and, like hypertension, occurs in the perfectionist preoccupied with achievement or success. The perfectionism leads to undue emphasis on efficiency and orderliness and sometimes to frigidity or disgust in the matter of sexual relations. Such persons are easily disturbed by conflict or stressful situations, and the migraine often serves as an adjustive mechanism to escape responsibility and the demands imposed by stressful situations.

Skin Disorders. Certain skin disorders including excessive perspiration, itching, urticaria, acne, and dermatitis nervosa, are common psychosomatic symptoms in the neurotic personality. These conditions are diagnosed as psychosomatic because they begin with or are aggravated by situations involving conflict or pressure and also because they are amenable to psychotherapeutic treatment. It must be recognized, however, that physical causes also play a part in some of these disorders. Typical of these skin conditions is *urticaria*, expressed as a fleeting rash and as a swelling and itching of the skin. Various studies have demonstrated the close relation between urticaria and emotional difficulties (Wittkower, 1953). The psychogenic background most often includes acute frustration of the need for acceptance and affection and the desire for attention. There is usually a picture of immaturity, fear of responsibility, and emotional dependence on others. Feelings of helplessness are also common, and there may be resentment and hostility against the forces that threaten the patient's security.

Similar personality factors are found in other skin conditions, such as *dermatitis* or *eczema*, an inflammation of the skin characterized by redness, itching, and sometimes the formation of small blisters. The term "neurodermatitis" is also used to indicate its "nervous" or psychological origin, when physical agents have been ruled out in diagnosis. Maslow and Mittelmann (1951) mention three emotional factors that play a role in determining this condition: desire for closeness and emotional warmth, aggression directed toward the self, symbolized by scratching, and erotization of the skin. The emotional basis of dermatitis is indicated by the fact that it responds readily to psychotherapy and occurs in persons with typical nervous traits. From a psychosomatic viewpoint, it seems to represent a desire for sympathy or for being cared for, traits that are in line with the immaturity and helplessness of the typical neurotic. One investigator reports that a group of twenty persons with acne differed significantly from a control group of the same number on four of the nine scales of the Minnesota Multiphasic Personality Inventory: hypochondriasis, hysteria, psychasthenia, and schizophrenia (Narciso, 1952).

Bronchial Asthma.   Disorders of the respiratory system are common among neurotic persons. For example, it was found that bronchial asthma increased as much as 40 percent among inductees in World War II, a significant increase in view of the fact that asthma was regarded as sufficient reason for noninduction. The condition is characterized by difficulties in breathing over which the patient has no control. Physically, the attacks represent an involuntary contraction of the muscles in the bronchia, which are mediated by the vagus nerve. Careful studies indicate that attacks of asthma are correlated with anger, hostility, and neurotic dependency, including the fear of rejection (French, 1939). Here again the illness reminds us of the immaturity and helplessness of the neurotic personality; it appears as a bid for attention, motherly care and affection, and reassurance of acceptance. Other studies have indicated that such respiratory disorders as pulmonary tuberculosis, respiratory infections, and vasomotor rhinitis are correlated with emotional disturbances. If nothing else, emotional difficulties and negative attitudes toward illness lower resistance to the point where recovery is made more difficult.

Peptic Ulcer.   Among the disturbances of the gastrointestinal system, peptic ulcer and colitis are perhaps the most closely associated with the neurotic tendency toward illness. Peptic ulcer is a small lesion that develops in the stomach or duodenum, the patient complaining of recurrent pains in the upper abdomen, especially when the stomach is empty, which is the reason why eating serves to relieve the pain. It is well known that peptic ulcer is closely correlated with emotional upset, particularly anger, anxiety, worry, shame, guilt, and embarrassment. Experimental studies on the effects of strong emotion on gastric functions have brought out clearly that relaxation is associated with a decrease in the secretion of hydrochloric acid, whereas during highly charged emotional discussions or situations the secretion is measurably increased. It has been noted also that, during such excitement, bile is regurgitated from the duodenum. Here we see a clear illustration of autonomic-glandular functioning induced by emotional reactions. Changes in the gastrointestinal system are also accompanied, significantly, by changes in the respiratory and cardiovascular systems. If these reactions become chronic, they cause the production of the ulcer, which, once established, is maintained or even reinforced by the worries and stresses of daily adjustments (Weiner *et al.*, 1961).

The literature on the psychogenic and neurotic background of peptic ulcer is very extensive. The student should see, for example, the study by Sullivan and McKell (1950), based on more than 1000 cases, which brings out clearly the personality factors in the development of peptic ulcer. According to the authors, 72 percent of the patients exhibited a typical "ulcer personality," including such traits as hyperactivity, ambitiousness, and tenseness. Another study, by Emery and Monroe (1935), is based on a study of 1435 cases of peptic ulcer. In a more recent study (Marquis, Sinnett, & Winter, 1952), which is defined as a psychological study of peptic ulcer patients, the authors distinguish a "primary" ulcer type and a "reactive" type, both of which, however, show marked oral fixations, dependency needs, sexual maladjustment, feelings of inferiority, and nervous tension. The types differ in their acceptance or denial of dependency needs. Other important sources are Draper (1942), Mittelmann and Wolff (1942), Szasz *et al.* (1947), Wolf and Wolff (1942), Robinson (1937), and Kapp, Rosenbaum, and Romano (1947).

Colitis. Colitis is a condition resembling ulcer, and, if it persists for a long time, it may terminate in ulcerative colitis. It is characterized by chronic constipation or frequent bowel movements and is accompanied by pain and a discharge of blood and mucus. As with other psychosomatic disorders, physical causes must be ruled out before it can be stated that colitis is a result of psychogenic or emotional difficulties. However, there is enough evidence available to indicate conclusively that conditions of the colon vary with emotional factors. For example, in a symposium on the influence of psychogenic factors on gastrointestinal disturbances, reported in the *Psychoanalytic Quarterly* for 1934, it is pointed out that the colon may become extremely tense or completely relaxed during periods of emotional stress. Similarly, mucous colitis is regarded as a psychosomatic disturbance since studies have shown it is correlated with various emotional states, such as anxiety, resentment, and guilt. Additional evidence comes from the fact that psychotherapy is often effective in the treatment of colitis.

Genitourinary Disorders. Finally, we may describe certain psychosomatic conditions associated with the genitourinary system. Of these perhaps the most common is enuresis, which is now regarded as almost entirely psychogenic in origin. Enuresis (involuntary voiding of urine) is variously interpreted as a failure or breakdown of control, lack of mature development, a desire to gain attention, or as a sign of hostility and retaliation against parental domination. Among enuretics are found the typical neurotic traits of excessive dependence, craving for affection, immaturity, and feelings of isolation and helplessness, any one or combination of which could help to account for the condition. Particularly is this true of immaturity, because this quality invariably includes lack of control. It is worth noting, too, that involuntary passing of urine is a typical reaction in extreme emotional seizures, such as terror, during which controls are broken down and the autonomic nervous system temporarily assumes command.

Biologically, the voiding of urine is an autonomic function that is brought under control only through conditioning and training. In situations of stress, therefore, there is a strong tendency to revert to the more primitive autonomic functioning.

Emotional stresses, conflicts, and frustrations find expression also in disturbances of the genital system. Changes in the menstrual flow, pseudocyesis (false pregnancy), dysmenorrhea (painful menstruation), sexual frigidity, and sexual impotence are common symptoms of emotional difficulties. Considering the intimate connection between such emotional states as fear and anxiety and the sexual functions, it is easy to understand why emotional conflicts should often find their locus in sexual difficulties, particularly in the type of psychological setting provided by the neurotic personality. Fear of pregnancy, feelings of disgust or guilt associated with sex, inadequacy and insecurity in the role of husband or wife, an over-developed or pathological sense of purity, all are fertile soil for the development of psychosomatic disturbances of the genital system. It is a truism of psychosomatics that the emotional difficulty or conflict will tend to express itself in that organ or part of the body that bears a symbolic relation to the nature of the conflict. Thus fears or anxieties regarding sex may be expected to result in symptoms associated with the genital system.

Mechanism and Development of Psychosomatic Disorders

The mechanism of psychosomatic disorders is not particularly difficult to understand and is substantially the same in the organ neuroses as in all other neurotic disorders in which physical symptoms of illness are determined by psychogenic factors. The general principle governing psychosomatic development is derived from the intimate connection between mental and physical functions already described in preceding pages; it is expressed in many nonpathological conditions, such as suggestion phenomena, fatigue effects, and the physiological concomitants of emotional experience. All these familiar phenomena are typically psychosomatic; familiarity with them should make it easier for us to understand the mechanism of neurotic illness.

The basis of neurotic illness is emotional conflict and the psychic tension of chronic frustration. In other words, in neurosis and psychosomatic illness there is always some kind of an emotional difficulty in which such emotions as fear, anger, guilt, hostility, isolation, and anxiety are predominant. It is well known, of course, that emotional responses are psychophysical, that is, they are psychic experiences or processes that affect the functioning of the thalamus, the autonomic system, and the glands of internal secretion. As a result, even normal emotional experiences are accompanied by somatic reactions, for example, sweating, increased heart beat, trembling, gastrointestinal changes, increased glandular secretions, and other intraorganic changes. These alterations are referred to as the "bodily resonance" of the emotional response and will not occasion distress or difficulty unless they occur too often or become chronic. In abnormal or neurotic personalities, emotional responses are excessive, pathological, and chronic, and thus the physical changes, which in themselves are normal, become excessive and pathological. A good illustration of this fact is the effect of anxiety. Normally, anxiety will bring about gastrointestinal changes, including increased digestive secretions, and these changes will abate when the anxiety is reduced. When, however, the anxiety becomes acute and chronic, the organic changes tend to persist, the end result of which may be peptic ulcer or colitis. Similarly, emotional conflicts lead to difficulties of breathing, migraine, and other typical psychosomatic reactions.

NEURASTHENIA AND HYPOCHONDRIA

Nature and Symptoms of Neurasthenia

Neurasthenia is another neurotic disorder that illustrates the flight into illness. *Its primary symptom and characteristic is chronic fatigue,* but there are other psychosomatic disturbances that are usually present, including headache, insomnia, digestive ailments, constipation, and vague aches and pains. Fatigue and exhaustion, however, are the predominant and continuous symptoms. These conditions often become chronic and may eventually result in invalidism. *The dominant emotional characteristic of neurasthenia is anxiety,* and the physical symptoms are an expression of the continuous emotional tension that the anxiety causes. One can see, therefore, that neurasthenia is closely related to the other neurotic conditions already described. For intensive studies of cases of neurasthenia and hypochondria the student is referred to Burton and Harris (1947) and Page (1947, Chapters VI and VII).

Background and Psychodynamics of Neurasthenia

The purposive and adjustive significance of neurasthenic symptoms is plain to see. They are clearly defensive and a definite bid for pity, attention, and sympathy. The neurasthenic craves being wanted and cared for, and the flight into illness is the most direct route to these goals. In many instances, the history of the patient includes favorable experience with illness, coddling, and parental overprotection. Feelings of inferiority and insecurity, and the characteristic neurotic sense of helplessness are other factors that are found in the background of the neurasthenic patient. In treatment, therefore, the primary aim should be the amelioration of the precipitating causes or situations, which involves giving the patient a chance to secure love, attention, and self-esteem in a legitimate way. Insight into the connection between symptoms and emotional difficulties is very helpful, although it is often difficult to get the patient to see this connection. In some cases, intensive character reorganization may be necessary for the patient to effect an adjustment.

Hypochondria

The term "hypochondria" has several meanings. It is used to refer to intense *fear or anxiety* regarding the state of one's health, and to a non-anxious but intense *preoccupation* with illness and symptoms. The word is usually used in the latter sense. The patient complains endlessly of backaches, pains or uncomfortable feelings in the stomach, head, and practically any other part of the body. Occasionally, there are no definite complaints at all but only an intense preoccupation with physiological functions. For this reason, health and diet faddists, who become preoccupied with vitamins, proteins, and so forth, are often classified as hypochondriacs. In all cases, *the essential characteristic is an intense or even morbid preoccupation with bodily health or functions.*

The hypochondriac, like all neurotics, exhibits distinctive personality characteristics. We might say that his neurosis is an *abortive* flight into illness for purposes of protection. Although he readily establishes social contact with others, he is psychologically isolated, preoccupied with his own life, and has little or no identification with other persons. Actually, the hypochondriac attempts to solve his frustrations and difficulties by increasing his isolation through an overdevelopment of self-interest. The symptoms are, of course, an expression of discomfort, illness, or suffering, and in that sense constitute a typical neurotic plea for attention, sympathy, affection, or help. At times, they may also serve the purpose of self-aggression or self-punishment for strong guilt feelings or hostility toward others. As has been stated, one of the basic characteristics of the neurotic personality is aggression directed toward self, and symptoms of illness often reflect this basic attitude. It is difficult to convince the real hypochondriac that his symptoms are psychologically determined, and for that reason he resists treatment. Like many neurotics, he clings to his symptoms as a protection against his own shortcomings, and psychotherapy is often ineffective. Insight and the development of feelings of being loved and wanted are necessary to break the hold of his symptoms.

CONVERSION HYSTERIA

Nature and Symptoms of Conversion Hysteria

Hysteria is the most complex of neurotic manifestations. It assumes many forms, ranging from simple "hysterics" to the most complex expressions of multiple personality. Here we are particularly interested in the type of hysterical manifestation that is reflected in some observable change in organic function. Considered broadly, *hysteria is the resolution of a mental conflict or personal difficulty by the adoption of some disease symptom*. In some instances, the emotional conflict is "converted" into a physical symptom or disability, a fact reflected in the term "conversion hysteria." It should be understood that in all cases of hysteria, regardless of the form, there is a common reaction pattern, which may be identified most simply and adequately as *autonomous functioning*. Whether the hysterical patient becomes anesthetic, paralyzed, or develops symptoms of amnesia and somnambulism, the essential feature is a failure in control over psychological or bodily functions (Thorpe & Katz, 1948, pp. 380–391).

Hysteria is a flight into illness or disability and manifests many of the characteristic features of the neurotic personality, particularly immaturity, helplessness, sensitivity, self-aggression, mental conflict, suggestibility, lack of self-control, and emotional instability. In many respects, the hysteric typifies the neurotic personality, and therefore hysteria expresses more of the characteristic features of neurosis than some of the other neuroses we have considered. Hysterical seizures must not be confused with *malingering*, which is a deliberate simulation of illness or disability in order to escape responsibilities or to evade the demands of a situation. The disabilities of hysteria are not consciously or deliberately determined; rather they represent an unconscious effort to resolve a mental conflict or to cope with an existing situation.

The range of symptoms in hysteria is extremely broad and may involve almost any aspect of personality. Prominent among them are the sensory disturbances, which include loss, impairment, or distortion of sensibility in all of the sensoria, but particularly touch and vision. Typically, the patient complains that he has no feeling in his hand ("glove" anesthesia) or leg ("stocking" anesthesia), or that all sensation is gone from one part of the body. The functional or psychogenic nature of these disturbances is made clear by the fact that the loss of sensitivity does not correspond to the anatomic distribution of the nerves. In addition, the anesthesia may transfer from one side of the body or from one limb to the other, which is impossible in the case of true organic lesions. Similarly, in hysterical blindness the optic mechanism is entirely normal, but the patient complains that he cannot see (Moore, 1948, Chapter XVI). Other sensory complaints include tingling or creeping sensations in different parts of the body (paresthesia), and excessive sensitiveness (hyperesthesia).

Related to these sensory disturbances are the motor symptoms—functional paralysis, excessive and unusual movements, or continuous contraction of the muscles. In some cases of long duration, muscular atrophy may occur, and even in the early stages of hysterical paralysis, the limb involved is cold and bluish. In addition to paralysis, motor symptoms include tremor, hysterical convulsion (a generalized twitching of the muscles that resembles the epileptic seizure), aphonia (the inability to talk above a whisper), and mutism.

Motor symptoms involve the voluntary musculature, but there are also disturbances of the autonomic functions. There may be difficulties in breathing, particularly short breath, loss of appetite, sensations of a lump in the throat (globus hystericus), coughing spells, hiccoughing, nausea, vomiting, constipation, urinary disturbances, excessive perspiration, and headaches. Each one of these symptoms is an expression of the hysterical tendency to exploit illness or physical disability for the sake of reducing tension or achieving adjustment.

Psychodynamics of Conversion Hysteria

As already indicated, the symptoms of hysteria are closely related to the personality structure of the patient. They represent in unmistakable terms his immaturity, helplessness, and feelings of emotional isolation. Like so many neurotics, the hysteric develops symptoms that call for sympathy, attention, and the care and emotional warmth of other persons. They function, therefore, as a defense against his own inadequacy and irresponsibility. As with the neurasthenic patient, there is usually a history of favorable experience with illness, parental coddling, and overprotection. There is also a strong fear of rejection, stemming from inconsistent or inadequate parental discipline, and an overevaluation of social approval.

The hysterical person is in many cases the prototype of the spoiled child, whose egocentrism feeds on the attention and care that he can extract from others. The immediate determinants of the hysterical reaction are, of course, situations involving stress or pressure in which the patient feels wholly inadequate, or deep-seated mental conflicts with which he is unable to cope successfully. The conflict is converted into physical symptoms of one kind or another, which helps to resolve the difficulty. The mechanism involved in this conversion is not essentially different from that which underlies other psychosomatic disturbances. If symptoms are not of long duration, psychotherapy is usually effective. Interview therapy, suggestion, and hypnosis have been used to good effect.

Here, then, is the picture of neurosis and the flight into illness. More than any other type of adjustive reaction, the flight into illness illustrates most clearly the dynamic force of human needs, frustrations, and conflicts. It points up also the deep significance of healthy parent-child relations, effective training, and adequate social development. It is the flight into illness, more than anything else, that gives the problem of mental health its epidemeological quality.

QUESTIONS AND PROJECTS FOR FURTHER STUDY

1. Explain the statement that all neuroses are psychogenic.
2. Write a critical and evaluative report on Karen Horney's *Neurosis and human growth*.
3. Explain why the flight into illness is characteristic of the neurotic personality.
4. Describe in your own words the difference between neurosis and psychosis.
5. Compare the characteristics of the neurotic personality with the criteria of adjustment and mental health outlined in Chapter 2.
6. Describe some common, everyday examples of obsessions, and compulsions.
7. Compare the concept of traumatic neurosis with that of organ neurosis, and give examples to illustrate the differences between them.
8. Explain the mechanism of psychosomatic disorders, and show how this mechanism is related to normal reactions.
9. Write a brief report of Flanders Dunbar's *Mind and body*.
10. To what extent are the backgrounds and syndromes of neurasthenic and hysterical patients similar? Explain this similarity.

SELECTED COLLATERAL READINGS

BURTON, A., & HARRIS, R. E. *Case histories in clinical and abnormal psychology*. New York: Harper & Row, 1947.

CATTELL, R. B., & SCHEIER, I. H. *The meaning and measurement of neuroticism and anxiety*. New York: Ronald, 1961.

GARRE, W. J. *Basic anxiety*. New York: Philosophical Library, 1962.

GOLDSTEIN, M. J., & PALMER, J. O. *The experience of anxiety: a casebook*. New York: Oxford University Press, 1963.

GRINKER, R. R., & ROBBINS, F. P. *Psychosomatic case book*. New York: Doubleday, 1954.

HOCH, P. H., & ZUBIN, J. (Eds.) *Anxiety*. New York: Grune & Stratton, 1950.

HORNEY, KAREN. *The neurotic personality of our time*. New York: Norton, 1937.

HORNEY, KAREN. *Neurosis and human growth*. New York: Norton, 1950.

MAY, R. *The meaning of anxiety*. New York: Ronald, 1950.

RUESCH, J. *Chronic disease and psychological invalidism*. Los Angeles: University of California Press, 1951.

SULLIVAN, A. J., & MC KELL, T. E. *Personality in peptic ulcer*. Springfield, Ill.: Charles C Thomas, 1950.

WINTER, J. A. *The origins of illness and anxiety*. New York: Julian Press, 1962.

PART FOUR

Mental Hygiene and Treatment

12

Background and Principles
of Mental Hygiene

In the foregoing sections of this book we have concerned ourselves with a descriptive analysis of the nature and criteria, the determinants and dynamics, and the structure and forms of adjustment and mental health. We included experimental and clinical data and representative viewpoints and theories from many disciplines in order to lay a secure groundwork for the understanding of mental health and the processes of adjustment. Now we turn our attention in this last part to mental hygiene and treatment—the application of tested principles and practices to the preservation of mental health or its restoration after disorder has set in. In this chapter we shall deal with the beginnings and development of mental hygiene and certain basic principles that govern mental hygiene practices.

CURRENT MENTAL HYGIENE CONCEPTS

Mental Hygiene and the Psychology of Adjustment

From what has been stated earlier in this text, we know that mental hygiene is specifically oriented to the problem of mental health, whereas the psychology of adjustment is directed toward studying the nature, determinants, and forms of response involved in the human organism's efforts to cope successfully with the demands of self and of the environment. That the mental status of the individual is directly involved in some of these behavioral efforts is a fact well known to all students in the field. At this point mental hygiene and the psychology of adjustment tend to merge, and the boundaries separating the two disciplines become less distinct. Thus it is not uncommon to speak of mental adjustments or to refer to mental disorders as a form of maladjustment. As we shall see, therefore, the principles of mental hygiene have much to do with the problem of good adjustment.

Nevertheless, there remains the distinction that the study of adjustment is much broader *in scope* and different *in aim* from mental hygiene. Marital adjustment, for example, is not just a matter of ironing out mental

343

quirks or difficulties. We may assume that mental health is a *sine qua non* of marital happiness, but there are other criteria that must be observed also. The same thing is true of academic, vocational, personal, and social adjustment, in each one of which mental health (and therefore mental hygiene) is a determining factor, but not the only one. Primarily, therefore, the study of adjustment is a scientific investigation to determine what these factors and criteria are in order that principles for the achievement and maintenance of good adjustment can be better formulated.

This idea gives us a clue to the nature of mental hygiene, and at the same time suggests that the psychology of adjustment is the basis for the principles that are utilized in any mental hygiene program. The study of adjustment, as we have tried to portray it, provides the facts, interpretations, and insights necessary to a formulation of practical rules for healthful living. These rules go beyond the scope of mental hygiene, but those relating to mental health, or more broadly, to the psychological well-being of the organism, constitute the framework of mental hygiene. In brief, therefore, *the term mental hygiene refers to the development and application of a set of practical principles directed toward the achievement and maintenance of the psychological well-being of human organisms and the prevention of mental disorder and maladjustment* (Bernard, 1951, pp. 17–18; Thorpe, 1950, p. 6).

Forms of Mental Hygiene

Preventive Mental Hygiene. From the definition made above it is clear that mental hygiene, like its counterpart physical hygiene, is essentially *prophylactic*; that is, it is aimed primarily at the development of mental and personality characteristics in such a way that mental difficulties, disabling symptoms, and maladjustments are largely precluded or at least minimized. Mental hygiene of this sort involves the application of principles that will ensure mental health and stability in the same manner as the application of physical hygiene principles safeguards physical health. Thus adequate rest is always urged as a necessary step in preserving physical well-being, and the healthful gratification of such basic needs as affection and security is set forth as a fundamental principle in the development and maintenance of mental health. The application of such principles, particularly in the home and school, is intended to prevent the onset of mental disability or disorder (Soddy, 1952; Ryan, 1953; Querido, 1954). Thus warm, accepting, and affectionate parents create a climate of interpersonal relations that helps produce happy, well-adjusted children, in whom the development of disabling symptoms or unacceptable behavior is unlikely. We realize, of course, that a great deal more than this is necessary; but, as we have noted, good parent-child relations are among the most important determinants of good adjustment (Stevenson, 1944).

Ameliorative Mental Hygiene.   Because many factors influence the development of personality and mental health, it is difficult to set up a pattern of relations and to develop methods of training and discipline that will guarantee fully adequate adjustment during the period of growing up. Mistakes will be made, and failure to provide the maturing child with all the requirements of good psychological development will occur in the normal course of events. Many children may, therefore, be expected to acquire behavior symptoms that stand in the way of good adjustment— nail biting, thumb sucking, crying, temper tantrums, hostile or aggressive behavior, biting, bed wetting, and the like. In such instances, the point of prevention has already passed, and it becomes necessary to utilize the principles of mental hygiene in an ameliorative fashion, that is, to improve personality and to raise the level of adjustment so that behavior symptoms and mechanisms are no longer necessary. Many children experience adjustment difficulties and failing mental health simply because they are inadequate to meet the demands and difficulties of daily living. Much of this inadequacy is attributable to immaturity, to the existence of such feelings as insecurity, isolation, or inferiority, or to the imposition of continuous frustrations, tensions, and irritations by unthinking parents, teachers, and others with whom they come in daily contact. As a result, they develop mental or behavior symptoms for purposes of protection or escape. In these instances, the application of principles of mental hygiene is directed toward greater maturity and the development of a better personality organization. This, too, is the primary goal of preventive mental hygiene. In some instances, however, this goal is not achieved, and the aim then becomes ameliorative.

Supportive Mental Hygiene.   The principles of mental hygiene may also be employed in a supportive manner so that whatever gains are realized by treatment may be safeguarded against the possibility of future setbacks as new difficulties, conflicts, and frustrations arise. Supportive mental hygiene is merely a continuation of the method of applying principles of adjustment that is begun with efforts to improve personality. It is easy for a person who has had psychological difficulties to slip back into the old pattern of handling his problems because symptomatic behavior is familiar, requires little effort, and provides a measure of safety and protection for the patient. Until, therefore, there is a profound reorganization of personality along the lines of greater maturity, a more adequate value system, and better habits, supportive hygiene is strongly indicated. Klein distinguishes prophylactic and meliorative mental hygiene, whereas Bernard uses a three-fold distinction similar to the one used here: conservative, preventive, and curative (Klein, 1944, pp. 14–18; Bernard, 1952, pp. 22–23). Regardless of adjustment level, every person is required to utilize all forms of mental hygiene at one point or another in his life, since even the most hardy personality cannot easily withstand the onslaughts against mental health of some of life's experiences and difficulties. In this sense, the principles of mental hygiene become universal in their application.

Mental Hygiene, Counseling, and Psychotherapy

The only real distinction between mental hygiene, counseling, and psychotherapy is the preventive aspect of the former discipline since both counseling and psychotherapy are methods of treatment directed toward the reduction of maladjustment and mental disorder once they have developed. But even these techniques can be utilized for prophylactic and supportive purposes, and in all counseling and therapeutic processes the principles of mental hygiene play an essential role. However, these disciplines are essentially *corrective*, whereas mental hygiene is essentially *preventive*. In Chapter 17 we shall discuss the nature and forms of counseling and psychotherapy.

Scope of Mental Hygiene

Usually, when we consider the application of psychological principles, we think only of the individual whose problems become the focal point of treatment. But here we must go beyond this restricted viewpoint, especially where mental hygiene is concerned. Admittedly, the principles of mental hygiene are directed primarily toward the individual who has problems of adjustment and mental health. It is important to recognize, however, that these principles can be applied with similar advantage to organized social units, such as the home and the school, and to the community. The mental hygiene of the home, for example, is as real and as important as the mental hygiene of the individual (Thorpe, 1950, Chapter XV; Schneiders, 1954, pp. 52–61). This idea is in line with the general psychological principle that personality and adjustment are conditioned throughout life by the environment and the psychological climate within which they develop. This fact was emphasized in Chapter 4 where we studied the conditions and determinants of adjustment (Lewin, 1946).

On the basis of the relations between personality and adjustment on the one hand and environment and psychological climate on the other, it is clear that the mental health and stability of the individual person will reflect, in part at least, the quality of the psychological context within which he functions. For example, if parent-child relations are unhealthy or damaging, if the marital situation is deteriorating, or if the general psychological climate in the home is one of hostility, jealousy, bickering, or immorality, the successful application of mental hygiene principles to the individual is largely precluded. In such instances, a sound, extensive program of mental hygiene for the home is even more important than one for individuals because, until the home situation is cleared up, there is little hope for an effective program of personal mental hygiene.

To a lesser degree, but of real importance, is the mental hygiene of the school. Maladjustment among teachers, damaging relations between school authorities and pupils, low morale, and unfair or discriminating practices on the part of school authorities are bound to impair the individual's chances for good adjustment. Furthermore, society in general could profit by the application of the principles of mental hygiene (Chapter 16). It is apparent, of course, that the individual is often caught up in a vicious circle, and perhaps the only way to break into this circle is by developing the mental health of the single person; in any event, until this circle is broken at one point or another, the principles of mental health and effective living cannot be used to the best advantage (Deutsch, 1949, pp. 409–510).

GROWTH OF MENTAL HYGIENE

Early Beginnings

In brief, some of the principles of mental hygiene have been known as far back as the pre-Christian era, but the development of mental hygiene as an organized body of knowledge and as a definite movement did not occur until the problem of mental health and disease was rescued from the superstitions and malpractices that characterized the period preceding the growth of psychiatry and abnormal psychology. As one writer says (Klein, 1944, p. 22):

> As a self-conscious movement with a novel name of its own, mental hygiene is only about thirty-odd years old. But in terms of its larger objectives it may be regarded as a new name for some very old ways of dealing with life's problems. . . . what our grandfathers and their forefathers called a *philosophy of life* was not altogether different from what we describe as sound mental hygiene. It is the same old quest for a wise, satisfying way of life. It is the same old quest for ways of meeting adversity without going to smash. It is the same old quest for enduring

values that will enable us to be brave and steadfast when the going gets tough. It is the same old quest for a type of training and education that will equip the child to make the business of living synonymous with the joy of living.

Needless to say, there is little room for the concepts of mental hygiene in the minds of persons who are convinced that mental disorder is the work of an evil spirit or a just chastisement for the commission of sins, not that sin cannot cause a great deal of mental difficulty. Our concept of mental disorder must include natural causes before we can begin to think of scientific means by which such disorders can be remedied (Curran, 1960). In earlier times, the unfortunate mental patient was cast into a dungeon or bound with heavy chains because of the way in which mental disorder was interpreted. It was not until the humanitarian efforts of men like Philippe Pinel of France and William Tuke of England, combined with the development of a more scientific attitude toward mental disorder, that a program of mental hygiene became possible.

Growth of Psychology and Psychiatry

In the background of the more humane consideration of the men-tally ill one can discern many different tendencies that gradually converge in a distinct program of treatment (Deutsch, 1949, pp. 484–505). There was, first of all, *the growth of a scientific attitude* toward all phenomena of nature; and it was inevitable that the diseases of the mind should finally come within the scope of this attitude. As modern science took definite form, medicine, and more particularly the field of psychiatry, emerged as scientific disciplines, gradually shaking off the chains of superstition, quack-ery, and charlatanism that had bound them for untold centuries. The same period witnessed the *growth of psychopathology*, within which the *psycho-genic concept* of mental disorder was able to assume a definite meaning; this formed the background for the growth of abnormal psychology and gave impetus to the development of such basic theories as psychoanalysis (Zilboorg & Henry, 1941). Just as the growth of a scientific psychiatry was necessary for the development of psychotherapy, or treatment of mental disorder, so the growth of the psychogenic concept was necessary for the development of mental hygiene. It is only with the realization that some maladjustments and mental disorders are caused by other than organic factors that the principles of mental hygiene can assume a definite meaning.

At the same time, there was *a growing interest in physiological research*, which complemented and lent support to *the growth of psy-chiatry* and helped to rescue abnormal psychology from the weaknesses of an overzealous psychogenic approach. These research efforts and findings led to a more precise understanding of the relation between the mental and the physiological and eventually paved the way for a better system of classification of psychological disorders. These trends laid the groundwork for *a scientific psychology of the abnormal,* which was a necessary prelude to the development of the concepts and principles of mental hygiene.

During this long period of scientific growth and emancipation there was a lively interest and a great deal of research and theorizing in the field of biology which, together with some of the trends already mentioned, led eventually to *the development of adjustment psychology.* Because the viewpoint in biology was functional and teleological, considerable emphasis was placed upon the ideas of adaptation and adjustment, and both structural and functional changes in the course of evolution were regarded as expressions of organic adaptation. Since the psychology of the period patterned itself after biology, psychologists came to regard behavior and mental life in terms of their adjustive significance, and from that time forward the concept of adjustment has played a leading role in psychological theories and explanations. Then, with the further development of abnormal psychology, psychiatry, and psychoanalysis, the psychology of adjustment broadened in scope and began to include failures in adjustment as well as the more normal adjustment processes. These ideas and developments also had a great deal to do with the formation of a mental hygiene point of view. In somewhat the same way as the greater maturity of the individual creates a better capacity to deal with personal problems, so the growing maturity of science paved the way to the handling of problems that had been largely excluded from scientific investigation and treatment.

Pioneers in Mental Hygiene

Added impetus in this direction came from the work and inspiration of several persons, notably Dorothea Dix and Clifford Whittingham Beers, both of whom dedicated their lives to the prevention of mental disorder and the care of the indigent and helpless. Dorothea Dix was a pioneer in the struggle to achieve more humane treatment of the insane poor in this country and abroad. Following her untiring efforts, twenty states established or enlarged mental hospitals; in all, she had a part in the founding or enlarging of thirty-two mental hospitals in the United States and in foreign countries. It has been said of her that she was one of the really great women of the age, and, judging by her prodigious accomplishments, from the age of fourteen, it is a compliment easy to accept.

Dorothea Dix belonged to the nineteenth century; she was born in 1802 and died on July 17, 1887. Her work helped to lay a solid groundwork for mental hygiene practices, but it was not until the present century, in the year 1909, that the mental hygiene movement was formally launched. The time was ripe for such a movement, for, during this decade (1900–1909), some of the most prominent associations for hygiene were established in this country, including the American Social Hygiene Association and the American Federation for Sex Hygiene.*

The mental hygiene movement might have been regarded as just another trend of the times, had it not been for the unique characteristics of the man who was its principal genius, Clifford Whittingham Beers. For Clifford Beers knew from anguished experience the deep significance of preventing mental disorder and of treating it in a charitable and humane fashion. He had spent several years in different mental hospitals as a patient, receiving in each one the harsh and crude treatment that was still all too prevalent. There was a great deal of ignorance concerning mental disorder, even in the early years of this century when Beers was first afflicted—ignorance not only of proper treatment but of the nature of mental disorder. Beaten and reviled by cruel attendants, and subjected for long periods to the agony of a strait jacket, he could well write the inscription found on the wall of his room, "God bless our Home, which is Hell."

Despite his mental difficulties, Beers was a strong-willed and aggressively independent person, and he rebelled against the harsh treatment meted out to unfortunate patients, the memory of which sustained him in his efforts for reform and enlightenment for the remainder of his life. After two years of hospitalization, he began to recover, and during his last year as a patient he conceived the idea of starting a world-wide movement for the protection of the insane. On his return to normal life, the idea for reform continued to grow and in 1908 found concrete expression in one of the most unusual publications ever written, A mind that found itself (Beers, 1937). In this book, acclaimed by the master psychologist William James, Beers set forth not only a thorough indictment of the treatment of mental patients in asylums but also a definite program of correction.

But reform of mental institutions was only part of the program suggested in Beers's book. His own illness, and the conditions surrounding it, had convinced him that mental disease was both preventable and curable in many cases. He therefore outlined a plan for a national society that would have as its aims (1) the development of reforms in the care and treatment of the insane, (2) the dissemination of information that would lead to a more intelligent and humane attitude toward mental patients, (3) the encouragement of research into the causes and treatment of mental disease, and (4) the development of practices for the prevention

* The history of the mental hygiene movement is recorded in Ment. Hyg., N.Y., 1933, 17, 529–568.

of mental disorders. The response to the program was immediate and sustained. Not only William James but eminent psychiatrists, such as Adolf Meyer, were attracted to the idea; in fact, it was Meyer who suggested the term "mental hygiene" for the new movement. The movement was launched shortly after the book appeared, and in 1908 the first unit of the new organization was founded, the Connecticut Society for Mental Hygiene. Less than a year later, on February 19, 1909, the National Committee for Mental Hygiene was established, and Beers was made secretary, a post that he filled almost continuously until his death in 1943.

We do not wish to create the impression that the concept of mental hygiene is associated exclusively with the name of Clifford Beers. In fact, as early as 1842, the Society for Improving the Condition of the Insane had been organized in London, and in 1880 the National Association for the Protection of the Insane and the Prevention of Insanity was formed in the United States. Though short-lived, the National Association did a great deal of good and paved the way for other movements that proved more successful. A quarter century after the failure of this society, conditions and attitudes regarding the mentally ill were still unfavorable, and thus, when Beers launched the mental hygiene movement in 1908, the time was ripe. The following chief objectives of the new organization, as quoted by Deutsch (1949, pp. 314–315), were:

> To work for the protection of the mental health of the public; to help raise the standard of care for those in danger of developing mental disorder or actually insane; to promote the study of mental disorders in all their forms and relations and to disseminate knowledge concerning their causes, treatment and prevention; . . . to coordinate existing agencies and help organize in each State in the Union an allied, but independent, Society for Mental Hygiene, similar to the existing Connecticut Society for Mental Hygiene.

How well the objectives of mental hygiene were realized is attested by the numerous societies and clinics that were established throughout the country. Deutsch describes the movement as follows (Deutsch, 1949, p. 318):

> The war and post-war period (World War I) witnessed a tremendous development of interest in mental hygiene, arising largely from the serious problems involved in the "war neuroses," and the demonstration of their diagnosis and treatment by the psychiatrists engaged with the military forces. The public's attention was increasingly directed to the problem of eliminating preventable mental disorders and of improving existing methods of treating such disorders. The mental hygiene movement rapidly extended its scope to include many new fields of activity. Within a few years after the World War it was being recog-

nized as an important factor, present or potential, in such varied fields as education, public health, general medicine, industry, criminology, penology, and social work. It was in the field of social work that the influence of the mental hygiene movement was most profoundly felt.

Other areas were similarly affected, particularly following the experiences and advances in treatment during World War II. In the field of child guidance, in the philosophy of family life, and in education the ideas and principles of mental hygiene have made a deep impression, so that the program of the movement is no longer concerned solely with persons who are or may become mentally ill; it is concerned with any agency or factor that can be utilized in the prevention and amelioration of mental difficulties. It draws upon many disciplines for its principles—child psychology, psychiatry, abnormal psychology, the psychology of adjustment, clinical psychology, sociology, and social work—because all of them have something to contribute to the understanding, prevention, and treatment of personality difficulties.

Continued Growth of Mental Hygiene

The mental hygiene movement has continued to grow—in scope, in importance, and in its effects on the people of this nation. On July 3, 1946, the President of the United States signed into law a measure of great importance to mental hygiene, the National Mental Health Act. This act is a blueprint for a comprehensive, long-range program directed toward the improvement of mental health among all persons. Section 2 of Public Law 487 (H.R. 4512) reads:

> The purpose of this Act is the improvement of the mental health of the people of the United States through the conducting of researches, investigations, experiments, and demonstrations relating to the cause, diagnosis, and treatment of psychiatric disorders; assisting and fostering such research activities by public and private agencies, and promoting the coordination of all such researches and activities and the useful application of their results; training personnel in matters relating to mental health; and developing, and assisting States in the use of the most effective methods of prevention, diagnosis, and treatment of psychiatric disorders.

To carry out some of these purposes, the act also provided for the creation of a National Institute of Mental Health, for which $7,500,000 was immediately appropriated for the erection and equipment "of suitable and adequate hospital buildings and facilities, including necessary living quarters for personnel, and of suitable and adequate laboratory buildings and facilities . . ." (Sec. 11). For a discussion of the history, organization, research programs, and related aspects of the National Mental Health Act as implemented by the National Institute of Mental Health, see the pamphlet published by the U.S. Public Health Service (1952).

In substance, therefore, the National Institute was to be a clinical research center for the investigation of problems relating to mental health. But more important perhaps are the grants-in-aid authorized by the National Mental Health Act. During the first three years of the program, grants for graduate and undergraduate training totaled approximately $5,700,000, in addition to research grants in the amount of $1,377,862 (Felix, 1950). To this account of advances should be added the fact that, in 1950, the National Association for Mental Health was formed, a merger of the nation's three leading voluntary organizations in the field of mental hygiene, the National Committee for Mental Hygiene, the National Mental Health Foundation, and the Psychiatric Foundation. Needless to say, all such developments portend well for the success of the mental hygiene movement since all of them are oriented as much to the concept of prevention as they are to diagnosis and treatment (Shore, 1950; Dribbin, 1954; Gamelin, 1963).

PRINCIPLES OF MENTAL HYGIENE AND ADJUSTMENT

What Mental Hygiene Principles Are

The principles of mental hygiene are rules or standards of behavior directed toward the maintenance or restoration of mental health and good adjustment and toward the prevention of psychological difficulties. For example, mental health requires ridding oneself of strong feelings of inferiority since they inevitably lead to defensive mechanisms or other interfering symptoms. These principles stem from the nature of mental health and adjustment, the criteria by which these conditions are evaluated, the nature of the human organism itself and its relations to reality situations, and from the experiences of both professional and nonprofessional persons in dealing with human problems in the home, school, clinic, social agencies, or consulting room. These latter factors have been studied intensively in preceding chapters since it is clear that we must know first what adjustment and mental health are before we can establish ground rules for their achievement. Similarly, we must define the connection between good adjustment and environmental determinants before we can determine what rules should be followed in applying principles of mental hygiene to the home, the school, or the community (Bernard, 1963).

Interrelation of Mental Hygiene Principles

The moralist, religionist, or sociologist is likely to ask how the principles of mental hygiene or effective living differ from moral standards, social rules and customs, and such religious principles as the Ten Commandments. Are these rules not intended to insure the welfare and contentment of the individual person, or for that matter, the family? Who is, or should be, the custodian of the good life? The priest, the minister, or rabbi? The academic moralist? The social scientist? The psychologist or psychiatrist? (Liebman, 1948, Part I; VanderVeldt & Odenwald, 1952, Chapters XI–XIII; Kaplan & Baron, 1952, pp. 397–401).

One can see how readily suspicions and hostilities can emerge when the welfare of man is claimed as a special field by many persons of divergent beliefs and convictions. For centuries the clergyman has been regarded as the primary source of advice and solace in the affairs of the mind and soul. Quite naturally, one took his stomach aches to the family doctor, and his heartaches to the family priest. And now the psychologist and psychiatrist threaten to usurp this age-old prerogative; and, if this were not bad enough, the psychiatric social worker has also entered the picture as a therapist of mental disorders and maladjustments. The pie is being cut many ways, and the role of the religionist tends to shrink in direct proportion to the growth of clinical psychology, psychiatry, and social work. The role of the psychologist in mental hygiene and psychotherapy has received a great deal of attention in recent years (Brown, 1952; Ellis, Nydes, & Reiss, 1955). These are only a few of many sources that deal with the growing scope of clinical and counseling psychology.

There are several ways in which to handle the conflicting claims made by many people involved with mental work. First, it should be pointed out that the problems of human beings, like personality itself, are many sided. Some are distinctively moral or religious and should be referred for treatment to persons trained in these areas; others are of a psychological nature and should be handled by the clinical psychologist, whereas those that involve serious disruptions of personality and behavior should be referred to the psychiatrist. These divisions of labor cannot always be observed, and there is bound to be a certain amount of overlapping; but the hope of an effective program of treatment and mental hygiene rests on mutual cooperation among the professional groups that are directly concerned in the handling of human problems (Keliher, 1949; Line, 1950). The latter author, stressing the need for universal principles of mental health, points out that all the various professions concerned with better human adjustments must cooperate in supplying data by which these principles can be validated. Anderson (1954) stresses the same point.

As O'Brien says in defining the relation between modern psychiatry and religion (O'Brien, 1950, p. 53), we must assume that

> the active, intelligent and sympathetic cooperation of all, who in any way contribute to the necessary treatment plan, is indispensable in any attempt to help an individual to maintain a state of total health, or to aid him in regaining a state of total health after he has lost one or more aspects of it because of deprivation, infection or trauma.

If we agree that the human personality is complex, then we can

> accept also the reasonable conclusion that any program committed to the understanding and treatment of the human being requires, by necessity in many situations, the cooperative participation of a varying number of well-trained and experienced individuals who are personally dedicated to and professionally capable of serving their fellow man (O'Brien, 1950, p. 57).

Other writers emphasize the same idea in many places. The promotion of mental health, according to Hayden (1950, p. 73),

> is a responsibility of all professional groups who serve people and those in the field of psychiatry can best contribute to this service by sharing their specialized knowledge of human behavior with them.

In addition to the relationship between mental hygiene and professionally trained people, it is important to recognize the close relation between principles of mental hygiene and moral, religious, and social codes. As we have seen, many of the principles of the former are derived from or are identical with those of the latter; certainly the person who lives a good moral, religious, and social life has taken a long step toward mental health and adjustment. The important moral virtues of justice, prudence, temperance, courage, thoughtfulness, or integrity are in themselves internal habits of effective living, and the more these virtues are put into daily practice, and allowed to dominate one's personal life, the more likely is he to reach a high level of psychological adjustment. Similarly, adherence to basic religious rules and practices, and bringing conduct into line with good moral and social principles, can be helpful in furthering adjustment and mental health. Are such principles and practices, then, part of mental hygiene? The answer to this question is clear. Since we cannot separate the mental or behavioral aspects of human nature from its moral, social, or religious qualities, all such principles can be used effectively for the promotion or the restoration of mental health (Godin, 1961; Schneiders, 1961; Van Buskirk, 1952).

However, it must be firmly emphasized that in many instances the principles described above are not enough because there are aspects of mental life or behavior that are not regulated by such principles. And even when they are, the problems that often arise in these areas have a psychological aspect to them that can be treated only in a psychological way. For example, there are several problems in the area of sexual adjustment that are clearly moral in character; but they are also psychological. The habit of masturbation is regarded by many persons as morally wrong, but it is also a problem in adjustment. In any single instance the problem may be more psychological than it is moral. Instead of reflecting moral weakness, as is usually thought, the difficulty may reflect immaturity, withdrawal, or rebellion. In such cases, a purely moral approach to the problem may serve only to deepen the difficulties that the behavior reflects.

Apart from such problems that lie on the border between morality and psychology, there are many others that do not present any moral aspect. A child may be exemplary in his moral conduct, but he may manifest many difficulties of a psychological nature, such as nail biting, nervousness, bed wetting, hostility, excessive daydreaming, truancy, or aggressiveness. These are the types of problems toward which the principles of mental hygiene are specifically directed; they are referred to as adjustment problems, personality difficulties, or mental disorders.

Let it be understood that the ramifications of personality difficulties are numerous and thus often reach into the moral, social, and religious aspects of daily life. The prevention or effective treatment of these difficulties can provide the psychological soil in which moral virtues and religious principles and ideals can develop more effectively (Schneiders, 1953). As many persons know from sad experience, it becomes increasingly difficult to achieve a high level of morality or religious experience within the framework of an inadequate personality. Where there is pervasive immaturity, hostility, feelings of inferiority, rebellion, hatred, aggression, or other signs and symptoms of the inadequate or disturbed personality, the path to moral goodness and to love of God and neighbor becomes more and more rugged. Mental hygiene and the psychology of adjustment, therefore, are *important complements to ethics and religion.* The psychologist, moralist, religionist, and psychiatrist all have a common goal—the "good life." They reach this goal and help their clients and patients reach this goal, by different paths, all of which converge toward a common point, whatever name we give it—adjustment, mental health, peace of mind, the good life, or just plain happiness.

PATTERNS OF MENTAL HYGIENE

The total spectrum of mental hygiene principles will emerge only as we consider the different patterns of mental hygiene. While there are certain general principles that can be applied to all persons or situations, it is important to realize that numerous principles are inseparably linked to the situation out of which they evolve. Thus, healthy attitudes are necessary to good adjustment regardless of time or circumstance, whereas good teacher-pupil relationships are an integral part of the mental hygiene of the school. It is possible therefore to distinguish between general and specific principles of mental hygiene.

The general principles of mental hygiene are derived from the analysis of adjustment and mental health such as we have developed in Chapters 2 through 11. The more specific principles will emerge as we study the patterns of mental hygiene (Tyson, 1951; World Federation for Mental Health, 1950, p. 53). These patterns, which will be studied in Chapters 13 through 16, include (1) personal mental hygiene, (2) the mental hygiene of work and marriage, (3) the mental hygiene of the home, school, and community, and (4) mental hygiene and religion. As we study these different patterns, we will encounter numerous principles for the maintenance of good adjustment and for the prevention of psychological difficulties.

GENERAL PRINCIPLES OF MENTAL HYGIENE

By way of recapitulation, and as a prelude to the study of specific mental hygiene principles, we will list in the briefest form those general principles that are widely regarded as basic to a program of mental hygiene. They are:

1. The physical well-being and integrity of the organism are basic to adjustment and mental health.
2. Human conduct should conform to the nature of man as a moral, intellectual, emotional, religious, and social being.
3. Personality integration and self-control are necessary to mental health and adjustment.
4. An expanding knowledge of self or self-insight is necessary to the achievement and maintenance of mental health.

5. Mental health requires a healthy self concept, which includes self-acceptance and a realistic appraisal of one's own worth.
6. Self-knowledge and self-acceptance must be complemented by continuous striving for self-realization.
7. Continuing moral development is important to effective adjustment and mental health.
8. Mental stability and adjustment require adaptability or the capacity to change in accordance with changing circumstances and changing personality.
9. Mental health and adjustment require maturity of thought, decisions, and conduct.
10. Learning how to deal effectively with conflicts, frustrations, and tensions is necessary to mental health.
11. Mental health and adjustment are dependent on healthy interpersonal relations.
12. A realistic attitude, which includes the acceptance of reality without distortion and a healthy objectivity, is basic to mental health.
13. Mental stability requires of each person a developing awareness of a reality greater than himself on whom he is dependent in a very real manner.
14. Mental health and adjustment are dependent on a fund of healthy attitudes and worthwhile habits.

The principles listed above are common to every situation in which human beings become involved. The interested student will find definitions of these principles in many different sources (Fosdick, 1943; Horney, 1950; Cole, 1944; Overstreet, 1949; Warters, 1949).

QUESTIONS AND PROJECTS FOR FURTHER STUDY

1. Write an evaluative report of Clifford Beers's book, A *mind that found itself*.
2. What is the difference between mental hygiene and psychotherapy?
3. Compare the principles of morality with the principles of mental hygiene.
4. Write a short biography of Dorothea Dix.
5. Describe some of the historical factors that contributed to the mental hygiene movement.
6. Explain the difference between the psychology of adjustment and mental hygiene.

SELECTED COLLATERAL READINGS

ALBEE, G. W.   *Mental health manpower trends.* New York: Basic Books, 1959.

BEERS, C. W.   *A mind that found itself.* New York: Doubleday, 1937.

CROW, L. D., & CROW, ALICE. (Eds.)   *Mental hygiene for teachers: a book of readings.* New York: Macmillan, 1963.

DEUTSCH, A.   *The mentally ill in America.* (2d ed., rev.) New York: Columbia University Press, 1949.

FOSDICK, H. E.   *On being a real person.* New York: Harper & Row, 1943.

GREEN, S. L., & ROTHENBERG, A. B.   *A manual of first aid for mental health in childhood and adolescence.* New York: Julian, 1953.

JOINT COMMISSION ON MENTAL ILLNESS AND HEALTH.   *Action for mental health.* New York: Basic Books, 1961.

OVERSTREET, H. A.   *The mature mind.* New York: Norton, 1949.

RENNIE, T. A. C., & WOODWARD, L. E.   *Mental health in modern society.* New York: Commonwealth Fund, 1948.

RIDENOUR, NINA.   *Mental health in the United States, a fifty year history.* Cambridge, Mass.: Harvard University Press, 1961.

SEIDMAN, J. M. (Ed.)   *Educating for mental health: a book of readings.* New York: Crowell, 1963.

SHORE, M. J., et al.   *Twentieth century mental hygiene.* New York: Social Sciences Publishers, 1950.

WARTERS, J.   *Achieving maturity.* New York: McGraw-Hill, 1949.

ZILBOORG, G., & HENRY, G. W.   *A history of medical psychology.* New York: Norton, 1941.

13

Personal Mental Hygiene

Having studied the nature and general principles of mental hygiene, it is now our task to investigate the different areas of mental hygiene and to define the specific principles related to each of these areas. We begin with personal mental hygiene which is oriented toward those principles that govern the mental health and the adjustment of the individual person. It is perhaps the most important aspect of mental hygiene because here these principles can be more readily put into actual practice.

THE SCOPE OF PERSONAL MENTAL HYGIENE

Principal Aspects of Individual Adjustment

The term "personal mental hygiene" refers to a set of principles for effective living that have to do with certain basic aspects of personal existence. These include physical health and the satisfaction of basic physical needs, emotional health and the gratification of psychological needs, the effective control of sexual impulses, behavior, and intersex relationships, the effective integration of moral concepts and mental health, the fitting of religious practices into the process of adjustment, and healthy adjustment to home and family, to school, and to the social order. This is not all there is to daily living; there are many incidentals of behavior and even of adjustment that would be excluded from this list. But certainly these various facets of personal life are the most important, and we can be sure that if the principles of mental hygiene governing personal existence are applied sensibly and consistently, some of the most basic aims of mental hygiene will be realized.

Interrelations among Adjustment Processes

It is important to recall that adjustment and mental health are both integral and total, so that difficulties in one area are likely to spread into other areas of behavior. Thus, in a simple case, the child who daydreams constantly in class, and as a result gets poor grades, is making a poor adjustment to the academic situation. Here the pattern of withdrawal influences one of the forms of adjustment. Similarly, the husband who

360

drinks excessively in order to escape from reality is endangering marital adjustment. By the same rule, there are important relations among the varieties of mental hygiene. It is well known that emotional health, perhaps the most important aspect of personal hygiene, has important implications for every other type of human response. Marital difficulties are likely to be reflected in adjustment to one's work. Sexual maladjustments will certainly disturb emotional balance. These relations underscore the fact that the starting point of effective mental hygiene is personal adjustment, and it is to this aspect that we now direct our attention.

PHYSICAL HYGIENE AND ADJUSTMENT

Because of the close connection between the physical and the psychological make-up of the organism, physical hygiene constitutes a first principle of mental health (Figure 21). Everyone is aware that chronic fatigue, physical dissipation, inadequate diet, and illness or disease stand in the way of healthy adjustment. You recall the old saying, "A sane mind in a sane body," which means simply that such factors as mental efficiency, good judgment, emotional stability, or clear-headed thinking vary with the physical condition of the organism. Students especially should be aware of this relation from their own experiences. Efficient studying and learning are not easily accomplished under conditions of fatigue or illness. Learning, concentration, and thinking—the essential tools of the student— *are dependent upon physical well-being.* Many other daily activities come under the same rule. Persons who are physically rundown, overweight, or chronically ill might well look to these factors for the explanation of their nervousness, irritability, or other signs of poor adjustment.

Physical hygiene is simply the application of well-established, valid rules and principles of health for the prevention of illness and disorder and for the achievement and maintenance of a high level of physical well-being. Among these principles are adequate rest, regularity in physical habits, exercise and recreation, and wholesome diet and weight control.

1. *Securing adequate rest* is one of the most important principles of physical hygiene. It means getting enough sleep, usually not less than seven or eight hours a day, the inclusion in one's schedule of rest periods throughout the day, regular periods of sleep, and the kind of rest that leads to the reduction of fatigue and the restoration of energy. Sleep, therefore, that is irregular or that is disturbed by the intrusion of conflicts, worries, or emotional upsets is not adequate to the requirements of physical health.

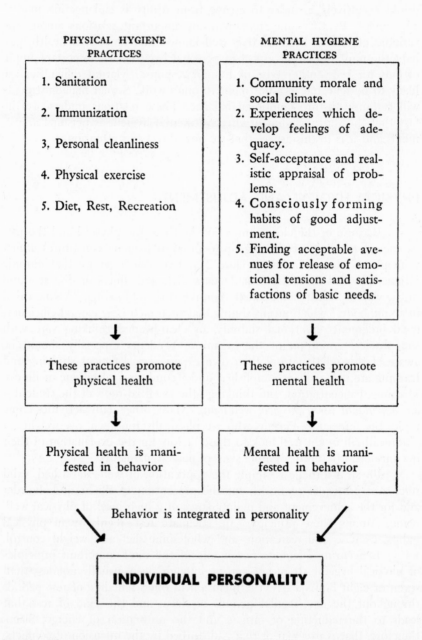

PHYSICAL HYGIENE
PRACTICES

1. Sanitation

2. Immunization

3. Personal cleanliness

4. Physical exercise

5. Diet, Rest, Recreation

MENTAL HYGIENE
PRACTICES

1. Community morale and social climate.
2. Experiences which develop feelings of adequacy.
3. Self-acceptance and realistic appraisal of problems.
4. Consciously forming habits of good adjustment.
5. Finding acceptable avenues for release of emotional tensions and satisfactions of basic needs.

These practices promote physical health

These practices promote mental health

Physical health is manifested in behavior

Mental health is manifested in behavior

Behavior is integrated in personality

INDIVIDUAL PERSONALITY

Fig. 21.   The integration of physical health and mental health. (Adapted by permission from Kaplan, L. & Baron, D. *Mental hygiene and life*. New York: Harper & Row, 1952, p. 37.)

2. *Regularity in physical habits*, such as eating, sleeping, elimination, and exercise, is important to good health because regularity is an essential feature of physical functions. It should therefore be carried through in the habits that grow out of these functions.

3. *Physical exercise and recreation* help to maintain good health. Exercise contributes to good appearance, to the maintenance of proper weight, to the stimulation of a healthy appetite, and to the toning up of the muscular system. The same benefits are gained from recreation. In addition, recreation serves the purpose of reducing emotional tensions and frustrations and of stimulating the development of interests and attitudes that are often important to good adjustment (Menninger, 1948; Gardner, 1952). A Medical Director of the United States Public Health Service has stated, "Not only are physical energy and vitality refreshed by active participation in games and sports, but mental tensions are relaxed, which is especially necessary in this age of mounting anxieties and frustrations. In order to retain a reasonable outlook, recreational outlets are equally as essential as a congenial occupation" (Schumacker, 1950, p. 3). Various investigators have pointed out that play, recreation, exercise, and rest promote relaxation and thus serve to reduce tensions; they have also indicated their value for therapy (Tyson, 1951, pp. 76–78; Wrenn & Harley, 1941; Schade, *et al.*, 1952). The more active forms of recreation, tennis, golf, swimming, and hiking, are particularly effective. Furthermore, these activities take place out-of-doors, where the organism's need for fresh air and sunshine are fulfilled in a healthful manner (Biddulph, 1954).

4. *Adequate diet and weight control* are basic to good health, buoyant energy, and zestful living. Underweight is correlated with chronic fatigue, lack of energy, and such pathological conditions as tuberculosis, whereas overweight is particularly detrimental to the cardiovascular system and robs the person of the energy and drive he needs to meet the tasks of daily life. An adequate diet includes the right kind and amount of food, proper vitamin intake, avoidance of excesses and dissipation, and a balanced diet. No one of these principles should become a fetish or an obsession, but with proper control of diet, weight control should offer little difficulty (unless, of course, there are glandular difficulties).

Comparing the principles of physical hygiene reveals that they are closely interrelated and that the successful application of one of them therefore will always be conditioned by the application of others. In short, *physical hygiene may be regarded as the wholesome expression of basic physical needs.*

The idea that physical health conditions mental health is complemented by the equally important observation that physical health bears directly on the more objective adjustments of the organism, especially motor skills and social responses. It is a truism of psychology that all behavior is conditioned by physical well-being, and certainly where motor skills are concerned it is easy to see the adverse effects of physical weakness, illness, or pathology. Even the relatively simple chores of housekeeping cannot be efficiently carried out under conditions of physical weakness and ill-health. Similarly, physical well-being influences social responses and relations. As an example, we may note the adverse effect on people of physical deformity, unsightly skin conditions, facial pallor, and excessive weight. It is difficult for people to react favorably to conditions of this kind. We are naturally attracted to persons who are healthy looking and just as naturally repelled by those who are not. Charity, of course, demands understanding and consideration, but this does not alter the fact that social feelings, attitudes, and relations are affected by physical characteristics. Thus it is the better part of social wisdom to do what we can to achieve and maintain physical well-being. Thorpe says (1950, p. 199):

> Society has placed a certain premium on physical characteristics in both the male and the female which handicaps children and youths who cannot measure up to them. The homely girl, the obese boy, the awkward youth, and the "runt" all feel the pain of social disapproval, and thus are likely to behave in ways induced by their resentment. The same may be said in the instance of physical defects—inadequate vision, loss of hearing, speech defects, and various crippling conditions increase children's dependability upon others and may lead to compensatory mechanisms in the form of daydreaming (fantasy) or over-aggressive behavior.
>
> This point was brought out forcibly in the course of the construction of a recent inventory for the diagnosis of psychological adjustment, the Mental Health Analysis. When scores on each of the ten categories of the inventory were correlated with scores for the instrument as a whole, the highest relationship for undesirable scores was that between the category concerned with the psychological effects of having one or more physical defects and the inventory as a unit.

EMOTIONAL HEALTH AND ADJUSTMENT

Because the maintenance of physical health is directly related to emotional health and adjustment, they are brought together in this section. From what we have said already regarding physical hygiene, it is clear that physical well-being is an important condition of emotional stability. This point was brought out in our discussion of the mechanism of psychosomatic development in Chapter 11, where it was emphasized that the emotions are psychophysical responses and thus closely bound up with the physical make-up and condition of the organism. It is well known that glandular disturbances, excessive fatigue, organic illness and pathology, and physical debilitation are emotionally disruptive, and in developing principles of emotional health, such factors must be considered.

Emotional health and adjustment imply three things: (1) emotional adequacy, (2) emotional maturity, and (3) emotional control.

Emotional Adequacy

The concept of emotional adequacy applies primarily to the content and range of emotional responses. When either of these aspects is distorted or inadequate, emotional maladjustment will result. It should be understood, first of all, that the majority of emotional responses are, in themselves, natural and wholesome, and therefore emotional health is jeopardized by their suppression or extinction. A stoical or phlegmatic attitude toward life and its problems is not a sign of good adjustment. On the contrary, the demands of daily living require an adequate range of emotional reactions, the content of which is neither damaging nor disagreeable, nor disruptive of personal, social, or moral adjustments. Emotional apathy and the absence or disintegration of capacities for love, sympathy, altruism, respect, kindness, and other ennobling emotions are contrary to the principle of emotional adequacy. In such instances, the content may be wholesome but the range is inadequate. Horney says of the neurotic, "There is in neurosis a general impoverishment of the emotional life showing in a diminished sincerity, spontaneity, and depth of feelings, or at least in a restricted range of possible feelings" (Horney, 1950, p. 164; also Kaplan & Baron, 1952, pp. 246–248).

Emotional health may also be disrupted by the content of emotional responses. Feelings of hostility, hatred, revenge, jealousy, inferiority, worthlessness, rejection, envy, and the like militate directly against emotional adequacy and adjustment. It is impossible for a jealous person or one consumed by feelings of hatred or revenge to achieve the calmness that is necessary to emotional health. His feelings are in a state of constant turmoil. What is more, this turmoil stands directly in the path of mental, moral, and social adjustment, which is why it is emphasized that at the core of every personality disorder there is emotional disruption or distortion.

The concept of emotional adequacy has one other aspect that must be noted—the direction of emotional response, or, more broadly, the object to which the response becomes attached. It is natural for two young people to fall in love, but, when the object of love is a person twice as old as the lover, or of the same sex, there are indications of emotional inadequacy. Often, some emotional reaction becomes attached to or conditioned by an object, situation, or person to which it has no essential or proper relation; all such reactions must be regarded as instances of poor emotional adjustment.

Emotional Maturity

Many of the difficulties encountered in the area of emotional response are related to the failure to achieve emotional maturity. We have noted repeatedly in preceding pages that maturity is one of the most important features of this general criterion (King, 1951, Chapters I–III). To be emotionally mature signifies the capacity to react in terms of the requirements that a situation imposes. Negatively, it means to avoid or eliminate responses that are not suited to these requirements. The child reacts with tears, temper tantrums, screaming, or vile language to threatening or frustrating situations because he is immature and does not know how to cope with them. But we also see "adults" react in these ways to similar situations, and we unhesitatingly classify the reaction as childish or immature. To be afraid of the dark or of thunderstorms, to "giggle" at the remarks of others, to be emotionally engulfed by a movie or soap opera, to engage in puppy-love relations in adulthood, to be envious of the good fortune of others, to enjoy spite or scandal, to cling to one's parents throughout adulthood, and to "adore" or idealize father or mother are common instances of emotional immaturity. The requirements of adult living render all such reactions inadequate and often damaging to good adjustment, and particularly to emotional health.

Emotional Control

A fundamental quality of emotional maturity is emotional control, without which adjustment and mental health are impossible. We have many terms to indicate lack of such control—rage, hatred, lust, terror, passion, avarice, and mania, for example—and all of them carry the implication of severe emotional disruption or even illness. Emotional control is a special phase of self-control, which is indispensable to maturity, adjustment, and mental health. It involves, among other things, the regulation and the ordering of feelings and emotions in terms of the demands imposed by external situations and in terms of inner standards related to values, ideals, and principles. Anger directed at a harsh or aggressive opponent, especially one who is unscrupulous and evil, is appropriate; but the rage of a parent against a child is a clear indication of breakdown in emotional control. The failure of some persons to regulate sexual feelings, to limit their fondness for material things, to place morality above momentary pleasure, or to desensitize themselves to aggravating stimuli and situations reveals poor emotional control. These failures are essentially like outbursts of rage or passion and tend to destroy emotional tranquillity. They represent a background of faulty training and self-discipline, of conflict and frustration, and a general psychological immaturity. Personal adjustment requires an effective and continuing discipline of feelings and emotions; this should be one of the primary goals of training, education, and mental hygiene programs.

The idea of emotional control should not be confused with emotional rigidity, which is as much opposed to emotional adjustment and health as lack of maturity or control. Some persons freeze emotionally in the presence of others, particularly members of the opposite sex; others find it impossible to react appropriately or in the right degree to emotionally toned stimuli or situations. As we have noted, the neurotic is typically lacking in a sense of humor. In a humorous situation, he finds nothing to laugh about. The delinquent or psychopathic person fails to experience sympathy or remorse. These people are emotionally rigid, owing to such factors as inadequate emotional development, overcontrol, traumatic experiences, insecurity. Perhaps the most typical example of the influence of such factors is sexual frigidity, a type of emotional rigidity that precludes adequate sexual adjustment. It clearly reflects faulty development, excessive inhibition, or damaging experiences, factors that make it extremely difficult for the organism to achieve a practical degree of emotional maturity; thus they stand in the way of adjustment and mental health. To achieve these aims one must strive constantly to reduce damaging or restrictive influences, and to raise the level of emotional adequacy, maturity, and control by whatever means are available (Franzblau & Franzblau, 1963).

SEXUAL ADJUSTMENT AND MENTAL HYGIENE

Nature and Characteristics of Sexual Development

Closely related to both physical and emotional adjustment is the mental hygiene of sexual behavior and relationships. Contemporary thinking, incidentally, no longer limits sexual development to the period between puberty and adulthood, although it is generally accepted that the major aspects of sexual adjustment are correlated with the maturing of the sex organs and the emergence of the secondary sex characteristics at puberty. The facts of sexual development and practice have received the most extensive treatment in Kinsey's two well-known volumes on sexual behavior in men and women (Kinsey, Pomeroy, & Martin, 1948; Kinsey *et al.*, 1953; also Ford & Beach, 1951). Evaluations of the Kinsey studies will be found in a number of places (Deutsch, 1948; Terman, 1948; Hyman & Barmack, 1954; Hiltner, 1953; Bergler & Kroger, 1954; Ellis, 1954).

Sexual development may be studied from the standpoint of theory and the standpoint of facts gathered by empirical studies. According to the most widely accepted theory, that of the Freudian school, sexual development and expression begin in infancy and continue throughout all stages of development. Supposedly, the organism passes through several stages of psychosexual development: the narcissistic stage, characterized by self-interest or self-love and oral needs and gratifications, the homosexual stage, in which the loved object is a person of the same sex, and the heterosexual period, in which love or sex desire is directed toward a member of the opposite sex (White, 1952, pp. 295–303). In Freudian theory, these periods are characterized by the development of the Oedipus and Electra complexes, fixation at one or another level of sexual development, emergence of the castration complex, and a certain amount of overt sexuality. Undoubtedly, some of these ideas are correct, but it is difficult to separate what is factual from the tangled skein of theoretical (and often slanted) interpretations. Some of the difficulties of sexual adjustment found in adolescence and adulthood are traceable to fixation or to unwholesome parent-child relations, but the Freudian theory involves too many broad and sometimes poorly grounded generalizations to be completely acceptable as a system of interpretation.

From the standpoint of empirical facts, it is clear that sexual behavior is often manifested prior to the onset of puberty, but what this means for psychosexual development is not at all certain. Such behavior usually takes the form of curiosity, self-exploration, or sexual play, which is often refered to as masturbatory activity. No one knows for sure what this behavior represents, whether it reflects pleasure seeking, frustration of basic needs, such as affection and security, incipient sex desire, accidental discovery of erogenous zones, or simply exploratory activity. At times, these activities create adjustment problems, as when the child develops a habit of "masturbation," but, for the most part, the real problem of sexual adjustment occurs during the adolescent period. For this reason, the application of principles of sex hygiene during childhood is important to later adjustment. The child who is adequately prepared for the difficulties of adolescence in matters of sex is not so likely to become sexually maladjusted as one whose preparation is grossly neglected.

Regardless of theory or of evidence relating to early sex behavior, the fact is that puberty ushers in a period of intense psychosexual development that is marked by profound physical changes, alterations in desires, imagery, feelings, and emotions, and modifications in social attitudes, interests, and aspirations. The groundwork of these changes is, of course, the growth and development of sex organs and functions, by which the organism becomes capable of reproduction. These changes are expressed in the secondary sex characteristics, which contribute importantly to the qualities, and to the personal conviction, of maleness and femaleness.

The changes in the sex organs and functions, referred to above, plus the situations and relations to which they give rise, create problems of sexual adjustment, especially when, as in our society, these changes take place in a cultural and moral setting that precludes frank expression of sexual desires and interests and that often fosters restrictive and damaging attitudes toward sexual realities. It is doubtful whether animals, and perhaps even some primitive tribes, are much bothered by problems of sexual adjustment. Animals, however, are not human and are not governed by moral law, social necessities and restrictions, or the demands of modern family life; nor are some primitive peoples faced with the same sexual realities that are part of modern society. Thus we are faced with the necessity of effecting a good adjustment in the area of sexual behavior, and, unless we do, the chances of effective mental and emotional adjustment are not good.

Premarital Sexual Problems

Here we shall confine ourselves to premarital sex problems because those that arise after marriage are a part of the general problem of marital adjustment, to which we shall turn in the following chapter (Schneiders, 1960b, Chapter VI). The two phases of the total problem are closely related, and what we have to say here has an important bearing on sexual adjustment in marriage. Prominent among premarital sexual problems are the following.

1. Inadequate or immoral sexual behavior, including masturbation, petting, necking, sexual intercourse, and adolescent crushes
2. Inadequate sex identification, which reflects immaturity in psychosexual development, and may involve tendencies toward homosexuality
3. Obsessive ideas and compulsions regarding sex, which often lead to sexual aberrations and unacceptable conduct
4. Restrictive and damaging sexual attitudes that preclude normal heterosexual relations and that often stand in the way of adequate social development

5. Feelings of anxiety, fear, and guilt regarding sex in all its forms
6. Deep-seated mental conflicts that center around sexual desires and behavior

One can see, of course, that these problems are closely interrelated. Improper sexual behavior gives rise to feelings of guilt or shame; inadequate sex identification may cause considerable anxiety; and obsessive ideas of sex lead to fear, conflict, or improper sexual conduct.

It is not an easy matter to formulate effective principles of sexual adjustment, because premarital sexual problems have many causes and many different ramifications. Sexual problems and maladjustments reflect in part the reactions of people to cultural and social demands and restrictions, failure to reach an adequate level of maturity, weakness in self-control, damaging and restrictive sexual attitudes on the part of parents, group pressures that enforce conformity, lax or poorly developed moral principles, and defective personality integration. In some instances, the difficulty may reflect inadequate physical development or fixation at an earlier response level. Poor sex identification is often associated with slowness or failure in the development of sex organs or of secondary sex characteristics. The adolescent boy, for example, may present feminine characteristics that make it difficult for him to identify adequately with his own sex. Fixation can produce the same effects, and both may be the forerunners of homoerotic tendencies, including crushes and frankly homosexual behavior. It should be understood, therefore, that some cases of sexual maladjustment, because of the nature of the cause, may be extremely resistant to treatment or to the application of principles of mental hygiene. Nevertheless, there are many instances in which such principles can be put to good use.

Principles of Sexual Adjustment and Hygiene

The formulation of acceptable principles of sexual adjustment will depend on the way such adjustment is interpreted. Some writers, for example, do not hesitate to suggest the free expression of sexual desire as a means of ridding oneself of sexual conflicts or frustrations. From our viewpoint, such a "solution" only complicates the problem, and thus falls outside the concept of adequate sexual adjustment. It is not by giving in to sexual impulses that adjustment is achieved; rather, it is knowing how to regulate them in an orderly, integrated manner that is most important from the standpoint of sex hygiene.

The concept of sexual adjustment is complex and many-sided, but basically it implies *the capacity to react to sexual realities—impulses, desires, thoughts, conflicts, frustrations, guilt feelings, and sex differences*

—in a mature, integrated, and disciplined manner that conforms to the demands of morality and society. This capacity requires sound, healthy attitudes regarding sex, the ability to defer sexual expression, and adequate heterosexual orientation, disciplined control of thought and behavior, and a healthy identification with the sex role one is supposed to play. This ideal is not easy to achieve, but knowing what constitutes it is a first step toward its achievement. On the basis of this interpretation, then, we can formulate several basic rules or principles for achieving sexual adjustment (Tyson, 1951, pp. 39–41; Fromme, 1950, pp. 85–89):

1. *Adequate sex information and knowledge* is the foremost principle. This knowledge should extend to the physical, psychological, social, and moral facts and implications regarding sex; it should be acquired gradually throughout childhood and adolescence and imparted by persons (usually the parents) who are qualified to give sex instruction. There is general agreement among the writers in the field of sex adjustment and hygiene that adequate instruction is essential to good adjustment (Kirkendall, 1950, Chapter II; Schneiders, 1960b, pp. 136–141; Brown 1952; Nash, 1948).

2. *The development of healthy, objective, desensitized, and moral attitudes* regarding sex and the problems associated with it should result from sex knowledge, correctly imparted. A healthy attitude is perhaps the most important principle governing sex hygiene because so many sexual difficulties stem from restrictive and damaging attitudes. Feelings of guilt, shame, and anxiety; sexual frigidity; chronic conflict; and a sense of frustration can be mitigated to an important degree by the development of wholesome attitudes based on an adequate knowledge of sexual development and behavior (Figure 22). We are not suggesting that guilt and shame in relation to sexual experience and behavior are always abnormal or damaging, but in many cases such feelings reflect lack of knowledge or poor attitudes rather than immoral behavior. Adolescents might experience any one of these feelings in connection with menstruation or nocturnal emissions because they do not understand these phenomena. Similarly, damaging information regarding the effects of masturbation often leads to deep-seated anxieties that are not justified by the actual facts, even though it is agreed that masturbation is morally wrong, psychologically detrimental, and results in feelings of shame and guilt. It is especially in matters of this kind that knowledge and perspective are basic to the preservation of emotional stability and sound mental health.

3. *The integration of sex desires and inclinations with moral principles and social responsibilities* is required by sound hygiene. This means that sexual tendencies and expressions must be brought into line with rules of right conduct. Magner says pointedly (1944, pp. 52, 53):

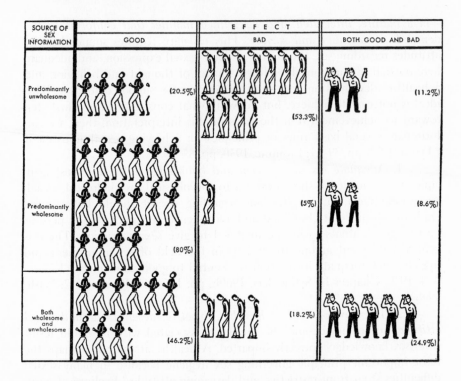

Fig. 22. Comparison of sex information with effects. Each figure represents 5 percent of the group supplying the information. It is clear from this illustration that unwholesome sex information can have widespread detrimental effects on young people. (From Fleege, U. H. *Self-revelation of the adolescent boy*. Milwaukee: Bruce, 1945. P. 281.

Of course, much depends upon our definitions. But if we define happiness as activity conformable to right order or the fulfillment of desire in accordance with our general good, we are immediately confronted with the problem of self-discipline. Self-discipline means governing onself and one's appetites according to good reason and judgment, and it applies both to persons and to things. . . .

Emphasis must be placed on *self*-discipline, for it is only on this basis that a person can live maturely and creatively. External guidance and correctives are generally necessary for the formation of character and the development of sane attitudes and habits; but unless this discipline, imposed from the outside, becomes assimilated by the individual for his own guidance and personal responsibility, its value is very small.

Sexual intercourse before marriage is precluded because it is morally and socially unacceptable. It is therefore damaging to the integrity of both persons. The integration of sexual life with moral principles is psychologically sound because it is a positive rather than a negative approach to the problem. To forego sexual expression *merely* because of social taboos, fear of pregnancy, or similar motives often aggravates emotional difficulties because it is likely to lead to conflict or frustration. To do so because it is *morally right*, however, is the most important step toward the resolution of conflict and the reduction of tension. When this step is taken, conflict becomes a means of reaching a higher level of integration and control.

4. *Sexual adjustment necessitates learning to defer sexual expression* in the interest of morality and good adjustment. This principle is not essentially different from the principle of integration, but it must be emphasized that in our society, where marriage is usually postponed for years after physical maturation has been reached, it is necessary to learn to defer sexual expression. This principle is not so important in societies where marriage follows closely on the heels of physical maturation. You will note that this principle of deferment is similar to the concept of frustration tolerance defined in Chapter 6. In our society, sexual frustration is unavoidable if one is to follow social and moral laws, and therefore deferment and tolerance become essential parts of sexual adjustment.

5. *Understanding the consequences and outcomes of sexual conduct* furthers the achievement of these various aims. Naïveté in the matter of sexual behavior and relations can easily lead to improper conduct and, what is often worse, emotionally damaging experiences. We may be sure that many unwed mothers did not understand the possible consequences of their conduct. The development of such understanding is, of course, an essential part of the program of sex education referred to earlier. Young, unmarried people, especially, need to learn about the social, moral, psychological, and even physical consequences of sexual behavior. They need to know about the possibility of pregnancy, why masturbation is psychologically as well as morally harmful, the evils of necking and petting, the dangers of venereal infection, the harmful effects of obscene literature and conversation, and the obsessive qualities of sexual imagery, thoughts, and desires. They need to know all these things so that they will become better equipped to control, defer, and integrate sexual tendencies and behavior in a way that is morally and socially acceptable, and at the same time, develop healthy, objective attitudes regarding sexual realities.

6. *The attainment of sexual maturity* is the final and most important principle of sexual adjustment (Overstreet, 1949, pp. 241–242). This principle is so important because it actually includes all the others. It means knowing the important facts about sex and understanding the consequences of sexual behavior; it means the control and integration of sexual thoughts, impulses, and acts; it means the adequate resolution of conflict and the reduction of tensions generated by sexual frustration; and it means

the achievement of healthy attitudes regarding sex. Just as adjustment itself, as we have noted repeatedly, requires maturity, so, too, does sexual adjustment. It is important for us to realize that the phenomena of sex, including the laws, mores, and taboos that regulate it, are an aspect of reality to which we must adjust as we do to other aspects of reality, and in all these adjustments maturity is a primary determining factor.

The foregoing principles have to do only with sex hygiene and adjustment and not with the entire complex problem of how sexual impulses may be controlled. This would involve another set of principles just as important as those already formulated. For example, it is a widely recognized principle that sexual difficulties can be avoided or reduced by eliminating the causes and conditions that contribute to sexual delinquency, including obscene literature, sexy movies, or persons and things that stimulate the sexual drive. It is also known that sexual urges can be effectively sublimated into channels of activity that are morally and socially acceptable. This is one of the most effective means of regulating sexual impulses. Vigorous physical activity in work and sports, intense preoccupation with hobbies and other recreational diversions, and social interests are also helpful in the reduction of sexual difficulties. Nor must we overlook the possibility of invoking strong moral principles and religious ideals and practices as effective instruments in the control of sex. These principles, however important and necessary to sex hygiene, are of a different kind than those originally stated, which were applied to the *psychological* conditions necessary to effective adjustment and hygiene in the area of sexual behavior.

MORAL AND RELIGIOUS ADJUSTMENT

Morality, Adjustment, and Mental Hygiene

A number of times in these discussions of human adjustment we have had occasion to emphasize the importance of moral principles for effective living and mental health. Just as we must observe principles of physical hygiene to maintain physical health, and principles of mental hygiene for the sake of mental health, so we must meet the demands of morality effectively in the interest of complete adjustment. *Moral laws are an important aspect of reality, and morality itself is an essential part of human nature.* Therefore, it is just as impossible to be morally deficient and at the same time well adjusted as it is to be emotionally disturbed and well adjusted. We must dispossess ourselves of the notion, supported by the Freudian theory of the superego, that morality is merely the incorporation of parental restrictions and social mores. On the contrary, moral laws are objective, and morality, in the best sense of the term, is a volitional disposition to accept and to act in terms of self-imposed moral laws and principles.

Morality can be interpreted, therefore, as a kind of adjustment. It is the capacity to meet the demands of living correctly in a manner that contributes to the well-being of the individual. Its relation to mental health is the same as that of any other aspect of human adjustment. Moral weakness or debilitation will disrupt mental and emotional stability, leaving in its wake feelings of guilt, shame, anxiety, inadequacy, and insecurity and giving rise to a great deal of conflict and tension. All instances of social and sexual delinquencies discussed in preceding pages reflect degrees of moral weakness or failure and therefore are a part of the general problem of moral adjustment. Conversely, the acceptance and application of moral principles and ideals can be instrumental in the effective resolution of mental conflict, in reducing the tensions created by frustration, and in preventing the development of such feelings as guilt and anxiety, which tend to impair mental stability. This is mental hygiene at its best.

The relation between morality, adjustment, and mental health is receiving much attention and support. Mowrer, for example (1950, pp. 31, 38), declares that a spurious dividing line has been drawn between the realm of fact and the realm of value, and thus

> the most crippling and really unscientific thing about contemporary social science in general is the extent to which we have tried to blink away certain perdurable social realities, notable among which is the fact that human development, both for the race and for the individual, importantly involves a *moral* struggle. . . .
> My own clinical experience leads me to the conclusion that it is not *id* but rather conscience which is being held down and denied by the neurotic and that the far more natural role for the therapist is to align himself with this part of the personality rather than with the *id*.

Writing of conscience further on, Mowrer says (1950, p. 39), "Thus the person who isolates and rejects this part of his personality stands in his own path to self-fulfillment and happiness. He feels and is, quite literally alone, cut off, lost." Moore (1944, pp. 134–135) expresses this relation in another way when he says that

> morality needs no customs for the source of its principles. Were all history destroyed, the fundamental relations of man to man in the existing social order would supply the material from which reason sitting in judgment on conduct would derive the necessary natural principles of the moral order. And action in accordance with these principles would constitute the essence of sound mental hygiene.

Moral adjustment in the best and fullest sense of the term requires (1) aceptance, introception, and continuous development of moral values, ideals, and principles, all of which are necessary to the growth of a mature, personal, and subjective morality, (2) integration of impulses, desires, and cravings with these moral values and principles, (3) constant application of values and principles to the effective resolution of mental conflicts, to the reduction of the tension of frustrations, and to the expression of truly moral conduct, (4) integration of moral values and principles with religious and spiritual values, and (5) a high degree of self-discipline by means of which values, principles, and ideals can be effectively expressed in moral conduct. If these requirements are met to even a reasonable degree in a person's daily affairs, his adjustment and mental hygiene will be greatly augmented (Cattell, 1950; Allport, 1950, Chapter IV).

Concept and Criteria of Religious Adjustment

The concepts of moral and religious adjustment are integrally and inseparably related, though we must recognize that there are instances in which morality and religion do not coexist in the same person. However, the more important point here is that moral adjustment is the most effective step toward a good religious orientation, and *religion is the most secure bulwark of a sound, effective, and mature morality*. Magner points out, "Religion becomes a personal and constructive force only when it is an integral factor in character formation and in the development of attitudes on life" (Magner, 1944, p. 144). VanderVeldt and Odenwald express the same idea. "Religion is effective in the implementation of moral standards, which, if sincerely followed up, would prevent a great deal of mental and emotional grief. In addition, religion gives the individual the reasons why he should conform his conduct to those standards" (VanderVeldt & Odenwald, 1952, p. 185).

The idea of religious adjustment must be examined and defined most carefully. We must not confuse the effects of religion on mental health (Chapter 15) with the concept of religious adjustment. It is generally conceded by counselors and therapists that religious experiences and practices can contribute to mental health, but we cannot conclude from this that persons who have benefited from religious experiences are therefore well adjusted religiously. As we saw in studying moral adjustment, we are dealing, in religion, with a special aspect of reality to which persons must adjust. If religion were purely subjective or a figment of imagination projected into reality, the question of religious adjustment would be empty of meaning. But the facts, as presented by religionists, are that God does exist, we are dependent on Him, the church is His instrument, the Incarnation is a historical fact, prayer is efficacious in helping people, and the human soul will continue to exist after death. These are some of the prominent realities of organized religion, and it is to these realities that adjustment must be made if religion is accepted as a part of life. It is for these reasons that mental hygienists and therapists often assert that an adequate philosophy of life, and therefore a good religious orientation, are the *sine qua non* of sound mental health and personal adjustment. Regarding this point, Steckle draws an interesting parallel between the teachings of Christ and the principles of good adjustment (1949, pp. 252–253). The student should also read Allport's chapter on the religion of maturity (1950, Chapter III) and the article by Angyal on the convergence of psychotherapy and religion (Angyal, 1952).

Religious adjustment, then, is a process and a style of life by which a person reacts adequately and wholesomely to religious realities and acquires the experiences, values, and practices necessary to a good religious orientation. Here, as in other phases of human adjustment we have studied, there are certain requirements that must be fulfilled in order to achieve the aims of mental hygiene.

1. *The first requirement is adequate knowledge of the basic facts or truths of religion and a willing acceptance of the implications and obligations that these truths impose.* To admit the existence of God is not enough for the religious person; he must also accept the implication of this fact for his own personal existence. Moore expresses this idea when he says that

> the love of God in its perfection is something more than freedom from sin. It is a positive turning to God with all one's heart and soul and mind and strength, that is to say, with all one's mental being, intellect, will, feelings, emotions, yearnings, and cravings (Moore, 1948, p. 417).

Thus, personal mental hygiene, from this viewpoint, requires that we should recognize our dependence on God, His personal interest in our welfare, the efficacy of divine grace, the obligations of love and sacrifice, and the reality of the promise of salvation. In terms of these acceptances, we should nurture a feeling of confidence in the supreme goodness and justice of God, and above all a love for Him as a person, friend, and Savior (Bernard, 1951, p. 368; Allport, 1950, p. 79).

2. *A good religious orientation requires a deep conviction of man's potentialities for religious experience and for personal salvation.* It is difficult, for example, to hold to the idea of a future life or of salvation when one is already committed to the principle of determinism. The capacity for self-determination is necessary for us to work and strive toward personal salvation. If such freedom does not exist, the ideas of a just God, eternal reward, meritorious conduct, commandments that must be obeyed, and

so on, become meaningless. Similarly, there must be a conviction that through prayer and other religious practices the graces of God can enter man's soul and transform it into a receptacle of deep religious experience. As Curran says (1952b, p. 34):

> We should note here that since the attainment of man's complete fulfillment in God cannot be achieved by his natural powers alone, prayer and Divine aid are absolutely essential. Counseling, by itself, no matter how skillful, as we shall discuss elsewhere may lead man to a temporary state of satisfaction and achievement, but it cannot bring him final and permanent happiness. God alone can do this.

3. *There must also be a keen awareness of man's relation to his fellow man.* Religion enjoins us to love our neighbor, to see in every man a brother, to forgive those who trespass against us, to see in our fellow man the handiwork of God. Hatred, revenge, hostility, scandal, gossip, and the like, therefore, stand directly in the path of a sound religious orientation and mental hygiene. Anything, in fact, that precludes the activation of one's relation to God, or that stands in the way of keeping His laws and commandments, or that mocks another person's relation to God is detrimental to good religious adjustment. Religion embraces human relations as well as the relations between man and God, and thus religious adjustment requires a satisfactory orientation and reaction to this pattern of relations and to the basic facts that serve as focal points (Van Buskirk, 1952, p. 106).

From what has been said, it is clear that good religious adjustment is of paramount importance to personal mental hygiene. All damaging feelings and attitudes, such as anxiety, inferiority, suspiciousness, hostility, anger, hatred, rejection, envy, jealousy, and revenge, which interfere with peace of mind, and all behavior that fosters mental conflicts, guilt feelings, and the sense of worthlessness and inadequacy are easy prey to a healthy religious outlook. Can one believe that he is created in the image of God and still feel inferior? Can one believe in the goodness and mercy of God and still despair? Can one think of the compassionate Christ and yet cherish revenge or hate his fellow man? Religion is the embodiment and the expression of the noblest virtues of the human mind and soul, and thus it tends of its nature to dissipate feelings, attitudes, and experiences that eat away at the nobility and the integrity of man. The integration of a sound religious outlook with other principles of mental health and adjustment is one of the surest steps toward mental hygiene (VanderVeldt, 1951; Beaven, 1951). And conversely, the sensible application of mental hygiene will contribute much to religious development.

SOCIAL ADJUSTMENT AND MENTAL HYGIENE

The three aspects of adjustment reserved for this section are so closely allied that the consideration of one almost necessarily involves the others. The home, school, and society are particular aspects of the social order and thus involve patterns of relations that bind each one closely to the other. In many instances, a bad home adjustment is quickly followed by difficulties in school or by inadequate social adjustment, and the inability to get along with classmates or associates may soon disturb the situation in the home.

Yet there are differences in these situations that must be observed. The home and family involve a special group of relations and situations that set them off from the school or society. Classmates, friends, and associates are different from brothers and sisters, and teachers, counselors, and other persons in authority are unlike parents in many important ways. It often happens that the child who has considerable difficulty adjusting to the demands and restrictions imposed by parents will accede readily to the commands of teachers and other authority figures. This sort of reaction clearly illustrates the uniqueness of parent-child relations. Similarly, the child who resents the leadership of an older brother or sister might submit meekly to the role of follower imposed by a playmate. Thus, adjustment to the home and family presents its own peculiar problems.

Adjustment to Home and Family

Social adjustment involving home and family imposes certain requirements, the foremost being *healthy relations among the members of the family group*. Evidently, bad feelings between parents and children or between siblings, such as resentment of parental discipline, rejection, favoritism, hostility, and jealousy, will make adjustment to the home situation difficult. The child who actively dislikes one of the parents or who is intensely jealous of the attention and affection bestowed on another child will find it impossible to meet the demands of family living. Numerous studies indicate that children who have such feelings invariably show serious adjustment problems.

The willing acceptance of parental authority is a second requirement. It is generally agreed among experts in family living that some parental authority is necessary for the stability of the family; it is one of the realities of family life to which adjustment must be made. The youngster who resents all parental discipline and regulation or who accepts it grudgingly only because he cannot do anything about it is courting mal-adjustment. To meet the demands of family life, children must learn that parental authority and discipline are not only necessary but actually de-sirable, and here again, empirical studies indicate that the most adequately adjusted children are those who have a good attitude toward parental dis-cipline. Conversely, many delinquents and children who have difficulty in adjusting to the requirements of school life express resentment toward and rejection of parental discipline, indicating that adjustment to authority in the family is an important first step toward adjustment in society.

The capacity to assume responsibility and accept restrictions is a third requirement. The acceptance of authority and discipline indicates a degree of maturity that is further reflected in the capacity to assume family responsibilities where necessary, and in the acceptance of whatever physical limitations the home imposes, and whatever restrictions on conduct may be necessary in the interest of a healthy family life. You will note that these requirements are simply particular instances of the criterion of maturity outlined in Chapter 2, and the concept of frustration tolerance described in Chapter 6. In fact, all the requirements described in this chapter on personal and social adjustment are special applications of the general cri-teria of adjustment. In the family connection, then, any member who resents or shirks necessary responsibilities, or who tries incessantly to break away from required restrictions, is adjusting poorly to the home situation. Responsibilities and restrictions are simply realistic aspects of normal family living to which adjustments must be made in the interest of individual members as well as the family group.

One must strive to help the family reach individual and group objectives, whether in achieving success in school, vocational aims, religious aspirations, economic security, the owning of a home, or recreational pur-suits. The older brother who is insensitive to the interests and strivings of the younger members of the family, who assumes a "devil-take-the-hind-most" attitude, is not measuring up well to the requirements of healthy family life. Similarly, many parents who show a lack of interest in their children's activities, school achievements, hobbies, and vocational aspira-tions are adjusting poorly to the demands of family living. In general, there-fore, family members need to develop mutual interest, cooperation, and continuing enjoyment in family activities and goals. Only in this way can a high level of adjustment to home and family living be secured. As one writer says (Magner, 1944, pp. 94–95):

> We come to tolerate, to understand, and to love people, not by waiting for them to serve us, much less by giving them an opportunity to dis-play their defects, but by assuming the active role ourselves and giving others positive reasons for tolerating and loving us. Nothing wins

friends so much as an unselfish concern on our part. Nothing makes us so worthy of friendship as developing ourselves, our resources, our personality by a program of friendliness and usefulness to others.

For the development of this program, certain fundamental realizations are necessary. The first is the conviction that the home and the family are the greatest and most abiding joy in life—that the home and all life stemming out from it can be made what we wish it to be, if we are willing to do our share in the cooperative enterprise. Nothing is too large and nothing is too small to contribute to this objective.

Gradual emancipation from the home and a growing independence on the part of the children in the family are also important, despite the necessity for cooperation and group participation. Parents for their part must learn to emancipate themselves from the emotional ties that bind them to the children, the reason being that emotional, intellectual, and volitional dependence, especially in later adolescence and early adulthood, fosters immaturity, which always stands as a threat to adequate adjustment. A certain amount of family affection, warmth, acceptance, and the feeling of belonging is necessary and beneficial to good family living. However, when family ties are too close, emotional strangulation occurs, and it becomes difficult for the persons involved to adjust effectively to whatever demands may arise. Such ties often get in the way of adequate relations between parents themselves and between parents and other family members, so that the whole pattern of family adjustment becomes adversely affected. In addition, where emancipation fails to occur, adjustment outside the home is generally impeded (Horney, 1950, Chapter X; Strecker, 1952, Chapter XV).

Adjustment to School

The adjustments demanded by life in school, aside from academic requirements, are not very different from those imposed by the home, although children react differently to the two. Respect for and acceptance of duly constituted authority, interest and participation in school functions and activities, adequate, friendly relations with classmates, teachers, and counselors, willing acceptance of limitations and responsibilities, and furthering the school's realization of both intrinsic and extrinsic objectives are ways in which adjustment to school life can be effectively realized. School life is simply a part of reality, and therefore such factors as lack of interest in school, truancy, poor emotional relations with teachers, rebelliousness, vandalism, and defiance of authority, constitute impediments to healthy adjustment. In general, it has been found that the child who is well adjusted to the home encounters few difficulties in meeting the demands of life in school (Crow & Crow, 1942, 1951; Hoyt & Norman, 1954).

Adjustment to Society

Since living in society is more or less a continuation of family living, wherein the basic pattern of social life is established, the concept of social adjustment offers little difficulty in the matter of definition. *Social adjustment signifies the capacity to react effectively to social realities, situations, and relations* so that the requirements for social living are fulfilled in an acceptable and satisfactory manner. As with every other aspect of human adjustment, these requirements are complex. Bernard (1951, pp. 245–254) lists the following "assets in social adaptation": altruism, understanding, sympathy, dependability, wide interests, conversational ability, and good personal appearance (See also Tyson, 1951, pp. 69–73). Following are some of the most important requirements.

1. *To recognize and respect the rights of other persons in society* is perhaps the most basic requirement. One can readily see that social conflict is the inevitable result of the failure to observe this fundamental principle.

2. *To be able to get along with other persons, and to foster lasting friendships* are important principles of effective social adjustment. Certainly, to be at odds always with our neighbors or to be friendless in a world of many potential friends is a sure sign of poor social hygiene. Every person has the innate ability to participate in social experiences and activities, and, therefore, when this ability is dormant or completely suppressed, it is meaningless to speak of social adequacy. The hermit, the recluse, the mysogynist, or the extreme introvert may prefer the excitement of his own company, but no one will pretend that these are good examples of the well-adjusted person (Bernard, 1951, pp. 231–245; Fine, Fulkerson, & Phillips, 1955).

On this point, psychologists are in good agreement. Notice the similarity of viewpoints in the following quotations.

There is now general agreement that many psychoneurotic disorders originate in poor interpersonal relationships. Modern civilization requires a high degree of socialization of every person. Within a span of less than 100 years, American culture has changed from a predominantly rural one . . . to a highly urban society in which every child is early exposed to large numbers of people in a socializing experience which is most demanding. In this type of culture, few people can be successful and be emotionally healthy until they have learned to adjust in the group and to build up congenial relationships (Tyson, 1951, p. 69).

Self-realization does not exclusively, or even primarily, aim at developing one's special gifts. The center of the process is the evolution of one's potentialities as a human being; hence it involves—in a central place—the development of one's capacities for good human relations (Horney, 1950, p. 308).

Improvement in mental health depends ultimately upon advance in *the understanding of human relations* and the practice of the principles to be discovered by social psychology and other allied sciences concerned with the general problem of how human beings can get along with one another to their mutual satisfaction. The task of achieving happiness is for each person a lifetime project, by its very nature both *personal* and *social* (Vaughan, 1952, p. 77).

3. *To be interested in the welfare of other people* (Figure 23). One must be sensitive to the problems and difficulties of persons around him,

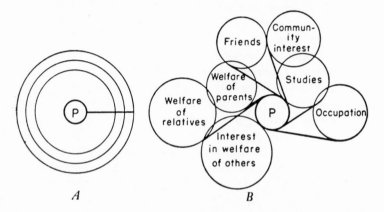

A　　　　　　　　　　　*B*

Fig. 23. Egocentric, selfish behavior contarsted with outgoing sociocentric behavior. Part A indicates how the world of the egocentric person is restricted; Part B illustrates the ever-expanding world and social relations of the person whose interests are tangents rather than concentric (egocentric) circles. (From Bernard, H. W. *Toward better personal adjustment.* New York: McGraw-Hill, 1951, p. 233. Used by permission of McGraw-Hill Book Company.)

and be willing, if possible, to lend a helping hand in the reduction of such difficulties; one must be interested also in the hopes and ambitions, the goals and aspirations of his friends and acquaintances and even take an active part in helping them achieve personal aims.

4. *To practice the virtues of charity and altruism diligently for the sake of healthy social adjustment.* Here again we are reminded of the fundamental relations among the different aspects of human adjustment. Charity and altruism are moral virtues, and their application is actually a part of good moral adjustment; yet they are unmistakably social in their implications and effects and thus enter into the concept of good social adjustment as well. In point of fact, *all human virtues bear this close relation to good adjustment,* including such diverse traits as chastity, courage, fortitude, honesty, kindness, veracity, and humility. All of them, ou

becoming an integral part of personality, contribute materially to mental stability, emotional health, and adjustment. It is because of this relation that character, morality, and adjustment are so intimately conjoined.

5. *To respect the value and integrity of the laws, traditions, and customs of society* is an important requirement that should complement all other requirements of good social adjustment. This does not mean a blind and undiscerning adulation of temporary fads, doubtful practices, or even laws whose morality is questionable. A person cannot be accounted socially maladjusted if he resists social pressures that require him to keep up with the Joneses, to wear freakish styles, or perform some foolish ritual. Nor should one be denied the individuality of deciding whether or not he wants to drink alcoholic beverages, or to eat pizza pie, or to drink tea instead of coffee. *Social adjustment is not the same thing as blind conformity.* There are times when social demands should be resisted with all the strength one can muster, for sometimes they are definitely wrong.

More often, of course, social laws and customs are basically right and good, and their violation leads to social maladjustment, delinquency and criminality being extreme examples. Lack of respect for the lawful demands of society and an unwillingness to abide by them marks the delinquent and criminal personality. But one does not have to be criminal in order to be socially maladjusted. Disdain for law and social propriety is often found in otherwise normal persons. There are persons, for example, the rugged individualists and iconoclasts, who refuse to recognize the traditional respect given to women, others who do not hesitate to violate lawful ordinances whenever opportunity permits, and still others who will not accept social practices that have been dignified by the stamp of time. Such persons must admit to the charge of social maladjustment. It is only by an intelligent appreciation of lawful requirements, plus a diligent, day-to-day application of them, that a good level of social adjustment can be achieved.

QUESTIONS AND PROJECTS FOR FURTHER STUDY

1. Explain in your own words why the mechanism of sublimation is important to good sexual adjustment.
2. Formulate five basic principles for achieving personal adjustment.
3. Explain and exemplify why physical hygiene is important to (1) emotional adjustment, (2) mental health, (3) sexual adjustment.
4. Select three basic principles of sexual adjustment and discuss their implications for personal and social hygiene.

5. Write a critical evaluation of Allport's *The individual and his religion* from the standpoint of mental hygiene.
6. Compare Fromme's *The psychologist looks at sex and marriage* with Kirkendall's *Sex education as human relations.*
7. Write a brief essay on "Basic Principles of Academic Adjustment."

SELECTED COLLATERAL READINGS

ALLPORT, G. W. *The individual and his religion.* New York: Macmillan, 1950.

CROW, L. D., & CROW, ALICE. *Sex education for the growing family.* Boston: Christopher, 1959.

FROMME, A. *The psychologist looks at sex and marriage.* Englewood Cliffs, N.J.: Prentice-Hall, 1950.

HOCH, P. H., & ZUBIN, J. (Eds.) *Psychosexual development in health and disease.* New York: Grune & Stratton, 1949.

KIRKENDALL, L. A. *Sex education as human relations.* New York: Inor, 1950.

LAIRD, D. A., & LAIRD, ELEANOR C. *The dynamics of personal efficiency.* New York: Harper & Row, 1961.

LINDGREN, H. C. *The art of human relations.* New York: Hermitage House, 1953.

O'BRIEN, J. A. *Sex-character education.* New York: Macmillan, 1953.

OVERSTREET, H. A. *The mature mind.* New York: Norton, 1949.

STECKLE, L. C. *Problems of human adjustment.* New York: Harper & Row, 1949.

STRECKER, E. A., & APPEL, K. E. *Discovering ourselves.* (2d ed.) New York: Macmillan, 1944.

TRAVIS, L. F., & BARUCH, D. W. *Personal problems in everyday life.* New York: Appleton, 1941.

VAN BUSKIRK, J. D. *Religion, healing and health.* New York: Macmillan, 1952.

14

Mental Hygiene
in Work and Marriage

We have just studied the conditions and principles of personal mental hygiene and included in this study the factors involved in promoting good social adjustment. These two areas of mental hygiene touch many points of a person's life, and it is clear that many of the principles governing personal and social adjustment reach into other areas of human behavior. This is particularly true of vocational and marital adjustment since each one is dependent to an important extent on personal mental hygiene and adequate social adjustment. In a sense, therefore, this chapter is a continuation of the study of specific mental hygiene principles as applied to particular situations.

BASIC MEANINGS AND RELATIONS INVOLVED
IN WORK AND MARRIAGE

Vocational versus Marital Adjustment

The areas of vocational and marital adjustment touch at many points. This does not mean that the world of work and the realities of marriage are basically alike. They are not, even though there are certain similarities worth noting. We should not put too narrow an interpretation on the concepts of vocation and vocational adjustment. Basically, the word "vocation" refers as correctly to marriage as it does to the kind of work or the profession one chooses as a livelihood, and it is this fact that brings together these two areas of human adjustment. Each one has its own requirements and distinctive characteristics, but there are basic similarities that enable us to subsume both under the concept of vocation. Both involve important responsibilities, interpersonal relations and adjustments, effort toward the realization of significant goals, and the achievement of personal satisfactions. In this sense, a vocation is a "calling," and it makes little difference whether one is engaged in ministering to the sick, raising children, or preaching the word of God—each one is truly a vocation. Generally, therefore, husbands have two vocations, their chosen field of endeavor and marriage, whereas many wives have only the one vocation, that of homemaking and rearing children. This difference in roles is often one of the basic determinants of marital difficulties and maladjustment. Though unavoidable, the duality of the husband's vocational role must be carefully and intelligently evaluated by both marital partners if a measure of marital adjustment and happiness is to be achieved.

Education as a Vocation

The concept of vocation, as outlined, should not be restricted to the field of work, marriage, or professional endeavor but should extend to any organized, goal-directed effort that is worthwhile and that leads to actual, personal achievement. Sometimes such efforts are referred to as *"avocations,"* as in the case of hobbies; the designation is a good one because it suggests a vocation that exists in addition to, or apart from the activity that constitutes the person's principal line of work. Using the term "vocation" in this broader sense, then, we can see that organized, educational effort is actually part of a person's vocation, or at least a necessary antecedent to the achievement of vocational aims. This is particularly true of education at the level of college and university, including, of course, professional schools. For the college and professional student, *his education (pro tem) is his vocation,* and in the majority of instances it is also a primary phase in the achievement of vocational goals that will dominate his life after the educational process is terminated. For this reason, we begin our analysis of vocational adjustment by studying the problems of academic adjustment, and we will see how fundamentally similar the vocational and educational aspects of adjustment are.

ACADEMIC ADJUSTMENT

Meaning of Academic Adjustment

Academic adjustment implies the abilities or processes by which the demands and requirements of academic life are fulfilled in an adequate, efficient, and satisfying manner. This concept will take on more meaning as we study the criteria by which such adjustment is evaluated; but, before going further, let us try to realize the degree to which this aspect of adjustment is related to, and dependent upon, other areas already studied. To be a good student it is necessary to achieve, first of all, a high level of personal adjustment, in which problems of a physical, emotional, sexual, moral, and spiritual nature are reduced to a minimum (Harris, 1961). The student who is caught between academic responsibilities and the throes of a disturbing love affair is not going to achieve academic adjustment; nor is the student racked by moral conflicts, frustrations, and indecisions, or the student incapacitated by chronic illness, likely to taste the fruits of academic success. This point is well illustrated in the following cases:

> The case of Carla is selected for presentation as fairly typical of maladjustments encountered at the college level. . . . Carla's academic work was initially very poor; she showed personality traits difficult for many of her teachers to handle; she was herself unhappy, anxious, lonely, and insecure beneath an assertive, almost boisterously cheerful front. Knowledge of her life history serves to clarify the origins of these undesirable patterns and to show their interrelatedness. Such a student fails academically for the same reasons which make her difficult as a member of the community, and personally distressed. She cannot "learn" so long as her energies are largely absorbed by rather frantic and inexpedient attempts to work out basic emotional problems (Munroe, 1947, p. 628; also Bordin, 1947, pp. 615–627).
>
> James was forced to drop out of college in his sophomore year because of poor grades and inability to keep up with the work, although he had performed successfully in his freshman year. Although only eighteen, James had been courting a girl steadily for three years and planned on an early marriage. The young lady's parents objected strenuously to these plans and insisted that the relationship be terminated. The resulting emotional turmoil made it impossible for James to concentrate on his school work, and his performance began to show the effects immediately. The parental opposition was mitigated by James's counselor, and he now plans to resume his college career (Author's files).

Similarly, students who are incessantly in conflict with parental demands and restrictions and who regard the home only as a prison and a source of frustration rather than a haven of security and affection are going to find the going difficult in the academic situation. Also, those who actively dislike school and strain continuously to escape its restrictions and responsibilities, in the vain belief that life outside the school contains all the potentialities of the good life, will not find it easy to achieve academic success. So, too, students who have failed to reach a satisfactory level of social adjustment will have difficulties in school. Maladjustments in these areas cause too much emotional upheaval, too many conflicts and frustrations, which stand directly in the path of intellectual effort, concentration, habits of study, and sincere academic interest. Adequate personal and social adjustment and the ability and willingness to learn to meet the requirements of home and school are of fundamental importance to academic success (Hoyt & Norman, 1954; Malleson, 1954). Here again we are reminded of the close relationships and interdependencies of the different facets of the total adjustment process.

Criteria of Academic Adjustment

Successful Performance.   If the student has not achieved successful performance, which is of primary importance it is difficult to see how one can speak of meeting academic demands in an adequate or satisfying manner. We must note, however, that the idea of successful performance varies to some extent from person to person, even though it is not to be determined on a subjective or emotional basis. An average grade of C may be good performance for one student and poor for another (Chandler, 1951; Witty, 1955).

Adequate Effort.   There are, as every teacher knows too well, countless students dominated by the "ideal" of mediocrity, who consider average performance as successful performance, even though it is far below their real capacities. If a student does as well as he can, his performance from the standpoint of adjustment must be evaluated as satisfactory, regardless of the grades he has achieved. If, despite his most sincere efforts, he achieves only failing grades, all that can be said is that his efforts should be directed toward other lines of achievement. It is the student who possesses the capabilities for good academic success and fails to achieve it who must be accounted academically maladjusted.

Acquisition of Worthwhile Knowledge.   To achieve academic success there is, of course, no substitute for the acquisition of knowledge to which, in some measure, all academic efforts are directed. This aim is automatically realized with the fulfillment of the first two criteria.

Intellectual Development.   But something more than acquisition of knowledge is necessary; there must also be real intellectual development, so that the student learns to use and to exploit facts, principles, and theories in an efficient and profitable way, to use intelligence in the solving of personal problems. The student who, in college or out, fails to apply his knowledge intelligently to the selection of a vocation, the solving of marital difficulties, the construction of a workable budget, or the maintenance of physical health cannot be regarded as an academic success. It is because of this failure in intellectual growth among students that education seems so often to fall short of its mark.

Achievement of Academic Goals.   Usually, the goals of academic effort include mastery of subject matter, integration of different fields of knowledge, enhancement of intellectual power and prestige, adequate preparation for a career or a livelihood, and graduation. To the extent that these several goals are achieved, the person comes closer to academic success and adjustment and also to the fulfillment of our sixth criterion, the gratification of needs, desires, and interests.

Satisfaction of Needs, Desires, and Interests. Academic success can go a long way toward satisfying the needs for status, recognition, achievement, social approval, and, to some extent, personal security and ego-identification. Similarly, the natural desires for knowledge, information, intellectual growth and stimulation, and power of expression can be realized through serious and successful academic effort. In making this effort the good student is motivated to an important extent by intellectual and vocational interests, and academic effort and achievement can provide an effective outlet for them.

From the standpoint of healthy adjustment, perhaps the most important aspect of these criteria is that, when they are met, frustrations and emotional tensions are likely to be few. Many students who might otherwise become the victims of emotional conflict find in academic achievement, particularly in the realization of cherished goals and the gratification of needs and interests, the means by which emotional stability and peace of mind can be maintained.

Principles and Practices Important to Academic Adjustment

In trying to realize academic goals and to fulfill the criteria of academic adjustment, there are several basic principles and practices that must be followed (Carter & McGinnis, 1950; Bennett, 1952).

1. *Understanding the aims and purposes of education is the first principle.* Without this understanding, the formulation of goals, the development and direction of interest, the formation of sound attitudes, and the application of worthwhile and sustained effort are almost impossible. If a student thinks of a college education as merely a stopgap between high school and lucrative employment, or as a means of achieving social and economic success, or as a continuation of the drudgery of high school lessons, there is little hope of real academic achievement. Education must be regarded as an adventure in intellectual growth, a preparation for effective living, and a cherished opportunity to rub elbows with the intellectual greats of the past and present. It must be thought of in terms of the truths, the knowledge, and the principles that it lays before the student for his enlightment, growth, and betterment.

2. *The basic aims of education must be brought into relation and integrated with the student's personal goals.* Or, to put it in another way,

personal goals should be formulated in terms of the purposes of education. Many students have a difficult time adjusting to the academic situation because of a basic conflict between what they want out of an education and what education is supposed to provide. This is especially likely to happen in a society like ours in which pragmatic values dominate the thinking of many young people. The high ideals cherished by the educator are often at complete variance with the concrete, cash-on-the-line aims of the student. One can see that it is difficult for a recent high school graduate to make the important distinction between education-for-a-living and education-for-life; ; yet this distinction must be made if the student hopes to understand the value and the importance of courses in English, history, philosophy, political science, art, music, and literature. These subjects are not so important in schools oriented toward practical training, but in a liberal arts college they form the backbone of the educational process.

3. *Students must learn, early in their academic career, to understand and appreciate the integrative character of education.* They must come to see that every course and program of study is integrally related to other courses and programs. They must grasp the intrinsic relations between philosophy and religion, between art and philosophy, between psychology and biology, between sociology and psychology, and so on. It is not enough to master the intricacies of the English language, or the sonnets of Shakespeare, or the differences between prose and poetry. What is more important is the clear perception of how learning in one field bears on things learned in another field. And all of this learning must be brought into relation with the aims of education and the personal goals toward which the student is striving. Only in this way can the student expect to measure up to the demands inherent in the educational process.

4. *Equally important is the development of worthwhile academic interests and attitudes.* Without a lively interest in one's subjects, it is almost impossible to learn and to study effectively. Interest creates a readiness for learning and motivates the learner to read, to study, and to do whatever research is necessary to the process of getting an education. It is of particular value in helping the student to accept the responsibilities of education and to develop the habits and skills necessary to academic success. Good attitudes are just as important. Attitudes toward education, programs of study, individual subjects, teachers, research, and class assignments will play an important part in converting a student into a scholar, an academic mediocrity, or, worse still, a failure. Not always realized is the important fact that interests and attitudes go hand in hand, that interests generate favorable attitudes, and that attitudes often sustain interest when other factors fail. Obviously, the attitude that academic success is not worth the effort, or that most teachers are incompetent, or that certain

subjects are a waste of time is not going to help matters when it comes to studying, attending class, and concentrating. In general, the mental perspective of the student will condition all his academic efforts, and it is therefore of real importance to develop an adequate perspective as early as possible in one's academic career.

5. *Allied to the development of academic interests is the development of resourceful academic habits.* Attending college is in some respects like having a job; there are certain obligations that must be met if one is to be allowed to continue. Among these obligations are attending classes regularly, fulfilling whatever requirements are imposed by individual instructors, using the library and other facilities when the need arises, and studying to the degree that is necessary. These obligations should become a matter of habit for the student, so that, like the worker or professional person, he learns to face obligations without regard for temporary wishes, distractions, or inertia, which so often lure the student away from the tasks he should do. Again, we may note certain basic relations important to academic achievement. Worthwhile interests and good attitudes will foster the development of these necessary academic habits. It is not difficult for the interested student to attend classes regularly or to do the amount of studying that is necessary; resourceful habits develop quickly and sustain him in all his academic efforts and goals. Similarly, the student with good academic attitudes will quickly acquire the habits that will help him to meet his responsibilities in an efficient manner.

6. *The development of efficient study skills and habits is also necessary to academic achievement.* We can do little more than suggest what these skills are, since limitations of space preclude a detailed description and discussion. Efficiency in studying requires, first of all, reading proficiency, which includes the ability not only to read rapidly but to understand what is being read. In many colleges today, facilities are available for the diagnosis of reading deficiencies and for instruction in how to read more efficiently. This skill must be complemented by the ability to develop a good set of notes for each class, whenever note taking is essential. Particularly important here is the ability to distinguish the essential from the nonessential and to shift quickly from the taking of notes to listening to the lecture or discussion (Mursell, 1951; Ephron, 1953; Preston & Botel, 1952).

Auxiliary to skill in taking notes is knowing how to study the textbook selected for the class. To read a text thoroughly is not enough. First of all, it is necessary to acquaint oneself with the text in all of its essential aspects—the nature and organization of content, the sequence of chapters, special study aids such as chapter summaries, questions, exercises, glossaries and indexes, and the particular mode of development that the author uses. Then, each chapter should be looked over quickly as the topic is brought up for discussion. This should be followed by a careful, critical reading, during which ambiguities and difficulties are noted, key sentences underscored, definitions committed to memory, and a quick test made to determine whether the essentials of the chapter have been learned. Once this is done, the material should be compared and integrated with the notes taken in class.

7. *Techniques of studying should be supplemented at all times by three important aids: thorough preparation for each class meeting, cumulative review of material learned, and periodic measurement of one's own progress in the course.* The majority of students having difficulties with their studies have never learned the necessity of getting ready to learn. They labor under the delusion that attending class and studying after class are enough. But this is not the case. The student should always prepare himself ahead of time for lectures and class discussions by reading over the material to be taken up in class. Such preparation provides him with a background in terms of which new material is more readily learned.

The second step in this phase of efficient learning is cumulative review, by which we mean periodic review of learned material from the very beginning. Review is essential to almost all learning, which follows the laws of frequency and use described in general psychology, but equally important is the habit of going over material that was learned three, six, eight, or ten weeks before. This principle makes use of both the law of currency and the law of frequency and is of primary importance to efficient learning. It brings old material up to date and obviates the inefficient practice of cramming for final examinations.

The third step, which involves periodic measurement of each individual's own progress in learning, is important because (1) it enables the student to discover weak spots, (2) it provides him with knowledge of performance, which is known to have a beneficial effect on continued learning, and (3) it stimulates interest and ambition with respect to further learning. Not knowing how much has been accomplished in any particular area of learning tends to lower interest in studies and to deprive the student of the incentive he needs to keep going. While there are many other things that reveal mental stability, certainly academic progress can be used as a yardstick of healthy mental development.

8. *The factors of concentration, critical thinking, and active participation directly influence progress.* Of all learning habits, the ability to concentrate is one of the most important. It is a special type of attention that is indispensable to understanding, to acquiring and developing ideas, and to grasping relations between various aspects of a subject, relations that must be known if a thorough knowledge of the subject is to be acquired. This is true whether a student is listening to a lecture or class discussion,

reading the textbook, or gathering material for a research paper. Therefore, the habit of concentration must be developed as early as possible in one's academic career.

An important adjunct of concentration is critical thinking, a process by which we examine ideas, data, statements, and theories to see whether or not they conform to standards of truth, objectively validated criteria, authority, or available evidence. If, for example, we come across the statement that "everyone is maladjusted to some degree," we should not accept it at face value; we should seek evidence or authority to support it. In every book, article, or lecture will be found statements whose validity should be carefully examined before we accept them. Moreover, critical thinking can be used to determine the validity or truth of our own knowledge, opinions, and beliefs, and to ascertain whether we actually comprehend the statements we hear or read. As you can see, a critical frame of mind, which must, of course, stop short of questioning and doubting everything, is an important tool in efficient learning. The student is referred to the section on thinking, wisdom, and mental health in Bernard (1951, pp. 276–281).

Both concentration and critical thinking are special instances of *active* learning, which is also indispensable to academic efficiency. Many students commit the fatal mistake of thinking that by merely listening or by reading passively they will learn. This is not the case because learning itself is inherently *an active process*. Therefore, whether attending a lecture or studying the text, the student should always actively participate in the learning process. He can do this by intense concentration, by critically analyzing what he reads, by asking himself or the instructor questions, by jotting down ideas, problems, and difficulties as he reads, and by entering into active discussion with the instructor or other members of the class. He will soon find that in this way learning becomes more thorough and retention a great deal easier. Active learning of this type is more likely to result in apperception—the integration of new knowledge with knowledge that is already familiar and accessible to recall. Too often, learning results in mere accretion, in which case it readily falls away and cannot be recalled when necessary.

9. *The student must learn to budget time efficiently* (Figure 24). Many students fail academically because they cannot seem to find the time necessary to fulfill the responsibilities involved in going to school. Budgeting time means simply the arrangement of waking hours in such a way that all duties are taken care of. At the same time, allowance is made for recreation and other activities that enter into a person's life. In the construction of a time budget, it is important to arrange study and recreation periods so that the aims of efficient studying are served best and to adhere to the arrangement as closely as possible without, however, allowing

Period	Sunday	Monday	Tuesday	Wednesday	Thursday	Friday	Saturday
8:00		Travel	Travel	Travel	Travel	Travel	
9:00	Church	Psych. Class	Prep.	Psych. Class	(Prep.)	Psych. Class	Library
10:00	Church	Prep. Review	Eng. 1 Class	Prep. Review	Eng. 1 Class	Eng. 1 Class	Library
11:00	Review	Art Class	Lunch	Art Class	Lunch	Prep. Rev.	Library
12:00	Review	Lunch	Religion Class	Lunch	Religion Class	Lunch	Lunch
1:00	Lunch	Prep. Review	History Class	Prep. Rev.	History Class	History Class	Recreat.
2:00	Review	Biology Class	Library	Biology Class	Review Prep.	Biology Class	Recreat.
3:00	Recreat.	Library	Biology Lab.	Recreat.	Biology Lab.	Recreat.	Study
4:00	Recreat.	Library	Biology Lab.	Recreat.	Biology Lab.	Recreat.	Study
5:00	Dinner	Dinner	Dinner	Dinner	Dinner	Dinner	Dinner
6:00	& Recreat.	& Recreat.	& Recreat.	& Recreat.	& Recreat.	& Recreat.	& Recreat.
7:00	Study	Study	Study	Study	Recreat.	Book Report	Recreat.
8:00	Study	Study	Term Paper	Review	Recreat.	Book Report	Recreat.
9:00	Recreat. Study	Recreat. Study	Term Paper	Review	Study	Recreat.	Recreat.
10:00	Study	Study	Term Paper	Review	Study	Recreat.	Recreat.
11:00	Retire	Retire	Retire	Retire	Retire	Retire	Retire

Fig. 24.   A typical time budget.

it to interfere with normal adjustments that must be made from time to time. When they adhere to these arrangements, students find that they have more time to do all the things they like to do than is the case when the distribution of available time is haphazard and inefficient. What is even more important, necessary work gets done when it should be done.

10. *The efficient distribution of time must be coupled with adequate working conditions.* These involve such factors as lighting, temperature, ventilation, materials, desk space, freedom from distractions, and the like. Efficiency of effort is always influenced by the environmental setting in which it occurs. It is obvious that excessive heat or humidity, bad lighting, annoying sounds, lack of necessary materials, and so on, will materially interfere with effective studying. Too often students fail to realize that efficient studying, like any other kind of work, requires optimum conditions. For this reason, the habit of using the library, where conditions are arranged for effective learning, is of great importance to the achievement of academic success. Thus, in the time budget that the student works out for himself, some time should be allowed for library study.

It is not an easy task to fulfill all these criteria and principles of academic achievement, but experience testifies conclusively that unless they are fulfilled to at least a reasonable degree, there is little chance that a student will achieve good academic adjustment.

VOCATIONAL ADJUSTMENT

Relation of Academic to Vocational Adjustment

Academic preparation and achievement are important milestones on the road to a career, but, even apart from this important connection, the requirements and principles governing most types of adjustment are so closely allied that their descriptions seem at times to be identical. However, some important differences will be brought out in our discussion of vocational adjustment.

Meaning and Criteria of Vocational Adjustment

To be adjusted to one's vocation or work means to act in such a way that all the essential requirements of the job or profession are fulfilled consistently in an efficient and satisfying manner. The vocationally well-adjusted person is satisfied with his work, makes reasonably good progress in it, and is usually capable of meeting whatever demands the work imposes. These ideas provide a starting point for defining the criteria of vocational adjustment.

Adequate Expression of Abilities, Aptitudes, and Interests. If, as often happens, the demands of the job are such that the person's intellectual abilities and special aptitudes are seldom called upon, there is small likelihood of his finding in the job the satisfaction he is looking for. This craving for expression is a definite human need, and when it is blocked or frustrated the possibilities of adjustment are limited. Similarly, the job that holds no interest will produce boredom rather than satisfaction and will rob the person of initiative and the drive to achieve his vocational goals. This is particularly the case when interests are well defined and closely related to personal goals. In this respect, the requirements of vocational adjustment are almost identical with those of academic achievement.

In his study of job satisfaction at various occupational levels, Centers found that the determinants of job satisfaction vary to some extent with the level of the occupation, but that interest, prestige, and self-expression are predominant factors. In answer to the question "Why are people satisfied with their jobs?" he says (Centers, 1948, p. 191):

> In terms of the responses of the most satisfied stratum of all, large business men, it is that their work is *interesting and varied*, that they enjoy working with or meeting people, or like the company of their associates, that makes them satisfied.
>
> The professional man says that he likes the people he works with also, but equally as often he says he likes his job because his work is *creative*, or permits him *self-expression*, and almost as often he says it is because he has an opportunity to be of service to others. The small businessman values above all his freedom and independence, and the farmer places the greatest emphasis of all upon this privilege. The white collar worker finds the people he meets or associates with at work and the *varied nature* of his activity the greatest source of pleasure.

Gratification of Basic Psychological Needs. The second criterion is that a vocation should lead to need gratifications, particularly the needs for status, achievement, security, and recognition. All these needs, as we have noted many times, are closely interrelated, and the chances are that when one is adequately satisfied the others will be, too. For example, if work leads to a sense of achivement, status will be enhanced, and achievement is likely to lead to recognition and security. In this area of adjustment, as in all others, the blocking or frustration of basic psychological needs is a first step toward maladjustment; therefore, if a job or vocation offers little hope of security, if it is unimportant or degrading in any way, if it never leads to recognition or to worthwhile accomplishment, there is little likelihood that the person will achieve good vocational adjustment (Lindgren, 1953, pp. 264–270). For these reasons, certain vocations, such as medicine, law, engineering, teaching, and the ministry, offer few difficulties in the way of adjustment, since they contain many opportunities for the expression of basic needs. As Centers points out (1948, p. 205):

> People in our culture desire, most of all, five sorts of gratifications; namely, independence, self-expression, security, a chance to serve others (social service), and interesting experience. They care, on the whole, much less about power, fame, esteem, leadership, and profit. The former, are, moreover, not only the most frequent and first choices, but they are the most frequent second and third choices as well.

Job Satisfaction and Achievement of Vocational Aims. If these two characteristics are lacking, it is difficult to see how a good level of vocational adjustment can be maintained. Needless to say, if a person's work allows for the expression of abilities, aptitudes, interests, and needs, there is not likely to be a problem of satisfaction and enjoyment. This interpretation reminds us that the criteria of vocational adjustment can be developed from the standpoint of the job itself or from the standpoint of the worker, and therefore whenever one set of criteria is fulfilled, the other is likely to be also. Carrying this idea one step further, we can readily see that when all the foregoing criteria are met, the realization of vocational aims is almost a certainty. It is inconceivable that a person should experience job satisfaction or the sense of achievement while basic vocational aims are continuously blocked.

Job Characteristics and Personality. Because the characteristics of the job and the personality of the worker must agree, for adequate vocational adjustment, these two aspects of a vocation are interrelated. It is a matter of common observation that some persons cannot achieve satisfaction or happiness in certain types of work. For example, if the accumulation of money or political power is important to them, then the professions of teaching or the ministry offer scant possibilities for vocational satisfaction. If they are extraverted, a research career would not be indicated. If they have little interest in the welfare of others, careers in psychiatry, social work, or the ministry would not be likely possibilities. In all the studies made on the problem of vocational adjustment, it has been found that personality characteristics are the most important factors in vocational success. This is to be expected in view of the close relation between personality characteristics and such factors as basic needs, interests, capabilities, and goals (Barahal, 1953; Small, 1953). It is to be expected also in view of the bearing of personality on all phases of the adjustment process.

Principles and Practices Important to Vocational Adjustment

In the light of the foregoing criteria, it is not difficult to formulate the main practical principles that must be followed in the interest of achieving vocational adjustment.

1. *Careful selection of a career that conforms closely to needs, interests, abilities, and characteristics is the first principle.* Several steps may be taken to achieve this objective. A good way to start is to become thoroughly acquainted with different vocations that are likely possibilities. This can be done by reading the books or monographs on various vocations that are available in high school and college libraries, discussing careers with vocational counselors or with persons successfully engaged in the kind of work being considered, or "sampling" the work during summer vacations, on part-time jobs, and the like. In other words, every effort should be made to find out as much as one can about the vocations in which he is interested (Calvert and Stelle, 1963).

Job possibilities can be narrowed down to some extent by taking advantage of vocational-guidance programs in high school or college, or by visiting a paid consultant. During vocational counseling, an effort is made to determine the capabilities, interests, and personality characteristics of the client and to bring these findings into line with the particular characteristics and demands of different vocations. These two approaches to the intelligent selection of a career emphasize the fact that the aspirant must know himself thoroughly and must know the potentialities and responsibilities of the vocation just as thoroughly before he can decide intelligently what line of work he should follow (Super, 1954).

2. *The second principle is the development of the knowledge, skills, and, later on, work habits necessary to functioning efficiently and successfully in the chosen field.* Without these qualifications there can be no vocational adjustment. This fact makes it doubly important to select a vocation as early as possible so that a curriculum can be chosen intelligently. If a student wishes to become a doctor, a science or premedical curriculum is the wisest choice; if a college teacher, then a regular liberal arts program is best, followed by graduate studies leading to an advanced degree. In any event, clear-cut vocational aims are of immense value in planning a school career as well as in planning a life after school.

3. *Continuous growth in the job or profession one has chosen for himself is the third principle.* It is not enough to possess the basic knowledge and skills demanded by our work; we must continue to grow with the vocation. Almost every type of work changes internally and externally over a period of time, and it is necessary to keep pace with these changes if

we are to meet the demands of the job. New knowledge, skills, and attitudes may become necessary; in many instances vocational aims and goals have to be revamped; in others basic changes in personality may be required. The necessity for growth is exemplified in situations where new inventions revolutionize accepted procedures, where new personnel and administrative officials are brought into the picture, where the person is shifted from one department to another or from one kind of job to another, and where he is promoted to a position of greater responsibility. Whenever growth does not occur, vocational maladjustment is likely to result.

4. *The development of personal qualities necessary to meet the demands of the vocation is the fourth principle.* We are thinking here of such qualities as ability to get along with others, consideration, understanding, cooperation, leadership, ability to accept suggestions and directions and to profit from job experiences. A few examples will serve to clarify this important principle. In the medical profession the knowledge of the human body, disease, and therapy must be thoroughly bulwarked with professional attitudes toward the patient and toward the science of medicine, with selflessness in the face of professional duty, with a bedside manner that instills hope and courage in the sick, and with humane considerations for the unfortunate. The profession of teaching often requires financial sacrifices, much tiresome work in the correcting of papers and examinations, and continuous research in order to keep abreast of new developments. All such requirements demand personal qualities that will enable the person to adjust to the limitations and difficulties inherent in any vocation. When such necessary qualities are lacking, we have the picture of the disgruntled, frustrated person who wishes he had never embarked on such a career. Because of this disturbing possibility the careful selection of a vocation constitutes the starting point of vocational adjustment.

ADJUSTMENT IN MARRIAGE

Implications of Marital Adjustment

The foregoing discussion of the problems of vocational adjustment is a good prelude to a consideration of the different problems of marital adjustment, the two being similar. Yet, as we shall see, marital adjustment has characteristics that set it apart and that require a separate and intensive study of the whole problem. A good start can be made by studying the implications of good and bad adjustment to marriage. There is, for example, the fact that in this country every year there are almost 400,000 divorces; and it is estimated that in a short time one out of every three marriages will terminate in divorce unless an effective remedy for marital discord is worked out. In addition, there are countless homes internally disrupted by incessant quarreling, dissension, hostility, jealousy, and similar characteristics. Divorced couples and psychologically broken homes represent appalling social waste and widespread marital and family maladjustments. It is obvious that where two people find it impossible to abide by marriage vows, or where the family is disrupted by internal conflict, it is impossible to speak any longer of good adjustment (Medalia, 1962).

Statistics of the Bureau of the Census indicate that in 1940 there were 264,000 divorces (including annulments) in the United States. By 1948, this figure had climbed to 408,000. The estimated figure for 1949 was 386,000, indicating a slight decline. This decline has continued in recent years and probably reflects the more stable marital conditions of the post-war years, after the time of hasty war marriages. Programs for better housing may also have played a part in the declining divorce rate. The National Office of Vital Statistics of the Public Health Service reports that in 1961 there were 1,547,000 marriages and 395,000 divorces, indicating that the picture is somewhat brighter than it was in previous years.

The number of persons involved in marital discord must run into the millions; and when to this figure we add the number of children adversely affected by the breakup of the family, the total is staggering. Nor is there much hope that children will in some way escape the effects of family discord; too many studies show a close relation between children's maladjustments and the breakup of the family. The unfortunate part of this relation is that unhappy and emotionally disturbed children become unhappy, disturbed adults. They in their turn contribute to the continuing increase of family disintegration, unless the principles of good marital adjustment are put into application on a wide scale. The effects of marital and family maladjustments on society are just as disturbing since *no society can be healthier than its individual members.* Unless, therefore, the vicious circle of maladjustment-breakup-maladjustment is broken at some point by a thoroughgoing mental-hygiene program, we can expect society to continue disintegrating at an accelerated rate.

The individual and social effects of marital and family discord are only the more obvious parts of the picture. Of even greater importance in numerous instances are the moral and religious consequences. Moral disintegration and loss of religious beliefs and practices often have their beginnings in the psychologically disrupted home. It is difficult for parents eternally at odds with each other to establish or to enforce moral and religious standards and practices. In such situations, authority and wholesome discipline rapidly disintegrate; the practice of setting good examples becomes an impossibility; and the healthy influence that parents can exert on children fails to materialize. The psychologically intact home, which must have its beginning in good marital adjustment, is indispensable to the realization of the social, moral, and religious aims of the members of the family.

Nature of the Problem of Marital Adjustment

Marital adjustment is different in several important respects from other aspects of human adjustment. We have many friends and acquaintances but only one husband or one wife. The greater the number of persons the better the chances of making an effective adjustment since, if we have difficulty in one group, we can turn to another for the expression of needs and interests or the reduction of frustration. The marital situation, in contrast, short of divorce or separation, demands continuous adjustment to the peculiarities, shortcomings, and vagaries of one individual, and there are relatively few people so sagacious, understanding, and considerate as to find this adjustment an easy task. But, as one writer remarks (Anderson, 1949, pp. 639, 640):

> persons who make good adjustments see the present situation in the light of its future outcome, and understand that the dynamic pattern of relations between individuals and within families is constantly changing and being recreated on new and different levels. What seems now to be a major difficulty turns out to be of minor significance if met with reasonable ease and patience. . . . Marriage itself is the means by which two persons work out a common way of life in order to achieve continuing happiness. If marriage is looked upon as the end, not the beginning of living, it can be a most unsatisfactory type of experience. It is more appropriately viewed as progressive growth and as an enlargement of the life space which will enhance personalities of both individuals through their relations with one another.

In his discussion of the causes of marital breakdown in the Catholic family, Thomas, too, emphasizes continuous adjustment. According to this investigator (Thomas, 1952, p. 450),

> too much emphasis is sometimes placed on the initial adjustment required in marriage to the neglect of pointing out that marriage is a dynamic union requiring constant adaptation along constantly changing lines. . . . The coming of children, changes in economic or social status, the influences of outside acquaintances, bad habits, all these and a variety of other things demand constant adjustment in the marriage cycle.

Second, the requirements of marriage are far more exacting and inescapable than is the case with other adjustment situations. If your friends begin to annoy you, all you have to do is not call on them in order to reduce the aggravation; however, the rigorous obligations of marriage preclude this easy solution when the wife or husband is annoying. Furthermore, social obligations are much less binding than marital ones. When the going gets difficult in marriage, a hasty retreat to one's club or a shrug of the shoulders is not an acceptable solution to the problem. The responsibilities of marriage make it mandatory to work at the problem until an acceptable solution is reached; otherwise, separation, divorce, or psychological breakdown of the marital relation is inevitable.

Third, marriage is distinctive in that emotional relations between husband and wife may be disrupted in the course of the gradual growth of the family, which, in many instances, gives rise to affectional rivalry or jealousy, and finally to estrangement and emotional impoverishment. Ideally, the addition of children to the family is supposed to enrich and cement existing relations, but often does not, with the result that the growth of the family has just the opposite effect.

The recognition of these three distinctive characteristics of marriage discussed above does not mean that marital adjustment is virtually impossible; rather, it is an effort to stress the fact that the probability of there being maladjustment in marriage is greater than it is in other areas of human adjustment. It is important for everyone, students of adjustment as well as married people, to have a clear understanding of the nature and magnitude of the problem.

Marital Adjustment and Marital Happiness

Another aspect of the problem of marital adjustment is the important distinction between adjustment and happiness in marriage. Far too many persons approach marriage and insist on thinking of it in terms of the happiness it is supposed to provide; then they find to their dismay that marital happiness is largely a will-o'-the-wisp. This expectation stands as a serious impediment to marital adjustment because it outruns the capabilities of marriage for providing happiness. Ideally, two persons, completely suited to each other and blessed with several children who are beautiful and perfectly adjusted, can be blissfully happy; but this sort of thing is strictly Hollywood and will seldom, if ever, be found in real-life situations. The most important requirement, where marriage is concerned is a realistic attitude that enables us to view marriage as it actually is, with all its trials, difficulties, disappointments, laughs, heartaches, shortcomings, and potentialities for happiness (Table 13). The idyllic view of marriage as a foun-

TABLE 13

Subjective Ratings of Marital Happiness by an Unselected Population,
Compared with Those by an Experimental Group of Married Couples

	UNSELECTED POPULATION		EXPERIMENTAL GROUP	
	Men N 902 %	Women N 644 %	Husbands N 792 %	Wives N 792 %
1. Extraordinarily happy	25.5	27.2	29.5	34.6
2. Decidedly more happy than average	29.4	28.0	36.8	35.9
3. Somewhat more happy than average	13.1	10.1	16.3	14.7
4. About average	18.2	16.3	12.9	9.2
5. Somewhat less happy than average	6.6	7.3	2.9	3.0
6. Decidedly less happy than average	3.2	4.0	1.6	1.8
7. Extremely unhappy	4.0	7.1	0.1	0.8
TOTAL	100.0	100.0	100.0	100.0

Source: Terman, L. M. *Psychological factors in marital happiness.* New York: McGraw-Hill, 1938. P. 78. Used by permission of McGraw-Hill Book Company.

tainhead of supreme bliss is the most common starting point of maladjustment. What people should strive for is a reasonable degree of adjustment in marriage, and the happiness will take care of itself (Christensen, 1950).

Meaning of Marital Adjustment

The concept of marital adjustment refers essentially to the art of living effectively and wholesomely within the framework of responsibilities, relations, and expectancies that constitute the state of marriage. It means the ability to meet the day-to-day demands, vicissitudes, and responsibilities of marriage with whatever degree of emotional equanimity and efficiency is required at the time. It involves getting along with and enjoying the companionship of the marital partner, participating in the interests and activities of the family group, accepting additional responsibilities as they arise, and changing one's style of life to correspond with changes in family life (Purnell, 1952). More than in any other area of human adjustment, meeting the responsibilities of marriage demands the ability and the willingness to change. This is so because of the continuous change that characterizes family living and because of the closeness of the relations that bind the members of the family together. Husband and wife change as they grow older; the family constellation is altered by the addition of children; the pattern of relations within the family constantly changes; the children grow up and in the process force continuous change in the style of living. These changes are gradual and often unobserved, but they are nonetheless real; and marital adjustment must keep pace with all of them. To fail in this is to make maladjustment inevitable.

Outcomes of Marital Adjustment and Happiness

The picture we have painted of marital adjustment makes it clear that it is a difficult goal to achieve and to maintain, but the outcomes are as worth striving for as the task is difficult. Marriage and family living have great potentialities for personal satisfaction and for the realization of worthwhile goals. Few vocations or modes of life can contribute so much to the sense of accomplishment and to the satisfaction of the need for affection, security, and the feeling of belonging. To be able to live intimately and successfully with one's spouse, to have children who grow up into well-adjusted and happy adults, to share in the interests, hopes, aspirations, and activities of the family are among the most satisfying and enriching of human experiences. This is a lesson that the self-appointed, ego-centered bachelor or spinster never learns, but it is one that most people find well worth learning.

Conditions Influencing Marital Adjustment

Premarital Adjustment. It is possible to isolate a number of factors that have a more or less direct bearing on success and failure in marriage and that shed considerable light on the problem of marital adjustment. The most prominent of these factors is the premarital adjustment level of husband and wife. If marriages are made in heaven, then just as certainly divorces are often made in childhood and adolescence, where future marital partners fail to achieve maturity, emotional stability, and ego security and where they become enmeshed in damaging family relations and conditions. Terman points out (1952, p. 380):

> The 10 background circumstances most predictive of marital happiness are (1) superior happiness of parents, (2) childhood happiness, (3) lack of conflict with mother, (4) home discipline that was firm, not harsh, (5) strong attachment to mother, (6) strong attachment to father, (7) lack of conflict with father, (8) parental frankness about matters of sex, (9) infrequency and mildness of childhood

punishment, (10) premarital attitude toward sex that was free from disgust or aversion.

Almost all of these basic factors have to do with successful family relations, which are so important to the achievement of maturity, security, and emotional stability. It is a patent fact that immature and insecure persons cannot meet the heavy responsibilities that marriage imposes since the realities of marriage are much more exacting than are other aspects of daily life (Stokes, 1952).

Of interest in this connection is a study by Hamilton and Wall (1948) of 100 female schizophrenics in a mental hospital. The average age of this group was twenty-eight, with a range of sixteen to fifty-two. The group was above average intellectually, educationally, and culturally. Fifty-four were catatonics, forty paranoids, and only six hebephrenics. In the background of many of these patients there was instability in the home, or homes broken by death, separation, divorce, or psychosis of the parents. Three fourths of the patients had emotionally inadequate parents. The fathers were characterized by rigidity, cruelty, and self-interest; the mothers were openly rejecting, neurotically self-centered, or smothering in their oversolicitousness. Forty-nine of the patients were married, but only thirty-two had children, and almost all of the mothers had made poor adjustments to their children. The authors remark (Hamilton & Wall, 1948, p. 347):

> The married women, as a rule, were unable to achieve the adult toughness necessary to stand the give and take of adjustment to marriage and parenthood. They were unprepared for this adjustment, often because their parents before them had not been healthy models for identification as mates and parents. Nine-tenths of the married women were described as "cold" and "frigid" in their sexual life or merely as "disgusted with sex." Of the 32 mothers, 25 became mentally ill within one year after a pregnancy, abortion, or childbirth. Seventeen married women had no children and several of these had induced abortions.

Many studies have emphasized the important relation between premarital adjustments and success in marriage. Burgess and Cottrell, for example, in discussing the prediction of success or failure in marriage, place considerable weight on the child's affectional relation with one or the other parent. If this relation was a happy one, the child tends to fall in love with a person who possesses characteristics similar to the loved parent; if unhappy, then he will likely choose a mate with characteristics opposite those of the parent. Also, the adult tends to relive his childhood affectional life in the marital situation (Burgess & Cottrell, 1939; Anderson, 1949, pp. 651–654; Tyson, 1951, pp. 51–52). Commenting on these observations, Steckle (1949, p. 197) says:

The responsibility of the family is clearly indicated. As we saw in the development of a normal personality as well as in the formation of basically neurotic patterns of behavior, the affectional relationships within the home are the deciding factors. Happy parents not only rear happy children, they also lay the groundwork for happy marriages. If, in the home, the child learns to love and to trust another, the prediction for his future marital happiness is that much better. If, however, he learns but attitudes of suspicion and antagonism, only trouble is ahead. The burden is squarely upon the shoulders of the parents; theirs is the choice. They may train the child to hate, or they may train him to love. The former is the easier, more emotional, less rational, way.

Family relations and experiences provide the background for the social development of the child, and, if the child fails to reach social maturity, his chances of marital adjustment are slight. Marriage and family are in part social institutions, and the failure to achieve social adjustment constitutes a serious impediment to successful family living.

What of sexual adjustment prior to marriage? Because of the importance of sex in marriage, one would think that good sexual adjustment during adolescence would have a direct bearing on marital adjustment (Baruch & Miller, 1962). The evidence, however, is inconclusive. For example, among the factors of slight importance to marital happiness, Terman lists adequacy of sex instruction, sources of sex information, amount of adolescent petting, and a history of sex shock on the part of the wife. Yet all such factors, as we saw in the preceding chapter, are important to adequate sexual adjustment. Terman does point out that a premarital attitude of disgust toward sex is unfavorable to marital happiness, particularly in men (Terman, 1952, p. 379). To the extent, of course, that the adolescent fails to attain sexual maturity, or develops habits of promiscuity and infidelity, or experiences deep-seated emotional conflicts over sexual excesses, we may expect preparation for marriage to be adversely affected. Sexual maturity and adjustment are certainly no less important to adequate marital relations than are social and emotional maturity. In fact, all aspects of maturity and adjustment are so closely interrelated that failure in one area is bound to affect the rest. If, therefore, the adolescent or young adult has learned how to cope successfully with sexual frustrations and conflicts, without damage to his spiritual, moral, and social ideals, he has a head start toward good marital adjustment. For other viewpoints, see Tyson (1951, pp. 56–58).

Attitude toward Marriage. A second condition that will certainly influence marital adjustment is the attitude toward marriage and its responsibilities. If marriage is regarded as an indissoluble union of husband and wife, the idea of separation or divorce is excluded, and more serious efforts will be made to adjust to difficulties and thus preserve the marital union. Undoubtedly, many marriages that finally turned into successful and happy partnerships might have been dissolved earlier if the way of divorce had been open to husband and wife. But many persons today accept and approve the idea of divorce and enter into marriage with the reservation that, if things do not work out, there is always the divorce court to fall back on. Such an attitude is certain to affect the person's *unwillingness to accept the responsibility of making marriage work*. According to J. T. and Mary G. Landis (1963, p. 281):

> As one studies large numbers of marriages that have lasted happily for years, the evidence becomes more and more convincing that successful marriages do not just happen. A conscious recognition of the need for working at building a successful marriage has proved to be the important factor in the success of many marriages, and the failure to recognize the necessity for working at it has resulted in unhappiness in many other marriages.

Of interest in connection with the foregoing discussion are the findings reported by Thomas in his study of the causes of marriage breakdown in the Catholic family. The main causes are indicated in Table 14 (also Thomas, 1953). It is clear that such factors as drink, adultery, and irrespon-

TABLE 14
Factors Involved in the Breakdown of Catholic Marriages

Factor	Percentage
Drink	29.8
Adultry	24.8
Irresponsibility	12.4
Temperament	12.1
Others	20.9

Source: Thomas, J. L. Marriage breakdown in the Catholic family. *Social Order*, 1952, 2, 447.

sibility, which seem to be the major causes of family breakdown according to this study, reflect thoroughly bad attitudes toward the responsibilities of marriage. Furthermore (Thomas, 1952, p. 448),

> The third largest category includes the cases in which irresponsibility, or, as some might prefer to call it, immaturity, was manifested in a marked degree by one or by both parties. Here are found individuals

who fail to recognize the basic obligations which they had assumed in the marriage contract.

Similarly, marital adjustment will be affected for good or ill by attitudes toward having and rearing of children, a fact that is partly reflected in the relation between divorces and size of family. In one study, cited by Moore, it was found that in families where there were no children the percentage of divorces was 63.0. In the one-child family, the percentage dropped to 20.5. In families of two, three, and four children, the percentages were 9.5, 3.9 and 1.7, respectively. Where there were five or more children the percentage of divorces dropped to 1.4. The obvious relation between distribution of divorces and size of family reflected in these figures indicates conclusively that the having of children has a stabilizing effect on the family. What is more, there seems to be a definable relation between the number of children and family stability. There are many persons who still regard the procreation and proper rearing of children as the primary end of marriage and who, therefore, freely and willingly accept this responsibility with the taking of the marriage vows. But if the wife or husband objects to this responsibility, the groundwork is laid for a great deal of discord. The wanton disregard for the welfare of children manifested by persons seeking divorce is testimony to their small concern for the responsibilities of marriage. Everyone today is acutely aware of the damaging effects of broken homes on children, yet the number of divorces continues at a very high rate. It is difficult to believe that such persons have a mature attitude toward the responsibilities of married life. As we noted earlier, the immature, poorly adjusted person has a generally inadequate sense of responsibility not only toward marriage but toward other basic aspects of life, and when this attitude is carried into marriage, maladjustment is inevitable.

If the acceptance of divorce is an impediment to successful marriage, so too is *the overidealistic attitude that marriage is a perpetual honeymoon.* The harsh realities of the marital union must be faced squarely from the very outset. The possibility of financial difficulties, of discovering unfavorable characteristics in the marital partner, of lack of consideration, of quarreling and disagreement, of petty annoyances, of forgetting important dates, and so on, must be taken into full account before and after the marriage ceremony. The likelihood of two people, who once were complete strangers, being perfectly suited to each other is so remote that it is not worth considering. In fact, one cannot be sure that it would be a good thing. The trials and difficulties of marriage, when successfully surmounted, contribute greatly to the growth of personality and to increase in the capacity for adjustment. It is not the conflicts and difficulties of married life that should cause us worry; it is the failure to surmount them.

Motivations Underlying Marriage.   The relation between attitudes and marital adjustment is closely paralleled by the motivations underlying marriage and their relation to adjustment. There are many reasons why people get married; some of them are distinctly bad and thus function as serious impediments to happiness and success in marriage. It is obvious that if a person marries for financial gain or security alone, without regard for love, the sacramental aspect of marriage, or the responsibilities of raising a family, the marriage is destined for failure from the outset. Similarly, if marriage is sought as a means of perpetuating unhealthy mother-son relations, so that the future wife is regarded as a mother surrogate rather than a partner, there is little hope of marital success.

In some instances, marriage is looked upon as a means of escape, or as a haven of security, or as one last chance to avoid staying single; in others, it is looked upon as a kind of adventure that one embarks on when he reaches adulthood, in still others, as a lawful means of sexual expression or release from sexual conflict, with little thought given to the solemn responsibilities of marriage, mutual love, and sacrifice. In all such instances, the marital craft is sure to run into stormy seas and hidden reefs that will threaten its destruction. These motives are no more adequate to the serious character and the responsibilities of marriage than the desire to attend football games or belong to a sorority is adequate motivation for going to college.

Only when marriage represents a sincere expression of mutual love and friendship, a deep craving for companionship, and a desire for children and family life is it adequately motivated. As Moore says (1944, p. 198), "the ideal marriage is going to look forward to a number of children and the establishment of a happy social group living together in peace and harmony, preparing to serve God and the social order by their life and work." That these ideas are not merely pious hopes is brought out in one study of why people marry. While many respondents in the group studied gave "being in love" as the reason for getting married, other factors were found to be more significant. Steckle reports (1949, p. 192):

> A survey of the reasons for marrying made upon over four hundred young women in our country revealed that companionship was given first place, a home of one's own second, while the desire for children and romantic love tied for third. Other factors, such as social and economic pressures, escape, loneliness, etc., followed.

Selection of a Mate.   Another important factor that has much to do with marital adjustment is the careful, intelligent selection of a mate. The only sensible rule to follow in the interest of marital happiness is to select someone who has the potentialities for meeting the crucial demands

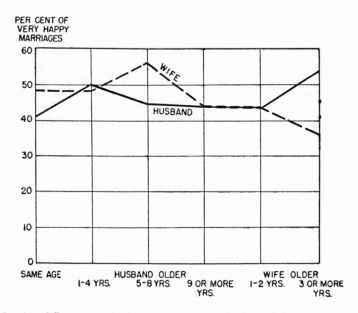

Fig. 25.   Age differences in husbands and wives and self-rated happiness in marriage. (From Landis, J. T. & Landis, Mary G. *Building a successful marriage*. Englewood Cliffs, N. J.: Prentice-Hall, 1948, p. 160. Reprinted by permission.)

and responsibilities of marriage. Why people are so meticulous about choosing a suit of clothes or a vacation spot when they are so careless about choosing a marital partner has never been explained. To be successful in marriage a woman has to be a good wife and a good mother, and she has to know or learn how to create a good home. It is not particularly important whether she can sew, write a novel, enjoy the opera, or make a *soufflé*. If she has an even disposition, good moral and religious principles, and a healthy attitude toward the responsibilities of married life, one can disregard her failure to look like a Conover model or the fact that she does not have a college degree (Landis & Landis, 1948, pp. 260–262). The potentially good husband must be a steady wage earner, considerate of his family, emotionally mature, and keenly aware of his marital responsibilities. It is not important whether he can play the piano or is not interested in mystery plays; but if he is egocentric, selfish, or immature in his attitudes toward women, there will be difficulties in the future. These facts point up the advantage of lengthier courtships, to give people a chance to find out what the other person is like, even though empirical studies indicate that length of courtship is not importantly related to marital happiness.

Factors of Little Significance.   As we have just indicated, there are many factors of little significance to marital adjustment. Investigators have

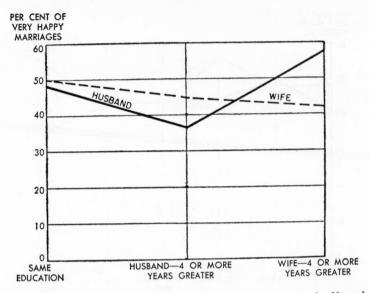

Fig. 26.   Educational differences of 409 husbands and 409 wives and self-rated happiness in marriages. (From Landis, J. T. & Landis, Mary G. *Building a successful marriage.*
Englewood Cliffs, N. J.: Prentice-Hall, 1948, p. 157. Reprinted by permission.)

found that family income, occupation, birth order, number of opposite-sex
siblings, adolescent popularity, and differences in age and schooling were
almost totally uncorrelated with happiness scores, although nearly all these
factors have been regarded as highly significant by one or another writer in
the field of marital adjustment (Figures 25 and 26). Even such conditions
as presence or absence of children and amount of religious training were
not significantly related to rated happiness, although in individual cases
both of them become highly significant.

Happiness in having children depends a great deal on the intensity of
the desire for a family and on the quality of early experiences with children.
The selfish wife who wants to possess her husband to the exclusion of other

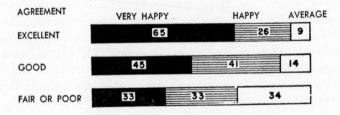

Fig. 27.   Agreement on religious expression and happiness in marriage. (From Landis,
J. T. & Landis, Mary G. *Building a successful marriage.* 4th ed. Englewood Cliffs, N. J.:
Prentice-Hall, 1963, p. 353. Reprinted by permission.)

affectional relations and the husband who hated his brothers and sisters or was jealous of them are not going to rate themselves as unhappy because of the absence of children. In fact, the advent of children would cause an avalanche of maladjustment.

Many persons with extensive religious training are miserably unhappy in the marital union not because of their training but because of personality factors that remain unaffected by their religious experiences and practices. If, to the contrary, religious training leads to a firm belief in the providence of God, attitudes of charity and humility, belief in the sacramental and grace-bestowing character of marriage, and the conviction that husband and wife should devote themselves to each other and to the welfare of their children, then, certainly, religious training is going to contribute much to marital happiness. This relation between religious practices and marital adjustment has been validated by empirical studies and has received emphasis in a number of studies on the conditions of marital adjustment (Figure 27). Burgess and Cottrell (1939, p. 123) found more favorable adjustment in marriage among those persons who attended Sunday school beyond the age of ten years and among those who were regular in their religious observances. J. T. and M. G. Landis suggest, too, that the person with a positive religious faith is more likely to have a well-integrated personality and is therefore a better risk as a marriage partner (Landis & Landis, 1963, pp. 356–357).

> The person who has a faith that "works" in his own life makes a good marriage partner. He will not be ready to do battle over nonessentials, but will rather strive to understand the viewpoint of the other person. He will show a willingness to compromise for harmony. He will respect the personality of the partner, refrain from ridicule or the belittling attitudes that are so devastating to the happiness of a wife or husband. He will build up the self-respect and self-confidence of his partner rather than destroy it. His own inner security will be a source of strength to those about him in the times of crisis that come to every family. He will be able to maintain a perspective on life and its values so that when trouble comes he will not go to pieces but will be able to withstand pressure.

Other factors that seem to be of little importance to marital happiness are present age of husband and wife, length of marriage, adequacy of income, age at marriage, circumstances of first meeting between the spouses, and length of premarital acquaintance. Nevertheless, it is significant that the number of divorces is much higher in the first ten years of married life than in any subsequent period, suggesting a strong relationship between adjustment and length of marriage (Landis & Landis, 1948, pp. 241–244). In his study of marital failure and duration, Thomas (1953)

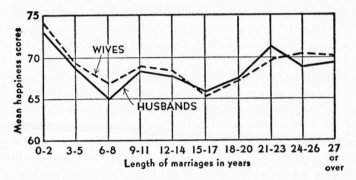

Fig. 28. Mean happiness scores according to length of marriage. (From Terman, L. M. Psychological factors in marital happiness. In R. G. Kuhlen & G. G. Thompson (Eds.), *Psychological studies in human development*. New York: Appleton, 1952, p. 375.)

reports that both drinking and adultery increase with length of marriage, each indicating marital maladjustment. An important point to note, however, regarding length of marriage (Figure 28), is the appreciable drop in mean happiness scores during the first six to eight years of marriage, which suggests that a considerable period of adjustment is required. On the more positive side, there is evidence that equality or near equality in mental ability is desirable and that strong attachments to either parent are favorable to marital happiness. "Marked mental superiority of husband makes for happiness in the wife but for unhappiness in the husband; marked inferiority of husband makes the wife unhappy but does not greatly affect the husband" (Terman, 1952, p. 379; also Landis & Landis, 1948, pp. 156–158).

Basic Requirements of Marital Adjustment and Success

Since we have already picked out several factors that seem to be positively related to marital adjustment, let us now take a closer look at those basic requirements that seem to be necessary for success and happiness in marriage. For practical, everyday principles of marital adjustment, see Fromme (1950); Hope (1943).

1. *One of the most significant requirements for successful marriage is compatibility.* However, contrary to what many writers have insisted, this does not mean sexual compatibility as much as it means *psychological* compatibility, which involves several areas of personality. Sexual factors are important, but they are far from being the most important determinants of marital success and, in some instances, are hardly correlated with happiness at all. Thus, sexual technique, preferred frequency of sexual relations, fear of pregnancy, wife's history of sex shock, and so forth, seem to have

little relation to happiness in marriage. However, the amount of pleasure experienced in sexual relations, overprudishness or excessive modesty regarding sex, the wife's orgasm adequacy, and differences in sexual drive between husband and wife are closely related to marital happiness. This is especially true of the last two factors, which seem to be genuine determinants of marital happiness (English, 1947, 1957; Anderson, 1949, pp. 657–660).

The influence of sexual factors on marital adjustment will be conditioned a great deal by personality characteristics of the couple, by attitudes toward sex, attitudes toward each other, and by the degree of psychological compatibility. As Freeman & Greenwald comment (1961, pp. 219–220):

> The happy marriage is not made in bed. It is a product of the entire aura of living. The husband who comes home from work and devotes the evening to pursuits of his own, scarcely speaking to his wife, cannot understand why, even though he does everything the sex manual commands, his wife acts cool to him when he tries to embrace her. . . . Similarly, the wife who has nagged all through supper may find herself disappointed when her husband does not wax duly romantic as the lights go off. Anger and sexual desire usually do not make good bed fellows.
>   If sexual intimacy grows out of a couple's whole life together, it becomes the spontaneous expression of the closeness of a man and woman rather than an ordered and prescribed ritual. There will be less possibility of the intrusion of emotions that interfere with spontaneity, such as rage, fear, or distrust.

Commenting on another aspect of the relationship, Terman remarks (1952, p. 382):

> Our data do not confirm the view so often heard that the key to happiness in marriage is nearly always to be found in sexual compatibility. They indicate, instead, that the influence of the sexual factor is at most no greater than that of the combined personality and background factors, and that it is probably less. The problem is complicated by the fact that the testimony of husband and wife regarding their sexual compatibility is influenced by their psychological compatibility. Couples who are psychologically well mated are likely to show a surprising tolerance for the things that are not satisfactory in their sexual relationships. The psychologically ill-mated show no such tolerance but instead are prone to exaggeration in their reports on sexual maladjustments. The two sexual factors of genuine importance are wife's orgasm adequacy and relative strength of sex drive in the two spouses.

To be psychologically well mated is a part of the general quality of compatibility found in some married couples and not in others. It refers to relative similarity in personality make-up, community of interests, ability to share activities and goals, and willingness to understand and sympathize with another's shortcomings, desires, and aspirations. Thus, there is little compatibility in marital situations where the husband wants to go bowling every time his wife is interested in a concert, or where the wife is disdainful of her husband's career, or where there is constant fault finding and bickering on the part of both spouses. Similarly, if one spouse is extremely dominating, egocentric, selfish, and inconsiderate, whereas the other is submissive, outgoing, and thoughtful, there can be little psychological compatibility (Eisenstein, 1956).

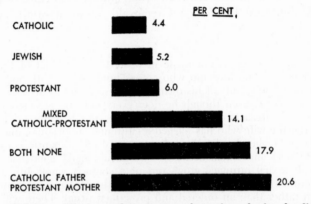

Religious affiliation and percentage of marriages broken by divorce or separation (4,108 marriages).

Fig. 29. Religious affiliation and percentage of marriages broken by divorce or separation (4,108 marriages). (From Landis, J. T. & Landis, Mary G. *Building a successful marriage.* 4th ed. Englewood Cliffs, N. J.: Prentice-Hall, 1963, p. 198. Reprinted by permission.)

The factor of compatibility is exempliefid very well in the matter of religion. It is well known that so-called mixed marriages, especially those involving Catholics and Protestants, are generally a bad risk (Figure 29). The emotional and intellectual gulf between the devout Catholic and the devout Protestant is often so great that even in instances where the marriage is relatively successful the feeling of incompatibility runs high. The good Catholic is bound in conscience to give his children a Catholic education, but can a Protestant be expected to understand and appreciate this fact? It is a matter of conscience also to attend Mass every Sunday, to receive the sacraments regularly, to support the Church and the pastor, but these things may have little meaning for the average non-Catholic. For the sincere communicant, religion is not simply a matter of ritual and practice; it runs deep and pervades many aspects of personality.

Thus two people of different faiths are going to find it extremely difficult to achieve compatibility. On such basic issues as the religious upbringing of the children, birth control, fidelity, divorce, and the validity of one's religion, they are miles apart, and even the great virtues of love and respect are often not enough to decrease this distance appreciably. Religious and psychological compatibility, far more than sexual gratification, is basic to a happy and successful marriage. Landis and Landis (1948, Chapter VII) discuss this problem at some length. They refer to Weeks's study, which analyzed the "marital status of 6,548 families of public and parochial school children in Spokane, Washington. He found a divorce rate of 3.8 among Catholics, 10.0 among Protestants, 17.4 in mixed marriages, and 23.9 if there was no religion. Howard Bell's analysis of the marital status of 13,528 families of mixed and non-mixed marriages in Maryland found a divorce rate of 6.4 among Catholics, 4.6 among Jews, 6.8 among Protestants, 15.2 in mixed marriages, and 16.7 if there was no religion in the home" (Landis & Landis, 1963, p. 198).

2. *Closely allied to compatibility is the factor of personality characteristics.* In the last analysis, all adjustment hinges upon the kinds of personalities involved in the adjustment situation. It is obvious that few people can live happily or successfully with a person who is highly neurotic or despondent, given to fits of temper, or lashed by a feeling of inferiority. Also, people who tend toward excessive drinking, extramarital relations, or punitive treatment of children will contribute little to marital success. Marriage involves a complex set of relations that will readily break down under the impact of characteristics and ways of behaving that are diametrically opposed to the harmony and compatibility necessary to marital happiness (Eisenstein, 1956, pp. 81–100).

From the positive viewpoint, marital adjustment requires the possession or development of personal characteristics that serve to strengthen the oneness of mind and spirit that is essential to marriage and to marital happiness. These characteristics are primarily moral virtues, and include such old stand-bys as kindness, selflessness, charity, consideration, sympathy, trust, faith, and tolerance. *The one basic element running through all these characteristics and absolutely necessary to a happy marriage is charity.*

But if charity with its multiple implications is the basic law of successful conjugal life, of paramount importance also are those personal characteristics that form the psychological groundwork of the moral virtues in man (Schneiders, 1953). This relation the moral theologian too often overlooks. Granted that the moral virtues are necessary to the good life, what is first of all necessary is a fertile soil in which they can grow. Can the egocentric husband, compensating for inferiority, be kind and considerate?

Can the wife who has strong feelings of inadequacy love and care for her children in a wholesome way? Factors such as jealousy, possessiveness, hostility, and anger, which destroy the moral virtues, and conjugal happiness along with them, grow out of psychological inadequacies in personality. For this reason, the only solution to many marital difficulties is marriage counseling or psychotherapy, by which inadequate personalities may be restored to a healthier condition.

3. *Continuous personal growth and advancement toward the goal of successful marriage is the third requirement of marital adjustment.* Marital adjustment is not something that can be attained in a month, a year, or five years. Because the conditions of the marital union constantly change, there must be *continuous adjustment*, which means not only adaptation to existing conditions but also growth in personality, in the qualities necessary to marital happiness, and in the capacity to meet the exacting demands of family life. We have seen this growth to be an essential part of all adjustment, and in marriage we have another special instance of the application of this general principle.

4. *Mutual love, respect, trust, and recognition of equality between husband and wife are of major importance for marital success.* It is doubtful whether marital happiness can be attained in any degree if one or another of these qualities is lacking. The concept of love used in this context does not refer to romantic attachment or infatuation, which may or may not be a part of marriage. Rather, it refers to that deep sense of oneness and of lasting friendship that is invariably associated with happy couples. More important than romantic attachment or interest are a sincere liking for each other, the desire to do things together, to share each other's experiences, hopes, disappointments, and joys, and to work together for the welfare of the family and for the realization of personal as well as common aims (Fromme, 1950, Chapter VI).

Love is bound to ensure mutual respect and trust because it develops an awareness of the worth and dignity of the marital partner as a person and leads to an appreciation of one another's moral integrity. Conjugal love that stimulates the sense of oneness and of belonging to each other leaves little room for suspicion, mistrust, jealousy, possessiveness, or envy, all of which work toward the destruction of marital joy; nor does it allow for the development of attitudes of superiority or domination, which militate against the feeling of equal rights and responsibilities in the marital relation. Both husband and wife should regard each other as partners in a common venture, not as master and servant. Christian doctrine insists that the father is the titular head of the home, and in him should rest the final decision on matters of importance, but this principle does not preclude the idea of equality, any more than the fact that the president is the head of the state precludes equality among the citizens, including the president himself. In marriage, there should be equality of rights and opportunities in the expression of opinion, in self-expression, and in activities; furthermore, there should be equality of duties and obligations. There should be an equitable, sensible division of labor based on mutual consideration and respect for the dignity of both husband and wife. Happiness cannot flourish in an atmosphere where the essential worth of human personality is degraded by attitudes of domination and superiority.

Practices Important to Marital Adjustment

As requirements for successful marriage, several important practices should be carefully defined and as carefully followed.

1. *Seek adequate premarital and marriage counseling.* Many of the pitfalls of marital adjustment can be anticipated and avoided through the knowledge and advice of experts in the field of marriage counseling (Clemens, 1951; Mudd, 1951; Lamson, 1951). No one can be expected to know the intricacies of a complex affair like marriage until he has learned by experience, or has made a careful study of it, or both. Young people, especially, should not assume that love and the solemn pronouncements of the marriage ceremony will by some special magic endow them with all the knowledge, skill, and qualities that a successful marriage demands. True, as a sacrament, marriage carries with it certain special graces that will enable them to surmount difficulties that arise; but there must be intelligent cooperation on the part of the married couple, and this cooperation requires knowledge and insight into the complexities of married life. Counsel should be sought also during marriage whenever difficulties arise that husband and wife cannot cope with. Steckle says (1949, p. 196),

> The use of premarital counseling services is fundamentally good, sound sense. Much is now known of the factors making for a happy marriage and to neglect them is to take unnecessary chances with future happiness. One thing is certain, the persons who make use of these services may rest assured that they have done everything humanly possible to be certain that their marriage is off to the best conceivable start.

2. *Have a thorough physical examination before marriage.* The premarital examination gives assurance of physical well-being to the prospective bride and groom and often brings to light certain physical defects that should be known to both. In one study, for example, the examination of 650 women prior to marriage showed that about fifteen of the group could not bear children; in another 130 the uterus was in an unusual position; and about seventy-five gave evidence of leukorrhea. Obviously, facts

such as these should be known if the marriage is to get off to a good start.

3. *Select a mate carefully.* In addition to the suggestions already offered for the wise choice of a mate, there are several cautions that should be observed. One should be wary of intense jealousy, insecurity, neurotic disabilities, tendencies to escape reality, immaturity, desire to make the other person over, and an incapacity for healthy love relations in a prospective mate. Any one of these weaknesses portend poor adjustment in marriage. One should also look for indications of mutual compatibility; if important interests, attitudes, values, and principles are antagonistic, the prognosis for happy marriage is poor. It is not wise to overemphasize the "for better or for worse" clause of the marriage ceremony. With an intelligent perspective during courtship, it is just as easy to do better as it is to do worse, and the dividends of this investment, paid off in the currency of happiness and adjustment, will be worth whatever effort or sacrifice is necessary.

4. *Learn to cope with marital requirements as they arise.* Premarital attitudes toward sex, children, and marriage itself, are seldom wholly adequate for the demands of married life. It is important to learn how to modify them. If certain aspects of sex are frightening or distasteful, learn to live with them by changing your attitude. If children seem more of a burden than a blessing, re-evaluate your attitudes toward the responsibilities of married life. If marriage itself turns out to be disappointing, remind yourself that, approached in the right way, it can offer many satisfactions as well as disappointments.

It is important also for married couples to learn how to work together as a team, to make necessary concessions to individual interests and peculiarities, not to take each other for granted, to understand each other thoroughly, and to develop mutual consideration. All these things have to be learned, and one must work at them constantly. The husband who exercises rigid control over the budget, without letting his wife in on the secrets of family financing, is setting an obstacle to marital harmony. The wife who refuses to recognize and tolerate any idiosyncrasies in her husband is asking for trouble. And the couple who begin to regard each other as part of the household furnishings instead of as living, dynamic human beings are certainly headed for discord.

Along the same lines, certain practices should be avoided by married people. Above all, learn to avoid nagging and criticizing because there is nothing that will destroy personal dignity and mutual respect as quickly as these vicious habits. Also, it is important to avoid excessive quarreling, and particularly is it necessary to avoid continuing a quarrel. Never let a day end without an amicable settling of differences; learn to swallow personal pride and to ask forgiveness and understanding. Finally, avoid the tendency toward possessiveness. Leave some room for individuality in marriage, whether in the matter of recreational activities or in the solitude of reading. The marital union must not be taken to mean complete surrender of all individuality. Of course, too much individuality of conduct and interest will tend to separate the couple, and this must be carefully avoided. However, there should always be some room for expression of individuality. As Magner states (1947, p. 219), husband and wife should not

> be so inseparable as to have no freedom of activity or individual personal and social interests. On the contrary, it is a good thing for them to go their separate ways occasionally, to dust off their mental cobwebs, and to learn through legitimate experience that "absence makes the heart grow fonder." Both parties must, in particular, be on their guard against that type of jealousy that makes all kind of independent action subject to suspicion and distrust.

The principles and practices discussed above certainly do not give the whole secret to marital adjustment and happiness; marriage has too many facets to be encompassed by a few principles. They are, however, among the most important rules for marital success and, if followed scrupulously, will take the well-meaning couple a long ways toward its goal of marital adjustment. In addition, they are essential to the mental hygiene of marriage.

QUESTIONS AND PROJECTS FOR FURTHER STUDY

1. Write a book report on one of the texts in the Selected Readings that deals specifically with the problem of marital adjustment.
2. Explain in your own words the relation between marital and vocational adjustment on the one hand, and vocational and academic adjustment on the other.
3. Describe in detail five basic principles important to the achievement of academic success.
4. In what manner is the gratification of basic human needs related to vocational adjustment? Cite at least five articles from the professional literature to substantiate your explanation.
5. What are four practices important to vocational success?
6. Write a brief essay on the conditions and requirements for good adjustment and success in marriage.
7. Compare and evaluate any two books on marriage counseling that are included in the References.

SELECTED COLLATERAL READINGS

BLOOD, R. O., JR., & WOLFE, D. M. *Husbands and wives: the dynamics of married life.* New York: Free Press, 1960.

BURGESS, E. W., & WALLIN, P. *Engagement and marriage.* Philadelphia: Lippincott, 1952.

CARTER, H. L. J., & MC GINNIS, D. J. *Building a successful college career.* Dubuque, Iowa: William C. Brown, 1950.

CHANDLER, J. R., *et al. Successful adjustment in college.* Englewood Cliffs, N.J.: Prentice-Hall, 1951.

FREEMAN, LUCY, & GREENWALD, H. *Emotional maturity in love and marriage.* New York: Harper & Row, 1961.

FROMME, A. *The psychologist looks at sex and marriage.* Englewood Cliffs, N.J.: Prentice-Hall, 1950.

HEALY, E. F. *Marriage guidance.* Chicago: Loyola University Press, 1948.

JOHNSON, D. *Marriage counseling: theory and practice.* Englewood Cliffs, N.J.: Prentice-Hall, 1961.

MC KINNEY, F. *Psychology of personal adjustment.* (2d ed.) N.Y.: Wiley, 1949.

SUPER, D. E. *Appraising vocational fitness.* (Rev. ed.) New York: Harper & Row, 1962.

WITTY, P. A. (Ed.) *Mental health in modern education.* Chicago: University of Chicago Press, 1955.

15

Religion and Mental Hygiene

It is readily recognized today that mental health has its roots in many different sources, for example, the home and school, the Church and society, and that mental hygiene, therefore, derives its support from many different agencies. One of the most important of these, according to a number of investigators, is religion. And just as, in the following chapter, we will study the relation between mental hygiene and the home and school, so here we wish to analyze the precise relation between religion and mental health. Is religion an essential part of mental hygiene? If so, is the nonbeliever or the atheist doomed to mental illness or maladjustment? What about guilt and scruples, anxiety and shame which are generated by religious attitudes and doctrines regarding sin, hell, and damnation? These are just a few of the questions that cry out for answers. Let us see what these answers may be.

RELIGION AND PSYCHOLOGICAL HEALTH

Cross-fire and Cross-currents

Much has been written, beginning early in the century, regarding religion and psychological health, but, as we noted above, there are many riddles still to be solved. William James's classic book, *Varieties of religious experience* (1902), is replete with many implications regarding the significant role which religious experience and behavior can play in promoting the emotional stability and personal growth of the individual, as are later books, articles, brochures, and pamphlets (Oates, 1955; Jung, 1933; Van Buskirk, 1952; Vaughan, 1962; Clark, 1958).

In recent years the same kind of thinking is reflected in the growing relationship between the transcendent science of theology and the practical arts of psychiatry and psychotherapy (Linn & Schwarz, 1958; Braceland, 1955; Fromm, 1950; Mowrer, 1961). Theologians in large numbers have overcome their anxieties and fears regarding psychoanalysis and dynamic psychiatry, and now vie with each other, most vigorously at times, in their efforts to assimilate and to exploit the complex and sometimes esoteric concepts of modern psychology, as well as to make use of the skills and

* Much of the material of this chapter on religion and mental hygiene is taken from the author's article, "Religion and psychological health—a new approach," published in the *Journal of Existential Psychiatry*, Vol. II, 1961. The author wishes to acknowledge the generous permission of the publishers to use this material.

knowledges of the psychiatrist and others engaged in the practice of psychotherapy whenever that step seemed desirable or necessary. For their part, the psychiatrists themselves, probably in smaller numbers, have also taken definite strides toward a better understanding and a firmer working relationship with the professional religionists (O'Doherty & McGrath, 1963).

This growing and often fruitful relationship between religion and psychology has assumed many forms in the past few years. Forums, conferences, institutes, and workshops have sprung up in large numbers in all parts of the country and in Europe, sometimes within the framework of a university setting, and at other times under the sponsorship of particular groups or organizations interested in exploring the relationship between religion and psychological health (Bier, 1962, 1963). Out of such efforts have emerged numerous publications that deal with the topic from one standpoint or another, adding to the list of books, brochures, and journal articles that come from other sources. This literature extends all the way from the superficial and platitudinous to the profundities of existential psychology, and therefore varies a great deal in its relationship to the problem. Almost all of it represents an effort to draw religion and the sciences of the mind as well as the healing arts closer together in the belief that religion and psychological health are in some way profoundly interdependent (Schneiders, 1961; Allport, 1963).

Attitudes of the Helping Professions

There are many expressions of the relationship between religion and psychological health in the literature of psychology and psychiatry. The classical example is the oft-quoted expression of Jung (1933, p. 264):

> I should like to call attention to the following facts. During the past thirty years, people from all the civilized countries of the earth have consulted me. I have treated many hundreds of patients, the larger number being Protestants, a smaller number of Jews, and not more than five or six believing Catholics. Among all my patients in the second half of life . . . there has not been one whose problem in the last resort was not that of finding a religious outlook on life. It is safe to say that every one of them fell ill because he had lost that which the living religions of every age have given to their followers, and none of them has been really healed who did not regain his religious outlook.

Compare this statement with that of another renowned psychiatrist, William Menninger. Christ Himself, says Menninger (1947),

> laid down one of the principles of mental health that we now recognize as of paramount importance. Matthew, Mark, and Luke all quoted Christ when they said in effect, "For whosoever will save his life shall

lose it, but whosoever will lose his life for My sake will save it." That sentence condenses in a nutshell the attribute of the mature individual. Some men can love others enough to derive more satisfaction from that than from being loved themselves. It is still a magnificent precept. If you can follow it, you will never have to make a date with a psychiatrist.

Statements such as those above can be found in scores of texts and treatises dealing with mental health, adjustment, and psychotherapy (Stern, 1948; VanderVeldt, 1951; Johnson, 1947). The relation between religion and mental health is based on the belief that religion, above everything else, is capable of supplying the values, beliefs, and practices that give meaning and stability to human life. Training, education, work, social experience, and group living play their respective and important roles in the inculcation of values, ideals, attitudes, and worthwhile habits, but in the nature of things, they cannot substitute for religion.

Yet the large effort on the part of both theology and the healing arts does not contain within itself the formula for its own success. Depth psychology, to which appeal is most often made by the eager theologian looking for answer to his parishioners' problems, may well serve to emasculate theology; or, if it leaves theology intact, it may emasculate the religious beliefs of the aspiring theologian. Theories of the unconscious, or of psychological dynamics, have a way of undermining belief in Divine Grace, the efficacy of prayer, or the value of the Sacraments. This point is particularly important in view of the widespread tendency in theological seminaries, particularly some of the Protestant denominations, to "bulwark" the theological training of their students with courses in abnormal psychology, psychological dynamics and diagnosis, mental hygiene, or essentials of psychiatry. It is still an open question whether a minister of souls can at the same time be a healer of minds. There are many clergymen today who are good counselors but not particularly effective ministers. By the same rule, there are many ministers who do a rather thorough job of bungling the counseling process (McCann, 1962).

All the observations made above point up the complexity and magnitude of the problem of defining the exact relationship between religion and psychological health. The injunction to "go and sin no more, thy faith hath made thee whole" carries such deep implications for this problem that it becomes an imperative demand to examine it from every possible point of view. The fact that professional religionists themselves often enter the ranks of the mentally ill and that many devoutly religious people are psychologically defunct, whereas just as many nonbelievers are psychologically intact, indicates with unmistakable clarity that our thinking about the relation between religion and mental health needs the most careful evaluation. Undoubtedly faith may at times make a man whole, but it seems also at other times to tear him apart (Oates, 1955, Chapter I). The principles and practices of religion should certainly be an important adjunct to the achievement and the maintenance of psychological health, but we cannot ignore the fact that in many instances they fail to do so. It is this strange paradox that suggests the most assiduous analysis.

Recent Developments Important to Mental Hygiene

Before going on, let us take note of some recent developments that have important implications for the growth of mental hygiene. Prominent among these developments are (1) the founding of two vigorous and rapidly growing organizations devoted to the study of religion and its impact on the individual and society—The Academy of Religion and Mental Health, and The Society for the Scientific Study of Religion, (2) the publication of four relatively new journals devoted to the study of problems germane to religion and mental health—*Pastoral Psychology* (1949), *Journal of Religion and Health* (1961), *The Journal for the Scientific Study of Religion* (1961), and *The Catholic Psychological Record* (1963), (3) the establishment of the Harvard, Loyola, and Yeshiva University Projects on Mental Health and the training of the clergy, all three of which were supported by substantial grants from the National Institute of Mental Health (Kobler, 1959), (4) the organization throughout the country of institutes for the clergy on problems in pastoral psychology (McDonnell, 1957), and (5) the appointment of permanent committees on religion and mental health in such organizations as the American Psychological Association and the American Psychiatric Association. These are some of the most significant trends that have developed within the past fifteen years. They augur well for the continued and growing *rapprochement* between religion and the helping professions and contain within themselves the promise of a deeper understanding of what religion means to mental health and what its implications are for the practical arts of mental hygiene, counseling, and psychotherapy (Academy of Religion and Mental Health, 1959; Miller, 1952; Bier, 1962, 1963).

DIFFICULTIES OF RELIGION FOR MENTAL HEALTH

Religion and Fear, Guilt, and Shame

If there is one thing that we can be certain of in this complex and uncertain area of human thought, it is that religion of and by itself *cannot guarantee* either the maintenance or the restoration of mental health. It may be used in some instances as a tool of mental hygiene or of psycho-therapy, but like the surgeon's scalpel, it can be used to destroy the patient as well as to heal him. As Oates points out (1955, pp. 3–4):

> Religion is just like dynamite, equally as dangerous as it is useful. Therefore, the psychiatrist is wise in recognizing that religion *can* be dangerous to his patients. . . . Personal acquaintance with mentally ill persons dramatically clarifies the "hindering powers" of religion as it appears in the lives of psychiatric patients. But even closer study of the needs of the patient enables one to re-evaluate the "helping power" of religious truth. Thereby the character of sound religion is better understood in the light of the prevention, amelioration, and healing of mental illness.

Undoubtedly, the sincere, devout practice of religion will at least promote if not guarantee the salvation of the human soul, but such practices may have little or no effect on the integration of the human mind. Witness the devout churchgoer or the daily communicant, confused and degraded by a sense of shame, guilt, and unworthiness, torn apart by the ambivalence of love and hate, or steeped in a pathological scrupulousness whose basic ingredient of senseless guilt reaches out to and engulfs every act no matter how sinless it may be. The following case illustrates this point very clearly.

> Helen, a graduate student, age 25, complained of compulsive handwashing which stemmed from a deep conviction of contamination. This sense of contamination was rooted in a pervasive feeling of guilt. Numerous objects made her feel contaminated and the contamination spread to everything that she touched. Her confessions consisted of relating "sins" of impurity that had to do mainly with offenses against cleanliness. Typically, the bodily functions of micturition and defecation were dirty and contaminating. If bodily needs manifested themselves while the patient was in church, God would be offended, and the entire ritual would become contaminated. She stated that if it were not for her religion and what God demanded of her, she would have no feelings of guilt and the compulsive tendencies would disappear. After three years of therapy, the guilt was still persistent.

Of course we cannot be too sure in such case as that above whether the "religion" of the seemingly devout worshipper is just so much symp-tomatology or whether it reflects a truly devout and total commitment to God. Religious devotion, prayers, rituals, and church-going are often symptomatic of an underlying psychic disturbance and are used by the patient to dispel his basic anxiety. For such persons, God is a projection of the father image or the expression of a primitive superego, and prayer is used as a device to prove that God (that is, the father) is unloving, unkind, merciless, and wholly rejecting (Oates, 1955, pp. 8, 18). For such persons, prayers are never answered, nor do they want them to be. If their prayers were answered, they would have to yield their neurotic feelings and the defensive system which they have carefully built up to protect their poorly structured ego from the demands and threats of reality. But even apart from this symptomatic aspect of religious devotion, the fact remains that religion of itself cannot guarantee mental health even when it is not used for defensive purposes (Schneiders, 1955, 1958, 1961).

If the practice of religion were a guarantee of good adjustment or mental health, there would be far fewer neurotics and psychotics in the world. Unfortunately, there are many deeply religious people who do not possess peace of mind or even emotional tranquility, and quite a few of them find their way into mental hospitals or require intensive therapeutic treatment. This fact can be readily understood when we remind ourselves that religion is only one determinant of adjustment. Often, therefore, its effects are not powerful enough to offset the influence of other factors working on personality and adjustment. In any single instance, it may be that the virtues and values of religion are not exploited thoroughly enough to be effective. As Moore states (1944, p. 234), "Religion as a therapeutic aid in mental difficulties is applicable only to those who have sincere and honest religious convictions. If a patient has no religious convictions he cannot be aided by religious concepts until he sees the truth and honestly adopts it." A religion that is based on family tradition, fear, habit, social pressure, and similar determinants, and is not an intrinsic part of one's personal life, cannot be expected to offset the effects of other determinants of adjustment and mental health. In fact, in such instances it may have a damaging effect because of the fear, anxiety, and guilt that it often generates. These effects are not so much the fault of religion but of the person's own inadequacies or misuse of religion. As in the case of family, school, or community influences, the ultimate effects of religion on adjustment and mental health will be determined by the total context, both personal and social, within which religion functions (Ausubel, 1955; Curran, 1960).

Complementing the fact that many devoutly religious people are neither well adjusted or mentally healthy is the observation that sanctity is no guarantee of mental health or emotional stability. One can examine the biographies of saintly men and women and find many instances of emotional turmoil and a lack of mental tranquility. It may be that the very effort to achieve a high level of sanctity is what causes so much anguish, guilt, a sense of worthlessness, and other disturbing mental conditions. Perhaps, as some people have observed, it is necessary to descend to the depths of mental anguish before sanctity or peace of mind can be attained. This possibility requires careful evaluation in determining the relation between religion and mental health (O'Doherty, 1959).

Not only is religion sometimes ineffective, but it may be seriously disruptive of mental health. Many persons who would otherwise be relatively normal are deeply troubled by the demands made on them by religious standards, beliefs, and practices. It is admittedly not an easy matter to measure up to the requirements of certain religious demands. Many persons certainly find the struggle against sin too much for their frail potentialities and are caught up in deep-seated conflicts, feelings of guilt, inadequacy, inferiority, and a sense of worthlessness in their striving to cope with the unending struggle between good and evil. As Ellis points out (1960, p. 190):

> The self-blaming person or individual with a pronounced sense of sin may say to himself (a) if I do this act it will be wrong; and (b) if I am wrong I am a worthless sinner. Then, being no angel and being impelled at times to commit the wrong deed, and being prepared to condemn himself mercilessly (because of the sense of sin) for his deeds, he will either refuse to admit that he has done the wrong thing or admit that he has done it but insist that it is not wrong. That is to say, the wrong-doer who has an acute sense of sin will either repress thoughts about his wrongdoing or psychopathically insist that he is right and the world is wrong.

Other persons find it difficult to accept or to live according to the requirements imposed by a church or religious group of which they are a member. For example, in the matter of confession, the need to reveal one's own weaknesses and wrongdoings to a confessor might be more than some persons can accept. Moreover, in the scrupulous individual, it is not uncommon to find that the guilt which led him to confession is compounded by the act itself, and he ends up in a worse mental state than before. Confession is good for the soul, but only when it resolves guilt rather than increases it. The following is a case in point.

> Jim, a twenty-three-year-old student, complained of intense scrupulosity, which was interfering with his religious practices. Of long standing, the scrupulosity became intensified after a general confession. In time, the patient stopped receiving the Sacraments altogether on the ground that it was impossible for him to make a truly good confession. This increased his sense of guilt. Typically, the scrupulosity developed to a point where everything was wrong. When he performed an act that was clearly wrong, he felt guilty; but if he did something good, he felt that this was also wrong because doing it gave him pleasure. He began to question basic religious concepts to which he had adhered all his life, and finally came to the conclusion that the God of his religion was not the true one and that his religion was permeated with error.

There are many aspects in the practice of religion that can serve to complicate the conflicts and frustrations that people experience. One can well imagine that the Catholic attitude regarding birth control, divorce, and similar practices has occasioned a great deal of anguish and guilt in the minds of many communicants. Mental health and emotional stability require that we meet the demands of reality in a straightforward, adequate, and healthy manner, but there are large numbers of people who are personally not equipped to meet the rigorous demands that religion often imposes. In this way, religion may complicate rather than help resolve the problems of mental instability.

We should note also that there are many nonreligious people who seem to be well adjusted, which requires us to examine carefully the asserted intrinsic relationship between religion and mental health. Here again, no one has provided an answer to the question of why this should be so. It is often suggested that even those people who seem to be nonreligious have substituted various gods for the God of religion. This may well be, but it seems like a weak answer to the question of how necessary religion is to mental health and adjustment (May, 1953b).

The Religious Neurotic

The deep and pervasive sense of shame, the pathological guilt, the self-rejection, and the feeling of worthlessness, as well as the typical symptomatology suggest that some persons are not only emotionally disturbed by their religious conflicts but are religiously neurotic (McKenzie, 1951). One of the clearest clinical expressions of this relationship occurs in the so-called obsessive-compulsive neurosis. Time and time again the clinician, working with religiously disturbed patients, is impressed with the consistency with which scrupulousness of the pathological type occurs within the framework of an obsessive-compulsive neurosis. The cases that we have described earlier are clear-cut instances of this type of religious neurosis, in which scrupulousness typically develops to the point where every act, every thought, feeling, or relationship is mortally sinful. Characteristically, these patients are tortured by pathological feelings of guilt, a deep sense of contamination, obsessive thoughts and fantasies regarding sex or bodily functions, and rigidly compulsive tendencies toward orderliness, perfectionism, and incessant ritualizing such as hand washing. In addition, there is present a typical neurotic pride and a total incapacity to deal with their problem on rational grounds.

Unlike other neurotic disorders where emotional disruption is a basic characteristic, in the pathologically scrupulous neurotic there seems to be a distinctive impairment of intellectual functioning, particularly that aspect referred to as moral conscience. The scrupulous person cannot distinguish between right and wrong, and his pervasive sense of guilt forces the conclusion that everything he does is wrong. No matter what he does, he feels that he has committed sin. Confession offers no relief whatever because he is sure that he has omitted telling something or that he has related his sins inadequately, or has confessed something that was not wrong, and thus every confession is a bad one. In place of peace of mind, which should come with reduction of guilt, he experiences additional guilt, self-recrimination, and mental torture. If he receives Communion, sacrilege is added on sacrilege, and his soul is tormented with unbearable guilt and self-recrimination (Schneiders, 1958).

Cases of the type described above clearly illustrate the relationship between religious conviction and neurotic development. Pathological scrupulousness, which seems to be common among Catholic penitents, invariably involves three elements that are complexly intermingled—the moral, the religious, and the sexual. In such cases one always finds a disordered conscience, an overdeveloped superego, sexual anxiety and confusion, unusual reduction of personal freedom, and a pathological attitude toward religious concepts and practices. The religious background is one of fear, repeated emphasis on the sinfulness of behavior, Jansenistic puritanism regarding sex, threat of hell and damnation, and ideas of an avenging God. Obviously, this sort of religiosity is directly contrary to the religion of love, which characterizes true Christianity regardless of its denominational form.

It is interesting to note that the kind of neurotic disorder developed in relation to religion is often linked to the religious symbolism that enters into the individual's early experience. This is particularly the case where the God concept is concerned. Scrupulous patients characteristically tend to disavow the God of their religion, and to rebel against Him as the real source of their anguish. Thus they may break away from religious practice altogether in rebellion against an avenging God, or invent a new God of their own. It is in this particularly peculiar reorientation toward religion that we see the influence of a damaging background on the content of the neurotic's symptomatology. The religious neurotic's sense of sinfulness, shame, and guilt is so unbearable that he has to redefine religious beliefs and to change the concept of God in a manner that will serve to relieve him of his anxiety and guilt. This fact conforms to the hypothesis that the form of neurotic disorder is often predetermined by the type of religious experience that preceded it. These relationships are extremely important in the understanding of certain neurotic developments without which it would be impossible to formulate a correct therapeutic procedure (Schneiders, 1958).

Religion and Escapism

Finally, we should note that religion, with its otherworld orientation, and its highly imaginative symbolism, lures many potentially neurotic or emotionally confused persons into an unrealistic attitude toward life and life's problems. For the insecure person, the inadequate or pathologically inferior person, and the one who cannot cope effectively with moral conflicts or guilt, the concepts of original sin, human depravity, personal weakness, and other ideas associated with certain religious beliefs have a particular attraction. Wrongdoing is typically rationalized as the result of original sin, neurotic suffering as the cross one must bear for having incurred God's displeasure, and the frustrations, conflicts, and difficulties of daily life as inevitable stumbling blocks on the road to eternal salvation. For such persons, too, there is a strong neurotic tendency to interpret every difficulty as Divine punishment, and every personal failure as a lack of Divine grace. For them, prayer is a demand for personal assistance rather than an act of love or adoration. When their prayers and supplications remain unanswered (at least as they see it), they unrealistically blame God for all of their neurotic misery and unhappiness.

For neurotic and emotionally confused persons, religion is truly an opiate. It is an escape from reality, rather than a means of coming to a firmer grip with the demands and problems that confront them in their daily lives. For the religious neurotic, religion is a mixture of fear, threat, shame, guilt, and vague promises that are supposedly realized through prayer or the possibility of a future life. This attitude is essentially escapist and unrealistic since it precludes a direct, straightforward approach to everyday problems and conflicts.

All the facts pointing up negative relations between religion and mental health should at least suggest considerable caution in our approach to the aspects of religion related to mental hygiene or its value for counseling and psychotherapy. We must face the issue squarely and determine, if we can, what the role of religion is in promoting or supporting mental health. Here we may discern a basic assumption, of considerable importance, that between religion and mental health there is a fundamental, intrinsic relation which, when activated in the right degree and in the right circumstances, and with just the right amount of skill and tact, will lead the individual sufferer back from the abyss of mental illness, or even better, further the growth of selfhood and personal integration. This assumption must be carefully examined in light of the facts pointed out relative to the negative effects of religious experience or practice (Godin, 1961).

RELIGION'S CONTRIBUTIONS TO MENTAL HEALTH

The Necessary Conditions of Religious Influence

When we analyze the assumption stated above and the supposed relationship between religion and mental health, we are quickly brought to the conclusion that religion is salutary to mental health and to counseling or psychotherapy only when it is able to furnish perdurable values that promote the process of personal growth and integration. As Moore has said (1944, pp. 244–245), "If religion has become an essential element of one's mental equipment, if it constitutes a plan of life that the individual has made a real part of his daily existence, if it is a practical ideal that he has adopted with enthusiasm, then it becomes a powerful inhibitory force in the development of unwholesome mental conditions." If this concept means anything, it means primarily that religion is something more than an emotional tranquilizer to which we have recourse when we encounter serious difficulties. If religion is nothing more than a personal subjective experience, it will fail miserably as a tool for mental hygiene or therapy. Experiences are evanescent, often fleeting, and have a way of being forgotten at crucial moments. They can be important, and in fact often are, but in order to play a significant role in promoting mental health they must be wrapped in a context of values that give them meaning and stability. When, therefore, we say that religion is something more than an emotional cathartic we mean to imply that it is an objective system of values that gives meaning and stability to daily life. This means also that the acceptance and practice of religion should preclude the development of deep-seated conflicts and frustrations that work toward the destruction of personality. This happens only when the basic and stable values of religion are integrated with the totality of a person's daily life.

Whereas there are some investigators who insist that religion has little or nothing to do with mental health, and has just as little therapeutic significance, there is too much evidence to the contrary to allow such a viewpoint to go unchallenged. It must be clear to anyone who takes the time to examine the issue that if religion, whether as a system of dogma or as a group of practices, or as personal experience, can gratify basic needs, help reduce conflicts and frustrations, modify anxiety, or bring peace of mind to the troubled penitent, then it is serving the aims of mental hygiene. In other words, if a person "feels better" for having made a confession, having prayed to God, or having experienced an upsurge of religious faith, we can certainly argue that the experience has had a salutary psychological effect. In similar vein, if religious experience or practice promotes self-realization, self-identity, selfhood, or even maturity, then it can be safely argued that it has some value for the psychological well-being of the individual (Allport, 1950, p. 79). Every clinician, psychiatrist, priest, minister, and counselor is aware of this possible effect, and religion is often exploited in the interest of maintaining or restoring mental health.

Religious experience is fundamentally no different than effective counseling, psychotherapy, or for that matter, pharmacologic therapy. The value and the efficacy of any experience or technique must be determined by the effect it produces. The logic of this proposition is simple: if religious experiences and practices further the aims and goals of counseling, psychotherapy, or mental hygiene, then religion can be said to have a salutary effect on psychological health, since all these disciplines are directed toward the goal of health. It can be argued just as forcibly that if drugs, exercise, or bed rest contribute to such goals, then they too are efficacious in the development of psychological health.

These statements do not imply that religion can be used for therapeutic purposes, nor is there any implication regarding the extent to which religion may affect mental health. They imply only the *possibility* of a cause-effect relationship between religion and mental health. And there is nothing in the concepts of counseling, psychotherapy, or mental hygiene to preclude this possibility. On the contrary, many persons report that religion was instrumental in stabilizing their lives, or helping them to achieve peace of mind, and these reports have to be taken at face value since there is no evidence to the contrary. We have here a situation similar to that of a person who takes aspirin to get rid of a headache. If the headache disappears when aspirin is taken internally, we are forced to conclude some relationship between the ingestion of the aspirin and the disappearance of the headache, even though we do not know exactly what effects the aspirin produced in the physiology of the organism, or "how it worked."

As an additional consideration, religion is universally regarded as a source of values or a philosophy of life, by means of which a person steers a straight course to the goals he sets for himself, whether in this life or in the next. For many persons it is a primary source or a guarantee of the purpose and meaning of life; for many others it is a powerhouse of love in which they find a haven of refuge from the difficulties, conflicts, hazards and threats of a complex world which they little understand and find extremely difficult to cope with. Now the disciplines of counseling, psychotherapy, and mental hygiene all recognize the importance of values, of a life philosophy, of meaning and purpose, and of love to psychological health. Here again, therefore, religion, insofar as it promotes these qualities in a person's life, is not essentially different from the healing professions. We thus arrive at a corollary to the foregoing proposition: to the extent that religion promotes a scale of values or a philosophy of life, and gives meaning to human striving, it tends to promote the stability, integration, and psychological health of the organism.

The Psychological Groundwork of Religion

It must be understood that, for religion to function as the corollary states, the psychological groundwork within the person must be properly disposed. It is very doubtful, for example, whether religion could be efficacious in a person with massive anxiety, pathological scrupulosity, or deep psychopathic trends. As with all helping processes, the "soil" within the human personality must be of a quality that will permit the seed to grow or the plant to sprout. The scrupulous person cannot use prayer to any real advantage because he fears and even despises God. The psychopath and the paranoid are so egoistic that a relationship of dependence between them and God would be impossible.

Even the simple neurotic will have great difficulty taking advantage of religious beliefs or practices because the soul is contaminated with anxieties, obsessions, defensive mechanisms and crippling feelings. This sounds very much as though the client or penitent must be mentally healthy before religion can help him achieve mental health, but we must not allow ourselves to fall into this trap. It is certainly true that in many instances the client or penitent may need specialized counseling or psychotherapy, or even shock treatment before he can utilize religion to his own personal advantage. The case comes to mind of a devoutly religious lady in the writer's community who ran afoul of religious practices because of a sudden psychotic outbreak. After a series of shock treatments, she was returned to the community and is today a very devoutly religious person, and has been so for the past five years. This situation is analogous to preparing a person for proper medication or a serious operation. Conditions must be favorable before an agent can be administered or an effect will take place.

This does not mean that a person has to be perfectly normal or mentally healthy to the nth degree for religion to work. The continuum of sound mental health and extreme mental disorder admits of n degrees, and no one can say at what point on the continuum religion will or will not be effective. It is only when the psychic condition of its nature *precludes* the influence of religious concepts and principles that remedy of some kind is first necessary. Thus, the confirmed homosexual, the nymphomaniac, the Don Juan, the alcoholic, or the obsessive-compulsive neurotic may find that religion is not only inefficacious but intolerable or even damaging. Such persons are quite likely to abandon their childhood religion altogether. In other instances of a less pathological nature religion may be quite effective.

The Effective Use of Religion

Despite the possible effectiveness of religion, we cannot ignore the real difficulties that surround the relationship between religion and mental hygiene. As we know it, and see it practiced, religion too often fails the individual person in his anxious striving for wholeness, integration, and healthful living. It often seems distressingly weak in the face of neurotic growth or psychotic outbreak. Hailed by some enthusiasts as an effective tool of counseling, it frequently fails to release hidden resources within the personality or even to provide the bulwark of values the client needs to withstand the pressures of daily life. We need, therefore, to take a fresh look at this problem. There must be something wrong in our interpretation of religion in relation to psychological health, or perhaps in our application of religious values and principles to the goals of mental hygiene. Being what it is, religion should provide a tremendous push toward psychological health or the good life. That it fails to do so must be attributable either to faulty concepts or to faulty application (Angyal, 1952).

Because religion does not lead to psychological health demands that we take a close look at the meaning of religion since our understanding of its relation to mental health will be determined to a great extent by our idea of what religion is supposed to be. For example, we may regard it as an organized body of truths, values, or dogma, in which case it may, for any individual, remain at a highly abstract and objective level that makes it ineffective in influencing psychological health. In many instances the religion of the Catechism, the Bible class, or of the exhortatory sermon belongs in this category. Persons exposed to such experiences may understand what is being said but fail to integrate this knowledge with everyday affairs. It may have little meaning for present anxieties, conflicts, guilt, or loneliness. Indeed, as often happens, religion of the dogmatic or exhortatory type may serve to deepen a person's anxieties, conflicts, or feelings of isolation and abandonment. It may also stimulate feelings of resentment and hostility against a code of behavior or a personal God that is too rigid or too demanding. This sort of thing is likely to happen in the neurotic personality, particularly one in whom there is a great deal of perfectionism, neurotic pride, or scrupulosity.

Religion may also be thought of as a special kind of experience, exemplified most clearly and strikingly in conversion phenomena, but also found in less dramatic situations. A person in church, for example, may experience a moment of ecstatic union with God, a feeling of closeness not ordinarily experienced, a sense of awe at the Divine presence, or a deep feeling of humility in the face of God's infinite power. These experiences are more likely to affect the psychic structure and the psychological health of the devout penitent than are sermons or lectures on sin, hell, and damnation. These experiences are personal and immanently psychic, whereas treatises, arguments, or exhortations are objective and external and may never reach the depth of immanence. In fact, it could be argued that religion will have very little if any effect on the psychic structure until it becomes immanent to some degree, which gives us a clue as to why religion often fails to exert a positive effect on the psychic life of the individual. To be really effective, experience must work its way through the encrusted layers of habits, dispositions, and resistances into the innermost core of the person's being. Only then will it stimulate the process of growth or change that results in psychological health.

There is a third characteristic of religion that is important to note, and that is its *developmental quality*. Religion as a personal way of life is obviously an acquired characteristic and is therefore subject to all the limitations and vagaries of development, just as are the emotions, drives, or physical characteristics of the human organism. If this development has been healthy, pervasive, and closely integrated with other phases of development, the chances are that new religious experiences or dogmatic pronouncements will fall on fertile ground. If, to the contrary, religious growth is encrusted with fears and threats, with false ideas of an avenging and wrathful God, with attitudes contrary to religious tenets, with harsh parental discipline, or with faulty identifications, it may have little import for psychological health or may act to undermine it. Failure to realize this developmental quality of religion makes it hard to understand the *inverse* relationship between religion and mental health so often observed even in persons who have dedicated their lives to the service of God. As a deepening relationship between man and God, or as a system of beliefs and practices, or as a deep personal conviction and affirmation, or as an enriching experience, religion certainly bears a positive relation to psychic health. But as a developmental encrustation that sets a limit to the immanence of experience or that hampers the freedom of the mind to reach out toward God, it may be much more of a hindrance than a help.

The foregoing discussion serves to remind us that religion and spirituality *are not the same thing*. Of itself, religion is *existential* and is thus limited and bound by all of the shortcomings of human existence. The spiritual quality in man, however, is *ontological*, as are the needs embedded in this quality. In many persons, religion functions only at the existential level and thus fails to reach down into the more immanent nature of the person. For this reason, religious needs and wants are often gratified, while the spiritual needs of the person remain barren and unfulfilled. To give this profound fact a different perspective, we may say that religion and religious training, as well as counseling and psychotherapy, often reach the *psyche* but seldom the *soul* of the person. The difference in these two terms is not merely semantic. Freud used the term *psyche* to signify the mental, topographic totality of id, ego, and superego. He certainly was not using the term to mean the spiritual soul.

The distinction between psyche and soul is of considerable importance in trying to understand the relationship between religion and psychological health. In neurotics, for example, the psyche is disturbed, distorted, immature, or inadequate to the task of facing reality and thus is overlaid with anxiety, feelings of inferiority and guilt, defensive reactions, faulty habits, inadequate values, and poor reality perceptions. Yet, even in such a person, spiritual values and wholesome religious experiences can work their way through these encrustations and uplift and enrich the human soul so that it can establish a firmer relationship with God. It is at this point that religion, understood as a spiritual growth or rebirth, can promote psychological health (Van Buskirk, 1952).

The Problem of Spiritual Needs

The stand that one takes regarding the efficacy of religion in a mental hygiene program will be determined in part by his attitude toward the problem of human needs. If religion is important to mental health, one should frankly face the question of whether there are spiritual as well as psychological needs in personality that bear on the problem of human adjustment. We noted earlier that man's physical, psychological, and social needs stem directly from human nature; therefore, to the extent that human nature is in any sense spiritual, or has a spiritual quality, we should expect to find basic needs that correspond to this spirituality. Just as the child needs the security and affection his parents can give him, and just as he needs the independence that underlies the process of growing up, so too he needs to know, to love, and to depend upon a Supreme Being. Much of what we have learned from wide experience, the psychological clinic, and psychiatric practice points to the necessity for most people of a sound religious orientation as a basis for the achievement of mental health and emotional stability. Therefore, as a part of the dynamics of human adjustment, it is important to recognize the existence of spiritual needs. The needs most often mentioned in this connection are the need to know and love God, the need for spiritual solace, the need for sympathy, understanding, and forgiveness, the need for purity of heart, and the need for salvation. It is these spiritual requirements that underscore the relation between religion and mental health.

Psychological Needs and Religious Experience

That spiritual needs of this kind are closely allied to and often parallel psychological needs is a fact that requires little emphasis. As we have pointed out several times, the personality of man is an integrated totality, and therefore we can expect the most basic interrelations among different aspects of personality. The need for affection so clearly manifested in child behavior is certainly akin to the need for love of God. The craving for security finds a close parallel in the need for salvation. And the need for belonging has a clear analogue in the desire for church membership. But here we should note that as the child grows toward maturity his world of reality expands, and the parents, who at one time were the primary source of need gratifications, no longer play so definite a role. The simple pattern of relations that provided the satisfaction of basic needs gives way before a continually expanding outlook on life and reality. Thus, as the child grows older and spiritual needs begin to function more noticeably, a more expansive orientation to reality takes place. No longer can parents, friends, or teachers provide all the answers that are necessary for effective living. Nor can one's wife, children, friends, or work always provide the solace that is required for peace of mind. Disappointments, failures, depression, discouragement, and conflicts require something more than human relations or the satisfactions that work can provide. It is then that spiritual needs are felt most strongly, and their gratification becomes as imperative as the need of the child to be loved and protected. Any program of mental hygiene must take note of these facts if the problems of adjustment and mental health are to yield to its principles.

Religion, by reason of its distinctive experiences, beliefs, and practices, is not only suited to the gratification of spiritual needs but also just as surely to the fulfillment of the basic psychological needs and to the reduction of damaging conflicts, feelings, and frustrations. Where, for example, can one find a greater source of love, status, and security than in the promise of God's providence or eternal salvation? Even more important is the fact that religion constantly reminds us of the intrinsic value and dignity of individual man, that he is created "in the image and likeness of God." What better way to offset the traumatic effects of inferiority or the feeling of personal worthlessness that we encounter so often in the helpless neurotic? When the unhappy penitent is torn by conflict, temptation, indecision, shame and sinfulness, he is assured of forgiveness and spiritual restoration. When guilt threatens to tear apart the delicate framework of a person's ego, and feelings seem beyond control, religion offers the tremendous solace of prayer or the Sacraments. In one's personal life, in marriage, and in relations with others, the influence of a deeply personal religion can be of inestimable value in meeting the demands that human nature, the social environment, or reality impose on the individual.

Religion and Personal Integration

The values and practices of religion have particular significance for the problem of personal integration. We have pointed out several times that personal integration is one of the most fundamental criteria of mental health, and therefore anything contributing to this unification of personality is of basic importance to mental hygiene. As Allport remarks (1950, p. 92), "All strongly ideal interests, we know, tend to unify the mind. But in principle, the religious interest, being most comprehensive, is best able to serve as an integrative agent." This idea is echoed in many places by persons who, as counselors and psychotherapists, have acquired an intensely intimate knowledge of the human mind. In his discussion of the same point, Moore says (1944, p. 243):

> Not only is religion of value in the sorrows of life . . . but it is also of particular importance in all mental conditions that are derived from the lack of a plan of life that is an integral part of one's mental equipment. . . . We have assumed also that religion has become the supreme moral virtue dominating thought and conduct. When this has come about in any individual his life is coordinated and directed to an end that has acquired in his mind a value with which nothing else can be compared.

It is this fact perhaps more than anything else, namely, that religion can provide the secure groundwork for an adequate philosophy of life, that defines its essential significance for mental hygiene. It is at this point that religion makes its most important contribution to a realistic outlook on life.

INTEGRATING DIFFERENT APPROACHES TO MENTAL HYGIENE

There are many roads to mental health, and religion is only one of them. From the standpoint of mental hygiene, religion can help to prevent the growth of unhealthy attitudes, crippling feelings of inferiority, worthlessness, or guilt, or the undermining of personal integration by unresolved conflicts or intolerable stresses (Bonnell, 1948). From the standpoint of counseling and psychotherapy, there is an obvious need to peel away the encrustations of bad experience, faulty training, of inadequate development, or of limited and distorting psychological mechanisms in order to make religious and spiritual values and practices more deeply and ontologically meaningful. It is at this critical point that religion on the one hand, and counseling and psychotherapy on the other, can join forces in an effective effort to restore and maintain psychological health (O'Doherty & McGrath, 1963). Counseling and therapy prepare the way by reducing existential limitations of the psychic structure, and religion completes the process of personal growth by furnishing the values and principles needed for psychological health.

QUESTIONS AND PROJECTS FOR FURTHER STUDY

1. Write a critical evaluation of one of the following books: Allport, *The individual and his religion*; Clark, *The psychology of religion*; Braceland, *Faith, reason and modern psychiatry*.
2. Discuss the paradoxical relation of religion to mental health, emphasizing the positive as well as the negative features of this relationship.
3. Compare James's classic book, *The varieties of religious experience* with Clark's *The psychology of religion*.
4. Write a research paper on the topic, "The Psychological Roots of Spiritual Development."
5. Is the practice of psychoanalysis contrary to Christian belief? Document your reply to this question with references from professional literature.
6. Write a brief essay on "Current Developments in the Area of Religion and Psychiatry."

SELECTED COLLATERAL READINGS

ACADEMY OF RELIGION AND MENTAL HEALTH. *Religion, culture, and mental health: Proceedings of the Third Academy Symposium, 1959.* New York: New York University Press, 1961.

ACADEMY OF RELIGION AND MENTAL HEALTH. *Religion and the developing personality.* New York: New York Unversity Press, 1960.

ALLPORT, G. W. *The individual and his religion.* New York: Macmillan, 1950.

AUMANN, J.   Sanctity and neurosis. In F. J. Braceland (Ed.), *Faith, reason and modern psychiatry*. New York: Kenedy, 1955, pp. 267–294.

CAVANAGH, J. R.   *Fundamental pastoral counseling*. Milwaukee: Bruce, 1962.

CLARK, W. H.   *The psychology of religion*. New York: Macmillan, 1958.

FROMM, E.   *Psychoanalysis and religion*. New Haven: Yale University Press, 1950.

JUNG, C. G.   *Modern man in search of a soul*. New York: Harcourt, 1933.

LINN, L., & SCHWARZ, L. W.   *Psychiatry and religious experience*. New York: Random House, 1958.

MEISSNER, W. W.   *Annotated bibliography in religion and psychology*. New York: The Academy of Religion and Mental Health, 1961.

MOWRER, O. H.   *The crisis in psychiatry and religion*. New York: Van Nostrand, 1961.

ZILBOORG, G.   *Psychoanalysis and religion*. New York: Farrar, Straus, 1962.

16

Mental Hygiene of the Home, School, and Community

In our opening chapter on the nature and principles of mental hygiene, we indicated briefly that the concepts of mental hygiene could be applied to institutions and groups as well as to individuals. It must be clear to anyone who studies the matter carefully that a great deal of maladjustment and mental illness could be prevented by wholesome home environments, healthy family relationships, effective parental models, and a sound program of discipline. It is equally clear that the aims of mental hygiene can be promoted through the medium of the educational system. Good schools, adequate recreational facilities, out-of-class activities, healthy peer-group experiences, and effective classroom techniques can all be exploited for mental hygiene purposes. It is to these aspects of mental hygiene that we now turn our attention.

MENTAL HYGIENE APPLIED TO INSTITUTIONS AND GROUPS

The Meaning of Community Mental Hygiene

We have emphasized many times the important fact that the human personality does not develop or function in a vacuum, that between each individual personality and the environment of physical conditions, cultural influences, interpersonal relations, and psychological climate there is a reciprocal influence that must be studied very carefully in order to understand the problems and intricacies of adjustment and mental health. We have emphasized repeatedly that the individual person is the focal point of mental hygiene, and certainly the majority of our interpretations have been slanted in this direction. But we have not neglected to emphasize also the environmental context within which the individual functions, and in this way we have laid the groundwork for a mental hygiene of the community (Felix, 1949; Seidman, 1963).

We are not referring here to community projects, such as urban renewal, slum clearance, or sanitation control. While such projects have definite implications for total mental health programs, we are concerned

443

chiefly with the import for mental health of two primary social agencies, the home and the school. These two social units are of particular importance because practically all children are exposed to the influences of both agencies for a period of many years. The majority of children in the United States reside in their own home prior to enrolling in school, and then do not leave school until they are at least sixteen years of age. In addition, millions of youngsters continue their schooling until they graduate from high school (usually at age eighteen), and another 4 million go on to college and graduate school. During most of these years, youngsters are exposed daily to the influence of the home, and during many of them they are similarly exposed to the influence of school life. Weighing the effects of these two primary social agencies on adjustment and psychological health, it can be said without fear of contradiction that no other extra-personal agencies can compare with these two in the extent and depth of their influence. It is here, therefore, that we shall put our emphasis in our study of the influence of social factors on mental hygiene programs.

Mental Hygiene in Group Living

Family life and school attendance are primarily *experiences in group living*, and we should indicate here what this means for effective mental hygiene. We anticipated this question in our discussion (Chapter 4) of the conditions and determinants of personality and adjustment. There we studied at length the social and environmental determinants of personal growth, and there we laid the groundwork for the mental hygiene of group living. The study of environmental-social determinants is simply the converse of the mental hygiene of group living.

It is from an analysis of the effects of group life that we can discover the principles that are necessary for an effective program of social mental hygiene. There are many instances that could be cited as illustrations of this point. Just as exercise, rest, and good food are important to physical hygiene, and just as need gratification and self-discipline are essential to personal mental hygiene, so a wholesome family life and adequate school experiences are necessary to support the aims of physical or mental hygiene. We all know that a sense of personal worth or the feeling of achievement are important to a child's mental health, but we also know that these important qualities are not likely to be realized in an unhealthy family environment or a school system that violates all principles of mental hygiene. This is another way of saying that group experiences are an essential part of daily living and that the more effective and enriching these experiences are, the more they serve the basic needs of the growing child; also, the more they promote personality development and integration, the better are the child's chances of growing into a mature, well-adjusted, and mentally healthy adult (Schneiders, 1954c, pp. 157–170).

THE HOME AND MENTAL HEALTH

Home, Family, and the Child

We do not wish to restate here what has already been said about the relationship between family living and personality development in Chapter 4. We wish merely to emphasize those characteristics of the home and family that must be developed, and those that must be avoided, if the aims of mental hygiene are to be achieved. This is essentially what the mental hygiene of the home means (Moore, 1944, Chapter X; Thorpe, 1950, Chapter XV; Schneiders, 1954b, pp. 52–61). As Overstreet says (1949, pp. 230–231):

> No social institution is more fateful for the human race than the home. In it the primary shaping of character takes place. In a good home, maturing gets quickly underway: the child is helped to grow from stage to stage of confidence, skill, affection, responsibility, and understanding. . . . If homes are psychologically sound, there is hope for our culture. If homes are psychologically unsound there is little hope; for in that case those who are born into those homes will merely grow from childhood into adulthood, not from immaturity into maturity. This puts upon all adults who create homes a large measure of responsibility for determining what our culture and the world culture is to be.

The home, therefore, with its distinctive structural characteristics may be regarded as a society in miniature that helps the child make the transition from ego-centered to socio-centered living. This is certainly mental hygiene at its best. All of the essential elements of the society and of social living are present in the ordinary home. Father and Mother may be regarded as the leaders and authority figures, aunts and uncles and grandparents as elder statesmen, and the children as the citizenry. As in any society, there are elements of authority, discipline, financing, conflicts and disagreements, debates and discussions, rebellion, submissiveness, and punishment. The larger the family the more it resembles the structure of society; the situation is more complex, effective leadership more necessary, discipline and law more complicated, and interpersonal relationships more varied.

In contrast, if we consider the only-child situation, or the childless couple, we see how unlike society the home can be. In such simplified structures, the mental hygiene of the home takes on an entirely different caste. The childless couple have only their own mental hygiene problems to worry about since children obviously are not involved, whereas in the only child situation mental hygiene problems can be compounded because the child is forced to live in and relate to an adult world for which he is poorly equipped. There is often too much attention, too much indulgence, too much protection, and too much "adultism" in the parents' attitudes toward the child. He may mature too early and become an adult in miniature, a somewhat pathetic social monstrosity that has the appearance of a child and the behavior or attitudes of an adult. This does not always happen by any means. We are merely using the only-child situation as an illustration of how the mental hygiene of the home can change with its particular structure.

Before leaving this consideration of the home as a miniature society and its implications for mental hygiene, let us look at several other features that can be important to the healthy growth of children and their later adjustment to society. For example, society is bisexual, heterosexual, and intersexual, and the more that family life or the structure of the family corresponds to these characteristics of society, the easier it will be for young people to fit into the social structure. A family of girls, with only the father available as a male figure, is not as advantageous as one in which there is a more or less even distribution of boys and girls. To learn to relate adequately to the opposite sex is one of the most important developmental tasks that face the growing child. Moreover, from the standpoint of personal mental hygiene, a boy growing up with sisters or a girl growing up with brothers has a better chance at developing healthy sex attitudes and a firmer sex identity than in a situation where other-sex peers are not a part of the family structure.

Above, we have discussed only a few of the implications for mental hygiene in the structural characteristics of the family, but they will serve to point up a relationship that is not always given due credit. However, there is inherent in this relationship a limitation that will reduce its value for mental hygiene. The structure of the family, unlike parental discipline, or interpersonal relations, cannot be as easily manipulated for purposes of mental hygiene. There are many things in the home and in the school that can be controlled for the sake of better mental hygiene; family structure is not one of them. However, for teachers and counselors interested in exploiting all situations for the promotion of better mental health, the facts that we have pointed out are in themselves significant and lead to a better understanding of the scope of mental hygiene.

Social-psychological Characteristics of the Family and Mental Health

The mental hygiene of the home may be defined as the application of tested principles of mental hygiene to the conditions and practices of home and family living so that the home will become a better place in which to realize personal, moral, social, and spiritual objectives. As a background for developing such principles as applied to the home situation, let us consider for a moment the concept of a psychologically healthy home environment. To do this, we should begin with the nature of the home itself. Here there are two considerations, both of which are integrally related, yet often regarded by many persons as distinct and separate. Quite generally, for example, the home is conceived of *as a place* where people, ordinarily bound together by ties of blood, mutual interests, and bonds of affection, work, live, play, and perhaps even pray together in the interest of healthy living, of achieving individual and common objectives, and of working out individual destinies. This concept is idealistic, but the chances are most people would agree at least that this is what a home should be like.

There is a second concept which regards the home *as a state of mind,* a deep-seated, pervasive attitude that is rooted in the natural human desires for a haven of rest, a place of unassailable security, and a source of warmth, dignity, and personal worth. In this sense, *home is where you find it*—in the ancestral mansion, the lowly tenement, the adobe hut, the suburban ranch house, the community shelter, the orphanage, or even, if we are to believe some newspaper accounts, the penitentiary. Both of the concepts of family described above are necessary to an adequate definition of the psychologically healthy home environment.

To achieve and maintain its own psychological integrity, then, the home must do at least three things. First, it must provide for the gratification of the natural desires for security, affection, dignity, and personal worth. Without this gratification of basic needs, the home becomes a building, an apartment, a shack, where one eats and sleeps more or less regularly, keeps his wardrobe, and glories in the fact that he has a fairly permanent base of operation. In counseling, one encounters young people, especially of college age, who quite frequently regard their home in just such a manner. Not infrequently they will insist on boarding at the college even though it is quite close to their home, or they will engage in countless activities that will keep them away from home as much as possible, or they will find work that will minimize their contacts with family members.

Barbara was a seventeen-year-old freshman in her home town university. She was referred to counseling because of a 65.4 average, even though her high school background and her College Board scores indicated that she was capable of doing much better work. In the first interview Barbara let go with a torrent of complaints against her parents, and stated that her family life was plain hellish, and had been for the past four years. Barbara did everything possible to stay away from home as much as she could. She studied in the library, went to parties, took summer jobs away from home, and secluded herself in her room when it was necessary for her to remain at home. Arrangements were made for her to board at the school, after which the conflict subsided and Barbara's grades began to rise perceptibly. Admittedly, this did not improve the mental hygiene of the home situation, but it did help Barbara in her academic pursuits.

Second, the home must provide a framework of wholesome interpersonal relationships within which enriching experiences, stable attitudes, character, and a healthy personality can develop. These experiences and attitudes will assume many different forms—emotional, religious, moral, social, and economic. The important thing is that they should have a chance to develop and to become a lasting, integral part of the character and personality of the individual.

Third, the home must function according to established principles of good adjustment and mental health. That is, there must be an effective, dynamic mental hygiene of the home which insures the realization of those qualities which the good home must develop (Zimmerman, 1949; Symonds, 1939).

The Importance of a Healthy Psychological Climate

This viewpoint of a dynamic mental hygiene points up the importance of creating within the home a healthy psychological climate for the development of mental health. Such a climate requires emotional stability in the parents, healthy interpersonal relationships among parents and children, healthy attitudes toward self and others, sound moral, spiritual, and social values, and a sense of humor that serves to temper family reverses, conflicts, frustrations, heartaches, and disappointments. On the negative side a healthy psychological climate in the home largely precludes incessant warfare among the members of the family, parental rejections of each other or of the children, neurotic behavior patterns, and the continuous exploitation of the family for selfish aims (Senn, 1948; Cavan, 1934). There is perhaps no factor of greater importance to the mental hygiene of the home than a healthy climate, and one can be sure that where the atmosphere is charged with the electricity of conflict, mutual rejections, hostility, hatred, and other negative feelings or relationships, the mental hygiene of the home becomes an empty catchword.

Factors that Disrupt the Home

The foregoing interpretation of the psychologically intact home offers an ideal toward which we can strive. But the brutal fact is that many homes do not come close to this ideal, principally because of negative influences in our society and culture that work ceaselessly toward the psychological disruption of the home. One of these factors is the attitude toward home life that many persons assume. Even for some parents the home is little more than a loosely organized entity of several individuals, to which only the most casual homage is paid. The term "homage" is particularly appropriate here. According to the dictionary it means respect or reverence, deference, obeisance, honor, allegiance, and fealty—ideas of fundamental importance to the integrity and the welfare of the home. Where such homage is lacking, the attitude toward home life is bound to be disruptive.

A second negative influence is the accepted breakup of the home in contemporary society. Divorce is no longer merely tolerated; it is accepted by many persons as a normal part of our way of life. If divorce or separation were regarded as a last resort, the home would have a much better chance for survival and integrity. Here again it is the attitude of persons involved that is the disrupting factor. The breakup of the family in modern society is a symptom more than a cause; it is a sign that healthy attitudes toward the integrity and the intrinsic value of the home have deteriorated to the point where family breakup is often accepted with little remorse and a disturbing equanimity.

Complementary to the social and cultural influences are the psychological conditions within the home itself (Kanner, 1949; Stagner, 1938). Far too many inadequate or neurotic parents exhibit and at the same time foster damaging attitudes, abuse privileges of authority and discipline, fail to provide the security, sanctuary, trust, and affection that children need, and contribute to feelings of jealousy, rivalry, rejection, and hostility among their children. This is what Overstreet refers to as a "bad" home (Overstreet, 1949, p. 230).

> In a bad home, maturing is variously arrested; the child is made to feel unwanted . . . or he is terrified by threats . . . or he is made the object of jealous competition between the parents; or he is forced to get everything he needs by such aggressive competition with other children that the word "enemy" soon has more meaning for him than the word "friend". . . . or he is introduced early, again by contention, to the beliefs that life has no meaning beyond the scramble to get the necessities.

Where psychological convictions of this nature exist, the integrity and the moral fiber of the home and the family are certain to reach a low ebb. No one can expect children to experience security, warmth, and the feeling of belonging in an atmosphere of rejection or carping criticism. How can there be serenity in a home dominated by a mother who is much more concerned about her neurotic symptoms than about the welfare of husband and children? How can there be dignity or a sense of personal worth in a home where the father bypasses the children because of his passion for television, poker, or night clubs? In the unwholesome atmosphere of the psychologically defunct home, the principles of mental hygiene have very little meaning.

QUALITIES OF A HEALTHY HOME ENVIRONMENT

If the foregoing analysis is substantially correct, what are the criteria by which we can evaluate the psychologically intact home, and which will serve as guides to thinking and planning for the mental hygiene of the home? There are many such criteria or characteristics, among which the following are of considerable significance.

1. *Wholesome inter-parent relationships* of mutual friendship, love, respect, and implicit trust. These relationships must dominate the home situation, and set the pattern for all other relations that emerge in the growth of home and family life (Brown, 1947).
2. *Healthy parent-child relationships* of mutual acceptance, warmth, and personal interest that guarantee a deep sense of belonging and safety to the growing child. This criterion excludes rejection, favoritism, jealousy, overprotection, and other damaging relationships.
3. *Authoritative discipline and training* set in a context of mutual affection, understanding, and trust. Such discipline must be always aimed at improvement, and should never be motivated by anger, revenge, or the parent's own sense of guilt.
4. *Adherence to democratic qualities,* a context within which discipline and training can work more effectively. In our society, which emphasizes the personal worth and integrity of the individual, a democratic attitude is more effective in the discipline and training of the children than one that is rigidly authoritative (Radke, 1946).
5. *Opportunities for group experiences and discussion,* which cor-

respond to and support a democratic setting. Children must be given opportunities to express their ideas and feelings in an open family forum so that they do not feel that they are regimented into behavior that is contrary to their own beliefs and ideals.

6. *Adequate sibling relations* of acceptance, friendliness, and mutual interest. This criterion offers considerable difficulty, and hinges on the success with which other criteria are applied. It should characterize the beginning of family life in order that hostility, jealousy, rivalry, etc., may be excluded or reduced.

7. *Common parental goals* that enrich and deepen the relations between the parents and that foster the oneness and solidarity of the marital union. These goals may be vocational, professional, spiritual, recreational, or financial but should not interfere with other family obligations.

8. *Common family goals* that promote the welfare of the family and individual members. These goals should be articulate and clearly understood, and should function in such a way as to increase the oneness and solidarity of the family group. They must, however, allow for the development of individual aims and aspirations.

9. *Sound religious, moral, and spiritual values* which will serve to support family goals and ideals and provide the kind of climate that contributes to healthy family life.

10. *Integrity, cohesiveness, and mutual support* which every social group needs in order to realize its own goals (Baruch, 1937, Torrance, 1945). Without these qualities, the family cannot function as a social group and provide the support that individual members need for their own security and other need gratifications.

11. *Adequate recreational facilities,* which are necessary for any social group from a mental hygiene point of view. We have already noted how these facilities are necessary to the effective use of leisure time.

12. *Family fun, humor, and healthy attitudes,* which we have emphasized earlier as being important to mental health and adjustment.

13. *Absence of damaging conflict,* which of course is the negative counterpart to a number of the criteria above. Mutual acceptance and respect, cohesiveness and integrity, and the striving for common goals cannot be achieved under the conditions of chronic conflict.

Admittedly, the criteria listed above portray an ideal picture of the home from a psychological point of view, but it is also a realistic one because it is based upon secure knowledge, empirically tested, of what is necessary for the psychological health and integrity of the home. If we are to succeed in developing a mental hygiene program for family living, we must determine the standards or criteria that govern such a program. The difficulties are enormous, but they should be accepted as a challenge by those interested in the mental hygiene of family life.

THE SCHOOL AND MENTAL HEALTH

Role of the School in the Process of Adjustment

If the home and the family are the primary socializing agencies in the life of the growing child, certainly the second most important agency is the school, and it is this socializing influence, along with certain other influences, that makes of the school an important tool for mental hygiene. We are referring here to the school as a social institution rather than to the classroom as a medium of education (Lippitt & Gold, 1963, Allinsmith & Goethals, 1962; Denemark, 1963). The school and the classroom stand in about the same relationship to the development of personality and mental health as do the home and the family. The home and the school may be regarded as primary social determinants of personal development and adjustment, whereas the family and the classroom may be thought of as essential implements for the application of mental hygiene principles. The school is the child's "home away from home," and the teacher is the authority figure *in loco parentis* (Olson & Wattenberg, 1955). The classroom becomes the substitute for the family, and the classmates become substitute siblings. These relationships are of considerable importance because they enable us to understand why for some children school life takes on a dimension that far exceeds in importance the influence exerted by the home and family. It is within the context of school life that some youngsters find for the first time a sense of belonging, the feeling of being accepted, or a deep sense of achievement. For some children school life is uninteresting, tedious, and boring (Jackson & Getzels, 1963); for others it is the means to a new life, to the discovery of self, to the achievement of status and dignity. These school experiences underscore the role of the school in the achievement of adjustment and mental health (Goldman, 1954; Peck & Mitchell, 1962).

Role Definitions in School

The foregoing comments remind us that life in school can play a basic part in helping a youngster to define present and future roles, which give him an added push toward the achievement of self-identity, social awareness, and a deeper orientation toward future self-realizations. The school offers countless opportunities for role definitions in the election of class officers, membership in student government, leadership in athletic events, working for the school paper, or emoting with the dramatic club. Many a budding politician, cub reporter, radio announcer, or actor first defined his later professional role in the halls of the local high school (Bonney, 1960).

We should not overlook the fact that other role definitions of significance for future growth and development often take form during high school or college years. The school environment and the activities associated therewith are often the starting point of social virtues and relationships that enforce the development of roles regarding self or the opposite sex. All marriages, and therefore the roles of husband and wife, mother and father, begin with intersex relations, dating, and similar practices. Boys and girls are forced by social activities or exigencies into roles that are suited to the situation. And these situations probably are more common and more numerous on the school campus than in any other setting. The school is a medium *par excellence* for social experience and the development of intersex relationships, which is often the start of role definitions (Fisher & Noble, 1960).

The School and Vocational Adjustment: The Development of Goals

It need hardly be emphasized that role definition is an important step forward in determining and defining personal goals that have such a direct bearing on personality integration and adjustment. This is a point that we emphasized much earlier in our study of the criteria of adjustment and mental health. On the face of it, there is not much difference between the anticipation of future roles and the definition of future goals. The goal of medicine for a young student becomes more and more realistic as he defines the role of the physician for himself. The two ideas should not be confused but their basic relations should be emphasized. It is obvious that the school can play a leading role in promoting awareness of goals, and in giving its students substantial help in moving realistically toward them. This can be done in the classroom, in the laboratory, in the counseling office, or on the playing field. Wherever it is done, or by whom, it represents a tremendous gain for the individual student in furthering his adjustment. The movement toward definite goals is an excellent demonstration of mental hygiene at work (Allinsmith & Goethals, 1962, pp. 219, 220).

The School and Recreation

We cannot ignore the role of the school in promoting physical hygiene through its athletic program, and its contributions to leisure-time activities. We have maintained several times the basic importance to mental hygiene of physical health and the value of wholesome recreational activities to mental health and adjustment. We do not wish to repeat those emphases here, but merely to point out the significance of these relationships and their implications for a total program of mental hygiene. Many a youngster has been rescued from maladjustment and personality difficulties by a stabilizing interest in sports or a healthy preoccupation with other recreational activities.

THE CURRICULUM AND MENTAL HYGIENE

Some Basic Issues Concerning the Profession of Teaching

The projection of the principles and practices of mental hygiene into the teaching situation has been regarded with considerable skepticism and even downright opposition by many educators who feel that the essential purpose of education is to develop the person intellectually, and perhaps morally, with small regard for other aspects of development. As Barzun says in his well-known essay, *The house of intellect* (1959, pp. 23–24), "Thus the school is not to teach, but to cure; body and mind are not to use for self-forgetful ends, but to dwell with Narcissus' adoring anxiety; the arts, not to give joy and light but to be scanned for a 'diagnosis' of some trouble, a solution of some 'problem,' or else exploited for the common good in occupational therapy. . . ." In this brief comment Barzun epitomizes with striking clarity the distaste of many educators for the indiscriminate mingling of the art of teaching with that of healing. Because of this dislike, we need to state our position carefully and see exactly how the principles of mental hygiene can fit into the classroom situation without doing violence to the business of teaching (Allinsmith & Goethals, 1962, pp. 12–13; Carroll, 1955). First of all, we do not need to subscribe to the idea that the classroom should be converted into a counseling or therapeutic situation. The primary and essential business of a school is to teach and to train, and to promote intellectual growth. Through this growth, the individual student *should* mature morally, spiritually, and socially. If he also matures emotionally, so much the better, but it is not the business of education to utilize the classroom situation for the purpose of emotional development. The classroom and the clinic, and the couch and the lectern are distinct entities with purposes and functions that belong to different aspects of human service. However, it is possible to use principles of mental hygiene in classroom instruction without doing violence to the essential purpose of the teaching art (Allinsmith & Goethals, 1962, Chapter 2).

There are certainly close relationships at times between mental health and learning. If a student, for example, is lacking in mental health, if he is mentally disturbed or emotionally confused, the teacher is likely to find it out before long because the student often acts in an unusual manner, disturbing the classroom situation. His attitude toward the teacher or toward classmates often indicates that there is something basically wrong. Such a student finds it hard to concentrate and to study and therefore does not learn efficiently. This type of situation indicates why mental hygiene should be brought into, and in some way integrated with the classroom situation (D'Evelyn, 1957).

Mental Health versus Adjustment in the Classroom Situation

In recent years there has been considerable objection raised to the intrusion of the concept of adjustment into the teaching situation. Many writers are critical of contemporary educational procedures and insist that students are not getting the education they require because we have forsaken the intrinsic goals of education and followed the precept of some educators for whom the adjustment of the child is the all important task of education. Certainly, if we were to organize our educational processes in such a way that the ideal of adjustment would replace the idea of sound intellectual growth, we would have taken a perilous step backward into the dark ages of education (Wall, 1960).

The difficulty of injecting adjustment into the educational process is not necessarily true of mental hygiene because mental health and adjustment are not the same thing. Mental hygiene is basically prophylactic rather than corrective or therapeutic, and in a number of ways it is possible to utilize hygiene principles without getting involved with the problem of adjustment. Mental hygiene in the classroom means simply the direct or indirect application of principles of mental health to the students and to student relationships in such a way as to *preclude* the development of undesirable or inefficient methods of thinking, feeling, or behaving. As we shall see, there are many ways in which these principles can be used without interfering with the proper aims of education. In fact, quite often it is possible to utilize them in a way to *promote* educational aims (Andrew & Middlewood, 1963).

MENTAL HYGIENE IN THE CLASSROOM

Teacher-Pupil Relations: The Primary Role of the Teacher

In determining the value of the classroom for mental hygiene, the first task that we must confront is to define the role of the teacher. What is he or she supposed to do? Obviously, if the role of the teacher precludes the use of mental hygiene principles, then the issue is settled since we should not inject anything into the teaching process that would undermine or disrupt his primary role. Many teachers do suffer role confusion (and also some parents). They begin as teachers and end up as counselors or therapists (Cook, 1956; Blos, 1953).

The primary role of the teacher is to be a custodian of truth and a purveyor of knowledge. This role has little to do, at least directly, with mental hygiene. But a second aspect of teaching comes closer to mental hygiene principles. Another role of the teacher, as a stimulant to the students and as a source of inspiration for total development, has more to do with mental hygiene (Baller & Charles, 1961, Chapter 15; Ryans, 1961). The teacher's effort goes beyond the student's intellect and moves more toward the will, emotions, social life, and other aspects of development. This type of teacher is the one usually referred to as "inspiring," the one who is always held up as a model and ideal for other teachers to emulate (Glaser, 1959; Gage, 1963). Certainly the teacher should, by his behavior in and out of class, by his principles and ideals, and by his relationships with others, inspire the students with whom he comes in contact and thus contribute importantly toward the development of each individual. And in enacting this role, the teacher is using mental hygiene principles of the highest order (Seidman, 1963; Barr, 1963; Novick, 1963).

Also, whether he likes it or not, the teacher functions *in loco parentis*, which is quite important for mental hygiene. The teacher is often a male figure with whom the student can identify, and quite frequently he also functions as a father figure for the student. He may even spend more time with the student than does the boy's real father, and thereby, if, in addition to teaching, he engages in faculty advising or counseling, he may develop an even more intimate, basic relationship with the student than do the parents themselves. The same situation applies to girls.

Relationships between student and teacher often begin in the class-room and are developed further as the student reaches toward an authority figure with whom he can identify or to whom he can take his problems and conflicts. Through such relationships the teacher lays the groundwork for promoting personality growth and character development. Probably no teacher sets out with a clear-cut, definitive goal of character formation, but often he molds character (Xavier, 1960).

Finally, the teacher *may become an ideal* for the individual student, which has implications for mental hygiene. The student should not neces-sarily emulate the teacher vocationally, but rather he may emulate the teacher *as a person;* there are countless students whose lives have been en-riched and perfected in some degree by reason of the teachers with whom they have come in contact. This influence of the teacher ideal can further mental hygiene considerably. The teacher who functions as a worthwhile ideal for the student will unconsciously promote mental health without ever intending to do so (Anderson, 1954).

Teachers as Models

This brief description of the teacher's role brings us even closer to the issue regarding the teacher and mental hygiene. As a person, the teacher can serve as a model of healthy adjustment, of self-discipline, of intellectual competence, and of respect for the integrity and dignity of others. Allin-smith and Goethals emphasize this point in the following statement (1962, p. 34):

> Riesman believes that the only solution for the teacher at the present time is to redefine his role in terms of what he knows he can and must do—instruct in subject matter—and let other agencies, such as home, Church, and the helping professions take over the heavy program im-plied by the mental health movement. "I would like to see teachers become more adult in the model of excellence they present to children, and hence in the demands they put on them intellectually, leaving the pal function to other agencies in the society, or to themselves on another occasion." Riesman, it must be emphasized here, is friendly to the idea of mental health, but he offers grave reservations about it as a central undertaking of teachers.

Allinsmith and Goethals, citing the opinions of teachers on the role of the teacher, point out that "Teachers agreed strongly that the teacher's role should include the primary functions of stimulating thinking and in-terest, guiding and assisting students in their learning experiences, and being a personal character model for the pupils" (1962, pp. 189–190). If, then, the teacher is a well-adjusted person in the best sense of this term, his performance in the classroom will be stable and well organized, he will not go to pieces over student rebellion or misbehavior, and he will not become involved in serious altercations with the principal, dean, or other faculty members (Berman, 1954; Solomon, 1960). The well-adjusted teacher likes his work, derives personal satisfaction from teaching, and gets along well with students. As a disciplined person, he knows how to play his role effectively as a teacher, how to function as a model for students, and how to develop healthy interpersonal relations. In this way the teacher exerts great influence on students and promotes their mental health most effectively.

Farnsworth expresses this same idea when he says that learning to conduct one's self with credit, satisfaction, and effectiveness is enormously complicated, but that (Farnsworth, 1957, p. 191):

> Exposure to and identification with persons who are emotionally mature is probably the most effective method of hastening one's own acquisition of mature attitudes. Hence, if a college takes seriously the task of teaching its students about emotions in such a way as to promote their own maturity, the faculty members will have as much or more influence because of what they are than because of what they know. A program for a proper understanding of the emotions is not one which affects the students alone, but instead concerns every person involved in the educational institution.

Here, then, we have a clear-cut definition of the way in which a teacher can play a definite role in implementing mental hygiene, even though he has never read a book on the subject, and knows little or nothing about the dynamics of behavior.

Still another way in which mental hygiene principles can be brought into the classroom without any formal effort is for the teacher to function as *a model of achievement and of competence*, especially for the superior student. The good teacher, by reason of his knowledge and personal achievement, his competence as a teacher, his enthusiasm for his subject matter and for his profession, and his zeal for the acquisition and development of truth, can inspire the better student to higher levels of achievement and personal growth. Moreover, such a teacher can help the student to define and to crystalize important goals and to make positive decisions in line with these goals. Mental health and good adjustment are directly dependent upon the ability to achieve, to realize personal potentialities, to actualize one's self, and to identify and work for attainable goals. Whenever a teacher helps students in this way, he is practicing mental hygiene without doing anything more than fulfilling his role as a good teacher (Abramovitz & Burnham, 1963).

Classroom Discipline and Mental Health

It is generally agreed that the good teacher maintains sound, healthy discipline in the classroom, and it is also agreed that discipline is essential to mental health. We must not confuse discipline with the techniques or methods of behavior control, particularly punishment. Essentially, discipline is the *achievement of order*. For the individual person it is the proper ordering of his life activities, and in the classroom it is bringing order into a complex and sometimes chaotic situation (Phillips, Wiener, & Haring, 1960). Here we see why the *method* of discipline can be *directly opposed* to discipline itself. If the teacher harshly punishes a child in class, because of hostility, anxiety, or inadequacy, with little regard for justice, he is not achieving order and therefore is not administering discipline. If, because of the method used, a student quits school, injures someone in his rage, or fails in his subjects, discipline fails completely.

Discipline is one of the most powerful tools for mental hygiene. Order in the classroom, in submitting assignments, in relation with others in the group or in students' thinking are all facets of a healthy, logical development; this is discipline of a high type.

> The world needs discipline. Our country needs discipline. Children need discipline. You cannot have a decent family or a decent business or a decent school or a decent town without discipline.
>
> Don't be afraid of the word. Don't be ashamed of it. "Discipline" is a *good* word. There is nothing old-fashioned about it. Discipline is as modern and as up-to-date as jet planes, as "miracle drugs." One of your very biggest jobs as a classroom teacher is to work for discipline. . . . There is nothing modern, nothing psychological, nothing progressive, nothing good about lack of discipline. When discipline is weak you can be sure that something somewhere, somehow has failed: home, school, church, community. When discipline is weak, you can be sure a child is unhappy. When discipline is weak, you can be positive: Everybody is in danger (Hymes, 1955, pp. 2, 3).

Discipline conceived in the manner described above is an essential part of mental hygiene. As a disciplinarian, but not in any sense as a punitive person, a teacher can play a basic role in promoting mental hygiene in the classroom. What is more, he does so naturally without particular regard for textbook arguments, educational theory, or behavior dynamics. In using discipline he is promoting the total development and mental health of the child. For this reason tardiness, excessive absences, failure to do assigned work, talking in class, and similar behaviors cannot be tolerated. These are clear signs of immaturity, which is diametrically opposed to discipline, adjustment, and mental health (Ausubel, 1963).

The Teacher as Counselor

The mental hygiene of the school can be carried one step further by the dedicated teacher as a confidant or counselor to the superior student who is seeking anxiously for adequate goals, the student whose intellectual capacities are below average, the underachiever, or the student who has problems of one kind or another, ranging from academic failure to emotional disability. Here the alert teacher can, and often does, bring principles of mental hygiene directly to the classroom situation or into his relationship with his students. Every teacher should develop an alertness to the relation between personality factors and achievement and to the dynamics of educational and vocational goals. He should learn to size up different students who indicate behavior problems or interpersonal difficulties: the chronically late student, the aggressive student, the bored student, the argumentative student, the absentee student, or the daydreaming student. All such factors are related to performance, and the alert teacher should be aware of what these behaviors mean.

Finally, the teacher can promote the aims of mental hygiene by using the technique of referral for students whose problems exceed the knowledge or skill of the teacher. The teacher in the classroom can be alert to signs of trouble and can often preclude more serious problems by referring the student to some person on the faculty, or on the counseling staff, who possesses particular skills in dealing with the kind of problem that the student manifests. When all these attitudes and procedures are added together, we have a complete program of mental hygiene for the classroom that in no way interferes with the primary business of teaching, which is the intellectual and personal development of the students (Bower, 1963; Poole, 1963).

Let us add just one brief negative note to one discussion, which should add to our perspective on the relation between mental hygiene and classroom experiences. Everyone is acquainted with the teacher who exemplifies in his behavior and his attitudes the reverse of mental health. Such teachers run the gamut from hostility to prejudice, from favoritism to suspiciousness, and from lack of self-confidence to chronic dissatisfaction. Their classroom behavior and their out of class relationships are replete with anger, blame, unfairness, inferiority, disdain for the teaching profession and for authority, chronic frustration, racial bias, lack of organization, an inadequate sense of humor, and projection of personal inadequacies. Such teachers destroy the possibility for practicing mental hygiene in the classroom. These negative qualities stand out sharply in teachers who actively dislike young people or those who are ashamed or disdainful of their own profession. In their dealings with youngsters they are impatient, sarcastic, hostile, and intolerant of any interference with established routine. In such instances it is obvious that the teacher cannot play the role of a healthy, well-adjusted, and self-disciplined authority figure. For them, the mental hygiene of the classroom does not exist (Kaplan, 1956).

Psychological Services in the School

As a final observation, let us note that the principles of mental hygiene can be most directly applied in the school situation through the organization of psychological services (or a guidance and counseling center), which makes available to needy students the knowledge and skills of professional personnel. A well-organized counseling center may utilize the services of academic advisers, a vocational guidance expert, a counseling psychologist, a teacher of remedial reading, a speech correctionist or therapist, and a psychiatrist. The organization of such services varies greatly from one school to another and from one community to another, depending on local conditions, availability of personnel, or educational policy. We wish merely to indicate the importance to mental hygiene of this adjunct to the educational process. Additional material and references on this topic will be found in the final chapter on the treatment of adjustment and mental health problems (Ullmann, 1957).

MENTAL HYGIENE AND THE COMMUNITY

Social Factors in Mental Health

It has long been recognized, and we have emphasized the fact several times in this text, that there is an important relation between individual adjustment and mental health on the one side and the social-cultural environment on the other. This recognition is nothing more than an extension of the proposition that ecology determines human behavior from the outside in much the same way that physiology or dynamics determine it from within (Plunkett & Gordon, 1960, p. 10).

> The health of the individual or of the species is the achievement of a dominance of positive adaptations to environment. Disease is the dominance of negative or unfavorable adaptations, a poor result of the dynamics of ecology, the extent and severity of which depend on the nature of the biological and social equilibrium between the human host and environment. Thus, the relative ascendancy of health or disease is a dynamic state, and the unfavorable adaptations that occur are assessed

in terms of the clinical nature, locale, and duration of the ensuing disease and the number of persons affected.

This is a clear and forceful statement of the relation in question. This relation has been studied by many investigators from many different points of view—the influence of culture on personality, effects of group membership on personality disorders, the relation between society and mental disorder, culture in relation to adjustment, society in relation to mental disease, and environmental factors influencing delinquency (Weinberg, 1952; Shaw & Port, 1953; Kardiner, 1953; Benedict, 1934; Kuhlen & Thompson, 1952). All such investigations help to pinpoint the influence of ecological factors on adjustment processes, mental health, or personality disorder. They help also to underscore the fact that, however healthy the individual may be *qua* individual, he may in time succumb to negative and damaging influences of the society in which he lives. To live in an insane society, as Erich Fromm has pointed out so strikingly (1955), is to risk sanity at every turn. Therefore, if we are to achieve individual mental health, we must also develop an effective mental hygiene of the community.

Community Programs for Mental Health

What does this term mean? How can the principles of mental hygiene be applied to a whole community? The answers to these questions are contained implicitly in the analysis of the relation between mental health and the social order made above. Just as mental health is to an important extent founded in physical health, so there must be a community hygiene in order to support mental health from without. Community efforts toward slum clearance, urban redevelopment, better school systems and better teachers, more extensive recreational facilities, youth programs, full employment, adequate wage scales, better and more efficient government, and better housing are typical instances of the application of mental hygiene to the community. That we have not achieved the millennium in this regard, despite massive efforts and the expenditure of billions of dollars is an all too obvious fact. But they are steps in the right direction, and we must continue the development of such community programs (Kotinsky & Witmer, 1955; Robinson, Demarsche, & Wagle, 1960; Ewalt, 1956).

The Church's Role in Mental Health

Prominent among social factors contributing to the mental hygiene of the community are the churches of all denominations. Not only do these institutions, through their services, contribute to the mental hygiene of religion, but they also function as agencies of social and mental hygiene through their many activities, group efforts, and organizations. The church sponsors numerous youth groups, social activities, public forums, and lectures that stimulate thinking for mental health; premarital as well as postmarital counseling, individual and family retreats, and many other activities and programs that contribute a great deal to individual gratifications, better family living, and a healthier society (McCann, 1960). All such programs deserve the interest and support of the community.

Public Health and Welfare Services

In addition to the efforts and agencies already described, there are numerous other resources for mental health that have developed over the past fifty years. There are countless mental health clinics, psychiatric outpatient services, psychological clinics associated with the courts, child welfare agencies, family service agencies, and many others too numerous to describe, all of which are directly or indirectly oriented toward the goal of mental health (Frost & Anderson, 1950; Shore, 1950; Lowry, 1953; Dribbin, 1954). These are some of the many facets of community mental hygiene. We are aware that, despite this massive effort, mental illness still remains the nation's number one problem. But we must recognize that, in the absence of these widespread community approaches, the mental health problem could be much greater than it actually is.

QUESTIONS AND PROJECTS FOR FURTHER STUDY

1. Make a careful study and write a full report on the mental hygiene services in your community.
2. Sample student opinion in your school in order to determine the essential characteristics of the good teacher.
3. Write a report on the National Institute of Mental Health.
4. What are the essential characteristics of the good home in relation to mental hygiene?
5. Write a term paper, documented by at least five pertinent sources, on the relations between classroom discipline and mental health.
6. Write a book report on Srole, *et al.*, *Mental health in the metropolis: the midtown Manhattan study*.
7. Compare the concept of the church's role in mental health with the concept of religion and mental health.

SELECTED COLLATERAL READINGS

ALLINSMITH, W., & GOETHALS, G. W. *The role of schools in mental health.* New York: Basic Books, 1962.

BERNARD, H. W. *Mental hygiene for classroom teachers.* New York: McGraw-Hill, 1952.

BROWN, E. J., & PHELPS, A. T. *Managing the classroom.* (2d ed.) New York: Ronald, 1961.

BUSH, R. N. *The teacher-pupil relationship.* Englewood Cliffs, N.J.: Prentice-Hall, 1954.

CROW, L. D., & CROW, ALICE (Eds.) *Mental hygiene for teachers.* New York: Macmillan, 1963.

D'EVELYN, KATHERINE. *Meeting children's emotional needs.* Englewood Cliffs, N.J.: Prentice-Hall, 1957.

FARNSWORTH, D. L. *Mental health in college and university.* Cambridge, Mass.: Harvard University Press, 1957.

FENTON, N. *Mental hygiene in school practice.* Stanford, Calif.: Stanford University Press, 1951.

INLOW, G. M. *Maturity in high school teaching.* Englewood Cliffs, N.J.: Prentice-Hall, 1963.

KOTINSKY, RUTH, & WITMER, HELEN L. *Community programs for mental health.* Cambridge, Mass.: Harvard University Press, 1955.

LANE, H., & BEAUCHAMP, MARY. *Human relations in teaching: the dynamics of helping children grow.* Englewood Cliffs, N.J.: Prentice-Hall, 1955.

LINDGREN, H. C. *Mental health in education.* New York: Holt, Rinehart and Winston, 1954.

PHILLIPS, E. L., WIENER, D. N., & HARING, N. G. *Discipline, achievement and mental health.* Englewood Cliffs, N.J.: Prentice-Hall, 1960.

REDL, F., & WATTENBERG, W. W. *Mental hygiene in teaching.* New York: Harcourt, 1959.

ROBINSON, R., DEMARSCHE, D. F., WAGLE, MILDRED K. *Community resources in mental health.* New York: Basic Books, 1960.

SMITH, H. T. *Psychology in teaching* (2d ed.) Englewood Cliffs, N.J.: Prentice-Hall, 1962.

SROLE, L., LANGNER, T. S., MICHAEL, S. T., OPLER, M. K., & RENNIE, T. A. C. *Mental health in the metropolis: the midtown Manhattan study.* Vol. I. New York: McGraw-Hill, 1962.

17

Treatment of Adjustment
and Mental Health Problems

Now that we have reviewed fairly extensively the different facets and applications of mental hygiene and its principles, we can conclude our study of personality dynamics and mental health with a brief statement on concepts and methods used in the treatment of adjustment and mental health problems. We have said that, whereas mental hygiene is essentially prophylactic, counseling and psychotherapy, as typical instances of the helping professions, are essentially corrective. They are processes directed against existing maladjustments, personality failures, and mental disorders. Taken together, therefore, the principles of mental hygiene and the techniques of counseling and psychotherapy can be used as effective broadsides against the encroachments of mental illness. Where mental hygiene leans on the age-old adage, "An ounce of prevention is worth a pound of cure," psychotherapy takes as its cue the idea that "A pound of cure is better than an ounce of mental disorder."

GENERAL PRINCIPLES OF TREATMENT

Treatment in Relation to the Problem

In the preceding chapters on mental hygiene, we studied the concepts and principles for the prevention of maladjustment and psychological disorder and for the achievement of good adjustment and mental health. These concepts and principles constitute the discipline of mental hygiene. We noted, too, that when a difficulty or disorder already exists, it becomes necessary to utilize principles and practices of treatment which serve to reduce the difficulty or to bring about more effective personality growth. Part of this area of treatment is taken up by *psychotherapy*, to which we shall turn later in this chapter. Problems have a way of determining the kind of treatment that is to be used, and, because psychological problems assume many different forms, there are different kinds of treatment to suit the various problems that are brought to the counselor or therapist (Woodward, 1951).

In many cases, the problem is simply one of adjustment to a local condition and does not involve deep-seated emotional difficulties or mental symptoms. Such, for example, is the kind of problem that is often involved in reading difficulties. The child is not getting along well in school and is referred to the clinic or school psychologist for diagnosis. Testing reveals that the child is a poor reader and so cannot keep up with the demands of school work. Treatment may involve nothing more than a number of sessions of special tutoring or remedial reading to bring reading efficiency to a higher level. If, of course, a problem of this kind is initiated by emotional difficulties, or leads to anxiety, rebellion, dislike of school, or isolation, the psychological implications become more important, and simple treatment may have to be complemented by intensive psychotherapy. Whether simple problems of adjustment are ever uncomplicated by emotional difficulties is problematical; yet there are many cases on record in which remedial treatment was enough to overcome the difficulty.

Again, there is the kind of problem that can be effectively resolved by information, advice, suggestion, or counsel. Many school problems and many difficulties that arise in marriage are of this kind. For example, a youngster may get into academic difficulties because he does not know how to evaluate a curriculum properly in terms of his ultimate aims, or he may need advice regarding the choice of the right vocation. Similarly, married couples often get out of difficulties by learning what they should have known regarding sex in marriage or by learning how to work out a satisfactory budget. There are countless problems in human adjustment that require nothing more than good sound advice, and any treatment that goes beyond this is predicated on the doubtful assumption that every human problem is at bottom an emotional one.

Types of Treatment

There are many adjustment difficulties, of the kind outlined in foregoing chapters, that require intensive and highly skilled treatment; difficulties of a mental and emotional kind that involve deep-seated personality factors, chronic conflicts and frustrations, or damaging trauma that will not respond to the simpler methods of treatment. In such instances some form of psychotherapy is indicated. If the condition is causally related to organic deficiency or pathology, treatment may have to assume a medical form, depending always on the exact nature of the difficulty. You can see, therefore, that the approach to psychological problems is varied.

On the basis of the foregoing analysis we can distinguish four basic methods of treatment: (1) *remedial,* when the difficulty involves some deficiency that can be remedied by instruction or training; (2) *informational* or *advisory* (guidance), when the problem is mainly peripheral and does not involve deep-seated psychological or organic failures; (3) *psycho-*

therapeutic (counseling), when there is personality maladjustment or mental disorder that is psychogenic in origin; and (4) *medical*, when treatment requires the use or manipulation of physical factors and agents. It is understood, of course, that any single problem may require the application of several or even all of these methods before treatment is fully effective. It is not uncommon to see medical and psychotherapeutic methods used with the same patient.

Steps in Treatment

Regardless of the treatment used, there are three essential steps involved in coping with psychological problems. The first of these involves the *accumulation of evidence* regarding both the patient (or client) and his difficulty. Second, there is the *diagnosis*, by means of which the problem is identified and classified. Third, there is the *process of treatment* itself, which aims primarily at a reduction of the difficulty by determining its precise nature and the causes or conditions that underlie it (Watson, 1949; Knapp, 1953). Although not necessary, the second step is often complemented by *prognosis*, which represents an attempt on the part of the counselor or clinician to predict the probable outcome of the disorder. Thus if the prognosis is favorable, the outlook for treatment is much better. In point of fact, prognosis can be used as a yardstick in determining the kind or intensity of treatment that is to be used. Just as treatment depends upon accurate diagnosis, so diagnosis itself relies upon the careful accumulation of evidence, which is the first step in handling human problems (Fisher, 1950, pp. 3–30).

Accumulation of Evidence

Recognition and Referral. The several processes necessary to get things started toward the reduction of a personal difficulty vary with the setting in which the problem occurs. In the usual clinical setting, whether in connection with a school system, juvenile court, or mental hospital, the referral of the patient or client is of importance because, if done carefully and skillfully, it can give the treatment process the right direction from the outset. Referral may be made by a teacher, school psychologist, medical practitioner, or other qualified person who has good opportunity to observe the behavior and reactions of the client. Indicated in the referral form are such useful items as the name of the person, class or school in which he belongs, sex, age, nature of the difficulty, and characteristic behavior patterns or psychological characteristics associated with the difficulty.

But prior to referral there is the important task of recognizing the problem or disorder. Here, much skill and careful observation may be required, not to mention intelligent evaluation of behavior. Many serious difficulties exist for a long time before they are recognized and long before they should have been referred for treatment. For this reason, teachers, counselors, and others who come in contact with possible problem cases, should be trained in those disciplines that will give them the ability to recognize difficulties and disorders whenever they arise. Many a seriously disturbed child has been dismissed by an unobservant parent or teacher as "merely shy," "stubborn," "disobedient," or "plain bullying," when actually they were face to face with a behavior disorder and did not know it. But it is just as serious a fault to discover in every childish prank or caprice the first signs of mental disorganization. To some extent, psychology and psychiatry have made us too symptom conscious, and we must be careful not to read into all behavior the signs of disorder or maladjustment.

Initial Interview. The first contact with client or patient is of particular importance not only as a source of vital information in the process of accumulating evidence but also as an opportunity to get the person in the right frame of mind for diagnosis and treatment. An attitude of sympathetic interest, friendliness, and acceptance can do a lot to break down the natural reserve most people have in a psychological interview. This applies particularly to children, since they have little understanding of the problems in which they become involved and considerable anxiety regarding treatment of any kind. With the data of referral available, the initial interview will provide a general impression of the patient, a clearer and more detailed picture of the problem or difficulty, and the opportunity for a rough classification of the problem so that procedures of diagnosis and treatment may be more efficiently organized. It is obvious that a school difficulty must be handled differently than a problem of extreme aggressiveness, neurosis, or sexual pathology. Often, the interview will bring to light factors and relations not contained in the original report. For example, what appears to be a simple school problem may turn out to be a serious problem in emotional adjustment, in which case different treatment procedures will have to be adopted (Kraines, 1948, pp. 141–144; Tyler, 1961, Chapter 3; Erickson, 1950; Gill, 1954). This point is illustrated in the following case.

The client, a twenty-two-year-old college senior, was referred to the counseling center because of academic difficulties that did not respond to the ordinary techniques of educational guidance. For the past two years, the student had been on the Dean's list, and then suddenly began to get poor grades in the majority of his subjects. The trouble began when the student was required to take a course in chemistry to fulfill a curriculum requirement. Despite intensive studying, the best the client was able to achieve was a grade of 48, and, after several of these discouraging performances, the entire academic record began to deteriorate.

Psychometric examination indicated that the student was well above average, a fact supported by his good performance in preceding semesters. Interviews, however, revealed that, in line with his father's wishes, the client had, early in his college career, attempted a pre-medical curriculum and had twice failed in chemistry courses, after which he changed to another curriculum. He felt his father's disappointment keenly, knowing that he had been expected to follow in the paternal footsteps. In his mind, chemistry, and science generally, stood as a symbol of failure, discouragement, and broken dreams. When this emotional block was removed by interview therapy, the student resumed his work and managed to complete all his courses successfully, including the course in chemistry. The problem, which at first seemed purely academic, was found to have its roots in deep-seated emotional difficulties that had to be resolved before the academic problem responded to treatment.

Developmental History. The process of gathering information is furthered by the developmental or case history technique, which serves to elicit and to bring together all pertinent facts in the client's background (Berg, 1954, pp. 91–127). You will recall that, in Chapter 4, we outlined the conditions and determinants of adjustment and mental health on the assumption that personality and the process of adjustment are continuously and often deeply affected by the physical-social-cultural milieu in which the individual develops and functions. The developmental history method is a concrete expression of this assumption. Early childhood experiences, parent-child relations, family constellation, breakup of the family, ages of parents at client's birth, school and work history, interests, hobbies, and aversions, history of emotional disturbance, incidence of psychological disorder in the client's family, and many similar factors are brought out in an effort to determine the conditions and pattern of the client's development and of his problem.

The etiological significance of background factors is often clear. For example, it is noted that the client's difficulties began soon after the death of the favored parent; or that a history of truancy is coincident with the parents' divorce; or that a long succession of childhood illnesses is correlated with a strong mother identification. Usually, interpretation and evaluation of background factors are not this simple; yet they may always be expected to shed some light on the personality of the client and on his problem. In some degree, every person reflects his past; and it is this relation that makes the developmental history technique an important part of treatment procedure. That this technique complements the referral and interview methods is obvious.

Physical Examination.   The mere existence of problems and disabilities, even those that seem to be purely psychological, demands a thorough physical examination. At the present stage of our knowledge regarding the psychosomatic structure of man, we can never rule out physical causes and conditions completely (Kraines, 1948, Chapter VI). Many a child has been censured for his lack of interest in school or for low grades when the only thing actually wrong was that he needed glasses or a hearing aid. Similarly, headaches have too often been diagnosed as psychosomatic or neurotic when actually the basic cause was some physical condition. In one case that was brought to the writer's attention, the patient presented the classical symptoms of neurasthenia along with periodic headaches that had all the earmarks of migraine; yet a thorough physical examination revealed the existence of an inoperable tumor at the base of the brain. In the absence of such an examination, and with the psychological tools presently available, there is no certain way in which we can determine whether the causes underlying symptomatic behavior or personality disorganization are physical or psychological. *The only reliable procedure includes a thorough physical examination.* Moreover, apart from the etiological significance and uses of a physical examination, it aids a great deal in building a complete picture of the client; and such a picture is of inestimable value to the psychologist or psychiatrist working with human problems.

Psychological Examination.   Parts of this picture are filled in by the psychological examination, which functions as a complement to the medical study of the client. Depending always on the character of the problem, or the facts brought out in the referral, interview, and case history, and on a preliminary diagnosis, it may become necessary to determine intelligence level, special aptitudes, peculiar disabilities, adjustment level, personality pattern and characteristics, the degree of unconscious motivation, level of maturity, range of interests, or scholastic achievement. In fact, every means that will throw some light on the personality of the patient and his problem should be explored. The psychologist has a large armamentarium—intelligence scales, aptitude and achievement tests, personality and adjustment inventories, perception tests, projective devices, and the like. Skillfully applied, these instruments can be very useful and often indispensable in preparing the way for effective treatment (Tyler, 1961).

Psychiatric Examination.   The medical and psychological study of the client is often regarded as part of the psychiatric examination, and it is not altogether wise to distinguish too sharply between these different approaches to a knowledge of the client and his problem. Nevertheless, the orientation of the psychiatrist is not the same as that of the physician or psychologist. The psychiatrist is interested primarily in telltale signs and symptoms of mental or personality disorganization (Strecker, 1952, Chapter III). He is on the lookout, as it were, for evidence of neurotic disability, psychopathic traits, psychotic or prepsychotic symptoms, signs of epilepsy or encephalitis, symptoms of organic pathology, and other cues that will enable him to identify the disorder and eventually to formulate a precise, differential diagnosis. In this procedure, the findings of the medical examiner and psychologist and the data revealed in the case history are of considerable value. In fact, a complete diagnosis and an effective treatment procedure would have to take all findings into account.

It is to be understood that this brief summary of steps involved in the accumulation of evidence regarding a patient and his problem is not typical of all treatment procedures. Some of these steps are eliminated when it becomes obvious that the problem is a simple one and can be resolved by simple procedures. A psychiatric examination is hardly indicated in cases where the problem is academic or vocational. Hence the need for a careful referral and preliminary interview, whereby simple problems may be screened out and those of a serious nature reserved for more intensive investigation.

The Process of Diagnosis

Diagnosis and Treatment.   All of the steps involved in gathering information are pointed directly toward an adequate diagnosis of the problem or disorder presented by the client. And diagnosis is oriented toward effective remedy or treatment. Diagnosis may be defined as a clinical procedure by which any disorder is identified, classified, and differentiated from other disorders of a similar or radically different kind by an analysis of available data, behavior, or symptoms. Thus, the physician studies the patient's symptoms and concludes with a diagnosis of measles, ulcers, or tuberculosis. Similarly, the psychiatrist diagnoses a patient's difficulty as traumatic neurosis, anxiety, or schizophrenia, using data from the case history and psychological examination, and the symptoms manifested by the patient. Without this identification and classification, treatment is handicapped since the method of treatment varies with the kind of disorder (Hunt, 1948; Cameron, 1953, pp. 33–45).

Identification and classification of the disorder are essential to diagnosis, but they are not enough; the disorder must be differentiated from others. Hence the term "differential diagnosis." It is not enough to discern that a disorder belongs to the class of psychosis; it is necessary also to determine *what form* of psychosis is involved. Manic-depressive reactions must be differentiated from schizophrenia, and the latter from paranoia. And even within the same class there must be differentiation. Neurasthenia must be distinguished from psychasthenia, and hypochondria from both. This is not an easy task since there is extensive overlapping of symptoms. Manic-depressive elements are often found in schizophrenic patients, and hypochondria is very similar to neurasthenia. Even in simple cases, one must be careful to differentiate between a true reading disability and intellectual deficiency that makes reading difficult. Thus, expert differential diagnosis, although often extremely difficult, is of great importance to adequate treatment (Weitz, 1954).

A good diagnosis is important also to *prognosis*, which is an attempt to predict the probable future of the disorder (Kraines, 1948, Chapter XIII; Bond & Braceland, 1937; Zubin & Windle, 1954; Rennie, 1953, pp. 66–79). For example, the prognosis in the case of neurotic disorder is generally more favorable than in the case of a psychosis, whereas the prognosis for psychopathic states or homosexuality is unfavorable. That prognosis has a direct bearing on treatment is obvious since the more favorable the prognosis, the brighter the outlook for therapy.

Organic versus Functional and Psychogenic Disorders. Whenever diagnosis indicates organic pathology, as in the case of paresis and traumatic psychosis, the prognosis and treatment will differ considerably from cases in which the disorder is essentially functional or psychogenic. In the development of diagnostic and treatment procedures, therefore, it is necessary to recognize this basic distinction. In speech pathology, for example, the difficulty may be purely functional and the result of faulty habits (baby talk, slurring of vowels, and so forth), or it may reflect an organic defect in the speech apparatus. In the one case, retraining is indicated, in the other some form of physical therapy or surgical treatment. Similarly, all neurotic disorders are regarded today as psychogenic, whereas some of the psychoses are clearly organic. As soon, therefore, as diagnosis indicates that the disorder is essentially neurotic, the implication is that it is also psychogenic, and treatment should take the form of psychotherapy.

A difficulty arises in the case of disorders that are classified as functional because they are often confused with those that are psychogenic. Among the psychoses, schizophrenia, manic-depressive reactions, and paranoia are regarded as functional in nature, as distinct from those psychoses that have a definite organic basis, such as paresis and senile dementia. The reason for the designation "functional" for disorders of this group is that no organic basis has been identified for them. Many attempts have been made to establish an organic basis but so far to little avail. Hence, in the absence of organic lesion or pathology of any kind, it has been assumed that the disorder reflects malfunctioning of some physical system, particularly the nervous system, or malfunctioning on the psychological level.

The logic of this assumption is substantially correct since disorders of function are as real as disorders of structure. This fact may be the essential reason why physical procedures like shock therapy or lobotomy are effective in reducing or at least altering functional disorders. If, however, the malfunctioning is psychological rather than physical, it is difficult to see how the disorder differs from those that are truly psychogenic; and it is at this point that considerable confusion exists. To avoid this confusion it would be better to restrict the term "functional" to disorders that reflect malfunctioning of some physical system, and the term "psychogenic" to disorders that are caused by psychological factors. In this sense, a difficulty that is caused by inferiority or guilt would be classed as psychogenic, whereas one caused by glandular imbalance (without structural impairment) would be diagnosed as functional. Thus the clinician would recognize three general classes of disorder: *organic* (structural), *functional*, and *psychogenic*. With this classification as a starting point, both diagnosis and treatment would have a more secure basis. The interested student is referred to the chapter on "functional" sickness in Strecker (1952). Strecker recognizes that the term "functional" is so broad in meaning that all sickness is functional insofar as it impairs the functions of the organism. However, he limits the term to disorders that are caused psychogenically. Other clarifications will be found in Heath (1952) and Degan (1952).

The classification of disorders as organic, functional, and psychogenic is not only logically sound, it has a basis in clinical experience. It is well known that some disorders do not occur unless there is structural impairment of some organ system, caused by lesions, injury, disease organisms, tumors, or toxic agents. We have already cited examples of this group. Similarly, there are disorders that are clearly functional in the sense introduced here. Examples are hyperthyroidism, involutional melancholia, and cretinism, in which the cause is malfunctioning of an organ system. There are also many disorders that are unquestionably psychogenic. Anxiety neurosis, hypochondria, hysteria, certain speech disorders, enuresis, nervousness, and obsessive-compulsive reactions are typical examples. Clinical experience, both diagnostic and therapeutic, has shown that the causes of such difficulties are psychological and not organic or functional. Effective therapy in such cases can be purely psychological in character.

These facts do not mean that every disorder can be neatly categorized for purposes of diagnosis and treatment. It is still uncertain where to place the "functional" psychoses like schizophrenia and paranoia. The fact that the former responds to psychotherapy suggests that it belongs with the psychogenic group, and this suggestion is supported by the fact that in the background of schizophrenia there is a consistent pattern of psychogenic causes. Still, this disorder also responds to convulsive therapy, which suggests a functional basis. Similarly, the spontaneous remissions of manic-depressive psychosis (a functional disorder) carry the implication of a psychogenic etiology; yet it, too, responds to physical treatment. To resolve these paradoxes, we need to know a great deal more about the etiology and development of functional disorders, and more about the rationale of certain forms of therapy.

We must keep in mind also the possibility of overlapping in the matter of etiology. Both psychogenic and organic causes may be involved in any single disorder. This fact is exemplified in the traumatic neuroses and, to some extent, in the organic psychoses; and it may be involved in other disorders about which we still know too little. In many cases, the remote cause of a traumatic neurosis is physical injury; the proximate cause is psychogenic, including such factors as insecurity and anxiety. Similarly, senile dementia is regarded as the outcome of organic deterioration; yet the pattern of this psychosis is determined in large part by psychogenic factors. The newer science of gerontology has shown that senile psychosis cannot be explained simply in terms of organic pathology; that attitudes, feelings, and personal history have to be taken into account if the disorder is to be adequately understood. As our knowledge of mental disorders and their causes increases, it is not unlikely that the science of etiology will be required to include both types of causes for at least the majority of adjustment difficulties.

Predisposing versus Exciting Causes. The foregoing discussion of etiology and classification of psychological disorders in relation to diagnosis and treatment requires a further statement regarding causes. Not only are causes psychogenic, functional, and organic, they are also classifiable as predisposing and exciting. Perhaps the term "condition" would be better than "predisposing cause" (Strecker, 1952, pp. 15–33).

In any event, the clinician must recognize that some causes or conditions prepare the ground, as it were, for the development of maladjustment or disorder, whereas others serve to precipitate it. In the understanding and diagnosis, as well as in the treatment of psychological difficulties, this distinction is of paramount importance. Among the predisposing causes are such factors as bodily constitution, heredity, chronic illness, inadequate personality, damaging interpersonal relations, chronic conflict and frustration, poor psychological climate, glandular malfunctioning, previous history of psychosis, and persistent failure. These factors are of a kind to favor the development of a mental disorder or maladjustment when the individual reaches a point where he can no longer cope with the demands and pressures of reality. It is then that he falls back on symptom formation or on defense and escape mechanisms.

The actual onset of the disorder is precipitated by causes that serve to initiate the reactions or symptoms by which it is recognized. It is highly probable that every psychological disorder involves both predisposing and exciting causes. Among the precipitating factors are traumatic experience, sudden loss of loved ones on whom the patient has been dependent, breakup of the home, unresolvable conflict or frustration, emotional shock caused by cataclysmic experience (train wreck, war atrocities, fire, and so forth), severe physical injury, such as cranial damage, loss of a limb or loss of sight, and sudden deprivation (of family, friends, job, or fortune). The fact that the majority of persons survive these experiences clearly suggests that some persons do not survive them because of the existence of predisposing conditions. For this reason, emphasis was placed in preceding chapters on the conditions of adjustment and the development of personality. Likewise, in our discussion of the principles of mental hygiene in the foregoing chapters, we stressed the importance of a wholesome environment and interpersonal relations in the prevention of maladjustment.

Multiple Causality as a Basic Principle of Interpretation.   By this time it should be clear that the diagnosis and interpretation of psychological disorders should not be oversimplified by reference to one type of cause or theoretical formulation. The cardinal error of the Freudian interpretation of mental disorder is its insistence on sexual conflict and frustration as the essential cause. Sexual conflicts and frustrations can and do play a part in the genesis of maladjustments; but they are only a part of the picture. First we must look to the background and history of the patient, then to the way in which his personality developed and became organized, then to his unique relation to reality, then to the manner in which he has learned to react to situations and people, and finally to the causes and events that seem to have precipitated the disorder. It is only when we know something about all such causes and conditions and have organized them into a coherent etiology that adequate diagnosis and treatment become possible.

Evaluation of Adjustment.   Throughout the process of diagnosis and the interpretation of the causes of psychological disorder, an effort is made to evaluate the adjustment of the patient. To assert, for example, that a particular mode of adjustment is good or bad is not especially meaningful for either diagnosis or therapy. Nor does it help a great deal to label behavior as normal, neurotic, or psychotic, unless everyone is agreed on what these terms signify. What the clinician needs to determine is the meaning of the adjustment for the patient. Why does he react in this unusual way? What is he getting out of his symptoms and mechanisms?

Is his peculiar adjustment consonant with his background and personality? Under the circumstances, is this the best possible adjustment or compromise that he could have worked out? If you will recall that all responses, whether normal or abnormal, acceptable or queer, adjustive or maladjustive, must be regarded as individual ways of reacting to and attempting to cope with situations and difficulties, you will understand the meaning of these questions. Patients are known to cling desperately to their symptoms and peculiarities, and the reason is that these symptoms have proved successful in reducing the tensions brought on by frustrations and conflicts. For the patient, therefore, they have a meaning and a value quite different from that which would be expected from an objective appraisal. Objectively, suicide or alcoholism are ridiculous solutions to a problem; but there is no denying the fact that such reactions can be very effective in the reduction of tensions.

In diagnosis, moreover, it is important to relate the form of adjustment to the degree of personality development and integration, maturity expectancy, innate capacity for objectivity and realistic thinking, and similar factors that bear on the meaning of the adjustment (Shostrom & Brammer, 1952). If a clergyman commits adultery, the maladjustment is a great deal more serious than for the ordinary layman because the clergyman can be reasonably expected to work out a better adjustment. Morally, it makes no difference who commits the wrong; but psychologically, we have a right to expect more from one person than from another. Similarly, the scientifically trained person has a greater capacity for objectivity than the factory worker who finds it hard to distinguish fact from fancy. These relations do not mitigate the seriousness of maladjustment—psychosis, for example, is a serious problem wherever it occurs—but they help a great deal in understanding and interpreting the adjustment; and this understanding is necessary for adequate diagnosis and treatment. Many persons, because of their personality organization, would have spent the remainder of their lives in a mental hospital if they had suffered the same disorder that Clifford Beers experienced. But in his case the outcome was vastly different and the possibilities of treatment and recovery entirely altered because of his distinctive personality. Cases such as these, and they are very numerous, exemplify the importance of a careful evaluation of adjustment.

The Process of Treatment

Guidance and Counseling versus Psychotherapy. At the start of this chapter, we noted that treatment processes vary as the nature of the adjustment problem varies; for this reason we must distinguish carefully between the forms of treatment. Guidance and counseling are not the same thing as psychotherapy, even though many writers fail to distinguish them (Rogers, 1942, pp. 3–4; Blum & Balinsky, 1951, pp. 15–17). The idea that these processes of treatment are identical stems from the assumption that all human problems that come to the attention of the psychologist or psychiatrist are basically emotional and psychogenic. This assumption is false. The field of vocational guidance, for example, has developed extensively in the past thirty years and to an important degree independently of psychotherapeutic advances. The main business of the vocational guidance expert is to help a person solve the problem of selecting the right vocation in which he can adequately express his capacities and interests and find satisfaction. In other words, the aim of vocational guidance is adequate vocational adjustment. To identify this activity with psychotherapy is only to compound the confusion in terms that already exists.

It is erroneous, also, to identify counseling and psychotherapy since very often both the aims and the techniques differ in these two approaches to human problems. After carefully defining psychotherapy, Fisher goes on to say (1950, p. x):

> Although readily distinguishable from it, and comprising broad fields of applied psychology in themselves, both psychological testing and psychological counseling are important adjuncts to psychotherapy. Psychological testing is an essential feature of diagnostic procedure and normally precedes the psychotherapy proper. Psychological counseling (vocational, marital, family, educational) is frequently included by the psychotherapist, particularly during the latter part of a course of treatment.

Thus, as this writer suggests, in the area of marital adjustment, there is a great amount of counseling that has little of the therapeutic in it (Hahn, 1953; Williamson, 1953). *Therapy means healing, and in guidance and counseling procedures the quality of healing may not enter at all.* To counsel is to give advice, impart information, or bring to bear on a problem insights and wisdom that the client himself does not possess. Curran says (1952b, p. 21),

> In our daily lives there is still the final problem of the choice of ways to fulfill the tasks to which education and guidance direct us. This means coping with and controlling the personal disorder within us as our particular instincts and emotional impulses tend to reach for satisfactions not in conformity with the reasonable needs of our whole person, the rights of others, and the demands of reality. . . . The individual on his own personal responsibility must be able to carry out the principles and practical information he has received. He must have acquired individual integration both in his ability to cope with the disorder within himself, the unreasonable impulses of his emotions and

instincts, and the disorder in the world, in other personalities and in reality itself. Knowledge must become activated in each individual's life as he copes with the single events in his daily actions. This is the function of *Counsel* as a part of each man's prudential judgment and action.

Counsel, therefore, goes one step beyond education and guidance, to both of which, however, it is closely related (Sanford, 1948; Williamson, 1950). These relations are illustrated in Figure 30.

There are many problems that require counsel without requiring healing. A wife may wish to know how better to understand her husband or children, how to develop a better attitude toward the raising of a family, how to work out an efficient family budget, or how to approach the question of sexual adjustment in marriage in a more wholesome manner (Adams, 1962). Questions such as these may occur to the most normal person; in fact, that they should be raised at all may be indicative of a good level of adjustment, a sincere desire to do whatever is necessary to secure marital happiness. In such situations, there is always the possibility that the counseling problem may be complicated by adverse psychological factors, such as immaturity, emotional instability, overcontrol, and negative ego feelings. Even the simplest problem in vocational guidance may involve factors of this kind. But the fact that this sometimes happens cannot be taken to mean that it always does. Until we have definite evidence to the contrary, we may assume that many problems can be resolved by the techniques of guidance and counseling, without psychotherapy (Curran, 1952a).

The three different approaches to problems in adjustment, however, are alike insofar as all are oriented toward the solving of problems and are involved with the procedures of collecting information and of diagnosis or evaluation by means of standard techniques, such as the interview, case history, intelligence testing, and personality measurement. In other words, in any problem situation, every effort is made to gather as much information as possible that will shed light on the difficulty and be of some help in diagnosis and in resolving the problem (Rotter, 1953). If it can be resolved by imparting information, advice, or suggestion, the procedure stops short of therapy; if, in contrast, because of serious conflicts, damaging feelings, or frustrations, the problem requires deep analysis of motivations, background factors, or personality characteristics, psychotherapy becomes necessary. To this type of treatment we now direct our attention.

Meaning of Psychotherapy. The term "psychotherapy" is used in different ways by different writers, and it is probably impossible to formulate a definition that would be generally acceptable (Rogers, 1961). The

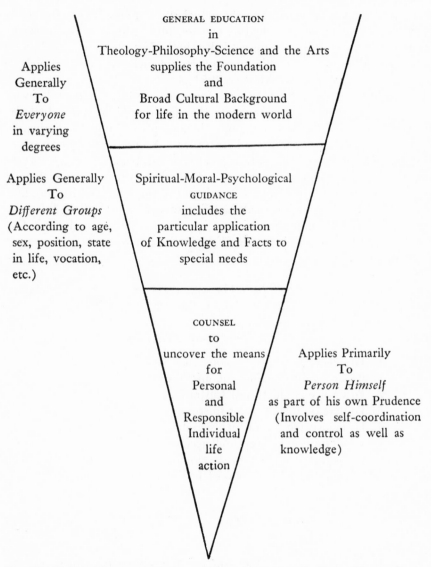

Applies
Generally
To
Everyone
in varying
degrees

GENERAL EDUCATION
in
Theology-Philosophy-Science and the Arts
supplies the Foundation
and
Broad Cultural Background
for life in the modern world

Applies Generally
To
Different Groups
(According to age,
sex, position, state
in life, vocation,
etc.)

Spiritual-Moral-Psychological
GUIDANCE
includes the
particular application
of Knowledge and Facts to
special needs

COUNSEL
to
uncover the means
for
Personal
and
Responsible
Individual
life
action

Applies Primarily
To
Person Himself
as part of his own Prudence
(Involves self-coordination
and control as well as
knowledge)

Fig. 30. Relations among education, guidance, and counsel. (From Curran, C. A. *Counseling in Catholic life and education.* New York: Macmillan, 1952, p. 18.)

process itself is a form of therapeutics, a term derived from the Greek, meaning literally to serve or to treat (medically). In general, it pertains to the art of healing, that is, to discovering and applying remedies for diseases, and has gradually come to signify that part of medical science which treats of the discovery and application of remedies for diseases. The term "therapy," then, refers to the actual application of remedies. A distinguishing prefix, such as hydro-, electro-, biblio-, and psycho-, indicates the kind of application being used. Psychotherapy, therefore, would refer to the application of psychic or psychological methods to the remedy of some disease or disorder (Mowrer, 1953).

There are, however, several forms of treatment called "psychotherapy" that would not square with the definition given above. Included are such diverse techniques as group therapy, play therapy, bibliotherapy, environment therapy, and shock treatment. All such techniques are regarded by one writer or another as psychotherapeutic, even though they do not employ psychological methods. Behind this attitude lies the thought that psychotherapy really means "treatment of the mind and its disorders" rather than "psychological treatment of disease or disorder." In this view, the particular technique used is not important; it is the end result that determines whether a technique is psychotherapeutic or not (Cumming & Cumming, 1962).

Aims of Psychotherapy.   The differences over what psychotherapy is can be resolved in part by defining the aims of psychotherapy. It has many aims, too many to enumerate here, but several of them are basic to the achievement of good results in therapy. They are:

1. To relieve pent-up tensions that stem from feelings such as anxiety, guilt, hostility, or inferiority
2. To resolve conflicts and frustrations
3. To develop tolerance for frustration and stress
4. To reduce (the need for) symptoms and defensive mechanisms
5. To increase self-esteem, self-acceptance, and security
6. To increase capacity for developing interpersonal relationships
7. Ventilation or expression of feelings (catharsis and abreaction)
8. To develop insight into personal motivations and psychological difficulties
9. To increase personal integration, growth, and striving toward positive goals

It is easy to see that the aims listed above are fundamentally psychological and that their achievement, which would improve the patient's attitude toward reality and his relations with people in such a way that symptomatic behavior and mechanisms would no longer be necessary, constitutes effective treatment (therapy) regardless of the method used. *Thus we may define psychotherapy as a clinical process, involving various specialized techniques, that is oriented toward healthful personal and social readjustment and toward growth of the individual patient through the re-*

duction of underlying causes and overt symptoms (Maslow & Mittelmann, 1951, Chapter XIII; Curran, 1952b, pp. 31, 36, 37; Hunt, 1948; Ewing, 1954; Barron, 1963). These techniques are of two broad types—the "psychological" and the physical—which can be further subdivided into specialized treatment procedures. The diagram in Table 15 outlines these techniques and their relations to one another.

TABLE 15

Techniques of psychotherapy in relation to one another

1. "Psychological"	a) Personal (involving direct interpersonal contact)	Interview therapy Client-centered therapy Psychoanalysis Hypnoanalysis Hypnosis and suggestion Rational psychotherapy Existential therapy Narcoanalysis
	b) Nonpersonal (expressive therapy)	Group therapy Play therapy Music therapy Psychodrama Bibliotherapy Art therapy Occupational therapy Environment therapy Recreational therapy Cinematherapy
2. Physical (psychosomatic)	a) Convulsive therapy b) Psychosurgery c) Chemotherapy d) Relaxational therapy	

As the table indicates, there are many techniques available for treatment of psychological disorders (Bychowski & Despert, 1952). Some of them are definitely physical in that they involve the use of a physical agent to bring about a psychological change. Prominent among these techniques is *convulsive therapy*, which, by means of a drug or electric shock, induces a convulsive seizure that may terminate in the remission of symptoms or even complete cure. The evaluation of such methods is still uncertain at the present time, although a great amount of research is being done to test their validity. It would seem that in some cases the technique is effective (Kalinowsky & Hoch, 1946; Kalinowsky, 1959; Hoch, 1959).

The majority of psychotherapeutic techniques are "psychological," that is, they do not involve the use of a physical agent and are dependent upon interpersonal relations, or the manipulation of psychological factors for the reduction of causes, conflicts, and symptoms. *Psychoanalysis* is a good example of the exploitation of interpersonal relations for therapeutic aims, and both *group* and *play therapy* exemplify the manipulation of psychological factors for therapeutic purposes. These two techniques are a part of *expressive therapy*, a group of methods in which basic tensions, conflicts, feelings, and frustrations are provided an outlet for expression and ventilation, on the theory that the free expression of such factors will bring about a reduction of symptoms and maladjustive behavior (Slavson, 1943; Bennett, 1963). Needless to say, our divisions of physical and psychological, and personal and expressive, are somewhat arbitrary and do not take into account the overlapping that exists among the various techniques. It is to be assumed that in a brief account of a very complex subject many things must be left unsaid. The interested student will find more extensive discussions in Powdermaker & Frank, 1953; Axline, 1947; Allen, 1942; Podolsky, 1954; Ellis, 1958; Shands, 1960; Ruesch, 1961.

Some Basic Principles of Counseling and Psychotherapy. In the treatment of psychological problems, as in professional work of any kind, there are several principles that should be carefully observed. These principles center around the therapist (or counselor), the therapeutic setting, the therapist-client relation, and the therapeutic process itself (Fromm-Reichmann, 1950).

1. *The effectiveness of treatment will always be conditioned to some extent by the quality of the setting in which it takes place.* Lighting, ventilation, and temperature should be carefully controlled, necessary facilities should be available, and the general surroundings should be pleasant, comfortable, and at the same time professional. The right kind of setting helps to instill confidence in the patient and to promote a good relation between patient and therapist. The wrong kind of setting can be depressing and often discourages the patient from continuing treatment.

2. *The therapist or counselor must possess the knowledge of and professional training in all fields important to his specialty.* These requirements vary considerably with the nature of the specialty. Marriage counseling, vocational guidance, and remedial work demand a different type of knowledge and training from that required for the practice of psychiatry. In all of them, however, a basic knowledge of psychology and related fields,

and specialized training in the philosophy and techniques of counseling and psychotherapy are important (Dollard & Miller, 1950; Tyler, 1961, Chapter XII).

3. *The personality characteristics of the counselor or therapist are important to treatment.* Among these the following are of primary significance.

    1. Emotional stability and high level adjustment
    2. Poise and self-confidence
    3. Prestige and the ability to inspire confidence in others
    4. Professional integrity, which includes sound ethical principles and right attitudes
    5. A wholesome respect for the worth and dignity of the patient as a human person
    6. A lively interest in people and their problems
    7. Objectivity in judgment and interpretation
    8. A good command of language
    9. The ability to be a good listener
    10. Good appearance

If these qualifications are fulfilled, the process of treatment has a good start toward success (Hiltner, 1952; Berdie, 1953; Schwebel, 1955).

4. *The relation between therapist and client must be adequate.* If this relation is not adequate, the chances of effective treatment are poor. On the part of the client or patient, there must be a willingness to undergo treatment and an attitude of acceptance and trust that will give the process of therapy a chance to work. Antagonism, rebelliousness, mistrust, or hostility set up difficult blocks in the path of effective treatment. On the part of the therapist, there must be acceptance, warmth, empathy, sympathetic interest, patience, and a degree of permissiveness that will encourage the patient to share his problem with the therapist, to express pent-up feelings, and bring to light whatever facts must be known for effective diagnosis and treatment. These qualities will lead to the development of *rapport* and, eventually, to a wholesome *transference* (in the broader, non-Freudian sense) by which feelings, frustrations, and conflicts can be ventilated, damaging causes brought to the surface, and symptoms rendered ineffective (Estes, 1948; Black, 1952; Johnson, 1953).

This kind of relation is necessary to an efficient and productive therapeutic or counseling process. Because of variation in psychological problems and disorders, in the background and training of the therapist, and in the personality of the client, this relation will vary from one situation to another. In some instances, nondirective or client-centered counseling is most effective; in others, direct suggestion or advice may work; and in still others, psychoanalysis, group therapy, or environment therapy may be indicated (Rogers, 1951; Rogers & Dymond, 1954). The therapist, therefore, must demonstrate initiative in adapting the technique to the requirements of the situation. He must be ready to exploit developments as they occur, and skillfully steer the process toward a successful termination. He must be conscious of the temporal limitations of the single interview as well as of the entire therapeutic relation, because a process of treatment continued for too long a period will foster dissatisfaction, loss of interest, or dependence, and thus defeat its own purpose. At all times in the treatment relation, the therapist should be guided by the primary aims of therapy and direct the process toward the development of insight, self-acceptance, more adequate perspective, sounder attitudes, and a general re-education of the personality toward integration, maturity, and a continuing adjustment. It is in this situation that the principles of mental hygiene can be exploited to the advantage of successful counseling and therapy.

Evaluation of Diagnosis and Treatment.   *Successful termination* of the therapeutic relation is the best criterion of adequate diagnosis, whereas the evaluation of treatment is determined by the degree to which the basic aims of therapy are realized. If the problem is effectively resolved, if symptoms are made ineffective or unnecessary, and if the patient develops greater maturity, insight, and perspective, the outcome of treatment may be regarded as satisfactory. The fact, however, that this fails to happen in countless therapeutic attempts indicates the need for constant evaluation of the techniques, concepts, and processes involved in psychological treatment. To this end, there should be unremitting research on the methods and outcomes of both diagnosis and therapy so that standards and criteria may be developed by which treatment procedures can be guided toward greater success (Hunt, 1952; Garfield & Kurz, 1952; Sells, 1952; Eysenck, 1952; Erickson, 1950, Chapter VIII; Wolff & Precker, 1952; Bromberg, 1962).

QUESTIONS AND PROJECTS FOR FURTHER STUDY

1. Explain in your own words the meaning of psychological diagnosis. How is diagnosis distinguished from etiology?
2. Write a brief essay on nondirective counseling, based on the work of Rogers and Curran.
3. What are the criteria by which counseling is distinguished from psycho-

therapy? Explain the relationships between education, guidance, and counseling.
4. Write a research paper on the principles and procedures of Alcoholics Anonymous and Recovery, Inc.
5. Describe in detail five personal qualities that are of particular value to effective counseling or psychotherapy.
6. Explain to what extent techniques of counseling or psychotherapy are determined by (a) the nature of the problem, (b) the characteristics of the client.
7. Write a book report on Axline's *Play therapy*, or Allen's *Psychotherapy with children*.

SELECTED COLLATERAL READINGS

ALLEN, F. H.   *Psychotherapy with children*. New York: Norton, 1942.

BERDIE, R. N.   (Ed.)   *Roles and relationships in counseling: Minnesota studies in student personnel*. Minneapolis: University of Minnesota Press, 1953.

BRAYFIELD, A. H.   (Ed.)   *Readings in modern methods of counseling*. New York: Appleton, 1950.

BUHLER, CHARLOTTE.   *Values in psychotherapy*. New York: Free Press, 1962.

DOLLARD, J., & MILLER, N. E.   *Personality and psychotherapy*. New York: McGraw-Hill, 1950.

ERICKSON, C. E.   *The counseling interview*. Englewood Cliffs, N.J.: Prentice-Hall, 1950.

LEVY, L. H.   *Psychological interpretation*. New York: Holt, Rinehart and Winston, 1963.

MC GOWAN, J., & SCHMIDT, L. D.   (Eds.)   *Counseling: readings in theory and practice*. New York: Holt, Rinehart and Winston, 1962.

ROGERS, C. R.   *On becoming a person: A therapist's view of psychotherapy*. New York: Houghton Mifflin, 1961.

SHOSTROM, E. L., & BRAMMER, L. M.   *The dynamics of the counseling process*. New York: McGraw-Hill, 1952.

TYLER, LEONA E.   *The work of the counselor*. (2d ed.) New York: Appleton, 1961.

WILLIAMSON, E. G.   *Counseling adolescents*. New York: McGraw-Hill, 1950.

Glossary

ABERRATION   Deviation from the usual or normal course.

ABNORMAL   Deviating from the usual, average, or normal in a quantitative as well as qualitative sense; also pathological.

ABNORMAL PSYCHOLOGY   A branch of psychology that studies deviant mental processes, conditions, and behavior, and unusual psychological phenomena.

ADJUSTMENT   The process of coping with internal and external demands, stresses, conflicts, frustrations, and problem situations by means of some personal response.

AMBIVALENCE   Contradictory feelings or attitudes toward the same person or thing, experienced simultaneously.

AMNESIA   A disorder of memory characterized by inability to recall past experiences or personal identity.

ANESTHESIA   Loss of sensation or sensitivity, either partial or total.

ANXIETY   Intense fearfulness or apprehension. When no real danger or threat exists, it is called neurotic anxiety.

APATHY   Emotional indifference; marked absence of feeling or emotion in situations that normally evoke such responses.

ATROPHY   Wasting away of a part of the body, for example, muscular atrophy.

AUTISTIC   Inordinately subjective or self-centered.

AUTOMATISM   An act or series of acts carried out without conscious volition.

AUTONOMIC NERVOUS SYSTEM   That part of the nervous system that regulates involuntary responses.

BEHAVIORISM   A system of psychology that emphasizes the study of objective responses to the exclusion of mental phenomena.

CENTRAL NERVOUS SYSTEM   That part of the nervous system that includes the brain and spinal cord.

CHRONIC   Pertaining to a condition or disorder that progresses slowly and persists over a long period of time.

CLINICAL PSYCHOLOGY   A branch of psychology concerned with the application of psychological facts, principles, and techniques to the solving of human problems.

COMBAT FATIGUE (war neurosis)   A term used to designate mental disorder precipitated by the stresses of battle.

COMPENSATION   A defense mechanism which tends to counterbalance or obscure any personal defect and inadequacy.

COMPLEX   An emotionally charged constellation of ideas, wishes, etc., usually unconscious.

COMPULSION   An irresistible impulse to act in a certain way, contrary to volition and judgment.

CONFLICT (mental)   A state of mind, often prolonged, that results from a clash between contrary motivations. It may be conscious or unconscious.

CONGENITAL   Present at or before birth, but not hereditary.

CONVERSION HYSTERIA   A neurosis characterized primarily by functional loss of sensory and motor functions.

CONVULSIVE THERAPY   The treatment of serious mental or personality disorders by means of metrazol, electric current, and other convulsants.

DEFENSE MECHANISMS   Adjustive reactions, usually unconscious, designed to protect the individual from personal limitations or from external stresses and frustrations.

487

DELINQUENCY   Socially nonconforming behavior committed by persons not legally of age.

DELUSION   A morbidly false belief usually resistant to logic or reason.

DEPRESSION   A mental condition involving emotional dejection, unpleasant feelings, and a sense of foreboding.

DETERMINISM   A theory of human conduct according to which all conduct is regarded as a necessary consequent of antecedent causes and conditions.

DEVELOPMENT   A process of progressive, internal change in the capacities and functions of living organisms directed toward complete maturation.

DIAGNOSIS   A clinical process by which the nature and classification of any disorder is determined by analysis of symptoms.

DIFFERENTIAL DIAGNOSIS   A technique of distinguishing between allied disorders by analysis of symptoms peculiar to one and not to the others.

DISORIENTATION   A state of confusion about place, time, or personal identity.

DISPLACEMENT   A mental mechanism by which emotions or feelings pertaining to one group of ideas are transferred to another (inappropriate) group.

DISSOCIATION   A mechanism by which a group of memories, ideas, etc., are functionally separated from normal mental life and thus function as a totality.

DYNAMIC PSYCHOLOGY   A branch of psychology that investigates the entire range of human motivations (needs, desires, and so on).

DYSFUNCTION   Disturbance, impairment, or abnormality in the functioning of an organ.

EGO   The whole person (I); that part of the person that mediates conscious experiences; in psychoanalysis, that part of the psyche that mediates between the id and reality.

EGOCENTRISM   A behavior mechanism used to force recognition and obscure inadequacy by boasting and self-aggrandizement.

EGO INTEGRITY   A quality of the ego that ensures internal harmony and consistency of response.

EGO SECURITY   A quality of the ego that ensures defense against thwarting, stress, and conflict.

EMERGENT   A property, quality, or reality that transcends its origin and cannot be predicted from the properties of its constituents.

EMOTION   A complex affective response characterized by feeling, excitement, and bodily changes.

EMPIRICAL   Pertaining to experience; applied to methods or subject matter based on observation.

ENDOCRINE GLANDS   A group of organs that secrete internally and pour their secretions directly into the blood or lymph.

ENURESIS   Involuntary discharge of the urine usually occurring at night and during sleep.

EROTIC   Of or pertaining to sex or sexual love.

ETIOLOGY   The scientific study of the causes of disease, mental disorder, or maladjustment.

EUPHORIA   Exaggerated feelings of well-being, often unfounded.

FANTASY THINKING   A mechanism by means of which one escapes from reality into a dream world where problems, conflicts, and frustrations are effectively reduced.

FEELING   The experience of pleasantness or unpleasantness.

FIXATION   Arrested (psychological) development at the child or adolescent level; persistence of outmoded responses.

FRIGIDITY (sexual)   Reduction or absence of sexual desire, usually caused by emotional disturbance.

FRUSTRATION   Blocking of motivational tendencies or behavior; hindrance in effecting adequate adjustment.

FUGUE   A flight. An amnesic (nonremembered) episode involving flight from familiar surroundings, usually of considerable duration.

FUNCTIONAL DISORDER   A disorder without known alteration or damage to underlying structure.

FUNCTIONAL PSYCHOSIS   A mental disease without known organic cause.

GERONTOLOGY, GERIATRICS   The scientific investigation of the characteristics and problems of old age.

GESTALT THEORY   A viewpoint in psychology that emphasizes the unitary character of experience and behavior as opposed to the analytic and elementaristic viewpoint.

GUILT, SENSE OF   The feeling or conviction of having contravened some principle, rule, or law. When unconscious and morbid, it is referred to as pathological guilt.

HEDONISM   The theory that the primary aim or determinant of human conduct is pleasure.

HORMONE   A specific chemical substance secreted by an endocrine gland that induces functional changes in other organs.

HOSTILITY   A feeling or attitude, often unconscious, involving behavior detrimental to individuals or groups against whom the hostility is directed.

HYPERESTHESIA   Excessive sensitivity of the skin or of one of the special senses.

HYPNOSIS   An artificially induced, trancelike state resembling sleep and characterized by heightened suggestibility; the process of inducing the hypnotic trance for experimental or therapeutic purposes.

HYPOCHONDRIA   Morbid concern about one's health.

HYSTERIA   A psychoneurotic disorder characterized by a wide variety of functional symptoms normally caused by organic diseases (such as anesthesia, amnesia, and so on). These symptoms are utilized for adjustive purposes in the reduction of conflict.

IDENTIFICATION   The unconscious assumption of identity with another person or a group for the enhancement of prestige or personal worth.

INFERIORITY, ATTITUDE OF   An attitude or complex, usually unconscious, engendered by feelings of inadequacy, lack of self-confidence, failure, and so on.

INSIGHT   In mental hygiene and psychotherapy, the understanding and evaluation of one's own characteristics, weaknesses, motivations, etc., by which mental health and adjustment are furthered.

INSOMNIA   Inability to sleep under normal conditions.

INSTINCT   An innate, unlearned, somewhat complex pattern of response characteristic of a given species. It differs from a reflex in that an instinct involves a need or impulse.

INTEGRATION   A process (or condition) whereby diverse elements in any structure or system are organized into a harmonious, coordinated whole. It is basic to mental health and adjustment.

INTROJECTION   A mechanism by which external qualities are adopted into the self.

INTROVERT   A person whose interests, attitudes, and activities are largely oriented toward self.

LIBIDO   A psychoanalytic term used to designate undifferentiated sexual energy or drive.

LOBOTOMY   A surgical technique for the relief of mental symptoms involving the frontal lobes of the brain.

MALADJUSTMENT   Inability to meet personal and environmental demands and to resolve conflicts and frustrations in a wholesome or efficient manner.

MALINGERING   The simulation of illness or disability.

MANIC–DEPRESSIVE (Psychosis)   A severe mental or personality disorder, characterized by alternating states of excitement and depression, and considerable impairment of intellectual functions.

MASCULINE PROTEST   In Adlerian theory, the desire to achieve masculine superiority as a cover up for inferiority, which is identified with femininity.

MATURITY   A state of growth and development that promotes the adequate adjustment of the organism.

MECHANISM   In psychology, an acquired response by which self-respect, ego-integrity, and so on, are maintained without the use of choice or deliberation.

MENTAL HYGIENE   The practical art of developing and utilizing principles and practices relating to mental health and adjustment and to the prevention of psychological disorders.

MIGRAINE   A psychosomatic disorder characterized predominately by severe headaches on one side and also by nausea and sensory disturbances.

MOTIVE   Any factor, intellectually evaluated, that stimulates volition of rational conduct.

NARCOANALYSIS   A therapeutic technique involving analysis while the patient is under the influence of a narcotic.

NARCOLEPSY   A condition of prolonged or pathological sleep or an uncontrollable desire for sleep.

NEED   A tension aroused in the organism by the absence or deprivation of some object, quality, or experience required for its well-being.

NEGATIVE IDENTIFICATION   The unconscious rejection of traits, attitudes, and so on, of another person or group with whom one is ordinarily closely related.

NEGATIVISM   An adjustment mechanism or disorder characterized by refusal, stubbornness, or rebellion.

NERVOUSNESS   A chronic emotional state marked by tenseness, restlessness, and irritability, and often manifested in behavioral symptoms (such as nail biting).

NEURASTHENIA   A psychoneurosis characterized by chronic fatigue, headache, insomnia, irritability, and vague aches and pains.

NEUROPSYCHIATRY   A branch of medicine which investigates and undertakes treatment of mental disorders, especially those involving the nervous system.

NEUROSIS   A relatively mild psychological disorder, the cause of which is psychogenic rather than organic; hence the term "psychoneurosis."

NEUROTIC   Pertaining to neurosis; a person suffering from a neurosis.

OBSESSION   An idea or idea complex with a strong emotional quality (usually disagreeable) that forces itself into and disturbs the normal processes of thought.

OEDIPUS COMPLEX   A psychoanalytic term to designate an excessive love relation between son and mother, which is accompanied by hostility toward the father.

ORGANIC PSYCHOSIS   A mental disorder or disease caused by injury to or pathology of the nervous system.

ORIENTATION   A particular outlook or viewpoint; also, good adjustment regarding place, time, and persons.

PARANOIA   A psychosis characterized by systematized fixed delusions, usually of a grandiose or persecutory nature.

PARESIS   Incomplete paralysis; a term used to indicate the mental disorder caused by syphilitic infection of the brain in which there is progressive mental and physical deterioration.

PATHOLOGY   A branch of medicine which treats of the essential nature of disease, particularly as it is reflected in structural and functional changes.

PERSONALITY   The organized, emergent totality of a human organism's individual characteristics, dispositions, values, and attitudes that regulate his adjustments to self and environment.

PHOBIA   A strong, morbid, persistent fear, usually of unknown origin.

PLAY THERAPY   A specialized therapeutic process utilizing play activities for the treatment of personality disorders in children.

PROGNOSIS   A prediction, based on diagnosis, of the probable outcome of a disease or disorder.

PROJECTION   A mechanism by which personal weaknesses, failures, and undesirable traits are attributed to external sources.

PROJECTIVE TECHNIQUES Specialized instruments (such as the Rorschach ink-blot test) for the investigation of personal traits and characteristics.

PSYCHASTHENIA A neurosis characterized by obsessions, scruples, phobias, and compulsive acts.

PSYCHIATRY A branch of medicine concerned with the diagnosis, treatment, and care of persons suffering from mental or personality disorders.

PSYCHOANALYSIS A theory and a method of treatment, originated by Sigmund Freud, relating to mental disorders.

PSYCHOGENIC Pertaining to causes or conditions that are psychological rather than physical in nature.

PSYCHONEUROSIS (See neurosis.)

PSYCHOPATHIC (Personality) Pertaining to mental and emotional disorders; a personality disorder characterized by weak character structure, impulsiveness, and emotional inadequacy.

PSYCHOSIS A severe mental or personality disorder, generally characterized by disorganization of personality and a progressive deterioration of mental functions. It may be organic or functional.

PSYCHOSOMATIC(S) Of or pertaining to mind and body taken as a unit; also, a specialized field of medical investigation that emphasizes the fundamental unity of mind and body.

PSYCHOSURGERY Brain surgery performed in the treatment of certain mental disorders.

PSYCHOTHERAPY Any clinical process involving psychological methods, such as psychoanalysis, used to treat mental disorders by the reduction of symptoms and their underlying causes.

RATIONALIZATION A mechanism by which an individual justifies doubtful attitudes, beliefs, or actions by giving spurious or inadequate reasons, and thus safeguards his own ego.

REGRESSION A reversion to an earlier and usually less adjustive pattern of response for purposes of preserving ego integrity or security.

REPRESSION In psychoanalysis, a mechanism by which emotionally toned experiences, wishes, feelings, and so on, are unconsciously forced out of or prevented from coming into consciousness because of their undesirable quality.

SADISM, SADISTIC Sexual abnormality in which sexual gratification is derived from the infliction of punishment or cruelty on another person.

SCHIZOPHRENIA A functional psychosis characterized by loss of contact with reality, disorganized thinking, and emotional apathy.

SELF–INSIGHT (See insight.)

SENILE DEMENTIA Mental disorder associated with old age or senility, and characterized by progressive mental deterioration, especially in memory functions.

SHOCK THERAPY A form of medical treatment of mental disorder which utilizes the shock effects produced by the injection of insulin for the alleviation of distressing symptoms and eventual cure.

SIBLING One of several offspring, of the same or different sex, produced by the same parents.

SOMATIC Organic or bodily as distinguished from mental or psychological.

SUBLIMATION A mechanism by which the energy of a drive or motive is redirected into other channels of activity.

SUPEREGO In psychoanalysis, that part of the mental make-up that functions as the conscience.

SYNDROME A more or less organized group of symptoms occurring together and characteristic of a certain disorder.

THERAPEUTIC Pertaining to the art of healing, or therapy.

TRAUMA, TRAUMATIC Of or pertaining to a wound or injury, whether physical or psychological.

UNCONSCIOUS Total absence of awareness. In Freudian psychology especially, mental processes that are inaccessible to the subject but still exert a dynamic influence on mental life and behavior.

WORRY Persistent nonadjustive thinking about personal problems, characterized by a strong, unpleasant emotional tone.

APPENDIX

Film Bibliography

I. GENERAL SOURCES

AMERICAN HOME ECONOMICS AS-SOCIATION. *List of films on family relations and child development,* 1960. Published by the Association.

FATTU, N. A., & BLAIN, B. B. *Selected films for teacher education: A bibliography.* Bloomington, Ind.: Indiana University, 1950.

GOVERNMENT PRINTING OFFICE. *Mental health motion pictures: A selective guide,* 1960. Washington, D.C.: U.S. Government Printing Office, 1960.

LEKKERKERKER, E. C. Films and mental health. *Bull. World Fed. Ment. Hlth.,* 1953, 5, 230–235.

NICHTENHAUSER, A., COLEMAN, M. L., & RUHE, D. S. *Films in psychiatry, psychology, and mental health.* New York: Health Education Council, 1953.

SPITZ, R. A. Films and mental health: Principles for the use of motion pictures for teaching mental health. *Bull. World Fed. Ment. Hlth.,* 1952, 4, 35–40.

U.S. DEPARTMENT OF HEALTH, EDUCATION, AND WELFARE. *A directory of 3660 16 mm. film libraries.* Washington, D.C.: Office of Education, 1959.

U.S. NATIONAL INSTITUTE OF MENTAL HEALTH. *Mental health motion pictures, 1952: A selective guide.* Washington, D.C.: U.S. Government Printing Office, 1952.

WORLD FEDERATION FOR MENTAL HEALTH. *International catalog of mental health films* (ed. 2), 1960. Published by the World Federation.

II. FILM PUBLISHERS AND DISTRIBUTORS

BA–VI Bureau of Audio-Visual Instructions, State University of Iowa, Iowa City, Iowa.

CF Coronet Films, Coronet Building, Chicago, Illinois 60601.

CMC Center for Mass Communication (Columbia University), 1125 Amsterdam Ave., New York, N.Y. 10025.

DHEW U.S. Department of Health, Education, and Welfare, Office of Education, Washington, D.C.

EBF Encyclopedia Britannica Films, 38 W. 32d St., New York, N.Y. 10001.

EGF Educators Guide to Free Films, Educators Progress Service, Randolph, Wisconsin.

IFB International Film Bureau, Inc., 332 S. Michigan Ave., Chicago, Illinois 60604.

MAMH Massachusetts Association for Mental Health, Inc., 38 Chauncy St., Boston, Mass. 02111.

MHFB Mental Health Film Board, Inc., 164 E. 38th St., New York, N.Y. 10016.

MHI Mental Health Institute, Inc., 25

W. 81st Street, New York, N.Y. 10024.

MHMC Mental Health Materials Center, 104 E. 25th Street, New York, N.Y. 10010.

MPD Motion Picture Division, Superintendent of Documents, Government Printing Office, Washington, D.C. 20402.

NAMH National Association for Mental Health, 267 W. 25th Street, New York, N.Y. 10001.

McGH McGraw-Hill Films, 330 W. 42d Street, New York, N.Y. 10036.

MOT March of Time, 369 Lexington Avenue, New York, N.Y. 10017

NFB National Film Board of Canada, Suite 819, 680 Fifth Ave., New York, N.Y. 10000.

NYU New York University Film Library, 26 Washington Place, New York, N.Y. 10003.

PCR Psychological Cinema Register, Pennsylvania State University, University Park, Pa. 16802.

SKF Smith, Kline and French Laboratories, 1500 Spring Garden Street, Philadelphia, Pa. 19101.

III. SELECTED FILMS (16 mm., sound)

Alcoholism (EBF). 22 min.

This film portrays alcoholism as a mental health problem and as an illness that can respond to treatment. The role of Alcoholics Anonymous in combating alcoholism is discussed. The film emphasizes the need for increased treatment facilities and for a better understanding of alcoholism as an illness.

Alcoholism: The Revolving Door (SKF). 30 min.

This film outlines the early treatment of alcoholism and the use of psychotherapy and drug therapy for the alcoholic. It illustrates conditions on "skid row" and the steps leading to alcoholism. A meeting of Alcoholics Anonymous is also shown.

Anger at Work (IFB). 21 min.

This film depicts one of the most common mental mechanisms, the displacement of anger onto other people. Techniques for handling such overwhelming feelings as anger, resentment, and frustration are explained.

Angry Boy (MHFB). 33 min.

The film depicts the problem of hidden hostility in a child that is expressed finally in terms of stealing. The hostility is traced to the home life of the child where a well-intentioned mother has been taking out her hostility toward her mother and her husband in an overprotective attitude toward the child. The film shows how the child is helped by guidance and counseling.

Anna M.: The Development of Emotional Problems in a Child Reared in a Neurotic Environment (NYU) 60 min. Silent.

This film shows a child of superior intelligence whose mode of adjusting is seen in her behavior. The interaction of her hereditary endowment with her neurotic parents, a sister, and grandparents results in a personality difficult to evaluate. The film gives the impression of a fairly healthy child with depressive, hysterical, and inhibited tendencies.

Beginnings of Conscience (McG-H). 16 min.

The social conscience of an adult client is traced back to his socialization as a child. The film indicates how the subject learns from parents, teachers, and school mates what is right and what is wrong.

Benefits of Looking Ahead (CF). 11 min.

By encouraging students to look ahead, this film helps them think constructively about immediate problems and about working toward achieving their future goals. It points up the fact that planning needs a long-range view supported by shorter-range objectives.

Bitter Welcome (MHFB). 36 min.

This film depicts the struggle of a discharged patient who overcomes the fears and prejudices of his fellow workers. His efforts to readjust to reality and to keep his job are depicted in the film. One main purpose is to help change community attitudes toward a person who has suffered a mental breakdown. Borderline (MHFB). 27 min.

This film dramatizes the use and mis-use of punishment, with sometimes tragic results, in the story of a rebellious fifteen-year-old girl. A skilled therapist at the resident treatment center helps this adolescent and her mother develop insight into their problems.

Breakdown (NFB). 40 min.

The film has to do with Ann, 23 years old, who has always been a model daughter. From a quiet, clever, and obedient child she has grown into a charming and responsible woman hold-ing a good job in the office of a family friend. But there is a seemingly unex-plainable deterioration in her work, and at home she remains away from meals, sulks in her room, refuses to see her friends, and is suspicious of all the food prepared at home. The film makes an appeal for the need to remove the stigma traditionally attached to mental illness.

Child Behind the Wall (SKF). 30 min.

Opening with reports from prominent leaders in the field of mental health, this "March of Medicine" documentary film emphasizes the lack of proper facil-ities and trained personnel for emotion-ally disturbed children, as well as the need for increased public understanding of their problems. The film shows a case study of a child undergoing treatment.

The Children of Change (IFB). 31 min.

Children of Change dramatizes one of America's most pressing problems— the special stresses and strains placed on children whose mothers work outside the home and who must adjust to two jobs. Considering that about thirty mil-lion American women are now employed outside their homes, of whom seven and one-half million have children under 18, the question of who takes care of the children during the day becomes crucial. Some of these questions and answers are depicted in Children of Change.

Community Mental Health (MHFB). 31 min.

The film shows how a community can achieve a broad mental health pro-gram.

Counselor's Day (McG-H). 12 min.

The film shows a counselor's day as a busy one with appointments, consulta-tion, teaching, extracurricular activities, and professional writing. It also shows the counselor's work relationship with the school staff and students. The film shows the counselor in his relationships to his family, and points to the fact that an understanding of home relations, as well as school relations, is essential to successful counseling.

David—The Profile of a Problem Drinker (NAMH). 27 min.

Some basic insecurities and danger signals leading to alcoholism are illus-trated in this film of a young architect whose dependence on alcohol disrupts his life. The use of drugs, psychother-apy, and hospitalization to combat the addiction are shown in the film.

Developing Self-Reliance (CF). 11 min.

In this film it is shown how depend-ency grows, and how necessary self-reliance is to successful endeavor and adjustment. It analyzes steps in develop-ing self-reliance, including assuming re-sponsibility, being informed, determin-ing the direction of personal strivings, and making personal decisions. A clear distinction is drawn between dependence and seeking advice or help.

Diagnosis and Planning Adjustments in Counseling (McG-H). 18 min.

This film outlines the techniques for diagnosing the case and illustrates meth-ods employed by the counselor to help the student work out his own personal adjustments. The film ends on a note of optimism as we see a gradual resolution of the client's problems.

The Drop-Out (MHFB). 29 min.

When the film opens, Joe has dropped out of school and is the envy of many former classmates because he has a job and a car. Flashbacks are used to show Joe's discontent with senior high school, his boredom in class, and the efforts made by his counselor to persuade him not to leave school. Joe's dislike of school began long before, and part of the blame is his home environment. Suggestions are offered for tackling the drop-out problem.

Emotional Health (McG-H). 20 min.

This film has three objectives, to as-sure people that emotional upsets are common, to indicate a need for professional counsel and care after disturbance is prolonged, and to explain in simplified language the basic techniques of psychiatric treatment. Through a case study, the film points out that emotional upset of the type depicted can be cured by bringing to the patient a better understanding of his problem.

Emotional Maturity (McG-H). 20 min.

The film dramatizes the immature behavior of a high school boy and shows some of the consequences of failure to channel emotions into positive actions and feelings.

Endocrine Glands—How They Affect You (McG-H). 15 min.

The film indicates how the endocrine glands secrete hormones that regulate the life processes in the body and influence appearance, personality, and behavior.

Eye of the Beholder (NYU). 26 min.

This film illustrates the idea that people often see what they want to see, what they are prepared to see, but not what actually exists. The film shows a series of incidents involving a young artist, described by his mother, a waiter, a cab driver, his landlord, a charwoman, and a model. In this way the film indicates the pitfalls of subjective interpretation of events and actions.

Facing Reality (McG-H). 12 min.

This film illustrates and explains some common defense mechanisms as well as typical escape mechanisms—rationalization, projection, negativism, daydreaming, identification, and malingering. A major part of the film describes the case of Mike Squires, a basically attractive boy who has developed a strong negativistic attitude.

Families First (RKO–NYU). 17 min.

The film takes the position that the home is responsible for child training and that when this is neglected delinquency is the result. It also indicates that the needs of the child cannot be met adequately by any institution outside the family.

Family Circles (NFB). 31 min.

Freddie Price, a first grader, is proud that his work will be shown on visitors' day, but his parents are too busy to share in his triumph or to realize what it means to him. Freddie's parents fail to realize that pride in his accomplishments must be shared by home and school alike. The film emphasizes throughout, by case studies, the importance of family living.

Fears of Children (MHFB). 30 min.

This is a film about Paul, a normal five-year-old, and his well-intentioned parents. In a series of episodes the film shows how Paul's fears of the dark, of being alone, of new situations, and so on, are related to his feelings about his parents. In a discussion between the parents, they reach a new understanding of Paul's behavior.

Feelings of Depression (NFB). 30 min.

The film relates the case history of John Murray, in his early 30's, who suddenly suffers periods of great depression. Neither John's wife nor his partner is aware that important factors, not of recent origin, underlie his depression. They are rooted deep in his emotional history and the end result of a long series of childhood events which helped shape his character. The film indicates that John may recover spontaneously, or, through the growing resources of psychiatry, may be helped to understand himself more fully.

Feeling of Hostility (NFB). 27 min.

This film is concerned with the problem of Clare, outwardly a successful, attractive young woman, sure of herself, but insecure and constrained in her personal relationships. The mechanism underlying her success is a feeling of hostility, unconsciously working to make her so successful that she will never need the love she finds so hard to give and to accept.

Feeling of Rejection (NFB). 23 min.

The film presents a case history of a young woman who learned in childhood not to risk disapproval by taking independent action. It shows the harmful effects of her inability to engage in normal competition and analyzes the causes of her trouble. Therapy methods that helped the girl to face and examine her problems are shown briefly.

Finding Your Life Work (NYU). 22 min.

This is one of a series of films on vocational guidance, aimed at young people. It summarizes a number of points under two headings: knowing one's self, and knowing the job situation.

Habit Patterns (McG-H). 15 min.

The film depicts the routine of a girl, Barbara, who is never prepared, never ready, never on time. Her room is always disorderly and her clothes are never neat. She has built up a pattern of sloppy habits that give her no time in which to be pleasant or civil at home. Because there is no planning, she has no time for interest in books, newspapers, or concerts. Throughout the film Barbara is contrasted with Helen, a girl who has learned to plan her tomorrow the day before, who knows what she wants to do and how she wants to look, and arranges her living so that she can achieve her goals.

He Acts His Age (NFB). 13 min.

The film describes the activities of children at different age levels and suggests that such activities are an index of emotional and mental development. It depicts the one-year-old, the two-year-old, the child at five, at nine, and at twelve years of age.

Heredity and Family Environment (McG-H). 9 min.

The film depicts a high school instructor illustrating the roles of heredity and environment in actual living. Using one of the class members, the film depicts her physical, emotional, and mental development and her genetic background. It concludes by pointing out that each person has a hand also in developing his own nature. Limitations are set by heredity, but within those limits there is room to grow and to develop one's own capacities.

The Hickory Stick (IFB). 29 min.

Many parents and teachers are caught between conflicting theories of discipline. This film provides insight into the building of character in young children, and considers the nature of good discipline in relation to permissiveness.

In Time of Trouble (McG-H). 14 min.

This is a film about marital difficulties, and concerns the wife who is worried about her husband's drinking. It shows, through the action of a pastoral counselor, how the wife's own personality is the real source of the problem.

It Takes All Kinds (McG-H). 20 min.

The film indicates that the right marriage partner need not be one's exact counterpart, but that a happy marriage does require that the two personalities must complement each other. The film shows a series of young people, each one reacting to an identical tense situation and each one disclosing the essential pattern of his own personality. The successful marriage will be one where the partners choose each other with care, and then accept each other for what they are.

The Lonely Night (MHFB). 62 min.

This is the story of a young woman's journey out of the dark hours of emotional disturbance, and depicts the process of psychiatric treatment candidly and completely. By contrast, it shows the kind of family life that can help build emotional strength leading to normal adulthood.

The Long Way Back (MHFB). 22 min.

This is a film designed to show lay persons how they can provide a link between the community and the patient in the mental hospital. It shows how a volunteer can help out in the area of recreation with the goal of drawing the patients out of themselves.

Marriage and Divorce (MOT). 15 min.

Emphasizing the extent of divorce, the film surveys the problem of broken homes and offers the opinion of experts about what should be done.

Marriage Series (McG-H). 5 Parts, 14 to 22 minutes each.

This is a series of five films that deal with marriage and divorce. Each one of the films depicts some aspect of marriage, including the relationship between marriage and divorce, the ideals and goals of marital life, and other aspects of marital life.

Maternal Deprivation in Young Children (NYU). 30 min.

This film shows the effects of maternal deprivation in young children. The children are between ages 1 and 2½ years. All have been reared in institutions that have not provided for stable and intimate relationships with one person. The question is raised how far serious damage at this critical age can be overcome. Many answers are left for further research.

Meeting the Needs of Adolescents (McG-H). 19 min.

This film describes ways in which parents may help prepare children for adulthood. It shows how the teenager's basic physical needs are met, how his mental development is stimulated and directed, how he is guided in his spiritual growth, and how parents can aid children in making a satisfactory adjustment in later life.

Meeting Emotional Needs in Childhood (NYU). 32 min.

This film is intended for parents and teachers and others interested in children. It focuses on the 7- to 10-year-old in school and home and is concerned with the attitude toward people and sense of community responsibility that the child develops as he grows to adulthood. The film suggests the ways in which parents and teachers may help these children meet these needs.

Mental Health (EBF). 12 min.

This presentation defines good mental health, its characteristics, and its importance to the individual and to society. It sets forth a series of simple, straightforward rules for keeping mentally fit and illustrates them with incidents from the lives of various members of the high school graduating class.

Mental Health Year (MHFB). 59 min.

This film is a visual survey of mental health over the world, which shows psychiatric treatment and facilities in twenty-two countries and emphasizes the contrast between modern therapeutic procedures and the restraint and confinement of past eras.

The Nation's Mental Health (MOT). 18 min.

This film emphasizes the dimensions of the mental health problem in the United States, and shows the facilities in the nation's largest training center at Topeka, and the work of the National Association of Mental Health in helping communities set up mental health clinics.

The Need to Work (SKF). 24 min. Color.

This film describes successful industrial therapy programs in two British mental hospitals. It shows clearly how patients benefit from this kind of work therapy. Patients with various forms of mental illness are seen performing a wide range of jobs.

The Ninety-First Day (SKF). 80 min.

This film, enacted by professional actors, is the story of a man's breakdown, his admission to a mental hospital, and his wife's subsequent struggle to get him the treatment he needs for a successful return to society. It is a production of high professional quality.

Out of Darkness (NYU). 55 min.

This film, a compelling and sensitive report of one woman's step-by-step recovery from mental illness, was produced by CBS Public Affairs in cooperation with the American Psychiatric Association and the National Association for Mental Health. It relates the story of a young woman, mute and withdrawn, who is hospitalized for a mental illness. After treatment, her indifference fades, she smiles for the first time, and speaks the first word.

Overdependency (NFB). 32 min.

This film describes the case of Jimmy, an attractive young man, whose life was crippled by behavior patterns carried over from a too-dependent childhood. The film indicates that Jimmy's illness has no physical cause, and that he finds it difficult to face and deal with the ordinary problems of life, taking frequent refuge in comfort by his wife and mother. Jimmy gradually begins to understand the emotional causes of his illness and his own fear and takes hold of life with new confidence.

Pathological Anxiety (IFB). 30 min.

This film is a study of psychoneurotic conditions and examines the effect of mental disorder on behavior. The effort of the patient to suppress his hostilities results in a sense of terror and panic that interferes with his leading a normal life.

Personality and Emotions (EBF). 13 min.

This film, designed for high school and college audiences, is a study in personality development and mental health and gives an overview of the development of the emotions from infancy through early childhood. It emphasizes the importance of emotional maturity to the development of personality.

Planning Your Career (EBF). 16 min.

This film is designed to show high school students who are thinking about their future careers the three basic steps of procedure: learning about yourself, learning about vocations that interest you, and comparing your own interests and abilities with the requirements of a selected vocation.

Preface to a Life (CMC). 29 min.

This film tries to show how attitudes influence adult actions and everyday situations, and how incidents that seem trivial can make a difference in the way a child develops. It promotes the idea that children must be understood and respected as individual, growing personalities with their own emotional needs and rights.

Problem Children (NYU). 20 min.

This is a film about two children, Roy and Jimmy, in the seventh grade of an American public school, who present special problems for the teacher. The film stresses the plea that there are problem children because there are problem homes, schools, and communities.

Problem Drinkers (MOT). 19 min.

This film presents the story of what has been done to date by such well-known organizations as Alcoholics Anonymous, and the Research Council on Problems of Alcohol. The film describes an alcoholic's downfall and his rehabilitation, and shows how he slips from moderate drinking into uncontrollable excess, how he is slowly rehabilitated, and his ultimate recovery.

Problems of Pupil Adjustment (2 Parts) (McG-H). 20 min. each.

These two films deal with the dropout and the stay-in in a typical high school situation. They have many suggestions for understanding the reasons for drop-outs and for overcoming the drop-out situation.

A Psychopath (IFB). 30 min.

This is a study of antisocial personality disorders. The film presents the case history of a psychopath whose criminal tendencies constitute a threat to the community. The patient in this case is a convicted burglar of high intelligence.

The Quiet One (NYU). 67 min.

This film tells the story of Donald Peters, who is an only child and a victim of a disrupted home in New York's Harlem section. Abandoned by his parents, Donald is forced to live with an unsympathetic grandmother. He makes no friends, never smiles, hardly ever speaks, and hides his bewilderment and bitterness within himself. At the age of ten he is sent to a special school, but eventually runs away. He returns to the school and is helped toward establishing a more hopeful future.

Roots of Happiness (MHFB). 25 min.

This is a film about family life which stresses the role of the father. Filmed in Puerto Rico, it carries a message that can apply to families everywhere. It dramatizes the contrast between a family in which the father respects and loves his wife and children and a family where discord and hostility prevail. It also shows how children can gain emotional strength from a family environment in which each person has dignity and an opportunity to be himself.

Search for Happiness (MOT). 17 min.

This film points out that the complicated machinery of modern living, which is intended to make life easier, seems on the whole to succeed only in making life more frustrating and complex. It shows modern man turning for advice and counseling toward whatever source is available, always certain that a miraculous solution to his problem is just around the corner.

Should I Go to College? (EBF). 29 min.

The film presents an interview with a distinguished university professor who answers many of the questions asked by students trying to decide whether or not to go to college. The film considers such issues as entrance requirements, prerequisites, costs, and self-support.

Shyness (NFB). 23 min.

This film deals with shyness in children, its causes, and how it may be dealt with by parents and teachers. From a description of the lonely existence of a shy adult, the film turns to a study of three children, all of whom exhibit a certain degree of shyness. The film emphasizes that confidence-destroying demands of parents have disposed these children to shyness. Together the teacher, psychiatrist, and parents bring about a change in the children's attitudes toward themselves and others.

Stress (NFB). 11 min.

This film introduces Dr. Hans Selye, noted researcher in the area of stress phenomena. The film clarifies his concept of stress in relation to disease. Discussing and illustrating the phenomenon of stress, the film concludes by showing the results obtained in the treatment of arthritis with a hormone substance, cortizone.

This Is Robert (NYU). 80 min.

This film traces the development of Robert, an aggressive, difficult, but very appealing child. His aggression is seen as a strong defensive counterattack against the whole encroaching world. The film was developed over a period of five years making it possible to show Robert's development in longitudinal sections and the continuing influence of guidance.

Ulcer at Work (NAMH). 23 min.

This film presents the case history of an ulcer patient and illustrates both the physical and the emotional aspects of the illness. The dynamics of psychosomatic disorders are indicated.

Unconscious Motivation (NYU). 38 min.

This film demonstrates how everyday thoughts, feelings, and actions may be influenced by unconscious motives. It also shows some standard psychological techniques used to detect the presence of troublesome repressed ideas. Emphasis is put in the film on an understanding of the dynamics of neurosis and the influence of such feelings as guilt and anxiety.

Understanding Aggression (NYU). 27 min.

The film describes methods used in a mental hospital to help nurses and attendants understand aggression in their patients. Emphasis is put on the staff understanding themselves and becoming more aware of their own feelings and reactions to the patients in order to work more effectively with them.

We, the Mentally Ill (SKF). 30 min.

This is a film report of the first public television program ever enacted and narrated by mental patients. Hospital pa-

tients perform in a historical drama about mental illness based on the life of Dorothea Dix, who crusaded for better care and treatment of the mentally ill. It also discusses the problem of crowded conditions and shortage of personnel in the large state mental hospitals and demonstrates therapies which have revolutionized the treatment of the mentally ill.

What Is Conscience? (CF). 11 min.

This film discusses the effects of conscience and how an understanding of the role of conscience can improve mental health. Explanations of conscience are presented and dramatic incidents of the implication of conscience are developed to provide a background for study and discussion.

Who's Delinquent? (RKO–NYU). 16 min.

The film action takes place in a typical American town in which there occurs an incident involving two boys who steal a car and nearly kill a local policeman. The city editor of the town's newspaper sets out to discover the causes of juvenile delinquency in this area. His reporters discover that delinquency usually begins at home, but that the whole town bears some responsibility. The film ends with the townspeople meeting in order to solve the problem.

Who Will Teach Your Child? (NFB). 24 min.

The film depicts a series of classroom situations which illustrate what teaching means to different persons. It is an excellent study of the teacher's vital role in the child's mental health and development.

Working and Playing to Health (MHFB). 35 min.

This film is a dramatization of the uses of recreational, occupational, and industrial therapy in a mental hospital. It was actually photographed in a state institution.

Youth and the Law (MHFB). 36 min.

This film dramatizes the role of the police as they work with the community organizations to guide youthful energies into constructive channels and to prevent delinquency. It is a valuable tool for professional personnel working with adolescents.

References

ABRAMOVITZ, A. B., & BURNHAM, ELAINE. Exploring potentials for mental health in the classroom. In L. D. Crow & Alice Crow (Eds.), *Mental hygiene for teachers: A book of readings.* New York: Macmillan, 1963. Pp. 16–23.

ABRAMS, E. N. A comparison of normals and neuropsychiatric veterans on the Rosenzweig Picture-Frustration Study. *J. clin. Psychol.,* 1953, 9, 24–26.

ACADEMY OF RELIGION AND MENTAL HEALTH. *Religion, science, and mental health.* New York: New York University Press, 1959.

ADAMS, J. F. *Problems in counseling.* New York: Macmillan, 1962.

ADLER, A. *Study of organ inferiority and its psychical compensation.* (Trans. by S. E. Jelliffe.) New York: Nerv. Ment. Dis. Publ. Co., 1917.

ADLER, A. The feeling of inferiority and the striving for recognition. *Proceedings of the Royal Society of Medicine,* 1927, 20, 1181–1186.

ALLEN, F. H. *Psychotherapy with children.* New York: Norton, 1942.

ALLERS, R. *The psychology of character.* (Trans. by E. B. Strauss.) New York: Sheed & Ward, 1943.

ALLINSMITH, W., & GOETHALS, G. W. *The role of schools in mental health.* New York: Basic Books, 1962.

ALLISON, J., & HUNT, D. E. Social desirability and the expression of aggression under varying conditions of frustration. *J. consult. Psychol.,* 1959, 23, 528–532.

ALLPORT, G. W. *Personality: A psychological interpretation.* New York: Holt, Rinehart and Winston, 1937.

ALLPORT, G. W. *The individual and his religion.* New York: Macmillan, 1950.

ALLPORT, G. W. The trend in motivational theory. *Amer. J. Orthopsychiat.,* 1953, 23, 107–119.

ALLPORT, G. W. *Pattern and growth in personality.* New York: Holt, Rinehart and Winston, 1961.

ALLPORT, G. W. Behavioral science, religion, and mental health. *J. relig. Hlth.,* 1963, 2, 187–197.

ALTSCHULE, M. D. *Bodily physiology in mental and emotional disorders.* New York: Grune & Stratton, 1953.

ANDERSON, J. E. *The psychology of development and personal adjustment.* New York: Holt, Rinehart and Winston, 1949.

ANDERSON, J. E. The relation of attitude to adjustment. *Education,* 1952, 73, 210.

ANDREW, GWEN, & MIDDLEWOOD, ESTHER L. The goals of mental-health education commonly selected by a group of experts. In J. M. Seidman (Ed.), *Educating for mental health.* New York: Crowell, 1963. Pp. 196–203.

ANGYAL, A. The convergence of psychotherapy and religion. *J. pastoral Care,* 1952, 5, 4–14.

APPEL, J. W. Incidence of neuropsychiatric disorders in the United States Army in World War II. *Amer. J. Psychiat.,* 1946, 102, 433–436.

ARNOLD, M. B., & GASSON, J. A. Feelings and emotions as dynamic factors in personality integration. In M. B. Arnold & J. A. Gasson (Eds.), *The human person.* New York: Ronald, 1954. Pp. 294–313.

ASHLEY MONTAGUE, M. F. *Prenatal influences.* Springfield, Ill.: Charles C Thomas, 1962.

ATKIN, E. L., in conjunction with the Staff of the Child Study Association. *Aggressiveness in children.* New York: Child Study Association of America, 1950.

AUSUBEL, D. P. *Ego development and the personality disorders: A developmental approach to psychopathology.* New York: Grune & Stratton, 1952.

501

AUSUBEL, D. P. Relationship between shame and guilt in the socializing process. *Psychol. Rev.*, 1955, 62, 378–390.

AUSUBEL, D. P. A new look at classroom discipline. In J. M. Seidman (Ed.), *Educating for mental health.* New York: Crowell, 1963. Pp. 264–274.

AXLINE, V. M. *Play therapy.* Boston: Houghton Mifflin, 1947.

BABCOCK, H. *Psychological and psychiatric concepts of normality.* Bull. No. 27. New York: Vocational Adjustment Bureau, n.d. Pp. 4–5.

BABCOCK, H. A neurosis? Or neurotic behavior? *J. Psychol.*, 1947, 17, 61.

BAILEY, SISTER AGNES THERESE. Aggressiveness in infancy and early childhood. *Cath. educ. Rev.*, 1946, 44, 421–429.

BALLER, W. R., & CHARLES, D. C. *The psychology of human growth and development.* New York: Holt, Rinehart and Winston, 1961.

BANDURA, A., & HUSTON, ALETHA C. Identification as a process of incidental learning. *J. abnorm. soc. Psychol.*, 1961, 63, 311–318.

BANDURA, A., ROSS, DOROTHEA, & ROSS, SHIELA A. Transmission of aggression through imitation of aggressive models. *J. abnorm. soc. Psychol.*, 1961, 63, 575–582.

BARAHAL, G. D. Personality problems and vocational planning. *Personnel guid. J.*, 1953, 31, 224–226.

BARKER, R. The effect of frustration upon cognitive ability. *Charact. & Pers.*, 1938, 7, 145–150.

BARKER, R., DEMBO, T., & LEWIN, K. *Frustration and regression: An experiment with young children.* Iowa City, Iowa: University of Iowa Press, 1941.

BARKER, R. G. Ecology and motivation. In M. R. Jones (Ed.), *Nebraska symposium on motivation.* Lincoln: University of Nebraska Press, 1960. Pp. 1–49.

BARKER, R. G., & WRIGHT, BEATRICE A. The social psychology of adjustment to physical disability. In J. F. Garrett (Ed.), *Psychological aspects of physical disability.* Bull. No. 210. Washington, D.C.: U.S.

Office of Vocational Rehabilitation, n.d.

BARKER, R. G., WRIGHT, BEATRICE A., MEYERSON, L., & GONICK, MOLLIE R. *Adjustment to physical handicap and illness.* Bull. No. 55, rev. New York: Social Science Research Council, 1953.

BARKER, R. G., WRIGHT, BEATRICE A., & GONICK, MOLLIE R. *Adjustment to physical handicap and illness.* Bull. No. 55. New York: Social Science Research Council, 1946.

BARR, A. S. Characteristics of successful teachers. In L. D. Crow & Alice Crow (Eds.), *Mental hygiene for teachers: A book of readings.* New York: Macmillan, 1963. Pp. 440–445.

BARRETT, L. The mature person. *Ment. Hyg., N.Y.*, 1962, 46, 98–102.

BARRON, F. *Creativity and psychological health.* Princeton, N.J.: Van Nostrand, 1963.

BARTHEL, C. E., & CROWNE, D. P. The need for approval, task categorization, and perceptual defense. *J. consult. Psychol.*, 1962, 26, 547–555.

BARUCH, DOROTHY W., & MILLER, H. *Sex in marriage.* New York: Harper & Row, 1962.

BARZUN, J. *The house of intellect.* New York: Harper & Row, 1959.

BATESON, G. The frustration-aggression hypothesis. *Psychol. Rev.*, 1941, 48, 350–355.

BATESON, G. Cultural determinants of personality. In J. McV. Hunt (Ed.), *Personality and the behavior disorders.* New York: Ronald Press, 1944. Vol. II, pp. 714–735.

BEACH, F. A. *Hormones and behavior.* New York: Harper & Row, 1948.

BEACH, F. A. The descent of instinct. *Psychol. Rev.*, 1955, 62, 401–410.

BEACH, F. A., & JAYNES, J. Effects of early experience upon the behavior of animals. *Psychol. Bull.*, 1954, 51, 239–263.

BEAVEN, R. J. Christian faith and the psychological study of man. *J. pastoral Care*, 1951, 5, 53–60.

BEERS, C. W. *A mind that found itself.* New York: Doubleday, 1937.

BELLER, E. K. Exploratory studies of dependency. *Trans. N. Y. Acad. Sci.*, 1959, 21, 414–426.

BELOFF, H. Two forms of social conformity: Acquiescent and conventionality. *J. abnorm. soc. Psychol.*, 1958, 56, 99–104.

BENDER, LAURETTA. Genesis of hostility in children. *Amer. J. Psychiat.*, 1948, 105, 241–245.

BENDER, LAURETTA (Ed.) *Aggression, hostility, and anxiety in children.* Springfield, Ill.: Charles C Thomas, 1953.

BENEDICT, R. Culture and the abnormal. *J. genet. Psychol.*, 1934, 10, 59–82.

BENNETT, E. *The search for emotional security.* New York: Ronald, 1959.

BENNETT, MARGARET E. *College and life.* (ed. 4.) New York: McGraw-Hill, 1952.

BENNETT, MARGARET E. *Guidance and counseling in groups.* (ed. 2) New York: McGraw-Hill, 1963.

BERDIE, R. F. (Ed.) *Roles and relationships in counseling.* Minnesota Studies in Student Personnel Work, No. 3. Minneapolis: University of Minnesota Press, 1953.

BERG, C. The fundamental nature of anxiety. *Brit. J. med. Psychol.*, 1951, 24, 232–241.

BERG, I., & FOX, V. Factors in homicides committed by 200 males. *J. soc. Psychol.*, 1947, 26, 109–119.

BERG, I. A. The clinical interview and the case record. In L. A. Pennington & I. A. Berg (Eds.), *An introduction to clinical psychology.* (ed. 2) New York: Ronald, 1954. Pp. 91–127.

BERGLER, E. Differential diagnosis between "normal" and "neurotic" aggression. *Quart. rev. Psychiat. Neurol.*, 1946, 1, 1–5.

BERGLER, E., & KROGER, W. S. *Kinsey's myth of female sexuality.* New York: Grune & Stratton, 1954.

BERKOWITZ, L. The expression and reduction of hostility. *Psychol. Bull.*, 1958, 55, 257–283.

BERKOWITZ, L. Anti-Semitism and the displacement of aggression. *J. abnorm. soc. Psychol.*, 1959, 59, 182–187.

BERKOWITZ, L. Repeated frustrations and expectations in hostility arousal. *J. abnorm. soc. Psychol.*, 1960, 60, 422–429.

BERKOWITZ, L., GREEN, J. A., & MACAULAY, JACQUELINE R. Hostility catharsis as the reduction of emotional tension. *Psychiatry*, 1962, 25, 23–31.

BERKOWITZ, L., & HOLMES, D. S. The generalization of hostility to disliked objects. *J. Pers.*, 1959, 27, 565–577.

BERLYNE, D. C. *Conflict arousal and curiosity.* New York: McGraw-Hill, 1960.

BERMAN, L. The mental health of the educator. *Ment. Hyg., N.Y.*, 1954, 38, 422–429.

BERNARD, H. W. *Toward better personal adjustment.* New York: McGraw-Hill, 1951.

BERNARD, H. W. *Mental hygiene for classroom teachers.* New York: McGraw-Hill, 1952.

BERNARD, H. W. Positive principles of mental hygiene. In L. D. Crow & Alice Crow (Eds.), *Mental hygiene for teachers: A book of readings.* New York: Macmillan, 1963. Pp. 108–115.

BERTOCCI, P. A. The psychological self, the ego, and personality. *Psychol. Rev.*, 1945, 52, 91–99.

BIBER, BARBARA. Schooling as an influence in developing healthy personality. In Ruth Kotinsky & Helen L. Witmer (Eds.), *Community programs for mental health: Theory, practice, evaluation.* Cambridge, Mass.: Harvard University Press, 1955. Pp. 158–221.

BIDDULPH, L. G. Athletic achievements and the personal and social adjustment of high school boys. *Res. Quart. Amer. Assoc. for Health & Physical Educ.* Mar. 1954, 25, 1–7.

BIER, W. C. (Ed.) *Problems in addiction: Alcoholism and narcotics.* New York: Fordham University Press, 1962.

BIER, W. C. (Ed.) *The adolescent: His search for understanding.* New York: Fordham University Press, 1963.

BINDER, H. The notion of normal in

psychology. *Dialectica*, 1956, 10, 31–44.

BINDRA, D. *Motivation: A systematic reinterpretation.* New York: Ronald, 1959.

BLACK, J. D. Common factors of the patient-therapist relationship in diverse psychotherapies, *J. clin. Psychol.*, 1952, 8, 302–306.

BLANCHARD, T. Adolescent experience in relation to personality and behavior. In J. McV. Hunt (Ed.), *Personality and the behavior disorders.* New York: Ronald, 1944. Vol. II, pp. 691–713.

BLOCH, H., & NIEDERHOFFER, A. *The gang: A study in adolescent behavior.* New York: Philosophical Library, 1958.

BLOS, P. Aspects of mental health in teaching and learning. *Ment. Hyg.*, N.Y., 1953, 37, 555–569.

BLUM, G. S. A study of the psychoanalytic theory of psychosexual development. *Genet. Psychol. Monogr.*, 1949, 39, 3–99.

BLUM, M. L., & BALINSKY, B. *Counseling and psychology.* Englewood Cliffs, N.J.: Prentice-Hall, 1951.

BOLLES, R. C. The usefulness of the drive concept. In M. R. Jones (Ed.), *Nebraska symposium on motivation, 1958.* Lincoln: University of Nebraska Press, 1958. Pp. 1–33.

BOND, E. D., & BRACELAND, F. J. Prognosis in mental disease. *Amer. J. Psychiat.*, 1937, 94, 263–274.

BONNELL, J. S. *Psychology for pastor and people.* New York: Harper & Row, 1948.

BONNEY, MERL E. *Mental health in education.* Boston: Allyn & Bacon, 1960.

BORDIN, E. S. Self-conflict as a source of vocational maladjustment. In A. Burton & R. E. Harris (Eds.), *Case histories in clinical and abnormal psychology.* New York: Harper & Row, 1947. Pp. 615–627.

BOWER, E. M. The emotionally handicapped child and the school. In L. D. Crow & Alice Crow (Eds.), *Mental hygiene for teachers: A book of readings.* New York: Macmillan, 1963. Pp. 162–173.

BOWLBY, J. *Maternal care and mental health.* Geneva: World Health Organization, 1951.

BOWMAN, K. M., & ROSE, M. A criticism of the terms "psychosis," "psychoneurosis," and "neurosis." *Amer. J. Psychiat.*, 1952, 108, 161–166.

BRACELAND, F. J. (Ed.) *Faith, reason & modern psychiatry.* New York: Kenedy, 1955.

BRACHFELD, O. *Inferiority feelings in the individual and the group.* New York: Grune & Stratton, 1951.

BRITT, S. H., & JANUS, S. Q. Criteria of frustration. *Psychol. Rev.*, 1940, 47, 451–459.

BROMBERG, W. Emotional immaturity and antisocial behavior. *J. clin. exp. Psychopath.*, 1947, 8, 423–452.

BROMBERG, W. *The nature of psychotherapy: A critique of the psychotherapeutic transaction.* New York: Grune & Stratton, 1962.

BROVERMAN, D. M., JORDAN, D. J., & PHILLIPS, L. Achievement motivation in fantasy and behavior. *J. abnorm. soc. Psychol.* 1960, 60, 374–378.

BROWN, A. W., MORRISON, J., & COUCH, G. B. Influence of affectional family relationships on character development. *J. abnorm. soc. Psychol.*, 1947, 42, 422–428.

BROWN, H. W. *Sex education in the home.* New York: Amer. Soc. Hyg. Ass., 1952.

BROWN, J. S. Pleasure-seeking behavior in the drive-reduction hypothesis. *Psychol. Rev.*, 1955, 62, 169–179.

BROWN, J. S., *et al. Current theory and research in motivation: A symposium.* Lincoln: University of Nebraska Press, 1953.

BROWN, W. T., PREU, P. W., & SULLIVAN, A. J. Ulcerative colitis and the personality. *Amer. J. Psychiat.*, 1938, 95, 407–420.

BRUETSCH, W. L. Mental disorders arising from organic disease. In Milbank Memorial Fund, *The biology of mental health and disease.* New York: Harper & Row, 1952. Pp. 302–322.

BRUNER, J. S., & GOODMAN, C. C. Value and need as organizing factors in perception. *J. abnorm. soc. Psychol.*, 1947, 42, 33–44.

BUCKLEW, J. *Paradigms for psycho-*

pathology. Philadelphia: Lippincott, 1960.

BUHLER, CHARLOTTE. School as a phase of human life. *Education*, 1953, 73, 219–222.

BURCHARD, E. M. L. Physique and psychosis. *Comp. psychol. Monogr.*, 1936, 13, No. 61.

BURGESS, E., & COTTRELL, L. *Predicting success or failure in marriage.* Englewood Cliffs, N.J.: Prentice-Hall, 1939.

BURTON, A., & HARRIS, R. E. (Eds.) *Case histories in clinical and abnormal psychology.* New York: Harper & Row, 1947.

BYCHOWSKI, G., & DESPERT, J. L. *Specialized techniques in psychotherapy.* New York: Basic Books, 1952.

CABOT, P. S. deQ. The relationship between characteristics of personality and physique in adolescents. *Genet. Psychol. Monogr.*, 1938, 20 (1).

CALDEN, G., MUNDY, R. M., & SCHLAFER, R. J. Sex differences in body concepts. *J. consult. Psychol.*, 1959, 23, 378.

CALVERT, R., & STELLE, J. R. *Planning your career.* New York: McGraw-Hill, 1963.

CALVIN, A. D., & HOLTZMAN, W. H. Adjustment and the discrepancy between self concept and inferred self. *J. consult. Psychol.*, 1953, 17, 39–44.

CAMERON, D. E. A theory of diagnosis. In P. H. Hoch & J. Zubin (Eds.), *Current problems in psychiatric diagnosis.* New York: Grune & Stratton, 1953. Pp. 33–45.

CAMERON, N., & MAGARET, ANN. *Behavior pathology.* Boston: Houghton Mifflin, 1951.

CANNON, W. B. *Bodily changes in pain, hunger, fear, and rage.* New York: Appleton, 1929.

CARROLL, H. A. *Mental hygiene: The dynamics of adjustment.* (ed. 2) Englewood Cliffs, N.J.: Prentice-Hall, 1951.

CARROLL, H. A. Motivation and learning: Their significance in a mental health program for education. *Fifty-fourth Yearbook.* NSSE (1955). Vol. III, 59–81.

CARTER, H. L. J., & McGINNIS, D. J. *Building a successful college career.*

Dubuque, Iowa: William C. Brown, 1950.

CARTER, L. F., & SCHOOLER, K. The effect of psychological need on perception. In R. G. Kuhlen & G. G. Thompson (Eds.), *Psychological studies of human development.* New York: Appleton, 1952. Pp. 246–252.

CASS, L. K. Parent-child relationships and delinquency. *J. abnorm. soc. Psychol.*, 1952, 47, 101–104.

CATTELL, R. B. The integration of psychology with moral values. *Brit. J. Psychol.*, 1950, 41, 25–34.

CATTELL, R. B., & SCHEIER, I. H. *The meaning and measurement of neuroticism and anxiety.* New York: Ronald, 1961.

CATTELL, R. B., & WENIG, P. W. Dynamic and cognitive factors controlling misperception. *J. abnorm. soc. Psychol.*, 1952, 47, 797–809.

CAVA, E. L., & RAUSH, H. L. Identification and the adolescent boy's perception of his father. *J. abnorm. soc. Psychol.* 1952, 47, 855–856.

CENTERS, R. Motivational aspects of occupational stratification. *J. soc. Psychol.*, 1948, 28, 191.

CHANDLER, J. R., BEAMER, G. C., WILLIAMS, C. C., & ARMSTRONG, V. L. *Successful adjustment in college.* Englewood Cliffs, N.J.: Prentice Hall, 1951.

CHILD, I. L., & WATERHOUSE, I. K. Frustration and the quality of performance: I. A critique of the Barker, Dembo, and Lewin experiment. *Psychol. Rev.*, 1952, 59, 351–362.

CHILD, I. L., & WHITING, J. W. M. Effects of goal attainment: Relaxation versus renewed striving. *J. abnorm. soc. Psychol.*, 1949, 45, 667–681.

CHODORKOFF, B. Self-perception, perceptual defense, and adjustment. *J. abnorm. soc. Psychol.*, 1954, 49, 508–512.

CHRISTENSEN, H. T. *Marriage analysis.* New York: Ronald, 1950.

CHRISTIE, P. Symbol, symptom, or state—the diagnostic problem of anxiety. *McGill med. J.*, 1951, 20, 16–27.

CLARK, W. H. *The psychology of religion.* New York: Macmillan, 1958.

CLEGHORN, R. A. Endocrine influence on personality and behavior. In Milbank Memorial Fund, *The biology of mental health and disease.* New York: Harper & Row, 1952. Pp. 265–273.

CLEMENS, A. H. Catholics and marriage counseling. In A. H. Clemens (Ed.), *Marriage education and counseling.* Washington, D.C.: Catholic University Press, 1951. Pp. 148–153.

COBB, S. Personality as affected by lesions of the brain. In J. McV. Hunt (Ed.), *Personality and behavior disorders.* New York: Ronald, 1944. Vol. I, pp. 550–581.

COLE, L. *Attaining maturity.* New York: Holt, Rinehart and Winston, 1944.

COOK, W. W, *et al.* Significant factors in teachers' classroom attitudes. *J. teacher Educ.,* 1956, 7, 274–279.

COUNCIL OF STATE GOV'TS. *The mental health programs of the forty-eight states.* Chicago, 1950.

COWAN, E. L. The influence of varying degrees of psychological stress on problem-solving rigidity. *J. abnorm. soc. Psychol.,* 1952a, 47, 512–519.

COWAN, E. L. Stress reduction and problem-solving rigidity. *J. consult. Psychol.,* 1952b, 16, 425–428.

CROW, L. D., & CROW, ALICE. *Mental hygiene in school and home life.* New York: McGraw-Hill, 1942.

CROW, L. D., & CROW, ALICE. (Eds.) *Mental hygiene for teachers: A book of readings.* New York: Macmillan, 1963a.

CROW, L. D., & CROW, ALICE. Defense mechanisms and adjustment. In L. D. Crow & Alice Crow (Eds.), *Mental hygiene for teachers: A book of readings.* New York: Macmillan, 1963b. Pp. 121–135.

CROW, L. D., & CROW, ALICE. Basic drives of the developing individual. In L. D. Crow & Alice Crow (Eds.), *Mental hygiene for teachers: A book of readings.* New York: Macmillan, 1963c. Pp. 95–102.

CRUICKSHANK, W. M. The relation of physical disability to fear and guilt feelings. *Child Developm.,* 1951, 22, 291–298.

CRUTCHFIELD, R. S. Conformity and character. *Amer. Psychologist,* 1955, 10, 191–198.

CUMMING, J., & CUMMING, ELAINE. *Ego and milieu: Theory and practice of environmental therapy.* New York: Atherton, 1962.

CURRAN, C. A. Guidance and counseling in education. *Education,* 1952a, 73, 223–228.

CURRAN, C. A. *Counseling in Catholic life and education.* New York: Macmillan, 1952b.

CURRAN, C. A. The concept of sin and guilt in psychotherapy. *J. couns. Psychol.,* 1960, 7, 192–197.

DAHLKE, H. O. Race and minority riots—a study in the typology of violence. *Soc. Forces,* 1952, 30, 419–425.

DALBIEZ, R. *Psychoanalytical method and the doctrine of Freud.* (Trans. by T. F. Lindsay.) New York: Longmans, 1941. 2 vols.

DAVIDS, A., & OLIVER, G. R. Learning, performance, and retention under stress in emotionally disturbed and normal children. *J. Pers.,* 1960, 28, 368–381.

DAVIES, J. T. *Sublimation.* New York: Macmillan, 1948.

DAVIS, K. Mental hygiene and the class structure. In P. Mullahy (Ed.), *A study of interpersonal relations.* New York: Hermitage, 1949. Pp. 364–385.

DAVIS, S. W. Stress in combat. *Scient. American,* 1956, 194, 31–35.

DEGAN, J. W. Dimensions of functional psychosis. *Psychometr. Monogr.,* No. 6, 1952.

DE GRAZIA, S. *Errors of psychotherapy.* New York: Doubleday, 1952.

DE MICHELE, J. H. The interpretations of anxiety by various psychotherapeutic schools. *J. consult. Psychol.,* 1954, 18, 47–52.

DENEMARK, G. W. Do schools have a role in adjustment? In L. D. Crow & Alice Crow (Eds.), *Mental hygiene for teachers: A book of readings.* New York: Macmillan, 1963. Pp. 288–296.

DEUTSCH, A. (Ed.) *Sex habits of American men: A symposium on the Kinsey report.* Englewood Cliffs, N.J.: Prentice-Hall, 1948.

DEUTSCH, A. *The mentally ill in America.* (ed. 2, rev.) New York: Columbia University Press, 1949.

DEUTSCH, A., & FISHMAN, HELEN. (Eds.) *The encyclopedia of mental health.* New York: F. Watts, 1963. 6 vols.

D'EVELYN, KATHERINE. *Meeting children's emotional needs.* Englewood Cliffs, N.J.: Prentice-Hall, 1957.

DODGE, R., & KAHN, E. *The craving for superiority.* New Haven: Yale University Press, 1931.

DOLLARD, J., & MILLER, N. E. *Personality and psychotherapy.* New York: McGraw-Hill, 1950.

DOLLARD, J., MILLER, N. E., DOOB, L. W., MOWRER, O. H., & SEARS, R. R. *Frustration and aggression.* New Haven: Yale University Press, 1939.

DOLORES, SISTER M. Physical factors underlying behavior patterns in children. *Education,* 1951, 72, 267–271.

DRAPER, G. Emotional components of ulcer susceptible constitution. *Ann. intern. Med.,* 1942, 16, 633–658.

DRIBBIN, I. S. Mental hygiene clinics of the Veterans Administration. *J. Amer. med. Ass.,* 1954, 155 (4), 331–335.

DUNBAR, H. F. The relationship between anxiety states and organic disease. *Clinics,* 1942, 1, 879–908.

DUNBAR, H. F. *Mind and body: Psychosomatic medicine.* New York: Random House, 1947.

DURBIN, E. F. M., & BOWLBY, J. *Personal aggressiveness and war.* New York: Columbia University Press, 1939.

DUREA, M. A. Personality characteristics of juvenile delinquents. II. Reliability of differentiating traits. *Child Developm.,* 1937a, 8, 257–262.

DUREA, M. A. The emotional maturity of juvenile delinquents. *J. abnorm. soc. Psychol.,* 1937b, 31, 472–481.

DUREA, M. A. The differential diagnosis of potential delinquency. *Amer. J. Orthopsychiat.,* 1939, 9, 394–398.

DUREA, M. A., & LOVE, L. L. The personal problems of college students. *Occup.,* 1939, 18, 21–27.

EATON, J. W. The assessment of mental health. *Amer. J. Psychiat.,* 1951, 108, 81–90.

EISENSTEIN, V. W. (Ed.) *Neurotic interaction in marriage.* New York: Basic Books, 1956.

ELLIS, A. (Ed.) *Sex life of the American woman and the Kinsey report.* New York: Greenberg, 1954.

ELLIS, A. Rational psychotherapy. *J. gen. Psychol.,* 1958, 59, 35–49.

ELLIS, A. There is no place for the concept of sin in psychotherapy. *J. couns. Psychol.,* 1960, 7, 188–192.

ELLIS, A., NYDES, J., & REISS, B. Qualifications of the clinical psychologist for the practice of psychotherapy. *J. clin. Psychol.,* 1955, 11, 33–36.

EMERY, E. S., & MONROE, R. T. Peptic ulcer, nature and treatment based on study of 1,435 cases. *Arch. intern. Med.,* 1935, 55, 271–292.

ENGLISH, O. S. Sexual adjustment in marriage. In M. Fishbein & Ruby J. R. Kennedy (Eds.), *Modern marriage and family living.* New York: Oxford University Press, 1957.

EPHRON, B. P. *Emotional difficulties in reading.* New York: Julian, 1953.

EPSTEIN, S. The measurement of drive and conflict in humans: Theory and experiment. In M. R. Jones (Ed.), *Nebraska symposium on motivation.* Lincoln: University of Nebraska Press, 1962. Pp. 127–206.

ERICKSON, C. E. *The counseling interview.* Englewood Cliffs, N.J.: Prentice-Hall, 1950.

ERICKSON, M. H. Experimental demonstrations of the psychopathology of everyday life. *Psychoanalytic Quart.,* 1939, 8, 338–353.

ERIKSEN, C. W. Defense against ego-threat in memory and perception. *J. abnorm. soc. Psychol.,* 1952, 47, 230–235.

ERIKSEN, C. W. The case for perceptual defense. *Psychol. Rev.,* 1954, 61, 175–181.

ERIKSEN, C. W. Unconscious processes. In M. R. Jones (Ed.), *Nebraska symposium on motivation, 1958.* Lincoln: University of Nebraska Press, 1958. Pp. 169–227.

ERIKSEN, C. W., LAZARUS, R. S., & STRANGE, J. R. Psychological stress and its personality correlates. *J. Pers.,* 1952, 20, 277–286.

ERIKSON, E. H. Identity and the life cycle. *Psychological Issues*, Monogr. No. 1, 1959.

ESTES, S. G. The therapeutic relationship in the dynamics of cure. *J. consult. Psychol.*, 1948, 12, 76–81.

EWALT, J. R. *Mental health administration*. Springfield, Ill.: Charles C Thomas, 1956.

EWING, T. N. Changes in attitude during counseling. *J. coun. Psychol.*, 1954, 1, 232–239.

EXPERT COMMITTEE ON MENTAL HEALTH OF THE WORLD HEALTH ORGANIZATION. *Bull. World Fed. Ment. Hlth.*, 1951, 3, 27–28.

EYSENCK, H. J. The organization of personality. *J. Personal.*, 1951, 20, 101–117.

EYSENCK, H. J. The effects of psychotherapy: An evaluation. *J. consult. Psychol.*, 1952, 16, 319–324.

EYSENCK, H. J. (Ed.) *Handbook of abnormal psychology*. New York: Basic Books, 1961.

FARNSWORTH, D. L. *Mental health in college and university*. Cambridge, Mass.: Harvard University Press, 1957.

FATERSON, H. F. Organic inferiority and the inferiority attitude. *J. soc. Psychol.*, 1931, 2, 87–101.

FEDERAL SECURITY AGENCY. *National Institute of Mental Health*. Washington, D. C., 1952.

FEIN, RASHI. *Economics of mental illness*. New York: Basic Books, 1958.

FELIX, R. H. Promoting mental health. *N.C. med. J.*, 1950, 11, 17–23.

FELIX, R. H. The technique of mass approach to the problems of mental health. *Neuropsychiat.*, 1952, 2, 48–62.

FELIX, R. H. Evolution of community mental health concepts. *Amer. J. Psychiatry*, 1957, 113, 673–679.

FELIX, R. H., & KRAMER, M. Extent of the problem of mental disorders. *Ann. Amer. Acad. polit. soc. Sci.*, 1953, No. 286, 5–14.

FENSTERHEIM, E., & TRESSELT, M. E. The influence of value systems on the perception of people. *J. abnorm. soc. Psychol.*, 1953, 48, 93–98.

FESHBACH, S. The drive-reducing function of fantasy behavior. *J. abnorm. soc. Psychol.*, 1955, 50, 3–11.

FESHBACH, S. The stimulating versus cathartic efforts of a vicarious aggressive activity. *J. abnorm. soc. Psychol.*, 1961, 63, 381–385.

FILER, R. J. Frustration, satisfaction, and other factors affecting the attractiveness of goal objects. *J. abnorm. soc. Psychol.*, 1952, 47, 203–212.

FINE, H. J., FULKERSON, S. C., & PHILLIPS, L. Maladjustment and social attainment. *J. abnorm. soc. Psychol.*, 1955, 50, 33–35.

FINESINGER, J. E. The needs of youth. *Psychiatry*, 1944, 7, 45–57.

FISHER, MARGARET, & NOBLE, JEANNE. *College education as personal development*. Englewood Cliffs, N.J.: Prentice-Hall, 1960.

FISHER, V. E. *Autocorrectivism: The psychology of nervousness*. Caldwell, Idaho: Caxton, 1937.

FISHER, V. E. *The meaning and practice of psychotherapy*. New York: Macmillan, 1950.

FLEEGE, U. H. *Self-revelation of the adolescent boy*. Milwaukee: Bruce, 1945.

FLETCHER, R. *Instinct in man, in the light of recent work in comparative psychology*. London: G. Allen, 1957.

FORD, C. S., & BEACH, F. A. *Patterns of sexual behavior*. New York: Harper & Row, 1951.

FOSDICK, H. E. *On being a real person*. New York: Harper & Row, 1943.

FRANK, L. K. The fundamental needs of the child. *Ment. Hyg.*, N.Y., 1938, 22, 353–379.

FRANZBLAU, ROSE M., & FRANZBLAU, A. N. *A sane and happy life: A family guide*. New York: Harcourt, 1963.

FREDERICSON, E. Competition: The effects of infantile experience upon adult behavior. *J. abnorm. soc. Psychol.*, 1951, 46, 406–409.

FREDERIKSEN, N. The effects of frustration on negativistic behavior of young children. *J. gen. Psychol.*, 1942, 61, 203–226.

FREEMAN, LUCY, & GREENWALD, H. *Emotional maturity in love and marriage.* New York: Harper & Row, 1961.

FRENCH, T. Psychogenic factors in asthma. *Amer. J. Psychiat.,* 1939, 96, 87–98.

FREUD, ANNA. *The ego and the mechanisms of defense.* (Trans. by C. Baines.) New York: International Universities, 1946.

FREUD, S. *The interpretation of dreams.* (Trans. by A. A. Brill.) London: Allen & Unwin, 1913.

FREUD, S. *Beyond the pleasure principle.* (Trans. from the 2d German edition by C. J. M. Hubback.) London: Hogarth, 1948.

FROMM, E. *Escape from freedom.* New York: Holt, Rinehart and Winston, 1941.

FROMM, E. Individual and social origins of neurosis. *Amer. sociol. Rev.,* 1944, 9, 380–384.

FROMM, E. *Psychoanalysis and religion.* New Haven: Yale University Press, 1950.

FROMM, E. *The sane society.* New York: Holt, Rinehart and Winston, 1955.

FROMME, A. *The psychologist looks at sex and marriage.* Englewood Cliffs, N.J.: Prentice-Hall, 1950.

FROMM–REICHMANN, FREDA. *Principles of intensive psychotherapy.* Chicago: University of Chicago Press, 1950.

FROST, D., & ANDERSON, G. A health department stimulates community thinking for mental health. *Amer. J. pub. Hlth.,* 1950, 40, 978–983.

FULLER, J. L. *Motivation: A biological perspective.* New York: Random House, 1962.

FUNKENSTEIN, D. H., KING, S. H., & DROLETTE, MARGARET E. *Mastery of stress.* Cambridge, Mass.: Harvard University Press, 1957.

FURSTENHEIM, W. Causes and motives of juvenile delinquency. *World ment. Hlth.,* 1954, 191–194.

GAGE, N. L. (Ed.) *Handbook of research on teaching.* Chicago: Rand McNally, 1963.

GAMELIN, F. C. Creative approaches to mental health. In L. D. Crow & Alice Crow (Eds.), *Mental hygiene*

for teachers: A book of readings. New York: Macmillan, 1963. Pp. 370–375.

GANTT, W. A. H. *Experimental basis for neurotic behavior.* New York: Harper & Row, 1944.

GARDNER, G. E. The mental health of normal adolescents. *Ment. Hyg., N.Y.,* 1947, 31, 529–540.

GARDNER, G. E. The emotional needs of the child. In J. L. Liebman (Ed.), *Psychiatry and religion.* Boston: Beacon, 1948. Pp. 69–90.

GARDNER, G. E. Recreation's part in mental health. *Recreation,* 1952, 45, 446–448.

GARFIELD, S. L., & KURZ, M. Evaluation of treatment and related procedures in 1,216 cases referred to a mental hygiene clinic. *Psychiat. Quart.,* 1952, 26, 414–424.

GARRETT, J. F. (Ed.) *Psychological aspects of physical disability.* Washington, D.C.: Federal Security Agency, n.d.

GARRISON, K. C. *The psychology of exceptional children.* (rev. ed.) New York: Ronald, 1950.

GATES, R. R. Genetics and normal mental differences. In Milbank Memorial Fund, *The biology of mental health and disease.* New York: Harper & Row, 1952. Pp. 277–281.

GIBSON, J. *The perception of the visual world.* Boston: Houghton Mifflin, 1950.

GILBERT, J. G. *Understanding old age.* New York: Ronald Press, 1953.

GILL, M. The present state of psychoanalytic theory. *J. abnorm. soc. Psychol.,* 1959, 58, 1–8.

GILL, M. M. *The initial interview in psychiatric practice.* New York: International Universities, 1954.

GLASER, JUDY. Teacher personality: The growth of assurance and authority. *Except. Child,* 1959, 26, 151–154.

GLIDEWELL, J. C. (Ed.) *Parental attitudes and child behavior.* Springfield, Ill.: Charles C Thomas, 1961.

GLUECK, S. The home, the school, and delinquency. *Harvard educ. Rev.,* 1953, 23, 17–32.

GLUECK, S., & GLUECK, ELEANOR.

Predicting delinquency and crime. Cambridge, Mass.: Harvard, 1959.

GODIN, A. Mental health in Christian life. *J. relig. & Hlth.*, 1961, *1*, 41–54.

GOLDFARB, W. The effects of early institutional care on adolescent personality. *Child Developm.*, 1943, *14*, 213–223.

GOLDFARB, W. Psychological privation in infancy and subsequent adjustment. *Amer. J. Orthopsychiat.*, 1945, *15*, 247–255.

GOLDFARB, W. Variations in adolescent adjustment of institutionally reared children. *Amer. J. Orthopsychiat.*, 1947, *17*, 449–457.

GOLDHAMER, H., & MARSHALL, A. *Psychosis and civilization.* New York: Free Press, 1953.

GOLDMAN, F. Breast feeding and character formation. II. *J. Personal.*, 1950, *19*, 189–196.

GOLDMAN, ROSE. Mental hygiene looks at education. *J. Nat. Assoc. Deans of Women*, 1954, *17*, 119–125.

GOLDSTEIN, M. J., & PALMER, J. O. *The experience of anxiety: A casebook.* New York: Oxford University Press, 1963.

GOULD, R. Repression experimentally analyzed. *Char. & Personal.*, 1942, *10*, 259–288.

GRAHAM, FRANCES K., CHARWAT, W. A., HONIG, A. S., & WELTZ, P. C. Aggression as a function of the attack and the attacker. *J. abnorm. soc. Psychol.*, 1951, *46*, 512–520.

GRINKER, R. R., & ROBBINS, F. P. *Psychosomatic case book.* New York: McGraw-Hill, 1954.

GRINKER, R. R., & SPIEGEL, J. P. *Men under stress.* New York: McGraw-Hill-Blakiston, 1945.

GUTHRIE, E. R. *The psychology of human conflict.* New York: Harper & Row, 1938.

HAHN, M. E. Conceptual trends in counseling. *Personnel guid. J.*, 1953, *31*, 231–235.

HAHN, M. E. Forgotten people: The normal individual and, in professional psychology. *Amer. Psychologist*, 1962, *17*, 700–705.

HAMBLING, J. Emotions and symptoms in essential hypertension. *Brit. J. med. Psychol.*, 1951, *24*, 242–253.

HAMILTON, D. M., & WALL, J. H. The hospital treatment of dementia praecox. *Amer. J. Psychiat.*, 1948, *105*, 346–352.

HANLON, T. E., HOFSTAETTER, P. R., & O'CONNOR, J. P. Congruence of self and ideal self in relation to personality adjustment. *J. consult. Psychol.*, 1954, *18*, 215–218.

HARRIS, I. D. *Emotional blocks to learning.* New York: Free Press, 1961.

HARTLEY, H. S. Conflict, frustration, and fatigue. *Psychosom. Med.*, 1943, *5*, 158–172.

HASTORF, A. H., & KNUTSEN, A. L. Motivation, perception, and attitude change. *Psychol. Rev.*, 1949, *56*, 88–94.

HAVIGHURST, R. J., ROBINSON, M. Z., & DORR, M. The development of the ideal self in childhood and adolescence. *J. educ. Res.*, 1946, *40*, 241–257.

HAVIGHURST, R. J., BOWMAN, P. H., LIDDLE, G. P., MATTHEWS, C. V. & PIERCE, J. V. *Growing up in River City.* New York: Wiley, 1962.

HAYDEN, J. J. The moral aspects of the new developments in mental hygiene. *Proc. Nat. Conf. Cath. Char.*, 1950.

HEALY, W., & BRONNER, A. F. Delinquency as a mode of adjustment. In R. G. Kuhlen & G. G. Thompson (Eds.), *Psychological studies of human development.* New York: Appleton, 1952. Pp. 480–489.

HEATH, R. G. The concept of functional versus organic disease: A critique. *Med. Clin. N. Amer.*, March 1952, 305–310.

HENDRICK, I. *Facts and theories of psychoanalysis.* (ed. 2) New York: Knopf, 1939.

HERR, V. V. Integration and self-ideal. In M. B. Arnold & J. A. Gasson (Eds.), *The human person: An integral approach to the theory of personality.* New York: Ronald, 1954. Pp. 283–293.

HERZOG, ELIZABETH. *Identifying potential delinquents.* Washington, D.C.: Government Printing Office, 1960.

HESTERLY, S. O. Deviant response patterns as a function of chronological age. *J. consult. Psychol.*, 1963, 27, 210–214.

HEWITT, L. E., & JENKINS, R. L. *Fundamental patterns of maladjustment: The dynamics of their origin.* Springfield, Ill.: Green, 1946.

HILL, W. F. Activity as an autonomous drive. *J. compar. physiol. Psychol.*, 1956, 49, 15–19.

HILTNER, S. *The counselor in counseling: Case notes in pastoral counseling.* Nashville, Tenn.: Abingdon-Cokesbury, 1952.

HILTNER, S. *Sex ethics and the Kinsey reports.* New York: Association Press, 1953.

HOCH, P. H. Experimental induction of psychoses. In Milbank Memorial Fund, *The biology of mental health and disease.* New York: Harper & Row, 1952. Pp. 539–546.

HOCH, P. H. Drug therapy. In S. Arieti (Ed.), *American handbook of psychiatry.* New York: Basic Books, 1959, II. Pp. 1541–1551.

HOCH, P. H., & ZUBIN, J. (Eds.) *Anxiety.* New York: Grune & Stratton, 1950.

HODGINS, D. R. Clinical manifestations of anxiety. *McGill med. J.*, 1951, 20, 12–15.

HODGKISS, M. The influence of broken homes and working mothers. *Smith Coll. Stud. soc. Wk.*, 1933, 3, 259–274.

HOFFMAN, J. Guilt feelings and psychiatry. *J. pastoral Care*, 1952, 6, 42–52.

HOGAN, R. A. A theory of threat and defense. *J. consult. Psychol.*, 1952, 16, 417–424.

HOKANSON, J. E. The effects of frustration and anxiety on overt aggression. *J. abnorm. soc. Psychol.*, 1961, 62, 346–351.

HOLLINGSHEAD, A. B. *Elmtown's youth.* New York: Wiley, 1949.

HOLLINGSHEAD, A. B., & REDLICH, F. D. Schizophrenia and the social structure. *Amer. J. Psychiat.*, 1954, 110, 695–701.

HONIGMANN, J. J. *Culture and personality.* New York: Harper & Row, 1954.

HORNEY, KAREN. Culture and neurosis. *Amer. sociol. Rev.*, 1936, 1, 221–235.

HORNEY, KAREN. *Our inner conflicts.* New York: Norton, 1945.

HORNEY, KAREN. *Neurosis and human growth.* New York: Norton, 1950.

HOYT, D. P., & NORMAN, W. T. Adjustment and academic predictability. *J. coun. Psychol.*, 1954, 1, 96–99.

HOPE, W. *Life together.* New York: Sheed & Ward, 1943.

HUNT, H. F. On goals, methods, and tactics in psychotherapy. *J. consult. Psychol.*, 1948, 12, 68–75.

HUNT, J. McV. (Ed.) *Personality and the behavior disorders.* New York: Ronald, 1944. 2 vols.

HUNT, J. McV. The problem of measuring the results of psychotherapy. *Psychol. Serv. Center J.*, 1949, 1, 122–135.

HUNT, J. McV. Toward an integrated program of research on psychotherapy. *J. consult. Psychol.*, 1952, 16, 237–246.

HYBL, A. R., & STAGNER, R. Frustration tolerance in relation to diagnosis and therapy. *J. consult. Psychol.*, 1952, 16, 163–170.

HYMAN, H., & BARMACK, J. E. Special review: Sexual behavior in the human female. *Psychol. Bull.*, 1954, 51, 418–427.

HYMES, J. L. *Behavior and misbehavior.* Englewood Cliffs, N.J.: Prentice-Hall, 1955.

INGLE, D. J. Endocrine function and personality. *Psychol. Rev.*, 1935, 42, 466–479.

JACKSON, P. W., & GETZELS, J. W. Psychological health and classroom functioning: A study of dissatisfaction with school among adolescents. In J. M. Seidman (Ed.), *Educating for mental health.* New York: Crowell, 1963. Pp. 140–156.

JACO, E. G. *The social epidemiology of mental disorders: A psychiatric survey of Texas.* New York: Russell Sage, 1960.

JAHODA, MARIE. *Current concepts of positive mental health.* New York: Basic Books, 1958.

JAMES, W. *The varieties of religious experience.* New York: Random House, 1902.

JANIS, I. L. *Air war and emotional stress.* New York: McGraw-Hill, 1951.

JANIS, I. L. Motivational factors in the resolution of decisional conflicts. In M. R. Jones (Ed.), *Nebraska symposium on motivation.* Lincoln: University of Nebraska Press, 1959. Pp. 198–231.

JAYASURIYA, J. E. Psychological needs of children. *J. educ. & Psychol.,* 1950, 8, 60–68.

JENKINS, R. L. Child-parent relationships and delinquency and crime. In W. C. Reckless (Ed.), *The etiology of delinquent and criminal behavior.* Bull. No. 50. New York: Social Sci. Research Council, 1943. Pp. 16–20.

JENKINS, R. L. Guilt feelings—their function and dysfunction. In M. L. Reymert (Ed.), *Feelings and emotions.* New York: McGraw-Hill, 1950. Pp. 353–361.

JENKINS, R. L. Motivation and frustration in delinquency. *Amer. J. Orthopsychiat.,* 1957, 27, 528–537.

JENSEN, A. R. Aggression in fantasy and overt behavior. *Psychol. Monogr.,* 1957, 71, No. 445.

JOHNSON, D. The understanding and use of the self in counseling. *Bull. Menninger Clin.,* 1953, 17, 29–35.

JOHNSON, G. The needs of youth. *Cath. educ. Rev.,* 1938, 36, 3–16.

JOHNSON, P. E. Religious psychology and health. *Ment. Hyg., N.Y.,* 1947, 31, 556–566.

JOHNSON, P. E. The problem of guilt in the adolescent. In J. L. Liebman (Ed.), *Psychiatry and religion.* Boston: Beacon, 1948. Pp. 126–143.

JONES, E. The concept of a normal mind. *Int. J. Psycho-Anal.,* 1942, 23, 1–8.

JUNG, C. G. *Modern man in search of a soul.* New York: Harcourt, 1933.

JUNG, C. G. *The integration of the personality.* New York: Holt, Rinehart and Winston, 1939.

KAGAN, J., & MOSS, H. A. *Birth to maturity: A study of psychological development.* New York: Wiley, 1962.

KALINOWSKY, L. B. Compulsive shock treatment. In S. Arieti (Ed.), *American handbook of psychiatry.* New York: Basic Books, 1959, II. Pp. 1541–1551.

KALINOWSKY, L. B., & HOCH, P. H. *Shock treatments and other somatic procedures in psychiatry.* New York: Grune & Stratton, 1946.

KALLMANN, F. J. Genetic aspects of psychoses. In Milbank Memorial Fund, *The biology of mental health and disease.* New York: Harper & Row, 1952. Pp. 283–298.

KALLMANN, F. J. *Heredity in health and mental disorder.* New York: Norton, 1953.

KANNER, L. The role of the school in the treatment of rejected children. *Nerv. Child,* 1944, 3, 236–248.

KANNER, L. Unwholesome parental attitudes and children's behavior. *Education,* 1949, 69, 263–270.

KAPLAN, L. *Mental health and human relations in education.* New York: Harper & Row, 1956.

KAPLAN, L., & BARON, D. *Mental hygiene and life.* New York: Harper & Row, 1952.

KAPP, F. T., ROSENBAUM, M., & ROMANO, J. Psychological factors in men with peptic ulcers. *Amer. J. Psychiat.,* 1947, 103, 700–704.

KARDINER, A. The relation of culture to mental disorder. In P. H. Hoch & J. Zubin (Eds.), *Current problems in psychiatric diagnosis.* New York: Grune & Stratton, 1953. Pp. 157–179.

KARDINER, A., & SPIEGEL, H. *War stress and neurotic illness.* New York: Harper & Row, 1947.

KATZ, B. The inferiority complex: Some essential causes. *Education,* 1949, 69, 293–295.

KATZENELBOGEN, S. Mental hygiene and personality problems. In M. J. Shore (Ed.), *Twentieth century mental hygiene.* New York: Social Sciences Publishers, 1950. Pp. 39–40.

KELIHER, A. V. Teamwork for maturity. *Ment. Hyg., N.Y.,* 1949, 33, 230–235.

KENNEDY, A. Obsessive states. *Practitioner,* 1951, 167, 122–133.

KEYS, A. Experimental induction of psychoneuroses by starvation. In Milbank Memorial Fund, *The biology of mental health and disease.* New York: Harper & Row, 1952. Pp. 515–528.

KEYS, A., *et al. Biology of human starvation.* Minneapolis: University of Minnesota Press, 1950.

KILBY, R. W. Psychoneurosis in times of trouble: Evidence for a hierarchy of motives. *J. abnorm. soc. Psychol.,* 1948, 43, 544–545.

KING, F. W. *Emotional maturity: Its nature and measurement.* Unpublished doctoral dissertation, Harvard University, 1951.

KING, G. M., & SCHILLER, M. Ego strength and type of defensive behavior. *J. consult. Psychol.,* 1960, 24, 215–217.

KING, S. H., & HENRY, A. F. Aggression and cardiovascular reactions related to parental control over behavior. In T. R. Sarbin (Ed.), *Studies in behavior pathology.* New York: Holt, Rinehart and Winston, 1961. Pp. 239–244.

KINSEY, A. C., POMEROY, W. B., & MARTIN, C. E. *Sexual behavior in the human male.* Philadelphia: Saunders, 1948.

KINSEY, A. C., POMEROY, W. B., MARTIN, C. E., & GEBHARD, P. H. *Sexual behavior in the human female.* Philadelphia: Saunders, 1953.

KIRKENDALL, L. A. *Sex education as human relations.* New York: Inor, 1950.

KISKER, G. W. (Ed.) *The psychopathology of international relations.* Englewood Cliffs, N.J.: Prentice-Hall, 1951.

KLEIN, D. B. *Mental hygiene.* New York: Holt, Rinehart and Winston, 1944.

KLEIN, G. S., SCHLESINGER, H. J., & MEISTER, D. E. The effect of personal value on perception: An experimental critique. *Psychol. Rev.,* 1951, 58, 96–112.

KLEIN, G. S., & SCHOENFELD, N. The influence of ego-involvement on confidence. *J. abnorm. soc. Psychol.,* 1941, 36, 249–258.

KLINEBERG, O. Cultural factors in personality adjustment of children. *Amer. J. Orthopsychiat.,* 1953, 23, 465–471.

KNAPP, R. H. *Practical guidance methods: For counselors, teachers, and administrators.* New York: McGraw-Hill, 1953.

KOBLER, F. J., WEBB, N. J., HERR, V. V., & DEVLIN, W. J. Loyola University NIMH project on religion and mental health. *Pastoral Psychol.,* 1959, 10, 44–46.

KOCH, S. The current status of motivational psychology. *Psychol. Rev.,* 1951, 58, 147–154.

KORCHIN, S. J., & BASOWITZ, H. Perceptual adequacy and life stress. *J. Psychol.,* 1954, 38, 495–502.

KORNER, A. F. *Some aspects of hostility in young children.* New York: Grune & Stratton, 1949.

KOROBOW, N. Reactions to stress: A reflection of personality trait organization. *J. abnorm. soc. Psychol.,* 1955, 51, 464–468.

KOTINSKY, RUTH, & WITMER, HELEN L. *Community programs for mental health.* Cambridge, Mass.: Harvard University Press, 1955.

KRAINES, S. H. *The therapy of the neuroses and the psychoses.* (ed. 3, rev.) Philadelphia: Lea & Febiger, 1948.

KRALL, V. Personality characteristics of accident repeating children. *J. abnorm. soc. Psychol.,* 1953, 48, 99–107.

KRASNER, L. Personality differences between patients classified as psychosomatic and as nonpsychosomatic. *J. abnorm. soc. Psychol.,* 1953, 48, 190–198.

KUHLEN, R. G., & THOMPSON, G. G. (Eds.) *Psychological studies of human development.* New York: Appleton, 1952.

LAMSON, H. D. Marriage counseling. *Education,* 1951, 72, 173–180.

LANDIS, C., & PAGE, J. D. *Modern society and mental disease.* New York: Holt, Rinehart and Winston, 1938.

LANDIS, C., *et al. Sex in development.* New York: Harper & Row, 1940.

LANDIS, J. T., & LANDIS, MARY G. *Building a successful marriage.* Englewood Cliffs, N.J.: Prentice-Hall, 1948 (ed. 4, 1963).

LANGNER, T. S., & MICHAEL, S. T. *Life stress and mental health.* New York: Free Press, 1963.

LANSKY, L. M., CRANDALL, V. J., KAGAN, J., & BAKER, C. T. Sex differences in aggression and its correlates in middle-class adolescents. *Child Develpm.*, 1961, 32, 45–58.

LAWRENCE, C. H. The endocrine factor in personality development. *Educ. Rec.*, 1942, 23, Suppl. 15, 83–94.

LAWSON, R., & MARKS, M. H. Frustration: Theory and experiment. *Genet. Psychol. Monogr.*, 1958, 57, 393–464.

LAZARUS, R. S. *Adjustment and personality.* New York: McGraw-Hill, 1961.

LAZARUS, R. S., & BAKER, R. W. Motivation and personality in psychological stress. *Psychol. Newsletter*, 1957, 8, 159–193.

LAZARUS, R. S., & BAKER, R. W., BROVERMAN, D. M., & MAYER, J. Personality and psychological stress. *J. Pers.*, 1957, 25, 559–577.

LAZAUS, R. S., VOUSEM, H., & ARENBERG, A. Hunger and perception. *J. Pers.*, 1953, 21, 312–328.

LEAVITT, H. C. Relationships between conditioned fear patterns and the development of anxiety. *Psychoanal. Rev.*, 1953, 40, 27–35.

LEIGHTON, DOROTHEA C., HARDING, J. S., MACKLIN, D. B., MACMILLAN, A. M., & LEIGHTON, A. H. *The character of danger: Psychiatric symptoms in selected communities.* New York: Basic Books, 1963.

LESSER, G. S. The relationship between overt and fantasy aggression as a function of maternal response to aggression. *J. abnorm. soc. Psychol.*, 1957, 55, 215–221.

LESSER, G. S. Conflict analysis of fantasy aggression. *J. Pers.*, 1958, 26, 29–41.

LEVIN, A. J. The fiction of the death instinct. *Psychiat. Quart.*, 1951, 25, 257–281.

LEVIN, H., & SEARS, R. R. Identification with parents as a determinant of doll-play aggression. *Child Develpm.*, 1956, 27, 135–153.

LEVINE, L. S. *Personal and social development.* New York: Holt, Rinehart and Winston, 1963.

LEVINE, R., CHEIN, I., & MURPHY, G. The relation of the intensity of a need to the amount of perceptual distortion. *J. Psychol.*, 1942, 13, 283–293.

LEVINE, S. Infantile experience in consummatory behavior in adulthood. *J. comp. physiol. Psychol.*, 1957, 50, 609–612.

LEVITT, E. E. Cognitive distortion and ego-involvement. *J. Pers.*, 1950, 18, 212–220.

LEVY, D. M. *Maternal overprotection.* New York: Columbia University Press, 1943.

LEVY, D. M. On evaluating the "specific event" as a source of anxiety. In P. N. Hoch & J. Zubin (Eds.), *Anxiety.* New York: Grune & Stratton, 1950. Pp. 140–149.

LEVY, D. M. Maternal overprotection. In R. G. Kuhlen & G. G. Thompson (Eds.), *Psychological studies of human development.* New York: Appleton, 1952. Pp. 387–394.

LEWIN, K. Behavior and development as a function of the total situation. In L. Carmichael (Ed.), *Manual of child psychology.* New York: Wiley, 1946. Pp. 791–844.

LIEBMAN, J. L. (Ed.) *Psychiatry and religion.* Boston: Beacon, 1948.

LINDGREN, H. C. *The psychology of personal and social adjustment.* New York: American Book, 1953.

LINDNER, R. *Prescription for rebellion.* New York: Holt, Rinehart and Winston, 1952.

LINE, W. Mental health and education. *Ment. Hlth., London*, 1950, 9, 92–93.

LINN, L., & SCHWARZ, L. W. *Psychiatry and religious experience.* New York: Random House, 1958.

LIPPITT, R., & GOLD, M. Classroom social structure as a mental health problem. In J. M. Seidman (Ed.), *Educating for mental health.* New York: Crowell, 1963. Pp. 117–140.

LITTMAN, R. A. Motives, history, and causes. In M. R. Jones (Ed.), *Nebraska symposium on motivation.* Lincoln: University of Nebraska Press, 1958. Pp. 114–168.

LIVSON, N., & MUSSEN, P. H. The

relation of ego control to overt aggression and dependency. *J. abnorm. soc. Psychol.*, 1957, 55, 66–71.

LLOYD, W., & HEINSTEIN, M. An experimental approach to mental health in the program of a children's hospital. *Ment. Hyg., N.Y.*, 1952, 36, 423–438.

LOTT, G. M. The prevention of neurosis. *J. Pediat.*, 1951, 38, 356–366.

LOWRY, J. V. Public mental health agencies, state and national. *Ann. Amer. Acad. Pol. & Soc. Sci.*, March, 1953, No. 286, 100–106.

LURIA, A. *The nature of human conflicts.* New York: Liveright, 1932.

MADISON, P. *Freud's concept of repression and defense: Its theoretical and observational language.* Minneapolis: University of Minnesota Press, 1962.

MAEDER, L. A. M. Diagnostic criteria: The concept of normal and abnormal. *Family*, 1941, 22, 171–179.

MAGNER, J. A. *Personality and successful living.* Milwaukee: Bruce, 1944.

MAGNER, J. A. *The art of a happy marriage.* Milwaukee: Bruce, 1947.

MAIER, N. R. F. *Frustration: The study of behavior without a goal.* New York: McGraw-Hill, 1949.

MAIER, N. R. F. Mechanisms in frustration. *Comp. psychol. Monogr.*, 1950, 20, 61–94.

MAILLOUX, N. Psychic determinism, freedom, and personality development. In M. B. Arnold & J. A. Gasson (Eds.), *The human person: An integral approach to the theory of personality.* New York: Ronald, 1954. Pp. 264–280.

MALLER, J. B. Size of family and personality of offspring. *J. soc. Psychol.*, 1931, 2, 3–27.

MALLESON, N. The mental health of the student. In *Health at the university.* Paris: International Universities, 1954. Pp. 51–58.

MANGUS, A. R. Family impacts on mental health. *Marriage and family living*, 1957, 19, 256–262.

MARCUSE, F. L. The nature of symptoms in the minor behavior disorders. *J. abnorm. soc. Psychol.*, 1953, 48, 151–152.

MARGOLESE, M. Mental disorders in childhood due to endocrine disorders. *Nerv. Child.*, 1948, 8, 55–77.

MARQUART, DOROTHY I., & ARNOLD, PATRICIA L. A study in frustration of human adults. *J. gen. Psychol.*, 1952, 47, 43–63.

MARQUIS, D. P., SINNETT, E. R., & WINTER, W. D. A psychological study of peptic ulcer patients. *J. clin. Psychol.*, 1952, 8, 266–272.

MARX, M. H. Some relations between frustration and drive. In M. R. Jones (Ed.), *Nebraska symposium on motivation.* Lincoln: University of Nebraska Press, 1956. Pp. 92–130.

MARZOLF, S. S. The disease concept in psychology. *Psychol. Rev.*, 1947, 54, 211–221.

MASLOW, A. H. Deprivation, threat and frustration. *Psychol. Rev.*, 1941, 48, 364–366.

MASLOW, A. H. The dynamics of psychological security-insecurity. *Charact. & Pers.*, 1942, 10, 331–344.

MASLOW, A. H. Conflict, frustration and the theory of threat. *J. abnorm. soc. Psychol.*, 1943a, 38, 81–86.

MASLOW, A. H. A dynamic theory of human motivation. *Psychol. Rev.*, 1943b, 50, 370–396.

MASLOW, A. H. Higher and lower needs. *J. Psych.*, 1948, 25, 433–436.

MASLOW, A. H. Self-actualizing people: A study of psychological health. *Personal.*, 1950, Symposium No. 1, 11–34.

MASLOW, A. H. *Motivation and personality.* New York: Harper & Row, 1954.

MASLOW, A. H., & MITTELMANN, B. *Principles of abnormal psychology.* (rev. ed.) New York: Harper & Row, 1951.

MASSERMAN, J. H. *Behavior and neurosis.* Chicago: University of Chicago Press, 1943.

MAY, R. *The meaning of anxiety.* New York: Ronald, 1950.

MAY, R. *Man's search for himself.* New York: Norton, 1953.

MAY, R. Religion—source of strength or weakness? *Pastor. Psychol.*, 1953, 4, 68–74.

McCABE, A. R. Meeting the emotional

needs of children. *Soc. Casewk.*, 1950, *31*, 332–339.

McCALL, R. J. The defense mechanisms re-examined: A logical and phenomenal analysis. *Catholic psychol. Rec.*, 1963, *1*, 45–64.

McCANN, R. V. *Delinquency: Sickness or sin?* New York: Harper & Row, 1957.

McCANN, R. V. *The churches and mental health.* New York: Basic Books, 1962.

McCLELLAND, D. C., ATKINSON, J. W., & CLARK, R. A. The projective expression of needs. III. The effect of ego-involvement, success, and failures on perception. *J. Psychol.*, 1949, *27*, 311–330.

McCLELLAND, D. C., *et al.* *The achievement motive.* New York: Appleton, 1953.

McDONNELL, K. Psychiatry and pastoral psychology: The experience of an institute for mental health. *Lumen Vitae*, 1957, *12*, 253–259.

McGRANAHAN, D. V. Critical and experimental study of repression. *J. abnorm. soc. Psychol.*, 1940, *35*, 212–225.

McKELL, T. E., & SULLIVAN, A. J. *Personality in peptic ulcer.* Springfield, Ill.: Charles C Thomas, 1950.

McKELLAR, P. The emotion of anger in the expression of human aggressiveness. *Brit. J. Psychol.*, 1949, *39*, 148–155.

McKENZIE, J. G. *Nervous disorders and religion.* London: Allen & Unwin, 1951.

McKINNEY, F. *The psychology of personal adjustment.* (ed. 2) New York: Wiley, 1949.

MEAD, M. Age patterning in personality development. *Amer. J. Orthopsychiat.*, 1947, *17*, 231–252.

MEDALIA, N. Z. Marriage and adjustment: In college and out. *Personn. guid. J.*, 1962, *40*, 545–550.

MELTZER, H. Students' adjustments in anger. *J. soc. Psychol.*, 1933, *4*, 285–309.

MENNINGER, W. C. *Meet your mind.* Lewellen's Productions, 1947.

MENNINGER, W. C. Recreation and mental health. *Recreation*, 1948, *42*, 340–346.

MERRILL, BARBARA. Mother-child interactions. In R. G. Kuhlen & G. G. Thompson (Eds.), *Psychological studies in human adjustment.* New York: Appleton, 1952. Pp. 402–409.

MEYER, V. Psychological effects of brain damage. In H. J. Eysenck (Ed.), *Handbook of abnormal psychology.* New York: Basic Books, 1961. Pp. 529–565.

MEYERS, C. E. The effect of conflicting authority on the child. *Univer. Iowa Stud. Child Welf.*, 1944, *20*, 31–98.

MILBANK MEMORIAL FUND. *The epidemiology of mental disorder.* New York: Milbank Memorial Fund, 1950.

MILBANK MEMORIAL FUND. *The biology of mental health and disease.* New York: Harper & Row, 1952.

MILE, H. H. W., COBB, S., & SHANDS, H. *Case histories in psychosomatic medicine.* New York: Norton, 1952.

MILLER, D. R. Responses of psychiatric patients to threat of failure. *J. abnorm. soc. Psychol.*, 1951, *46*, 378–387.

MILLER, D. R., & SWANSON, G. E. The study of conflict. In M. R. Jones (Ed.), *Nebraska symposium on motivation.* Lincoln: University of Nebraska Press, 1956. Pp. 137–174.

MILLER, J. G. *Unconsciousness.* New York: Wiley, 1942.

MILLER, N. E. Experimental studies of conflicts. In J. McV. Hunt (Ed.), *Personality and the behavior disorders.* New York: Ronald, 1944. Vol. I, pp. 431–465.

MILLER, N. E. Effects of drugs on motivation: The value of using a variety of measures. *Ann. N.Y. Acad. Sci.*, 1956, *65*, 318–333.

MILLER, N. E., *et al.* The frustration-aggression hypothesis. *Psychol. Rev.*, 1941, *48*, 337–342.

MILLER, S. H. Exploring the boundary between religion and psychiatry. *J. pastoral Care*, 1952, *6*, 1–11.

MILT, H. *Basic facts about mental illness.* New York: Science & Health Publications, 1957.

MITTELMANN, B., & WOLFF, H. G. Emotions and gastroduodenal function: Experimental studies on patients with gastritis, duodenitis and peptic ulcer. *Psychosom. Med.*, 1942, *4*, 5–61.

MOHSIN, S. M. Effect of frustration on problem-solving behavior. *J. abnorm. soc. Psychol.*, 1954, *49*, 152–155.

MOORE, T. V. *Personal mental hygiene.* New York: Grune & Stratton, 1944.

MORGAN, A. E. *The needs of youth.* New York: Oxford University Press, 1939.

MORGAN, C. M. Factors related to personal adjustment in old age. In R. G. Kuhlen & G. G. Thompson (Eds.), *Psychological studies in human adjustment.* New York: Appleton, 1952. Pp. 511–522.

MORGAN, C. T. Physiological mechanisms of motivation. In M. R. Jones (Ed.), *Nebraska symposium on motivation.* Lincoln: University of Nebraska Press, 1957. Pp. 1–35.

MORGAN, D. H. Emotional adjustments of visually-handicapped adolescents. *J. educ. Psychol.*, 1944, *35*, 65–81.

MOSSE, E. P. *The conquest of loneliness.* New York: Random House, 1957.

MOWRER, O. H. Discipline and mental health. *Harvard educat. Rev.*, 1947, *17*, 284–296.

MOWRER, O. H. What is normal behavior? In L. Pennington & I. Berg (Eds.), *An introduction to clinical psychology.* New York: Ronald, 1948. Pp. 58–88.

MOWRER, O. H. Pain, punishment, guilt, and anxiety. In P. H. Hoch & J. Zubin (Eds.), *Anxiety.* New York: Grune & Stratton, 1950. Pp. 27–40.

MOWRER, O. H. The therapeutic process. III. Learning theory and neurotic fallacy. *Amer. J. Orthopsychiat.*, 1952, *22*, 679–689.

MOWRER, O. H. *Psychotherapy: Theory and research.* New York: Ronald, 1953a.

MOWRER, O. H. Motivation and neurosis. In *Current theory and research in motivation: A symposium.* Lincoln: University of Nebraska Press, 1953b. Pp. 162–184.

MOWRER, O. H. Changing conceptions of the unconscious. *J. nerv. ment. Dis.*, 1959, *129*, 222–234.

MOWRER, O. H. "Sin" the lesser of two evils. *Amer. Psychologist*, 1960, *15*, 301–304.

MOWRER, O. H. *The crisis in psychiatry and religion.* New York: Van Nostrand, 1961.

MUDD, E. H. *The practice of marriage counseling.* New York: Association Press, 1951.

MULLAHY, P. *Oedipus: Myth and complex.* New York: Hermitage House, 1948.

MUNROE, RUTH L. A maladjusted college student. In A. Burton & R. E. Harris (Eds.), *Case histories in clinical and abnormal psychology.* New York: Harper & Row, 1947. Pp. 628–649.

MUNROE, RUTH L. *Schools of psychoanalytic thought.* New York: Holt, Rinehart and Winston, 1955.

MURPHY, L. B. Childhood experience in relation to personality development. In J. McV. Hunt (Ed.), *Personality and the behavior disorders.* New York: Ronald, 1944. Vol. II, pp. 652–690.

MURSELL, J. L. *Using your mind effectively.* New York: McGraw-Hill, 1951.

MUSSEN, P. H. Long term consequences of masculinity of interests in adolescence. *J. consult. Psychol.*, 1962, *26*, 435–440.

MUSSEN, P. H., & NAYLOR, H. K. The relationships between overt and fantasy aggression. *J. abnor. soc. Psychol.*, 1954, *49*, 235–240.

MUSSEN, T., & DISTLER, L. Masculinity, identification, and father-son relationship. *J. abnorm. soc. Psychol.*, 1959, *59*, 350–356.

NARCISO, J. C. Some psychological aspects of dermatosis. *J. consult. Psychol.*, 1952, *16*, 199–201.

NASH, E. Mental hygiene and sex education. *Understand. the Child*, 1948, *17*, 111–112.

NATIONAL INSTITUTE OF MENTAL HEALTH. *Patients in mental institutions, 1948.* Washington, D.C.: Federal Security Agency, 1951.

NATIONAL INSTITUTE OF MENTAL HEALTH. The teacher and

mental health. In L. D. Crow & Alice Crow (Eds.), *Mental hygiene for teachers: A book of readings.* New York: Macmillan, 1963. Pp. 445–451.

NEUMEYER, M. H. *Juvenile delinquency in modern society.* New York: Van Nostrand, 1949.

NEWELL, N. L. Mental health and ill-health among youth. *Understand. the Child,* 1947, *16,* 3–6.

NISSEN, H. W. Instinct as seen by a psychologist. *Psychol. Rev.,* 1953, *60,* 291–294.

NISSEN, H. W. The nature of the drive as innate determinant of behavioral organization. In M. R. Jones (Ed.), *Nebraska symposium on motivation.* Lincoln: University of Nebraska Press, 1954. Pp. 281–321.

NORMAN, R. D., & AINSWORTH, P. The relationships among projection, empathy, reality and adjustment. *J. consult. Psychol.,* 1954, *18,* 53–58.

NOVICK, R. G. How teachers can build mental health. In L. D. Crow & Alice Crow (Eds.), *Mental hygiene for teachers: A book of readings.* New York: Macmillan, 1963. Pp. 385–391.

NOWLIS, V. The development and modification of motivational systems in personality. In *Current theory and research in motivation: A symposium.* Lincoln: University of Nebraska Press, 1953. Pp. 114–138.

NUNNALLY, J. C. *Popular conceptions of mental health: Their development and change.* New York: Holt, Rinehart and Winston, 1961.

NUTTIN, J. *Psychoanalysis and personality.* (Trans. by G. Lamb.) New York: Sheed & Ward, 1953.

OATES, W. E. *Religious factors in mental illness.* New York: Association Press, 1955.

O'BRIEN, F. J. Modern psychiatry and religion. *Proc. Nat. Conf. Cath. Char.,* 1950.

O'DOHERTY, E. F. Mental health and sanctity: An interview. *Ave Maria,* Jan. 10, 1959.

O'DOHERTY, E. F., & McGRATH, S. D. (Eds.) *The priest and mental health.* New York: Alba House, 1963.

OFFICE OF EDUCATION. *Evaluating guidance procedures: A review of the literature.* Washington, D.C.: Federal Security Agency, 1949.

O'KELLY, L. I., & MUCKLER, F. A. *Introduction to psychopathology.* (ed. 2) Englewood Cliffs, N.J.: Prentice-Hall, 1955.

O'KELLY, L. I. The psychophysiology of motivation. *Ann. Rev. Psychol.,* 1963, Vol. 14, 57–92.

OLSON, W. C., & WATTENBERG, W. W. The role of the school in mental health. *Fifty-fourth Yearbook.* NSSE, 1955, Part 2. Pp. 99–124.

OPPENHEIMER, O. The functional autonomy of motives. *J. soc. Psychol.,* 1947, *25,* 171–179.

OPPENHEIMER, O. Freedom and mental health. *Educ. Theory,* 1952, *2,* 222–224.

OSTOW, M. The biological basis of human behavior. In S. Arieti (Ed.), *American handbook of psychiatry.* New York: Basic Books, 1959, I. Pp. 58–87.

OUTLAND, G. E. The home situation as a direct cause of boy transiency. *J. juven. Res.,* 1938, *22,* 33–42.

OVERSTREET, H. A. *The mature mind.* New York: Norton, 1949.

PAGE, J. D. *Abnormal psychology.* New York: McGraw-Hill, 1947.

PALMER, S. Frustration, aggression, and murder. *J. abnorm. soc. Psychol.,* 1960, *60,* 430–432.

PAPANEK, HELEN. Ethical values in psychotherapy. *J. individ. Psychol.,* 1958, *14,* 106–166.

PARSONS, T. Certain primary sources and patterns of aggression in the social structure of the western world. *Psychiatry,* 1947, *10,* 167–181.

PARTRIDGE, E. D. *Social psychology of adolescence.* Englewood Cliffs, N.J.: Prentice-Hall, 1938.

PASAMANICK, B. Patterns of research in mental health. *Psychiat. Quart.,* 1952, *26,* 477–589.

PECK, R. F., & MITCHELL, J. V. *Mental health.* Washington, D.C.: National Education Association, 1962.

PECK, R. F., & MITCHELL, J. V. Effect of teacher's mental health on pupil learning. In L. D. Crow & Alice Crow (Eds.), *Mental hygiene for teachers: A book of readings.*

New York: Macmillan, 1963. Pp. 344–349.

PEPITONE, A. Motivational effects in social perception. *Hum. Relat.*, 1950, 3, 57–76.

PETERSON, D. R., QUAY, H. C., & CAMERON, C. R. Personality and background factors in juvenile delinquency as inferred from questionnaire responses. *J. consult. Psychol.*, 1955, 23, 395–399.

PFEFFER, A. Z. *Alcoholism.* New York: Grune & Stratton, 1958.

PHILLIPS, E. L., WIENER, D. N., & HARING, N. G. *Discipline, achievement, and mental health.* Englewood Cliffs, N.J.: Prentice-Hall, 1960.

PLUNKETT, R. J., & GORDON, J. E. *Epidemiology and mental illness.* New York: Basic Books, 1960.

PODOLSKY, E. (Ed.) *Music therapy.* New York: Philosophical Library, 1954.

POOLE, FLORENCE. The child with social and emotional problems. In L. D. Crow & Alice Crow (Eds.), *Mental hygiene for teachers: A book of readings.* New York: Macmillan, 1963. Pp. 150–158.

POSTMAN, L. Perception, motivation, and behavior. *J. Personality*, 1953, 22, 17–30.

POSTMAN, L., & BROWN, D. R. The perceptual consequence of success and failure. *J. abnorm. soc. Psychol.*, 1952, 47, 213–221.

POSTMAN, L., & BRUNER, J. S. Perception under stress. *Psychol. Rev.*, 1948, 55, 314–323.

POWDERMAKER, F. B., & FRANK, J. D. *Group psychotherapy.* New York: Commonwealth Fund, 1953.

PRATT, DALLAS. Making the environment respond to basic emotional needs. *Psychiatry*, 1952, 15, 179–188.

PRESTON, R. C., & BOTEL, M. The relation of reading skill and other factors to the academic achievement of 2,048 college students. *J. exp. Educ.*, 1952, 20, 363–371.

PRONKO, N. H., & LEITH, W. R. Behavior under stress: A study of its disintegration. *Psychological Reports*, Monogr. Suppl. No. 5, 1956, 205–222.

PURNELL, P. The interests of happily married couples. *Marr. fam. Liv.*, 1952, 14, 276–280.

QUERIDO, A. Mental health at the university. In *Health at the university.* Paris: International Universities, 1954. Pp. 27–31.

RADKE, M. J. *The relation of paternal authority to children's behavior and attitudes.* Minneapolis: University of Minnesota Press, 1946.

RADO, S. Psychodynamics as a basic science. *Am. J. Orthopsychiat.*, 1946, 16, 405–409.

RAPAPORT, D. On the psychoanalytic theory of motivation. In M. R. Jones (Ed.), *Nebraska symposium on motivation.* Lincoln: University of Nebraska Press, 1960. Pp. 173–247.

RASEY, M. I. *Toward maturity.* New York: Barnes & Noble, 1947.

RATHS, L. Eight basic needs of all children. In L. D. Crow & Alice Crow (Eds.), *Mental hygiene for teachers: A book of readings.* New York: Macmillan, 1963. Pp. 32–33.

RECKLESS, W. C. *The etiology of delinquent and criminal behavior.* Bull. No. 50. New York: Social Science Research Council, 1943.

REDL, F., & WINEMAN, D. *Children who hate.* New York: Free Press, 1951.

REES, L. Constitutional factors and abnormal behavior. In H. J. Eysenck (Ed.), *Handbook of abnormal psychology.* New York: Basic Books, 1961. Pp. 344–392.

REIK, T. *The need to be loved.* New York: Farrar, Straus, 1963.

RENNIE, T. A. C. Prognosis in the psychoneuroses: Benign and malignant developments. In P. H. Hoch & J. Zubin (Eds.), *Current problems in psychiatric diagnosis.* New York: Grune & Stratton, 1953. Pp. 66–79.

RETHLINGSHAFER, DOROTHY. Experimental evidence for functional autonomy of motives. *Psychol. Rev.*, 1943, 50, 397–407.

RIBBLE, MARGARET A. *The rights of infants: Early psychological needs and their satisfaction.* New York: Columbia University Press, 1943.

RIBBLE, MARGARET A. Infantile experience in relation to personality development. In J. McV. Hunt (Ed.), *Personality and the behavior disorders.* New York: Ronald, 1944. Vol. I, pp. 621–651.

ROBBINS, L. L. Unconscious motivation. *Menninger Quart.*, 1956, *10*, 24–28.

ROBINSON, R., DeMARSCHE, D., & WAGLE, MILDRED K. *Community resources in mental health.* New York: Basic Books, 1960.

ROBINSON, S. C. Role of emotions in gastroduodenal ulcers. *Illinois med. J.*, 1937, *71*, 338–347.

ROGERS, C. R. *Counseling and psychotherapy.* Boston: Houghton Mifflin, 1942.

ROGERS, C. R. *Client-centered therapy.* Boston: Houghton Mifflin, 1951.

ROGERS, C. R. *On becoming a person: A therapist's view of psychotherapy.* Boston: Houghton Mifflin, 1961.

ROGERS, C. R., & DYMOND, R. F. (Eds.) *Psychotherapy and personality change.* Chicago: University of Chicago Press, 1954.

ROSENZWEIG, S. Types of reaction to frustration: An heuristic classification. *J. abnorm. soc. Psychol.*, 1935, *29*, 298–300.

ROSENZWEIG, S. Frustration as an experimental problem. VI. General outline of frustration. *Charact. & Pers.*, 1938, *7*, 153.

ROSENZWEIG, S. An outline of frustration theory. In J. McV. Hunt (Ed.), *Personality and the behavior disorders.* New York: Ronald, 1944. Vol. I, pp. 379–388.

ROTTER, J. B. Clinical methods: Psychodiagnostics. *Ann. Rev. Psychol.*, 1953, *4*, 295–316.

RUBINS, J. L. Psychodynamics and psychosomatic symptoms. *Amer. J. Psychoanal.*, 1959, *19*, 165–187.

RUESCH, J. *Chronic disease and psychological invalidism.* Los Angeles: University of California Press, 1951.

RUESCH, J. *Therapeutic communication.* New York: Norton, 1961.

RYAN, W. C. Mental health in education. *Bull. World ment. Hlth.*, 1953, 136–138.

RYANS, D. G. Some relationships between pupil behavior and certain teacher characteristics. *J. educ. Psych.*, 1961, *52*, 82–90.

SALTER, A. *The case against psychoanalysis.* New York: Holt, Rinehart and Winston, 1952.

SANFORD, R. N. Psychotherapy and counseling: Introduction. *J. consult. Psychol.*, 1948, *12*, 65–67.

SARBIN, T. R. (Ed.) *Studies in behavior pathology: A reader in experimental psychology of the abnormal.* New York: Holt, Rinehart and Winston, 1961.

SARGENT, S. S. Reaction to frustration—a critique and hypothesis. *Psychol. Rev.*, 1948, *55*, 108–114.

SAUL, L. J. Physiological effects of emotional tension. In J. McV. Hunt (Ed.), *Personality and the behavior disorders.* New York: Ronald, 1944. Vol. I, pp. 269–305.

SAUL, L. J. The nature of neurotic reactions. *Amer. J. Psychiat.*, 1950, *106*, 547–548.

SAUL, L. J. Inferiority feelings and hostility. *Amer. J. Psychiat.*, 1951, *108*, 120–122.

SAUL, L. J. *Emotional maturity.* (ed. 2) Philadelphia: Lippincott, 1960.

SCHADE, M., HRUZA, T., WASHBURNE, A., & CARNS, M. Relaxation as an adjunct to psychotherapy. *J. clin. Psychol.*, 1952, *8*, 338–346.

SCHAFFER, H. R. Behavior under stress: A neurophysiological hypothesis. *Psychol. Rev.*, 1954, *61*, 323–333.

SCHNEIDERS, A. A. Emotional development in children. *Education*, 1951, *72*, 216–223.

SCHNEIDERS, A. A. The psychological bases of the moral virtues. Presidential Address read at the seventh annual meeting of the Amer. Cath. Psychol. Assoc., Cleveland, Ohio, September 6, 1953.

SCHNEIDERS, A. A. Psychology as a normative science. In M. B. Arnold & J. A. Gasson (Eds.), *The human person: An integral approach to the theory of personality.* New York: Ronald, 1954a. Pp. 373–394.

SCHNEIDERS, A. A. The child and the family. In E. J. Schmiedeler (Ed.), *The child and problems of today.* St. Meinrad, Ind.: Grail, 1954b. Pp. 1–14.

SCHNEIDERS, A. A. Mental hygiene of the home. In E. J. Schmiedeler (Ed.), *The child and problems of today.* St. Meinrad, Ind.: Grail, 1954c. Pp. 52–61.

SCHNEIDERS, A. A. Family culture, child training and development. In E. J. Schmiedeler (Ed.), *The child and problems of today.* St. Meinrad, Ind.: Grail, 1954d. Pp. 157–170.

SCHNEIDERS, A. A. Personality needs, religion and psychotherapy. *Intern. rec. Med.,* 1955, *168,* 790–792.

SCHNEIDERS, A. A. Religious symbolism and neurotic disorder. *Intern. rec. Med.,* 1958, *171,* 745–792.

SCHNEIDERS, A. A. Clinical manifestations of guilt. In W. C. Bier & R. J. McCall (Eds.), *Three joint symposia from the ACPA–APA meetings of 1957, 1958, 1959.* New York: Fordham University Press, 1960a. Pp. 7–18.

SCHNEIDERS, A. A. *Personality development and adjustment in adolescence.* Milwaukee: Bruce, 1960b.

SCHNEIDERS, A. A. Religion and psychological health—a new approach. *J. existent. Psychiat.,* 1961, *2,* 93–104.

SCHNEIDERS, A. A. *The anarchy of feeling.* New York: Sheed & Ward, 1963a.

SCHNEIDERS, A. A. Counseling and moral values in the church-related college. *J. coll. stud. Personnel,* 1963b, *5,* 35–39.

SCHUMACHER, H. C. The importance of recreation to mental health. Second Annual California Recreation Conference, February, 1950.

SCHWARTZ, C. *Neurotic anxiety.* New York: Sheed & Ward, 1954.

SCHWEBEL, M. Some ethical problems in counseling. *Personnel & Guid. J.,* 1955, *33,* 254–259.

SCOTT, J. P. *Aggression.* Chicago: University of Chicago Press, 1958.

SCOTT, W. A. Research definitions of mental health and mental illness. In T. R. Sarbin (Ed.), *Studies in behavior pathology.* New York: Holt, Rinehart and Winston, 1961. Pp. 8–22.

SCULL, A. J. The challenge of the "well child." *Calif. Med.,* 1952, *77,* 285–292.

SEARS, PAULINE S. Problems in the investigation of achievement and self esteem motivation. In M. R. Jones (Ed.), *Nebraska symposium on motivation.* Lincoln: University of Nebraska Press, 1957. Pp. 265–339.

SEARS, R. R. *Survey of objective studies in psychoanalytic concepts.* Bull. No. 51. New York: Social Science Research Council, 1943.

SEARS, R. R. Effects of frustration and anxiety on fantasy aggression. *Am. J. Orthopsychiat.,* 1951, *21,* 498–505.

SEARS, R. R. The relation of early socialization experiences to aggression in middle childhood. *J. abnorm. soc. Psychol.,* 1961, *63,* 466–492.

SEARS, R. R. Dependency motivation. In M. R. Jones (Ed.), *Nebraska symposium on motivation.* Lincoln: University of Nebraska Press, 1963. Pp. 25–64.

SEARS, R. R., MACCOBY, E. E., & LEVIN, H. *Patterns of child rearing.* New York: Harper & Row, 1957.

SEARS, R. R., PINTNER, M. H., & SEARS, PAULINE S. The father's influence on children's behavior patterns. In R. G. Kuhlen & G. G. Thompson (Eds.), *Psychological studies in human development.* New York: Appleton, 1952. Pp. 395–401.

SEGEL, D. *Frustration in adolescent youth.* Washington, D.C.: U.S. Office of Education, Bull. No. 1, 1951. Pp. 29–30.

SEIDMAN, J. M. (Ed.) *Educating for mental health: A book of readings.* New York: Crowell, 1963.

SELLS, S. B. Problems of criteria and validity in diagnosis and therapy. *J. clin. Psychol.,* 1952, *8,* 23–28.

SELYE, H. *The stress of life.* New York: McGraw-Hill, 1956.

SENN, M. J. E. Constructive forces in the home. *Ment. Hyg.,* N.Y., 1948, *32,* 382–391.

SEWARD, J. P. How are motives learned? *Psychol. Rev.,* 1953, *60,* 99–110.

SEWARD, J. P. A neurological approach to motivation. In M. R. Jones, (Ed.), *Nebraska symposium on motivation.*

Lincoln: University of Nebraska Press, 1956. Pp. 180–208.

SHAFFER, L. F. *The psychology of adjustment.* Boston: Houghton Mifflin, 1936.

SHAFFER, L. F., & SHOBEN, E. J., Jr. Results of defensive behavior. In L. D. Crow & Alice Crow (Eds.), *Mental hygiene for teachers: A book of readings.* New York: Macmillan, 1963. Pp. 135–139.

SHANDS, HARLEY C. *Thinking and psychotherapy.* Cambridge, Mass.: Harvard University Press, 1960.

SHAPIRO, D. S. Perceptions of significant family and environmental relationships in aggressive and withdrawn children. *J. consult. Psychol.,* 1957, 21, 381–385.

SHARMA, SOHAN L. Personality under stress: Survey of the literature. *J. educ. Psychol.,* 1955, 13, 143–154.

SHAW, F. J., & ORT, R. S. *Personal adjustment in the American culture.* New York: Harper & Row, 1953.

SHEERER, E. The relationship between acceptance of self and the acceptance of others. *J. consult. Psychol.,* 1949, 13, 169–175.

SHELDON, W. H., & STEVENS, S. S. *The varieties of temperament.* New York: Harper & Row, 1942.

SHERIF, M., & CANTRIL, H. *The psychology of ego-involvements.* New York: Wiley, 1947.

SHERMAN, H. C. *The nutritional improvement of life.* New York: Columbia University Press, 1950.

SHERMAN, M. *Mental conflicts and personality.* New York: Longmans, 1938.

SHERMAN, M. *Basic problems of behavior.* New York: Longmans, 1941. Courtesy of David McKay Company, Inc.

SHIELDS, J., & SLATER, E. Heredity and psychological abnormality. In H. J. Eysenck (Ed.), *Handbook of abnormal psychology.* New York: Basic Books, 1961. Pp. 298–343.

SHNEIDMAN, E. S., & FARBEROW, N. L. (Eds.) *Clues to suicide.* New York: McGraw-Hill, 1957.

SHOBEN, E. J. Toward a concept of the normal personality. *Amer. Psychologist,* 1957, 12, 183–189.

SHOCK, N. W. Physiological factors in behavior. In J. McV. Hunt (Ed.), *Personality and the behavior disorders.* New York: Ronald, 1944. Vol. I, pp. 582–618.

SHOCK, N. W. Physiological manifestations of chronic emotional states. In M. L. Reymert (Ed.), *Feelings and emotions.* New York: McGraw-Hill, 1950. Pp. 277–283.

SHORE, M. J. The bondage of stability. In M. J. Shore (Ed.), *Twentieth century mental hygiene.* New York: Social Sciences Publishers, 1950. Pp. 433–440.

SHOSTROM, E. L., & BRAMMER, L. M. *The dynamics of the counseling process.* New York: McGraw-Hill, 1952.

SIEGEL, S. The relationship of hostility to authoritarianism. *J. abnorm. soc. Psychol.,* 1956, 52, 368–372.

SIEGMAN, A. W. Personality variables associated with admitted criminal behavior. *J. consult. Psychol.,* 1962, 26, 199.

SINGER, J. M., & ROWE, R. An experimental study of some relationships between day-dreaming and anxiety. *J. consult. Psychol.,* 1962, 26, 446–454.

SINGER, R. D., & FESHBACH, S. Some relationships between manifest anxiety, authoritarian tendencies and modes of reaction to frustration. *J. abnorm. soc. Psychol.,* 1959, 59, 404–408.

SLAVSON, S. R. *An introduction to group therapy.* Cambridge, Mass.: Harvard University Press, 1943.

SMALL, L. Personality determinants of vocational choice. *Psychol. Monogr.,* 1953, 67, (Whole No. 351).

SMART, M., & SMART, R. *An introduction to family relationships.* Philadelphia: Saunders, 1953.

SMITH, M. B. Optima of mental health. *Psychiatry,* 1950, 13, 503–510.

SMITH, M. B. Mental health reconsidered: A special case of the problem of values in psychology. *Amer. Psychologist,* 1961, 16, 299–306.

SNYGG, D., & COMBS, A. W. *Individual behavior.* New York: Harper & Row, 1949.

SODDY, K. Mental health and the maladjusted child. *Ment. Hyg.*, N.Y., 1952, *36*, 383–393.

SODDY, K. (Ed.) *Mental health and infant development.* New York: Basic Books, 1956. 2 vols.

SODDY, K. (Ed.) 1. *Identity.* 2. *Mental health and value systems.* Chicago: Quadrangle Books, 1962.

SOLOMON, J. C. Neuroses of school teachers. *Ment. Hyg.*, N.Y., 1960, *44*, 79–90.

SOLOMON, P., *et al.* (Eds.) *Sensory deprivation: A symposium held at Harvard Medical School.* Cambridge, Mass.: Harvard University Press, 1961.

SONTAG, L. W. The genetics of differences in psychosomatic patterns in childhood. *Amer. J. Orthopsychiat.*, 1950, *20*, 479–489.

SOPCHAK, A. L. Parental "identification" and "tendency toward disorders" as measured by the Minnesota Multiphasic Personality Inventory. *J. abnorm. soc. Psychol.*, 1952, *47*, 159–165.

SPALDING, W. B., & MONTAGUE, J. R. *Alcohol and human affairs.* New York: World Book Company, 1949.

SPITZ, R. A. Personal emotional adjustment during infancy. In R. G. Kuhlen & G. G. Thompson (Eds.), *Psychological studies of human development.* New York: Appleton, 1952. Pp. 490–495.

SROLE, L., LANGNER, T. S., MICHAEL, S. T., OPLER, M. K., & RENNIE, T. A. C. Mental health in the metropolis: The Midtown Manhattan Study. New York: McGraw-Hill, 1962. Vol. I.

STAGNER, R. The role of the parents in the development of emotional instability. *Amer. J. Orthopsychiat.*, 1938, *8*, 122–128.

STAGNER, R. The psychology of personality. (ed. 2) New York: McGraw-Hill, 1948.

STECKLE, L. C. *Problems of human adjustment.* New York: Harper & Row, 1949.

STELLAR, E. The physiology of motivation. *Psychol. Rev.*, 1954, *61*, 5–22.

STERN, K. Religion and psychiatry. *Commonweal*, 1948, *49*, 30–33.

STERN, K. *The third revolution.* New York: Harcourt, 1954.

STEVENSON, G. S. The prevention of personality disorders. In J. McV. Hunt (Ed.), *Personality and the behavior disorders.* New York: Ronald, 1944. Vol. II, pp. 1165–1184.

STOCK, D. The self-concept and feelings towards others. *J. consult. Psychol.*, 1949, *13*, 176–180.

STOKES, W. R. The concept of emotional maturity as related to marriage counseling. *Marr. fam. Liv.*, 1952, *14*, 127–131.

STRAUSS, A. L. *Mirrors and masks: The search for identity.* New York: Free Press, 1959.

STRECKER, E. A. *Fundamentals of psychiatry.* (ed. 4) Philadelphia: Lippincott, 1947.

STRECKER, E. A. *Basic psychiatry.* New York: Random House, 1952.

STRECKER, E. A., & APPEL, K. E. *Discovering ourselves.* (ed. 2) New York: Macmillan, 1944.

SULLENGER, T. E. Juvenile delinquency: A product of the home. *J. crim. law Criminol.*, 1934, *24*, 1088–1092.

SULLENGER, T. E. *Social determinants in juvenile delinquency.* New York: Wiley, 1936.

SULLIVAN, A. J., & McKELL, T. E. *Personality in peptic ulcer.* Springfield, Ill.: Charles C Thomas, 1950.

SUPER, D. E. Career patterns as a basis for vocational counseling. *J. coun. Psychol.*, 1954, *1*, 12–20.

SUTTIE, I. D. *The origins of love and hate.* New York: Julian, 1952.

SYMONDS, P. M. *The psychology of parent-child relationships.* New York: Appleton, 1939.

SYMONDS, P. M. *The dynamics of human adjustment.* New York: Appleton, 1946.

SYMONDS, P. M. *Dynamic psychology.* New York: Appleton, 1949.

SZASZ, T. S., KIRSNER, J. B., LEVIN, E., & PALMER, W. L. The role of hostility in the pathogenesis of peptic ulcer. *Psychosom. Med.*, 1947, *9*, 331–336.

SZASZ, T. S. The myth of mental illness. *Amer. Psychologist*, 1960, *15*, 113–118.

SZASZ, T. S. *The myth of mental illness.* New York: Harper & Row, 1961.

TAYLOR, C., & COMBS, A. W. Self-acceptance and adjustment. *J. consult. Psychol.*, 1952, 16, 89–91.

TAYLOR, J. A. Drive theory and manifest anxiety. *Psychol. Bull.*, 1956, 53, 303–320.

TAYLOR, J. G. *The behavioral basis of perception.* New Haven, Conn.: Yale University Press, 1962.

TERMAN, L. M. *Psychological factors in marital happiness.* New York: McGraw-Hill, 1938.

TERMAN, L. M. Kinsey's "Sexual behavior in the human male": Some comments and criticisms. *Psychol. Bull.*, 1948, 45, 443–459.

TERMAN, L. M. Psychological factors in marital happiness. In R. G. Kuhlen & G. G. Thompson (Eds.), *Psychological studies in human development.* New York: Appleton, 1952. Pp. 373–382.

TERMAN, L. M., & MERRILL, MAUDE A. *Measuring intelligence.* Boston: Houghton Mifflin, 1937.

THIBAUT, J. W. The concept of normality in clinical psychology. *Psychol. Rev.*, 1943, 50, 338–344.

THOMAS, J. L. Marriage breakdown in the Catholic family. *Social Order,* 1952, 2, 450.

THOMAS, J. L. Marital failure and duration. *Social Order,* 1953, 3, 24–29.

THORNE, F. C. Life record criteria of psychological health. *J. clin. Psychol.,* 1958, 14, 123–132.

THORPE, L. P. *The psychology of mental health.* New York: Ronald, 1950.

THORPE, L. P., & KATZ, B. *The psychology of abnormal behavior.* New York: Ronald, 1948.

THURSTON, J. R., & MUSSEN, P. H. Infant feeding gratification and adult personality. *J. Personal.,* 1951, 19, 449–458.

TOBY, J. The differential impact of family disorganization. *Amer. sociol. Rev.,* 1957, 22, 505–512.

TORRANCE, P. The influence of the broken home on adolescent adjust-ment. *J. educ. Sociol.,* 1945, 18, 359–364.

TRESE, L. J. *101 delinquent girls.* Notre Dame, Ind.: Fides, 1962.

TROUTON, D., & EYSENCK, H. J. The effects of drugs on behavior. In H. J. Eysenck (Ed.), *Handbook of abnormal psychology.* New York: Basic Books, 1961. Pp. 634–696.

TUREK, E. V., & HOWELL, R. J. The effect of variable success and failure situations on the intensity of need for achievement. *J. soc. Psychol.,* 1959, 49, 267–273.

TYLER, LEONA E. *The work of the counselor.* (ed. 2) New York: Appleton, 1961.

TYSON, R. Current mental hygiene practice. *J. clin. Psychol.,* Monogr. Suppl. No. 8, January 1951.

ULLMANN, C. A. *Identification of maladjusted school children.* Public Health Monograph No. 7. Washington, D.C.: U.S. Public Health Service, 1957.

UNITED STATES DEPARTMENT OF HEALTH, EDUCATION & WELFARE. *Facts on mental health and mental illness.* Publication No. 53, 1962.

UNITED STATES PUBLIC HEALTH SERVICE. *National Institute of Mental Health.* Washington, D.C.: Federal Security Agency, 1952.

VAN BUSKIRK, J. D. *Religion, healing, and health.* New York: Macmillan, 1952.

VANDERVELDT, J. H. Religion and mental health. *Ment. Hyg., N.Y.,* 1951, 35, 177–189.

VANDERVELDT, J. H., & ODEN-WALD, R. P. *Psychiatry and Catholicism.* New York: McGraw-Hill, 1952.

VAUGHAN, R. P. *Mental illness and the religious life.* Milwaukee: Bruce, 1962.

VAUGHAN, W. F. *Personal and social adjustment.* New York: Odyssey, 1952.

VINACKE, W. E. The drive-modification theory of human motivation. *J. genet. Psychol.,* 1960, 96, 245–268.

VINACKE, W. E. Motivation as a complex problem. In M. R. Jones (Ed.), *Nebraska symposium on motivation.*

Lincoln: University of Nebraska Press, 1962. Pp. 1–46.

VOGEL, W., BAKER, R. W., & LAZARUS, R. S. The role of motivation in psychological states. *J. abnorm. soc. Psychol.*, 1958, 56, 105–112.

VOGEL, W., & LAUTERBACH, C. G. Sibling patterns and social adjustment among normal and psychiatrically disturbed soldiers. *J. consult. Psychol.*, 1963, 27, 236–242.

VOGEL, W., RAYMOND, S., & LAZARUS, R. S. Intrinsic motivation and psychological stress. *J. abnorm. soc. Psychol.*, 1959, 58, 225–233.

VROOM, V. H. Personality determinants of the effects of participation. *J. abnorm. soc. Psychol.*, 1959, 59, 322–327.

WALDSCHMIDT, R. Relationships among the need for positive regard, the need for self regard, and positive regard for others. *Amer. Psychologist*, 1960, 15, 391.

WALKER, E. L., & HEYNS, R. W. (Eds.) *An anatomy for conformity.* Englewood Cliffs, N.J.: Prentice-Hall, 1962.

WALL, B. D. Education's mental hygiene dilemma. *Ment. Hyg.*, 1960, 44, 569–576.

WARTERS, J. *Achieving maturity.* New York: McGraw-Hill, 1949.

WASHBURN, W. C. The effects of physique and intrafamily tension on self concepts in adolescent males. *J. consult. Psychol.*, 1962, 26, 460–466.

WATSON, R. E., PRITZKER, L., & MADISON, P. Hostility in neurotics and normals. *J. abnorm. soc. Psychol.*, 1955, 50, 36–40.

WATSON, R. I. (Ed.) *Readings in the clinical method in psychology.* New York: Harper & Row, 1949.

WEIL, R. J. Problems of interdisciplinary research in mental health. *Bull. marit. psychol. Assoc.*, December 1952, 29–36.

WEINBERG, S. K. *Society and personality disorders.* Englewood Cliffs, N.J.: Prentice-Hall, 1952.

WEINER, H., THALER, MARGARET, REISER, M. F., & MIRSKY, I. A. Etiology of duodenal ulcer. In T. R. Sarbin (Ed.), *Studies in behavior pathology.* New York: Holt, Rinehart and Winston, 1961. Pp. 273–282.

WEININGER, O. The effects of early experience on behavior and growth characteristics. *J. comp. physiol. Psychol.*, 1956, 49, 1–9.

WEITZ, H. Semantics in diagnosis. *J. coun. Psychol.*, 1954, 1, 70–73.

WHILES, W. H. The nervous or "highstrung" child. *Med. Pract.*, 1951, 113, 362–365.

WHITE, R. W. *The abnormal personality.* New York: Ronald, 1948.

WHITE, R. W. *Lives in progress.* New York: Holt, Rinehart and Winston, 1952.

WHITE, R. W. Motivation reconsidered: The concept of competence. *Psychological Rev.*, 1959, 66, 297–333.

WIENER, D. N. Personality characteristics of selected disability groups. *Genet. Psychol. Monogr.*, 1952, 45, 175–255.

WILLIAMSON, E. G. *Counseling adolescents.* New York: McGraw-Hill, 1950.

WILLIAMSON, E. G. Counseling: Therapy and diagnosis. *Ann. Rev. Psychol.*, 1953, 4, 343–360.

WILNER, D. M., *et al.* *The housing environment and family life: A longitudinal study of the effects of housing on morbidity and mental health.* Baltimore: Johns Hopkins University Press, 1962.

WINDER, C. L., & RAU, LUCY. Parental attitudes associated with social deviants and pre-adolescent boys. *J. abnorm. soc. Psychol.*, 1962, 64, 418–424.

WINTER, J. A. *The origins of illness and anxiety.* New York: Julian, 1962.

WITTENBORN, J. R. Symptom patterns in a group of mental hospital patients. *J. consult. Psychol.*, 1951, 15, 290–302.

WITTENBORN, J. R., & HOLZBERG, J. The generality of psychiatric syndromes. *J. consult. Psychol.*, 1951, 15, 372–380.

WITTKOWER, E. D. Studies of the personality of patients suffering from urticaria. *Psychosom. Med.*, 1953, 15, 116–126.

WITTY, P. A. (Ed.) *Mental health in modern education.* Chicago: University of Chicago Press, 1955.

WOLBERG, L. R. Adjustment problems in male adolescents. *Nerv. Child,* 1945, *4,* 129–134.

WOLF, S., & WOLFF, H. G. Evidence on the genesis of peptic ulcer in man. *J. Amer. med. Ass.,* 1942, *120,* 670–675.

WOLFF, H. G. The mind-body relationship. *J. religion & Health,* 1961. *1,* 12–30.

WOLFF, W., & PRECKER, J. A. (Eds.) *Success in psychotherapy.* New York: Grune & Stratton, 1952.

WOODWARD, J. L. Changing ideas on mental illness and its treatment. *Amer. sociol. Rev.,* 1951, *16,* 443–454.

WORLD FEDERATION FOR MENTAL HEALTH. *Annual Report,* 1950, 53.

WORLD FEDERATION FOR MENTAL HEALTH. *Bulletin,* 1951, *3,* 27–28.

WRENN, C. G., & HARLEY, D. L. *Time on their hands: A report on leisure, recreation, and young people.* Washington, D.C.: Amer. Council on Education, 1941.

WRIGHT, M. E. The influence of frustration upon the social relations of young children. *Character & Pers.,* 1943, *12,* 111–122.

WURTZ, K. R. Some theory and data concerning the attenuation of aggression. *J. abnorm. soc. Psychol.,* 1960, *60,* 134–136.

XAVIER, SISTER MARY. The influence of the teacher. *Cath. educ. Rev.,* 1960, *58,* 580–588.

YATES, A. J. *Frustration and conflict.* New York: Wiley, 1962.

YOUNG, P. T. *Emotion in man and animal.* New York: Wiley, 1943.

YOUNG, P. T. The role of hedonic processes in motivation. In M. R. Jones (Ed.), *Nebraska symposium on motivation.* Lincoln: University of Nebraska Press, 1955. Pp. 193–238.

YOUNG, P. T. The role of affective processes in learning and motivation. *Psychol. Rev.,* 1959, *66,* 104–125.

YOUNG, P. T. *Motivation and emotion.* New York: Wiley, 1961.

ZILBOORG, G. *Psychoanalysis and religion.* (Edited with an introduction by Margaret Zilboorg.) New York: Farrar, Straus, 1962.

ZILBOORG, G., & HENRY, G. W. *A history of medical psychology.* New York: Norton, 1941.

ZIMMER, H. Self-acceptance and its relation to conflict. *J. consult. Psychol.,* 1954, *18,* 447–449.

ZIMMERMAN, K. A. The importance of the family in the prevention of mental illness. *Milbank Mem. Fund quart. Bull.,* 1949, *27,* 133–142.

ZUBIN, J., & WINDLE, C. Psychological prognosis of outcome in the mental disorders. *J. abnorm. soc. Psychol.,* 1954, *49,* 272–279.

ZUCKERMAN, M. The effect of threat on perceptual effect in a group. *J. abnorm. soc. Psychol.,* 1951, *46,* 529–533.

Index of Names

Abrams, E. N., 309
Academy of Religion and Mental Health, 426
Adams, J. F., 478
Adler, A., 23
Ainsworth, P., 249
Alexander, F., 53
Allen, F. H., 107, 113, 482
Allers, R., 221
Allinsmith, W., 452, 454, 455, 457
Allport, G. W., 40, 42, 43, 51, 52, 69, 82, 86, 154, 309, 313, 376, 377, 434, 440
Altschule, M. D., 329
American Federation for Sex Hygiene, 350
American Social Hygiene Association, 350
Anderson, J. E., 5, 37, 50, 168, 355, 401, 406, 415, 456
Angyal, A., 377, 436
Appel, J. W., 6, 210, 214, 249, 317
Arnold, Magda B., 50
Atkin, E. L., 256, 257
Ausubel, D. P., 68, 428, 459
Axline, Virginia M., 482

Babcock, H., 47, 48, 309
Baker, R. W., 161, 170
Baller, W. R., 456
Bandura, A., 112
Barahal, G. D., 398
Barker, R. G., 98, 225, 271
Baron, D., 80, 143, 155, 168, 169, 183, 354, 362, 365
Barrett, L., 43, 69
Barron, F., 481

Baruch, Dorothy W., 407, 450
Barzun, J., 454
Bateson, G., 119, 269
Beach, F. A., 101, 368
Beers, C. W., 349, 350, 351, 476
Bell, H., 417
Beller, E. K., 145
Bender, Lauretta, 257, 268
Benedict, Ruth, 119, 462
Bennett, E., 145
Bennett, Margaret E., 390, 482
Berdie, R. F., 483
Berg, I., 469
Bergler, E., 256
Berkowitz, L., 264, 269
Berlyne, D. C., 173
Bernard, H. W., 40, 42, 97, 344, 346, 353, 377, 382, 383, 394
Bertocci, P. A., 65
Biber, Barbara, 117
Biddulph, L. G., 363
Bier, W. C., 424, 426
Binder, H., 54
Blanchard, T., 122
Bloch, H., 14
Blos, P., 456
Bond, E. D., 472
Bonnell, J. S., 441
Bonney, Merl E., 453
Bordin, E. S., 388
Bower, E. M., 460
Bowlby, J., 144
Braceland, F. J., 423, 472
Brachfeld, O., 223
Brammer, L. M., 476
Britt, S. H., 179, 197
Bromberg, W., 281, 484

527

Subject Index